"As the culture wars intensify, parents must become increasingly vigilant. If you want to protect the hearts and minds of your children, read this book."

R.C. Sproul, Jr.

"A comprehensive overview of the benefits of home schooling."

The New American

"Here is a book that gives you the facts. If you are thinking about taking the first step toward home education, then the best place to start is with *Home Schooling: The Right Choice.*"

Gary DeMar,
President of American Vision

"Written in an easy, conversational style, with splashes of humorous anecdotes. Klicka covers home schooling from all perspectives, historical, academic, biblical, practical, and legal...One word of warning, though, to prospective readers: Don't read this book unless you plan to home school—otherwise you will."

Debra Brett,
Book review for *Charisma,* September 1993

"I love it! It is the perfect book for the ignorant, the new home schooler lacking confidence, the parent trying to make a decision to home school, and the individual who is preparing to speak to a legislative committee. I am recommending it to everyone. Although the book reads easily, it is like a reference book. Imagine having all the quotes referring to home and public education and its history right at your fingertips, along with the statistics and the findings from the research. Great job! Thank you!"

Phil and Mary Lou Sampley,
Indiana Association of Home Educators

"Just wanted to let you know how much we love the book. It's so complete. Unfortunately, we may never get to see it again—we have so many people waiting to borrow it."

Dave and Deb Richards,
home schoolers

Home Schooling:
The Right Choice

An Academic, Historical, Practical, and Legal Perspective

by

Christopher J. Klicka

BROADMAN
&HOLMAN
PUBLISHERS

Nashville, Tennessee

Home Schooling: The Right Choice
© 2002 Christopher J. Klicka

Published by Broadman & Holman Publishers, Nashville, Tennessee
First published in 1995 and revised in 2000 by Loyal Publishing, Inc.

0-8054-2585-3

All Scripture quotations, unless indicated are taken from the New American Standard Bible. © 1975 by the Lockman Foundation (Anaheim, California: Foundation Press). Used by permission.

Scripture references marked KJV are from the Holy Bible: Authorized King James Version.

Scripture references marked NIV are from the Holy Bible, New International Version, copyright © 1973, 1978, 1984 by International Bible Society. Used by permission.

The cartoons in this work were drawn by Matthew Arnold, AlA © 1995 1544 Brookshire, Reston, Virginia 22090 and Chris Loope.

Cover design by David Uttley Design, Sisters, OR.

Note: The information in this book is not intended to be, and does not constitute, the giving of legal advice. Many states have unclear compulsory attendance statutes, and the courts of those states often vary in dleir interpretation of the statutes. Therefore, there is no guarantee that any particular court or state authority will accept the interpretations of the law explained in this book. This book is not intended to be a substitute for individual reliance on privately retained legal counsel.

1 2 3 4 5 6 7 8 08 07 06 05 04 03 02

Dedication

To all home schooling parents who love the Lord and are dying to themselves in order to diligently train their children according to God's law, despite legal or financial hardship or the criticism of others.

Contents

Foreword

by *D. James Kennedy, Ph.D.*

From the earliest days of my ministry, I have held the conviction that apostasy and anarchy can dominate the life of any nation if the coming generation fails to share the beliefs and ethical values of godly parents. This very day, I am shocked by the realization that, although our Pilgrim Fathers stated in the Mayflower Compact that they would create schools to teach their children the Word of God, it is now unlawful for children in the public schools to read or hear the Word or even to pray publicly to the God of the Bible.

That is why I began a Christian school, deliberately placed under the oversight of the elders of Coral Ridge Presbyterian Church, and with a school board made up of parents who were members of the congregation. In 1971, that was considered a drastic step, but the success of Westminster Academy over the years has placed it in the forefront of Florida's total educational effort.

For the same reason, I welcome this exciting new book by Dr. Klicka, *Home Schooling: The Right Choice*, a subject which is considered by many to be as drastic an innovation. You will be convinced by the urgent need for and the invaluable contribution by home schooling as analyzed and prescribed in this scholarly volume.

Let me warn you that the brilliant research which went into the compilation of the facts presented in this book will astound you and shock you. It is difficult for most of us to understand just how insidious and how tireless have been the efforts of secular humanism in the rewriting of curricula and textbooks for the purpose of indoctrinating an entire generation of young people in America's public school systems today.

If you are concerned, and desire authoritative information on what is right about carefully structured Christian home schooling, you will not find a more reliable and enlightening source book than this outstanding work written by the senior counsel for the Home School Legal Defense Association.

Few Americans realize that, from 1620 when the Pilgrims landed until 1837, virtually all education in this country was private and Christian. *Home Schooling: The Right Choice,* squarely based on historical principles, brings us to examine the roots that made America great.

Acknowledgments

My first thanks goes to the Lord who has saved me for all eternity and has brought me to the place where I am today. I praise Him for freely giving me the blessing and privilege of having such a wonderful wife and children. I thank my heavenly Father for allowing me to work at the Home School Legal Defense Association since 1985, for a cause I believe in with all my heart.

I give special thanks to my wife, Tracy, who supported me throughout this three-year project (and subsequent revisions) and encouraged me to complete it. I also thank my children; Bethany, Megan, Jesse, Susanna, John, and the twins, Charity and Amy, for helping me realize that children are a gift from God and one of the greatest privileges and responsibilities we have on earth. The training of their hearts and minds in the Lord and their education are priorities which demand my wife's and my time and should not be delegated to those who do not know God.

The twins especially helped me realize that we might not have our children with us very long. So, every minute counts. The doctors predicted Amy and Charity would die but God mercifully saved them. I have learned to not take my family for granted and to make every minute count.

I want to thank Gregg Harris, my original publisher and friend, who made this book possible.

I am grateful to my former publisher, Matt Jacobson, for his friendship and steady support. His encouragement has helped me to keep writing.

I also want to thank Matt Arnold, home schooling dad and Chris Loope, home school graduate, who provided the illustrations.

I would like to give special thanks to Mike Farris, president of the Home School Legal Defense Association, and Mike Smith, vice president. I thank both of them for their vision in establishing the Home School Legal Defense Association, their love and godly training of their children, their hearts in desiring to protect families from an ever- encroaching state, and their constant friendship, advice, and encouragement to me since 1983.

A word of appreciation goes to attorney John Whitehead who got me involved in writing this book, reviewed the original draft in 1990, and encouraged me to have it published.

Finally, I want to give a special tribute to my close friend and legal assistant, Kimberly Wray, who was killed in a car accident with Angela Yerovsek, another of our legal assistants, on May 29, 1994. Her love for the Lord, love for home schoolers, and faithful service to me at HSLDA will never be forgotten. (See Appendix D for a tribute to Kimberly.)

Christopher Klicka
January 2000

Preface

Home schooling is an age-old educational method that has experienced a resurgence, beginning in the 1970s in the United States. This resurgence indicates a definite trend away from conventional schooling and standardized educational methods, and a return to the traditional tutorial process involving individualized instruction and apprenticeships. Furthermore, the home schooling movement is representative of a desire of parents to personally teach their own children at home in order to restore the traditional Christian values in education and bring unity to the family. These parents, for the most part, are seeking to train their children in God's principles so they will grow up to love and obey God.

In short, families who are home schooling are making the "right choice." In many ways home schooling is a moral and spiritual revival where children are being seriously trained in God's Word to not only believe as Christians but to think and live as Christians. Home schooling is a return to parent-controlled education with an emphasis on learning the basics and achieving academic excellence. The home school movement is led by parents willing to take responsibility and to commit themselves to thoroughly educating their children in spite of the sacrifice. Home schooling is producing skilled and academically talented children with moral fortitude and leadership abilities.

This educational movement, however, has been misunderstood and often condemned by the state and public school officials. These officials are convinced that, as representatives of the state, they are guardians of the children and therefore know what is best for the children. As a result, this attempt to restore effective parent-controlled education continues to meet opposition as home schooling parents are prosecuted under state compulsory attendance and educational neglect laws. This conflict can be narrowed down to one basic issue: to what extent may the state restrict the constitutional right of parents to direct the education of their children? This question is still in the process of being answered, as hundreds of courts and dozens of legislatures debate the subject of home schooling.

I am a home schooling parent and a full-time home schooling attorney. As I have worked to protect home schoolers in the courts and legislatures, I have witnessed firsthand the academic successes and legal struggles of home schoolers. I believe the preservation of the right of parents to teach their children at home is vital to the preservation of freedom in general and especially to parental and religious freedom. As the moral foundations of our nation are steadily eroded by textbooks and valueless training which children are receiving through the public school system, the home school movement is applying biblical principles and absolute truths to each area of academic discipline. Grounding the children in the fundamental truths on which our country was founded is the only way that we, as a nation, will continue to enjoy the liberty that our forefathers secured for us.

In addition, the home schoolers are providing a solution to the educational crisis generated by the incredible failure of the public school system, as the home school children consistently, on the average, academically outperform their public school counterparts. Home school children are becoming more and more in demand, both in universities and in the workplace.

Since home school children have a strong moral and academic foundation, I am convinced they will be the leaders of tomorrow who will be able to fill the vacuum being created by the public schools.

The home school families are accomplishing these goals, family by family. Through the growth of the home school movement, families, which provide the backbone of our nation, are being preserved and strengthened.

In the following pages, I expose the modern academic, moral, and philosophical crisis in the public schools and thoroughly explore the solution of home schooling. The chapters include a historical account of home schooling, with a chapter on famous home schoolers of the past. The success of home schooling, the benefits, and the reasons why more and more parents are turning to home schooling will be presented and documented. I will give a thorough account of how home schoolers are faring in college: both academically and socially. I will explain the discrimination they sometimes face and how they overcome it.

Also I summarize the biblical principles involved, in order to challenge the readers to make the raising of our children in the Lord a priority and to persuade them that the modern public schools are no place to send our children.

For parents wanting to start home schooling, I share seven simple steps.

Furthermore, I describe the conflict taking place between home schoolers and the state's attempt to restrict their freedom. I show how God has sovereignly protected home schoolers time and time again, against great odds. I will share many true stories of miracles God performed on behalf of home schoolers. Some chapters cover encounters with child welfare investigators, illegal home visits by school officials, the myth of teacher qualifications, and identification of the educational elite who are working to abolish parental rights. I discuss the rights of home schoolers in the military and the rights of parents home schooling handicapped children.

In addition, I touch on the constitutional defenses and legislative trends involved in preserving the liberty of parents in this crucial area. Parents need to be familiar with their God-given parental rights. The last few chapters describe some practical tips on how to deal with the media, state legislatures, and Congress with a special section on the miraculous defeat of HR6 by home schoolers in 1994. Also an index to state home schooling organizations is included.

I hope parents will assign this book as required reading for their junior high and high school students. I believe this book will help them appreciate the parents' commitment to home schooling as they consider the advantages of home schooling, its heritage, and the chaos in the public schools. My hope is that our children will want to home school their children and continue from generation to generation. Toward this goal, I have written a special introduction for the home school student.

The future of liberty in our country and the very survival of the family may depend on our commitment to home schooling in both preservation and practice in the coming years. Let us, therefore, make the "right choice" and do all we can to protect this right to teach our children and commit ourselves to training our children in the Lord. A nation and future generations are at stake.

Christopher J. Klicka
January 2000

Introduction

An Introduction for the Home School Student

This book was written not only for parents, but also for home school students. I believe it is vitally important for you, the student at home, to be aware of your heritage as a home schooler and the purpose of home schooling. As you read portions of this book, you will become aware of the extraordinary benefits of home schooling that many youth will never enjoy.

You will begin to see why your parents have chosen this "different" form of education and hopefully will come to appreciate more fully the commitment and sacrifice they have willingly taken upon themselves. When most parents at this time are selfishly seeking their own careers and personal satisfaction, your parents are devoting their time to you. Many other parents send their children to a day care center and then to twelve years at the public school, unaware of the damage they are inflicting on their children emotionally, spiritually, and mentally. By home schooling you, your parents show they care about you and your future.

If you read the first three chapters, you will see what you are "missing" in the public schools. You will see both the blatant problems and the subtle deceptions. God, our Creator and Redeemer, is mocked or ignored in the public schools. Immaturity and selfishness are encouraged. The curriculum teaches that wrong is right, and right is wrong. The academic training in the public schools has brought us shame and is a joke to other industrial nations. By participating in home schooling, you are avoiding wasting a lot of time!

Part Two will show the history and tremendous success of home schooling. You will see renowned scientists, presidents, statesmen, lawyers, businessmen, artists, preachers, educators, and many more men and women from the past who were home schooled. You can take pride in this heritage. I encourage you to study the lives of many of these men and women who lived for the Lord. You will also read about the commands that God has given to your parents to raise you and teach you thoroughly in biblical principles. In order to be obedient to God, they cannot send you to the public schools.

As you read the many advantages of home schooling and the consistent academic success of home school students throughout the nation, you will come to realize that home schooling really works. Many home schooled students have pioneered ahead of you, gaining entrance into colleges and universities throughout the country. This, of course, requires much self-discipline and diligence in your studies now. Without your commitment to learn and your desire to prepare for your future, the benefits of your home schooling will be limited.

The rest of the book will help you see the legal rights and risks of home schooling. You will begin to understand the real legal dangers faced by your parents as they teach you themselves. You will become aware of the forces that are committed to break up your family and take over the minds of the nation's youth. You will see how far we have come in the struggle to restore our rights to be free from excessive governmental intrusions into our families. If you are interested in studying law, you will learn much about the Constitutional protections of our freedoms and the legal strategies used to preserve our rights.

You are participating in an important historical movement. You make up, in many ways, the hope of the future of our nation. You and hundreds of thousands of home schooled students around the nation are being grounded in biblical truth and established in academic excellence. You will be able to lead, while many of those in public schools will be floundering. If you love the Lord with all your heart, soul, and mind, you will be wise and you will be blessed. Hopefully, you will begin to develop a vision of where you are going after you leave home and how you can make a difference for the Lord's Kingdom.

Therefore, count yourself privileged to have this opportunity to be home schooled in this day and age. I encourage you to dedicate yourself, first, to seeking the kingdom of God and, second, to disciplining yourself to diligently study and learn. Jesus tells us "Seek first the Kingdom of God and His righteousness and all these things shall be added unto you" (Matt. 6:33). Make this your life's goal and you won't go wrong. God honors those who honor Him. May God bless you as you serve Him with your whole heart, soul, and mind.

Christopher J. Klicka

1

The Incredible Failure
of Public Education

One of the major reasons why people are turning to home schooling is because the state-run public school system has become both academically and morally bankrupt. Since 1963 public schools have virtually been in a "tailspin" with SAT (Scholastic Aptitude Test) scores consistently declining, academic performance dropping, illiteracy increasing, morality slipping, and violence escalating. The educational empire and virtual monopoly of the public school system is crumbling. The bankrupt philosophy behind the public school "movers and shakers," both past and present, has led the whole massive system into a moral and academic disaster for millions of students.

Home schooling parents are saying, "We can do a better job ourselves," and they are doing just that! In Part Two it will be shown that the educational restoration process of home schooling is taking place in the midst of a national educational crisis.

These next three chapters will describe the poor condition of the public school system in which over 40 million children in the United States are presently being trained.

It is important to note that the academic, moral, and philosophical crisis is clearly affecting all public schools. The following documentation will demonstrate this universal failure of the public schools. It is intellectual dishonesty to believe your local public school is exempt from these destructive influences. The question you must ask yourself is, "How can I prevent my child from becoming one of these statistics of failure?"

The Academic Crisis in Public Education

"Bill Bennett thinks the schools ought to get five more years to get back to where they were in 1963. 'If they're still bad,' he says, 'maybe we should declare educational bankruptcy, give the people their money and let them educate themselves and start their own schools.'"[1]

"We must do better or perish as the nation we know today."[2]

Former Secretary of Education Lauro Cavazos

These two former Secretaries of Education give a startling description of the crisis in education in the public school empire in which over forty million children are being taught. A child who attends public school from kindergarten to twelfth grade will spend about fifteen thousand hours there. Since 1963 the public school system has experienced a steady decline in literacy.

Hopefully, these warnings and the alarming statistics below will convince you that sending your children to the modern public school system involves a tremendous risk. Your child could become one of these statistics of failure.

Public Schools Are Failing in 1982

In 1982, the federal government decided the public school system needed a thorough examination. President Reagan formed the National Commission on Excellence in Education which published its findings in the report, "A Nation at Risk: The Imperative for Education Reform." The report stated:

> The educational foundations of our society are presently being eroded by a rising tide of mediocrity that threatens our very future as a Nation and a people.... If an unfriendly foreign power had attempted to impose on America the mediocre educational performance that exists today, we might well have viewed it as an act of war. As it stands, we have allowed this to happen to ourselves. We have even squandered the gains in student achievement made in the wake of the Sputnik challenge. Moreover, we have dismantled essential support systems which helped make those gains possible. We have, in effect, been committing an act of unthinking, unilateral educational disarmament.[3]

Furthermore, according to the National Commission on Excellence in Education study, public school children in the United States fall short of those in other industrialized countries by nineteen measures of academic achievement. The most significant areas of decline have been in math and reading skills and logic and the ability to draw inferences. One writer commented on the results of the study:

> One of the most shocking findings is that only one-fifth of the seventeen-year-olds in public education can write a persuasive essay; only one-third can solve a mathematical problem requiring several steps; and 13 percent, by the simplest tests of reading, writing and comprehension, are functionally illiterate. [4]

Moreover, the study found that 27 million illiterates were in our nation, most of them churned out by our public school factory. The estimate for functionally illiterate people is at 45 million.

Once the country was alerted, federal and state reforms were begun, and the amount of funds channeled to public education was almost doubled. After all these years, however, no significant change has occurred. The public school system, both academically and morally, is still failing. In fact, it is destroying America's youth.

After "Reforms," Public Schools Are Still Failing in 1988

On April 26, 1988, Secretary of Education William Bennett released a report assessing America's educational progress since 1983, when the National Commission on Excellence in Education declared the United States to be a "nation at risk." The secretary concluded, "We are still at risk."[5]

This 1988 report discussed results from various statistics gathered from the National Assessment of Educational Progress (NAEP). Concerning writing the report states, "The general picture for all students is still no better than it was in 1974." NAEP's evaluation of its most recent writing assessment is that "performance in writing in our schools is, quite simply, bad."[6]

The results in literature surveys conducted by the NAEP found that children in the public schools knew little about the subject. Less than 50 percent of seventeen-year-olds knew that Byron, Keats, and Wordsworth were poets. Less than 17 percent knew that Tocqueville wrote *Democracy in America*.[7]

In math, the report documents that American first and fifth graders were found to be lagging badly behind similar groups of students in Japan, Taiwan, and China.[8] Knowledge of history was particularly discouraging according to the "Education for Democracy Project," which was reviewed in Bennett's report. The Project issued this statement, "Many students are unaware of prominent people and seminal ideas and events that have shaped our past and created our present."[9] Bennett's report reviewed the NAEP's 1986 assessment which exposed the glaring lack of historical knowledge by seventeen-year-olds in the public schools. More than two-thirds of them did not know when the Civil War occurred while three-fourths of them could not say within twenty years when Abraham Lincoln was president.

> More than one-fifth of the students could not identify George Washington as the commander of the colonial forces during the Revolution. Almost one in three did not know Lincoln was the author of the Emancipation Proclamation. And nearly half failed to recognize Patrick

Henry as the man who said "Give me liberty or give me death." ...Half the students did not know the meaning of the Monroe doctrine.... Almost 70 percent did not understand what Jim Crow laws were designed to do.[10]

Ignorance of history will cause disaster for the United States because the public school children will be condemned to repeat the mistakes of the past, once they are in positions of authority.

History Rewritten

One reason the public school students are not learning important history is because the textbook publishers have purposely rewritten history. The American Federation of Teachers, in a study released September 13, 1989, found the most important facts missing out of high school textbooks for public school students. Former AFT President Albert Shanker explained that while public school history textbooks have some good points, "there's a lot that is missing, and what's missing is important.... There is little to convey the ideas, passions, religious views, and values that would give students a greater sense" of America's beginnings.[11] Paul Gagan, one of the historians commissioned to review the textbooks, said the books "fail to make explicit enough the sacrifices, hard thought, hard work, and high cost of producing and sustaining democracy in America."[12]

The study criticized the high school textbooks for providing little to no biographical detail on key leaders. For example, one book summarizes Abraham Lincoln's and George Washington's lives in approximately six lines each. Also, the books "contain little about the impact of religion and religious beliefs in history. Texts rarely discuss the religious ideas shared in communities and the religious convictions that motivated many leaders."[13]

Numerous Historical Errors in the Textbooks

A further problem that plagues history instruction in the public schools: lack of accurate textbooks. For instance, the Texas Board of Education was in the process of adopting new history textbooks when Mel and Norma Gabler announced they had found 231 "definite, unmistakable, undetected errors of fact."[14] Some of the errors in the public school textbooks included claims that the atomic bomb ended the Korean War (instead of World War II) and that only 53,000 rather than 126,000 Americans were killed in World War I. Also the wrong dates were given for numerous events, including the invention of the telegraph, the first moon walk, the bombing of Pearl Harbor, and the assassination of John F. Kennedy[15] Each year the Gablers catch hundreds of errors in textbooks designated to be used in the Texas public schools.

Bias against Free-Market Economics

Meanwhile, the schools are consistently producing graduates with little to no understanding or appreciation of America's successful free-market system. Columnist Warren Brookes recounts the conclusion of Milton Friedman:

> I asked Nobelist economist Milton Friedman why most American students still graduate from high schools not only with low performance but also with such a socialist perspective…His answer was characteristically clear: "Because they are products of a socialist system. How can you expect such a system to inculcate the values of enterprise and competition, when it is based on monopoly state ownership?"[16]

Friedman is absolutely right. America's public education system is a Socialist system in which the government takes money from those who do not send their children to public school (and who still must pay to educate their children privately) and uses that money to endlessly support a bloated educational monopoly. The public schools hate competition, so how can they teach it?

Even general economic knowledge is sorely lacking. In 1989 the Joint Council on Economic Education administered a basic economics test to 8,205 high school juniors and seniors. Overall, the students answered only 40 percent of the questions correctly on a standard multiple choice test. Only 25 percent demonstrated a clear understanding of inflation, only 34 percent could define profits, and only 39 percent could define the Gross National Product.[17]

Geography Crisis

Geography is not much better. A 1988-89 Gallup Poll, commissioned by the National Geographic Society, found that American students ages eighteen to twenty-four came in last among ten countries tested in geography. Half of the American students did not know the Panama Canal cuts sailing time between New York and San Francisco.[18]

Public Schools Are Still Failing in Reading and Writing in 1990

In January 1990, Secretary of Education Lauro Cavazos released the results of two nationwide tests in reading and writing. The Secretary remarked that the reading and writing skills of children in the public school are "dreadfully inadequate," despite a decade of "education reforms."[19] The NAEP report found 58 percent of seventeen-year-olds cannot understand a twelfth-grade academic textbook or comprehend many articles in the *Wall Street Journal, Time,* or *Newsweek.* Ninety-five percent of the seventeen-year-olds do not have the reading skills to understand college-level textbooks. Forty-two percent of thirteen-year-olds and 14 percent of seventeen-year-olds cannot read at the eighth grade level, which is about the level of *People* magazine.[20]

Furthermore, in the area of writing, the NAEP test results demonstrated that 85 percent of fourth graders cannot write a well developed story, and 72 percent of eleventh graders cannot write an adequate, persuasive article. Meanwhile, eighth graders showed a significant, steady decline in the last four years.[21]

Public Schools Are Still Failing Math

Since 1973, national math tests have shown consistently dismal results. The most recent statistics, after years of "reform," were released in the 1990 Nation's Report Card. The results were so poor that Education Secretary Lamar Alexander declared a "math emergency," saying, "None of the states are cutting it. This is an alarm bell that should ring all night in this country."[22] The secretary should have added that this alarm should continue to ring every day and night until Americans wake up.

The math test was given to 126,000 students in grades four, eight, and twelve, and it caused one commentator to remark:

> How bad are eighth graders' math skills? So bad that half are scoring just above the proficiency level expected of fifth-grade students. Even the best students did miserably; at the top-scoring schools, the average was well below grade level.

> Hardly any students have the background to go beyond simple computation; most of these kids can add but they have serious trouble thinking through simple problems.[23]

Only 14 percent of eighth graders scored at the seventh grade level or above, regardless of whether the students were in a wealthy suburban system or a poor school system.[24]

It seems apparent from these math test results and the many other studies described above that the longer children are in public school, the worse they perform academically. In the Nation's Report Card, for example, 72 percent of fourth graders tested at or above the third grade level, and 11 percent scored at or above the fifth grade level. However, only 46 percent of twelfth graders could perform *seventh grade work* and only 5 percent could do pre-calculus work![25]

This has been documented in many other studies, including one study released on February 11, 1992, concerning the failing public schools in the District of Columbia. The study demonstrated that in reading, children were scoring on the average 52nd percentile in the sixth grade, 42nd percentile in ninth grade, and 32nd percentile in the eleventh grade. Similarly, in math, children in sixth grade scored in the 67th percentile, in the ninth grade the 50th percentile, and in the eleventh grade the 42nd percentile.[26] The longer the children are in the public schools, the worse their academic achievements. Does that tell us something about the methods of teaching in the public schools?

On September 30, 1991, the nation's governors released the "National Educational Goals Report" which documented math skills to be even worse. The report found only 15 percent of fourth graders, 18 percent of eighth graders, and 16 percent of twelfth graders reached a "competent" level on a 1990 math survey test.[27]

After Fifteen Years of "Reforms," Public Schools Are Worse

On January 31, 1992, the U.S. Department of Education released a report that showed that the reading skills of nine-year-olds worsened during the 1980s when schools were supposed to be getting better due to massive reforms.[28] The study was based on a review of twenty years of NAEP tests. For example, in 1980, 68 percent of nine-year-olds could summarize the main idea of a passage. By 1990, only 59 percent of nine-year-olds could summarize it.[29] On April 27, 1995, the 1994

Reading Report Card was released by the National Assessment of Educational Progress (NAEP). This report brought more of the same bad news: only 25 percent of fourth graders, only 28 percent of eighth graders and only 34 percent of high school seniors were "proficient" in reading—able to analyze and react to what they read![30]

Meanwhile, a study was released in February 1992, which found U.S. students were below the world average in math and science.[31] The survey of 175,000 students worldwide was funded by the Department of Education, the National Science Foundation, and the Carnegie Foundation. In math, American thirteen-year-olds only averaged 55 percent correct answers, while Taiwan and Korea students averaged 73 percent correct, and the Soviet Union averaged 70 percent correct.[32] In science, American thirteen-year-olds scored on the average 67 percent, while Korea and Taiwan scored 78 percent. Some of the other countries that scored above the United States were Slovenia, France, Spain, Hungary, Italy, Israel, Scotland, and Canada. The survey also showed that longer school years and more money spent on education and teachers did not make a measurable difference on student achievement. Hungary, for example, only requires 177 days of instruction, and yet their students scored with the top five countries in both math and science.[33]

According to the Science Report Card, fewer than half of twelfth grade students could operate at a level of being capable of analyzing scientific procedures and data, and less than 10 percent reached the highest level which is the ability to integrate scientific information.[34]

This pattern is present in nearly all other areas of public education. Public school children are memorizing basic facts: look-say reading, science facts, etc. However, many children cannot think or process those facts into coherent paragraphs. They cannot analyze or integrate the scientific information.

According to a special education report which appeared in *Fortune Magazine,* November 29, 1993, public education is continuing to decline. The article commented on the release of two reports from the Department of Education in November 1993. The 1992 *Reading Report Card* surveyed tests of 140,000 students. The survey demonstrated more than two-thirds of fourth, eighth and twelfth graders are not proficient readers. The second report indicated that only 9 percent of high school seniors can solve math problems that require more than an educated guess!

The Decline Continues Unbroken for Nearly 20 Years

In September of 1999, the results of the National Assessment of Educational Progress (NAEP) in writing was officially released. The report shocked the education establishment. "The average, or typical, American student is not a proficient writer. Instead, students show only partial mastery of the knowledge and skills needed for solid academic performance in writing," said Gary W. Phillips, Acting Commissioner for NCES.

Three-quarters of the 60,000 students (in 35 states), who took part in the test on writing ability did not perform at levels considered proficient for their grade in school. Only 22 percent of 4th graders, 25 percent of 8th graders, and 21 percent of 12 graders were proficient in writing. Only 1 percent of students in all grades were counted as showing advanced proficiency for their grade level. It is significant to note that the longer in school, the worse the writing ability. Only one in five seniors was proficient in writing![35]

How much more evidence will it take for parents to wake up and realize the academic dangers facing their children in the public schools?

Lack of Competency in Public School Teachers

One of the contributing factors to the academic decline in public schools is the training and competency of teachers. For instance, according to a study released in July 1991 by the Carnegie Commission on Science, Technology, and Government, more than 80 percent of math instructors are deficient in math![36] Also the study found more than two-thirds of elementary school science teachers lacking adequate preparation in science.[37]

Rita Kramer documents in her recently released book *Ed School Follies: The Miseducation of America's Teachers,* that most future teachers who are trained in the nation's teacher colleges primarily receive indoctrination in politics rather than learning.[38] She explains, "Almost nowhere did I find teachers of teachers whose emphasis was on the measurable learning of real knowledge."[39] She spent a year touring fifteen teachers' colleges from Columbia to UCLA. Kramer concludes that America's schools of education are appalling. She found that among teacher-educators today, "the goal of schooling is not considered to be instruction, let alone intellectual, but political."

The aim is not to produce individuals capable of effort and mastery, but to make sure everyone gets a passing grade. The school is to be remade into a republic of feelings—as distinct from a republic of learning—where everyone can feel he deserves an A.…

What matters is not to teach any particular subject or skill, not to preserve past accomplishments or stimulate future achievements, but to give everyone that stamp of approval that will make them "feel good about themselves." Self-esteem has replaced understanding as the goal of education.[40]

Kramer discovered teacher colleges do not teach knowledge but rather four years of methods. As a result, they are "producing for the classrooms of America, experts in methods of teaching with nothing to apply those methods to." She says teachers are no longer being taught to teach reading, writing, history, science, math, or literature—rather they are being trained as counselors, psychotherapists, social workers, babysitters, and policemen.[41] The "educators" are not educated in knowledge, nor do they love learning, and, as a result, they cannot instill a desire to learn in their students.

She soundly exposes the new emphasis in teacher training on "multiculturalism" and "globalism." She says such teaching is often nothing more than "a thinly disguised rejection of individualistic democratic values and institutions and of the very idea that underneath all our variety of cultural backgrounds, we Americans have been and should continue to become one nation, one culture."[42]

She blames much of the failure of the public schools on those who teach the teachers.

Next to the media in general and the television in particular, our schools of education are the greatest contributor to the dumbing down of America. They have been transformed into agencies for social change, mandated to achieve equality at all costs, an equality not of opportunity but of outcome. No one can be tested because no one must fail.[43]

Kramer concludes by identifying exactly what the institutions that teach the teachers have become:

The most prestigious of them are largely concerned with academic reputation within the university setting, competing for funds with the professional schools of law and medicine, and cranking out enormous amounts of research, much of it trivial, with much faculty time and energy writing grant proposals and designing model projects. Little of this helps the classroom teacher.

The worst of them are certification mills where the minimally qualified instruct the barely literate in parody of learning. Prospective teachers leave, no more prepared to impart knowledge or inspire learning than when they entered.[44]

This poor training of future teachers is apparent in the low standards set by states for teachers to be certified to teach. In fact, fifteen states use exams supplied by the Educational Testing Service in Princeton, New Jersey and set cut-off scores that range from 35 to 55 percent.[45] In Kentucky, the low qualifying score for math certification is 35 percent. Other examples of cut-off scores are 40 to 45 percent in science, 40 to 55 percent in chemistry, and 40 to 60 percent in physics. These types of low scores would be an F or a D for students who took exams in these subjects. Yet, these same people teach thousands of children throughout the public school system every day.

The students attending teachers' colleges and pursuing education degrees are, on the average, below average on SAT scores. Consistently, these students who are planning to major in education scored below the national average. Such students' average verbal score is 406 (out of a possible 800; national average is 422) and their math score average is 441 (out of a possible 800; national average is 474).[46]

National Endowment for the Humanities Chairman Lynne V. Cheney released a report on November 11, 1991, concerning the failing educational practices in the public schools, including teacher training.[47] Her report concluded that future teachers would be better off spending more time on subject matter and less on "how-to-teach" courses.[48] She identified these failed educational practices as "tyrannical machines" and recommended encouragement of "alternative systems of education" and parents' right to choose.

Public School Teachers Know Something
Most Americans Don't

It is no surprise that many of these public school teachers send their children to private schools. They know firsthand how bad the public schools have become. For example, the deputy mayor of education of Chicago, Lourdes Monteagudo, says she is sending her eldest daughter to a suburban private academy because the quality of education in Chicago public schools is poor. "I could not support her staying in Chicago until the school system can be reformed because the system is bad."[49]

In fact, a U.S. Department of Education study demonstrates that public school teachers are more likely to send their children to a private school than any other group. The study shows that:

> In Albuquerque, 30 percent of the public school teachers send their children to private schools, compared with 14 percent of the population at large. In Houston and Denver, the ratio is 22 to 13; in San Francisco, 28 to 19; in Baltimore, 27 to 16; in Los Angeles, 29 to 17; in Atlanta, 25 to 14; in Austin, 25 to 13. The cities with the highest private school enrollment of public teachers' children were New Orleans (50 percent), Washington, D.C, (40 percent), and Detroit (35 percent).[50]

Could the public school teachers know something about the condition of American public schools that the majority of Americans don't?

The Failure of the Look-Say Method of Reading

Another reason public schools have had difficulty teaching children to read is because the educational elite have abandoned time-tested educational techniques and have replaced them with new and inadequate methods. For instance, the teaching of phonics has been abandoned almost completely throughout the public school system. Educational expert Samuel Blumenfeld discovered this rejection of phonics to be to the detriment of millions of public school children:

> In the course of researching this book, I made a shocking, incredible discovery: that for the last forty years the.... children of America have been taught to read by a method

(look-say) originally conceived and used in the early 1800s to teach the deaf how to read, a (experimental) method which has long since been discarded by the teachers of the deaf themselves as inadequate and outmoded. The result has been widespread reading disability.[51]

The U.S. Department of Education verifies the success of phonics:

Classroom research shows that, on the average, children who are taught phonics get off to a better start in learning to read than children who are not taught phonics.[52]

In 1837 Horace Mann developed a reading system based on the *look and say* method of memorization for the deaf that was applied in the Boston schools. Although it was rejected after six years by the Boston Board of Education, it was adopted later by John Dewey at the University of Chicago and Arthur Gates at Columbia Teachers' College. Now the faulty system has become almost universally used throughout the United States, to the detriment of millions.[53]

The look-say method teaches children to memorize words in context by initially using pictures or clues. According to look-say promoters:

A child taught this method should be able to recognize 349 words by the end of the first grade; 1,094 by the end of the second; 1,216 by the end of the third grade; and 1,554 by the end of fourth grade.[54]

The phonics method, on the other hand, teaches children how to sound out and blend the letters that make up words in a specific sequence. The child is taught simple words first and works up to the complex words. This method basically gives the child the skill and logic to understand virtually any word in the English language. By the end of fourth grade, a child will generally be able to read and understand at least 24,000 words![55]

Rudolf Flesch, author of *Why Johnnie Still Can't Read*, summarized the difference between the two methods of teaching reading as follows:

Learning to read is like learning to drive a car. You take lessons and learn the mechanics and the rules of the road.

After a few weeks you have learned how to drive, how to stop, how to shift gears, how to park, and how to signal. You have also learned to stop at a red light and understand road signs. When you are ready, you take a road test, and if you pass, you can drive. Phonics-first works the same way. The child learns the mechanics of reading, and when he's through, he can read. "Look and say" works differently. The child is taught to read before he has learned the mechanics—the sounds of letters. It is like learning to drive by starting your car and driving ahead.... And the mechanics of driving? You pick those up as you go along.[56]

In spite of a lack of research supporting the look-say method, the public schools applied and continue to apply the faulty method of reading. Can the public schools be trusted to teach the children in America even in the mechanics of learning?

Nose-dives in Student Test Scores

On August 27, 1991, the SAT scores released by the College Board showed a continued decline. In fact, in the past five years, verbal averages dropped eight points to 422 (out of a possible 800) and math went down to 474 (out of 800) for a total of 896 out of a possible 1600.[57] Even the elite students have not avoided the consequences of lower standards in the public schools. Since 1972 the share of students scoring above 600 on the verbal SAT (on a scale of 200 to 800) has dropped from 11 percent to approximately 7 percent.[58] This is quite a drop from the years 1951 to 1961, when the SAT score total average was 972 out of a possible 1600—76 points higher than the average total score today.[59]

One way of solving the SAT "nose-dive" is to "dumb-down" the SAT. Believe it or not, that is exactly what they did in 1995! The College Board "recentered" its test scores. The recentering was accomplished by adding 80 points to individual scores on the verbal section of the SAT and 30 points to scores on the mathematics section. In other words, the SAT scores are going up, but not because students are getting smarter. It is simply because each student gets extra points added to his score in order to play a numbers game to lift the average SAT score from 423 to 500. To cover for the public schools' failures, the academic standards of the Scholastic Aptitude Test is being "dumbed down!"[60]

Cost of Public Education Rises While SAT Scores Decline

During the 1991-92 school year for example, the U.S. Department of Education reported $248.6 billion will go to public elementary and secondary schools. This means that the per-pupil spending in public schools is approximately $6000 per student. Diane Ravitch, former assistant secretary for the Office of Educational Research and Improvement stated: "Spending is up and achievement is down."[61] Even the average teacher salary for public school has risen to its highest ever of $34,814. This is for working nine to ten months out of each year.[62]

Therefore, from 1982 to 1992, per-pupil spending has nearly doubled from approximately $3000 per student to just under $6000 per student. However, the SAT scores declined, causing former U.S. Education Secretary Lamar Alexander to remark: "We in the 80s went from spending $160 billion to $400 billion [on education on all levels] without much improvement in results."[63] In fact, from kindergarten through the twelfth grade, the United States spends more per student than any other country, except Switzerland.[64] More money is obviously not the answer since spending doubled but academic results steadily declined. Americans are over-investing in a failing monopoly of public education.

This is further supported by numerous independent studies[65] and by the results of the NAEP math study described above. The study showed that North Dakota ranked the highest on math scores, but was thirty-second in per-pupil spending, while D.C. ranked second to the last on the math scores, but is the highest in per-pupil spending.[66] Research overwhelmingly demonstrates that there is no correlation between spending levels and educational performance.

Myron Lieberman, in his book *Public Education and Autopsy,* reviewed the real cost of public education.[67] He discovered that per pupil expenditure often estimated between $5000-6000 per student in the country does not factor in other huge expenditures for public education.

Lieberman documents how per pupil expenditure of $5000 to $6000 does not include pensions for teachers, social security, textbooks, administrative costs, school district labor relations, judicial costs, and non-educational agencies performing K-12 services. He also demonstrates that the per pupil expenditure does not include local school district expenditures, such as capital equipment, interest, capital outlay and facilities already paid for. Furthermore, the per pupil expenditure does not include donations and contributions in grant money from private and business sources.

Lastly, it does not include many of the federal expenditures for education, including the Headstart funds, which are approximately $2 billion. Therefore, the per pupil expenditure often estimated for public schools is in reality close to double the cost: $10,000 per pupil expenditure! There is no doubt; home schoolers are saving taxpayers billions of dollars.

As a further indictment of the bureaucratic, government-run public school system, only 60 percent of this money even gets to the classroom. At least 40 percent of the money goes to the bureaucracy. According to Albert Shanker, past president of the American Federation of Teachers (second largest teachers' union):

> One of the major differences between American schools and all others in the world is that we spend half of our money on bureaucracy, whereas the other schools in the world don't spend more than 20 percent.... You know, we have about one teacher to every twenty-five kids in the country *but we have one supervisor for every six teachers.*[68]

In California, 40 percent of the $25 billion a year spent on education goes to layers of bureaucracy at state, county, and local levels.[69] Former Secretary of Labor William Brock emphasized that public education is a failing bureaucracy out of control:

> We have public education at the elementary and secondary level that ranks below every industrial competitor we have in the world.... Education is the most backward single institution in all the U.S. It is not for lack of money. It's lack of intelligence and will and competence. It is bureaucratic inertia that is unbelievable and inexcusable. Between thirty-eight cents and forty-one cents of our education dollar gets to the classroom. That is an act of irrationality.... In the city of New York there are more administrators than there are in all of France. In the state of New York, there are more administrators than there are in all of the European Community, and the E.C. has twelve countries and 320 million people.[70]

Illiteracy out of Control

On December 9, 1993, the U.S. Department of Education released the National Adult's Literacy Survey which was performed by the Education Department's National Center for Educational Statistics. The "Adult Literacy in America" study was set in motion by Congress in 1988. The cost of this study was $14 million and involved lengthy interviews with 26,000 adults.

According to this study, a diploma does not mean a person is functionally literate! More than half of high school graduates were found to have restricted abilities in math and reading.[71]

According to this study, 40 million adults operate in the lowest literacy level. "These adults are unable to locate a single piece of information in a passage, if the passage requires an inference or background information unless the wording in the question is identical and there are no distracting items present." The report goes on to state "they are also unable to perform a single arithmetic operation unless the numbers are already in place and the operation is specified."

In addition some 50 million adults, or 25 percent of the adult population, demonstrate skills in the second lowest literacy level. "This group could not perform tasks beyond, for example, calculating the total cost of a purchase, determining the difference in price between two items, locating an intersection on a street map, or entering background information on a simple form." According to the study in each of these two categories, between 16 percent and 20 percent of the 51 million adults with high school diplomas (or about 10 million people) perform no higher than the lowest level. Between 33 percent and 38 percent perform at the second lowest level, and only 10 percent to 13 percent of adults with high school diplomas reach the two highest levels.[72]

In conclusion, the survey found that 90 million adults in this country do not have the literacy skills they need to function in our increasingly complex economic system. The 90 million figure represents 47 percent of the nation's 191 million adults.[73]

The Business World Is Shocked by the Public School Product

Jonathan Kozol, author of *Illiterate America,* estimates that U.S. corporations alone lose $25 billion a year in lost profits, lower productivity, reduced international competitiveness, and increasing remedial training.

David Kearns, chairman of Xerox Corporation, stated, "Public education has put this country at a terrible disadvantage. The American workforce is running out of qualified people." He, too, estimated the tremendous loss the poor performance of public schools will cost American business:

> The American work force is in grave jeopardy.... If current demographic and economic trends continue, American business will have to hire a million new workers a year who can't read, write or count. Teaching them how, and absorbing the lost productivity while they are learning will cost industry twenty-five billion dollars a year for as long as it takes.... It is a terrible admission, but twenty-five billion dollars a year for remedial training has become a necessary added cost of doing business.[74]

Gerald Greenwald, vice chairman of Chrysler Corporation, expressed his concern with the ill-prepared students coming out of the public schools to work for Chrysler:

> You want to know what Chrysler's most harrowing private nightmare is? Our nightmare will be finding people capable of running that sophisticated plant in the years to come. I'm talking long-term as our current work force retires. We'll have to replace them with the very kids whose performance constitutes that depressing data from Secretary Cavazos. And if they can't read, and if they can't write, and if they can't do simple basic calculations, they're not going to be able to run that billion dollar plant to anywhere near its world class potential....
> Did you know that you and I and all the rest of American industry together spend more money each year teaching remedial math to U.S. workers than all the grade schools, high schools. and colleges in this country combined? Chrysler alone is already spending $120 million a year training our workforce, and at least 10 percent of it goes to teach our employees the Three R's that they should have learned in school.[75]

A few other examples include the Metal Fab Corporation of Florida, which estimated that it could save $1.2 million a year if its employees had been properly trained in reading and math. If this were so, the corporation would avoid tremendous waste in misreading blueprints and inaccurately measuring production materials.[76] In 1990, Citicorp Savings Bank of Illinois had to reject 840 of every 1000 applicants because most of them could not fill out the application form.[77] As the result of frequent American worker mistakes on insurance forms, New York Life began sending its insurance forms to Ireland for processing.[78] One study reported in *USA Today*, found: "High school graduates entering the workforce can't read, write, or reason well, according to 64 percent of human resource officers for major U.S. companies. This poll of officers of twelve hundred of USA's major companies shows that the educational skills of graduates has declined in the last five years."[79]

A Louis Harris and Associates poll was conducted of employers throughout the country. The results demonstrated the low level of preparation for the job market of recently hired high school graduates. Only 33 percent of employers said their recently hired high school graduates were able to read and understand written and oral instructions. Only 25 percent found their high school graduate employees to be capable of doing math functions. Furthermore, only 20 percent of employers found their high school graduate employees to show a sense of dedication to work, and only 19 percent stated that the recent high school graduates were disciplined in their work habits.[80]

In light of the tremendous drain of barely literate public school graduates on American businesses, where will America be in twenty years?

Businesses are worried, but they realize parental involvement in education is the key. According to *Fortune Magazine*,

> In a recent *Fortune* survey on corporate efforts to improve education, 89% of the CEOs that responded said the biggest barrier to reform was the lack of parental involvement. Study after study shows that the #1 indicator of success for a child is a good relationship with a nurturing adult. Yet, says Adam Urbanski, head of a local teacher's union in Rochester, New York, "parents are abandoning

their children too much, not only in our poorest communities, but also in our wealthiest. Left alone these children are rudderless and they are inventing values that are scaring the hell out of us."[81]

As more time passes, big business will begin to realize that home schooling is an answer to its problem because of the maximum parental involvement and tremendous track record.

The Public School Product Not Ready for College

Colleges are finding that they cannot give many of their students a college education because the students from the public schools are not prepared for college and need remedial training.

For example, a survey of state colleges in New Jersey found that 73 percent of all incoming freshman were not proficient in verbal skills, and 69 percent were not proficient in the minimal standards of computation.[82] A survey of five thousand college faculty members by the Carnegie Foundation for the Advancement of Teaching found that between 70 and 80 percent of them agreed that there is "widespread lowering of academic standards and grade inflation at their institutions." The faculty members concluded that the majority of students enrolled in their schools are poorly prepared in the basics, reluctant to work hard, and willing to cheat to get good grades.[83]

The Southern Regional Education Board surveyed 826 campuses in fifteen states and discovered that one-third of all freshmen need remedial training in reading, writing, or math and are not ready to begin regular college courses.[84] It seems that at least one-third of public high school students are suffering from educational malpractice.

According to a Gallup Poll, of 696 college seniors, a quarter of them believed Christopher Columbus first landed in America sometime *after* 1500, and over a third of them believed that the Magna Carta was signed by the Pilgrims on the Mayflower. Many of them confused excerpts of the Communist Manifesto with the U.S. Constitution, and over 40 percent could not determine when the Civil War occurred.[85] Al Shanker, former president of the American Federation of Teachers, honestly summed up the problems in colleges this way:

We have huge numbers of kids in colleges and universities who are basically getting their elementary and high school education and calling it a Bachelor of Arts degree.[86]

Even the colleges are having to "dumb down" their standards in order to admit public high school graduates.

We Must Act Now

Modern public education has been in trouble for over forty years and, instead of getting better, the problems have grown worse. The problems documented above can be personified and summed up in the experience of a recently retired public school teacher.

Edward Rauchut, who for fourteen years was a public high school English teacher, quit his job as a teacher in a high school reputed to be one of the best academic schools in the Midwest (Omaha, Nebraska). In a February 1992 "Comment" in *Teacher Magazine*, he related his experience:

> With very few exceptions, I watched for fourteen years as student after student entered and left high school having learned next to nothing during his or her four year term. And the problem is not in someone else's backyard, not in someone else's school district: It's systemic. *My experience has convinced me that if the purpose of the public schools were to prevent children from acquiring an education, they could not do a better job than they are right now, at this very moment, in classrooms all across the nation.*
>
> Ours is an educational system that labels children "learning-disabled" and then calls for more tax dollars to remediate the problem it created. It is an anti-intellectual, morally bankrupt system whose values-clarification classes and bogus drug and sex education programs contribute to the very addictions they sanctimoniously claim to solve. It is a system that crushes our children's intellectual curiosity and then demands that they learn anyway.[87] (emphasis added)

Public schools are failing, and parents need to realize the danger of sending their children to public school. Home schooling is an alternative that is available to parents if they are seriously committed to having their children educated and taught the traditional, biblical values on which this country is founded. If we do not get our children out of the failing public school system, we will lose a generation of children. As parents, we cannot afford to be apathetic or neutral on the issue of public schools. We must act now!

Notes

1. Suzanne Fields, *Detroit News,* October 6, 1989.
2. Education Department's sixth annual report on public schools, May 3,1989.
3. National Commission on Excellence in Education, "A Nation at Risk: The Imperative for Education Reform" (1982), 20. Reprinted in 129 Congressional Record S 6059, S 6060 (daily ed. May 5, 1983).
4. Emmett, "American Education: The Dead End of 80s," *Personal Computing,* August 1983, 96, 97.
5. William Bennett, "American Education; Making It Work," U.S. Department of Education, April 26, 1988, 1.
6. *Ibid.,* 10. The report continues, "Fewer than one-fourth of all seventeen-year-olds tested in 1984 were able to perform at an "adequate" level on writing tasks considered essential to academic study, business, and professional work. Only about 20 percent of them, when asked to write a letter to their principal requesting permission to take a particular schedule of classes, handled this relatively simple assignment satisfactorily. A similarly small percentage performed adequately when asked to write an imaginative passage describing a hypothetical situation and their reactions to it."
7. *Ibid.,* 12.
8. *Ibid.,* 12.
9. *Ibid.,* 13.
10. *Ibid.,* 13.
11. "History Textbooks Don't Portray Democracy Fully, Study Says," *Education Daily,* Vol. 22, No.178, September 14, 1989, 4. The study was entitled, "Democracy's Half-told Story: What History Textbooks Should Add."
12. *Ibid.*
13. *Ibid.*
14. Debbie Graves, "More Than 200 Errors Prompt Panel to Fail Books," *Austin American-Statesman,* November 8, 1991, A9. Also see "Textbook Errors," *Dallas Morning News,* November 12, 1991.
15. *Ibid.*
16. Warren Brookes, "Socialism: A Failure in Public Education" *Washington Times,* September 25, 1989.
17. "Common Measures," *The American School Board Journal,* October 1989, A18.
18. Samallis, "Quick! Name Togo's Capital," *Time,* July 6, 1990, 53. For further description and commentary on the results see "The Phyllis Schlafly Report," Vol 23, No.11, June, 1990, Alton, IL.
19. Carol Innerst, "U.S. School Children's Reading, Writing Skills Inadequate," *Washington Times,* 10 January 1990, A5.
20. *Ibid.*
21. *Ibid.*
22. Pat Wingert and Barbara Kantrowitz, "A Dismal Report Card," *Newsweek,* June 17, 1991, 64.
23. *Ibid.*
24. *Ibid.,* 65.
25. *Ibid.,* 65. Also see *Educational Leadership,* Vol. 47, No. 3, November 1989, 5. Published by Association for Supervision and Curriculum Development, Alexandria, \Virginia). This documents that 40 percent of seventh and eighth graders have trouble reading and understanding their textbooks. The article shows that many students, however, do well at age nine but get "lost" during the next four years.
26. Matt Neufeld, "D.C. Schools Fail Two-year Checkup," *Washington Times,* February 12, 1992, B3.
27. James W. Brosnan, "Today's Student 20 Years Behind," *Washington Times,* October 1, 1991, AI.
28. Carol Innerst, "Reading Skills Fell Despite Reforms," *Washington Times,* February 1, 1992, AI.
29. *Ibid.*
30. Denise Kelly, "Kid's Scores for Reading in Trouble," *USA Today,* April 28, 1995, AI.

31. Mary Jordan, "Students Test Below Average," *Washington Post*, February 6, 1992, A1.
32. *Ibid.*, A4.
33. *Ibid.*
34. "The 1990 Science Report Card: NAEP's Assessment of Fourth, Eighth and Twelfth Graders," prepared by the Educational Testing Service for the National Center For Education Statistics, Office of Educational Research and Improvement, U.S. Department of Education, released March 1992.
35. Alan Borsuk, "Only 25% Tested Are Proficient in Writing," *Milwaukee Journal*, September 29, 1999, 1.
36. Tim Bovee, "If Johnny Can't Learn, Maybe Teacher Didn't," *Washington Times*, July 16,1991, A1.
37. *Ibid.*
38. Rita Kramer, *Ed School Follies: The Miseducation of America's Teachers* (New York: The Free Press, 1991), 211.
39. *Ibid.*, 209.
40. *Ibid.*, 210.
41. *Ibid.*, 212.
42. *Ibid.*, 211.
43. *Ibid.*, 213.
44. *Ibid.*, 220.
45. "Need for Teachers Keeps Passing Scores Low," *Daily Oklahoman and Times*, July 14, 1990.
46. "SAT Scores Decline," *Teacher Magazine*, November/December 1991, 21.
47. Carol Innerst, "Teachers Urged to Focus on Subjects," *Washington Times*, November 12, 1991.
48. *Ibid.*
49. *"City Educator Shuns Chicago High School,"* *Washington Times*, March 28, 1990.
50. William Jasper, "Not My Kids," *New American*, May 19, 1986, 47. The Department of Education study was done under a contract with the American Enterprise Institute and was based on the Census Bureau's data for twenty-two major cities. The researchers were Doyle and Hartle. Also in November 1993, researchers at the University of Wisconsin Extension in Madison conducted a computer analysis of census data to learn where public school teachers send their children to school. These statistics showed that 49.7 percent of public school teachers in Milwaukee Central City sent their children to private school rather than public school. See Richard P. Jones, *Milwaukee Journal*, November 14, 1993, B1.
51. Samuel Blumenfeld, *The New Illiterates* (Boise, Idaho: Paradigm Co., 1988), 9-10.
52. "Becoming a Nation of Readers," U.S. Department of Education publication, 1989.
53. "Illiteracy: An Incurable Disease or Education Malpractice?" An educational research report published by the U.S. Senate Republican Policy Committee, Senator William Armstrong, chairman. September 13, 1989, 5.
54. *Ibid..*, 3-4.
55. *Ibid..*, 4.
56. *Ibid.*, 1.
57. Carol Innerst, "Taxpayers to Invest $414 billion in Schools," *Washington Times*, August 29, 1991, A5.
58. Robert Samuelson, "School Reform Fraud," *Washington Post*, October 23, 1991.
59. David Barton, *America: To Pray or Not to Pray* (Aledo, TX.: Wallbuilder Press. 1988), 58. Data derived from the College Entrance Exam Board.
60. Carol Innerst, "College Board Halts Slide in SAT Scores," *The Washington Times*, April 1, 1995, A3.
61. Carol Innerst, "Taxpayers to Invest," A5.
62. *Ibid.*
63. Lee Mitgang, "Survival, Not Reform, Is Agenda for Nation's Public Schools," *World*, September 14, 1991, 5.
64. Paul Craig Roberts, "U. S. Overinvesting in Education," *Washington Times*, February 26, 1990, D3.
65. For instance, see *American School Board Journal*, June 1991, 12. This article summarizes two studies (by Urban Policy Research Institute of Ohio and the Utah Taxpayer's Association) which showed that lower-spending school districts tended to have higher student achievement scores.

Their conclusion was that more spending is not necessarily the answer to each state's educational problems.

66. *Newsweek*, June 17, 1991, 65.
67. Myron Lieberman, *Public Education and Autopsy*, (Cambridge, Massachusetts; Harvard University Press, 1994), 119.
68. Albert Shanker, from the text of a speech he delivered to a conference of teachers and school administrators sponsored by the Gates Foundation in Denver, Colorado, September 20-23, 1989.
69. *The Sacramento Union*, October 27, 1990.
70. *Time*, September 23, 1990.
71. Mary Jordan, "90 Million Lack Simple Literacy," *Washington Post*, September 9, 1993, Al.
72. Carol Innerst, "America's Illiteracy Increasing," *Washington Times*, September 13, 1993.
73. "Nearly Half of Adults Read Poorly," *The Milwaukee Sentinel*, September 9, 1993, lA.
74. *Milwaukee Journal*, October 1986 and Warren Brookes, "Why An Education President?" *Washington Post*, April 25, 1988, Dl; also see David T. Kearns, Dennis Doyle, "Winning The Brain Race," Institute for Contemporary Studies, San Francisco, California, 1988.
75. Gerald Greenwald, vice chairman of Chrysler, was speaking to the National Association of Black Automotive Suppliers, *Detroit News*, May 4, 1989.
76. "Businesses Teaching the Three R's to Employees in Effort to Compete," *Wall Street Journal*, May 1, 1988, 29. For more details on the cost of illiteracy to business see Kerry Knobelsdorff, "Corporations Take Aim at High Cost of Worker Illiteracy," *Christian Science Monitor*, March 10, 1988, 12.
77. Patrick Keleher, Jr., "Business Leadership and Education Reform: The Next Frontier," Heritage Lecture No. 257, April 28, 1990, 1.
78. David Gergen, "Sending Companies to School," *U.S. News* and *World Report*, November 6, 1989, 112.
79. "Firms Find Grads Lacking in Basic Skills," *USA Today*, July 16, 1990.
80. "Passing School, Flunking Life," chart appeared in *Washington Times*, January 3, 1992, A3.
81. Nancy Perry, "School Reform", *Fortune*, November 29, 1993.
82. Ronald Nash, *The Closing of the American Heart*, (Dallas, Texas Probe Books, 1990), 46.
83. Carol Innerst, "Students Stumble, Despite Reforms," *Washington Times*, November 11, 1989.
84. "Remedial R's Aid Many Freshman," *Washington Times*, 7 August 1991, A6. Also see "Help Required," *Teacher Magazine*. October 11, 1922, where Virginia's first statewide study of high school students entering college was reported. It found that nearly one in seven freshman in college last year required remedial classes in math, English, or reading. At one Virginia university 79% of the freshman required such remedial courses!
85. The National Endowment for the Humanities commissioned the Gallup Poll of the college students' history and literature knowledge. The test used was designed for seventeen-year-olds by the National Assessment of Educational Progress. The summary of this study appeared in *Washington Times*, April 3, 1990, A1.
86. Albert Shanker, Speech at Gates Foundation conference.
87. Edward Rauchut, "I Quit: A Teacher Refuses to Be Part of a Dysfunctional System," *Teacher Magazine*, February 1992, 26. Rauchut is an associate professor at Bellevue College in Nebraska.

FIRST DAY OF SCHOOL...   ...LAST DAY OF SCHOOL...

2

The Moral Crisis in Public Education:
If It Feels Good, Do It

"I am as sure as I am of Christ's reign that a comprehensive and centralized system of national education, separated from religion, as is now commonly proposed, will prove the most appalling enginery for the propagation of anti-Christian and atheistic unbelief, and of antisocial nihilistic ethics, individual, social and political, which this sin rent world has ever seen." [1]

Dr. A. A. Hodge of Princeton over 100 years ago

Although the academic crisis documented in the previous chapter is extremely damaging to our children, economy, and nation, the moral crisis in the public schools is far more insidious and far more devastating.

When the moral backbone of a nation is removed, a nation will surely collapse. The public schools have abandoned the absolute moral values and biblical morality on which our country was founded and have replaced them with the religion of humanism, where man is the measure of all things and values are determined by the individual. [2] Therefore, when the bankrupt philosophy of humanism is adopted, and biblical morality is removed in the public schools, only chaos will reign.

This chapter will summarize the results of this rejection of absolute moral values beginning with censorship of religion in the curriculum.

Removal from the Public Schools of Virtually All References to Religion

Dr. Paul Vitz conducted a study funded by the National Institute of Education and found an unsettling censorship of nearly all religious events in history textbooks. His study found that in fifth-grade U.S. history textbooks, "the treatment of the past 100 years was so devoid of reference to religion as to give the impression that it ceased to exist in America."[3] After examination of all the most popular public school textbooks for grades one through six, Vitz discovered "religion, traditional family values, and many conservative positions have been reliably excluded from children's textbooks."[4] One of his most disturbing conclusions was that *"none* of the books had a single text reference to a primary religious activity occurring in contemporary American life.... For all intents and purposes, religion is excluded from these basic readers."[5]

In his study of eleventh and twelfth-grade history textbooks, Vitz found:

> For all practical purposes, religion is hardly mentioned as existing in America in the last seventy-five to one hundred years; in particular, none of these books include any serious coverage of conservative Protestantism in this century....There is not one book that recognizes the continuity of the revival and evangelical movements throughout American history since the Colonial Period.... One indication of the biased treatment of religion in American history is the universal tendency to omit from the lists of important historical events almost all dates referring to religion, especially in the last one hundred years.[6]

Vitz also found, after reviewing forty social studies textbooks used in the public schools for grades one through four, that no mention is made even once of "marriage," "wedding," "husband," or "wife." A "family" is commonly defined as "a group of people." Families are routinely depicted without a father, without a mother, or as a couple without children. Marriage is never mentioned as the foundation of the family and yet these books are supposed to be textbooks which introduce the child to an understanding of contemporary American society. There is no doubt, as Vitz explains, that these textbooks clearly foster the notion of family without marriage.[7]

In a conference conducted by the American Family Association in the summer of 1990, Vitz stated that no real change had occurred in the textbooks. He stated, " Although I published my study four years ago, the problem is still there."

Another study was undertaken by Bryce Christensen, associate editor of "Chronicles: A Magazine of American Culture." Christensen found that public school literature books consistently exclude famous works by playwrights, poets, and novelists who wrestle with the meaning of life from a Judeo-Christian standpoint, such as John Bunyan, T. S. Elliot, C. S. Lewis, Walker Percy, John Milton, Flannery O'Connor, and Gerard Manley Hopkins.[8] Instead, stories such as E. E. Cumming's repudiation of the Resurrection in "O Sweet Spontaneous," Ernest Hemingway's nihilism in *The Sun Also Rises,* and Conrad's inaccurate comparison of paganism and Christianity in *Heart of Darkness,* are studied by public school children. In addition, literary attacks on biblical beliefs by humanistic writers such as John Steinbeck, Theodore Drieser, and A. E. Housman are frequently taught.[9] Christensen explains that " American high schools offer relatively few Bible-as-literature classes, but they do offer hundreds of literature-as-Bible classes."[10]

Christensen, as a teacher of literature at the secondary and college levels, saw firsthand the consequences of such irreligious and biased literature classes in the public schools. One student wrote in an essay: "I believed in God until my high school teacher helped me become smarter." This child was raised as a believer. Another student informed Christensen that his high school English teacher had taught him that the only standards he had to live by and be accountable to were those of his own making. Another young girl explained that the literature she studied in public high school made her "feel suicidal."[11]

This censorship of the impact of religion in the history and accomplishments of our nation deceives our children by making them think religion is ineffectual and outmoded. This is intellectually dishonest, in light of the many historical documents and contemporary historians that demonstrate the tremendous significant effect biblical Christianity has had on every aspect of our nation. In fact, our legal and governmental systems were founded on biblical principles. The well-known Alexis de Tocqueville wrote in the 1840s of his observations of visiting this country:

> The religious atmosphere of the country was the first thing that struck me on my arrival in the United States. The longer I stayed in the country, the more conscious I became of the important political consequences resulting from this novel situation....
>
> Religion, which never intervenes directly in the government of American society, should therefore be considered as the first of their political institutions....
>
> I do not know if all Americans have faith in their religion—for who can read the secrets of the heart? But I am sure that they think it necessary to the maintenance of republican institutions. That is not the view of one class or party among the citizens, but of the whole nation; it is found in all the ranks....
>
> For the Americans, the ideas of Christianity and liberty are so completely mingled that it is impossible to get them to conceive of the one without the other. [12]

Our children are being lied to every day in the public schools, and this is causing the very fabric of our nation to unravel before our eyes.

This removal of religion and prayer from the public schools was, in effect, the removal of God and His standards. This is by far the most devastating cause of the decline of public schools. David Barton, in his book *America: To Pray or Not to Pray?*, documents the connection between the removal of prayer from the public schools in 1962 by the U.S. Supreme Court in *Engel v. Vitale* and the drastic decline in the public schools. He demonstrates how, beginning in 1962, SAT scores suddenly plummeted and teen pregnancies, teen sexual diseases, teen suicides, violent crimes among youths, teen alcohol and drug abuse, use of pornography among students, and illiteracy rates abruptly increased 200 to 300 percent.[13] His book is based on statistics gathered from the Departments of Education, Justice, Health and Human Services, Labor, and many other sources and studies. Of course, the removal of prayer in 1962 was followed by a long line of court cases that removed nearly every vestige of the Christian religion from the public schools. Barton's research indicates that when God was removed from the public schools, chaos set in. Is this a coincidence or a connection?

Now let us look further at the practical impact which the removal of absolute moral values has had on the youth who have "graduated" from the public schools, or who are presently in the public schools.

Violence in the Halls of Education

In 1940 the top discipline offenses, according to educators, were talking, chewing gum, making noise, running in the halls, getting out of turn in line, wearing improper clothing, and not putting paper in wastebaskets. However, by 1982 the top discipline offenses had become rape, robbery, assault, burglary, arson, bombings, and murder. This does not even count the prevalence of extortion, drug abuse, abortion, and sexual diseases.

Throughout the public school system in America violence has become a way of life—something the students just have to get used to. I have talked with hundreds of school officials across the nation who are critical of home schooling because it "shelters" the children from the "real" world. They explain that violence, sex, and negative peer pressure are things children need to confront and deal with so that they will be prepared for the world. It is revolting to hear highly educated men excuse such violence and immorality. Yet millions of parents fall for such reasoning and continue to put their children at risk by sending them to the public schools.

The Center for Disease Control and Prevention performed a school-based survey designed to produce a nationally representative sample of risk behaviors among students in grades 9-12. In 1997, the Youth Risk Behavior Survey reported that 18.3 percent of students carried a weapon during the 30 months preceding the survey and 7.4 percent of high school students were threatened or injured with a weapon on school property during the 12 months preceding the survey. Approximately one third (32.9 percent) of students nationwide had property (car, clothing, or books) stolen or deliberately damaged one or more times during the 12 months preceding the survey. Of particular interest is the Center for Disease Control and Prevention finding that during the years of August 1995 to June 1998, there were an average of five multiple homicide victim events per year compared to an average of one multiple homicide victim event per year from 1992 to 1995.

In 1999, the multiple victim shootings increased even more. Let us look at some of the most infamous of these school violence incidents.

In what may prove to be the watershed act of school violence in U.S. history, on April 20, 1999, two Columbine High School students went on a shooting spree through their school in Littleton, Colorado. In their massacre Eric Harris and Dylan Klebold killed 12 students and a teacher (injuring several others) before committing suicide.

At Heritage High School in Conyers, Georgia, 15-year-old T.J Solomon brought a .22 caliber rifle to school and began firing it into a crowd of students on May 20, 1999. Six students were injured and several stated that Solomon was the last person "they thought was capable of such a violent act." If the difference between right and wrong is not taught and children are told "if it feels good, do it," is it any surprise our public schools are creating "time bombs" ready to blow at any moment?

On December 6, 1999, a 13-year-old boy firing a 9mm semiautomatic handgun wounded four classmates at rural Fort Gibson Middle School. Police are not sure of the student's motive. Students were once again shocked, describing the suspect as "nice to everyone," "intelligent," and "an honor student."

On December 14, 1999, a ninth-grader at Archbishop Curley Notre Dame High School in Miami pulled two guns on his biology class and held it hostage for several minutes. A team of teachers was able to talk the boy into releasing the class.

Many American teenagers believe a shooting rampage like the one in Littleton, could happen at their school and think they know students who might be troubled enough to carry one out. According to a new *Washington Post*-ABC News poll of teenagers and parents. . . About a third of the teenagers have heard a student threaten to kill someone, and few of them reported the threats to a teacher or other adult. Four out of 10 say they know students troubled enough to be potential killers. [14]

The National Institute of Education released its "Safe Schools" report. Some of its findings were: 1) the risk of violence to teenagers is greater in public schools than elsewhere; 2) over 5,200 secondary school teachers were physically attacked per month, with at least 1,000 of them seriously injured, requiring medical attention; 3) each month 282,000 secondary school students are physically attacked; 4) about 11 percent of secondary school children, 2.4 million, are victims of robbery or theft in a given month; 5) there are about 2,400 acts of arson in schools each month; and 6) more than one-fourth of all schools are subject to vandalism in any given month.[15]

The U.S. Bureau of Census undertook the National Crime Survey and found that nearly 184,000 students, teachers, and visitors were injured as a result of violent crime in one year.

In May 1991 the National Crime Survey was released by the U.S. Department of Justice's Bureau of Justice Statistics. This study showed that crime on school grounds or in school buildings is becoming more serious. Assaults are much more frequent. Almost three million violent crimes and thefts occur on public school campuses annually. This equals approximately sixteen thousand incidents per school day, or one every six seconds.[16]

The National Crime Survey indicated that about sixty-seven students of every thousand teenagers, or 1.9 million, are victims of a violent crime, including rape, robbery, assault, and murder each year. Annually, approximately 483,764 of these violent crimes against youth occurred at school or on school property. However, the survey estimated that at least a third of all violent crimes are not reported, making the actual figures much higher.[17] The covering up of crime statistics was exposed by one commentator:

> No one really knows the number of teachers who are victims of violence nationwide. Relatively few districts report campus crime; of those that do, say some sources, under reporting or camouflaging school violence is not uncommon. High crime figures make for bad public relations.[18]

The National Educational Goals Panel released a report in October 1991 and announced:

> Substantial numbers of twelfth graders are victims of violent acts at school. During 1990, 25 percent were threatened and 14 percent were injured without a weapon being used, while 13 percent were threatened and 6 percent were injured with weapons. In addition, 42 percent reported their property stolen and 29 percent reported their property vandalized.
>
> Nearly one out of five public school teachers reported being verbally abused by students in the previous month.

Eight percent reported being physically threatened, while 2 percent reported being physically attacked during the previous year.[19]

Some of the violent crimes involve students robbing other students in order to steal their designer sneakers, sunglasses, and athletic jackets. Students who resist are often beaten and sometimes killed.[20] For example, in Chicago, in the middle of winter, a student was robbed of his $61 sneakers and forced to walk home barefoot. In Detroit a child was shot for his $135 goose-down jacket. The rash of assaults over clothing has prompted many schools to adopt dress codes.

As a result of shootings, some students are wearing bulletproof vests to school. One former New York policeman, who now sells bulletproof vests for children, summed it up this way: "The fact that New Yorkers and people throughout the world need protective clothing, especially for children, is a terrible reflection of the collapse of law and order in our society."[21]

In Washington, D.C., drugs and violence were such a problem in one elementary school, that the principal banned regular recess, and children are only allowed to play outside in a pit enclosed by eight-foot concrete walls, or on a small section of the playground monitored by the police.[22]

Many students drop out of school or become truant in order to avoid becoming victims of continual crime and harassment. Parents often are further frustrated when disruptive children, caught with weapons or caught victimizing students, are simply allowed back into the public school system.[23]

Rape is becoming another common problem among juveniles attending public schools. The FBI documents that one out of every five rapes committed throughout the country is committed by a juvenile.[24] In Montgomery County, Maryland, there were four reported rapes on public school grounds during a five-month period.[25] In the same article, D.C. authorities were alarmed with the growing number of sex crimes committed by juveniles.

After a close look at the immoral teachings in the public schools, as outlined in this chapter, it does not take much imagination to discover the real cause behind the rise in sex crimes on and off public school campuses. For over twenty years, the public schools have been drilling into the heads of forty million students, "If it feels good, do it!" and, "There are no moral absolutes—everything is relative."

The Annie E. Casey Foundation and the Center for the Study of Social Policy issued, on March 23, 1992, a report called the "Kids Count Data Book." This study demonstrates that in the last ten years the chances that a juvenile would violently die as the result of murder, suicide, or accident has increased from sixty-two to sixty-nine deaths per 100,000 children ages fifteen to nineteen. The number of children ages ten to fifteen who were required by juvenile courts to be put in juvenile homes as a result of committing crimes, rose from 142 to 156 per 100,000 youth.[26]

After a study was released of thirty-one city and suburban public schools in Illinois which showed 26.5 percent of the suburban school students were victims of theft and 9.7 percent were assaulted, one official drew the "startling" conclusion:

> There are indications that crime in the schools seems to be affecting the learning process. Students are afraid of being victimized. Teachers are afraid of staying late after school. Those things can only detract from the learning process.[27]

I wonder how long it will take the educational elite to realize that runaway crime, which is encouraged by the public schools' valueless curriculum, may actually detract from the learning process!

In California, the most recent data shows that 174,478 crimes took place during the 1988-89 school year, up 5 percent from the previous year. Assaults increased 16 percent to 69,191 and armed assaults rose 25 percent to 1,830. In Philadelphia, the number of school crime incidents jumped from 5,861 crimes in 1987 to 7,505 crimes in 1990. In Dade County Public Schools in Florida, assaults rose 9 percent to 1,889.[28]

On August 30, 1992, the FBI released its twenty-five year study on juvenile violence as part of its annual survey of U.S. crime statistics. The report demonstrates how juvenile crimes have soared "to an unprecedented level" affecting not only "disadvantaged minority youth in urban areas but [is] evident in all races, social classes, and lifestyles" in all parts of the country.[29] The study documents how the white juvenile arrest rate for violent crimes rose 44 percent during the 1980s.[30] Attorney General William Barr, commenting on the alarming rise in juvenile crime, suggested a solution:

It requires strengthening those basic institutions—the family, schools, religious institutions, and community groups-that are responsible for instilling values and creating law-abiding citizens.[31]

It is apparent from the other statistics described throughout this chapter that the public schools are not only failing to instill values in our nation's youth, but they are already reaping the results of their self-centered and valueless curriculum by the uncontrolled crime occurring on their own campuses.

Children are not the only ones victimized in the public school; many teachers are becoming crime statistics. In New York City the United Federation of Teachers reported 2790 crimes committed against teachers during the 1989-90 school year. At least one-third of the crimes against teachers were serious violations including assaults, robberies, and sexual offenses.[32]

Teacher Magazine devoted its cover story to violence against public school teachers, dispelling the myth that violence only occurs in the big city schools. It stated: "Every day, thousands of teachers are attacked or threatened in schools. If you think it happens only in New York, Chicago, or Los Angeles, you're wrong."[33] The article documented how violence is prevalent throughout the country's public schools, citing several examples: In Abilene, Texas, a high school student shot a teacher in the head for giving him a low grade; in Florida's Pinellas County, students killed an assistant high school principal and injured another administrator and teacher; in Goddard, Kansas, a fourteen-year-old boy gunned down two teachers and a junior high school principal; in Fort Worth, Texas, a teacher was stabbed to death and a twelve-year-old student confessed to the crime. The writer concluded, "The list is horrifyingly long."[34]

Crime is running rampant on public school campuses and taxpayers are now forced to pay the tremendous costs for high tech security devices and security guards and dogs. A fifty-state check by the Associated Press found the annual security costs of major school systems, including the following: $60 million on security by New York City public schools; $26 million in Los Angeles; $10.3 million in Dade County, Florida; $10.4 million in Philadelphia; and $2.2 million in Boston. Chicago's school system, the nation's third largest, spends $12.5 million a year on security and has 723 security positions. The check of districts in all fifty states found that the cost of security throughout the nation's public schools is in the hundreds of millions of dollars.[35]

Public schools have "sown the wind" by not teaching absolute moral values and are "reaping the whirlwind" as crime escalates while students do "what feels good." Do you want your child to become a "statistical blip" on next year's national crime survey? He has the same chance if you either send him to your local public school or let him loose to roam the streets at night.

Drugs and Alcohol: The Ultimate Insider Trading

Children in the public schools are using drugs and alcohol in record numbers. In fact, drug abuse has become a national crisis. The National Institute on Drug Abuse has found that this nation's high school students have a greater involvement in illegal drugs than those in any other industrialized nation.[36] With the prevailing philosophy of values clarification in the public schools, it is not surprising that children are turning to drugs. Why not? It feels good.

The Texas Commission on Alcohol and Drug Abuse released the results of a statewide study of drug and alcohol use among secondary school students. According to a sampling of junior high and high school students in thirty-eight school districts in Texas, the most popular substance used is alcohol—76 percent of all secondary students drink. That number jumps to 86.4 percent for high school seniors. Furthermore, 45.7 percent of high school seniors have used marijuana, and 26.3 percent of eighth graders have used inhalants.[37]

In 1988, according to a national study by the National Institute of Drug Abuse, 33.1 percent of high school seniors used marijuana, 7.1 percent used inhalants, 1.2 percent used PCP, 7.9 percent used cocaine, 3.1 percent used crack, .5 percent used heroin, 85.3 percent used alcohol, and 4.7 percent used tranquilizers (not prescribed by a doctor).

Excessive alcohol consumption leads youth to violence and sex, according to Surgeon General Antonio Novello. She drew public attention to the Justice Department statistics which reveal that alcohol consumption is connected with 37 percent of all robberies committed by youth, 27 percent of all murders, 33 percent of all property offenses, and 31 percent of all rapes committed by youth. It also contributes from one-third to two-thirds of all "date rapes."

The Surgeon General was also "shocked" by a survey of high school students which found nearly 20 percent of all girls and 40 percent of all boys thought it was "okay to force sex if a girl was drunk."[38]

On June 30, 1993, Surgeon General Antonia Novello released statistics demonstrating that binge drinking (taking five drinks in a row) is a habit for approximately one half million U.S. teenagers in seventh to twelfth grade. The surveys show that nearly 14 percent of the nation's 8th graders already are binge drinkers. Of the 20.7 million seven to twelfth grade students nationwide, 8 million of the students drank alcohol weekly, drank when upset, drank when bored.[39]

Over one third of the children in public schools are using drugs. Over 80 percent of public high schoolers drink alcohol. Over 40 percent of high school boys think it is not wrong to force sex on a girl who is drunk. Are these children being taught any worthwhile values in the public school? Is the risk of sending our children to such a school system really worth it?

Sex and the Single Student

Virtually all sex education textbooks used in public schools throughout the country teach that any kind of sex is all right; such as premarital sex, adultery, masturbation, homosexuality, and lesbianism. The basic principle children are taught about sex is "do whatever is comfortable for you."

Mel and Norma Gabler have been reviewing hundreds of public school textbooks for years and report these findings in their book, *What Are They Teaching Our Children?*[40] They found many common but disturbing themes throughout the "health" textbooks used in public schools. One widely used ninth and tenth grade textbook states: "In many societies, premarital intercourse is expected and serves a useful role in the selection of a spouse. In such societies, there are seldom negative and psychological consequences."[41] In another textbook, students are told that "research shows that homosexuals can lead lives that are as full and healthy as those of heterosexuals." The statement is under a picture of two men embracing.[42] Masturbation is also commonly taught as an acceptable sexual option.[43]

Another researcher, Dr. Donald Oppenwal, confirms similar findings in his survey of textbooks. One example which typified the textbooks he reviewed, declared, " Although homosexual acts have been traditionally characterized as deviant or unnatural, there is no evidence that they are any more or less so than heterosexual acts."

This same book uses statistics of the frequency of such activity and uses the phrases "experts say" and "most authorities agree" to support homosexuality, masturbation, and premarital intercourse. He found other textbooks that make value-laden statements supporting incest and sadism and masochism.[44]

The Michigan Model, a program being used throughout the state of Michigan, encourages explicit sexual instruction to children starting at age five. One of the exercises requires fifth graders to submit anonymous essays about their sexual experiences. A fifth grade sex education film, "Boy to Man," declares masturbation to be "natural and normal." This film and the film "Girl to Woman," graphically depict male and female genitalia, breast development, and the growth of pubic hair. In other aspects of the program, homosexuality is graphically pictured and described in a favorable light, which is basically nothing more than a form of pornography. The definition of "monogamy" is "one partner at a time."[45] A lawsuit has even been filed against one Michigan school district after seventh through eleventh graders received instruction in "Self-Pleasuring Techniques" that involved techniques in masturbation, and descriptions of sexual fantasies involving group and homosexual acts.[46]

The murder of unborn children is also encouraged in many textbooks. The Gablers document states, "Abortion is discussed as an aspect of birth control in biology and health and homemaking books."[47] Nothing is said in these textbooks of the large amount of research which clearly establishes that life begins at conception and abortion is extermination of a baby's life.

In summary, all teaching of sex in the public school textbooks ignores absolute moral standards. Nearly all forms of sex are acceptable. The children's inhibitions are gradually eroded and their teaching from home and church is soundly and "clinically" rejected.

In addition to the immoral instruction in the textbooks, immoral school policies are also being passed. For instance, the Massachusetts State Board of Education, in October 1991, enacted a policy to encourage local school boards to adopt a condom-distribution policy for high school students.[48] These types of policies are spreading across the public schools in this country, and the effect has been to encourage illicit sexual activity between unwed teens.

Is it healthy for our children to be exposed to such training in the area of sex? Is it fair to them to be forced to learn this sinful and destructive behavior?

Can the Public Schools Teach Moral Values?

The public schools are being run by teachers' unions that annually pass resolutions supporting all types of immorality, including sex before marriage, homosexuality, abortion, and lesbianism. For instance, the National Education Association, the American Federation of Teachers, and the Association for Supervision and Curriculum Development, passed resolutions asking school districts to acknowledge the special needs of homosexual students, provide support services to them, and adopt anti-harassment guidelines.[49]

The Maryland State Teachers' Association supported these resolutions and urged similar protection for gays because "when they hide their feelings…their emotional and sexual development languishes." The teachers' union simply recognizes homosexuality and bisexuality as the natural result of being human since "our capacity to relate emotionally and physically to other human beings is not limited to the other gender…we are diverse sexual creatures."[50] The immoral and deadly lifestyle of homosexuality is readily embraced by the teachers' unions rather than condemned.

These groups promoting immorality in our nation's public schools represent the teachers who are teaching the children! The question comes to mind: Can public school teachers teach moral values in the first place? A quick look at the statistics demonstrates that many teachers are out of touch with traditional Judeo-Christian moral values and even out of touch with the American public.

The majority of public school teachers find nothing wrong with teaching and encouraging sexual immorality. Do you want your children taught by these teachers who hold to the following beliefs?

The Connecticut Mutual Life Insurance Company did a nationwide survey of thousands of members of the public and of leaders in various fields, such as education, law, business, etc. This report is entitled "The Connecticut Mutual Life Report on American Values in the 80s: The Impact of Belief." Concerning abortion, 65 percent of the general public believed abortion to be wrong while only 26 percent of teachers believed it is wrong. In the area of premarital sex, 40 percent of the public believed it is wrong while only 27 percent of the educators found it objectionable. Concerning homosexuality and lesbianism, at least 70 percent of the public opposed it on moral grounds while only 30 percent of the educators opposed it.

Regarding viewing pornographic movies, 68 percent of the public believed it to be morally wrong while 50 percent of the educators found no moral problem with pornography. Seventy-one percent of the public opposed having sex before age sixteen while 54 percent of the educators believed there is nothing wrong with premarital sex. In the area of the mother working, 72 percent of the public believed the mother should not work outside the family while only 46 percent of the educators are morally opposed to mother working.[51]

Teachers Abusing Children

As seen above, a high percentage of public school teachers hold to a moral standard of living that is contrary to God's absolute moral values. As if it is not bad enough that they attempt to convince the students to embrace the same immorality as they themselves hold and the curricula teaches, some of them even practice their immoral beliefs on the students!

For instance, in an issue of *West Education Law Reporter,* a weekly law journal which reports on new education cases, five cases of teacher abuse of students appeared: 1) In Montana a public school teacher was convicted of having sexual intercourse with an eighth grade girl; 2) in Florida, a public school teacher's aide was convicted of lewd assault upon an eight-year-old autistic school boy; 3) in Wisconsin, parents were suing a local public school for not detecting or preventing a teacher's homosexual assault on their son; 4) in Pennsylvania a public school woodshop teacher hit a student on the head with a chisel; and 5) in Ohio a teacher made a student do twenty-five pushups naked.[52]

Teacher abuse of students is widespread as illustrated by the following examples. In Chicago, sexual molestation of students by teachers has become a major problem. In one week, four public school teachers were arrested for sexually abusing children in their classes. One of the teachers was photographed performing homosexual acts on two male high school students. He admitted to the police he was trading sex for grades.[53] In Los Angeles, an elementary public school teacher was sentenced to twelve years in prison for sexually molesting four boys that he taught.[54]

In Montana a public high school teacher was convicted of sexually molesting four students and was sentenced to twenty years in prison. The county attorney said he knows that the teacher sexually molested at least forty-five students over the last three decades and others believe the number may be in the hundreds. Many other public school officials knew he was a homosexual and knew of students who repeatedly accused him of sexual molestation. He was a model employee in every other respect, as he donated part of his salary back to the school and volunteered many hours to paint and fix up the school during the summers.[55]

In Cooke County, Illinois, a high school principal was convicted of trading sex for grades with several male and female students over several years. He would even call students out of class and have sex with them in his office. Some students who needed better grades were required to have sex with him in his office two and three times a week.[56] An elementary school teacher in Maine was found unfit to teach after admitting maintaining a sexual relationship with a psychologically disturbed fifteen-year-old high school student.[57] In Oklahoma, an elementary school teacher committed sexual molestation against three fifth-grade boys. The teacher had a history of molestation from previous teaching jobs.[58]

A public school teacher in Oregon was denied renewal of his teaching certificate for sexual misconduct toward his female students in his sixth-grade class, which included fondling private parts.[59] In Alaska, a public school music teacher regularly had intercourse in his office with a thirteen-year-old student teacher's aide. She became pregnant and had a miscarriage. Two other students in eighth grade also came forward, claiming he sexually abused them, too. He was convicted of a felony and sentenced to five years of prison.[60] Another public school teacher in Maine was convicted of committing unlawful sexual contact with a fifth-grade student.[61] In North Carolina a student was charged with truancy because she refused to go back to school, where a public school principal had sexually assaulted her. This same principal had resigned from another school after sexually assaulting a student there.[62]

In Fairfax, Virginia, a substitute teacher who had been teaching in the public schools for over two months was actually a convicted murderer who had escaped from prison! The principal in one of the public schools in which the murderer did substitute teaching said the killer was "very organized, very thorough," with "very good rapport with students and staff."[63] I guess you can never know who might be teaching your children in the public school!

Even more frustrating is that, even though these teachers are caught abusing students or discovered to be incompetent teachers, they cannot be easily fired. On March 25, 1992, the *Detroit Free Press* released a report entitled "Shielding Bad Teachers." The report was based on four *Free Press* education writers who interviewed more than 300 people and reviewed 611 cases that went to the Michigan Teacher Tenure Commission. The findings are disturbing, to say the least.

The report found:

> Michigan's costly, arduous system for firing bad teachers sometimes encourages school districts to simply transfer problems from one school board to another. Or teachers and school boards make secret deals to pay the teacher to go quietly away, running the risk that the teacher could end up in another district.
>
> It's a system designed to protect teachers from arbitrary and vindictive school boards, unions say.
>
> *But* no *protections are built in for the state's 1.5 million public school students, who can suffer physical, sexual or educational abuse.*[64] (emphasis added)

The report gave many examples of public school teachers who were caught abusing their students, and the school district quietly negotiated a deal which allowed the teacher to transfer to another school district. Also situations were documented in which the school district looked the other way even though evidence continued to mount, in one case for nineteen years, showing that the teacher was making improper sexual advances to students. In 1980 a teacher was found to be sexually fondling students and exposing himself. He appealed, and in 1992 the appeal is still not resolved. It has already cost the Ann Arbor School District $156,437.49 in legal fees. Meanwhile, the teacher has been tried and convicted of murdering his wife with an ax![65]

The report found that a school district spends, on the average, $100,000 or more to fire a teacher, and the process usually takes seven years. As a result, many school districts make secret deals and "pay questionable teachers thousands of dollars and spare them from public exposure of complaints against them."[66] These settlements are rarely disclosed in public. One school board member called it a "conspiracy of silence." Teachers do not inform parents of the abuse of students, physically or educationally.

Even if bad teachers are caught, many times they work out a deal and merely go teach somewhere else. This is frightening.

This list is only the "tip of the iceberg" of the reported incidences of public school teachers who abuse their students. Also many of these incidences go unreported due to the shame that the children bear or the fear of teacher retaliation. A heavily documented review of many cases of teachers abusing public school students appeared in *West Education Law Reporter.* The survey concluded that the number of cases involving teachers improperly touching students is steadily on the rise. The author of this survey states:

> One can conclude that the problem is far more prevalent than the data reported. There is no way of knowing how many teachers resign each year when their dismissal is threatened for sexual abuse of students.[67]

Knowing the immoral philosophy embraced by many public school teachers today and the immorality which is encouraged in the public school curricula, we should not be at all surprised that so many public school teachers would practice this immorality on the students.

Of course, there are many public school teachers and administrators who would never commit such acts against the students. However, the immorality is still being consistently taught through the curricula. Either way, the children are the ones who suffer as a result of this "anything goes" philosophy. How well do you know the teachers and administrators in your local public school? Could they be practicing the immorality they preach in their public schools?

Sexual Promiscuity Among Teens: Reaping What We Sow

Has this immoral instruction in the public schools had any effect on our youth? The answer is yes, and the effects are devastating.

In 1990 researchers at the Guttmacher Institute in New York and the Urban Institute in Washington analyzed federally funded surveys of teens. This is what they discovered concerning the sexual activity among unwed teens according to age group: 1) among fifteen-year-olds,

33 percent of the boys and 27 percent of the girls were sexually active; 2) among sixteen-year-olds, 50 percent of the boys and 34 percent of the girls have had sex; 3) among seventeen-year-olds, 66 percent of the boys and 50 percent of the girls had engaged in sex; 4) among eighteen-year-olds, 72 percent of boys and 69 percent of girls were sexually experienced; 5) among nineteen-year-olds, 86 percent of boys and 75 percent of girls were sexually active.[68]

For nineteen-year-olds this means that three out of four unmarried women and five out of six unmarried men were sexually experienced! Many had been having sex for several years with several different partners. No wonder the cases of sexual diseases and AIDS are so high among teenagers.

The survey also showed that many students are under constant intense pressure to join the sexually promiscuous crowd.

The National Center for Health Statistics supports these findings and released comparisons between sexually active teens in 1980 and in 1988. For instance, in 1980, 17 percent of fifteen-year-old girls were sexually experienced, compared with 26 percent in 1988; and in 1980, 36 percent of seventeen-year-old girls were sexually active, compared to 51 percent in 1988.[69]

In some public school systems the statistics are even worse. In D.C., for example, the U.S. Centers for Disease Control reports that 89.5 percent of tenth grade boys and 63.9 percent of tenth grade girls had engaged in intercourse. Of these students, 66.6 percent of the boys and 17.9 percent of the girls had four or more sex partners.[70]

Not surprising, sexual diseases are rampant among teens in D.C. Among fifteen to nineteen-year-olds in 1990, there were 4,135 cases of gonorrhea and 138 cases of syphilis. These diseases can cause birth defects and several other damaging side effects. Based on 11,481 blood samples taken of teens treated in D.C. hospitals, 1 out of 77 teens is infected with AIDS.[71]

In addition, one out of every six babies in the nation in 1981 was born out of wedlock, and among unmarried teens there are three live births for every five abortions.[72] The public schools, which advocate abortion as a form of birth control, are training our children to kill innocent babies.

The consequences of this immoral teaching advanced in the public schools is even more devastating to future generations. The Alan Guttmacher Institute released a survey in April 1993 that found that one out of five Americans now suffers from a sexual disease! In other words, 56 million people in the United States are infected with a sexually transmitted disease, and more than half of those sufferers have sexual diseases that are incurable.

The study estimated that one hundred fifty thousand women every year become infertile as a result of sexual diseases. The report warns "if current trends continue, 1/2 of all women who were 15 in 1970 will have had pelvic inflammatory disease, which causes infertility, by the year 2000."[73] It is hard to believe we have come this far!

The public schools' lack of moral instruction and the public school teachers' lack of values are devastating our youth and destroying traditional families. This gradual destruction of our families will inevitably lead to the destruction of our nation.

Humanism: One of the New Religions in Public School

With all the censorship of religion and traditional values from the public schools, a vacuum has been created. This "values vacuum" is being filled by two other value systems: the religion of humanism and the religion of the New Age occultism.

The religion of humanism is quite easy to identify. Humanism simply means that man, rather than God, is the measure of all things. Humanism does not recognize God or His absolute moral values, but instead asserts that each person can set his own values and control his own destiny. Professor Donald Oppewal, who participated in the study of public school textbooks used throughout the public school system, along with Paul Vitz, summarized the basic tenets of humanism as described in *Humanist Manifesto* I and *Humanist Manifesto* II:

1. Humanism holds to an evolutionary explanation of both human rights and development.
2. Humanism believes that the scientific method is applicable to all areas of human concern and is the only means of determining truth.
3. Humanism affirms cultural relativism, the belief that values are grounded only in a given culture and have no transcultural normativity. [In the words of *Humanist Manifesto* II, third thesis, it says, "We affirm that moral values derive their source from human experience. Ethics is autonomous and situational, needing no theological or ideological sanction."]

4. Humanism affirms an anthropocentric and naturalistic view of life [i.e., there is no supernatural God and man has no soul].

5. Humanism affirms an ethic of individualism, one in which personal values take precedence over community standards for behavior. [*Humanist Manifesto* II, sixth and seventh theses, advocates any type of sexual behavior between consenting adults, euthanasia, and the right to suicide.]

6. Humanism affirms cultural determinism, the belief that values in a given society are largely determined by environmental circumstances.

7. Humanism believes in the innate goodness and perfectibility of man.[74]

Professor Oppewal then proceeds to demonstrate, through numerous examples of textbooks, how these concepts of humanism pervade public school textbooks.

Of course, as these humanistic concepts completely saturate modern public school textbooks in every subject, God and biblical values have been systematically replaced with the values of humanism. One example of humanism in the public school textbooks is readily apparent in the widespread teaching of "values clarification." This instruction teaches children that everything is relative, and they alone can determine what is right and wrong for themselves. The Gablers document this type of education throughout public school textbooks in their chapter entitled "Children Adrift." The Gablers state: "The students' 'convictions' are determined on the basis of situation ethics and peer pressure."[75]

The "Problem Solving with People" (PSP) program is a typical example of values clarification taught in the public schools. G. Wes Rowlader, head of a parent group trying to expose this destructive instruction, described PSP as it is used in Michigan:

Five- to thirteen-year-olds are coerced to use child intuition to solve problems dealing with divorce, death, drugs, etc.—all by voting for the "desired" solution. The teacher, by Model standards, is not to influence a solution. PSP is a decision-making technique for children that determines "right" from a majority vote of peers using feelings to determine solutions. One major problem with PSP—no answer is wrong. This undermines parental authority by implying that all responses are valid.[76]

Also included in this "values clarification" methodology is "death education."[77] Death education teaches death apart from God and ignores the concepts of heaven and hell. Suicide is often discussed and studied as an option that is not necessarily wrong. Studies are coming out that "death education" may be linked to the runaway suicide rate among teens in America. In 1990, an eight-year-old child in the public schools committed suicide. He killed himself the day after he was forced to watch a movie about a boy who tries to kill himself.[78] The movie was part of the Michigan Model and was shown in the context of an exploration of feelings, including a list of twenty-five bad feelings that the children are supposed to "get in touch with." Of course, the class is taught "free of values." This boy had an I.Q. of 130, was obedient, and was very active in sports and the arts. He should not even have been thinking of suicide. Dr. William Coulson, who investigated the incident, concluded:

> His parents did not know the movie was shown. The teachers did not prescreen the movie. But I have since looked at the curriculum and been told by the director of the elementary education in that district that the movie was shown as part of a unit on feelings and self-esteem. And I think it's not going to be the last such tragedy that emerges from this model.[79]

In fact, 400,000 adolescents attempt suicide each year. This suicide rate among fifteen- to nineteen-year-olds rose 44 percent from 1970 to 1984, compared to an increase of only 2.6 percent for the nation as a whole.[80]

Another example of humanism is the teaching of evolution. Evolution is a scientific theory which requires the child to develop "blind faith" in science since the formation of the world cannot be observed. Evolution systematically destroys the concept of God and reduces man to an animal. The biblical truth that man is made in the image of God, has worth in Him, and is given by Him unchanging rules by which to live, is replaced with man being nothing more than an expendable animal with no standard to follow. Evolution destroys the values of life and encourages extermination of the unborn. Infamous Communist leaders such as Lenin, Stalin, and Mao Tse-tung, who were responsible for the massacre of millions of their countrymen, were all dedicated evolutionists who believed that men were animals and had no individual worth beyond the "good of the state." With the role of God scientifically explained away by evolution, which is taught as a "fact," children begin to accept the humanistic notion that God is a fable and develop a disrespect for human life.

On the other hand, Scientific Creationism, which scientifically exposes evolution as false and defends the truth that this world was created, is forbidden to be taught in public school.[81] The home schooler may be encouraged to know, however, that the Institute of Creation Research has developed scores of heavily documented textbooks and teaching aids for students, that expose the myth of evolution and defend biblical creation.[82]

The teaching of sex education and health courses, which are described earlier in this chapter, directly follow the tenets of humanism by blessing any and all forms of deviant sexual practices. The removal of God and His standards in every subject reflects the humanistic belief that God does not exist and man is autonomous and innately good. The evidence is overwhelming that the religion of humanism has pervaded the public schools in every subject. Sadly, forty million children in America are captive audiences to these lies.

New Age and Occult Influence

The New Age religion has also seeped into the public schools but it is a little more difficult to identify.

Examples of the New Age practices are Progressive Relaxation, Guided Imagery, Deep Breathing, and Meditation. Progressive Relaxation is the serial relaxation of the major muscles of the body by direction of the teacher, which involves a process of first tensing and then relaxing major muscle groups in a certain order. Often this practice is accompanied by soothing music. I have seen several hypnotists at work, and this technique is always used.

One book utilized as part of the deceptively named "Family Life Education" program, adopted in Virginia, instructs the student:

> Let's take a moment to use our imagination. Relax and get comfortable with both feet on the floor. Let your shoulders

relax, and let your arms and hands rest in a comfortable way. Let your head relax. You can let it fall forward a little if that helps you relax. Let your whole body work as if it were in slow motion. Close your eyes, but not tight. Take slow deep breaths. When you let your breath out, you might feel as if you could sink into your chair.[83]

These "mind control" practices are commonly used throughout the public school system.

Guided Imagery involves the use of images communicated to the student by the teacher while the student is in a relaxed state or a hypnotic state. In the program described above in Virginia, a imaginary figure named "Pumsy" is created for the students. This figure is "someone" for the child to go to for comfort, friendship, counsel, etc. In Session 3 and 12 of the curriculum it says:

You may return to spend time with Friend and Pumsy any time you wish by creating your own Mind Picture whenever you like [Session Twenty-four]. You can come visit your clear pond any time you like. It's as near to you as your own mind, as close to you as your own heart. No one can stop you from going there.[84]

...After you have decided what to do with your magic cup, you can start wiggling your fingers, and then when you're ready you can move your arms around a little bit. Next, you can begin to open your eyes and say with me in a clear, strong voice... 'I am me, and I am enough. I am me, and I am enough. I am me, and I am enough.' [85]

Developing this imaginary person in the student's mind is supposed to build the child's self-esteem. However, it clearly has its roots in the New Age and occult practice of "channeling" and communicating with the spirit world. It also replaces God and leads the children to trust either totally in themselves or develops a dependency on this imaginary person. This can and has led children right into the occult.

A similar program is currently being used in the Michigan public schools. In this program children are encouraged by their teacher or counselors to picture something in their minds like a clear, blue pond, which is safe and warm. Often the exercise ends after fifty minutes of sitting in a darkened classroom with music tapes playing in the background. Children are then told to open their eyes and repeat: "I can choose how I feel. I can choose how I feel."

The Deep Breathing practice commonly used in public schools encourages students to breathe regularly, being aware of the diaphragm and the lungs. Usually, students are directed to use imagery during these breathing exercises.

Meditation involves repeated exposure of students to words or sounds, directed by the teacher, in order to create a relaxed or altered mental state.

Let me give you two more examples of curricula that apply these New Age techniques. First, the *Impressions* readers are frequently used in the public schools for kindergarten through sixth grades in language arts classes. Harcourt Brace Jovanovich publishes this series through its subsidiary, Holt Rinehart and Winston. It is presently being used in twelve hundred public schools in thirty-four states.[86]

Portions of this series are responsible for thousands of children learning how to create and cast spells to effect change, how to do circle chanting within a witchcraft or magic paradigm, and how to encounter creatures who lust for the flesh of children. One example is the story of "Zini and the Witches," in which Zini discovers the bones and bodies of murdered victims and realizes that his wife is a witch. The chief witch finds out that Zini knows and will only spare him if he brings her the hearts of his mother and sister.[87]

In the *Impressions* curricula, children are also forced to read anthologies that describe violent ritual practices, including a poem by Jack Pretlutsy called "The Sorceress." This poem describes the sorceress casting spells, entering trances, and sending souls to hell, where the demons rejoice with the arrival of each additional soul.[88]

Children are also required to role play as witches, and the program applies the symbols, belief systems, and practices of witchcraft and neo-paganism.

Many experts agree that the *Impressions* curricula is saturated with the occult and New Age. Former Wiccan high priest and witch, William Schnoebelen, states that *Impressions* exercises "promote the practices, rituals, and belief systems of witchcraft and neo-paganism." Dr. Carl Raschke, an internationally recognized expert on religion, finds the *Impressions* program to be a "thorough and consistent means of advocacy" and "religious indoctrination" for "witchcraft,

Wicca, and neo-paganism."[89] Thomas C. Jensen, an investigator of occult crimes, states *Impressions* teaches rituals and symbols used in Wicca, Satanism, and Santeria which is a blend of Catholicism and the Aruba religion.[90]

Children in public schools have been reliably prohibited from learning any kind of aspect of Christianity (except to degrade it), in the name of avoiding the "establishment of religion." However, the empty moral vacuum has been filled to the brim with warped occult practices and the tenets of humanism. If that is not an "establishment of religion," I do not know what is!

Another curriculum designed to promote the elusive "self-esteem" of the children is "Developing an Understanding of Self and Others" (DUSO). This program uses forty-two guided imagery exercises. The children are told to lie on their backs or put their heads down on the table while the teacher plays a tape which leads them through various relaxing exercises. The children are introduced to the secret world of " Aquatron" which is inside each of them. Then the children are told to picture "Duso the Dolphin" and "Sophie the Sea Otter," who will help them work through the problems which they may be facing.[91] This is very similar to the other types of programs being used in public schools but are given a different name.

One more example of blatant New Age teaching is in the S.O.A.R. curriculum, which has been used in the Los Angeles public schools among others. One exercise in this program states:

> This lesson introduces school children to their psychic workshop and two spirit guides who will help them make decisions. Teacher says, "How would you like a special or custom-built house to go to anytime you want to, with anything you want in it? You could have any person you want come and visit you. It wouldn't matter if he or she was dead or alive, real or imaginary. After today, you will always have this special place and special way of being with anyone you want. Be sure to use them....
>
> "First, you will see your male helper. He is behind the sliding door in your elevator. Use the control panel on the arm of your chair to make the door of your elevator open.... Now look at your male helper.... He is now real and alive, and he comes into your workshop. This is your

male helper. Say 'hello' and ask him his name. Show him around your workshop and tell him how glad you are that he is there with you."[92]

Programs such as these are becoming more and more prevalent throughout the public school system. The *Impressions* program, the Michigan Model, and some of the others, are currently under litigation for violating the establishment clause. Other New Age programs in the public schools have been moderated after concerned citizens have objected. However, the same practices have only appeared elsewhere in the curriculum. The curriculum publishers and creators of the programs, in fact, have developed training seminars for teachers to instruct them on how to counter parental objection to these insidious programs. In spite of minimal public outrage, these types of programs continue to inflict untold damage on our youth.

The Solution

The public schools are in deep trouble. Since the public school system is responsible for teaching over forty million students in this country, its influence and immoral instruction is being felt throughout our society. The moral crisis in the public schools is acute, and we as a nation are already reaping the consequences in the rise of violence, crime, sexual diseases, divorce, selfishness, various forms of paganism and the occult, and a growing rejection of God's absolute moral standards. In the name of "neutrality," the public schools are steadily and many times subtly assaulting the traditional family and destroying the minds of our youth.

We, as adults, should do all we can to "clean up" the public schools, but can we afford to lose our children in the process? The public schools' curriculum and atmosphere clearly oppose God and His laws. Christians armed with this information can no longer be held guiltless in regard to their children's education. By God's grace, in America, there is an alternative that is working and is allowing children to be raised in the "nurture and admonition of the Lord." That solution is the subject of this book: home schooling.

Notes

1. Archibald A. Hodge, *Popular Lectures on Theological Themes* (Philadelphia: Presbyterian Board of Publications, 1887), 283-84.
2. Appendix A in this book gives the reader a brief comparison between humanistic education and Christian education, as summarized by scholar and theologian, R. J. Rushdoony.

3. Paul C. Vitz, "Religion and Traditional Values in the Public School Textbooks: An Empirical Study," "Report of NIE Grant: Equity in Values Education: Do the Values Education Aspects of Public School Curricula Deal Fairly with Diverse Belief Systems?" (NIE 6-84-0012; Project No. 2-0099).
4. *Ibid.*
5. *Ibid.*
6. Paul Vitz, *Censorship: Evidence of Bias in Our Children's Textbooks* (Ann Arbor, Mich.: Servant Books, 1986), 56-57.
7. *Ibid.*, 37-38.
8. *Ibid.* Appendix B, 122-23.
9. *Ibid.*, 123.
10. *Ibid.*, 126.
11. *Ibid.*, 122-23.
12. Alexis de Tocqueville, *Democracy in America*, J. P. Mayer, ed., trans. G. Lawrence (Garden City, NY: Doubleday, 1969), 290-300.
13. David Barton, *America: To Pray or Not to Pray*, (Aledo, TX.: Wallbuilder Press, 1988).
14. Hanna Rosin and Claudia Deane, "Teens Nationwide See Signs of Potential School Violence," *Washington Post*, April 27, 1999, A1.
15. "Safe Schools," a report released in 1978 by the National Center of Education.
16. "Annual Study Shows 3 Million Crimes on School Campuses," National School Safety Center News Service, Pepperdine University, California, October 1991, Dr. Ronald Stephens, Director. This newsletter provides a review of the "National Crime Survey of 1991."
17. Ibid.
18. Denise Foley, "Danger: School Zone," *Teacher Magazine*, May 1990, 58.
19. "National Goals Report; Building a Nation of Learners," released in October 1991 by the National Educational Goals Panel. Also see excerpts printed in *Education Week*, October 2, 1991, 18.
20. "Youths Merely Robbed of Clothes Considered Lucky, By Comparison," *Washington Times*, April16, 1990, A3.
21. *Education Week*, Vol. X, No. 3, September 19, 1990.
22. "Crime Curtails School Recess," *USA Today*, February 20, 1990.
23. Carol Innerst, "Pistol-Packing Kids Put School on Alert," *Washington Times*, August 23, 1992, A16.
24. Kristan Metzler, "Two Charged in Girl's Rape-All Age Eleven," Washington Times, 21 March 1992, A9.
25. *Ibid.*
26. Spencer Rich, "Report Card on Youth: Downward Trends Dominate," *Washington Post*, March 24, 1992, A17.
27. George Papajon, "School Crime Study Deflates Some Myths," *Chicago Tribune,* March 22, 1991, DuPage Section.
28. Annual Study Shows 3 Million Crimes on School Campuses," National School Safety Center News Service, Pepperdine University, California, October 1991, Dr. Ronald Stephens, Director.
29. Andrew Glass, "Juvenile Crime Soaring, FBI Reports," *The Sunday Oregonian*, August 30, 1992, A17 .
30. *Ibid.*
31. Jerry Seper, "Violent Crime Hits Record Levels, *Washington Times*, August 30, 1992, A15.
32. *Ibid.*, 7.
33. Denise Foley, "Danger: School Zone," cover page.
34. *Ibid.*, 57-58. In Detroit alone, attacks on public school teachers increased 900 percent in five years. Seventy public school employees were victims of reported physical assaults by students during the 1989-90 school year. See " Attacks on Teachers Skyrocket," *Detroit News*, June 20, 1991, 1A, 12A.
35. "Security Becomes Priority in Schools Across Nation," *Washington Times*, August 29, 1989.
36. "America on Drugs," *U.S. News and World Report*, July 28, 1986, 48.
37. Barbara Linkin, "High Drug Use Found in Schools," *The Daily Texan*, September 1, 1988, results released by the Texas Commission on Alcohol and Drug Abuse.

38. Paul Taylor, "Surgeon General links Teen Drinking to Crime, Injuries, Unsafe Sex," *Washington Post*, April 14, 992, A12.
39. Dr. Antonia Novello, "Beer: Teens Drug of Choice," *USA Today*, June 30, 1993, A11.
40. Mel and Norma Gabler, *What Are They Teaching Our Children?* (Wheaton, Ill.: Victor Books, 1986). Their latest research can be obtained by contacting them at P.O. Box 7518, Longview, Texas, 75607.
41. *Ibid.*, 66.
42. *Ibid.*, 66-67.
43. *Ibid.*
44. Paul Vitz, Censorship, Appendix A, 108-110. This Appendix reprints the research findings of Dr. Oppenwal, Professor of Education of Calvin College, Grand Rapids, Michigan.
45. G. Wes Rowlader, "Michigan Model," *Jackson Citizen Patriot*, March 14, 1991, A14.
46. Action newsletter, published by the Rutherford Institute of Charlottesville, Virginia, June/July 1990, 4.
47. Mel and Norma Gabler, *"What Are They Teaching Our Children?"* 69.
48. *Teacher Magazine*, November/December 1991, 21.
49. "Helping Students Understand and Accept Sexual Diversity," MSTA Action line, February 1992, 8, published by the Maryland State Teachers' Association.
50. *Ibid.*
51. "The Connecticut Mutual life Report on American Values in the 80s: The Impact of Belief," conducted by Research and Forecasts, Inc., New York, 1981, commissioned by Connecticut Mutual life Insurance Co., 219-25.
52. West' s Education Law Report, June 11, 1987.
53. William Jasper, *The New American*, March 24, 1986, 36.
54. *Ibid.*
55. "Protected: Town Kept Teacher's Dirty Secret," *The Milwaukee Journal*, November 25, 1990, A10.
56. *People v. Moffat*, 560 N.E. 352 (1990).
57. *Elvin v. City of Waterville*, 573 A2d. 381 (1990).
58. *D. T. v. Independent School District No.16 of Pawnee County*, 894 F.2d. 1178 (1980).
59. *Reguero v. Teacher Standards Commission*, 789 P.2d. 11 (Or. App. 1990).
60. *Osterback v. State of Alaska*, 789 P.2d. 1037 (Alaska App. 1990).
61. *Martin v. City of Biddefard*, 568 A.2d. 1103 (Me. 1990).
62. *Medlin v. Bass*, 386 S.E.2d 80 (1989).
63. Maria Koklanaris, "Escaped Killer Nabbed Teaching at Fairfax School," *Washington Times*, May 16, 1992.
64. "Shielding Bad Teachers, A Special Three Part Report," *Detroit Free Press*, March 15, 1992, lA.
65. *lbid.*, 10A.
66. *lbid.*
67. Terri Regotti, "Negligent Hiring and Retaining of Sexually Abusive Teachers," 73 ed., *West Education Law Reporter* 333, May 21, 1992.
68. Kim Painter, "Fewer Kids Save Sex for Adulthood," *USA Today*, March 5, 1991, ID-2D.
69. Barbara Vobejda, "Teen Birthrates Reach Highs Last Seen in 70's," *Washington Post*, January 19, 1992, A3.
70. Amy Goldstein, "D.C. Teens' High Sex Rate Risks Pregnancy, Disease," *Washington Post*, November 24, 1991, A1, A11.
71. *lbid.*, A11.
72. *Time*, November 9, 1981, 67.
73. Phyllis Schlafly, "Data that Refutes Safe Sex Slogans," *Washington Times*, April 17, 1993.
74. Paul Vitz, *Censorship*, 101-104.
75. Mel and Norma Gabler, *What Are They Teaching Our Children?*, 105. See entire chapter, 98-114.
76. G. Wes Rowlader, "Michigan Model," A14.
77. *lbid.*, 90.
78. American Family Association Newsletter, September 1990, Jackson, Michigan.
79. *lbid.*

80. *U.S. News and World Report,* November 12, 1984 and Herbert Kohl, "What Teenage Suicide Means," *Nation,* May 9, 1987, 603.
81. *Ibid.,*131-48.
82. Institute of Creation Research, P.O. Box 2667, El Cajon, CA 92021. If you contact them at his address, they will be happy to send you a catalogue of their materials and put your on their newsletter list.
83. Jill Anderson, *Pumsy in Pursuit of Excellence* (Timberline Press, 1987, Eugene, Oregon). These "mind picture" sessions occur in Sessions 3, 6, 9, 12, 15, 18, 21, and 24.
84. *Ibid.,* Session 24 and 3.
85. *Ibid.,* Session 12, 148.
86. Kimberly Parker, "New Age in the Public Schools," *The Teaching Home,* April/May 1991, 77.
87. *Ibid.*
88. *Ibid.,* 79.
89. *Journal of the American Family Association,* March 1992, Tupelo, MS, 13.
90. "New Age in the Public Schools," *The Teaching Home,* April/May 1991, 77.
91. *Ibid.*
92. *Ibid.*

3

The Philosophical Crisis in Public Education:

The Battle for Our Children's Minds

"The public school has become the established church of secular society."[1]

Ivan Illish

Why do I take time to write a chapter on the modern philosophy behind education? Does the philosophy behind our educational system have any relevance to our present crisis in education? This chapter will show how the philosophy behind public schools has everything to do with why our public school system is in chaos today. I will demonstrate how the philosophical basis of the public schools and the agenda of those who created it have brought us the problems we face today.

For the most part, I will let the "movers and shakers" of the public school movement do the talking. The reader need only compare the philosophy and agenda of these public school advocates to the present condition of the public schools in order to understand the "cause and effect" of their destructive philosophy.

The Christian, especially, needs to take a hard look at this philosophy and determine if it is compatible with God's Word. Chapter 4 discusses at length what the Bible says about parents' responsibility in education. We must ask ourselves: "Can we fulfill these biblically mandated responsibilities and still send our children to public school?"

In order to accurately understand the impact of the public schools' philosophies of education, we need to first define education.

Definition of Education

What is education? In simple terms, education is the transmission of basic skills and values to the next generation. It is inescapably religious, and it cannot be neutral.

So why is education so important? At present, over forty million students are being taught in the public school system. How we educate our youth, therefore, is crucial for the future of our nation.

Furthermore, education, in a general sense, comprises every area of life. This training of our minds ultimately affects all our actions in this life. In fact, the average child spends approximately twelve hundred hours per year in formal education at school. While in kindergarten through twelfth grade, the child spends over seventeen thousand hours in school, which is approximately one-third of all his or her waking hours. God tells us we must redeem the time. Are we doing that in our present educational system?

There is a very valid and often repeated phrase that states "a mind is a terrible thing to waste." The wasting of our children's minds is truly terrible, and the wasting of forty million minds of children in the public school is devastating.

Many of the leaders of the public school system, past and present, recognize the importance of education. They realize how millions of students can be mass manipulated to conform to one certain pattern. At present, forty million students are being conformed to a clearly humanistic philosophy, which has smothered our public school system.

Battle for our Children's Minds

Taking place at this moment is a major battle for our children's minds. This is a philosophical battle which has significant spiritual ramifications. The battle for our children's minds is being waged by those who have a Christian mindset (requiring the teaching of

Scripture as the basis of all knowledge), and the humanists (who believe man is the measure of all things). As I have already stated, education is never neutral. Someone's values will be applied to each and every subject.

Scripture, as I demonstrate in chapter 4, explains that all knowledge and wisdom come from God. Knowledge owes its very existence to God. True knowledge, as a result, cannot be fully understood unless one looks through the lenses of Scripture.

On the other hand, the humanist view of education, as we find in the modern public school system, holds that knowledge exists in its own right. According to the humanists, knowledge can be truly interpreted without reference to God and His constant involvement in all of history. The humanists' goal, as envisioned by many of the founders and present operators of the public school system, is to use education to manipulate and control masses of students. In light of these two battling philosophies, the reader needs to determine for himself which system of philosophy is consistently being taught in the public schools, and which system of philosophy is demanded of all believers to be applied to the education of their children.

In this chapter are several quotes by men of the past and present who have warned us what the public school system will become. You will also find that their warnings have come true. Furthermore, you will read numerous quotes from influential men in the public school community who have clearly revealed their agenda and their desire to eradicate God and His principles from the instruction of our youth. In chapter 6 we find that home schooling and family education was the major form of education for the first one hundred years of our country's existence. I document how this form of education worked, and how it resulted in a moral populace dedicated to building a nation founded on godly principles. This moral and godly foundation forms the basis of the freedoms we enjoy in this country today. In fact, even the literacy rates were close to the 99th percentile before compulsory education laws.

Today, we see the direct "cause and effect" of the public school system on our youth and our nation. These statistics are documented in chapters 1 and 2. I encourage you to carefully consider the major philosophical crisis that is presently taking place in our public school system and act now to remove your children from the public school system or encourage others to do so before it is too late.

The Philosophy and Agenda of the Public School Founders and Leaders

State education, as we know it today, did not begin to exist in the United States until the 1840s in Massachusetts.[2] It was not until the early 1900s that state education became widespread.

As a result, by the early 1900s the authority and responsibility for education shifted from the parents to the state. This shift was the beginning of the decaying process of American education. No longer would children be considered sinful and responsible for their behavior but rather "innately good." Education would be manipulated by the elite educational establishment to "save our society." Instead, the "man is the measure of all things" educational philosophy, along with the denial of absolute values, has brought our country into the chaos and crisis occurring today.

Horace Mann, called "the father of public education," led the crusade to establish a public school system throughout the country when he became the first secretary of the newly established Massachusetts Board of Education in 1837. Mann, who was a Unitarian, called himself a Christian and was a "thorough believer in the doctrine of the perfectibility of man." [3] He further believed that children had a "right" to an education, and that right needed to be guaranteed by the state.[4] The education of the child, and not the child himself, was responsible for his action as an adult. He held that "society in its collective capacity, is a real...godfather for all its children."[5] His goal was to create a nonsectarian school system, and he envisioned that education would bring salvation to society. He wanted to establish "a new religion, with the state as its true church, and education as its Messiah."[6]

Mann stated further:

> What the church has been for medieval man the public school must become for democratic and rational man. God will be replaced by the concept of the public good.... The common [public] schools...shall create a more far-seeing intelligence and a more pure morality than has ever existed among communities of men.[7]

Horace Mann had a view of education in which the elite must manipulate and conform the masses in order to create an ideal society. The state, not the parents, knows what is best for the children. There is little room left for God in Mann's philosophy of public education.

The second most important man in the modern public school movement was John Dewey. He was also a signer of the *Humanist Manifesto* and first president of American Humanist Association. The major tenets of the *Humanist Manifesto* are listed in chapter 2 of this book. These tenets, which Dewey affirmed with his signature, flatly reject God and all absolute values and embrace reason, relativism, and science as the controlling forces in society. Christian values have no place in society.

Humanism, as described in the *Humanist Manifesto*, does not recognize God or His absolute moral values but, instead, asserts that each person can set his own values and control his own destiny. The *Humanist Manifesto* affirms the theory of evolution which teaches that man has no soul, and reduces man to simply an animal. Since values are determined by the individual, any type of sexual perversion between consenting adults, euthanasia, and suicide are all proper. In fact, the 6th and 7th theses of the *Humanist Manifesto* II, advocate exactly this.

John Dewey, the author of the modern public school system, helped author and signed the *Humanist Manifesto*, consenting to these false principles. He did not even quietly agree with the humanists. He boldly and publicly signed their "statement of faith." This same man applied the principles of the *Humanist Manifesto* to America's public school system.

Dewey believed that man is not a reflection of God, but that society and education must be "socially planned" by the state. Dewey stated "...all *aims* and values which are desirable in education are themselves moral."[8] In other words, humanism is a religion, and its tenets are the only acceptable source of moral principles. He believed that these principles of humanism, as outlined in the *Humanist Manifesto*, must be infused in all public education.

Like Mann, Dewey believed in the "messianic character of education," a phrase coined by scholar R. J. Rushdoony.[9] For Dewey, humanism is the religion and the public school teachers are the prophets. Dewey stated:

> I believe all education comes through the stimulation of the child's powers by the demands of the social situations in which he finds himself.... Education is the fundamental method of social progress and reform [religion being

by-passed].... Every teacher should realize the dignity of his calling; that he is a social servant set apart for the maintenance of proper social order and the securing of the right social growth.... In this way the teacher is always the prophet of the true god and the usherer of the true kingdom of god.[10]

This is frightening. But this is exactly what Dewey was working toward. The True God and His absolute moral principles did not fit into Dewey's plans for the public school. Only the religion of humanism would be taught in his school system. This next statement by John Dewey is even more explicit:

Faith in the prayer-hearing God is an unproved and outmoded faith. There is no God and there is no soul. Hence, there are no needs for the props of traditional religion. With dogma and creed excluded, the immutable truth is also dead and buried. There is no room for fixed, natural law or moral absolutes. [11]

Dewey also emphasized "social unification" as the goal of the public schools in order to promote "state-consciousness."

The American people is conscious that its schools serve best the cause of religion in serving the cause of social unification; and that under certain conditions schools are more religious in substance and in promise without any of the conventional badges and machinery of religious instruction than they could be in cultivating these forms at the expense of a state-consciousness.[12]

Other humanist leaders recognized and applauded the change that was taking place in the public schools. They knew the humanist agenda was coming to fruition. For example, Paul Blanshard, contributing author of the magazine called *The Humanist*, declared the success of their goals:

I think that the most important factor moving us toward a secular society has been the educational factor. Our schools may not teach Johnny to read properly, but the fact that Johnny is in school until he is sixteen tends to lead toward the elimination of religious superstition. The average American child now acquires a high school education and this militates against Adam and Eve and all other myths of alleged history.... When I was one of the editors of the *Nation* in the 20s, I wrote an editorial explaining that golf and intelligence were the two primary reasons why men did not attend church, perhaps I would now say golf and a high school diploma.[13]

To Blanshard, Christianity is nothing more than "religious superstition," and the public schools, back in 1976, had already become the most influential vehicles for eradicating belief in Christianity. Look how much further we have come since then!

John Dunphy, another writer for *The Humanist*, agreed that in the public schools a war is taking place for the minds of our children.

The classroom must and will become an arena of conflict between the old and the new—the rotting corpse of Christianity, together with all its adjacent evils and misery, and the new faith of humanism. [14]

In the late 1980s Dr. John Goodland wrote a report for the National Education Association arguing that one of their goals is to re-educate children to turn away from the values of their parents. He said:

Our goal is behavioral change. The majority of our youth still hold to the values of their parents and if we do not resocialize them to accept change, our society may decay.[15]

The agenda of many public school leaders is to manipulate the masses of students in the American public school system to reject absolute values. This is not just an empty allegation. This agenda is revealed in the public school leaders' own writings.

Another set of convincing quotes are those from many of the professors of schools of education which teach the teachers. For instance, Harvard professor Dr. Chester M. Pierce in 1973, representing The Association For Childhood Education International, declared war on traditional values, challenging teachers to help make well all the "sick" children who hold to godly values:

> Every child in America entering school at the age of five is mentally ill because he comes to school with certain allegiances toward our founding fathers, toward our elected officials, toward his parents, toward a belief in a supernatural being, toward the sovereignty of this nation as a separate entity. It's up to you teachers to make all of these sick children well by creating the international children of the future.[16]

However, you might challenge this one college professor as being a little extreme. Well, let us review several professors from teachers' colleges, such as Columbia University and Ohio State University, and other influential educators involved in the public school movement. In fact, scholar R .J. Rushdoony, in his book *The Messianic Character of American Education* thoroughly reviews the writings and teachings of many of these public educators and managers from the middle 1800s until the late 1960s. He sums up the humanistic philosophy of these educators:

> The state is the order of liberty and the school is the means whereby citizens are prepared for the good life. The state has become the saving institution, and the function of the school has been to proclaim a new gospel of salvation. Education in this era is a messianic and a utopian movement, a facet of the enlightenment hope of regenerating man in terms of the promises of science and that new social order to be achieved in the state.[17]

This messianic and humanistic philosophy is evidenced in the writings of many of these "movers and shakers" in the public schools.

For instance, James G. Carter, who worked along with Horace Mann, to develop state control over schools, believed that as a result of state funding and control "the whole earth will then constitute but one beautiful temple, in which may dwell in peace, all mankind."[18] He also advocated state institutions for educating teachers:

> An institution for this purpose would become by its influence on society, and particularly on the young, an engine to sway the public sentiment, the public morals, and the public religion, more powerful than any other in the possession of government.[19]

Carter, like Mann, saw state education as the "savior" and understood the tremendous power that the enlightened elite could wield, once such a state system was in place throughout the country.

John Swett, who served as the state superintendent of California from 1863 to 1868, helped create the state system of public schools. Swett strongly believed that "the property of the State should be taxed to educate *the children of the State*"[20] [emphasis added]. To make clear his position, Swett declared, "Children arrived at the age of maturity belong, not to the parents, but to the state, to society, to the country."[21] John Swett worked hard to regulate private schools making it a crime for parents to send their children to private schools without the approval of the local school district. Swett was particularly proud of the idea and function of state schools and sincerely believed "no prophets of evil can convince the American people that vice, crime, idleness, poverty, and social discontentment are the results of free public schools."[22]

Chapters 1 and 2 of this book show that what Swett believed state education would cure, it has actually caused: namely vice of every kind, out-of-control crime, and academic decline which contributes to poverty and social unrest. Once state education is divorced from biblical, moral values, and the parents' God-given role is usurped by the state, chaos will result. Faith in the intellectual elite managing the public school system has failed.

Colonel Francis Wayland Parker was called "the father of the progressive educational movement" by John Dewey.[23] Parker was basically an existentialist who believed in the natural divinity of the child.[24] He taught that children gravitated toward good, and that discipline and punishment were harmful for children because they interfered with the child's self-education and his spontaneity.[25] Parker believed that children can be "conditioned" like animals. He stated that salvation of all children could be obtained through state schools.

> We must know that we can save every child. The citizen should say in his heart: I await the regeneration of the world from the teaching of the common schools of America.[26]

Salvation through education is becoming a familiar refrain, being sung by the public school founders and managers. Parker even went so far as to say, "Every school in the land should be home and heaven for children."[27] Because of his complete faith in public education, he opposed private education and referred to those maintaining private education as practicing "bigotry."[28]

It is clear from many of these leaders in the public school system that they have little room for tolerating private education or the God-given rights of parents.

The educational elite also commonly believe that children can be conditioned, much like Pavlov's dog. William James, Lyman Bryson, and S. L. Pressy held to this view. James, a humanistic psychologist and educator, taught that "habits" would create how a child would believe, rather than the reverse, which is commonly held by Christians.[29]

Bryson, a professor who taught many new teachers over his nearly twenty years at Columbia University, held that "by molding and forming the varied adaptable nature of the young people in any society, education aims to make normal persons out of them."[30] Whose definition of "normal"? As far as Bryson was concerned, and many other past and present public school leaders, it certainly did not include the Christian view of "normal."

S. L. Pressy, professor of educational psychology at Ohio State University, taught his future teachers:

> People are what the world has made them. In character, in usefulness, in happiness, they are the product of forces which can be controlled. And the chief agency for such control must be education.[31]

Pressy instilled in his students the understanding that they, as teachers, could mold the children, since the children are just the "product of forces which can be controlled." With proper conditioning, teachers could save our future generations.

Another professor of education at Ohio State University was Boyd Henry Bode. He wrote:

> Authoritarianism places these values in the acceptance of certain habits for the guidance of belief and conduct. Democracy stresses the importance of keeping intelligence free. For the continuous remaking of beliefs...intelligence

should function as a means of the abundant life and not as a means of the discovery of eternal and immutable truth.[32]

In other words, teaching absolute values restricts true education and is not democratic. Remaking of beliefs is essential to true freedom.

George S. Counts was known for his advocacy of a planned economy and his work to use the public schools to help implement this planned economy which was nothing more than socialism. He had a "messianic" view of education in which state education would usher in the "new order." "Education is identified with the work of the school. As a consequence, the faith in education becomes a faith in school, and the school is looked upon as a worker of miracles. In fact, the school is the American road to culture."[33] Like many of the other public school educators, Counts considered that the teachers were "the spiritual leaders of the masses of people," and that the "teacher is a bearer of culture and a creator of social values."[34]

Counts, like many of the public school leaders discussed above, had a faith in "public education" as being the "salvation" of our nation. Counts and the others eagerly put aside academics in the public schools and replaced it with a social agenda which involved a remaking of our culture and a rejection of our system of traditional values. In 1958 one dean of a teachers' college explained his school's goal: "An educated man is one who is well adjusted and helpful in his community." When asked if such a man could still be considered educated without being able to count his fingers or write his name the dean answered, "Yes."[35] Humanist editor Paul Blanshard, whom I quoted earlier, said that "Johnny" may not be learning to read in the public schools, but he is learning the Bible is nothing but superstition. Literacy is secondary to the social agenda. Time has proven this to be true since millions of children graduate from the public schools illiterate, and yet the crime statistics in chapter 2 show the Christian values of our youth have nearly been obliterated.

These "movers and shakers" of the public school system openly admit that their agenda, from the beginning of the public schools, was to manipulate and "condition" the masses of children in order to change their traditional value systems. The goal of literacy and learning basic skills was replaced by a social agenda. This agenda of the public school leaders supports the tenets of the *Humanist Manifesto*, which is clearly a slap in the face of God.

This was recently confirmed by Rita Kramer in *Ed School Follies* who documents how the teacher colleges concentrated on teaching future teachers politics rather than academic knowledge. In chapter 1 I summarize her book in greater detail.

This philosophy pervades the modern public school system. Chapters 1 and 2 demonstrate where this valueless philosophy is taking us.

Former Proponents Verify the Philosophical Failure of the Public Schools

In case you think my conclusions concerning the public school philosophy are somewhat exaggerated, I document below accounts from modern public school leaders who have abandoned the system and are exposing its failures.

For instance, John Taylor Gatto taught for over thirty years in the public school system and was even elected the New York Teacher of the Year in 1989. Gatto independently describes the influence of Horace Mann and others. In his speech while accepting the award, Gatto stated:

> Schools were designed by Horace Mann and by Sears and Harper of the University of Chicago and Thorndyke of Columbia Teacher's College and some other men to be instruments of scientific management of a mass population. Schools are intended to produce through the application of formulae, formulaic human beings whose behavior can be predicted and controlled.... The products of schooling are, as I have said, irrelevant...useless to others and useless to themselves.[36]

In another example, psychologist W. R. Coulson, who holds two doctorates—one in philosophy from the University of Notre Dame and the other in counseling psychology from the University of California at Berkeley—was even more critical than Gatto. During the 1960s, Coulson was an associate of Carl Rogers and Abraham Maslow, gurus to a generation of psychologists and educators and both winners of the "Humanist of the Year Award." It is interesting to note that both Rogers and Maslow finally acknowledge the educational failure of encounter groups, sensitivity training, and values clarification.

In an interview, Coulson remarked:

> American education has experienced a "meltdown" because it has "wimped out on substance." Teachers have "lost their nerve." Furthermore, the public schools are highly secularized and seek to "convert" children to a "humanistic" ethic. Moreover, the sex and anti-drug education the schools dish out only encourages young people to have sex and use drugs.... Coulson believes that we have "given in" to the "religion of psychology," particularly in the area of education, which has become too therapeutic." He is critical of "lifestyle" programs which take away from academic achievement. The educational system has in his view fallen into such bogus offerings as "visualization" and "relaxation"—because today's teachers often can't deliver the academic goods. "Teachers are not learning to teach," Coulson says, but instead are becoming "facilitators." In that capacity, they "make students feel good about their disablement."
>
> Such trends Coulson sees as proceeding, not just from prominent humanist John Dewey, but from Horace Mann and the fathers of mass education in America. The system, he says, is essential "Unitarianism in the classroom." What the schools are forking out now is not only religious, Coulson contends, but it is "religious trash," and in that judgment he is not alone.[37]

The public schools are "religious," but it is a religion devoid of values. It is a religion of humanism. It has been designed that way since Horace Mann. It has not changed. It has only become worse.

Even the Harvard Educational Review recognizes the value-laden nature of modern public schools:

> Parents, social commentators, anthropologists, sociologists, psychologists, and others who have done research on schooling have all understood its value-laden nature.... Whatever their values, most parents seem to realize that a good deal of child rearing will take place at school and a great many basic values will be foisted on children there. The

school is a social environment in which a child may learn much more than that which is in the formal curriculum.[38]

Another highly reputed educational journal analyzes one of the most destructive and humanistic aspects of the modern public schools' instruction:

> Values clarification appears, at least by default, to hold the view that all values are equally valid.... The moral point of view imbedded in values clarification is that of the ethical relativist. In its simplest definition, ethical relativism holds that one person's views are as good as another's; everyone is entitled to his own morality, and when it comes to morality, there is no way of showing one opinion is better than the other. The fundamental objection to ethical relativism is that it can be used to justify virtually any activity in which an individual or society wishes to engage.[39]

The evidence is overwhelming for an indictment against the leaders of the public school system, past and present, for imposing their devastating agenda on our country's youth.

Unheeded Voices of the Past that Predicted the Results of Secular State Schools

History is a valuable tutor. If we can learn from the mistakes of the past, we can avoid repeating them. Let us briefly review the critique of godly men and other scholars of the past who understood the consequences and warned us about secular, state education. I will let them speak for themselves on this issue.

For instance, Archibald Hodge, pastor and theologian nearly one hundred years ago, warned:

> I am as sure as I am of the fact of Christ's reign that a comprehensive and centralized system of national education, separated from religion as is now commonly proposed, will prove the most appalling enginery for the propagation of anti-Christian and atheistic unbelief, and of anti-social nihilistic ethics, individual, social, and political, which this sin rent world has ever seen.[40]

Timothy Dwight, president of Yale University from 1795 to 1817, was a man of God and home schooled by his parents. He, too, understood the importance of Christian education:

> Education ought everywhere to be religious education...parents are bound to employ no instructors who will not instruct their children religiously. To commit our children to the care of irreligious persons is to commit lambs to the superintendency of wolves.[41]

Similarly, Noah Webster echoed this truth:

> In my view, the Christian religion is the most important and one of the first things in which all children, under a free government, ought to be instructed.... No truth is more evident to my mind than that the Christian religion must be the basis of any government intended to secure the rights and privileges of a free people.[42]

During the Reformation, Martin Luther warned us:

> I am afraid that the schools will prove the very gates of hell, unless they diligently labor in explaining the Holy Scriptures and engraving them in the heart of the youth.[43]

R. L. Dabney, a reformed preacher and writer during the time of the Civil War and following, noticed that with the growth of public schools, crime increased. He also made some very prophetic statements in his book *On Secular Education*, describing the inevitable censorship of religion:

> But the result of public education is to bring a larger number of children into primary schools, and reduce the illiteracy somewhat—which is a great delight to shallow philanthropists. But the number of youths well educated above the mere rudiments and especially those brought under daily Christian training is diminished.
>
> So, the actual and consistent secularization of education should not be tolerated. But nearly all public men and

preachers declare that the public schools are the glory of America. They are a finality, and in no event to be surrendered. We have seen that their complete secularization is logically inevitable. Christians must prepare themselves then, for the following results: all prayers, catechisms, and Bibles will ultimately be driven out of the schools.[44]

Responding to his critics who said we need public schools because some people may not educate their children, Dabney said:

…But may parents nevertheless neglect or pervert the power? Yes, but does the State never neglect and pervert its powers? With the lessons of history to teach the horrible and almost universal abuses of power in the hands of civil rulers, that question is conclusive. In the case of an unjust or Godless state, the evil would be universal and sweeping. There is no doubt that God has deposited the duty [to train the children] in the safest place [the parents].[45]

Historian Philip Schaff remarked in 1888:

It is impossible to draw the precise line between moral and religious education. Absolute indifference of the schools to morals is impossible; it [education] must be either moral or immoral, religious or irreligious…. An education that ignores religion altogether would raise a heartless and infidel generation of intellectual animals.[46]

Other leaders of the past saw the advent of public schools as a way for the state to control education nationwide. For example, free market economist John Stuart Mill warned:

A general state education is a *mere contrivance* for *molding people* to be *exactly* like one *another*: and as the mold in which it casts them is that which pleases the predominant power in the government or [the will of] the majority of the existing generation; in proportion as it is efficient and successful, it establishes a *despotism* over the *mind*, leading by natural tendency to one over the body.[47] (emphasis added)

Mill, who was home schooled, had a point that has been proven over and over again. For example, Hitler said, "Let me control the textbooks, and I will control Germany." And he did. Hitler's government also outlawed private education. "Recalcitrant parents were warned that their children would be taken away from them and put in orphanages or other homes unless they enrolled."[48]

In 1923, author and professor at Westminster Theological Seminary, J. Gresham Machen, sounded the alarm concerning the direction of attendance at the public schools becoming compulsory:

> When one considers what the public schools of America in many places already are—their materialism, their discouragement of any sustained intellectual effort, their encouragement of the dangerous pseudo-scientific fads of experimental psychology—one can only be appalled by the thought of a commonwealth in which there is no escape from such a soul-killing system. But the principles of such laws and their ultimate tendency are far worse than the immediate result.
>
> The public school system in itself is indeed of enormous benefit to the race, but is a benefit only if it is kept healthy at every moment by the absolutely free possibility of the competition of private schools. A public school system, if it means the providing of free education to those who desire it, is a noteworthy and beneficent achievement of modern times. But once it becomes monopolistic, it is the most perfect instrument of tyranny which has yet been devised.
>
> Freedom of thought in the Middle Ages was combated by the Inquisition, but the modern method is far more effective. Place the lives of the children in their formative years, despite the convictions of the parents, under the intimate control of experts appointed by the state, force them to attend schools where the higher aspirations of humanity are crushed out and where the mind is filled with the materialism of the day, and it is difficult to see

how even the remnants of liberty can subsist. Such a tyranny, supported as it is by a perverse technique used as the instrument in destroying human souls, is certainly far more dangerous than the crude tyrannies of the past, which despite their weapons of fire and sword permitted thought, at least, to be free.

The truth is that the materialistic paternalism of the present day, if allowed to go unchecked, will rapidly make of America one huge "Main Street" where spiritual adventure will be discouraged and democracy will be regarded as consisting in the reduction of all mankind to the proportions of the narrowest and least gifted of the citizens.[49]

Machen was right. All of these men were right about the dangers of a wide-spread public educational system. Chapters 1 and 2 of this book are overflowing with evidence. These voices may have been from the past, but they ring true today. We would do well to heed their warnings.

The Philosophy and Agenda of the Public Schools Was Fulfilled at the Expense of Our Youth

Who is winning the battle for the minds of our children? It is obvious from reading chapters 1 and 2 and this chapter that the humanists are winning. Here are a few more comments from contemporaries, describing the present condition of the public schools.

A professor at Pepperdine University condemned the public school product when he stated:

I believe that the decline in education is probably responsible for the widespread use of drugs. To live in the midst of a civilized society with a level of knowledge closer perhaps to that of primitive man than to what a civilized adult requires (which, regrettably, is the intellectual state of many of today's students and graduates) must be a terrifying experience, urgently calling for some kind of relief, and drugs may appear to many to be the solution....

This is no longer an educational system. Its character has been completely transformed and it now clearly reveals itself to be what for many decades it has been in the process of becoming: namely an agency working for the barbarization of youth.[50]

John Taylor Gatto, mentioned earlier in this book, said he quit teaching because he didn't want to "hurt" kids anymore. In addition, he declared "government schooling…kills the family by monopolizing the best times of childhood and by teaching disrespect for home and parents."[51] In an earlier speech on January 31, 1990, in accepting an award from the New York State Senate naming him "New York City Teacher of the Year," Gatto gave more details:

> We live in a time of great school crisis. We rank at the bottom of nineteen industrial nations in reading, writing, and arithmetic. At the very bottom. The world's narcotic economy is based upon our consumption of this commodity: If we didn't buy so many powdered dreams the business would collapse-and schools are an important sales outlet. Our teenage suicide rate is the highest in the world and suicidal kids are rich kids for the most part, not the poor. In Manhattan, 70% of all new marriages last less than five years. So something is wrong for sure…. [52]
>
> I don't think that we'll get rid of schools any time soon, certainly not in my lifetime, but if we're going to change what's rapidly becoming a disaster of ignorance we need to realize that the school institution "schools" very well but it does not "educate"—that's inherent in the design of the thing. It's not the fault of bad teachers or too little money spent. It's just impossible for education and schooling ever to be the same thing.[53]
>
> The daily misery around us is, I think, in large measure caused by the fact that, as Paul Goodman put it thirty years ago, we force children to grow up absurd. Any reform in schooling has to deal with its absurdities.
>
> It is absurd and anti-life to be part of a system that compels you to sit in confinement with people of exactly the same age and social class. That system effectively cuts you off from the immense diversity of life and the synergy of variety; indeed it cuts you off from your own past and

future, sealing you in a continuous present much the same way television does....

Two institutions at present control our children's lives: television and schooling, in that order; both of these reduce the real world of wisdom, fortitude, temperance, and justice to a never-ending, non-stop abstraction. In centuries past, the time of the child and adolescent would be spent in real work, real charity, real adventures, and the realistic search for mentors who might teach what you really wanted to learn. A great deal of time was spent in community pursuits, practicing affection, meeting and studying every level of the community, learning how to make a home, and dozens of other tasks necessary to become a whole man or a whole woman.[54]

The public schools are in sad shape. In America, by God's grace, we have alternatives to sending children to public school. Please, read the next section of this book about the tremendous academic and moral success of home schooling.

Knowing This, Can We Risk Sending Our Children to Public School?

I will close with three more quotes, which sum up the modern philosophical crisis in the public school.

Author Charles Francis Potter who wrote the book *Humanism: A New Religion*, saw humanism rushing into the public school system.

Education is thus a most powerful ally of humanism, and every public school is a school of humanism. What can the theistic Sunday school, meeting for an hour once a week and teaching only a fraction of the children, do to stem the tide of a five day program of humanistic teaching?[55]

Educational writer Elmer Town, declared:

The public schools have a singular adherence to secular humanism, and defined as a total lifestyle without reference to or need of God...the public schools are not neutral, it is anti-Christian. For a Christian to send his children to the public school is just as consistent as sending them to a Unitarian Sunday school: they are learning the opposite of what is taught in the Word of God.[56]

Finally, Robert Thoburn, author and administrator of a large Christian school, tells us about "Satan's big lie."

> Obviously the schools are not Christian. Just as obviously they are not neutral. The Scriptures say that the fear of the Lord is the chief part of knowledge; but the schools, by omitting all reference to God, give the pupils the notion that knowledge can be had apart from God. They teach in effect that God has no control of history, that there is no plan of events that God is working out, that God does not foreordain whatsoever come to pass....
>
> The public schools are not, never were, can never be, neutral. Neutrality is impossible.
>
> The big lie of the public schools is that the God of the Bible is irrelevant. The textbooks never mention Him. Everyone assumes that children do not need to know anything about God, God's law, and God's Word in order to become educated people. This is Satan's own lie.[57]

How much longer will we fall for Satan's lie?

Notes

1. Ivan Illich, *New York Review of Books,* Vol. 13, No.6, October 9, 1969, 12-15.
2. Samuel I. Blumenfeld, *NEA: Trojan Horse in American Education* (Boise, Idaho: Paradigm Company, 1984), 1.
3. E. I. F. Williams, *Horace Mann, Educational Statesman* (New York: Macmillan, 1937), 205.
4. Rousas J. Rushdoony, *The Messianic Character of Education* (Nutley, N.J.: Craig Press, 1968), 21.
5. *Ibid.,* 24.
6. *Ibid.,* 32.
7. *Ibid.*
8. John Dewey, *Democracy in Education* (New York: MacMillan, 1918), 360.
9. Rousas J. Rushdoony, *The Messianic Character of Education* (Nutley, N.J.: Craig Press, 1968).
10. John Dewey, *My Pedagogic Creed* (Washington D.C.: Progressive Education Association, 1897), 6, 15, 17.
11. John Dewey, "Soul-Searching," *Teacher Magazine,* September 1933, 33.
12. John Dewey, *Characters and Etlents, Popular Essays in Social and Political Philosophy,* Vol. II (New York: Holt, 1929), 515.
13. Paul Blanshard, "Three Cheers for Our Secular State," *The Humanist,* March/April 1976, 17. (A publication of the American Humanist Association which is based in Amhurst, New York.)
14. John Dunphy, *The Humanist,* January/February 1983.

15. Dr. John Goodland in a report written for the National Education Association entitled, "Schooling For the Future." This passage was quoted by Dr. D. James Kennedy in a sermon entitled "A Godly Education," delivered to the Coral Ridge Presbyterian Church in Ft. Lauderdale, Florida.
16. Statements made by Harvard University Professor Dr. Chester M. Pierce in a written address delivered to over 2,000 teachers at a child education seminar in Denver, Colorado in 1973. See *Schooling Choices*, (Portland, Oregon: Multnomah, 1988), 131.
17. Rousas J. Rushdoony, *The Messianic Character*, 4.
18. James G. Carter, "Letters to the Honorable William Prescott on the Free Schools of New England, with Remarks upon the Principles of Instruction" (Boston: Cummings, Hilliard &Co.,1824), 123.
19. James G. Carter, "Essays upon Popular Education" (Boston: Bowles and Dearbom, 1826), 49-50.
20. John Swett, *History of the Public School System of California* (San Francisco: Bancroft, 1876), 113.
21. Ibid., 115.
22. John Swett, *American Public Schools, History and Pedagogics* (New York: American Book Company, 1900), 168.
23. Rousas J. Rushdoony, *The Messianic Character*, 97. This title was given to Parker in an article in the July 9, 1930, *New Republic*.
24. Francis Wayland Parker, *Talks on Pedagogics* (New York: John Day, 1937), 18.
25. *Ibid.*, 265-71.
26. *Ibid.*, 328.
27. Ida Cassa Heffron, *Francis Wayland Parker, An Interpretive Biography* (Los Angeles: Deach, 1934), 41.
28. "The School of the Future," *NEA Journal*, 1891, 82-89.
29. William James, *Talks to Teachers on Psychology* (New York: Henry Holt, 1907), 202.
30. Lyman Bryson, *An Outline of Man's Knowledge* (Garden City: Doubleday, 1960), 374.
31. S. L. Pressy, *Psychology and the New Education* (New York: Harper, 1933), 6.
32. Boyd Henry Bode, *Educational Freedom and Democracy* (New York: D. Appleton-Century, 1938), 15.
33. George Counts, *The American Road to Culture* (New York: John Day, 1930), 16.
34. George Counts, *A Call to the Teachers of the Nation* (John Day Pamphlet No. 30,1933), 19-25.
35. John Keats, *Schools Without Scholars* (Boston: Houghton Mifflen, 1958), 19.
36. John Taylor Gatto, *Dumbing Us Down* (Philadelphia: New Society Publishers, 1992), 26.
37. "Psychologist Unloads on Religious Trash in Nation's Schools," *World*, October 27, 1990, 10. This is based on an interview with W. R. Coulson.
38. Stephen Arons, "The Separation of School and State: Pierce Reconsidered," *Harvard Educational Review*, Vol. 46, No.1 (February 1976), 98.
39. Alan B. Lockwood, "Values Clarification," *Teachers College Record*, Vol. 77, No.1 (September 1977), 46-47.
40. Archibald A. Hodge, *Popular Lectures on Theological Themes* (Philadelphia: Presbyterian Board of Publications, 1887), 283-4.
41. Timothy Dwight, President of Yale, 1795-1817.
42. Noah Webster, *An American Dictionary of the English Language*, reprint of the 1828 edition (San Francisco: Foundation for American Christian Education, 1967), 12.
43. Manin Luther, *What Luther Says*, Vol. I, 449.
44. R. L. Dabney, *On Secular Education*, ed. Douglas Wilson (Ransom Press, 1989), 28.
45. *Ibid.*, 30-33.
46. Philip Schaff, "Progress of Christianity in the United States," *Princeton Review*, Ser. 4, Vol. 4 (September 1879), 228
47. John Stuart Mill, *American State Papers: On Liberty*, pub. Benton William (Chicago: Encyclopedia Britannica, Inc., 1972), 318.
48. William Shirer, *Rise and Fall of the Third Reich* (New York, Simon and Schuster, 1960), 255.
49. J. Gresham Machen, D.D., *Christianity and Liberalism*, (Grand Rapids, MI: Eerdmans Publishing Co., 1923), 13-14
50. George Reisman, *The Intellectual Activist*, as quoted in the "Blumenfeld Education Letter," (Boise, ID: August 1990), 8.

51. Carol Innerst, "N.Y. Teacher of Year Walks Out on System," *Washington Times,* October 22, 1991, A1.

52. John Taylor Gatto, *Dumbing Us Down,* 23-24.

53. *Ibid.,* 26.

54. *Ibid.,* 28.

55. Charles Frances Potter, *Humanism: A New Religion* (New York: Simon & Schuster, 1930).

56. Elmer Town, *Have the Public Schools Had It?* (New York: Thomas Nelson, 1974), 101-104.

57. Roben Thoburn, *The Children Trap, Difficult Principles for Education* (Fort Worth, TX: Dominion Press, 1986), 34.

II

The Rising Hope
of Home Schooling

Many families are turning to home schooling as the solution to the decaying public school system. However, home schooling is not a new idea—it is the restoration of an old and successful idea. It is not only a return to effective, parent-directed education; it is a moral and spiritual reformation.

Part Two will discuss the historical perspective of education in our country, demonstrating that Christian private education and, particularly, home education, was the predominant form of education in our country until the early 1900s. This section will also present the "Home Schooling Hall of Fame," briefly describing the lives of many famous home schoolers of the past. A thorough account of the modern home school movement will show the tremendous academic, economic, social, and spiritual advantages of home schooling. Since much of the home school movement is in the midst of a spiritual revival, the biblical principles will be identified and applied. The lengthy review of Bible verses dealing with education, and the parents' responsibilities to train their children in God's ways, leave little doubt as to whether or not we should send our children to public schools.

In short, home schooled children are generally both academically literate and biblically literate, preparing them to become leaders of tomorrow. The home education movement is providing a lasting solution to the failing public school system. This academic and moral revival is being achieved independently of the government or any national organization. It is being achieved family by family as the Holy Spirit impresses parents' hearts to take seriously their responsibilities before God to train their children.

This note that John Taylor Gatto received after speaking in Nashville, Tennessee, summarizes the problem with the public schools and the hope of home schooling. Mr. Gatto recounts this in his book, *The Empty Child*.

> "We started to see Brandon flounder in the first grade. He had developed hives, depression, and he died every night after he asked his father, 'Is tomorrow school too?' In second grade the physical stress became apparent. The teacher at the public school pronounced his problem Attention Deficit Syndrome. My happy, bouncy child is now looked at as a medical problem, by us as well as the school.
>
> A doctor, psychiatrist, and a school authority determined he did have this affliction. Medication was stressed along with behavior modification. If it was suspected that Brandon had not been medicated, he was sent home. My square peg needed a bit of whittling to fit their round hole, it seemed.
>
> I cried as I watched my parenting choices stripped away and my ignorance of options allowed Brandon to be medicated through second grade. The tears and hives continued another full year until I couldn't stand it, and I began to home school Brandon. It was his salvation. No more pills, tears, or hives. He is thriving. He never cries now and does his work eagerly."

The note was simply signed, *Debbie*.

> "And he will restore the hearts of the fathers to their children, and the hearts of the children to their fathers, lest I come and smite the land with a curse" Malachi 4:6.

The Biblical Principles:

A Support for Home Schooling and an Indictment of Public Education

"I am afraid that the schools will prove the very gates of hell, unless they diligently labor in explaining the Holy Scriptures and engraving them in the heart of the youth." [1]

Martin Luther

With a majority of school-aged children attending public schools, education in America has primarily become a function of the state. This public school system is failing miserably, both academically and morally, as demonstrated in previous chapters. If we are honest with ourselves, we cannot escape the fact that the public schools are no longer a safe place for children academically, physically or, most important of all, spiritually. The state, meanwhile, not content to control only public schools, constantly encroaches on the freedoms of private schools and home schools through various case precedents, regulations, and statutes. As a result, many public school authorities have come to believe that they are the guardians of all of the children. Frequently, when I negotiate with public school superintendents, they refer to the children in their school district as "our" children. It is apparent that superintendents sincerely believe they know what is best for "their" children and feel obligated to try to control home schools.

Many home schooling parents, however, take offense to this presumption by superintendents. In the tradition of their forefathers, as seen in chapter 6, these parents believe that God, not the state, has given parents the sole authority and responsibility for the education of their children. Approximately 85 percent of the estimated 450,000 home schooling families in the United States are Bible-believing Christians. Therefore, the Word of God is recognized as the source of all truth and the standard by which all things are measured. These parents want their children not only to believe as Christians, but to develop minds so they can think as Christians. They want their children to be biblically literate.

When the United States was formed, the framers of the Constitution and many of the citizens had a biblical mindset. All of them may not have had a personal relationship with Jesus, but they respected the Bible as defining right and wrong and providing a foundation on which to build the country. For this reason, the country prospered. Today, the biblical mindset has been replaced by a secular mindset. Public schools are teaching the children to be biblically *illiterate* and to ignore God's absolute moral values. The negative effects are being felt throughout the country, as seen in chapters 1 and 2 of this book. In many ways we have "sown the wind and now reap the whirlwind," as we allow children's minds to be wasted in the public schools, void of godly values and truth. Home schoolers are working to restore that biblical mindset in their children and trying to fulfill the commands of God concerning the education of their children.

The following is a summary of the biblical principles of education which support Christian home schooling. In these verses the reader will find that God has delegated to the parents *first,* the authority *and* responsibility to teach and raise children. We can delegate the authority to train our children to someone else, but we can never delegate the responsibility.

A close and prayerful study of these verses will demonstrate that sending your children to a public school is no longer an option. But do not take my word for it. Carefully read the verses yourself and let God speak to your heart.

The Scripture states, to "everyone who has been given much shall much be required" (Luke 12:48). Since we have a free choice in this country to *not* send our children to an ungodly public school, we will, all the more, be responsible.

The Raising of Children Is Delegated to Parents by God

According to the Bible, children belong to God, but the responsibility and authority to raise and educate them is delegated to their parents. For example, in Psalm 127:3-5 it says children are a gift from the Lord to the parents:

> Behold, children are a gift of the Lord; The fruit of the womb is a reward. Like arrows in the hand of a warrior, so are the children of one's youth. How blessed is the man whose quiver is full of them; they shall not be ashamed when they speak with their enemies in the gate.

Our children are a reward! They are a blessing from God. What wonderful gifts they are to us.

Also God describes our children as arrows in the hands of a warrior! Consider that for a moment. What kind of arrows are we making as we educate and train our children? Are our "arrows" straight or slightly bent? Are our "arrows" completely finished and ready, able to endure their tasks ahead? Or are they half made, weak, and not properly balanced? Have we diligently crafted our "arrows" so they can be trusted to hit their target as we launch them into the world? Or have we simply worked on our "arrows" here and there when we can fit time into our busy schedules?

Have we personally guaranteed our "arrows" are the most carefully crafted and have the sharpest point, or did we hire some stranger ignorant of the way the Creator demands that arrows be made? Are we training our children to be the best-prepared warriors for God? What kinds of "arrows" are the public schools crafting? These are questions we must ask ourselves as we raise our children—the never-dying souls whom God has entrusted to us.

In Genesis 33:5, Jacob introduces his children to his brother Esau as "the children whom God has graciously given me," and similarly in Isaiah 8:18, the prophet says, "I and the children whom the Lord has given me." (Also see Hebrews 2:13 and Genesis 48:8-9.) Nowhere in

Scripture can a reference be found in which God delegates to the state the authority to raise and educate children.

The only time that God's people were educated by the state was when they were occupied by a heathen nation which left them no alternatives. Some of the more well-known examples are Moses, Joseph, and Daniel. God, nonetheless, has clearly delegated the *responsibility and authority to teach and raise children to the parents first.* Parents can delegate their *authority* to raise and teach their children to someone else (i.e., tutor or church school or private or public school), but they can *never delegate their responsibility to teach their children to anyone else.* In other words, God will always hold parents responsible for the education their children receive. For this reason parents need to be aware of who is teaching their child, what is being taught verbally in class by both the teacher and the peers, and what is being taught in all textbooks and supplemental books and projects. Many home school parents take this responsibility so seriously that they believe they must be the primary teachers of their children.

Children Still Belong to God

Although God has "given" children to parents, children are a "gift of stewardship," which means that parents do not really "own" their children. Parents, therefore, are not free to raise their children any way they want because God gives the parents certain "conditions" that must be met. God still considers the children to be His children. God refers to Jacob's children as "the work of My hands" in Isaiah 29:23. David gave thanks to God for being "fearfully and wonderfully made" while in his mother's womb in Psalm 139:13-14. (Also see God's claim to unborn children whom He has made and called while they are in their mother's womb in Jeremiah 1:5; Psalm 139:13-16; Job 10:8-12; Isaiah 49:1-5; and Luke 1:41-44.)

In Ezekiel 16:20-21 the Lord emphasizes again that the children are His.

> Moreover, you took your sons and daughters whom you had born to Me. and you sacrificed them to idols to be devoured. Were your harlotries so small a matter? You slaughtered My children and offered them up to idols causing them to pass through fire.

God judged these parents severely because they did not meet God's conditions for raising His children. They gave their children up to an idolatrous system which hated God. As a result, home schooling parents, aware of the anti-God curriculum and complete lack of absolute values in the public schools, cannot sacrifice their children to such a system.

The Bible states further that parents must "render to Caesar [the state] the things that are Caesar's, and to God the things that are God's" (Matthew 22:21). In fact, in some of the cases that I have handled, the prosecutor has asked the home school parent on the stand why he is not obeying the law, since he says that he believes the Bible, and the Bible commands: "Render to Caesar the things that are Caesar's." Of course, he never finishes the verse. Since the children are not Caesar's in the first place, but rather God's, parents do not have any obligation to render their children to the public school by enrolling them in public school or complying with excessively restrictive state controls of their children's education and training.

God's Conditions for Educating Children

Part of the parents' stewardship responsibility in raising children is that certain commands and conditions set by God must be followed in raising and educating His children. For example, concerning children's education: "Fathers, do not provoke your children to wrath, but bring them up in the nurture and admonition of the Lord" (Ephesians 6:4). This is a heavy command to fathers! In verses 1 and 2 of the same chapter, God gives commands concerning both mothers and fathers. However, in Ephesians 6:4, the command is to fathers only. We, as fathers, therefore, definitely carry the heaviest responsibility in training our children. The word "nurture" involves loving, providing for, and carefully instructing them. Of course, the instruction must be "in the Lord."

The word "admonition" is the same word as "discipline," and it involves using the biblical methods of spanking and other admonitions in order to ensure our child's obedience and ability to "stay the course." We must not "provoke" our children by acting hypocritically, ignoring them, or being preoccupied with our work. I believe we are "provoking" our children when we send them to public schools to learn the ways of the world, outside of godly training and nurture. Let us train our children diligently in order to sear the truth of God into their very souls.

Furthermore, in Deuteronomy 6:6-9, the Lord, after restating His moral law, declares:

> And these words which I am commanding you today, shall be on your heart; and you shall teach them diligently to your sons and shall talk of them when you sit in your house and when you walk by the way and when you lie down and when you rise up. And you shall bind them as a sign on your hand and they shall be as frontals on your forehead. And you shall write them on the doorposts of your house and your gates.

(Also see parallel passages in Deuteronomy 4:9, 11:18-21; Psalm 78:1-11.) In other words, God's commands and truth must be taught to the children by the parents, and they must be taught *diligently*. Children are to be brought up in the "instruction" of the Lord. How can this be achieved if a child spends six to seven hours a day receiving a public education that teaches him to think as a non-Christian?

It is clearly the parents' primary responsibility to teach their children "so that your days and the days of your sons may be multiplied" (Deuteronomy 11:21). These commands to educate our children, of course, cannot be accomplished once a week at Sunday school. It involves a comprehensive approach to education on a *daily* basis. The commands of God should be taught to our children when we sit in our homes, when we rise up, lie down, and when we travel. *In other words, all the time.*

This comprehensive educational program is to be based on God's commands. Two of the goals of godly education, therefore, are that children will put their confidence in the Lord, and that they will keep His commandments.

> For He established a testimony in Jacob, and appointed a law in Israel which He commanded our fathers that they should teach them to their children that the generation to come might know, even the children yet to be born, that they may arise and tell them to their children, that they should put their confidence in God and not forget the works of God, but keep His commandments (Psalm 78:5-7).

Many other verses emphasize that parents have the weighty responsibility of teaching their children what God has done so that the children will not forget (see Exodus 13:8, 14; Joshua 4:20-22, 24). In Proverbs 22:6, God commands, "Train up a child in the way he should go, even when he is old, he will not depart from it." We need to thoroughly train our children now so they will follow the path of righteousness as adults.

Of course, the children also have some responsibility. They must obey the commandments of their parents who, in turn, are obeying God:

> My son, observe the commandments of your father, and do not forsake the teaching of your mother; bind them continually on your heart; tie them around your neck. When you walk about, they will guide you; when you sleep, they will watch over you; and when you awake, they will talk to you. For the commandment is a lamp, and the teaching is light; and reproofs for discipline are the way of life (Proverbs 6:20-23).

Teaching these commands of God comprehensively to our children is "light" to our children and leads them to "the way of life." A side effect of a biblical education, then, can be the salvation of our children's souls for all eternity. Learning God's Law and His principles "tutors" and "leads us to Christ" (Galatians 3:24). If the very souls of our children are at stake, should we risk having them taught thousands of hours of information that is contrary to God's truths and in an atmosphere that denies God's existence?

In addition, our children will receive a tremendous blessing, according to Isaiah 54:13: "And all your [children] will be taught by the Lord; and great will be your children's peace" (NIV). It seems apparent that the "children's peace" will affect the parents by contributing to a peaceful home and minimal rebellion. No wonder so many parents who send their children to the public school for six or more hours a day of ungodly instruction have chaotic homes in which the children regularly challenge the parents' authority and mistreat siblings.

Commands to Train Our Children's Minds

None of us want to waste the minds of our children. Unfortunately, Christians do exactly this when they send their children to the modern public school.

God commands His people in Jeremiah 10:2: "Learn not the way of the heathen" (KJV). The public schools are teaching the children the "way of the heathen," while ignoring God's ways.

Furthermore, David explains that we need to "meditate" on God's Law, day and night (Psalm 1:2). How can our children meditate on God's Law, when they are never even taught God's Law in the public schools? In fact, Christians are to "take every thought captive to the obedience of Christ" (2 Corinthians 10:5).

This responsibility is immense. Parents must train their children to think God's thoughts after Him. A godly education, therefore, is learning not only to believe as a Christian (for salvation), but to *think* as a Christian. Christian home schooling teaches children to think as Christians. Unfortunately, public schools and some private schools are teaching children who believe as Christians to think as non-Christians. Since Christian parents in the past have neglected their *duty* to follow this comprehensive approach to education, generations of adult Christians now apply ungodly principles in their lives and workplaces, while simultaneously believing as Christians. In essence, many parents are raising humanistic Christians, many of whom are "lukewarm" and not thinking God's thoughts after Him.

Proverbs 23:7 states, "For as [a man] thinks within himself, so he is." If a child is trained to think as a humanist, he will tend to act and live as a humanist. Moreover, Scripture states, "Everyone, after he has been fully trained, will be like his teacher" (Luke 6:40). This passage continues by describing the blind who lead the blind into the pit. This is why it is so important that parents teach their children to *think* as Christians and that children be taught by godly teachers. Parents must not let their children be conformed to the pattern of this world, but they must be transformed by the renewing of their *minds,* that they may prove what is good, and acceptable, and the perfect will of God (see Romans 12:2). Unfortunately, public schools are working to conform our children's minds to the pattern of this world.

In Matthew 16:23, Peter, thinking like a humanist, told Jesus that He would not have to die. Jesus' response to him was harsh: "Get behind Me, Satan! You are a stumbling block to Me: for you are not setting your *mind* on God's interests, but *man's.*" Parents are casting a stumbling block before their children by having them trained to think man's thoughts, instead of God's thoughts, over thirty hours a week.

"Keep seeking the things *above*, where Christ is…. Set your *mind* on things above, not on the things that are on earth" (Colossians 3:1-2). The Bible and its principles are things from above—the blueprint that God has given to show us how we are to live. In Matthew 22:37-38, Jesus commanded, "You shall love the Lord your God with all your heart, and with all your soul, and with all your *mind*. This is the great and foremost commandment." How can children love God with their minds when the public school and some private schools train their minds to ignore God's principles and to think as humanists?

Home schooling enables families to properly and comprehensively train their children's minds to think God's thoughts and to develop a biblical mindset rather than a secular mindset. However, it is important to make sure you are using a good curriculum and books which are grounded in God's Word. Even a home schooled child's mind can be wasted if the parents, for instance, just "baptize" humanist textbooks. By this I mean that sometimes parents use humanistic textbooks and merely pray over those books or try to do "damage control." With all the excellent Christian textbooks available and countless Christian books covering every subject, we are without excuse to give our children the most truth we can while they are being educated under our roofs. They will only be stronger and more grounded in God's principles, until truth becomes second nature to them.

In Appendix A, I have reprinted an excellent comparison between a Christian education and a humanistic education so that the reader can determine the type of education his children are receiving, whether at home, private school, or public school.

Negative Socialization in School

Even though parents are commanded to give their children a biblical education, they must also protect them from "negative socialization." The Scripture warns, "Do not be deceived: Bad company corrupts good morals" (1 Corinthians 15:33). Proverbs 13:20 states, "He who walks with wise men will be wise, but the companion of fools will suffer harm."

The public schools fail miserably in the area of socialization, with the abundance of crime, drugs, immorality, and gang warfare rampant in the school system. Home schooling enables parents to fulfill this responsibility by fostering positive socialization.

Content of True Education

It is clear from the passages above that God delegates to the parents the authority and responsibility for teaching children. God requires us to make certain that His Word and principles are applied in a daily, comprehensive manner to the education and upbringing of our children. Furthermore, He will hold us responsible for how we direct the education of our children. We must be careful not to "cause one of these little ones who believe in Me to stumble" by subjecting them to an ungodly education. Christ explains "it is better for him that a heavy millstone be hung around his neck, and that he be drowned in the depth of the sea" (Matthew 18:6; also see the consequences of disobedience in Colossians 3:25).

Therefore, parents must be careful to provide their children with an education in which the *content* is based on His Word.

> ...from childhood you have known the sacred writings which are able to give you the wisdom that leads to salvation through faith which is in Christ Jesus. All scripture is inspired by God and profitable for teaching, for reproof, for correction, for training in righteousness; that the man of God may be adequate, equipped for every good work (2 Timothy 3:16-17).

"The fear of the Lord is the beginning of knowledge" (Proverbs 1:7; also see Psalm 111:10). "The Lord gives wisdom; from His mouth come knowledge and understanding" (Proverbs 2:6; also see 9:10). In fact, James 1:5 affirms that in Christ are all the treasures of wisdom. Further, in James 3:13-18, it says wisdom which is not from above is earthly, natural, and demonic. Wisdom from above (which is found in the heavenly blueprint, the Bible) is "pure, then peaceable, gentle, reasonable, full of mercy and good fruits, unwavering, without hypocrisy." Which form of wisdom is being taught? Public schools and some private schools certainly are not teaching the wisdom from above.

The goal of true education is found in Psalm 119:97-101: To train children in God's laws so they can govern themselves, be wiser than their enemies, have more insight than their teachers, and understand more than the aged. If we train our children this way God will no doubt find us faithful stewards of the children He has placed in our care.

Scripture speaks to every area of life. It is clear that education is inescapably religious. Every subject, as a result, needs to be studied through the lens of God's Word. If parents do this, their children will be equipped for *every* good work and able to apply God's principles to every area of life. Their beliefs will not be separate from their thoughts and actions, as is so often the case with "Christians" today.

Does Sending Our Children to Public School as Missionaries Make it Right?

Many Christian parents rationalize that they are sending their children to public school in order for them to be "missionaries" to the unsaved children. However, there are no biblical examples of children being used as missionaries, but rather adults are always the missionaries. This means it is important for adult Christians to become public teachers and administrators, school board members, truant officers, and social workers.

As far as our children are concerned, God commands us, as seen in this chapter, to provide our children with a comprehensive education based on His principles. Sending our children to public school to "save souls" while they receive six or more hours of secular brainwashing does not relieve us of our responsibility before God. Disobeying God by doing something in the name of God does not justify our sin.

For instance, in 1 Samuel 15:1, 23, King Saul directly disobeyed God's command to destroy all of the Amalekite animals by sparing the animals and then offering them as sacrifices to the Lord. God rebuked Saul through Samuel, saying,

> Has the Lord as much delight in burnt offerings and sacrifices, as in obeying the voice of the Lord? Behold, to obey is better than sacrifice, and to heed than the fat of rams. For rebellion is as the sin of divination, and insubordination is as iniquity and idolatry (1 Samuel 15:22-23).

Are we trying to make a "sacrifice" to God by sending our children to public school to "save souls" while disobeying God's commands to us concerning raising our children? We must remember to obey is better than sacrifice.

These Biblical Principles Apply to Children in High School

Sometimes families are tempted to educate their children only *until* high school. At that point, they rationalize that their child is ready to be trained in a secular setting or elsewhere. The biblical principles discussed above, however, still apply to high-school-aged children. In fact, the high school years are generally the most difficult and formative years for a child. Therefore, consistent, biblical training is more important than ever.

Also the high school years are crucial for the training of the child's mind in God's principles and teaching him how to apply those principles in his life and in the world around him. A high-school-aged child is more mature and often ready for learning the weightier matters of God's laws and principles. The four high school years should be the final phase of training the child for adulthood so that he can thoroughly think as a Christian and apply biblical solutions to his future work, family, or college. These years are too valuable to waste and much too risky, considering the peer pressures and subtle humanistic training. God calls our children "arrows" and we need to be sure they are "finished" arrows that are straight, sharp, and sure of their mark. We do not want to shoot into the secular world partially finished arrows that are not fully sharpened. Such "arrows" will often miss their mark and make no impact.

In appendix C, Elizabeth Smith, a veteran home school mother and teacher, has prepared "15 Reasons to Home School in the High School Years." The reader is encouraged to review and consider these reasons as your children reach high school age.

Home Schooling Is a Biblical Form of Education

It is beyond dispute that home schooling has much support from the Word of God. I am convinced it is the best way that parents can fulfill God's commands to provide their children with a comprehensive biblical education while restoring and preserving their families. The goal of home schooling is to raise the children so that each of them will "be diligent to present [himself] approved to God as a workman who does not need to be ashamed, handling accurately the word of truth" (2 Timothy 2:15).

As seen from the verses above, God's truth and His principles are the foundation of all knowledge. Our children must not only be taught to *believe* as Christians but also to *think* as Christians. God's principles must be taught to children in a comprehensive manner on a daily basis. God's truth speaks to every academic discipline. Does modern public education even come close to these commands?

Sending our children to the public school violates nearly every biblical principle described above. It is tantamount to sending our children to be trained by the enemy. No doubt that if Satan had his choice as to which school system he would want us to send our children to, he would choose the public school system. Sending them to public school, knowing what we know the public schools have become, is like playing Russian Roulette with their souls! Yet the vast majority of Christians still send their children to public schools.

We need to encourage our pastors to start preaching these truths from the pulpit. Until pastors start to take the lead to urge an exodus from the public schools, the minds of many children from Christian families will be wasted and, in some instances, their hearts will be lost. You may want to give a copy of this book, or at least this chapter, to your pastor and encourage him to take a stand on this issue for the sake of our children. I have also prepared a short outline in appendix B, summarizing this chapter, entitled "Biblical Principles of Education," for you to photocopy and give to your pastor and fellow Christian parents who have their children in public schools. God's Word will not return void.

As parents, we cannot escape the responsibility for how our children are trained and educated. God will hold us responsible for the choices we make in regard to our children and to whom we delegate the authority to teach our children.

Home schooling is truly a biblical form of education. It is clear that God is raising up the home school movement from which properly trained children will one day assume leadership. God is blessing the home schooling movement, not because families are home schooling for home schooling's sake, but because the families are faithfully teaching their children to obey and glorify God! God will bless you as you "seek first His kingdom and righteousness" in the education and training of your children, and "all these things shall be added unto you" (Matthew 6:33).

It may not be easy for you to start home schooling. Once you start, the road will not always be smooth. But, remember that God will honor those who honor Him! By making your children and their training a priority, God will bring many invaluable blessings. In chapter 5, you will see the remarkable academic blessings from God. Throughout this book, you will see the legislative and court victories with which God has blessed home schoolers.

However, most important of all is our children's souls. Some day I would much rather have my children Bethany, Megan, Jesse, Susanna, Charity, Amy, and John standing with me in heaven than having them live as geniuses in terms of their secular education and lost forever in hell. John said it all when he said: "1 have no greater joy than this; to hear of my children walking in the truth!" (3 John 4). This is why I home school. This is my hope. I trust it is yours as well.

Notes

1. Martin Luther, *What Luther Says*, Vol. 1, 449. 99.

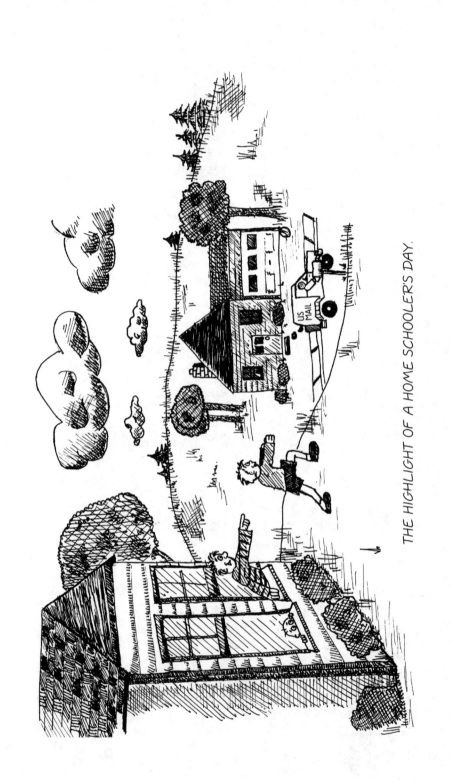

THE HIGHLIGHT OF A HOME SCHOOLER'S DAY.

Chapter
5

The Many Benefits
of Home Schooling

"Education: comprehends all that series of instruction and discipline which is intended to enlighten the understanding, correct the temper, and form the manners and habits of youth, and fit them for usefulness in their future stations. To give children a good education in manners, arts, and science, is important; to give them a religious education is indispensable; and an immense responsibility rests on parents and guardians who neglect these duties."

Definition from Noah Webster's First *Edition of an American Dictionary of the English Language,* 1828[1]

Sometimes, when people first hear of home schooling, they shudder and express doubt that a child could receive an adequate education at home. This reaction is normal since most Americans were trained in an institutional school and the majority of those attended a public school. I must admit I was initially one of these doubters.

This bias has been nurtured even further by the teacher unions and other pro-public school organizations which propagate myths, such as the necessity of certification of teachers and the claim that the government knows what is best for our children. As a result, many people, at first impression, are quickly ready to dismiss home schooling as a viable option for educating children.

However, once a person can put aside his bias and review the tremendous advantages of home schooling, these advantages speak for themselves. Nearly every week a new study is released which exposes the failing condition of the public school system, in spite of numerous reforms. Studies on home schooling, on the other hand, reveal academic excellence on the part of these students along with possession of a disciplined lifestyle and a moral foundation.

This chapter is intended to provide documentation to convince the doubter, and to give encouragement and "ammunition" to the home schooler, to counter criticism. Home schooling has many advantages, but the most convincing is that it really works.

What Is Home Schooling?

Home schooling is exactly what the name implies: a school in the home. The Illinois Supreme Court defined a school as "a place where instruction is imparted to the young."[2] The teachers in a home school are generally the parents, and it is estimated that at least 50 percent of them only have a high school diploma.[3] One element which all the home school parents seem to have in common is a commitment to making the necessary sacrifices to personally provide an education for their children.

As more and more people become aware of the advantages of home schooling, the ranks of home schoolers continue to swell. Between 1982-1987, approximately 1 million students were being home schooled nationwide. By 1997, the number of home schooled students was estimated to be at least 1.23 million which is more than the total amount of children enrolled in the public schools in Wyoming, Vermont, Delaware, Rhode Island, North Dakota, Alaska, South Dakota, Montana and Hawaii combined![4] Based on the rate of growth of home schooling in the states, membership with HSLDA, enrollments in correspondence schools and purchases by curriculum providers, I estimate that the amount of home schools has risen to 1.5 to 2 million home schoolers in the year 2000.

One example of the incredible increase in home schooling is reflected in a study of home schoolers in Wisconsin by the Wisconsin Policy Research Institute. The study demonstrates that when home schooling was officially legalized in the state in 1985, the number of children whom parents reported as being home schooled was 1,126. By 1998, the total number of home schooled children reached 18,712, an increase of 1,562%. It also is likely there are numerous students being home schooled without the state being notified. According to the researcher of this study, Robert V. Luebke, if all the home schooled students were considered part of a single school system, it would be the sixth largest district in the state.[5]

Luebke also explained that the research shows that home schooled children have active social and extracurricular lives. Although lack of such things has often been raised as a concern by critics of home schooling, Luebke said there is no research to support the claim.

As described on the front page of *USA Today*, home schooling is one of the ten major trends which carried us into this new century according to Gerald Celente, director of The Trends Research Institute, Rhinebeck, NY, and publisher of the *Trends Journal*. He says, "More parents working at home combined with dissatisfaction in public schools will swell the ranks of children being home schooled."[6]

Approximately 85 to 90 percent of the home schooling families are doing so for religious reasons.[7] One study of over 2,000 home school families found that 93.8 percent of the fathers and 96.4 percent of the mothers described themselves as being "born again" Christians.[8] These parents believe that God has given them the responsibility and the authority to educate their children.[9] In essence, I believe the modern home school movement is a spiritual revival which has embraced the Puritan and colonial understanding of the centrality of the family in education as described in chapter 6.

Christian Home Education News compiled results from a survey of 2,444 home school families in all fifty states. Approximately 25 percent of those surveyed lived in Florida. The findings showed that home school families tend to have more children than the national average: 10 percent had one child, 33 percent had two, 29 percent had three, 17 percent had four, and 11 percent had five or more. This means 57 percent of home school families had three or more children!

Concerning the method of teaching, the survey showed that out of the 2,244 families surveyed, 556 families used traditional text-books, 497 used workbooks, and 855 families used the unit study method. This method integrates the study of history, geography, math, language arts, science, and religion around one particular event or theme.[10]

The educational establishment initially tried to squelch the home school movement, and the public was generally against it. They claimed that home schooling would hamper a child's growth, and they asserted that parents with merely a high school diploma could never successfully teach their children. By God's grace the home schoolers proved them wrong. Home schooling does work, and the end product is children who academically excel and who readily are accepted into universities.

In this chapter, several advantages of home schooling will be identified in order to demonstrate why home schooling is a solution to today's educational crisis.

Spiritual Life: Home Schooling Teaches What Really Matters

The most important benefit of home schooling is the spiritual aspect. It has been said: "After this life is past, only our life in Christ will last." Since most home schooling parents profess a personal relationship with Christ and a belief that the Bible is the inspired Word of God, these families are teaching their children that living for Jesus, in accordance with the Word, is their most important priority. Public schools, on the other hand, ignore God and refuse to acknowledge the fact that everyone needs a Savior or they will eternally perish. Public schools also ignore God's laws and are churning out millions of students who are biblically illiterate.

In home schooling, parents can fulfill the commands in Scripture to teach their children God's truths throughout each day (see chapter 4 and appendix A and B for further discussion). Biblical principles can be applied to each and every subject. Erroneous and humanistic philosophies can be exposed, such as evolution, inaccurate historical revisions, situational ethics, amoral sex education, and New Age influence. The home schooled child can be consistently and carefully nurtured and trained in the admonition of the Lord so that he develops a strong moral foundation for his life. A comprehensive Christian education can be given to the home schooled child in response to the biblical commands in Scripture.[11] The parents have the opportunity to concentrate on establishing godly character in their children.

In appendix D, I thoroughly explain the need for all of us to accept Jesus Christ as our personal Lord and Savior. We all are going to die, and we need to be prepared. By home schooling, we can prepare our children and tend to their souls. Home schooling teaches what really matters.

Quality of Life: A Family Who
Schools Together Stays Together

The family also benefits from the home school in terms of cohesiveness and increased time spent together. Parents are able to spend hours interacting, teaching, sharing, and nurturing their children. Fathers, no matter what their work hours, can spend much more time with their children because the children's instruction can be adjusted. This time is far above the national average of parents spending approximately seven minutes a day with face-to-face contact with their children, according to a study from Stanford University. The children also do not become segregated from their brothers and sisters by age differences but are able to relate to all age groups.

In my work, I have learned of hundreds of families who were beginning to fragment or whose marriages were dissolving. However, after home schooling, these family relationships were restored and major problems overcome.

In addition, many home school mothers forsake careers and do not work outside the home. This gives the mother enough time to not only thoroughly train her children in academic and spiritual matters, but to spend time with her infant or preschool children. Home school mothers who stay home to teach their children do not place their infants and toddlers in day care centers. This is a major benefit to her children since children in day care centers are developing various types of negative side effects. Research for the last ten years demonstrates that infants raised in day care centers "are more prone to behavioral problems as young children than their home-reared cousins."[12]

According to Jay Belsky, a child care expert at Penn State's College of Health and Human Development, the research is compelling:

> There was this slow, steady trickle of disconcerting evidence. It looked like kids who were exposed to 20 or more hours a week of nonparental care in their first year of life…seemed to be at elevated risk. They were more likely to look insecure in their relationships to their mothers, in particular at the end of their first year of life. [They were also likely to show] aggression and noncompliance or disobedience between the ages of 3 and 8. That's it in a nutshell.[13]

On February 6, 1995, researchers from the University of Colorado in Denver, the University of California at Los Angeles, the University of North Carolina, and Yale University in Connecticut released results of a two and a half-year study. Researchers studied four hundred day-care centers in four states, evenly divided between for-profit and non-profit programs. Each of the centers had state licenses. A complete total of 749 infant, toddler, and preschool classrooms were studied. The study found that the quality of most daycare centers is so poor that it interferes with the emotional and intellectual development for thousands of young children. The study stated,

> babies in poor quality rooms are vulnerable to more ill-ness because sanitary conditions are not met for diapering and feeding; are in danger because of the safety problems that exist in the rooms; miss warm, supportive relation-ships with adults; and lose out on learning because they lack books and toys required for physical and intellectual growth.

The report stated that approximately 10 million children under the age of five are cared for by someone other than the parents. Of the infant and toddler classrooms observed, only 8 percent were consid-ered of good quality, while 40 percent were rated less than minimal. The rest were mediocre. The average fees charged by the centers per month was $450 for infants and $371 for preschoolers. The study found that only one in seven centers provides good quality care that encourages a child's healthy development. In one in eight, the chil-dren's health and safety were actually threatened.[14] Parents who home school can avoid this "parent trap" of day care centers for their pre-school children, that is commonly accepted today.

In this fast-moving technological age, time with the family is harder and harder to come by and there is constant pressure pulling the family apart. Our time with our children is precious. In fact, raising children is one of the greatest privileges and responsibilities God gives us. We never know how long our children will be with us. This point can best be made by the following excerpt from a letter which HSLDA received from a home school family in Michigan. Their thirteen-year-old son collapsed suddenly after getting off a ride at Disneyland. He had taken a trip to see his grandparents. His mother writes:

They took him immediately into surgery, but there was nothing they could do. The aorta wasn't just torn; it was shredded. God took Jim to be with Him three days before Jim's fourteenth birthday.

Jim was surrounded with Christian nurses at the hospital. My mom and dad were allowed to stay in the room with him. My parents had prayed with him, along with one of his nurses, even before they knew how serious Jim's condition was. My mom says that right after the prayer Jim's eyes and face just glowed and a peace and calm came over Jim which never left him. God was with Jim every step of the way.

How thankful we are that we have home schooled Jim and our other two boys for the last six years! We have seen Jim grow and mature in a way most parents never experience. We were able to spend many hours a day with him. We have so many keepsakes and memories.

My brother-in-law, who had gone on many of the Disneyland rides with Jim said, "Jim had an innocence about him. You could tell he was untouched by the world."[15]

No doubt every moment counts with our children—especially concerning the time cultivating their spiritual life. Unlike many families in our society, home schoolers have the time to make certain each day counts.

Socialization: Home Schoolers Are in the Real World

Academically, the home schoolers have generally excelled, but some critics have continued to challenge them on an apparent "lack of socialization" or "isolation from the world." Often there is a charge that home schoolers are not learning how to live in the "real world." However, a closer look at public school training shows that it is actually those public school children who are not living in the real world.

For instance, public school children are confined to a classroom for at least 180 days each year with minimal opportunity to be exposed to the workplace or to go on field trips. The children are trapped with a group of children of their own age with little chance to relate to children of other ages or adults. The children spend their time pooling their ignorance. They learn in a spiritual and moral vacuum where there are no absolute standards. They are given little to no responsibility, and everything is provided for them. The opportunity to pursue their interests and to apply their unique talents is stifled. Actions by public students rarely have consequences, as discipline is lax and passing from grade to grade is automatic. The students are not really prepared to operate in the home (family) or the workplace, which comprise a major part of the "real world" after graduation.

Home schoolers, on the other hand, do not have the above problems. They are completely prepared for the "real world" of the workplace and the home. They relate regularly with adults and follow their examples rather than the examples of foolish peers. They learn, based on "hands-on" experiences and early apprenticeship training. In fact, the only "socialization" or aspect of the "real world" which they miss out on by not attending the public school is unhealthy peer pressure, crime, and immorality. Of course, the average home schooler wisely learns about these things from afar instead of being personally involved in crime or immorality or perhaps being a victim.

Since the great majority of parents home school their children because of Christian beliefs, these parents consider it paramount to train their children in learning to serve others. They take seriously Jesus' command to love your neighbor as yourself. As a result, home schoolers are very involved in ministering to others in their respective communities. For instance, the LIFE Support Group in Gainesville, VA, is involved in a local Habitat for Humanity project. The home school children are participating in the rebuilding of a city block in Baltimore, MD. Home schoolers will also often minister to people in elderly care centers and help needy families in their community and church.

Apparently, home schoolers carry these principles of service they have developed into the college years. For instance, in the fall of 1994, Mike Mitchell, Dean of Enrollment Management of Oral Roberts University in Tulsa, Oklahoma, conducted a survey of home schooled students enrolled at the university. The survey revealed that of the 212 home schooled students enrolled at Oral Roberts University, 88 percent of these home schooled students were involved in one or more outreach ministries to the community, i.e., helping orphans, handicapped, elderly, prison ministries, and many more.

Practically, home schoolers overcome the potential for "isolation" through heavy involvement in church youth groups, community activities, 4H clubs, music and art lessons, Little League sports participation,

YMCA, Scouts, singing groups, activities with neighborhood children, academic contests (spelling bees, orations, creative and research papers), and regular involvement in field trips. In fact, one researcher stated, "The investigator was not prepared for the level of commitment exhibited by the parents in getting the child to various activities.... It appeared that these students are involved in more social activities, whether by design or being with the parent in various situations, than the average middle-school-aged child."[16]

In nearly every community throughout the country, local "home school support groups" have been formed in addition to the state-wide home school associations.[17] These local support groups sponsor, in many areas, weekly and monthly activities for the home school students, including physical education classes, special speakers, sports, camping, and trips to museums, industries, farms, parks, historic sites, and hundreds of other activities. Also regular contests are held including spelling bees, science fairs, wood working contests, and geography contests. Home schoolers in many localities have formed home school choirs, bands, sports teams, bowling leagues, educational and activity clubs of every kind, and many types of resource libraries. The state home school associations generally sponsor a major conference where home school children can attend and the older children perform plays, assemble year books, and participate in graduation ceremonies for eighth and twelfth grades. A review of the state home school association and local support group newsletters testify of the many social activities available. Home school families, as a whole, do not raise their children in social isolation.[18]

In addition, several studies have been done to measure home schoolers' "self-concept," which is the key objective indicator for establishing a child's self-esteem. A child's degree of self-esteem, of course, is one of the best measurements of his ability to successfully interact on a social level. One such study was by John Wesley Taylor, using the Piers-Harris Children's Self-Concept Scale to evaluate 224 home schooled children. The study found that 50 percent of the children scored above the 90th percentile, and only 10.3 percent scored below the national average.[19]

Another researcher compared private school nine-year-olds with home school nine-year-olds and found no significant differences in the groups in virtually all psycho-social areas. However, in the area of social adjustment, a significant difference was discovered: "private school subjects appeared to be more concerned with peers than the home-educated group."[20] This is certainly an advantage for home schooled children who can avoid negative peer influence.

Dr. Linda Montgomery studied home school students between the ages of ten and twenty-one and concluded that home schooled children are not isolated from social activities with other youth. She also concluded that home schooling may nurture leadership at least as well as the conventional schools do.[21]

Thomas Smedley prepared a master's thesis for Radford University of Virginia on "The Socialization of Home School Children." Smedley used the Vineland Adaptive Behavior Scales to evaluate the social maturity of twenty home schooled children and thirteen demographically matched public school children. The communication skills, socialization, and daily living skills were evaluated. These scores were combined into the "Adaptive Behavior Composite" which reflects the general maturity of each subject.

Smedley had this information processed using the statistical program for the social sciences and the results demonstrated that the home schooled children were *better socialized and more mature* than the children in the public school. The home schooled children scored in the 84th percentile while the matched sample of public school children only scored in the 27th percentile.

Smedley further found:

> In the public school system, children are socialized horizontally, and temporarily, into conformity with their immediate peers. Home educators seek to socialize their children vertically, toward responsibility, service, and adulthood, with an eye on eternity.[22]

Dr. Larry Shyers compared behaviors and social development test scores of two groups of seventy children ages eight to ten. One group was being educated at home while the other group attended public and private schools. He found that the home schooled children did not lag behind children attending public or private schools in social development.

Dr. Shyers further discovered that the home schooled children had consistently fewer behavioral problems. The study indicated that home schooled children behave better because they tend to imitate their parents while conventionally-schooled children model themselves after their peers. Shyers states:

> The results seem to show that a child's social development depends *more* on *adult contact* and less on contact with other children as previously thought.[23]

Dr. Brian Ray reviewed the results of four other studies on the socialization of home schoolers and found:

> Rakestraw, Reynolds, Schemmer, and Wartes have each studied aspects of the social activities and emotional characteristics of home schooled children. They found that these children are actively involved in many activities outside the home with peers, different-aged children, and adults. The data from their research suggests that home schoolers are not being socially isolated, nor are they emotionally maladjusted.[24]

J. Gary Knowles, University of Michigan Assistant Professor of Education, released a study done at the University of Michigan which found that teaching children at home won't make them social misfits. Knowles surveyed fifty-three adults who were taught at home because of ideology or geographical isolation. He found that two-thirds were married, which is the norm for adults their age. None were unemployed or on welfare. He found more than three-fourths felt that being taught at home had helped them to interact with people from different levels of society. He found more than 40 percent attended college and 15 percent of those had completed a graduate degree. Nearly two-thirds were self-employed. He stated, "That so many of those surveyed were self-employed supports the contention that home schooling tends to enhance a person's self-reliance and independence." Ninety-six percent of them said that they would want to be taught at home again. He stated, "Many mentioned a strong relationship engendered with their parents while others talked about self-directed curriculum and individualized pace that a flexible program of home schooling permitted."[25]

As mentioned earlier, the greatest benefit from home school socialization is that the child can be protected from the negative socialization of the public schools associated with peer pressure, such as rebellious attitudes, immaturity, immorality, drugs, and violent behavior. This is becoming more of a factor as the crime rate continues to soar in the public schools, as documented in chapter 2.

Effective Instruction: One-on-One Tutoring

Home schooled children are being taught with the most effective method of instruction: the tutorial method. Some of the benefits of this superior form of education are mentioned below.

For instance, a common difference between public schools and home schools is the amount of time parents need to spend per week instructing their children. It is clear that one-to-one instruction or tutoring by the parents of their child is far more efficient than the time spent in institutional schools. As a result, the average home schooler only needs to spend, on the average, three to four hours per day receiving formal instruction.[26] Unlimited learning can take place beyond formal instruction by spending "time on task" with various projects and "hands-on" experiences.

Richard Rossmiller of the University of Wisconsin studied elementary and secondary students throughout the country and discovered some interesting facts on how much time is wasted each year in institutional schools. According to his research, the typical student annually spends 367 hours (more than two hours a day) in activities such as lunch, recess, attendance-taking, and class changing, and 66 hours in "process activities" during which teachers answer questions, distribute material, and discipline students. In addition, the average pupil is absent from the classroom approximately 108 hours annually and loses about 54 hours to inclement weather, employee strikes, and teacher conferences.[27]

This leaves approximately only 485 hours of instructional time left in the average institutional school year of 1080 hours. Since the average home schooler spends about three to four hours a day in actual instruction over at least one-hundred-eighty days, he is spending a total of 540 hours to 720 hours in actual instruction time. This far exceeds the actual instructional time students spend in public schools.

This study further documents the differences between the tutorial method (home schooling) and the institutional school. From a legal perspective, home schools should not be required to fulfill institutional schools' hourly requirements without taking into account the inefficient use of time in the classroom.

Other benefits of home schooling include one-on-one instruction in which the parent can develop his child's gifts and overcome the child's weaknesses. This can be done much more accurately and in much less time than in the conventional schools. Gifted children are free to excel and slower students are not left behind.[28]

Also the child can be allowed to focus on what he is most interested in and to excel in his unique talents. The curriculum can be individually geared to the child's needs. Education can be flexible, maximizing the benefits for the child.

In addition, the children can be involved in apprenticeships, and experience much of their education firsthand, instead of only receiving their education through books. Without standardized education as offered in the public schools, the home school can provide unlimited hands-on learning tasks, field trips, and service projects. This practical aspect of learning is often lacking in institutional schools.[29]

Economics: Can the Family Survive on One Income?

Finances are always an important consideration for most families. Many people question whether home schooling is really practical, in light of the high cost of living. Keeping the mother at home to teach the children means the mother will most likely have to give up any job or career she has outside the home. In light of this, is home schooljng affordable? A recent study seems to indicate that the average working mother does not really bring home much income, after all the expenses are deducted.

On July 2, 1990, a study was released by the House Democratic Study Group in Washington, D.C.[30] The study revealed that the added income of a working mother was offset by increased work expenses, so that the family's usable income was only marginally increased. Although the average additional income that a working mother brings home is approximately $10,000, the actual *usable* income from a working mother averaged only $1,000 to $1,500 per year, after the expenses of taxes, transportation, child care, clothes, and meals were deducted. The study estimated that "one-third to one-half of the apparent increase in women's earnings was eaten up by work expenses and taxes."

The original purpose of the study was to determine how much better off families were because the mother worked. It compared two-parent families, factoring in mothers who worked full-time and part-time with the six to seven million mothers who were not employed outside the home. The financial plight of the American family was confirmed by the study, as the average earning of the approximately twenty-five million fathers in two-parent families fell from $31,973 in 1978 to $30,766 in 1988 (measured in constant 1990 dollars).

The average earnings of the working mothers increased because more of them were working and they were working more hours. Combined family income increased from $38,439 to $40,711, a modest gain, given the difficulty and sacrifices families must make to allow a mother to work outside the home.

The 18.1 million working mothers, on the average, make only a marginal increase in usable income from their jobs outside the home. Is the strain and fatigue of an outside job coupled with the small financial gain really worth the cost to their family life and their children's spiritual and mental well-being?

Based on this study, it would seem that home school mothers are not losing that much by forsaking careers for their children's sakes. In fact, many home school mothers start and operate home businesses in which the children can even participate after home school studies are completed. Most importantly, these mothers are placing a priority on the nurturing and discipline of their children, which cannot be measured in dollars and cents.

The "Nationwide Study of Home Education" which involved over two thousand home schooling families found that the average per-pupil expenditure for education is $488.00. Home schooling is very affordable. In addition, by home schooling one child, we save approximately $3,987.00 in tax dollars. Otherwise if we send our child to public school at least $3,987.00 will be spent on that child on the average.[31]

Academic Advantage: Home Schoolers on the Average Above Average

Many studies over the last few years have established the academic excellence of home schooled children. Not only can home schooled students compete with children in public school, but they excel, on the average, well above average. The one-on-one tutorial approach to education, which also is centered in the family unit, is a time-tested and winning combination. Below is a brief summary of some of these studies that support the academic success of home schooling.

Home Schooling Works Regardless of Race, Income or Grade Level

Most of the studies discussed below involve tests using the "norm referenced" system of scoring. This simply means the child's achievement is measured against a norm, or set of scores, established by a group of students thought to be typical of the nation as a whole. For example, if home schooled children in a particular study scored in the 80th percentile, that means that the home schooled children, on the average, did better than 80 percent of the national sample of the population on whom the test was normed.

In 1982, Dr. Raymond Moore studied several thousand home schooled children throughout the United States. His research found that these children had been performing, on the average, in the 75th to the 95th percentile on Stanford and Iowa Achievement Tests.[32] Additionally, Dr. Moore did a study of home schooled children whose parents were being criminally charged for exercising their right to teach their own children. He found that the children scored, on the average, in the 80th percentile.[33]

In 1986, researcher Lauri Scogin surveyed 591 home schooled children and she discovered that 72.61 percent of the home schooled children scored one year or more above their grade level in reading and 49.79 percent scored one year or more above their grade level in math.[34]

In 1988, Dr. Brian Ray, president of the National Home Education Research Institute, reviewed over sixty-five studies concerning home education. He found that home schoolers were performing average or above on testing.[35]

In 1990, the National Home Education Research Institute issued a report entitled "A Nationwide Study of Home Education: Family Characteristics, Legal Matters, and Student Achievement." This was a study of over 2,163 home schooling families.

The study found the *average* scores of the home school students were at or above the 80th percentile in all categories. This means that the home schoolers scored, on the average, higher than 80 percent of the students in the nation. The home schoolers' national percentile mean was 84 for reading, 80 for language, 81 for math, 84 for science, and 83 for social studies.

In 1997, a study of 5,402 home school students from 1657 families was released. It was entitled, *Strengths of Their Own: Home Schoolers Across America.* The study demonstrated that home schoolers, on the

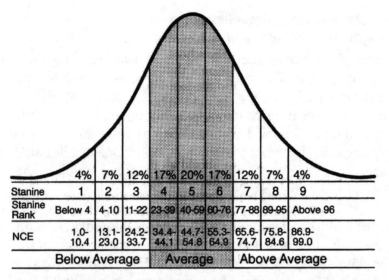

			4%	7%	12%	17%	20%	17%	12%	7%	4%
Stanine			1	2	3	4	5	6	7	8	9
Stanine Rank			Below 4	4-10	11-22	23-39	40-59	60-76	77-88	89-95	Above 96
NCE			1.0-10.4	13.1-23.0	24.2-33.7	34.4-44.1	44.7-54.8	55.3-64.9	65.6-74.7	75.8-84.6	86.9-99.0
		Below Average			**Average**			**Above Average**		

A Normal Distribution of Stanines, Percentile Ranks, Normal Curve Equivalents, and Performance Classification.

average, out-performed their counterparts in the public schools by 30 to 37 percentile points in all subjects. A significant finding when analyzing the data for 8th graders was the evidence that home schoolers who are home schooled two or more years score substantially higher than students who have been home schooled one year or less. The new home schoolers were scoring on the average in the 59th percentile compared to students home schooled the last two or more years who scored between the 86th and 92nd percentile.[36]

This was confirmed in another study by Dr. Larry Rudner of 20,760 home schooled students which found the home schoolers who have home schooled all their school-aged years had the highest academic achievement. This was especially apparent in the higher grades.[37] This is a good encouragement to families to catch the long-range vision and home school through high school. (See appendix C for "15 Reasons to Home School Through High School.")

Another important finding of *Strengths of Their Own* was that race of the student does not make any difference. There was no significant difference between minority and white home schooled students. For example, in grades K-12, both white and minority students scored, on the average, in the 87th percentile. In math, whites scored in the 82nd percentile while minorities scored in the 77th percentile. In the public schools, however, there is a sharp contrast. White public school eighth grade students nationally scored in the 58th percentile in math and the 57th percentile in reading. Black eighth grade students, on the other hand, scored on the average at the 24th percentile in math and the 28th percentile in reading. Hispanics scored at the 29th percentile in math and the 28th percentile in reading.[38]

These findings show that when parents, regardless of race, commit themselves to make the necessary sacrifices and tutor their children at home, almost all obstacles present in other school systems disappear.

Another obstacle that seems to be overcome in home schooling is the need to spend a great deal of money in order to have a good education. In *Strengths of Their Own*, Dr. Ray found the average cost per home school student is $546 while the average cost per public school student is $5,325. Yet the home school children in this study averaged in 85th percentile while the public school students averaged in the 50th percentile on nationally standardized achievement tests.[39] Similarly, the 1998 study by Dr. Larry Rudner of 20,760 students, found that eighth-grade students whose parents spend $199 or less on their home education score, on the average, in the 80th percentile. Eighth grade students whose parents spend $400 to $599 on their home education also score on the average, in the 80th percentile! Once the parents spend over $600, the students do slightly better, scoring in the 83rd percentile.[40]

The message is loud and clear. More money does not mean a better education. There is no positive correlation between money spent on education and student performance. The public schools advocates could refocus their emphasis if they learned from this lesson. Loving and caring parents are what matter. Money can never replace simple, hard work.

Also watching less television also seems to be distinguishing characteristic of home schoolers. Only 1.6 percent of fourth-grade home schoolers spend four to six hours watching TV on a daily basis compared to 40.5 percent of fourth graders nationwide. Television is a powerful force in reshaping the minds of children and doing their thinking for them. It is inhibiting their desire to apply themselves to their studies while teaching them to think like non-Christians. In our family, we decided in1995 to cut the cable and discontinue all television watching. We have never regretted it. We have wondered, however, how we ever had time to watch TV. Our seven children's tender hearts and minds are being protected from the very worldly influences of the television and they are being taught to learn without having to be entertained.

The last significant statistic from the *Strengths of Their Own* study regards the affect of government regulation on home schooling. Ever since I started working at the Home School Legal Defense Association in 1985, school officials and social workers have been telling our members and me, "the government, not the parents, knows what is best for our children." Your response is probably the same as mine: "What audacity! Who do they think they are? Where were they when our children were sick in the night? Where were they when we taught our children to walk and talk?" Yet, that remains the prevailing philosophy among public school officials and social workers. As seen in chapter 10, these government officials still believe home schoolers are not regulated enough.

The statistics give a very different story. Dr. Brian Ray compared the impact of government regulation on the academic performance of home school students and he found know positive correlation. In other words, whether a state had a high degree of regulation (i.e., curriculum approval, teacher qualifications, testing, home visits) or a state had no regulation of home schoolers, the home schooled students in both categories of states performed the same. The students all scored on the average in the 86th percentile regardless of state regulation.[41]

Home school freedom works. Home schoolers have earned the right to be left alone. These and many more studies documented in this chapter repeatedly prove what our experience in our own home school already demonstrates.

The research below reflects studies of home schoolers residing in certain states. This demonstrates that home schoolers do equally well regardless of their locality.

For example, in South Carolina, the National Center for Home Education did a survey of sixty-five home school students and found that the average scores on the Comprehensive Test of Basic Skills were 30 percentile points higher than national public school averages. In math, 92 percent of the home school students scored above grade level, and 93 percent of the home school students are at or above grade level in reading. These impressive scores are "being achieved in a state where public school SAT scores are next-to-last in national rankings."[42]

In Pennsylvania, 171 home schooled students took the CTBS Standardized Achievement Test. The tests were all administered in group settings by Pennsylvania certified teachers. The middle reading score was the 89th percentile, and the middle math score was the 72nd percentile. The middle science score was the 87th percentile, and the middle social studies score was the 81st percentile. A survey was conducted of all these home school families who participated in this testing which found that the average student spent only sixteen hours per week in formal schooling (i.e., structured lessons that were preplanned by either the parent or a provider of educational materials).[43]

In North Dakota, Dr. Brian Ray conducted a survey of 205 home schoolers throughout the state. The students scored, on the average, at the following percentiles: the reading score was the 84th percentile, language was the 81st percentile, science was the 87th percentile, social studies was the 86th percentile and math was the 81st percentile.

Further, Dr. Ray found no significant statistical differences in academic achievement between those students taught by parents with less formal education and those students taught by parents with higher formal education.[44]

In West Virginia over four hundred home school students, grades K-12, were tested with the Stanford Achievement test at the end of the 1989-90 school year. The Psychological Corporation scored the children together as one school. The results found that the typical home schooled students in eight of these grade levels scored in the "somewhat above average" range (61 to 73 average percentile), compared to the performance of students in the same grade from across the country. Two grade levels scored in the "above average" range (80 to 85 average percentile) and three grade levels scored in the "about average" range (54 to 59 average percentile).[45]

In Washington State, a survey of the standardized test results of 3,634 home schooled students, over a period of five years, found that the median cell each year varied from the 64th percentile to the 68th percentile on national norms. The Washington Home School Research Project concluded that "as a group, these home schoolers are doing well."[46]

In Idaho, fifty-four home school students were tested with the Iowa Basic Skills Tests and treated as a separate school district. A comparison based on the overall performance of students in the public schools in Boise with the home schooled students was performed. The data, based on the averages of each grade tested, demonstrated that in the complete composite home schoolers scored in the 89th percentile, and the Boise public school students scored in the 66th percentile.[47]

A survey of home schoolers in Montana was conducted by the National Home Education Research Institute in 1990. The test results of the Montana home schoolers which were used by the Institute were supplied by the Bob Jones University Testing Service based in South Carolina. The results of the Institute's survey indicated:

> On average, the home education students scored above the national norm in all subject areas on standardized achievement tests. These students scored, on average, at the 73rd percentile in terms of a combination of their reading, language, and math performance. This is well above the national average.[48]

Another significant study was released by the National Center of Home Education on November 10, 1994. According to these standardized test results provided by the Riverside Publishing Company of 16,311 home school from all 50 states K-12, the nationwide average for home school students is at 77th percentile of the basic battery of the Iowa Test of Basic Skills. In reading, the home schoolers nationwide grand mean is at the 79th percentile. This means, of course, that the home school students perform better in reading than the 79 percent of the sample population on whom the test is normed. In the area of language arts and math, the typical home schooler scored in the 73rd percentile. (See graphs on the next page).

These 16,311 home school students scores were not self-selected by parents or anyone else. They represent all the home schoolers, whose tests were scored through the Riverside Publishing Company. It is important to note that this rollup of home school achievement test scores demonstrates that 54.7 percent of the students in grades K-12 are achieving individual scores in the top quarter of the population of students in the United States. This figure is more than double the number of conventional school students who score in the top quarter.[49]

State Department of Education Statistics on Home Schoolers

Several state departments of education or local school districts have also gathered statistics on the academic progress of home schooled children.

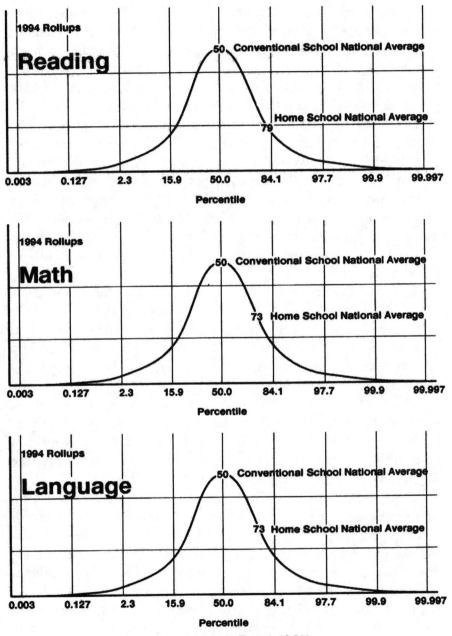

Number of Students Tested: 16,311

In the spring of 1987, the Tennessee Department of Education found that home schooled children in second grade, on the average, scored in the 93rd percentile, while their public school counterparts, on the average, scored in the 62nd percentile on the Stanford Achievement test. In eighth grade the home schooled students scored, on the average, in the 87th percentile in reading and in 71st percentile in math, while their public school counterparts scored in the 75th percentile in reading and the 69th percentile in math.[50]

Similarly, in 1986, the State Department of Education in Alaska, which had surveyed home schooled children's test results every other year since 1981, found home schooled children to be scoring approximately 16 percentage points higher, on the average, than the children of the same grades in conventional schools.[51] In Oregon, the State Department of Education compiled test score statistics for 1,658 home schooled children in 1988 and found that 51 percent of the children scored above the 71st percentile, and 73 percent scored above the 51st percentile.[52]

In North Carolina, the Division of Non-Public Education compiled test results of 2,144 home school students in grades K-12. Of the 1,061 home school students taking the California Achievement Test, they scored, on the average, at the 73rd percentile on the total battery of tests: 80th percentile in reading, 72nd percentile in language, and the 71st percentile in math.

The 755 home school students who took the Iowa Basic Skills test scored at the 80th percentile in the total battery of tests: 81st percentile in reading, 77th percentile in language, and 77th percentile in math. The remaining students who took the Stanford, scored, on the average, in the 73rd percentile in the whole battery.[53]

In Arkansas, for the 1987-88 school term, home school children, on the average, scored 75 percent on the Metropolitan Achievement Test 6. They outscored public school children in every subject (reading, math, language, science, and social studies) and at every grade level. For example, at the tenth-grade level, public school children scored an average of 53rd percentile in social studies, while home school children scored at the 73rd percentile. In science, an area in which home schoolers are often criticized for lack of facilities, the home schoolers scored, on the average, 85th percentile in fourth grade, 73rd percentile in seventh grade, and 65th percent in tenth grade. The public school students, on the other hand, scored much lower in science: 66th percentile in fourth grade, 62nd percentile in seventh, and 53rd percentile in tenth.[54]

According to the Arizona State Department of Education, 1,123 home schooled children in grades 1 through 9, on the average, scored *above* grade level in reading, language arts, and math, on standardized tests for the 1988-89 school year. Four grades tested were a full grade level ahead.[55]

Home Schoolers' Scores Top National Averages in Canada

The results of a formal study released on July 5, 1994, shows that Canadian home schooled students score at or above the 76th percentile on national norms in reading, listening, language, math, science, social studies, basic battery, and complete battery scores. Many factors were examined for their relationship to the students' academic performance; only a few are significant. Educational attainment of the fathers is a weak predictor of reading and language scores, and the longer a child has been home educated, the better his language score. Commissioned by the Home School Legal Defense Association of Canada and conducted by Dr. Brian Ray of the National Home Education Research Institute (NHERI), the study represents 808 home-educating families and 2,594 children. In addition to examining the academic performance of home schooled students, the study also collected and analyzed information on the parents' educational background, family income, family size, age of children being taught at home, previous education experience in either private or public education, family's religious affiliation, and the legal status of their home school.[56]

Conclusion of the Studies: Home Schooling Works!

These statistics point to one conclusion: home schooling works. Even many of the State Departments of Education, which are generally biased toward the public school system, cannot argue with these facts. Not only does home schooling work, but it works without the myriads of state controls and accreditation standards imposed on the public schools.

Home Schooling Is Not a Passing Fad

Overall, the success of home schoolers seems to be due to one-to-one instruction, tailoring instruction to the needs and ability of each individual child, more individual responses, and an absence of negative socialization pressure. These advantages, as summarized above, continue to fuel the rapid growth of the home schooling movement.

Notes

1. Noah Webster, *American Dictionary of the English Language* (San Francisco: Foundation for American Christian Education, 1980) reprinted from the original A. & C. Merriam Company, 1828.
2. *People* v. *Levisen,* 404 11. 574, 90 N.E.2d 213, (1950). *Black's Law Dictionary* defines the term "school" as "an institution *or place* for instruction or education."
3. In July 1986, Lauri Scogin, B.S., M.A., an independent educational research consultant, did a random survey of three hundred home school families from across the states and found that 45 percent of the parents had a college degree or higher, 50 percent had high school diplomas, and the remainder had below high school. See "Home Schoolers Excel," *The Home School Court Report,* Vol. 3, No.1, January-February, 1987.
   This finding is supported by a recent study of 199 home schoolers conducted by Donald Wynn, Sr., which found that 54 percent of home school parents had college degrees or higher. See "A Study of the Development of Home Schools As an Alternative to Public School Education," as appeared in the *Home School Researcher* (Seattle: Home School Researcher, 1989), Vol. 5 No.1, 18. (Now located in Salem, Oregon as of 1991.)
4. Dr. Brian Ray, *Strengths of Their Own: Home Schoolers Across America,* National Home Education Research Institute, Salem, OR, 1997.
5. The Wisconsin Policy Research Institute study is a private, nonprofit research organization based in Thiensville, Wisconsin. The home school study was written by Robert V. Luebke, an independent educational researcher from Middleton with a doctoral degree in educational administration. The study was released July 1999.
6. Anita Manning, "Life in '94 Will Offer Glimpse Into Next Century," *USA Today,* December 22, 1993, 1.
7. This conclusion has been drawn from the applications of over fifty thousand home school families across the nation who have joined the Home School Legal Defense Association since 1985, and from conversations with state home school leaders.
   Also the North Carolina Department of Education released a study for the 1988-89 school term and found that out of 1,385 home schools registered with the state, 1,085 designated themselves as "religious" schools. North Carolina Home School Enrollment by Ages and Statewide Statistical History" (Raleigh: Division of Non-Public Education, December 1, 1989).
8. Dr. Brian Ray, "A Nationwide Study of Home Education: Family Characteristics, Legal Matters, and Student Achievement," National Home Education Research Institute, Seattle, Washington, 1990. (Now located in Salem, Oregon as of 1991.)
9. Many home school authors echo these profound Christian beliefs concerning education, which are commonly held throughout the home school movement. For example, see Blair Adams and Joel Stein, *Wisdom's Children,* (Austin, TX: Truth Forum, 1989), 88-130; Gregg Harris, *The Christian Home School* (Brentwood, TN.: Wolgemuth & Hyatt, 1988), 61-80; J. Richard Fugate, *Will Early Education Ruin Your Child?* (Tempe, AZ: Alpha Omega, 1990), 3-13; Theodore Wade, Jr., *The* Home *School Manual* (Auburn, CA.: Gazelle, 1991), 177-86.
10. Survey conducted by Roy Lind, editor of the *Christian Home Education News,* reported in Vol. 3, No.4, 1994, Special Edition, 1-6.
11. See chapter 4 for a detailed review of biblical mandates on education.
12. Daniel Wattenberg, "The Parent Trap," *Insight* magazine, Washington D.C., March 2, 1992, 7.
13. *Ibid.*
14. "Daycare Study Finds Centers Inadequate, *Washington Times,* Associated Press, February 7, 1995, A5.
15. "What's Worth Fighting For?" *The Home School Court Report,* May-June 1991, Vol. 7, No.3, 20.

16. "Socialization Practices of Christian Home School Educators in the State of Virginia," a study of ten Virginia home school families, performed by Dr. Kathie Carwile, appeared in *Home School Researcher*, Vol. 7, No.1, December 1991.

17. For an extensive list of many of the state home school associations see listing in the back of this book.

18. R. Meighan, "Political Consciousness and Home-Based Education," *Educational Review*, 36 (1984): 165-73.

19. Dr. John Wesley Taylor, *Self-Concept in Home Schooling Children* (Ann Arbor, MI.: University Microfilms International), Order No. DA8624219. This study was done as part of a dissertation at Andrews University. The results of the testing of the 224 home schooled students was compared to the testing results of 1,183 conventionally schooled children.

20. Dr. Mona Delahooke, "Home Educated Children's Social/Emotional Adjustment and Academic Achievements: A Comparative Study," unpublished doctoral dissertation, California School of Professional Psychology, Los Angeles, 1986, 85.

21. Dr. Linda Montgomery, "The Effect of Home Schooling on Leadership Skills of Home Schooled Students," *Home School Researcher* (5)1, 1989.

22. Thomas C. Smedley, M.S., "Socialization of Home Schooled Children: A Communication Approach," thesis submitted and approved for Master of Science in Corporate and Professional Communication, Radford University, Radford, Virginia, May 1992. (Unpublished)

23. Dr. Larry Shyers, "Comparison of Social Adjustment Between Home and Traditionally Schooled Students," unpublished doctoral dissertation at University of Florida's College of Education, 1992. Dr. Shyers is a psychotherapist who is the Chairman of the Florida Board of Clinical Social Work, Marriage and Family Therapy, and Mental Health Counseling.

24. Dr. Brian Ray, "Review of Home Education Research," *The Teaching Home*, August/September 1989, 49. See Rakestraw, "An Analysis of Home Schooling for Elementary School-Age Children in Alabama," Doctoral dissertation, University of Alabama, Tuscaloosa, AL, 1987; Reynolds, "How Home School Families Operate on a Day-to-Day Basis: Three Case Studies," Unpublished doctoral dissertation, Brigham Young University, Provo, UT, 1985; and Schemmer, "Case Studies of Four Families Engaged in Home Education," unpublished doctoral dissertation, Ball State University, Muncie, IN, 1985.

25. University of Michigan, Ann Arbor, study of home school adults by Assistant Professor of Education, J. Gary Knowles, Associated Press article entitled, "University Study Says Home-taught Children Won't Become Social Misfits," appearing in the *Grand Haven Tribune*, March 9, 1993.

26. Dr. Brian Ray found home school students, on the average, spend three to four hours a day on formal instruction. Ray further found no statistically significant relationship between hours per day in formal education and academic achievement. Brian Ray, Ph.D. *Home Education in Oklahoma: Family Characteristics, Student Achievements, and Police Matters*, NHERI, Salem, Oregon.

27. Richard A. Rossmiller, "Time-on-Task: A Look at what Erodes Time for Instruction," National Association of Secondary School Principals (NASSP) Bulletin Vol.67, No.465, 45-49, October 1983.

28. See note 8 of this chapter for a list of books that describe the benefits of home schooling.

29. See note 8 for a list of books that describe the benefits of home schooling.

30. *Washington Post*, July 2, 1990.

31. Dr. Brian Ray, "A Nationwide Study of Home Education," National Home Education Research Institute, Seattle, Washington, 1990. (Now located in Salem, Oregon as of 1991)

32. Dr. Raymond Moore "Research and Common Sense: Therapies for Our Home Schools," *Teachers College Record*, Columbia University, Vol. 84, No.2, 1982, 372.
    For further documentation of the academic success of home schooling see N.J. Linden, "An Investigation of Alternative Education: Home Schooling." Ph.D. dissertation, East Texas State University, 1983.
    Also see Dr. Brian Ray, "A Comparison of Home Schooling and Conventional Schooling: With a Focus on Learner Outcomes" (a paper presented at Oregon State University, 1986). The author concluded, based on reviewing eleven studies which addressed the achievement of home school children, home schoolers were matching, and in many cases, excelling the average school achievement.

33. " Home Schooling: An Idea Whose Time Has Returned," *Human Events*, September 15, 1984.

34. "Home Schoolers Excel," *The Home School Court Report*, Vol. 3, No.1, January-February, 1987.

35. Dr. Brian Ray, *Education and Urban Society*, Vol.21, No.1, November 1988 (Newbury Park, CA), 16-31.

36. Dr. Brian Ray, *Strengths of Their Own: Home Schoolers Across America*, National Home Education Research Institute, Salem, OR, 1997.

37. Lawrence M. Rudner, Ph.D., Director of the ERIC Clearing House on Assessment and Evaluation, *Home Schooling Works: The Scholastic Achievement and Demographic Characteristics of Home School Students in 1988*, published by the Home School Legal Defense Association, Purcellville, VA 20134, www.HSLDA.org. ERIC is sponsored by the National Library Services of the U.S. Department of Education.

38. Dr. Brian Ray, *Strengths of Their Own: Home Schoolers Across America*, National Home Education Research Institute, Salem, OR, 1997.

39. *Ibid.*

40. Rudner, *Home Schooling Works: The Scholastic Achievement and Demographic Characteristics of Home School Students in 1988*.

41. Dr. Brian Ray, *Strengths of Their Own: Home Schoolers Across America.*

42. Statistics compiled by the National Center For Home Education, P.O. Box 125, Purcellville, Virginia 22129, in 1990.

43. "PA Homeschooled Students Score High!" *Pennsylvania Homeschoolers* newsletter, Issue 33, Fall 1990, 1.

44. "ND Research Shows Home Schoolers Do Very Well." *North Dakota Home School Association Newsletter*, Vol. 6, Issue 4, April 1991, 1. The complete study is entitled "Home Education in North Dakota: Family Characteristics and Student Achievement," 1991, National Home Education Research Institute (NHERI) Western Baptist College, 5000 Deer Park Dr. S.E., Salem, Oregon 97301.

45. Psychological Corporation, San Antonio, Texas.

46. Jon Wartes, "Five Years of Home School Testing within Washington State: 1986-1990." This report, concluded in December 1991, is the result of the findings of the Washington Home School Research Project which is conducted by thirteen public school educators and home schoolers. (Available from the Washington Home School Research Project, 16109 NE 169 Pl., Woodinville, Washington 98072.)

47. Res Peters, Idaho Home Educators, Boise, Idaho, 1991.

48. "Study Shows Homeschoolers Ahead in Achievement," *The Grapevine: Montana* Home *School News*. January 1991, 6. The complete study is entitled "'Home Education in Montana: Family Characteristics and Student Achievement," 1991. It was conducted by NHERI (see note 22).

49. This study was released by the National Center for Home Education, November 10, 1994, Purcellville, Virginia.

50. Office of the Commissioner, Tennessee Department of Education, *Home School Student Test Results: 1986 and 1987* (Nashville, 1987).

51. *Method:* Alaska *Perspectives*, Vol. 7, No.1 Juneau, Alaska Dept. of Education, 1986.

52. "March 1, 1988 Oregon Home School Data Report," *Line Upon Line*, Vol. 11, No.5 (Beaverton, OR, 1988). The data was compiled from information submitted from the Educational Service District and County Units in Oregon between September 1987 and March 1988. Office of Policy and Program Development, Oregon Department of Education, Les Marten, December 1, 1986, *Home School Data Report* (Salem: 1986). Showed in 1986 that of 1,121 home schoolers, 76 percent were above the 50th percentile.

53. "North Carolina Home School Nationally Standardized Achievement Test Results 88-89 School Term" (Raleigh: Office of the Governor, Division of Non- Public Education, December 1, 1989).

54. "Standardized Test Results," *Update*, Vol. 7, No.1 (Little Rock, Arkansas Christian Home Education Association, September 1988). This newsletter reported on test results compiled by the Arkansas Department of Education of 760 home schooled students.

55. Arizona Department of Education, *Students Taught at Home 1989 Average Grade Equivalents*, compiled by Steve Stephens, State Testing Coordinator, July 1989.

For earlier statistics for Arizona home schoolers' success on standardized tests, see article by Patricia Lines, "States Should Help, Not Hinder, Parents' Home Schooling Efforts," *Education Week*, May 15, 1985.

56. This Canadian study may be obtained from HSLDA of Canada, #203, 1601 Dunmore Rd., S.E., Medicine Hat, Alberta TIA IZB, Canada; 403-528-2704.

Wherefore, seeing we also are compassed about with so great a cloud of witnesses, let us run with patience the race that is set before us.

—Hebrews 12:1

Chapter
6

The History of Home Schooling in America

All government originates in families, and if neglected there, it will hardly exist in society...The foundation of all free government and of all social order must be laid in families and in the discipline of youth.

...The education of youth, [is] an employment of more consequence than making laws and preaching the gospel, because it lays the foundation on which both the law and gospel rest for success."[1]

Noah Webster

Home schooling is not, by any means, a new phenomenon in our country. It is a time-tested and very successful form of education that has been used since the 1600s. When the public schools were formed and compulsory attendance laws were passed throughout the country in the early 1900s, home schooling almost died out. Not until the 1970s was the modern home school movement born. A glance at the history of "family education" in the home, where many Americans were taught during the first 250 years of their presence on this continent, follows.

Education in Early America Primarily Took Place in the Home

From the founding of this country by the Pilgrims in 1620 and the Puritans in 1630 to the late 1800s, most education took place in homes, with either the parents or a tutor (usually a pastor) providing the instruction.

> Education was mainly a family responsibility in colonial America, and the extent of it was largely left up to the individual. There were no compulsory attendance laws enforced by governments. Most children got at least their early education in the home, where they might be taught to read, write, and figure, but most certainly would be trained in housekeeping...and in many of the tasks of making a living.[2]

The colonists were heirs to common law and biblical traditions "stressing the centrality of the household as the primary agency of human association and education."[3] They were "instructed—indeed harangued—by Puritan tracts and sermons proclaiming the correctness and significance" of family education.[4] As a result, individual reading, responsive reading, and community reading were daily activities in the colonial household. After analyzing colonial education, historian Lawrence Cremin concluded: the "family was the most important agency of popular education."[5]

The Role of the Bible in Home Education

This principle of home education came from the colonists diligently reading and applying the Bible. The cornerstone of education was their belief that children are a gift and blessing from the Lord to the parents.[6] Parents were to train their children in the "nurture and admonition of the Lord" and apply biblical principles to every area of life. Education was not a responsibility of the civil government.

In fact, historians agree that the Bible was "the single most important cultural influence in the lives of Anglo-Americans."[7] Alexis de Tocqueville, in his travels throughout the colonies and the frontier, found the Bible to be in nearly every household.[8] Consequently, the most important reason the colonists wanted their children to be literate was so they could read the Bible and thereby learn the principles of living as commanded by God.[9] For that reason, the Bible itself was used as a major textbook in most homes.

> Doubtless, many a colonial youngster learned to read by mastering the letters and syllables phonetically and then hearing Scriptural passages again and again, with the reader pointing to each word until the relationship between the printed and oral passages became manifest.[10]

The Bible was further revered and applied by the textbook writers of that period. The most popular textbooks were *The New England Primer* and Noah Webster's books, *A Grammatical Institute of the English Language* and *The American Spelling Book*. One hundred million copies of *The American Spelling Book* were sold in early America.[11] All of these books were made up of spiritual rhymes and biblical principles, further evidencing the impact of the Bible on education.[12]

Noah Webster explained the importance of the Bible in education: "The Bible is the chief moral cause of all that is good, and the best corrector of all that is evil, in human society; the best book for regulating the temporal concerns of men, and the only book that can serve as an infallible guide to future felicity."

Twofold Purpose of Home Education

In colonial America, home education by the immediate family, or in some instances, the extended family, had two basic purposes. First, "sustained and systematic instruction" was normally given in order to achieve literacy. Second, vocational education was provided in order to enable the children to learn to be self-sufficient. This same twofold interest of the parents has now been usurped by the state, by declaration of the United States Supreme Court.

Literacy education involved daily parental instruction of the children in reading and writing. The reading materials would include the Bible, religious primers, some of the classical writings, history books, and almanacs.

The vocational education included daily household chores which "provided a continuous general apprenticeship in the diverse arts of living."[13] Many times children would work along side their father and mother, learning usually diverse skills. If a child desired a trade or skill other than their parents' skills, he would acquire a formal apprentice-ship with another businessman or tradesman. Such apprenticeships were commonplace, whether learning carpentry, iron making, medi-cine, or law.[14] As a result,

> For many, formal schooling was simply unnecessary. The fine education they received at home and on the farm held them in good stead for the rest of their lives, and was sup-plemented with Bible reading and almanacs like Franklin's *Poor Richard's*.[15]

The grammar schools that existed were privately run and mere extensions of the home and church. Most children who entered these grammar schools at age eight or nine, however, were already substan-tially taught at home in reading and writing.[16]

College education was something many of our forefathers did not want or need. Degrees were unimpressive because men were mostly judged by their character and experience. At least nine colleges were quickly established in the middle 1700s, including Yale, Harvard, and Princeton. All of them were founded on Christianity and emphasized biblical and classical studies.[17] The entrance requirements for these colleges were stiff. A freshman in the College of William and Mary in the 1700s had to "be able to read, write, converse, and debate in Greek."[18] The King's College in New York required applicants to translate the first ten chapters of the Gospel of John from Greek into Latin.[19] Yet John Jay entered college at the age of fourteen,[20] John Cotton, Ezekiel Rogers, Reverend Witherspoon, and Jonathan Edwards, at the age of thirteen,[21] and Thomas Jefferson,[22] John Adams, and James Monroe at age sixteen.[23]

Home education provided a complete education for children, making them both literate and self-sufficient, and also prepared those who wanted to proceed to grammar schools and college.

The Founders Never Intended State Education

Thomas Jefferson's beliefs concerning public education and state control reflected our forefathers' fear of such education:

> It is better to tolerate the rare instance of a parent refusing to let his child be educated than to shock the common

feelings and ideas by the forcible asportation and education of the infant against the will of the father.[24]

State education, as we know it today, did not begin to exist in the United States until the 1840s in Massachusetts.[25] It was not until the early 1900s that state education became widespread.

As a result, the authority and responsibility of education shifted, by the early 1900s, from the parents to the state. This shift, as seen in Part One of this book, was the beginning of the decaying process of American education. No longer would children be considered sinful and responsible for their behavior. Education would be manipulated by the elite educational establishment to "save our society." Instead, the "man is the measure of all things" educational philosophy, along with the denial of absolute values, has brought our country into the chaos and crisis occurring today.

Home Education in Early America Was Successful

As a result of home education and private grammar schools during the first seventy-five years of our country, the overall literacy rate was much higher than it is today.[26]

For example, DuPont de Nemours surveyed education in America in the early 1800s, and discovered a nearly 99 percent literacy rate:

> Most young Americans…can read, write, and cipher. Not more than four in a thousand are unable to write legibly-even neatly—while in Spain, Portugal, and Italy, only a sixth of the population can read; in Germany, even in France, not more than a third; in Poland, about two men in a hundred; and in Russia not one in two hundred. England, Holland, and the Protestant Cantons of Switzerland, more nearly approach the standard of the United States, because in those countries the Bible is read; it is considered a duty to read it to the children…. In America a great number of people read the Bible.[27]

John Adams discovered in 1765 that a "native of America, especially of New England, who cannot read and write is as rare a Phenomenon as a Comet."[28] Jacob Duche, the Chaplain of Congress in 1772, said of his countrymen, "almost every man is a reader."[29]

Similarly, Daniel Webster confirmed that the product of home education was near-universal literacy, when he stated "a youth of fifteen, of either sex, who cannot read and write, is very seldom to be found."[30] An example of the success of home schooling was the ability of the average citizen to read and understand *The Federalist Papers*, which was specifically written for the common man but is rarely comprehended today.

The desire to read resulted in most households building personal libraries that contained as many as four thousand volumes. According to Benjamin Franklin, the American libraries have improved the general conversation of Americans, made the common tradesman and farmers as intelligent as most gentlemen from other countries, and perhaps have contributed in some degree to the stand so generally made throughout the colonies in defense of their privileges.[31]

The home education of many early Americans was supplemented by sermons each Sunday. These sermons were given by pastors who would spend eight to twelve hours in study daily, researching and praying over their weekly sermons. The major impact of this Calvinistic clergy in shaping the Christian culture and biblical government of our country is documented by many historians[32]

> Thus, without ever attending a college or seminary, a churchgoer in colonial America could gain an intimate knowledge of Bible doctrine, church history, and classical literature.[33]

Home Schooling Has a Proven Track Record

The message is clear. Education at home achieved literacy and self-sufficiency. The colonists understood that the God-given responsibility of training children rests with the parents. The biblical principle that they applied was the principle that the parents had sole control of the process of education. America produced several generations of highly skilled and literate men and women who laid the foundation for a nation dedicated to the biblical principles of freedom, moral law, and self-government. In chapter 7, I will give the reader many accounts of individual success stories of home schoolers in history.

The recent revival of home education, beginning substantially in the 1980s, "is actually the closing of a circle, a return to the philosophy which prevailed in an earlier America."[34]

Notes

1. *Noah Webster's First Edition of an American Dictionary of the English Language,* 12 of Preface by Rosalie J. Slater (San Francisco: Foundation for American Christian Education, 1980).
2. Clarence Carson, *The Colonial Experience* (Wadley, AL: American Textbook Committee, 1987), 124-25.
3. John Bamard and David Burner, editors, *The American Experience in Education,* chapter 1 by Lawrence Cremin, "Education in the Households and Schools of Colonial America" (New York: Franklin Watts, Inc., 1975), 3.
4. *Ibid.*
5. *Ibid.,* 12.
6. See chapter 4 for a summary of the Scripture verses supporting the parents' roles in education which are often quoted throughout the writings of the Puritans and many of the early educators and leaders. Also see Levi Hart, "The Importance of Parental Fidelity in the Education of Children" (Norwich, 1792) and Reverend John Witherspoon, "Letters on Education of Children" (1797), both reprinted in Vema Hall, editor, *Christian History of the American Revolution,* (San Francisco: The Foundation for American Education, 1982), 213-45.
7. Lawrence Cremin, *American Education: The Colonial Experience,* 1607-1789 (New York: Harper and Row, 1970), 40.
8. Alexis de Tocqueville, *Democracy in America,* trans. George Lawrence, ed. J.P. Mayer (Garden City, NY: Doubleday and Co., 1969), 290-315.
9. Bamard and Burner, *The American Experience,* 8. Another historian summarized that colonial education's "chief purpose was to support revealed religion." Clinton Rossiter, *Seedtime of the Republic: The* Origin *of the American Tradition of Political Liberty* (New York: Harcourt, Brace, 1953), 120.
   Another reason the colonists encouraged family education was to protect their country from tyranny. "Education is favorable to liberty. Freedom can exist only in the society of knowledge. Without learning, men are incapable of knowing their rights, and where learning is confined to a few people, liberty can be neither equal or universal." Dr. Benjamin Rush, one of the framers of the Constitution, in an essay written in 1786, quoted in Hamilton Abert Long, *The American Ideal of 1776* (Philadelphia: Your Heritage Books, Inc.), xix.
10. *Ibid.,* 8. Also see Pierre Samuel DuPont de Nemours, *National Education in the United States of America* (Newark: University of Delaware Press, 1923), 329-330.
11. Noah Webster, *American Dictionary of the English Language,* preface by Rosalie Stater (San Francisco: Foundation for American Christian Education, 1967), 13.
12. ed. Vema Hall *Christian History,* 21. Webster further explains his views on education, typifying the philosophy of education prevalent in his time: "In my view, the Christian religion is the most important and one of the first things in which all children...ought to be instructed. No truth is more evident to my mind that the Christian religion must be the basis of any government intended to secure the rights and privileges of a free people.... When I speak of Christian religion...I mean primitive Christianity in its simplicity as taught by Christ and His apostles, consisting in belief in the being, perfection, and moral government of God; in the revelation of His will to men, as their supreme rule of action; in man's accountability to God for his conduct in this life; and in the indispensable obligation of all men to yield entire obedience to God's commands in the moral law and in the Gospel." *American Dictionary of the English Language,* 12. Also see J. Richard Fugate, *Will Early Education Ruin Your Child?* (Tempe, AZ: Alpha Omega Publications, 1990), 58 (or 23 in 2nd Edition, 1992).
13. Barnard and Burner, *The American Experience,* 6.
14. Carson, *The Colonial Experience,* 125 and Barnard and Burner, *The American Experience,* 11-12.

15. Robert A. Peterson, "Education in Colonial America," *The Freeman* (New York: Irvington-on-the-Hudson, 1983), 6. Also see Samuel Eliot Morison, *The Intellectual Life of New England* (Ithaca: Cornell University Press, 1965), 71- 72.
16. Peterson, "Education in Colonial America," 5.
17. Carson, *The Colonial Experience*, 124.
18. John Eidsmoe, *Christianity and the Constitution* (Grand Rapids, Mich.: Baker Book House, 1987), 22.
19. *Ibid.*
20. *Ibid.*
21. Fugate, *Will Early Education Ruin Your Child?*, 60-62.
22. Eidsmoe, *Christianity and the Constitution*, 218.
23. *The American Heritage Book of the Presidents* (New York: Dell Publishing, 1967), 62 (also page 160 in II).
24. Saul K. Padover, *Jefferson* (New York: Harcourt-Brace 1942), 369.
25. Samuel Blumenfeld, *NEA: Trojan Horse in American Education*, (Boise, Idaho: Paradigm Company, 1984), I.
26. Samuel Blumenfeld, *Is Public Education Necessary?* (Old Greenwich, CN.: Devin Adair, 1981), 27 -30 and Rousas John Rushdoony, *The Messianic Character of American Education* (Nutley, NJ: The Craig Press, 1979), 330.
27. See Nemours, *National Education in the United States of America* (Delaware: University of Delaware Press, 1923), 3-5.
28. Butterfield, ed., *Diary and Autobiography of John Adams* (Cambridge, MA.: Harvard University Press, 1961).
29. Carl and Jessica Bridenbaugh, *Rebels and Gentlemen* (New York: Oxford University Press, 1982), 99.
30. "Discourse on Education," *The Works of Daniel Webster* (Boston: C.C. Little & J. Brown Co., 1851), 125.
31. Max Farrand, ed. *The Autobiography of Benjamin Franklin*, (Berkley, CA: 1949), 86. See Carson, *The Colonial Experience*, 125, for a description of many of the colonial household libraries.
32. Peterson, "Education in Colonial America," 8. For further description of the crucial role of the Calvinistic clergy in educating the people of early America through their verbal and written sermons, see John Whitehead, *The American Dream* (Westchester, IL, Crossway Books, 1987), 35-43 and Eidsmoe, Christianity and the Constitution, 17-38.
33. *Ibid.*
34. Beshoner, "Home Education in America: Parental Rights Reasserted" (Kansas City: University of Missouri Law Review 191, 1981), 49.
    For instance, in the Plymouth Colony, "most of the heads of families were not only fully competent to teach their own sons and daughters, but found it no severe hardship to give their time to the training of the few whose parents had either died or were needy." See William T. Davis, *History of the Town of Plymouth* (Philadelphia: J.W. Lewis & Co., 1885), 52.

7

The Home School
Hall of Fame

"It is better to tolerate the rare instance of a parent refusing to let his child be educated, than to shock the common feelings and ideas by the forcible asportation and education of the infant against the will of the father."[1]

Thomas Jefferson

As seen in chapter 6, family education has established a successful track record during the history of the United States. Much of this family-centered education was directed by the parents, and took place in the home.

Thus far, I have only presented general historical information as to the excellence of this form of education from both an academic and a moral perspective. I believe such general information, however, is hard to fully appreciate without specific examples of individuals positively affected by home schooling.

In this chapter, therefore, I will provide the reader with short descriptions of many renowned leaders, businessmen, statesmen, inventors, scientists, writers, educators, artists, lawyers, and presidents who were successfully home educated for most or all of their childhood education. These true accounts of real men and women from history who were home schooled can serve as an encouragement to both parents and home schooled children alike.

I encourage you to assign your children further study into the lives of these men and women in order to appreciate their contribution in their various fields. A special emphasis should be placed on the majority of these men and women who relied on the Lord for their strength and wisdom.

Below is a very short list (by no means exhaustive) and descriptions of some of these famous home schoolers who serve as further evidence of the success of parental commitment to home schooling.

Presidents Taught at Home

At least ten presidents were substantially taught through home schooling. For instance, George Washington, often called the "father of our country," received most of his education at home by his father and mother, at least until his father died when George was eleven.[2] His mother carefully and consistently provided him with religious teaching from the Bible.[3] Throughout his remaining childhood, he was taught primarily by family members and experience. He was "a man of hands…not without brains, but with hand and brain moving together." This resulted in a basic education in accounting, math, geometry, geography (surveying), and astronomy.[4] Washington later became a brilliant general, businessman, statesman, and the first president of the United States.

Thomas Jefferson was taught to read and write by his father at home.[5]

> The father also set his impressionable boy [Thomas Jefferson] an example of vigorous physical out-of-doors life. Thomas learned to ride, to shoot, to paddle a canoe on the Rivanna, and to hunt deer and turkey….
>
> Tom did not ride and shoot and canoe only; he also studied diligently. His education consisted of the typical classical curriculum of the period.
>
> Tom mastered languages, both classical and modern, with great ease. He read Homer in his canoe trips down the Rivanna and Virgil while lying under an oak tree.[6]

Thomas Jefferson later became the third President of the United States and was responsible for drafting the Declaration of Independence.

James Madison was taught to read and write by his mother, and his father taught him his obligations to community service.[7] Primarily his mother and grandmother taught him at home until the age of eleven when he was tutored at home by Reverend Thomas Martin.[8] Of course, he later served as the fourth President of the United States and became a strong protector of religious freedom.

John Quincy Adams was completely home schooled until he was twelve years old. He entered Harvard at the age of fourteen.[9]

His mother, Abigail Adams, had accepted the responsibility for keeping up the education of her children—especially of her oldest son, John Quincy Adams.... First came instruction in the Word of God. So well did his mother commit the Word to young John Quincy's heart that it became for him both compass and anchor in a long life of service.

> From his mother he was also led into the love and inspiration of literature. He learned the poetry of Pope, read the plays of Shakespeare, struggled with Milton, and generally devoured the family library. He listened to his mother's talk of the economic concerns of the war.... Duty and service were both ingrained in his parents. He learned much from their example and personal conduct.... In addition to his studies in the Bible and his reading in the family library, Abigail Adams directed John Quincy's thoughts towards a knowledge of history.[10]

This godly instruction by his mother and commitment and sacrifice by his parents to personally train their child, helped to produce the integrity and wisdom in John Quincy Adams to enable him to serve as the sixth president of the United States.

Likewise, President Abraham Lincoln received all of his education, except one year, through home instruction.[11] Since his own library was limited, Abraham Lincoln would walk to other households, reading nearly every book within a fifty mile radius. His godly character was instilled in him through his family education, helping him serve as president during the Civil War.

President John Tyler was "tutored at his father's knee."[12] According to several historians, there is no record of him attending school before he enrolled in college at William and Mary at the age of twelve.[13] "Judge John Tyler raised young John to manhood and by all surviving accounts, he did an excellent job of it."[14]

Presidents William Henry Harrison,[15] Theodore Roosevelt,[16] and Franklin Roosevelt were also taught at home. Theodore Roosevelt received an excellent education from his family through home schooling and travel. As a result, he became one of the few presidents who was endowed "with an encompassing intellectual curiosity and with a real sympathy for and enjoyment of literature and the arts."[17] Franklin D. Roosevelt was taught at home where he received a thorough education and was trained in French and German. At age fourteen, he was enrolled in Groton school and four years later entered Harvard.[18]

President Woodrow Wilson received most of his pre-college instruction through home education.[19] His father, Joseph Wilson, would take young Woodrow on regular field trips to neighboring cities, cotton gins, mills, and factories. Afterward, Joseph Wilson would ask his son questions and have him write down what he saw and learned.[20]

Modern home schooling applies many of the characteristics of home schooling which most of these presidents received: regular field trips, hands-on learning, apprenticeships, development of a love for reading, regular interaction with adults, and emphasis on teaching biblical principles.

Many Delegates of Constitutional Convention Were Taught at Home

At least seventeen of the total delegates to the Constitutional Convention were schooled at home. These men drafted the most significant Constitution in the history of the world to protect and preserve liberty and harness the power of government. Two of the home schooled delegates, Washington and Madison, whose home schooling experiences are described above, later became presidents of the United States.

Another delegate was Reverend John Witherspoon, Calvinist and Presbyterian pastor, member of the New Jersey Senate, and president of the College of New Jersey (later called Princeton University). He was taught to read by his mother at age four and was eventually able to recite much of the New Testament and Watt's *Psalms and Hymns*.[21] He received much of his teaching at home, with some in grammar school, and he entered the University of Edinburgh at age thirteen.

Witherspoon dedicated his life to applying the Word of God to everything he did. He especially focused his attention on training college students in God's principles, and they then used those principles to form our nation.

Witherspoon was president of the College of New Jersey from 1768 to 1794. In those twenty-six years, 478 young men graduated—about eighteen students per year. Of those 478 graduates, 114 became ministers; 13 were state governors; 3 were U.S. Supreme Court judges; 20 were United States Senators; 33 were U.S. Congressmen; Aaron Burr, Jr. became Vice-President; and James Madison became President.[22]

I'm sure that Mrs. Witherspoon never dreamed that her son, whom she was training at home, would end up training so many leaders of our country.

Delegate Benjamin Franklin, printer, author, inventor, and U.S. minister to France, was home schooled. He received all of his schooling at home from his family, except for one year in grammar school and one year with a private tutor when he was between the ages of eight and ten.[23] He learned the highly skilled trade of printing through apprenticeship and ended up teaching himself science so well that he placed himself on the cutting edge of many new scientific discoveries.

Several of the other delegates were educated entirely at home except for college. Some of these men include William Samuel Johnson, president of Columbia College and a U.S. senator from Connecticut;[24] George Clymer, signer of the Declaration and U.S. representative of Pennsylvania;[25] Charles Pickney, III, governor of South Carolina, U.S. senator and representative;[26] and John Francis Mercer, Maryland delegate and U.S. representative.[27] George Wythe, signer of the Declaration, justice of the Virginia High Court of Chancery, and professor of law, was taught at home by his mother,[28] and William Blount, speaker of the Tennessee Senate and U.S. senator, was instructed at home and in the businesses of his father, real estate and politics.[29] Delegate Richard Dobbs Spaight, governor of North Carolina and a U.S. representative, was orphaned early and educated at home by relatives.[30] John Rutledge, chief justice of the U.S. Supreme Court, was taught by his father until age eleven.[31]

Other delegates were taught at home for much of their early education, such as William Livingston, lawyer and governor of New Jersey;[32]

Richard Basseti, lawyer, governor of Delaware, and U.S. senator;[33] William Houston, lawyer;[34] and William Few, justice and U.S. senator from Georgia, who only received two years of formal schooling.[35] George Mason, the principal author of the Virginia Declaration of Rights and member of the Virginia Legislature, had some training in grammar schools, but "his most important teacher was his mother, from whom he learned the art of being master of a great plantation and the necessity of personal management, planning, and careful accounts."[36]

Famous Women Who Were Home Schooled

Many renowned women in early America were also successfully taught through home education, such as Abigail Adams,[37] who, in turn, taught her son John Quincy Adams at home; Mercy Warren;[38] Martha Washington,[39] who married a home schooled husband; and Florence Nightingale.[40] In fact, Nightingale and her sister were instructed by their father, who taught them English grammar, history, philosophy, Latin, French, Greek, German, and Italian. He even taught her to read the Bible from the Greek text.[41] Furthermore, the black author, Phyllis Wheatley, was also primarily educated at home.[42]

Famous Lawyers, Educators, and Preachers Taught at Home

Patrick Henry, orator (the famous advocate for independence— "Give me liberty or give me death!"), framer, lawyer, and governor of Virginia, went to school for a few years but was pulled out at age ten to be home instructed by his father. His father taught him math, Greek, Latin, Bible, and the classics.[43] Patrick Henry was a consistent Christian throughout his life, acquiring his love for the church from his father, and his zeal for the Lord and Calvinist doctrine from his Scottish Presbyterian mother. His mother would have him repeat the sermon text and summarize the sermons he heard on the way home from church.[44] His grandson later explained that Patrick Henry spent one hour each evening in private devotion and prayer. Henry studied the Bible at length and developed his political beliefs in the necessity of limited government (because of man's sin nature) and in his recognition and desire to preserve God-given rights. He read sermon notes to his family every Sunday night, and afterward his family sang sacred songs while he accompanied with the violin.[45]

John Jay, one of the authors of *The Federalist Papers*, Chief Justice of the U.S. Supreme Court, and Governor of New York, was taught at home for several years. He was taught by his mother reading, grammar, and Latin, in his early years, and at age eight he was enrolled in grammar school.[46]

John Marshall, soldier, lawyer, diplomat, and also Chief Justice of the U.S. Supreme Court by age forty-five, was home schooled. Until he was age fourteen, he was taught by his father and mother entirely in his own home in Fauquier County, Virginia.[47]

> The father worked hard with the son. "My father possessed scarcely any fortune," wrote John Marshall, "and had received a very limited education; but was a man to whom nature had been bountiful, and who assiduously improved her gifts. He superintended my education, and gave me an early taste for history and poetry. At the age of twelve, I had transcribed Pope's *Essay* on *Man,* with some of his moral essays." Thomas, being a surveyor, had a rudimentary understanding of mathematics and astronomy. He also gradually acquired a library of history and literature. All of this he shared with his son [John Marshall].[48]

Timothy Dwight, grandson of Jonathan Edwards, was entirely taught by his mother at home until he entered Yale at age thirteen. He became born-again at age fifteen and in 1795 became the president of Yale University, which at that time was a school of higher learning dedicated to advancing the cause of Christ.[49]

John and Charles Wesley, renowned preacher during the Great Awakening and missionary/song writer, respectively, were taught at home by their mother, Susanna Wesley. In fact, Susanna taught all of her children at home.

> In her "Household School," for six hours a day through twenty years, she taught her children so thoroughly that they became unusually cultured. There was not one of them in whom she did not instill a passion for learning and righteousness.
>
> When her husband, in exasperation, asked her: "Why do you sit there teaching that dull child that lesson over the twentieth time?" she replied calmly: "Had I satisfied

myself by mentioning the matter only nineteen times, I should have lost all labor. You see it was the twentieth time that crowned the whole."[50]

Although she was thorough in instructing them in academics, the spiritual welfare of her children mattered most, and she consistently trained her children in the Word in spite of many trials, including the deaths of ten of her nineteen children.[51]

Jonathan Edwards, a Calvinist preacher, theologian, and author, was educated entirely at home by his father.[52] He and his sisters received a superior education from their father.

> The course of his education may in this way have been less systematic, indeed, and less conformed to rule, than that ordinarily given in the school. At the same time it was more safe; forming him to softer manners, gentler feelings, and purer affections. In his circumstances, also, it was obviously more comprehensive and universal; and while it brought him acquainted with many things which are not usually communicated until a later period, it also served to unfold the original traits of his mind, and give it that expansion, which is the result of information alone.[53]

Jonathan Edwards went on to become one of the most effective and influential preachers during the Great Awakening.

William Carey was taught by his father.[54] He was instilled with a desire to read everything, and spent much time collecting specimens, as he studied insects and plants.[55] He became a cobbler, scholar, linguist, botanist, and a missionary to India. He is known today as the "father of modern missions."

Dwight L. Moody, famous evangelist, had the equivalent of a fifth-grade education with the rest of his learning taking place at home or at work.[56]

American Generals Instructed at Home

In addition to George Washington, General Robert E. Lee, a brilliant southern general, president of Washington and Lee University in Virginia, and dedicated Christian, was taught at home by his mother.[57]

At his mother's knee, that divinely appointed school whose instruction no other teacher can impart, and whose lessons when faithfully given are worth all others we receive, he learned his obligations to his maker and his fellow man.[58]

From her he learned to practice self-denial and self-control, as well as the strictest economy in all financial concerns, virtues which he retained throughout his life.[59]

It was from her lips he learned the Bible, from her teaching he drank in the sincere belief in revealed religion which he never lost. It was she who imbued her great son with an ineradicable belief in the efficacy of prayer and in the reality of God's interposition in everyday affairs of the true believer.[60]

Thomas "Stonewall" Jackson, another famous southern General, man of God, and contemporary of Lee, was taught at home by his mother until age seven when he was orphaned.[61] He lived most of his remaining youth working, although he did attend a country school for a time.

Two other successful American generals who were primarily educated at home were George Patton,[62] who grew up in a remote part of Texas, and Douglas MacArthur, who grew up on a succession of army posts.[63] Patton served in World War II, winning many victories against Hitler. General MacArthur served in World War II, leading American soldiers to victory over the Japanese. He also served in the Korean War, in which he masterminded the surprise attack which led to the defeat of North Korea.

Renowned Home Schooled Scientists, Businessmen, Authors, and Artists

Booker T. Washington, scientist and founder and president of Tuskegee Normal and Industrial Institute, taught himself to read by using Noah Webster's "blue back speller" and by the constant support and common sense of his mother. By age thirteen he was prepared enough through his self-taught home education to enter an agricultural institute.[64]

Moreover, industrialist Andrew Carnegie[65] and inventor Thomas Edison[66] were schooled primarily through home education.

It is interesting to note that Thomas Edison was expelled from public school at age seven because he was considered "addled" by his public school teacher.[67] He lasted only three months in formal schooling. Over the next three years, his mother taught him the basics at home, and as Edison himself stated, "She instilled in me the love and purpose of learning."[68]

> When he [Edison] was an overly tender 10 years old, his mother introduced him to an elementary book on physical science, and that marked the beginning of his lifelong effort to teach himself. He set up his own chemistry laboratory in the basement. Since he was crushed by the overwhelming disadvantage of poverty and had no welfare net to save him, he went to work at the age of 12 and became self-supporting while continuing to educate himself and carry on his own experiments that eventually helped to revolutionize the world.[69]

Famous author Mark Twain,[70] who wrote many American classics including *The Adventures of Huckleberry Finn* and *The Adventures of Tom Sawyer*, was taught primarily at home. Also authors Agatha Christie,[71] who wrote popular mystery novels, and Pearl S. Buck[72] were educated at home, as was George Bernard Shaw.[73] Irving Berlin quit school in second grade and became a self-taught musician.[74]

Photographer Ansel Adams, a "hyperactive" child, was removed from school and taught by his father at home.[75] In his autobiography, Ansel Adams gave tribute to his father's instruction:

> I am certain he established the positive direction of my life that otherwise, given my native hyperactivity, could have been confused and catastrophic. I trace who I am and the direction of my development to those years of growing up in our house on the dunes, propelled especially by an internal spark tenderly kept alive and glowing by my father.[76]

Several renowned artists were taught at home by their parents, including John Singleton Copley and Rembrandt Peale. Copley was taught by his stepfather until age thirteen.[77] He then opened up his own painting and engraving shop. He soon became famous for his lifelike portraits of contemporary leaders of the colonies during the Constitutional Debate period in the 1700s. Rembrandt Peale received his early education from his father and later dropped out of school at age thirteen to devote himself completely to his art.[78] He painted numerous portraits of well known contemporaries, such as George Washington, Thomas Jefferson, Andrew Jackson, and Marquis de Lafayette, many of which are presently on display in Washington D.C.

Newell and Carol Wyeth removed their son Andrew from the public school after only two weeks and instructed him at home.[79] Newell Wyeth reassured his son, "No first rate painter ever came out of college." Andrew Wyeth's father taught him his comprehensive theory of painting and trained him in his studio. Andrew Wyeth went on to become a famous painter who has been given "one-man shows by prestigious museums, including New York's Metropolitan Museum of Art, Washington's National Gallery of Art, and London's Royal Academy of Arts."[80]

Home Schooled Leaders in Other Countries: Scientists, Authors, Composers, Economists, and Preachers

Some famous foreign men and women who were home schooled were Blaise Pascal, scientist, who invented the calculating machine (forerunner of the computer), discovered the theory of probability and the principle of the vacuum, and helped shape the field of calculus.[81] Author C. S. Lewis was taught by his mother until she died when he was ten. She had already taught him French and Latin, preparing him well for preparatory school which he entered at age thirteen.[82] He became a strong Christian who wrote *The Chronicles of Narnia, Screwtape Letters, Mere Christianity,* and many other popular works, both fiction and nonfiction.

Author Charles Dickens was taught reading and writing and Latin from his mother and began working at age twelve.[83] Among some of his more well-known books are *The Christmas Carol,* which extols the godly virtue of charity, and *David Copperfield.*

John Owen was home schooled by his father during his early education and was later transferred to a private academy.[84] He became a respected Puritan pastor, authoring many great works on theology. He also served as chaplain to Oliver Cromwell in England.

Philosopher Charles Louis Montesquieu, who authored "L' Esprit des Lois," the political treatise which influenced the writer of the U.S. Constitution, was educated first at home and then entered the College de Juilly when he was eleven.[85]

William the Silent, Prince of Orange and Protestant leader who founded the Dutch Republic, was taught by his mother at home, along with his sixteen brothers and sisters. His mother was a devout Lutheran, "practicing a rigid moral code, sincere, generous and simple, her energetic example and spoken precepts molded the characters of all her children."[86]

Artist Claude Monet said, "It was at home that I learned the little that I knew."[87]

John Newton, hymn writer and London preacher, was taught at home by his mother until age seven when she died.[88] Afterward, he was sent to school for approximately three years and then went to sea with his father. His most well-known song which he authored is "Amazing Grace." John Newton recounts his early home instruction:

> The tender mercies of God toward me were manifested in the first moment of my life. I was born, as it were, in His house and dedicated to Him in infancy. My mother....was a pious, experienced Christian.... I was her only child.... Almost her whole employment was the care of my education.... At not more than three years of age, she herself taught me English. When I was four years old I could read with propriety in any common book. She stored my memory, which was then very retentive, with many valuable pieces, chapters, and portions of Scripture, catechisms, hymns and poems.... In my sixth year, I began to learn Latin.[89]

Free-market economist John Stuart Mill was taught entirely at home by his father until age fourteen.[90] He was the eldest of nine children. His father started him in Greek at age three and by eight he had read Herodotus and Plato in the original. At age twelve, he was seriously studying logic.[91]

Many famous composers were taught primarily at home. Wolfgang Amadeus Mozart, born in Vienna, was primarily taught by his father, who historians agree was an excellent teacher.[92] His education began when he was four, and he began his international travel when he was five, causing him to spend nearly half of his time from age five to fifteen on tour. In his travels, Mozart came in touch with every type of music of his day, resulting in a well-rounded cultural and musical education. In fact, his own music became a perfect blend of Italian, German, and French styles. At six, Mozart wrote his first minuet, by nine he wrote his first symphony, at eleven he wrote his first oratorio, and by twelve he composed his first opera.[93]

Composer Anton Bruckner was born in Austria and was one of eleven children. His father was a school teacher and his mother was a singer. By the time he was four years old, he displayed a precocious interest in music which his parents encouraged.[94] He learned at home until age eleven and then lived with his grandfather for two years to continue his musical education. When he was fourteen he went to school at a local monastery.[95] Bruckner considered the Lord to be his best friend, and one contemporary stated that he was "perhaps the only great composer of this century [nineteenth] whose entire musical output is determined by his religious faith."[96] Bruckner was extremely well-read in the Bible and always spent time in prayer before composing or teaching.[97] He is known especially for *Te Deum* and composed nine famous symphonies.

Felix Mendelssohn's first teacher was his mother who, among other subjects, taught him music, the tradition of hard work, and self-denial, until he was tutored at age eleven.[98] Mendelssohn became a renowned composer and conductor, an excellent artist in drawing and painting, and an all-round athlete.[99] He is known for his oratorios *Elijah* and *St. Paul,* and many symphonies, including the *Reformation Symphony.* He knew his Bible well and worked to the glory of God.[100]

Also, composer Francis Poulenc received most of his early education from his mother and father. His mother taught him music, beginning with piano lessons at age five, and his father made sure he completed his academic studies.[101] After his mother taught Francis all that she knew, she had him taught by tutors at least by age fifteen.

Conclusion

These many famous men and women of the past who were taught by their parents at home lends further credence to the effectiveness of this tutorial form of education. The modern home schooling movement, which blossomed in the 1980s and continues unabated, is confirming the same results, as it begins to produce highly trained and successful graduates. This list of famous home schoolers is just beginning.

Notes

1. Saul Padover, *Jefferson* (Harcourt-Brace, 1942), 369.
2. John C. Fitzpatrick, *George Washington Himself* (Indianapolis: Bobbs-Merrill Co., 1885), 19, and also see John Eidsmoe, *Christianity and the Constitution* (Grand Rapids, Mich.: Baker Book House, 1987), 125-27.
3. William Johnson, *George Washington the Christian* (Arlington Heights, Ill.: Christian Liberty Press), 19-22.
4. *The American Heritage Book of the Presidents and Famous Americans,* Vol. 1 (New York: American Heritage Publishing Co., 1967), 11.
5. Saul K. Padover, *Jefferson: A Great American's Life and Ideals* (New York: Mentor Books, 1942), 10-14; Eidsmoe, *Christianity and the Constitution,* 218.
6. *Ibid.,* 11.
7. *The American Heritage Book of the Presidents,* Vol. 2 (New York: Dell Publishing, 1967), 133.
8. *James Madison 1751-1836,* ed. Ian Elliot (Dobbs Ferry, N.Y.: Oceana Pubs., 1969), 1.
9. *Memoirs of John Quincy Adams,* ed. Charles Francis Adams (Philadelphia: J.B. Lippincott, 1874), 7.
10. *The Christian History of the American Revolution,* compiled by Verna Hall, "The Education of John Quincy Adams," Rosalie Slater (San Francisco: Foundation for Christian Education, 1982), 603-604.
11. Benjamin P. Thomas, *Abraham Lincoln: A Biography* (New York: Alfred A. Knopf, 1952), 7-8, 12; Albert J. Beveridge, *Abraham Lincoln* (New York: Houghton- Mifflin Co., 1928), 63.
12. Robert Seager, III, *And Tyler Too* (Norwalk, Conn.: Easton Press, 1963), 53.
13. *Ibid.,* 50.
14. *Ibid.,* 48.
15. *World Book Encyclopedia* (1986). Harrison received his early education at home and entered Hampden Sidney College at age fourteen.
16. *Encyclopedia Britannica,* Vol. 19 (Chicago, Ill.: William Benton, 1968), 606.
17. *Ibid.*
18. *Ibid.,* 600 and see *F.D.R: His Personal Letters,* ed. Elliott Roosevelt (New York: Duell, Sloan & Pearce, 1947), 5.
19. Ray S. Baker, *Woodrow Wilson: Life and Letters* (Garden City, N.Y.: Doubleday, Page & Co., 1927), 37.
20. Arthur Walworth, *Woodrow Wilson* (Norwalk, Conn.: Easton Press, 1958), 9-10.
21. Martha Lou Lemmon Stohlman, *John Witherspoon: Parson, Politician, Patriot* (Philadelphia: Westminster Press, 1897), 17.
22. Eidsmoe, *Christianity and the Constitution,* 83, and Stohlman, *John Witherspoon,* 172.
23. John Bigelow, *The Life of Benjamin Franklin, Written by Himself* (Philadelphia: J.B. Lippincott, 1957), 99. John Eidsmoe, *Christianity and the Constitution,* 192.
24. M. E. Bradford, *A Worthy Company* (Marlborough, N.H.: Plymouth Rock Foundation, 1982), 30. The footnotes 24 through 36 are taken from Bradford's book. He gives at least eight sources, including a number of biographies for each of the delegates, as supporting his research.
25. *Ibid.,* 97.
26. *Ibid.,* 212.
27. *Ibid.,* 123.
28. *Ibid.,* 176.
29. *Ibid.,* 187.
30. *Ibid.,* 193-94.
31. *Ibid.,* 197.

32. *Ibid.*, 59.
33. *Ibid.*, 110.
34. *Ibid.*, 218.
35. *Ibid.*, 220.
36. *Ibid.*, 155.
37. Charles W. Akers, *Abigail Adams: An American Woman* (Boston: Little, Brown & Co., 1980), 8.
38. Alice Brown, *Mercy Warren* (New York: Charles Scribner's Sons, 1903), 8.
39. Alice Curtis Desmond, *Martha Washington; Our First Lady* (New York: Dodd, Mead &Co., 1963), 7.
40. Mary Lewis Coakley, "The Faith Behind the Famous Florence Nightingale," *Christian History* (Carol Stream, Ill.: Christianity Today, Inc.), Issue 25, 38 and David Collins, *God's Servant on the Battlefield; Florence Nightingale* (Milford, Mich.: Mott Media, 1985).
41. Edith Deen, *Great Women of the Christian Faith* (Westwood, N.J.: Barbour and Company 1959), 214.
42. G. Herbert Renfro, *Life and Works of Phyllis Wheatley* (Freeport, N. Y.: Books for Libraries Press, 1972), 11-12, and Benjamin Brawley, *The Negro in Literature and Art in the United States* (New York: Duffield & Co., 1939), 17-18.
43. Robert Douthat Meade, *Patrick Henry; Patriot in the Making* (Philadelphia: J.B. Lippincott, 1957), 51. Also see Eidsmoe, *Christianity and the Constitution*, 298-99.
44. Eidsmoe, *Christianity and the Constitution*, 308.
45. *Ibid.*, 307-315.
46. *Ibid.*, 165.
47. Leonard Baker, *John Marshall; A Life in Law* (New York: Macmillan Publishing Co., 1974), 13.
48. *Ibid.*, 12-13.
49. *The Christian History of the American Revolution*, compiled by Vema Hall (San Francisco: Foundation for American Christian Education, 1982), 559.
50. Edith Deen, *Great Women*, 143. Also see *Encyclopedia Britannica, op. cit.* , Vol. 23, 414.
51. *Ibid.*, 142, 144.
52. *The Works of Jonathan Edwards*, ed. Edward Hickman (Edinburgh, England: Banner of Truth Trust), XVI.
53. *Ibid.*
54. Basil Miller, *Men of Faith: William Carey, Father of Modern Missions* (Minneapolis, MN: Bethany House, 1980), 10.
55. *Ibid.*, 8.
56. Virginia Lieson Brereton, "The Popular Educator," which appeared in *Christian History*, ISSN 0891-9666 (Carol Stream, IL: Christianity Today, Inc.), Issue 25, 26.
57. William Johnson, *Robert E. Lee: The Christian* (Arlington Heights, IL: Christian Liberty Press, 1989), 26-29.
58. *Ibid.*, 27.
59. Emily V. Mason, *Popular Life of General Robert E. Lee* (Baltimore, Md.: J. Murphy and Co., 1874), 22.
60. Viscount Wolseley, *General Lee* (Rochester, NY: George P. Humphrey, 1906), 13.
61. R. L. Dabney, *Life and Campaigns of General T.J. (Stonewall) Jackson* (Harrisonburg, VA.: Sprinkle Publications, 1977), 10-13.
62. Harry H. Semmes, *Portrait of Patton* (New York: Appleton Century Crofts, 1955), 4-5.
63. I. D. Clayton James, *The Years of MacArthur* (Boston: Houghton Mifflin & Co., 1970), 53. Also see Brian Mitchell, "More Military Families Opting for Home Schools," *Navy Times*, October 24, 1988, 15.
64. Booker T. Washington, *Up From Slavery: An Autobiography* (Boston: Western Islands, 1965), 14-16, 22-23.
65. Burton J. Hendrick, *The Life of Andrew Carnegie* (Garden City, NY: Doubleday, Doran & Co., 1932), 21.
66. Matthew Josephson, *Edison* (New York: McGraw-Hill, 1959), 21.
67. *Ibid.*, 20-23.

68. "Thomas Alva Edison," *The New Encyclopedia Britannica*, Vol. 6, Macropaedia (Chicago: University of Chicago Press, 1983), 308. Also see Gerald M. King, "Home Schooling: Up from Underground," *Reason*, April, 26.

69. Jack Douglas, "Only Freedom of Education Can Solve America's Bureaucratic Crisis of Education," *Policy Analysis*, June 17, 1991, Cato Institute, Washington D.C., 6. Also see Wyn Wachhorst, *Thomas Alva Edison* (Cambridge: MIT Press, 1981), 180-83.

70. DeLancey Ferguson, *Mark Twain: Man and Legend* (New York: Bobbs-Merrill and Co., 1943), 21, 24, 29.

71. Agatha Christie, *Agatha Christie: An Autobiography* (New York: Dodd, Mead &Co., 1977),19-20.

72. Paul A. Doyle, *Pearl S. Buck* (New York: Twayne Publishers, 1965), 24.

73. Hesketh Pearson, *George Bernard Shaw: A Full Length Portrait* (New York: Harper & Bros., 1942), 11.

74. Michael Friedland, *Irving Berlin* (Stein and Day, 1974).

75. Teresa Amabile, "Personal Glimpses: To His Own Beat," *Reader's Digest*, 1990, 19.

76. *Ibid.*

77. *The Christian History of the American Revolution,* complied by Verna Hall (San Francisco: Foundation for American Christian Education, 1982), 579.

78. *Ibid.*, 584.

79. Richard Meryman, "The Wyeth Family: American Visions," *National Geographic*, Vol. 180, No. 1, July 1991, 100.

80. *Ibid.*

81. "Genius with a Heart of Faith," *Glimpses* (Worcester, PA: Christian History Institute, 1989), Number 2.

82. Clyde S. Kilby, *The Christian World of C. S. Lewis* (Grand Rapids, MI: Eerdmans, 1978), 14.

83. Angus Wilson, *The World of Charles Dickens* (Viking, 1970), 43.

84. *The Works of John Owen,* ed. William Goold, Vol. 1 (Edinburgh, England: Banner of Truth Trust, 1981), XXII.

85. *Encyclopedia Brittanica*, Vol. 15 (Chicago: William Benton, 1968), 785.

86. C. V. Wedgewood, *William the Silent* (New York: Norton and Company, 1968), 10-11.

87. Sheridan Morely, *A Talent to Amuse: Noel Coward* (New York: Doubleday, 1969).

88. John Newton, *Out of the Depths* (Grand Rapids, Mich.: Kregel Publications, 1990), 21-23.

89. *Ibid.*, 21.

90. Michael St. John Packe, *The Life of John Stuart Mill* (London: Secker & Warburg, 1954), 19-20.

91. *John Stuart Mill: Autobiography* (New York: Collier and Son, 1909), 3.

92. Jane Stuart Smith and Betty Carlson, *The Gift of Music* (Westchester, Ill.: Crossway Books, 1987), 55.

93. *Ibid.*, 56.

94. *Ibid.*, 126.

95. *Ibid.*

96. *Ibid.*, 127.

97. *Ibid.*, 130.

98. *Ibid.*, 84-85.

99. *Ibid.*, 86.

100. *Ibid.*, 88.

101. *Ibid.*, 264.

The Right Choice:
Teach Them at Home

More and more parents are becoming serious about the training of their children. They are realizing the public schools are failing their children both morally and academically.

Parents are waking up to the truth that their children are *not* disposable commodities to be blindly turned over to daycare centers and mass educational systems. Rather, children are gifts from God and the preservation of the family unit is one of our utmost priorities.

One chapter in this section will explain to you how you can start home schooling your own children. You will discover that *any* parents who are willing to sacrifice their time and possibly their careers for their children's sake can succeed at home schooling. Both new and veteran home schoolers will learn from the tips on teaching your children at home and how to incorporate a biblical worldview. Without such a biblical foundation, your educational program will be incomplete.

The other chapter will investigate the area of college admission and practical steps on how home schoolers can overcome certain obstacles.

God will honor those who honor Him in their commitment to training their children in His ways.

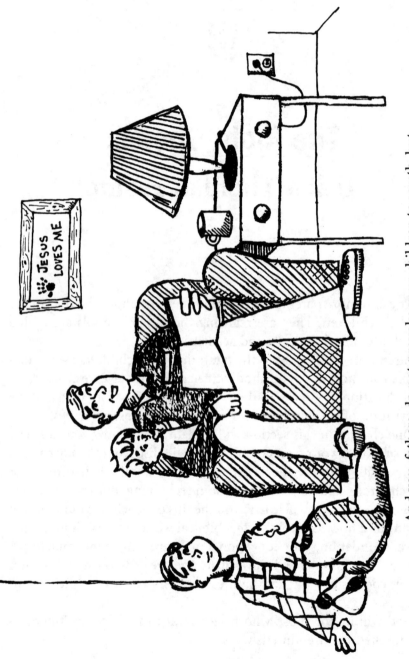

And you, fathers, do not provoke your children to wrath, but bring them up in the training and admonition of the Lord.

—Ephesians 6:4

8

Seven Practical Steps to Successful Home Schooling

"Be steadfast, immovable, always abounding in the work of the Lord, knowing your labor is not in vain in the Lord."

1 Corinthians 10:37

You might be thinking, "I'm convinced that there is no place like home to teach my children...but, how do I start?" You also might have nagging doubts deep down inside, making you wonder, "Will I ever be able to successfully home school my children?" Believe me, after working with home schoolers since 1984, these questions are common to most parents. I truly believe that while home schooling is not for everybody, it is for anybody.

Remember, we veteran home schoolers continue to experience these same doubts. We, too, wonder if our home schooling will be successful. Although my wife and I have home schooled for many years, we still have moments when we wonder if we can continue.

In 1994, I was diagnosed with Multiple Sclerosis, and my wife discovered she had an incurable disease called ulcerative colitis. To make matters more complicated, we have seven children and I have a very intense job at the Home School Legal Defense Association. With this combination of factors, my wife and I feel very weak and very inadequate. But God has reminded us repeatedly that this is where He wants us to be. He wants us to lean only on Him as He promises in Second Corinthians 12:9-10, "My grace is sufficient for you; for power is perfected in weakness. Most gladly, therefore, I will rather boast about my weaknesses that the power of Christ may dwell in me. Therefore, I am well content with weakness, with insults, with distresses, with persecutions, with difficulties for Christ's sake. For when I am weak, then I am strong." My wife and I know that while we are weak, God is making us strong.

God also promises that those who honor Him He will honor (1 Samuel 2:30). As you strive to please God in training your children according to His Word, God will honor your efforts. Sometimes you will not see the fruit immediately—it takes repetition and endurance.

You might say, "How long must I repeat that lesson to my child?" As parents fulfilling their responsibility before God, our answer must be, "Until he gets it!" God wants us to walk by faith and not by sight. (2 Corinthians 5:7). We walk much closer to the Lord when we do not know what is ahead. Faith enables us to trust in the Lord our God and lean not on our own understanding. This is where we find ourselves as we home school. We do not know what lies ahead. However, we trust in a sovereign and loving heavenly Father who is always faithful.

So, can you home school? The answer is, "Yes, if you are willing to sacrifice the time and effort that is necessary for success." This involves a tremendous love for your children and a willingness to die to yourself. I am convinced from the Word of God and my own experience that our own children are one of the most valuable gifts that God has given us. Teaching my children to love the Lord our God with their whole heart, soul, and mind is worth the sacrifice and time.

Below are seven steps you can take to start your home schooling and keep it going strong.

1. Seek First the Kingdom of God.

Jesus promises us in Matthew 6:33, "Seek first the kingdom of God and His righteousness, and all these things shall be added unto you." In that same passage, God reminds us that we are not to worry, but to lean completely on Him, putting our entire trust into His capable hands.

Before you begin home schooling, you must seek God's face and ask for His blessing. Most of all, ask for His strength and His wisdom. In order to have a successful home school, both academically and spiritually, it is essential that you build your home school on the foundations of God's Word and Jesus Christ. In this vein, I urge you to carefully read the many Bible verses listed in chapter 4.

Be thoroughly familiar with Psalm 127:3-5, so you remember that children are a gift from the Lord and are like arrows in the hand of a warrior. Memorize Ephesians 6:4, "Fathers, provoke not your children to wrath, but bring them up in the nurture and admonition of the Lord." Don't ever forget God's command to you as a parent in Deuteronomy 6:6-9, where He tells us that we must teach God's principles to our children diligently—virtually all the time. A comprehensive view of Christian education is demanded by our God. Jeremiah 10:12 tells us, "Learn not the way of the heathen." Public schools cannot be an option. We must pray for the Holy Spirit's power to help us commit to training our children according to these commands. Home schooling is not easy, but its rewards are great.

Like Davy Crockett once said, "Be sure you are right: then go ahead." Similarly, we need to make sure we are right by reading God's Word and praying diligently. Then we can proceed to the next step

2. Attend a Home School Conference.

There are various types of home school conferences which take place several times each year.

Every state has at least one major annual statewide convention, which includes both special speakers and an exhibit hall for the home school education materials. These conferences are particularly important, since they will enable you to hear firsthand from speakers who are practicing home schoolers. They will provide answers to your questions. The keynote speakers furthermore will provide inspiration and encouragement to you as you embark on home schooling. The workshops that are available will cover many of the "nuts and bolts" of home schooling. Attending the state home school convention is a must.

In addition to the statewide convention, you can also find book fairs, which are organized exclusively for the buying and selling of home school books. Usually there are no special speakers and the home school parents come for the sole purpose of shopping. These events provide a fantastic opportunity to see books firsthand, page through workbooks, and check out new educational software.

In order to learn more about a home school convention scheduled in your state, review appendix G in this book for the contact information for the state home school organization nearest to you. By contacting the state home school association, you can find out the date and time of the next convention and they can inform you of any book fairs which may also be scheduled.

Visiting a home school convention will help you to appreciate how large the home school movement has grown and understand that you are not alone. It is also encouraging to see the endless resources that are available to help the home school mother and father succeed.

3. Choose a Curriculum.

Choosing a curriculum is probably the most important task to be a successful home schooler. I recommend that you contact a number of the major home school publishers or correspondence courses and request their latest catalog. Although I have not had the opportunity to check all products of home school publishers and organizations, I can without hesitation recommend the following publishers and home school correspondence courses as a partial list:

Curriculum: **Covenant Home Curriculum**
Publisher: Covenant Home Curriculum
              PO Box 267
              Sussex, WI 53069-0267
Phone: 800.578.2421/ 414.246.4760
Fax: 414.246.4827
Web: www.covenanthome.com
This is an excellent, classical curriculum and correspondence course. It is a home school program you can trust. The founder is my former pastor when I lived in Wisconsin. It has a solid biblical worldview.

Curriculum: **Christian Liberty Academy**
Publisher: Christian Liberty Academy
              502 W. Euclid Ave.
              Arlington Heights, IL 60004
Phone: 847.259.4444 (Inquiries Only)
Fax: 847.259.2941
Web: www.homeschools.org

This is one of the oldest and largest Christian home school programs. They have both a correspondence course plan and an individual family plan where you can assemble your own program. I grew up with many of the employees and I know the leadership well since I attended and graduated from the Christian Liberty Academy's sister school in Milwaukee. This is a time-tested program. This program presents a coherent biblical worldview.

Curriculum: **KONOS**
Publisher: KONOS, Inc
          PO Box 1534
          Richardson, TX 75083
Phone: 972.924.2712
Web: www.konos.com
This is one of the best unit study home school programs available. I know the founders well. For the creative home school mom, this is excellent. We have used portions of this program over the years together with several families in our home school support group.

Curriculum: **A Beka Correspondence School**
Publisher: A Beka Book Publications
          A Beka School Services
          Box 18000
          Pensacola, FL 32523-9160
Phone: 877.223.5226/ 850.478.8933
Fax: 800.874.3593
Web: www.abeka.com
A Beka publishes good Christian textbooks. They also provide written and video home school correspondence courses.

Curriculum: **Advanced Training Institute**
Publisher: Advanced Training Institute
          Box One
          Oak Brook, IL 60522-3001
Phone: 630.323.ATIA
Fax: 630.323.6746
Web: www.atia.iblp.org

This is a very comprehensive Christian home school program with a major emphasis on godly character training.

Curriculum: **Alpha Omega LIFEPACs, Switched-On Schoolhouse, Bridgestone Online Academy**
Publisher: Alpha Omega Publications
PO Box 3153
Tempe, AZ 85282
Phone: 800.622.3070/ 602.438.2717
Fax: 602.785.8034
Web: www.home-schooling.com

Curriculum: **Bob Jones University Press**
Publisher: Bob Jones University Press
Greenville, SC 29614
Phone: 800.845.5731
Fax: 800.525.8398
Web: www.bjup.com
This publisher in particular has excellent science textbooks with an emphasis on creationism.

Curriculum: **Christian Light Education**
Publisher: Christian Light Education
PO Box 1212
Harrisonburg, VA 22801-1212
Phone: 540.434.1003
Fax: 540.433.8896

Curriculum: **Rod and Staff Publishers**
Publisher: Rod and Staff Publishers
PO Box 3
Highway 172
Crockett, KY 41413-0003
Phone: 606.522.4348
Fax: 800.643.1244/ 606.522.4896

If you are home schooling for the first time, you may want to enroll in a correspondence course in order to get a solid start into home schooling. After a year or two, you will be familiar enough with home schooling that you may want to embark on your own customized home school program.

It is very important that you have your new curricula in place before you withdraw your children from school so you will be defensible in the event of a challenge by the school district.

4. Join a Local Home School Support Group.

What exactly is a home school support group? It is two or more families who gather together in order to exchange ideas and experiences on home schooling. Home school support groups consist of a half dozen to more than 500 families. In many ways, local support groups are the backbone of the home school movement. Local support groups enable you to get acquainted with veteran home schoolers who can help guide you along the way. Support groups offer practical learning experiences such as field trips to museums, dairy farms, factories, quarries, zoos, and many more places. Local support groups will often hold project fairs, where home schooled children in the support group can submit their favorite invention, collection, engineering project, or historical object for the opportunity to win an award and recognition.

Our support group is called Lifetime. It is operated under the auspices of our church elders, but it is open to any home school family who shares a belief in Jesus Christ as their Lord and Savior and willing to sign a statement of faith. We have nearly 100 families enrolled in Lifetime, many from outside our church. Every other Friday we have a half day of classroom sessions at our church. The children can supplement their education with classes in advanced writing, biology, biblical worldview, or whatever is offered in a given semester. Our Lifetime group also sponsors field trips and is involved in local community projects.

Some home schoolers, or potential home schoolers, have asked me whether they should join a home school support group that has a statement of faith. I personally believe that local home school support groups should have a statement of faith espousing the basic tenets of the Christian faith. This is necessary at the local level in order to ensure that our children will be socializing and making friendships with other godly children. There are many values-laden issues discussed at the local support group level, such as methods of instruction, types of curricula, and child discipline. In order to fulfill God's command to us as parents to train our children in the way they should go, I am convinced that we should primarily participate with the activities of a local home school support group that has a solid Christian foundation.

At the state level, however, all home schoolers must work together to provide a united front in battle to protect our freedom to home school, both in the legislatures and in the courts. This is one of the reasons the Home School Legal Defense Association membership is open to all home schoolers. We rise and fall together.

Local home school support groups provide both new and veteran home schoolers with encouragement and physical support. The new home schoolers have access to veteran home schoolers, which helps them avoid many potential obstacles and problems. A local support group oftentimes holds used curriculum fairs to enable members of the home school support group to buy textbooks and materials at a very low cost. Our local support group is a tremendous blessing, as they consistently hold our family up in prayer and offered frequent help during our difficult times.

Participating in support group functions provides an opportunity for your children to develop friendships and receive positive socialization. Proverbs 13:20 indicates, "He who walks with wise men will be wise, but the companion of fools will suffer harm." A Bible-believing support group will offer the opportunity for your children to walk with other wise children.

Remember the road to successful home schooling is fraught with difficulties and hardships. However, the value of our children is so great in God's eyes that it is worth the sacrifice to die to ourselves and perform our home school responsibilities with diligence. It is helpful, nonetheless, to have encouragement along this way. Participating in a support group and developing relationships with veteran home schoolers will keep you going when the going gets rough. The support that support groups give is often all we need to endure and persevere when we feel like quitting. It is also an opportunity to learn from others and avoid their mistakes in order for our home school to be even more successful.

5. Establish Discipline in the Home.

If you want your home school to succeed, you will have to make certain that discipline is established in your home. Proverbs 13:24 says, "He who spares his rod hates his son, but he who loves him disciplines him diligently." The Scriptures are filled with references to the importance of parents disciplining their children. Proverbs 23:13, "Do not hold back discipline from a child. Although you beat him with the rod, he will not die. You shall beat him with the rod and deliver his soul from hell." Proverbs 22:15 reveals to us the sin nature of a child, "Foolishness is bound up in the heart of a child, but the rod of discipline will remove it far from him."

God has ordained parents to have authority over their minor children. God requires that we "train up a child in the way he should go and when he is old he will not depart from it" Proverbs 22:6. In chapter 4, I summarize many of the commands in Scripture which require parents to train up their children in the nurture and admonition of the Lord.

I spend many hours as a father verbally exhorting and correcting my seven children. I diligently teach the principles of the Word of God to them. I make certain that I come alongside them and shepherd their hearts. Nevertheless, my children still have a sin nature. Although they listen intently and seem to understand the truths of the Word of God and how they must live, they regularly disobey and try to transgress the boundaries which my wife and I have set for them. If we want to follow God's recipe for child training, discipline is a necessary ingredient.

When we compare our relationship to God and the relationship of our children to us, we see many similarities. We are constantly attempting to transgress the boundaries God has laid for us. We know what is right, but we often do the wrong thing. We sin everyday. Of course, we confess that sin and repent and try again to turn away, but old habits die hard. God, by His grace, intervenes in our lives to discipline us in various ways to keep us on the straight and narrow path which leads to heaven.

Likewise, we as parents must not spoil our children. These passages from Proverbs indicate that we must use the rod to discipline our children, for it has a spiritual consequence. God uses the rod in discipline to "deliver our children's souls from hell." There is spiritual blessing associated with using the rod. Of course, these passages also indicate we must use the rod diligently. We cannot use it now and then, or after every fourth or fifth offense. We need to be willing to be diligent in our application of discipline.

In the same manner, we want God, our Father, to diligently discipline us so that we do not go astray. Proverbs 3:11-12, "My son, do not reject the discipline of the Lord or loathe His reproof; for whom the Lord loves, He reproves even as a father the son in whom he delights." If we truly love our children as the Lord loves us, we must reprove them and discipline them. If we truly love our children we must not spare the rod. Inconsistent discipline simply means, in God's eyes, that we hate our children. Therefore, we as fathers must especially take the lead. In my house, whenever I come home from work, I take over all discipline from my wife so that my children know that I support her 100 percent. I also allow my wife at extremely busy times of the day to simply write a mark under the child's name on the refrigerator, so that when I come home I can follow through with the discipline that needs to be administered.

You may be wondering why I spend so much time in this area. We have a culture today that has rejected the need for disciplining children. They believe a false philosophy that dictates that children should be allowed to establish their own moral values. Many homes in America are child-centered. This, of course, contradicts the Word of God and God's ordained authority in the family.

The most important aspect of being consistent in discipline is for the sake of our children's souls. That is paramount. I am certain you would agree that our highest goal is that one day our children will stand in heaven with us. We pray and hope they will fight the good fight, run the course, and finish the race. For the home schooler, the second most important aspect of discipline is to create a learning environment for our children. Our children will not listen to their mother's instruction if there is no discipline to support her. In order for home schooling to work, almost everything in the home needs to be done "decently and in order."

Parents will burn out quickly trying to home school their children if they don't establish a firm hand of discipline. With discipline, your learning environment will be peaceful, and your children will be able to learn. Discipline will enable you to make sure that they complete their lessons and learn how to work hard and efficiently.

This disciplining I'm describing takes time. Often in the midst of a task, we don't want to take the time to discipline an unruly child or bad attitude. Nonetheless, we must make the time, because the problem will only become worse as the days and weeks and months go by. It is also important that we do not discipline our children in anger. Scripture says that the wrath of man does not achieve the righteousness of God.

We want to always pray for God's strength and mercy to enable us to peacefully discipline our children without giving in to anger. We cannot take the offense personally. It is important that each time we discipline our children that we make them tell us why they were disciplined so they understand the offense. We must ask them then to repent and pray to God for His forgiveness. I also forgive them and pray for them that they will be able to learn from this lesson and not repeat the sin. We end with a hug. Without love accompanying the discipline, the children will have a difficult time receiving the discipline.

I am convinced God will bless you and your home school as you apply these God-ordained principles.

6. Develop and Apply a Biblical Worldview.

The term *biblical worldview* is often used among Christian circles, but do we really understand what a biblical worldview is? The scriptures says in Ephesians 4:14-15, "We are no longer to be children to be tossed here and there by waves and carried about by every wind of doctrine by the trickery of men, by craftiness and deceitful scheming, but speaking the truth in love." God wants us to know His truth. He wants us to have view of the world looking through His eyes. God wants us to apply to the world His heavenly blueprint. Where can we obtain this heavenly blueprint? It is in His Word.

A biblical worldview can be illustrated in two ways. Consider your worldview to be a pair of glasses. Are you wearing rose-colored glasses that make everything look all right and any type of belief or opinion is acceptable? Or do you look through a pair of lenses that is multi-colored and everything in the world is not to be taken seriously? You look for ways to avoid responsibility and simply have fun. The main goal of your world view is to satisfy yourself.

Do you look through dark glasses at the world? You have no hope. You are cynical. You believe things will only get worse and there is nothing you can do about it.

Or do you look through the lenses of Scripture? You understand that God made the world, that He controls and sustains all things. You see that God is the sovereign Lord of the universe. You also understand, by looking through the lenses of Scripture, that He has sent His Son to be our Redeemer so that we have everlasting hope. You have joy in the knowledge that God is preparing a place in heaven for all those who love Him. You understand that "all things work together for those who love God and are called according to His purpose" Romans 8:28.

As you look though the lenses of Scripture, you begin to see that God has something to say about economics. As you search the Scripture, you find numerous examples of economic principles that God teaches from the concept of private property, to the importance of tithing, to paying a fair wage.

As you peer through the lenses of Scripture, you see that God has ordained all of history and His Providence personally guides every detail towards the ultimate consummation when His Son, Jesus Christ will return to this earth. You understand that nothing happens by accident or by chance, but that God is in control.

As you look through the lenses of Scripture at science, you see that God made the world and that His laws of gravity, entropy, and many other laws, harness the earth. You can see the glories of God's creation as you study a small insect or a huge volcano. You see the power of God throughout creation, and how all creation gives glory to Him. You gaze upon the principles of mathematics and see that God has ordained the numerical orders. You see the Trinity explained through the mathematical principle of $1 \times 1 \times 1 = 1$.

You can also depict a biblical worldview as a map through life. A map drawn by the Architect of the World: the God who made us in His image. Are you going to follow the map of the world or of some vain philosophy, or will you follow the map that is laid forth in the Word of God as to how we should live? Are you following the biblical map that tells us to steer clear of abortion but demonstrates life begins at conception? The biblical map shows us how we must love our wives as Christ loves the Church and train our children in the nurture and admonition of the Lord. As we follow the biblical map, we must walk on the path of disciplining our children rather than avoiding discipline as the world would tell us. As we study this biblical map, we find that we must help the poor and die to our own selfishness as we journey though this world on the narrow path to heaven.

These principles are no doubt elementary, but we need to consciously think and teach them to our children. This requires that we find a curriculum that applies God's principles to every area of life. There are so many secular books that Christian schools simply baptize and pray over, but the children are still learning the way of the world. We want our children to not only *believe* as Christians but also to *think* as Christians. We do not want our children to believe as Christians but then think like the pagans. Jesus commands us to "Love the Lord your God with all your heart, soul, and mind. This is the greatest and foremost commandment" Matthew 22:37-38. We cannot divorce our children's minds from their hearts. We need to train our children's minds to love the Lord: that is why teaching them and helping them adopt a biblical worldview is a necessity.

Thus, we must be self-conscious in how we teach our children the academic subjects. We must teach them from the foundation of God's truth: His Word.

As one of the most important tools for providing your children with a biblical world view, I strongly recommend home school families to obtain the *Encyclopedia of Bible Truths for School Subjects* (Ruth Haycock, Association of Christian Schools International: Colorado Springs, Colorado; 800-367-0798). This is an invaluable resource that demonstrates how the biblical principles apply to virtually every academic discipline. Each chapter in this book covers a different subject: e.g., art, math, science, grammar. The biblical principles are clearly outlined and thoroughly supported by hundreds of Scripture passages. This book serves as an index to the Bible as to what God says about the academic subjects you are teaching your children. This will provide your children with a sound understanding of the biblical foundations for most areas of life. This will help them see the relevancy of Scripture to society and describe to them, in practical terms, how the Bible is the source of all knowledge and wisdom. Your children can better learn the standard (the Bible) by which they must live by and judge all things. I think *the Encyclopedia of Bible Truths for School Subjects* is especially helpful for your home school students who are in junior high and high school levels.

Another good resource is from David Quine. He has created a biblical worldview curriculum called the Cornerstone Curriculum. He has recently written a book called, *Let Us Highly Resolve*. Information on his biblical worldview materials can be obtained from the Cornerstone Curriculum Project in Richardson, Texas, www.cornerstonecurriculum.com, or 972-235-5149.

If you want to provide your high schooler with some intensely practical, biblical worldview training, contact the Summit Ministries, 423-775-7599 or 719-685-9103 or www.summit.org. You can also obtain *Understanding the Times* by David Noebel from Summit

Ministries. It compares the reasonableness of the biblical worldview to three other prominent worldviews, covering theology, philosophy, biology, ethics, ecology, sociology, politics, economics, law, and history. This is a must for every home school library.

Another important resource is *American Christian History: The Untold Story* by Gary DeMar, which you may obtain through American Vision at 770-988-0555. This provides a thorough review of the history of our country from a Christian perspective. American Vision also offers a wonderful biblical worldview magazine that I highly recommend you subscribe to and have your children read.

I recommend *Proverbs for Parenting: A Topical Guide to Child Raising from the Book of Proverbs,* by Barbara Decker of Lynn's Bookshelf, Boise, ID, copyright 1989. This is an excellent book for helping you work through the book of Proverbs which gives so much practical biblical worldview instruction for your children. *Shepherding a Child's Heart* by Ted Tripp (Shepherd Press, Wapwallopopen, PA, 1995) is an insightful book for teaching your children in the Lord and providing godly discipline. His brother, David Tripp, has written a book, *Age of Opportunity: A Biblical Guide to Parenting Teens* (P&R Publishing, Phillipsburg, NJ, 1997). This book provides an excellent resource for training your teenagers in the Lord. Everyone with children of any age will benefit from this book.

A professionally designed magazine for keeping yourself and your family up on current events from a biblical perspective is *World* Magazine, 800-951-6397. This weekly magazine looks at the world's events from a biblical perspective. You can assign various articles for your teens to read and summarize enabling them to practice analyzing issues from a biblical perspective.

A biblical worldview is foundational. Make certain that a consistent biblical worldview is incorporated in your home school.

7. Join the Home School Legal Defense Association.

Your right to home school is too precious to lose. Without it we cannot train our children in the way God has called us. The fight to obtain the freedom to home school has been a difficult one over the last 15 years. God in His mercy has granted us many victories.

The Home School Legal Defense Association is dedicated to protecting the rights of parents to choose home schooling. God has blessed us in many ways with the knowledge and experience to provide a good defense and, in some cases, a good offense in order to protect your rights. As you have seen from various parts of this book, the prejudices against home schooling abound among the educational elite.

We need to have solidarity with one another. As Benjamin Franklin once said, "If we do not hang together, we shall surely hang separately." Joining Home School Legal Defense Association is an investment in the freedom to home schooling, not only in our country, but around the world as we work in other nations spreading the good news of home schooling. For more information on the Home School Legal Defense Association and how to join, please consult chapter 24 of this book and review our web page at www.hslda.org, where you can join on line.

Ready, Get Set, Go!

These seven steps will enable you to get a good start on home schooling. If you feel overwhelmed, that's OK. It is an overwhelming task. But God would not have given you children if He did not also give you the ability to train up your children and educate them. Remember, "we can do all things through Christ who strengthens us" (Phillipians 4:13). We need to persevere. It is important we start out strong. But it is even more important we finish strong. May God bless you as you glorify Him by diligently training your children according to His Word.

9

Can Home Schoolers Succeed in College?

"Do you see a man skilled in his work? He will stand before kings; he will not stand before obscure men."

Proverbs 22:29

At Home School Legal Defense Association, we receive calls or letters virtually everyday from home schoolers seeking admission to college. Among the most frequently asked questions are: "How can my home schooled child meet the documentation requirements and still be admitted to college?" "Does my child have to take a GED or an SAT II exam?" "How can I persuade the college of our choice not to discriminate against home schoolers?" "Do home schoolers succeed in college?" "What colleges are home school friendly?"

If you have some of these same questions, read on.

Discrimination of Home Schoolers

Home schoolers are growing up! And in the process they are experiencing growing pains. As more and more home schoolers are becoming college age, the inquiries received by universities around the country are increasing. Some colleges are responding by streamlining their admission standards to cater to home schoolers while others are erecting roadblocks such as requiring GEDs, higher SAT scores, accredited diplomas, or additional SAT II exams. Many are treating home schoolers on a case by case basis.

In order to remedy the situation, we at HSLDA's National Center for Home Education are working at the state and federal levels to improve admission procedures for home schoolers at colleges and universities across the country. The National Center also has persuaded national college organizations to help develop guidelines for colleges to deal with home schoolers seeking admission and worked with hundreds of colleges on an individual basis to adjust their policies in favor of home schoolers. On a regular basis, I personally represent home schooled students as they face problems with college admission with nearly universal success.

The Winning Argument: Home Schooling Works

As I talk with college officials and speak at college admission conferences, I always emphasize that home schooling works. I explain that the track record of home schoolers over the last 15 years is so exemplary that the risk to the college is virtually negligible. In fact, these are students who will enhance the overall image of the college. I often share the following.

First, home schooling has a proven academic success record at the elementary and secondary level. For example, standardized test results for 16,000 home educated children, grades K-12, were analyzed in 1994 by researcher Dr. Brian Ray. He found the nationwide grand mean in reading for home schoolers is at the 79th percentile; for language and math, the 73rd percentile. This ranking means home-educated students perform better than approximately 77 percent of the sample population on whom the test was normed. Nearly 80 percent of home schooled children achieve individual scores above the national average and 54.7 percent of the 16,000 home schoolers achieved individual scores in the top quarter of the population, more than double the number of conventional school students who score in the top quarter.[1] These same basic results of this study commissioned by HSLDA have been confirmed again and again. Most recently in the 1999 study of over 20,000 home schooled students' test scores analyzed by Dr. Larry Rudner, Director of the ERIC Clearinghouse on Assessment and Evaluation. (See generally chapter 5 for more statistics on the success of home schoolers.)

Secondly, research demonstrates that home schoolers tend to score above the national average on their college entrance exams.

According to the 1998 ACT High School Profile Report, 2,610 graduating home schoolers took the ACT and scored an average of 22.8 out of a possible 36 points. This score is slightly higher that the 1997 report released on the results of 1,926 home school graduates and founding home schoolers maintained the average of 22.5. This is higher than the national average, which was 21.0 in both 1997 and 1998.

The results continue. In 1999, ACT tracked 3,257 home school students and found they scored, on the average, 22.7 in comparison to the national average of 21.0. This average of the home schoolers was higher than the average of Rhode Island whose students scored the highest on the ACT.

Thirdly, home schoolers perform above average on the average in the college setting: both academically and socially.

1994 Oral Roberts University Study

For instance, in the fall of 1994, Oral Roberts University (OK) Dean of Enrollment Management Mike Mitchell found that 212 home school students were enrolled, comprising about 10 percent of the student body. The average home schooler had an ACT score of 24 and an SAT score of 1005, consistent with the average score for all ORU students, but higher than the national average. Mitchell's report also found that the average ORU home schooler's GPA was 3.02, while the overall average ORU student's GPA was 2.76.

Mitchell reported that 88 percent of ORU home schooled students were involved in one or more outreach ministries. Many served as chaplains in the dorms and virtually all embraced the ORU honor code as an already adopted way of life. In addition, over 90 percent of ORU home schoolers participated in intramural sports and nearly 80 percent in various campus clubs and organizations. Home schoolers were active in all areas of college life, debunking the myth that home schoolers are largely unsocialized.

1997 Galloway/Sutton Study

On October 10, 1997, Drs. Rhonda Galloway and Joe Sutton released the results of a four-year study to find out how home schoolers fared in the college setting as compared to Christian and public school graduates. The study tracked 180 students, 60 graduates from each home schooling, public school, and Christian school. Five success indicators were used in the study: Academic, Cognitive, Spiritual, Affective-Social, and Psychomotor.

Galloway and Sutton found that in every success category except psychomotor, the home school graduates excelled above the other students. Out of 12 academic indicators, the home schoolers ranked first in 10. Out of 11 spiritual indicators, home schoolers ranked first in seven. In cognitive skills, home schoolers ranked first in 17 of the 23 indicators. Out of 63 total indicators, home schoolers ranked first in 42.

Home Educated Athletes

The National Center for Home Education has worked for several years with the National Association of Intercollegiate Athletics (NCAA) to establish guidelines to help standardize eligibility for homeschooled athletes. According to the guidelines, home schooled athletes who have sufficiently high standardized test scores and proof that they took at least 13 courses that meet the association's core-course standards may be automatically awarded freshman eligibility. John Morris, NCAA spokesman, said that during the 1998-1999 school year, of the 49 home schooled students applying for waiver of initial academic-eligibility for Division I, everyone was approved. Likewise, all 20 applicants for Division II were approved as well.

Home School Scholarships

This tremendous track record of the academic and social success of home schoolers has encouraged various colleges to offer scholarships to home schoolers. Oral Roberts University has established a $6,000 scholarship especially for home school graduates. Belhaven College in Mississippi grants $1,000 a year to qualified home educated students. Nyack College (NY) says their "experience with home schoolers has been a positive one" and awards up to $12,000 to home schoolers: $1000 for each year they were home schooled.

Federal and State Solutions

Some state legislatures and departments of education, recognizing the abilities and achievements of most home educated students, have written laws or regulations addressing the problems a home schooler may face at college entrance, specifically prohibiting discrimination. HSLDA works with state legislatures to pass these types of laws on all colleges receiving state funds. Some of the states with such laws or policies are New Mexico, North Carolina, Arizona, Montana, and South Dakota. The New Mexico statute that passed in 1997 reads:

> In determining the standard of requirements for admission to their respective institutions, boards of regents [for institutions of higher education] shall not require a student who has completed the requirements of a home-based or non-public school educational program and who has submitted test scores that otherwise qualify him for admission to that institution, to obtain or submit proof of having obtained a general education development certificate. In determining requirements for admission, boards of regents shall evaluate and treat applicants from home-based education programs or non-public school fairly and in a nondiscriminatory manner.[2]

North Carolina House Bill 746 (1997) directed the University of North Carolina Board of Governors to review the University's admissions procedures, practices and requirements regarding applicants from home schools in compliance with North Carolina law. The new policy stated there will be "no discrimination...against applicants for admission regardless of whether they attended a public or non-public school." Further the policy states that "no additional information will be required from any applicant based on the type of high school they attend."

The South Dakota Board of Regents policy referring to home-educated students allows a composite score of 18 on the ACT test as the only academic requirement of admission.

During the 105th Congress, I crafted report language for both the United States House of Representatives and Senate Committee Reports accompanying the Higher Education Act of 1999, which encourages colleges and universities, receiving federal funding, to discontinue their discrimination against home schoolers. The House Report specifically recommends that colleges and universities change any admissions policies which force home schooled students to take additional tests beyond what is required of traditionally schooled students, including the GED and the SAT II exams:

> The Committee is aware that many colleges and universities now require applicants from non-public, private, or nontraditional secondary programs (including home schools) to submit scores from additional standardized tests...(GED or...SAT II) in lieu of a transcript/diploma from an accredited high school. Historically,...the SAT II was not designed for, and until recently was not used to determine college admissions. Given that standardized test scores (SAT and ACT) and portfolio- or performance-based assessments may also provide a sound basis for an admission decision regarding these students, the Committee recommends that colleges and universities consider using these assessments for applicants educated in non-public, private, and non-traditional programs rather than requiring them to undergo additional types of standardized testing. Requiring additional testing only of students educated in these settings could reasonably be seen as discriminatory....
>
> The Committee believes that college admissions should be determined based on academic ability of the student and not the accreditation status of the school in which he or she received a secondary education.[3]

This report language of the Higher Education Act evidences the Congress's intent and enables us to negotiate with colleges from a much stronger position.

While lobbying Congress, the National Center for Home Education also met with both the American Council on Education (ACE) and the American Association of State Colleges and Universities (AASCU) and negotiated for them to contact their member colleges and request these colleges change their policies regarding home schoolers. As a result, the ACE and the AASCU both sent letters to their members, encouraging them to not discriminate against home schoolers by requiring GED or SAT II tests. (U.S. Representative Bill Goodling (R-PA), Chairman of the House Committee on Education and the Workforce, wrote a letter to the ACE, urging them to carry out their agreement with us.)

Stanley Ikenberry, president of the ACE, states in his letter:

> The General Educational Development (GED) and Scholastic Aptitude Test subject area (SAT II) examinations...have been criticized by some in the home school community as discriminatory and unnecessarily burdensome.
>
> I urge you and admissions personnel at your institution to engage in a dialogue with providers of nonpublic, nontraditional programs in forming admissions policies regarding their graduates.

The AASCU letter to its Council of State Representatives said:

> AASCU's view is that the setting of college and university admission standards is a responsibility that belongs with the institutions themselves and their governing entities. At the same time we urge colleges and universities to address this issue if they have not already done so . . .
>
> The policies by which these [home schooled] students are admitted must balance the need for accurate assessment of their academic preparation with a sensitivity to their special circumstances and attributes.

Their guidelines carry much weight with thousands of colleges across the United States.

Federal Financial Aid

In times past, colleges and universities have insisted that home schoolers obtain a General Equivalency Diploma (GED), not only for financial aid, but also for admission. However, the Higher Education Act Amendments of 1998 (Pub. L. No. 105-244) enacted in early October 1998, changed this requirement by adding my language which I drafted for the Senate Education Committee.

Section 483 simply states that, in lieu of an accredited high school diploma or GED, a student is eligible for federal financial aid if the student has completed a secondary school education in a home school setting that is treated as a home school or a private school under state law. [Pub. L. No. 105-244 amending 20 U.S.C. Sec. 1091(d)] Fulfillment of this requirement is usually accomplished during the college admissions process when a student supplies a college with a transcript and other evidence of meeting the credit hour requirements for the completion of a high school education.

No more wasting time obtaining a GED in order to qualify for college financial aid. This way home schoolers can avoid the stigma of being a dropout. Ever since passage of this amendment, I have been able to solve every HSLDA member's problem regarding obtaining financial aid.

National Center For Home Education Recommendations

Home-educated high school graduates offer an academically creative and socially diverse background. Home schoolers' strong work ethic and high moral values contribute to their success in college. More and more colleges and universities are recognizing their unique capabilities and circumstances. In light of the proven success of home education at the elementary, secondary, and post-secondary levels, the National Center for Home Education recommends that colleges adopt specific written home school admission policies which reflect the following:

1. Home-educated applicants should not be required to submit an accredited diploma or GED. Accreditation does nothing to measure a student's knowledge or what he was taught, it only reflects *where* he was taught. In addition, GED carries with it the stigma of being a high school drop-out. Home schoolers are not drop-outs, but talented, conscientious students who have completed their high school education. They should not be treated as drop-outs by being required to obtain a GED.

2. If a transcript is required, colleges should have flexible guidelines for records and documentation of the basic credit hours for high school completion. Some colleges supply home schoolers with a "Home School Credit Evaluation Form" that may be completed in lieu of a transcript.

3. As the primary instructors, parents should be recognized as capable of evaluating their student's academic competence in letters of recommendation. Schools frequently ask

for an additional evaluation from someone outside the home.

4. SAT/ACT scores and portfolios or performance-based assessments provide schools with a solid basis for admission. Furthermore, home schoolers should not be required to achieve higher college entrance test results than their public school counterparts.

5. Mandatory SAT II testing in specific subjects is an unnecessary roadblock. Requiring only home school students to take these tests, in addition to the SAT, is discriminatory. Colleges will discourage home schoolers from seeking admission by holding them to this unreasonable standard. SAT/ACT testing is more than enough to indicate the academic proficiency of the student.

6. A bibliography of high school literature and an essay are two admission criteria that accurately evaluate a student's life experience and thinking skills.

7. Interviews and a review of extracurricular activities are two ways to determine overall student proficiency and leadership qualities.

The above criteria also summarize the type of documentation home schoolers seeking college admission should prepare ahead of time. This should increase the likelihood of obtaining admission to the college of your choice.

Survey of Admissions Personnel

In general, how are college admission personnel receiving home schoolers? On the whole, very well.

In 1997, Dr. Irene Prue, Assistant Director of Admission of Georgia Southern University, released a nationwide survey of admissions personnel's knowledge, attitudes and experiences with home-educated applicants. In general, a total of 210 (out of the 1,289 surveyed) respondents to the study reported:

1. Home schoolers are academically, emotionally, and socially prepared to succeed at college.

2. Parental motivations and involvement are in the best interest of their children.

3. While documentation and evaluation of home schooled applicants is problematic, it is not insurmountable.

A Positive College Experience

A 1996 survey of over 60 colleges and universities in all fifty states, conducted by the National Center for Home Education, revealed the following anecdotal accounts of home schoolers in college:

> A Harvard University (MA) admissions officer said most of their home-educated students "have done very well. They usually are very motivated in what they do." Results of the SAT, an essay, an interview, and a letter of recommendation are the main requirements for home educated applicants. [Transcripts are] irrelevant because a transcript is basically a comparison to other students in the school.

The *Wall Street Journal* confirms Harvard's positive experience with home schoolers:

> Many colleges now routinely accept home schooled students, who typically present portfolios of their work instead of transcripts. Each year Harvard University takes up to 10 applicants who have had some home schooling. "In general, those kids do just fine," says David Illingworth, senior admissions officer. He adds that the number of applications and inquiries from home schoolers is "definitely increasing."

In addition to Harvard, prominent schools like Yale (CT), Princeton (NJ), Texas A&M, Brown University (RI), the Carnegie Mellon Institute (PA), the universities of Arizona, Maryland, Virginia, Hawaii and many others all have flexible transcript criteria, accept parental evaluations, and do not require any accreditation or a General Equivalency Diploma (GED). At Kansas State University and others like Lipscomb University and Middlebury College, transcripts are optional.

In 1996 Birmingham-Southern College (AL) had only one home school applicant, but the admissions officer said the college "would be glad to have many more just like him!"

Roughly 50 home schoolers attended the University of Montana. "The home schoolers in this state seem to be up to date and well organized. We even have home schoolers in our honors programs. I know of one student for sure. She is one of our top students," remarked one admissions official.

Bruce Walker at the University of Delaware said one home educated student who "had an exceptional SAT score was invited to be considered for a full scholarship!"

"Home schooling is becoming more and more prevalent," said Mark Wheeler of Boise State University (ID). "We're all trying to work together."

Pennsylvania State University had 20 home school applicants in 1995, double the previous year. They prefer a portfolio with as much information as possible, including extracurricular activities that demonstrate leadership. "Home schoolers show strongly in that," said the admissions officer for Penn State.

Lewis and Clark College (OR) has a method of application called the "Portfolio Path where a student can bypass standardized tests and instead be reviewed on a myriad of things that would point to, and measure academic performance." The universities of Minnesota and Mississippi also look at the all-around abilities demonstrated in a home schooler's portfolio. University of Kentucky home school applicants all have to provide a portfolio of what they have done throughout their high school years that is "creative and informative." A UK admissions officer also said, "Our home schoolers (about 50) tend to be very bright, and have scored very high on standardized tests."

The Dartmouth College (NH) admissions officer explained, "The applications I've come across are outstanding. Home schoolers have a distinct advantage because of the individualized instruction they have received."

University of Alaska/Fairbanks has had over 300 home-educated students in the last few years, several of which were in their honors program. The program director, Mary Dicicco commented, "They have been wonderful students on the whole."

Staff from Geneva College (PA) and Belhaven College (MS) are actively recruiting home schoolers by going to home school conferences and book fairs to talk to parents and students about admissions.

"Home schoolers have to work harder thereby increasing student productivity," Jeff Lantis said of the 75-90 home schoolers at Hillsdale

College (MI). "Home schoolers are consistently among our top students, in fact home schoolers have won our distinct Honors Program the last three years in a row. We tend to look very favorably upon home schoolers applying to our college."

USA Today reported on October 28, 1996, that the University of North Carolina-Chapel Hill's dean of admissions, James Walters, has enrolled about 20 home educated students, all of whom "are performing above average academically."

A letter sent in 1991 to home school leaders in Massachusetts from Thomas M. Rajala, Director of Admissions at Boston University is another example of the recognition institutions of higher learning are showing home schoolers' academic achievements:

> Boston University welcomes applications from home schooled students. We believe students educated at home possess the passion for knowledge, the independence, and the self-reliance that enable them to excel in our intellectually challenging programs of study.

Wheaton College Director of Admissions Dan Crabtree says that "Nearly ten percent of our current freshmen were home schooled at one point, and about a dozen were home schooled through high school."

The Message: Home Schooling Works

The conclusion of the matter is "Home Schooling Works!" Home schoolers will continue to advance and succeed in college as each student diligently applies himself in his studies.

[For more this information in a form to present to a college in your area which has not yet adopted a home school admissions policy, obtain our "College Packet" available from HSLDA at 540-338-5600 or www.hslda.org]

Notes

1. *Home Schoolers Score Significantly Above National Average*, National Center for Home Education Press Release, December 7, 1994.
2. *New Mexico Statutes Annotated* section 21-1-1(B).
3. 105th Congress, *2d Session*, House of Representatives, Report 105-481, Higher Education Amendments of 1998, April 17, 1998, 147.

IV

A Desperate Foe:
The Attack of Social Workers, School Officials, and Child Right's Advocates

Home schooling, in the eyes of many public school officials and educational interest groups, such as the National Education Association, is threatening. It is a blatant challenge to their virtual monopolistic control over education in the United States. Additionally, it is a repudiation of their philosophy, which holds that the state and the educational elite know what is best for our children.

While home schooling is in the process of restoring education, it is simultaneously exposing the corruption and failure of the public school system. Home schooling is also embarrassing the public schools since "mere parents," on the average, are performing a better job teaching their children than the public school system. Home schooling is a reassertion of parental rights, which is considered to be a rebellion by many public school officials and education union leaders who are accustomed to nearly complete control of children.

As seen from the attempts of school officials to teach home school parents "who is boss" through legal intimidation, the resolutions of the education organizations which condemn home schooling and the results of polls of school officials, it is apparent that many of them do not approve of home schooling in the least. As long as there is a public school system and compulsory attendance laws, this conflict between home schoolers and the state (and educational unions) will not end.

The most subtle undermining of home schooling which is on the horizon is government vouchers. Government money brings government controls. Acceptance of these handouts will effectively return the home schoolers "back to Egypt." A portion of chapter 10 thoroughly discusses this danger.

In this section the reader will be made aware of this conflict in many different areas and the position of the educational elite groups concerning home schooling. Much documentation in this section will show that the law, the Constitution, and the statistics are generally on the side of home schoolers, but the numbers, dollars, and child welfare bureaucracies are on the side of the state and unions. Even so, home schooling, as a minority right, continues to gain greater recognition and protection.

chapter 10

The Continuing Battle for the Child:

From Teacher's Unions to Vouchers

"A general state education is a mere contrivance for molding people to be exactly like one another: and as the mold in which it casts them is that which pleases the predominant power in the government or [the will of] the majority of the existing generation; in proportion as it is efficient and successful, it establishes a despotism over the mind, leading by natural tendency to one over the body."[1] *(emphasis added)*

John Stuart Mill

In spite of the impressive academic record of home schoolers and the numerous benefits of this type of tutorial education, certain groups usually representing the educational establishment continue to oppose home schooling in the legislatures. Also families across the nation are routinely harassed by their local school district or law enforcement officials.

I am convinced that the conflict with home schoolers has nothing to do with education. Home schoolers have consistently proved that it works as documented in chapter 5. In fact, in every single case in which the Home School Legal Defense Association has been involved since its inception in 1983, the children have been proven to be progressing academically often above average. It is apparent that the real issue involves who has the authority to mandate how the children must be educated. Do the parents or the public schools have this authority?

As a result, home schoolers are on the "front lines" of the battle for liberty in the United States. If they lose, the Christian schools, churches, and families will soon follow suit.

The Clash Between Competing Financial Interests

The main opposition to home schooling is made up of public school officials and teachers' unions. This should be expected since the public school officials and teachers have a financial interest ($3,000 to $4,000 in tax monies per child for their school district from the state and federal governments) in whether or not home schoolers are allowed to exist. Sometimes, their jobs may even be on the line. This is a strong financial incentive, especially for small school districts, to disapprove home schools and get the children back in public school. This financial interest, of course, makes it very difficult for the school authorities to remain neutral when determining whether or not a home schooler should be allowed to operate freely. I have had numerous experiences with school officials coming to the door of new home schoolers and telling them that they are causing the school district to lose thousands of dollars in funding since they pulled their children out of school. However, the education of the children is not even mentioned. Chapter 18 discusses many examples of school officials who were worried more about the financial loss to their school district than about children being taught at home. Chapter 18 also provides documentation as to the amount of money each child is worth in state and federal tax dollars, and the constitutional implications.

The Clash Between Educational Philosophies

In addition, there is a philosophical reason for opposition to home schooling. In my experience of talking with thousands of school officials, I found that many actually believe that they are the "guardians of the children" and, as such, they need sufficient controls over all the children within the boundaries of their school district. They sincerely believe that since they often have had seven years of higher education, they know what type of education is best for the children. They cannot understand how a parent can teach the children. They do not recognize that God has delegated the right to teach children to the parents, not the state.

This combination of both the philosophy of control and the financial and competitive interest makes clear to public school authorities that they must do something about home schooling. Several of the powerful education unions and associations have begun vocalizing their opposition to home schooling in recent years. The following are several examples of the opposition's position reflecting the strong philosophical bias they have against home schooling.

For instance, the National Education Association, a teachers' union, with a budget exceeding 200 million, has consistently opposed home schoolers in the legislatures. Below are excerpts from the 1999 resolutions of the NEA:

> B-65. The National Education Association believes that home schooling programs cannot provide the student with a comprehensive education experience. When home schooling occurs, students enrolled must meet all state requirements. Instruction should be by persons who are licensed by the appropriate state education licensure agency, and a curriculum approved by the state department of education should be used.
>
> Home schooling should be limited to the children of the immediate family, with all expenses being borne by the parents.[2]

If the NEA had its way and every state required parents to be state-certified and have their curriculum approved, at least 90 percent of the home schoolers in the country would be outlawed. On the issue of teacher certification, the NEA ignores the hundreds of studies that have been performed which demonstrate no positive correlation between teacher qualifications and student performance.

Some of the comments quoted in a *USA Today* article demonstrate just how threatened NEA members feel by home education. The president of the Maryland State Teachers Association, Beverly Correlle, told the reporter that law makers in her state are "caving in to the zealots who push home schooling allowing them to operate with few restrictions." Texas teachers said, "Up to 20 percent of students are being taught at home" in rural Texas.[3]

Annette Cootes of the Texas State Teachers Association declared, "My own personal opinion is that home schooling is a *form of child abuse* because you are isolating children from human interaction. I think home schoolers are doing a great discredit to their children."[4] A quick look at the condition in public schools as documented in Part One of this book will demonstrate that sending children to public school, not teaching them at home, is the real child abuse.

Another national organization is less polite concerning its opposition to home schooling. It would like to see home schooling completely prohibited. The National Association of Elementary School Principals (NAESP) is urging local and state associations to promote legislative changes that will "enforce compulsory school attendance and prohibit home schooling as a substitute for compulsory school attendance." The NAESP's platform lists eight reasons why home schooling is inferior to the traditional classroom setting. The platform states:

Such schooling:

1. Deprives the child of important social experiences;
2. Isolates students from other social/racial/ethnic groups;
3. Denies students the full range of curriculum experiences and materials;
4. May be provided by non-certified and unqualified persons;
5. Creates an additional burden on administrators whose duties include the enforcement of compulsory school attendance laws;
6. May not permit effective assessment of academic standards of quality;
7. May violate health and safety standards;
8. May not provide the accurate diagnosis of and planning for meeting the needs of children with special talents, learning difficulties, and other conditions requiring atypical educational programs.[5]

It is interesting to note that the worst harassment that home schoolers receive from school districts, in my experience in representing home schoolers, is usually directly from the principal.

Another organization which is diametrically opposed to home schooling is the National Parent Teachers Association. At their 1987 national convention, they passed these resolutions:

WHEREAS National PTA believes that all children should have access to equal educational opportunities; and

WHEREAS, the National PTA has consistently supported a quality education for all students; and

WHEREAS, the number of home schools and other non-approved schools has increased significantly in the last five years; and

WHEREAS, there are no uniform standards that home schools and other non-approved schools must meet, such as hours and days of instruction, curriculum, teacher certification, and reporting;

NOW THEREFORE be it resolved that the National PTA encourages state PTAs to urge state boards of education and/or state legislators to require home and other nonapproved schools to meet the same minimum educational standards as *public schools.*

This organization claims to be operating for parents.

Thomas Shannon, executive director of the National School Boards Association, in an interview, calls the home schooling trend "a giant step backward into the seventeenth century." He stated further in the interview:

We are very concerned that many parents who think they are qualified to teach their youngsters, simply are not....The youngsters are getting shortchanged.... Society ultimately has to pay for any mistakes, not to mention the loss of a child who might otherwise have made a maximum contribution.[6]

If he had not said he was talking about home schooling, it would seem apparent that he was describing the failure of the public school system. There is certainly no documentation to support his assertion concerning home schooling.

Bureaucrats in the various state education departments usually are influenced by the teachers' unions. For instance, Wisconsin's state superintendent, Herbert Grover, tried to push for legislation restricting home schoolers. He declared that home schools should be required to "meet all expectations of the public schools. These children are neglected and abused. That is wrong."[7] He also made claims that thousands of home schooled children were not being educated. However, like many critics of home schoolers, he offered no documentation to back his allegations. I was able to minimize his attack on home schooling by supplying a special legislative committee whose purpose was to scrutinize home schooling with numerous studies which proved the success of home schooling. The result was that the legislative committee rejected the state superintendent's allegations and recommended no changes to the home school law in Wisconsin.

It is clear the educational elite are protecting their vested interest and ignoring the academic statistics which expose the failure of the public schools and the consistent success of home schoolers.

The Public Wants More Controls on Home Schools: Especially If They Receive Government Vouchers

Phi Delta Kappa International released the results of the 1999 Phi Delta Kappa/Gallup Poll entitled, "Of the Public's Attitudes Toward the Public Schools." The poll surveyed 1,103 adults (18 years of age and older) throughout the continental United States. Included among this year's questions were a couple of questions which demonstrate how the general public does not understand that home school freedom works.

For instance, 92 percent of those polled favor requiring home schoolers to take all the state and national assessment tests that public school students are required to take. This means that the fight to be free from government regulation is not over. Public opinion still wants home schoolers to be accountable to the government. The public seems to believe the government knows better than individual parents do. They do not understand what it is to be free. This survey is a reminder to us that we cannot count on the public to help us in our battle to remain free.

Second, 77 percent of respondents think that private or church-related schools that accept government tuition payments should be accountable to the state in the same way that public schools are accountable. In a related question, 74 percent think nonpublic schools that receive public funding should be required to accept students from a wider range of backgrounds and academic ability than is now generally the case. This statistic should serve as a warning against government vouchers, since public opinion believes that those who receive government money should also be bound by government regulations. In the first question, the general public believed all home schoolers should be tested—but when it comes to receiving government voucher money, the 77 percent of people believe nonpublic schools (which includes home schools) should be regulated the same as public schools. If this were came to pass, home schools who received government money would be reduced to nothing more than ineffective, compromised, little public schools in the home.

But supporters argue that vouchers would cause public, private, and home schools to compete against one another for students, thereby improving education. Why will schools compete for students? Because students bring government money with them. So private and public schools would compete for government money. What makes a private school "private" is that the "public" (at large) is not involved. Private schools have consumers; public schools have constituents.[8] When private schools accept government money, they become obligated, not to their consumers, but to their constituents. The government dictates this duty toward the public constituents. Private schools, therefore, would be obliged to comply with government mandates concerning hiring quotas, curriculum standards, etc. In other words, private schools, that accept students with public vouchers, will become essentially "public."

I believe vouchers are one of the great temptations and threats faced by home schoolers. We all pay double for our children's education: for our own private home schooling and for the ailing public schools. It is not fair. But if we have vouchers, those of us who take them will be gradually strangled with government strings, which always come. Look at history. As Benjamin Franklin once said: "Those who give up essential liberty to purchase a little temporary safety, deserve neither liberty or safety."

Secretary of Education, Richard Riley, summarized the need for "strings" to accompany vouchers. He gave these warnings:

> You have to be accountable with public tax dollars...when it comes to taking federal tax dollars and giving those to parents and then having the absence of accountability as far as their children's education...If you have accountability, then you lose the private and parochial nature of those schools...It's bad, we think, for private schools and parochial schools. It takes away from them the private and

parochial strength, which is being totally free from any federal regulations...[9]

[Vouchers] threaten the very nature of private and parochial schools. It makes them less private and less parochial.[10]

Conservative government education officials echoed the same sentiments that should serve as "red flags" to any home schoolers thinking of supporting education vouchers. Lamar Alexander, former Secretary of Education under George Bush, declared, "A public school would become any school that receives students who brought with them public monies..."[11] Chester Finn Jr., former Assistant Secretary of Education under Ronald Reagan, explained his concern simply: "There is no doubt in my mind that there will be some new regulations with voucher plans."[12]

But some will say, "We need the money." William Pitt responded to this reasoning, "Necessity is the excuse of tyrants and the creed of slaves." Freedom is too precious to lose over government money. God honors those who honor Him. He will provide for us so we can fulfill His commands to us concerning the training of our children.

Furthermore, those of us who refuse government vouchers will be triple taxed: we will have to pay for our own private home schooling, public schools, and all private and home schools receiving tax funded vouchers! I believe this is, as economist Frederic Bastiat once coined, "legal plunder."

Voucher proponents, on the other hand, will argue that a voucher system would produce fierce competition between education providers, thus driving education costs down. However, a study conducted by Columbia University Professor Henry Levin[13] reveals that the federal government would actually spend more money under a school voucher plan than under the current system.

In his study, Professor Levin, arguing that tuition should not be the only factor considered when comparing education costs, examined experimental school voucher programs in Milwaukee and Cleveland. He found that the public schools provided many free services such as food and transportation, which the voucher schools provided for an extra fee.

Some of the additional hidden expenses that Levin said a voucher system would incur are the following:

- $20 billion to $33 billion for students currently attending private schools who would also be eligible for vouchers;
- $2.5 billion for maintaining school attendance records, and certifying and monitoring the voucher schools;
- $42 billion for transportation, since a greater number of students would attend schools outside their neighborhoods. In Cleveland's voucher experiment, Levin found that approximately 1,100 students take taxicabs to school, accounting for $9,900 of public funds every week;
- $1.8 billion to inform families about the schools available to them; and
- $1.8 billion for settling disputes involving students who want to change schools or schools that want to expel students.

There are over 5.5 million children who do not attend public schools in this country. If these children suddenly began using money from the state's treasury for their schooling, taxes would have to be raised to generate the additional revenue. Ed Doerr, Executive Director of Americans for Religious Liberty, predicts that vouchers would cost Americans 33 billion dollars annually in increased taxes.[14]

From the numerous accounts in this book, you can see the heavy sacrifices paid by many home school families who risked all to make home schooling free from government control. When I began my work at the Home School Legal Defense Association, it was only legal in about 5 states. Now after hundreds of court battles and legislative struggles, many of which I was involved in, it is legal in all 50 states. Home schooling has come too far in its struggle to be free from government control to crawl back on its knees to drink from the public trough! I predict if we take the course of government vouchers, we will lose the precious freedom we have gained as home schoolers.

If home school parents forget the struggle for freedom to home school—the emotional and economic sacrifices, the fear and uncertainty, the threats to children, harassment, school board inquisitions, criminal truancy charges served late at night on innocent parents, lengthy trials, appellate arguments, legislative hearings packed with home schoolers trying to repeal onerous restrictions of their freedom and the losses and the victories—they will be tempted to compromise. They are in danger of becoming selfish and complacent. They will look once again to the government for their free benefits and entitlements. They will demand their share of the "government's tax-funded pie." They will ignore the impact and loss of freedom for future generations.

Unless we repeat the stories of these sacrifices and remind ourselves and our children of God's deliverance of the home schoolers, we will be tempted and enticed back into government dependence. Ultimately, the most important thing will be for us to run the race while" keeping our eyes fixed on Jesus Christ, the Author and Finisher of our faith." We must never relegate Christ to second in the home school movement.

The following scenario should serve as a warning to us. This is the way of great civilizations and the way of great movements. Historian Sir Alexander Fraser Tyler wrote in the early 1800s:

> The average age of the world's greatest civilizations has been 200 years. These Nations have progressed through the following sequence:
> From bondage to spiritual faith,
> From spiritual faith to great courage,
> From courage to liberty,
> From liberty to abundance,
> From abundance to selfishness,
> From selfishness to complacency,
> From complacency to apathy,
> From apathy to dependency,
> And from dependency back into bondage.

Home schoolers need to be careful they are not undermined from within. We need to depend on God rather than depend on government or we will return to bondage.

I have personally observed the consequences of home schoolers receiving government money in other nations. I serve as Vice Chairman of the Board of the Home School Legal Defense Association of Canada. The province of Alberta had always been one of the least regulated provinces to home school in until, in the early 1990s, legislation was passed to give all home school parents a government voucher of $500 per child. The very next year, complex requirements were enacted for all home schoolers, transforming Alberta into one of the most regulated provinces. When questioned, the Alberta Minister of Education explained the new regulations were necessary since they had to know about the home schoolers since many were receiving the voucher money.

Let us not give the government an excuse to regulate us and return us under its yoke. Neither let us allow the government to take credit for home schoolers' success because it gives us money. Abraham in Genesis 14 was offered a government handout by the king of Sodom who he and his men rescued from an invading army. Abraham simply replied, "I have sworn to the Lord God Most High, possessor of heaven and earth, that I will not take a sandal thong or anything that is yours, lest you should say, 'I have made Abraham rich'"(Genesis 14:22-23).

The Battle Is Not Over: Public School Authorities Are Not Convinced

It is easy to assume that now that home schooling is legal in every state, the public school authorities support home schooling. A recent survey by *The American School Board Journal* gives a very different picture.

The Xavier University research team joined *The American School Board Journal* to conduct a national survey of nearly 1000 public school executives including superintendents and principals.[15] Surprisingly, 55 percent of the public school officials believe that home schoolers do not meet the academic standards set by the state and 24 percent admit they have no idea whatsoever how home schoolers perform.[16]

When asked to rank the alternatives to public schools, 95 percent of the public school officials believe anything is better than home schooling! And when it comes to regulation of home schooling, 71 percent of superintendents believe home schoolers are not regulated enough.[17] Finally, a whopping 1 percent of public school officials believe home school students perform better than public schools.

It is clear from these statistics that the prejudices remain. The majority of public school officials is presently being held at bay by the law and court cases won by the home schoolers. But their hearts have not been won. As soon as they have the chance, they will implement methods to regulate and curtail home schooling. Let's not give them any excuse such as clamoring for government money in the form of vouchers.

Mike Farris, Mike Smith, and I actually thought we would work ourselves out of business at HSLDA once all the battles were won over the right to home school. But our experience proves otherwise. Public school officials continue to harass home schoolers and attempt to intimidate them to stop home schooling in one way or another. Our staff of seven lawyers and nine legal assistants at HSLDA are engaged full-time in protecting home schooler rights in spite of the improvement in state laws. We are convinced there will always be trouble for home schoolers as long as the public school officials have authority to enforce truancy under the compulsory attendance laws.

One of our goals at HSLDA remains the eventual repeal of compulsory attendance laws. Then and only then will parents be truly free to home school without interference by prejudiced school officials.

The Clash Between Parental Rights and State Control

This bias against home schooling by the educational establishment and many school authorities results in numerous legal conflicts across the country each year.

During the 1998-99 school year, nearly two thousand negative legal contacts were handled by HSLDA. These contacts involved various degrees of harassment, ranging from actual or threatened prosecution to the attempted imposition of restrictions in excess of the law.[18]

Misapplication of the law even plagued the thirty-seven states that had home school legislation. Single parents or parents with handicapped children received the worst treatment. For example, families were threatened with a termination of their right to home school by school districts trying to impose false notification deadlines, testing or evaluation procedures, curriculum requirements, or in some instances, qualification requirements.

In states where home schools either have to be approved by the school district or operate as private schools, the challenges were more intense. Many members of HSLDA were faced with illegal home visits, curriculum approval, and excessive qualification requirements. In many of these states the law is somewhat vague, which contributes to the arbitrary treatment of home schools.

As a result, we at HSLDA must daily counsel members as to appropriate action and then, when necessary, intervene on their behalf. This often involves writing lengthy legal letters to the school districts or making numerous phone calls. In 10 percent of the situations where the school districts refuse to back off, the families are charged with educational neglect or criminal truancy.

The reason these home school families are harassed usually is connected to either the school official's philosophical bias or the school district's financial interest.

The Battle Is Intensifying

Home education, one of the most important liberties, is protected by the First and Fourteenth Amendments. However, the opposition realizes the danger of this growing movement and is seeking to regulate home schooling out of existence or, at least, into conformity.

This battle has two important fronts remaining: the spiritual battle and the legal battle. The academic battle has already been won with numerous studies documenting the success of home schooling.

As a result, home schoolers must remain committed to prayer for protection and committed to train up the children to think and believe as Christians. Furthermore, parents must remain eternally vigilant in order to fight any legislative attempts to undermine parental liberties. Parents must also have solidarity with home schoolers throughout the nation by supporting ministries such as HSLDA, which is dedicated to defending the rights of all home schoolers at the local, state and federal levels. (Chapter 24 gives information on how to join HSLDA.)

Notes

1. John Stuart Mill, *American State Papers: On Liberty* (Chicago: Benton William, Publisher, Encyclopedia Britannica, Inc., 1972), 318.
2. "The 1999 Resolutions of the National Education Association."
3. *USA Today*, July 8, 1988.
4. Ann Zimmerman, "Is Anybody Home?" *Dallas Observer*, November 21, 1991, 20.
5. National Association of Elementary School Principals 1987-88 platform, 3.
6. Mary Esch, "Home Schooling Good or Bad, More Parents Are Willing to Try It," *State Journal Register*, June 30, 1991.
7. *Milwaukee Journal*, June 7, 1990.
8. Keven B. Smith and Kenneth J. Meier, "School Choice, Panacea or Pandora's Box," *Phi Delta Kappan*, December 1995, 314.
9. Richard Riley, U.S. Secretary of Education during a September 20, 1995 radio interview, "The Diane Rehm Show," National Public Radio.
10. Richard Riley, U.S. Secretary of Education, "Third Annual State of American Education Address," Maplewood-Richmond Heights Senior High School; St. Louis, Missouri; February 28, 1996.
11. Lynda Friesen, "Vouchers: Free Ride or Hidden Trap?" *Home School Court Report*, July/August 1992, 4.
12. John J. Miller, "Opting Out," *The New Republic*, November 30, 1992, 13.
13. Laureen Lazarovici, "National Voucher System Could Be Costly, Study Says," *Education Daily*, February 23, 1998, 1.
14. Ed Doerr, "School Voucher Programs Can't Stand Close Scrutiny," *Washington Times*, October 11, 1995, A18.

15. James Booth, Leo Bradley, Michael Flick, and Susanne Kirk, "No Place Like Home," *The America School Board Journal*, February 1997, pp. 38-41. A research team from Xavier University in Cincinnati, Ohio conducted the Journal's survey of public school executives. The questionnaire was mailed to a stratified random sample of 6,102 public school officials from an administrator population of more than 125,000. The overall response rate was 16 percent or 983 responses.

16. *Ibid.*, 39.

17. *Ibid.*

18. Record of the Home School Legal Defense Association, Purcellville, Virginia. Also see back and future issues of the Home School Court Report for a chronological account of harassment faced by home schoolers around the nation

11

United Nations Convention on the Rights of the Child:

The Anti-Parents' Treaty Which Never Dies

"You are not to say 'It is a conspiracy!'…And you are not to fear what they fear or be in dread of it. It is the Lord of Hosts whom you should regard as Holy. And He shall be your fear. And he shall be your dread."

Isaiah 8:12-13

"Behold the nations are as a drop from a bucket…All the nations are as nothing before Him, they are regarded by Him as less than nothing and meaningless."

Isaiah 40:15, 17

After years of debate within the international community, child's rights activists reached an agreement in 1988 which created a comprehensive charter advancing the agenda of the children's "liberation" movement. What the child's rights advocates have for over two decades been unable to accomplish through the normal legislative process may now be realized in one sweeping blow.

If ratified by the U.S. Senate, the United Nations Convention on the Rights of a Child would undermine families by granting to children a list of radical "rights" which would be primarily enforced against the parents. These new "fundamental" rights would include "the right to privacy," "the right to freedom of thought and association," and the right to "freedom of expression." Such presumptions subvert the authority of parents to exercise important responsibilities toward their children. Under the U.N. Convention, parental responsibility exists only in so far as parents are willing to further the independent choices of the child.

Declaration of War on Parents' Rights

On February 14, 1995, the Clinton Administration, through Hillary Clinton, declared war on parents' rights in America. On that day, Hillary Clinton announced that the United States would sign the U. N. Convention on the Rights of the Child and send it to the U.S. Senate for ratification. Hillary Clinton described the Convention as advancing a "noble cause, to promote the wellbeing and protect the basic rights of children throughout the world."[1]

On February 23, U.N. Ambassador Madeleine Albright signed the U.N. Convention on the Rights of the Child for the President. Commenting on the move by the President, Senator Bill Bradley of New Jersey stood up that same day in the U.S. Senate and declared,

> This marks a small, but long overdue step toward improving the lot of the world's children. I urge the President to take a much larger, and equally overdue step, and submit the Convention at once to the Senate for advice and consent to ratification...The lives of children are at stake until we ratify this Convention, we will be unable to exert the leadership necessary to make a difference in the lives of the world's children. President Clinton has done the right thing by instructing Ambassador Albright to sign the Convention. He should now submit it to the Senate and we should ratify it without delay.[2]

The pressure is on. The U.N. Convention on the Rights of the Child was unanimously adopted by the General Assembly of the United Nations on November 20, 1989. The Convention drafting process spanned ten years, during which the United States was an active participant. The year 1995 was targeted by UNICEF for universal ratification. At this point, 176 nations, including the Vatican and virtually every major industrialized nation are signatories to the Convention. The United States is one of the last nations which has not ratified this Treaty.

The President is embarrassed and is being subjected to extraordinary international pressure from the child's rights organizations. In fact over 150 groups have indicated their support for the U.N. Convention on the Rights of the Child and are urging Clinton to send it to the Senate. These include the National Education Association, the National Council of Churches, the Children's Defense Fund, American Council for Social Services, the National Committee for the Rights of the Child, the National Council for Child's Rights, Planned Parenthood, International School of Psychology Association, the National School Board Association, the American Bar Association, the International Council on Social Welfare, and more.

One of the groups urging passage of the Treaty is the American Academy of Pediatrics, which represents 40,000 pediatricians. They wrote to President Clinton stating,

> Opponents of the Convention, many of whom oppose the portions of the Treaty banning corporal punishment for minors and home schooling, have been contacting Senate offices. Therefore, it is critical that the Senators and the President hear that there is broad-based, grassroots support for the treaty. Fellows are encouraged to contact their Senators and the President in expressing support for the Convention...

The path is set and the push has begun for the U.N. Convention on the Rights of the Child to be ratified by the U.S. Senate. Even if it does not come before the Senate any time soon, or even if the Senate defeats the Convention on a floor vote, it still will not die. Treaties like the U.N. Convention on the Rights of the Child never die. At a moment's notice, it can be resurrected and considered by the Senate Foreign Relations Committee. Therefore, we have to stay vigilant, informed, and ready to fight to prevent the U.N. Treaty from being ratified by the U.S. Senate.

What Difference Does the Treaty Make as Far as Affecting our Parental Rights in America?

According to the Supremacy Clause in Article VI of the U.S. Constitution, a treaty directly applies to all citizens in the United States. Article VI, Section 2 states:

> All treaties made, or which shall be made, under the
> authority of the United States, shall be the supreme law of
> the land; and the judges in every state shall be bound
> thereby, anything in the constitution of the laws of any
> state to the contrary notwithstanding.

Therefore, otherwise valid state laws pertaining to education and parents' rights throughout the states which conflict with the provisions of the Treaty will be nullified by our own U.S. Constitution. In *Missouri v. Holland,*[3] the Supreme Court held that a treaty made by the President of the United States with the required concurrence of two-thirds of the Senate, is under the Supremacy Clause of Article VI, Section 2, and becomes part of the supreme law which takes precedent over contrary state laws. In other words, if the U.N. Convention on the Rights of the Child is sent to the U.S. Senate and ratified by two-thirds of the senators, the U.N. Convention on the Rights of the Child becomes the supreme law of the land. Therefore when aspects of the Treaty conflict with present federal precedence on parents' rights, it will be up to the courts to balance and resolve a conflict. The state laws, however, will simply be superseded.

Why is the Convention on the
Rights of the Child so Dangerous?

In compliance with the Treaty, the United States will be obligated to "ensure" various rights of children. Howard Davidson, Director of the American Bar Association Center on Children and Law, and Cynthia Price Cohen, member of the Ad Hoc Non-Governmental Group on the Drafting of the Convention on the Rights of the Child, have written a treatise which was published by the American Bar Association in 1990. The book is entitled, "Children's Rights in America: U.N. Convention on the Rights of the Child Compared with United States Law." On page 35 of the book, Davidson and Cohen comment on the meaning of the word "ensure" and how it binds signatory nations:

> In the accepted hierarchy of treaty terminology, a State
> Party's promise to "ensure" a right denotes the highest
> degree of obligation. The word "ensure" requires more
> than mere non-interference with the exercise of a right; it

requires a state party to take positive measures, legislative and otherwise, to make sure that the right can be effectively exercised.

The authors mention that the word "ensure" is used thirty-two times in the substantive portion of the Convention and that "its frequency reflects the degree of seriousness and commitment that delegates gave to the rights of the child" (p. 36).

If the United States ratifies the U.N. Convention on the Rights of the Child, the U.S. government will be obligated to "ensure" the following:

1. That every child shall be registered by the government immediately after birth Article 7 (1). Government tracking of all children will be required.
2. That every child shall receive the highest attainable level of health care services Article 24 (1). In chapter 11 of the American Bar Association book by Davidson and Cohen, they state that this provision indicates that a mandatory federal health insurance plan would be necessary to comply with the Treaty.
3. That no child is subjected to corporal punishment. Article 28.2 states that all schools must be prohibited from using corporal punishment. In Article 19.1, and in Article 37 (a), it not only prohibits school authorities from administering corporal discipline, but it also applies it to "parents, legal guardians, or any other person who has care of the child." This Treaty will essentially outlaw spanking.

In fact, Canada, one of the signatories of the U.N. Convention on the Rights of the Child, is presently reviewing its criminal code to see if parents can legally spank their children. According to the Justice Minister, Alan Rock, "As a signatory to that Convention, Canada became obligated to review its own domestic laws to ensure that they reflect that international principle of basic decency." Canada is presently on course of attempting to ban spanking as a result of its attempts to implement the U.N. Treaty.[4] Who says this Treaty is cosmetic?

4. Under the U.N. Treaty, the United States will be required to ensure that children are vested with "freedom of expression."

Section 1 states that a child has a right to "seek, receive and impart information of all kinds, regardless of frontiers, either orally in writing or in print, in the form of art, or through any other media of the child's choice." This essentially gives children the right to listen to rock music, watch television, and even have access to pornography.

5. Furthermore, children are guaranteed the "freedom of thought, conscience, and religion." This will give children the right to object to their parents' religious training and participate in religious services of other cults.

6. The child under the Treaty would have the "right to freedom of association." Parents would be prevented from prohibiting their children from associating with certain other children or gangs.

7. A child will be given a "right of privacy," which of course would open the door for children to get access to abortion over their parents' objection. This would virtually invalidate all parental notification laws concerning abortion.

8. Public education for the first time would be a "right" to all children of the United States under the U.N. Convention. Parents interfering with the child's right to choose public education would be violating his rights and could be subject to prosecution.

In Article 29, the American Bar Association treatise by Cohen and Davidson indicates this Article would force the public schools of America to adopt "federally prescribed curriculum content" (p.177). Furthermore, the curriculum would "prescribe certain values which the State Parties agree to transmit to the children through education." Each child would be required to be prepared to be a responsible citizen by having "the spirit of understanding, peace, toleration, equity of sexes, and friendship for all peoples, ethnic, national and religious groups of indigenous origin" (Article 29).

Cohen and Davidson further comment, "It is conceivable that the Court could someday move toward prescribing some values content in private school curriculum" (p.182). They assert that private schools "must conform to certain standards, specifically those enumerated in Article 29 and such minimum standards may be laid down by the state" (p. 180). They specifically criticize curriculum used by

Accelerated Christian Education (ACE) and the teaching in Bethany Baptist Academy in Illinois, since their teachings of Christianity as the only true religion "flies in the face of Articles 29.1(b),(c),(d)" (p. 182).

9. Under the Treaty, governments must enforce the right of the child to "freely participate in cultural life and arts."

10. Cohen and Davidson in the American Bar Association treatise indicate that Article 27 would require the United States to increase massive social welfare programs for children. They state: the Convention should be required as requiring the U.S. to move progressively toward child support, social insurance, parental support and income maintenance policies and practices that ensure that every child in the U.S. has, in the words of Article 27, a standard of living adequate for the child's physical, mental, spiritual, moral, and social development. The U.S. Congress and the President must in this decade attack the problem of child poverty with the same vigor as their predecessors attacked the problem of elderly poverty.... Improvements in the minimum wage, the availability in the amount of tax credits, education, job training, and job creation efforts, social insurance programs and benefits and safety net programs are all necessary (p. 214).

The cost of the ratification of the U.N. Convention on the Rights of the Child and its subsequent implementation would be staggering.

It is clear from these few examples above that this Treaty would virtually undermine parents' rights as we know them in the United States. Parents no longer would have the basic right to control what their children watch on TV, whom they associate with, and what church they attend. Parents could be prosecuted and children be taken away simply because they spank their children or refuse to honor the various rights that the children are guaranteed as cited above.

There is no doubt that this Treaty is completely devastating to the traditional parents' rights upon which our nation was founded. The U.N. Convention on the Rights of the Child is the perfect vehicle to fulfill all the goals of the child's rights organizations and bureaucrats that have presently surrounded Washington D.C. and are working for an agenda that would eradicate parents' rights.

The U.N. Convention on the Rights of the Child makes it clear that a new standard will prevail as to determining whether or not action taken for or against the child is proper. In Article 3, Section 1, the provision gives the state the power to make all decisions regarding the welfare of the child by divesting parents of their right to determine what is in the best interest of the child and transferring this right to government. The Treaty states, "In all actions concerning children, whether undertaken by public or private social welfare institutions, courts of law, administrative authorities or legislative bodies, the best interest of the child will be a primary consideration." The best interest of the child is a completely subjective standard which will be determined by social workers and not parents.

The Juvenile Officers Association of Michigan enacted a joint resolution on July 14, 1994 condemning the U.N. Convention on the Rights of the Child since it has the potential of wreaking havoc in the administration of juvenile justice. In part they state,

> Whereas the U.N. Convention on the Rights of the Child presumes that a parental responsibility exists only in so far as parents are willing to further the independent choice of the child; Whereas the U.N. Convention on the Rights of the Child though in part but in acceptance of its entirety, undermines parental rights and the autonomy; Whereas the U.N. Convention on the Rights of the Child subverts the role of the parent and diminishes the role of law enforcement, police juvenile officers and juvenile court personnel and other representative professionals, all of whom through cooperation and partnership guide, direct, and counsel and protect the child under the laws of the state of Michigan in the United States of America.

The executive board and board of directors of the Juvenile Officers Association of Michigan resolved, in representation of its members, to oppose the U.N. Convention on the Rights of the Child. Even the juvenile officers, which include sheriff departments, police departments and juvenile courts, understand the utter devastation the U.N. Convention on the Rights of the Child will bring upon the ability of law enforcement officials to punish juvenile offenders.

Will this Treaty Actually be Enforced in the United States?

In Article 4 of the Treaty, it makes clear that the signatory nations are bound to "undertake all appropriate legislative, administrative, and other measures for the implementation of the rights" specified in the convention. Furthermore, the Convention would require the United States, if it ratifies the Convention, to "undertake measures to the maximum extent of available resources…within the framework of international cooperation" to revamp our present structure to the specified child's rights.

In Article 43, an international committee of ten experts has been established to oversee the progress of the implementation of the Treaty. Davidson and Cohen state:

> ultimately, no law, whether it is local, national, or international can be understood until it has been interpreted and applied to a given set of circumstances by some authoritative source….In the case of the U.N. Convention on the Rights of the Child, that authoritative source would be the Committee on the Rights of the Child. The Committee will be made up of ten experts of high moral standing and recognized competence in the field covered by the Convention" (p. 33).

For the first time, America will have its domestic policy subjected to foreign control through the arbitrary whims of this Committee of Ten. It drastically subverts the sovereignty of our nation.

An example of the Committee's oversight of the various nations that have ratified the U.N. Convention on the Rights of the Child is a recent report by the Committee in its eighth session, dated January 1995. The report is called, "Concluding Observations of the Committee on the Rights of the Child Concerning United Kingdom of Great Britain and Northern Ireland." The Committee heavily criticizes Britain for not implementing many aspects of the Treaty. The Committee states,

> In relation to the possibility for parents in England and Wales to withdraw their children from parts of the sex

education programs in schools, the Committee is concerned that this and other decisions, including exclusion from school [this could include home schooling], the right of the child to express his or her opinion is not solicited. Thereby the opinion of the child may not be given due weight and taken into account as required under Article 12 of the Convention.

This seems to be a direct attack on parents' rights to choose the form of education and content of education for their children. It also implies that some parents are excluding their children from school, which would impact those families who choose not to send their children to school and teach them at home instead.

Furthermore, the report by the Committee of Ten states,

...the Committee is deeply worried about the information brought to its attention regarding judicial interpretations of the present law permitting the reasonable chastisement in case of physical abuse of children within the family context. Thus the Committee is concerned that legislative and other measures relating to the physical integrity of children do not appear compatible with the provisions and principles of the Convention, including those of its Articles 3, 19, and 37. The Committee is equally concerned that privately funded and managed schools are still permitted to administer corporal punishment to children.

Essentially the Committee is pointing out that spanking is still allowed in Britain, which is a violation of the U.N. Treaty. Furthermore, the Committee found, "In this connection the Committee observes in particular that the principal for the best interest of the child appears not to be reflected in legislation in such areas as health, education, and social security, which have a bearing on the respect for the rights of the child."

In another instance in 1997, when one of the delegates from Australia argued that the Convention did not specifically forbid spanking, the Committee in its "Concluding Observations of the Committee on the Rights of the Child" disagreed stating,

> [T]he Convention should be interpreted holistically taking into consideration not only its specific provisions, but also the general principals which inspired it.

In other words, the Convention means whatever the Committee says it means! If the Committee wants the treaty to prohibit spanking, it prohibits spanking. There is no opportunity for recourse.

Equally disturbing is the 1998 "Concluding Observations of the Committee on the Rights of the Child" report on Japan which states,

> [T]he convention on the Rights of the Child has precedence over domestic legislation and can be invoked before the domestic courts...

These reports further confirm the position of the United Nations that all nations which sign the Children's Convention are obligated to apply its mandates, thereby overriding the country's own domestic law. This is clearly a usurpation of national sovereignty.

The power and scrutiny of this foreign Committee of Ten to criticize other nations is very dangerous and attacks the sovereignty of that nation. The result of any nation which does not follow the recommendations of the Committee of Ten could easily result in the United Nations enacting some type of sanctions on that nation. The other way the Committee of Ten's critique could affect Britain is if Britain's government feels obligated along with its court system to implement these changes by legislation or court decisions. Who says this U.N. Treaty is harmless?

In the United States, since the Treaty is the supreme law of the land, the authorities in the government and the courts have an obligation to apply correctly the provisions of the Treaty and will thus be forced into following recommendations of the Committee.

Can the U.N. Convention on the Rights of the Child be Amended by the United States?

The U.N. Convention on the Rights of the Child can only be amended through an eight-step process. First, at least one-third of the nations must favor a conference even to discuss an amendment. Once a conference is convened, a majority of the nations present at the conference must vote to adopt the amendment. Then it must be submitted to the full General Assembly for approval. If the amendment is approved by the General Assembly, it must then be accepted by two-thirds of the participating nations. The great difficulty in amending this Treaty is unthinkable. To bind ourselves with such a treaty dictating domestic policy by foreign powers would simply weaken our own national sovereignty while creating no benefits whatsoever for our nations and its citizens.

Doesn't the U.N. Convention on the Rights of the Child Promote the Primacy of Parents in the Life of the Child?

Senator Bill Bradley, when proposing that the Senate immediately ratify the U.N. Convention, indicated that the Convention is explicit on the primacy of the parents in the life of the child. He quoted Article 5, which states, "State Parties shall respect the responsibilities, the rights and duties of parents....to provide, in a manner consistent with the evolving capacities of the child, appropriate in the direction and guidance in the exercise by the child of the rights recognized in the present Convention."

A close look at this Article and other examples of the U.N. Treaty referring to the primacy of the parents indicates that it is nothing more than "lip service." In other words, although the terminology is used, in actuality, the parents' rights are subservient to "the evolving capacities of the child" and exercised in conjunction with "the rights recognized in the present Convention." The Convention so undermines the rights of parents their rights are already taken away. The fact that the parents' rights are still recognized in their limited capacity has no relation to the present capacity of parents' rights in America today. Under the U.N. Convention on the Rights of the Child, a parent's right to control the religion, health, and training of his child is virtually nonexistent. Social workers will play the key role in determining the best interest of the child.

We Do Not Need This Treaty

The U.N. Convention on the Rights of the Child clearly gives children the fundamental rights of freedom of association, freedom of expression, freedom of religion, the right to choose their education, the right of access to media materials, the right to abortion, the right to be free from spanking, the right to health care and many more rights which do not presently exist. Furthermore, the Treaty would put Christian schools at risk since they teach a curriculum that would be outside the requirements of the Treaty.

The Treaty makes it clear that infringement on a child's rights in any of these areas could cause the parents to be prosecuted with the possibility of having the child removed from the home. This Treaty, if it becomes the law of the land in the United States, once it is ratified by the U.S. Senate, will have to be balanced by the federal courts and will be used to empower child's rights advocates in our already uncontrollable welfare system. The rights which the Treaty gives children are in direct opposition to those parents' rights and will only wreak havoc by causing untold litigation in our country.

The bottom line is that we do not need the U.N. Convention on the Rights of the Child in the United States. We already have a massive child welfare system in place throughout the country. In a few countries, the U.N. Convention on the Rights of the Child prohibits such things as slave labor of children. To be sure, this is of great significance in lesser-developed nations where child slave labor may be prevalent, *but in the United States it is not relevant!* We do not need to sign this Treaty to maintain our position as a world power, nor is our signing of this Treaty necessary to influence other nations to clean up their human rights records for both adults and children. To sign the Treaty for this purpose is completely illogical, especially when it poses such a terrible risk to the parental rights and freedoms of U.S. citizens.

Since the United States takes treaties seriously, we will have to implement these aspects of the Treaty by the mandates of our own Constitution under the Supremacy Clause. The Treaty is better designed for nations like China and Iraq. In fact, China willingly signed on to the Treaty. However, it means nothing to China since China does not have any provisions in its constitution which makes treaties the supreme law of the land. It is purely cosmetic. Entering into a treaty of this type is virtually irrelevant for all those nations that most need to protect children at least as far as we already do in the United States.

Stay Informed and Be Prepared

Home schoolers and parents throughout the United States must stay informed and be ready to sound the alarm to everyone if the time comes. This Treaty will devastate our nation in many ways. We must educate our neighbors.

Even if this Treaty is defeated in the Senate, *it will never die.* Treaties can be brought up indefinitely in subsequent years for as long as the Treaty exists. This effort for all of us is a continuing effort from which we can never rest. The price of freedom is eternal vigilance, particularly in this instance. We, as home schoolers, as parents and as lovers of freedom, must not be ambivalent or apathetic concerning the U.N. Convention on the Rights of the Child. This Treaty must be opposed and it must be stopped.

It only takes thirty-four U.S. Senators to block the ratification of this Treaty, and that is possible. Senator Dole, on February 24, 1995, stood before the Senate and condemned the U.N. Convention on the Rights of the Child. Thousands of phone calls from home schoolers responding to HSLDA's nationwide alert is what got him on his feet! (In fact, many other U.S. Senators changed their position or committed in writing to oppose the treaty as a result of HSLDA's phone blitz and lobbying efforts in 1995.) Dole stated,

> Mr. President, in the past several days, I have received thousands of calls from all over the country in opposition to this Convention. My office has not received one call for it. These contacts have raised many serious problems that need to be examined. They have raised questions about Articles 13, 14, and 15, which grant children the freedom of speech, thought, conscience, religion, association, and assembly. Could these articles be interpreted to limit the ability of parents to decide for themselves how best to raise their children? Should U.S. citizens be subject to some sort of international committee that enforces compliance with Article 28 (2) which states: "State Parties shall take all appropriate measures to ensure that school discipline is administered in a manner consistent with the child's human dignity and in conformity with the present Convention"?

Under Article VI of the Constitution, Senate ratification of this Treaty would make it the supreme law of the land. Would the Convention then supersede federal and state laws? What would the effect of the convention be on the Tenth Amendment? Is the convention merely a symbolic exercise, or will it actually require the United

States to take actions? These are sincere questions from sincere people. They deserve answers...

> ...I also believe we in the United States have made significant progress in protecting the rights of the child through federal, state, and local laws. These laws are better equipped to deal with the varying challenges posed by the issue of child rights. If there is one thing this election taught us, it is the need to get excessive government out of people's lives. This applies to the federal government, and it certainly applies to the multilateral, quasi-government that is the U.N.[5]

Dole's response is proof we can make a difference! Stay ready and stay informed! The best way to stay informed is to join the Home School Legal Defense Association. We lobby the U.S. Senate annually educating them and urging them to oppose ratification. We also monitor the Committee of Ten's reports from the U.N. regarding the treaty's implications in other countries. Contact HSLDA for the latest updates at 540-338-7600.

Notes

1. John Harris, "U.S. to Sign U.N. Pacts on Childs' Rights," *Washington Post*, February 11, 1995, A3.
2. *Congressional Record*, page S-292, 55 lines.
3. *Holland*, 252 U.S. 416.
4. *Rapid City Reporter*, "Senators Question Wisdom of Children Rights Treaty," August 2, 1994, quoting a press release from the Evangelical Press Association.
5. *Congressional Record*, page S-3081.

"EXCUSE ME, I CAN'T UNDERSTAND YOU WITH ALL THAT NOISE."

"HOW CAN A MERE MOM DO AS GOOD OF A JOB AS OUR PUBLIC SCHOOL SYSTEM?"

The Myth of Teacher Qualifications

"Some of the worst teachers I've ever seen are highly certified. Look at our public schools. They're full of certified teachers. What kind of magic is that accomplishing? But I can take you to the best teachers I've ever seen, and most of them are uncertified…. We don't have evidence at all that what we do in schools of education makes much difference in teacher competence."[1]

Dr. Donald Ericksen, UCLA

How many times have you been asked, "Are you qualified to teach your children?" or "Don't you have to have a teaching certificate or a degree to home school?" I have heard those questions hundreds of times as I talk to people on airplanes, at stores, and in my neighborhood.

This idea that all teachers must be professionals is ingrained in our minds by the powerful teachers' unions. In order to teach at most colleges now, professors must have a Ph.D. To teach at law school, professors must have a JD. Neither college professors nor law professors can technically teach at local public schools because they must have a teaching certificate. Something is wrong with this picture! Businessmen, former legislators, generals, scientists, etc. are not considered qualified to teach at public elementary or secondary schools.

The thought of a home school mom, with only a high school diploma, teaching her children is even more radical to modern teacher unions and education "professionals."

Most education officials publicly claim that teachers need special "qualifications" in order to be effective. As a result, public education organizations often promote legislation or an interpretation of the law which would require home school parents to have one of three qualifications: 1) a teacher certificate, 2) a college degree, or 3) pass a "teacher's exam." Although this seems reasonable on the surface, such requirements not only violate the right of parents to teach their children as guaranteed by the First and Fourteenth Amendments, but virtually all academic research documents that there is no positive correlation between teacher qualifications (especially teacher certification requirements) and student performance.

It also seems apparent that Americans in general are seeing through the "smoke screen" of teacher qualifications. On July 23, 1991, the results of a public opinion poll were released by the Washington-based Belden and Russonello public opinion research firm. It found that three out of four Americans disagreed with the notion that teacher certification requirements in public schools assure high-quality teachers. The poll also found that 71 percent do not believe that the lack of teacher certification in private schools means that their teachers are less qualified than public school teachers.[2]

Only the National Education Association and some of the other members of the educational establishment continue to defend teacher certification and high qualification standards for home schoolers, in spite of the overwhelming research against the need for such teaching standards. Their vested interest in certified teachers may explain their blindness to the facts.

I have talked with hundreds of school officials who cannot understand how a "mere mother" with a high school diploma could possibly teach her own children. These officials literally take offense that parents would try to teach their children and actually think that they will do as well as teachers in the public school who have at least four years and sometimes seven years of higher education. Unfortunately, critics in the media have also believed this myth and will question the validity of home schooling by asking, "But are the parents qualified?" What is so laughable about this belief in teacher qualifications by public school authorities are the statistics which show the appalling decline in competency among certified public school teachers and the failure of the teacher colleges. Chapter 1 documents many of these statistics.

Since 1983, HSLDA has been battling teacher qualifications for home school parents in the legal arena. I have fought hundreds of school districts which have misapplied the laws in states such as Alabama, Massachusetts, Pennsylvania, Ohio, Kansas, Maryland, Michigan, California, and South Carolina. These school districts often used the vagueness of the law to impose college degree or certification requirements on home school parents, which, if successful, would shut down over half of all home schools. As of the printing of this book, the battles have been won in most of these states, either in the courts or in the legislature. Other states such as Iowa, North Dakota, Michigan, Florida, Virginia, and Washington applied more explicit laws requiring home schoolers to be certified teachers. Most of these laws were finally defeated or repealed, but many families ended up in court in the process. For over ten years, virtually every HSLDA family that was discovered by a school district in North Dakota was taken to court for not being certified.

Home schoolers need to remain constantly informed. For example, a few years ago, the Kansas School Board Association made an unsuccessful attempt to get House Bill 2392 passed which would have required home schoolers to be certified.[3] Home schoolers, as a result of these continuing attacks by school officials, lobbyists, and the media, need to be familiar with the statistics in this chapter in order to expose the "myth of teacher qualifications" so that no qualifications will be placed on home school parents.

This chapter summarizes research and opinions of professional educators, confirming the absence of a positive correlation between teacher qualifications and student performance. There is also a clear trend in the legislatures and the courts away from enacting or enforcing certification and other teaching standards to restrict home schoolers.

Research and Researchers Which Expose the Myth of Teacher Qualifications

One of the most significant studies in this area was performed by Dr. Eric Hanushek of the University of Rochester, who surveyed the results of 113 studies on the impact of teachers' qualifications on their students' academic achievement. Eighty-five percent of the studies found *no positive correlation* between the educational performance of the students and the teacher's educational background.

Although 7 percent of the studies did find a positive correlation, 5 percent found a *negative impact.*[4] Those who push for legislation requiring certain teacher qualifications for home schoolers have no research to support the necessity of such standards. The results of these 113 studies are certainly an indictment on proponents of certain teacher standards for home schoolers. Higher teacher qualification does not make better students.

Dr. Sam Peavey, professor emeritus of the School of Education at the University of Louisville, earned advance education degrees from Harvard (Master of Arts) and Columbia (Doctor of Education) and was involved in the preparation of thousands of prospective teachers for state certification. He has served on numerous committees and commissions dealing with the accreditation of schools and colleges. On September 30, 1988, Dr. Peavey testified before the Compulsory Education Study Committee of the Iowa Legislature on the subject of teacher qualifications, citing numerous studies. He stated:

> May I say that I have spent a long career in developing and administering programs for teacher certification. I wish I could tell you that those thousands of certificates con-tributed significantly to the quality of children's learning, but I cannot.... After fifty years of research, we have *found no significant correlation between the requirements for teacher certification* and *the quality of student achievement.*

Later in his testimony, Dr. Peavey explained that he has found only *one* valid way of identifying a good teacher:

> However, in spite of years of frustration, I am pleased to report to you there has been discovered one valid, legal, honest, professional, common sense way to identify a good teacher. As far as I know there is only one way, and it is about time for legislators to recognize it and write it into school law. It involves a simple process. Step one is to *stop looking at the teachers* and *start looking at the students.* Step two is to determine how well students are learning what they are supposed to be learning. The quality of learning provides the only valid measure of the quality of teaching we have yet discovered [emphasis added].

Dr. Peavey concluded his testimony with practical examples of excellent student achievement results by students who were being taught by their parents, most without degrees or certificates. He explained that many studies demonstrate that home schooled children "commonly score a year or more above their peers in regular schools on standard measures of achievement."[5]

Another expert, Dr, Donald Ericksen, professor of education for the University of California at Los Angeles, stated in a recent interview:

> Some of the worst teachers I've ever seen are highly certified. Look at our public schools. They're full of certified teachers. What kind of magic is that accomplishing? But I can take you to the best teachers I've ever seen, and most of them are uncertified.... We *don't have evidence at all that what we do in schools of education makes much difference in teacher competence* [emphasis added].[6]

In a well known case before the Michigan Supreme Court concerning a Christian school's challenge to the state's teacher certification requirement, Dr. Ericksen testified as an expert witness on teacher certification. There he explained that extensive research has established that no significant correlation exists between certification (or teacher qualifications) and student learning, and that student testing is a far superior method of determining teacher effectiveness. Dr. Lanier, an expert who testified on the side of the state in favor of teacher certification, admitted under oath that she was unaware of any verifiable evidence establishing any correlation between teacher certification requirements and student learning or teacher competence.[7]

Two education researchers, R. W. Heath and M. A. Nielson, surveyed forty-two studies of "competency-based" teacher education. Their findings were that no empirical evidence exists to establish a positive relation between those programs and student achievement.[8]

Four other education researchers, L. D. Freeman, R. E. Flodan, R. Howsan, and D. C. Corrigan, did separate studies in the effectiveness of teacher certification requirements. They all concluded that there is no significant relation between teacher certification and student performance in the classroom.[9]

The 1990 Science Report Card surveyed almost twenty thousand students in grades four, eight, and twelve. The survey demonstrates that there is no relationship between the science achievement of students and the certification level or advanced degrees of their teachers. For instance, eighth graders taught by teachers who had finished six or more college physics courses had virtually the same proficiency as those teachers who had no courses in physics.[10]

C. Emily Feistritzer, director of the private National Center for Education Information, claimed that she does not know "of a single study that says because a teacher has gone through this or that program, he or she is a better teacher." Supporters of teacher training programs "argue eloquently that teachers need to be grounded in all of these things, but there has yet to be a study that shows that in fact this is the case."[11]

In July 1999, the Thomas Fordham Foundation published a study entitled; "Better Teachers, Better Schools," a 250-page study edited by Chester Finn & Marci Kanstoroom. This study report was broken into several sections including, "Teacher Licensing and Student Achievement." The researchers employed data from the National Educational Longitudinal Study of 1988 (NELS), a nationally representative survey of about 24,000 eighth-grade students conducted in the spring of 1988. A subset of these students were resurveyed in tenth (1990) and twelfth grades (1992).

The following two questions were the key questions of the study:

> 1) Do teachers with "standard" certification outperform teachers with alternative or probationary credentials in terms of the achievement of students?
> 2) Are different components of a state's system of licensure systematically related to student achievement?

After careful comparison of the teachers' certification or lack of certification with the students' performance, their findings confirmed the results of the many other studies the teachers' unions do not like to talk about. The authors explain:

> Although teacher certification is pervasive, there is little rigorous evidence that it is systematically related to student achievement. Contrary to conventional wisdom, mathematics and science students who have teachers with emergency credentials do no worse than students whose teachers have standard teaching credentials, all else being equal. This result should, at the very least, cast doubt on

assertions that standard certification should be required of all teachers. [12]

The study also found that having a degree in education has no impact on student science test scores and, in mathematics, having a BA in education actually has a statistically negative impact on scores in math!

So don't worry, Moms! All the studies demonstrate your "hands-on" degree in home schooling your own children is much more effective than spending all that time for a BA in education.

John Chubb, a fellow at the Brookings Institute (a liberal think tank), extensively studied various popular reforms including the push to professionalize teaching, toughen teacher certification standards, and implement more extensive teacher evaluation systems. As a result, he authored a book with Terry Moe, *Politics, Markets, and America's Schools* on the subject of reform of education. Mr. Chubb found "no correlation between student achievement and any of the variables on which school reformers have been concentrating so much time, effort, and money." He continues, "There is little reason to believe" that these actions will improve student achievement and "there is considerable reason to believe they will fail."[13]

Dr. Brian Ray of the National Home Education Research Institute released a report entitled, "A Nationwide Study of Home Education: Family Characteristics, Legal Matters, and Student Achievement." This was a study of over two thousand home school families in all fifty states. The research revealed that there was no positive correlation between the state regulation of home schools and the home schooled students' performance. The study compared home schoolers in three groups of states representing various levels of regulation. Group 1 represented the most restrictive states, such as Michigan, which at the time of the study required home schoolers to use certified teachers; Group 2 represented slightly less restrictive states including North Dakota; and Group 3 represented unregulated states, such as Texas and California, which have no teacher qualifications. Dr. Ray concluded:

> No difference was found in the achievement scores of students between the three groups which represent various degrees of state regulation of home education.... It was found that students in all three regulation groups scored

on the average at or above the 76th percentile in the three areas examined: total reading, total math, and total language. These findings in conjunction with others described in this section, do not support the idea that state regulation and compliance on the part of home education families assures successful student achievement.[14]

Furthermore, this same study demonstrated that only 13.9 percent of the mothers (who are the primary teachers) had ever been certified teachers. The study found that there was no difference in students' total reading, total math, and total language scores based on the teacher certification status of their parents:

> The findings of this study do *not* support the idea that parents need to be trained and certified teachers to assure successful academic achievement of their children.[15]

Whether the home school parent had a teaching certificate, a college degree, or a high school diploma or less, did not make any difference—all their children scored, on the average, in the 80th percentile.

This study has been confirmed by two other studies of the qualifications of home school parents. Dr. J. F. Jakestraw surveyed the student performance of home schoolers in Alabama and reported:

> This finding suggests that those children in Alabama whose parent-teachers are not certified to teach perform on standardized achievement tests as well as those whose parent-teachers are certified to teach. Therefore, it is concluded that there is no relationship between the certification status of the parent-teacher and the home schooled children's performance on standardized achievement tests.[16]

Jon Wartes performed a similar study on home schoolers over three years in the state of Washington and reached the same conclusion. [17]

On the whole, home schoolers' achievements are ranked above average on standardized achievement tests as demonstrated by the numerous studies summarized in chapter 5. Dr. Ray and others have found that only 35 percent of teaching mothers have a college degree or higher, and yet their children score no higher on standardized achievement tests than those being taught by mothers without a college degree.

The Evidence Is In: Teacher Qualifications Do Not Make Better Students

Nearly all existing research on teacher qualifications or state regulations demonstrates that they have no significant relation to student performance. In fact, teacher qualification requirements have no positive correlation with even *teacher* performance. In the end, as the Coleman Report (U.S. Office of Education, 1964) pointed out, families are the most important factors in determining a student's academic performance.

Statutory Trend Lessening Teacher Qualification Requirements

The trend across the United States is to remove all teacher qualifications standards for home schoolers. The emphasis seems to be on protecting parental rights and, in several states, focusing on student performance through an annual test or portfolio evaluation.

As of January 2000, forty-one states do not require home school parents to have any specific qualifications. Home schoolers in these states can home school without proof of any particular educational qualifications. In fact, of the nine states that do have qualification requirements, seven of them require only a GED or high school diploma. The states in this category are North Carolina, Ohio, Pennsylvania, Georgia, South Carolina, Tennessee, and New Mexico. Of the remaining two states, only North Dakota presently requires the passage of a "teacher's test," college degree, or high school diploma if monitored by a certified teacher for two years. West Virginia requires parents to have four years of education beyond their oldest student.

South Carolina previously required a college degree or passage of a teacher's examination. Michael Farris of HSLDA challenged the law and on December 9, 1991, the South Carolina Supreme Court struck down the test, making a high school diploma the only qualification necessary for parents to home school.[18] New Mexico required a Bachelor's Degree, but this requirement was repealed due to efforts of the grass roots home schoolers and HSLDA. Michigan, the last state to require home school parents to have teaching certificates or use a person with a certificate to teach the children, recently changed. On May 25, 1993, the Michigan Supreme Court struck down the teacher certification requirement as unconstitutional in *People v. DeJonge,* as case I handled for eight years (See chapter 17 for details). Many of the other states which formerly had a law like Michigan's also abandoned such teacher qualifications requirements.[19]

Major Cases on Teacher Qualifications for Home Schools and Private Schools

Below are summaries of several cases in various states that dealt with the issue of teacher qualifications and found teacher certification requirements or college degree requirements to be excessive or unconstitutional.

In New York, according to its compulsory attendance statute in section 3204, instruction "elsewhere" must be given by a "competent" teacher. The court, in the case *In re Franz,* interpreted "competent" to *not* mean "certified."[20] Furthermore, home school regulations adopted in June 1988 do not require home school parents to have any qualifications. Home school parents are "competent" as long as they file a notice of intent, quarterly reports of progress, and test results every other year beginning in third grade.

New Jersey law allows *"equivalent* instruction elsewhere than at school."[21] Regarding the interpretation of the word "equivalent," the New Jersey Supreme Court in the *Massa* case stated: "…perhaps the New Jersey Legislature intended the word equivalent to mean taught by a certified teacher elsewhere than at school. However, I believe there are teachers today teaching in various schools in New Jersey who are not certified…. Had the legislature intended such a requirement, it would have said so."[22]

Ohio law requires home school teachers to be "qualified."[23] State Board of Education regulations define "qualified" as a GED or high school diploma.[24] Prior to these regulations, in *Ohio v. Whisner,* the Ohio Supreme Court struck down Ohio's Minimum Standards which required teacher certification, stating, "Equally difficult to imagine, is a state interest sufficiently substantial to sanction abrogation of appellants' [parents'] liberty to direct the education of their children."[25] The Court pointed out that the state "did not attempt to justify [prove] its interest in enforcing the minimum standards [which included teacher certification requirements] as applied to non-public religious schools."[26]

On May 25, 1993, Michigan's teacher certification requirement for home schools was struck down by the highest court of the state. In a four-to-three decision of the Michigan Supreme Court, four Justices found: (See chapter 17 for details.)

> In sum, we conclude that the historical underpinnings of the First Amendment to the U.S. Constitution and the case law in support of it compels the conclusion that the imposition of the certification requirement upon the DeJonges violates the Free Exercise Clause. We so conclude because we find that the certification requirement is not essential to nor is it the least restrictive means of achieving the State's claimed interest. Thus, we reaffirm that sphere of inviolable conscience and belief which is the mark of a free people. We hold that the teacher certification requirement is an unconstitutional violation of the Free Exercise Clause of the First Amendment as applied to families whose religious convictions prohibit the use of certified instructors. Such families, therefore, are exempt from the dictates of the teacher certification requirements.[27]

Indiana presently allows home schools under its law which exempts children from compulsory attendance if they are "provided with instruction *equivalent* to that given in public schools."[28] A federal court in the *Mazenac* case, when trying to interpret the word "equivalent," stated: "…it is now doubtful that the requirements of a formally licensed or certified teacher…would pass constitutional muster."[29] The Court would not interpret "equivalent instruction" as requiring certified teachers because of the constitutional problems involved.

In Massachusetts, "a child who is otherwise instructed in a *manner approved in advance* by the superintendent…" is exempt from attending public school.[30] When establishing guidelines for approving home schools, the Massachusetts Supreme Judicial Court stated, in the *Charles* case, that the superintendents or local public school committees could *not* require the parents to be certified or have college degrees. The Court said: "While we recognize that teachers in public schools must be certified, certification would *not* be appropriately required for parents under a home school proposal.…Nor must parents have college or advanced academic degrees."[31] In fact, the home school mother in this case, in whose favor the Court ruled, did not even have a high school diploma.[32]

In Kentucky, home schools operate as private schools. When private schools were required to use certified teachers, even though the statute was unclear, the Kentucky Supreme Court, in the *Rudasill* case, ruled that teacher certification did not apply to private schools and could not be mandated.[33]

In Hawaii, according to its regulations, "parents teaching their children at home shall be deemed *qualified* instructors."[34] In other words, parents are qualified because they are parents. No certain degrees or diplomas are necessary for parents to be able to successfully educate their children.

In South Dakota, a child is allowed to be "otherwise provided with instruction."[35] The statute further explains that "the individuals [who give instruction] are not required to be certified."

In North Dakota, Nebraska, and Iowa, teacher certification requirements were upheld by the courts in the *Shaver, Faith Baptist,* and *Fellowship Baptist* cases.[36] In each of these cases no expert testimony or evidence was given to prove teacher certification was necessary or essential for children to be educated. In fact, the state could also not prove, with evidence, that teacher certification was the "least restrictive means" for children to be educated.

Furthermore, the legislatures in all three of these states have mooted these cases and vindicated home schooling parents by repealing the teacher certification requirements. Nebraska and Iowa have created an option in their compulsory attendance statutes to allow parents to home school without any qualifications. North Dakota allows parents to pass a "teacher test" or produce a college degree in order to opt out of teacher certification.[37]

The Need For Teacher Qualifications Is a Myth

Educational research does not indicate any positive correlation between teacher qualifications and student performance. Many courts have found teacher qualification requirements on home schoolers to be excessive or not appropriate. The trend in state legislatures across the country indicates an abandonment of teacher qualification requirements for home school teachers. In fact, Americans, in general, are realizing that the necessity of teacher qualifications is a myth. The teachers' unions and other members of the educational establishment make up the small minority still lobbying for teacher certification in order to protect their disintegrating monopoly on education.

Notes

1. "The ABC's of Reform: Give Parents a Choice," *Insight,* September 24, 1990, 13.
2. Carol Innerst, "Parents Prefer Private Schools," *Washington Times,* July 24, 1991, A3.
3. "Worst Home School Bill in the Nation Introduced in Kansas," *Home School Court Report,* March/April 1991, 5. Also "Kansas Teacher Certification Bill Shelved," *Home School Court Report,* May/June 1991, 6.
4. Dr. Eric Hanushek, "The Impact of Differential Expenditures on School Performance," *Educational Researcher,* May 1990.
5. Dr. Sam Peavey, testimony at a hearing before the Compulsory Education Study Committee of the Iowa Legislature, September 30, 1988. Dr. Peavey made similar statements in an interview with *Insight,* September 24, 1990, 13.
6. "The ABC's of Reform: Give Parents a Choice," *Insight,* September 24, 1990, 13.
7. *Sheridan Road Baptist Church v. Department of Ed.,* 396 N.W. 2d 373, 419 fn. 64 (1986).
8. "The Research Basis for Performance-Based Teacher Education," *Review of Educational Research,* 44, 1974, 463-84.
9. See W. R. Hazard, L.D. Freeman, *Legal Issues in Teacher Preparation and Certification,* ERIC, Washington, D.C. 1977; R. E. Flodan, "Analogy and Credentialing," *Action in Teacher Education,* Spring/Summer 1979; R. Howsam and D.C. Corrigan, *Educating a Profession* (Washington D.C., American Association of Colleges for Teacher Education, 1976).
10. "The 1990 Science Report Card: NAEP's Assessment of Fourth, Eighth, and Twelfth Graders," prepared by the Educational Testing Service for the National Center for Education Statistics, Office of Education Research and Improvement, U.S. Department of Education released March 1992.
11. "The ABC's of Reform: Give Parents a Choice," *Insight,* September 24, 1990, 13.
12. Chester Finn & Marci Kanstoroom, editors, "Better Teachers, Better Schools," (Washington D.C.: Thomas Fordham Foundation, July 1999) p. 97. Quote is from a chapter by Dan Goldhaber and Dominic Brewer, "Teacher Licensing and Student Achievement." http://www.edexcellence.net
13. *Ibid.,* 17. Also see John Chubb and Terry Moe, *Politics, Markets, and American Schools* (Washington, D.C.: Brookings Institution, 1990), 202-205.
14. Dr. Brian Ray, "A Nationwide Study of Home Education: Family Characteristics, Legal Matters, and Student Achievement" (Seattle: National Home Education Research Institute, 1990), 53-54.
15. *Ibid.,* 53.
16. Dr. J. F. Jakestraw, "An Analysis of Home Schooling for Elementary School-age Children in Alabama," Doctoral dissertation at the University of Alabama, 1987.
17. Jon Wartes, "Washington Home School Research Project," Woodinville, Washington, 1987-1989.
18. "Home Schoolers Win EEE Case," *Home School Court Report,* January/February 1992, 1; *Lawrence v. South Carolina Board of Education,* 412 S.E.- 2d 394 (1991).
19. See, e.g., Florida, F.S.A.§ 232.02 (4) (1982), and Florida Admin.Reg.6A- 1.951 (1974); New Mexico, N.M.S.A.§ 22-10-3 (1981); Virginia, Virginia Code § 22.1-254 (1980); Washington, R.C.W.§ 28A.27.010 (1980); Iowa Code Ann. section 299.1 (1988); North Dakota: Century Code section 15-34.1-04 (1987).
20. *In re Franz,* 55 A 2d 424, 427 (1977).
21. New Jersey Statutes Annotated § 18A:38-25.
22. *New Jersey v. Massa,* 231 A.2d 252,256 (1967).
23. Ohio Rev. Code Ann. § 3321.04(A)(2).
24. See Ohio State Board of Education Administrative Code chapter 3301-34.
25. *Ohio v. Whisner,* 47 Ohio St.2d 181, at 214 (1976), 351 N.E. 2d 750.
26. *Ibid.,* 217.
27. *Michigan v. Delonge,* 501 N.W. 2d 127 at 144 (Mich. 1993).
28. Ann. lnd. Code § 20-8.1-3-34.
29. *Mazenac v. North Judson-San* Pierre *School Corporation,* 614 F.Supp. 1152, 1160 (1985).
30. Ann. Law of Mass. ch. 76, §1.
31. *Care and Protection of Charles,* 504 N.E.2d 592, 602 (Mass. 1987).
32. *Ibid.,* 504 N.E.2d at 594, ftn. 2.
33. *Kentucky State Board v. Rudasill* 589 S. W.2d 877, 884 (1977).
34. Dept. of Ed. Regs. 4140.2(D)(2).
35. S.D. Cod. Laws Ann. §13-27-3.
36. See *North Dakota* v. *Shaver* 294 N.W. 2d 883 (1980), *Nebraska v. Faith Baptist Church,* 301 N.W. 2d 571 (1981), and *Fellowship Baptist Church* v. *Benton,* 815 F.2d 485 (1987).
37. See Revised Stat. of Nebraska §79-1701(3); N.D. Century Code §15-34.1-03; and Iowa H.F. 455(1991).

WHICH SITUATION HAS NEVER RESULTED
IN A CHILD ABUSE INVESTIGATION?

1 KIDS (GASP!) LEARNING AT HOME.

2 KIDS PLAYING (OH MY!) IN THE YARD.

3 DISHES (MY GOODNESS!) IN THE SINK.

A: **4** (!)

4 PUBLIC SCHOOL-BASED HEALTH CLINIC.

Surprise Attack:

What Can You Do When a Social Worker Comes to Your Door?

"In too many cases, Child Protective Services cannot distinguish real abuse from fabrication, abuse from neglect, and neglect from poverty or cultural differences."[1]

San Diego County Grand Jury

You are at home diligently teaching your children when you hear an unwanted knock at the door. You hope it is just a salesman but you know deep inside it is probably a public school official. You offer a prayer, answer the door, and instead of only a truant officer, you find a child welfare agent. The agent accuses you of child neglect and demands entry into your home and insists on being allowed to interrogate your children alone. When you refuse, the agent threatens to get a court order. But you are innocent! What should you do?

This scenario may sound dramatic, but this is exactly the type of contacts more and more home schoolers are receiving throughout the country. I have handled thousands of legal conflicts since 1985 between home schoolers and the state, and each year there have been more child welfare and social service investigations than the previous year. At HSLDA, we used to talk to a child welfare agent every other month, but now we talk to at least six agents every week.

Why is there such an increase in child welfare contacts? It seems apparent that some school districts are starting to play "hardball" with home schoolers. They see the child welfare and social service agencies as a "back door" way of closing down home schools. In several instances, I have tracked down referrals of home schoolers to child welfare agencies to the local principal or truant officer.

I believe another reason that more home schoolers are referred to social service is because of the availability of "child abuse hotlines" throughout the country. Although these "hotlines" can be used for a good purpose, they can also be used to harass home schoolers. Nasty neighbors who resent the fact that a particular family is home schooling can make an anonymous call to a "hotline" and fabricate some story about child abuse going on at the home of the home schooler. In most states, the child welfare worker has an obligation under law to investigate all referrals, even if based on an anonymous tip, within twenty-four or forty-eight hours. As a result, home schoolers are being subjected to some very intimidating confrontations with child welfare agents.

Of course, what makes child welfare and social service agents so intimidating is that, unlike truant officers, they are known to routinely take children from their parents.

In every instance of fabricated abuse or neglect, we have been successful, by God's grace, to resolve the investigations favorably by counseling the family or intervening directly with the child welfare agent. In HSLDA's entire history since 1983, we have never had any children taken from the home over home schooling, nor have any families ever had to stop home schooling.

Although we have been successful thus far, the intensity of contacts by social service agents is increasing. The harassment is continuing. In this chapter I will summarize some of the confrontations that innocent home schoolers have had with social workers in which I was involved, review the statistics that show the child welfare system is abusing the children, and offer some practical suggestions on how to handle visits by social workers.

Are Any States Safe from these Investigations?

I have found that home schoolers from both favorable and unfavorable states toward home schooling have experienced child welfare investigations. For example, in Georgia, normally a favorable state, one family following its religious convictions concerning home educating was harassed by the local truant officer. After a while the truant officer decided to turn them over to a social worker for educational neglect. A group of families in another county was intimidated by a social worker who attempted to circumvent the home school law and impose illegal requirements on them. Another HSLDA member in Georgia was a single parent who lived in subsidized housing. Since she was poor, the social worker assumed she could not home school her children and even threatened to take the children.

In Colorado, a family was investigated by a social worker under somewhat bizarre circumstances. In the middle of the night, the family heard someone trying to break into their house. They called the police who came into the house to inspect the door to which forced entry was attempted. Instead of writing a report on the attempted burglary, the police officer started asking questions concerning the children. After he left, he contacted a social worker to investigate the family for child abuse. The allegations were that clothes were seen lying around the house, dishes from the night before were still in the sink, and there was a strange odor in the house. With four children it was true that there were some clothes lying around, and the family had figured that they were too tired that night and, as a result, would do dishes in the morning. As for the odor, it was the middle of winter and the family had just had an Italian dinner that night. Sure sounds like major child abuse to me! We all are child abusers if this constitutes child abuse.

In Virginia, a family was turned over to the child welfare agency even though it was operating under a religious exemption as allowed by statute. The child welfare agent tried to intimidate the family in order to meet with the children privately. I refused on behalf of the family, and I persuaded a superior to convince the agent to close the case. In Oklahoma, a child welfare agent came to the door as the result of a neighbor turning the home school family over for child abuse because they were home schooling.

In Indiana and Illinois, home schoolers were reported to child welfare by neighbors who fabricated stories about child abuse. In Michigan, child welfare and social service agents are more plentiful than virtually any other state. On numerous occasions, home schoolers have been turned in to child welfare by their school officials who have been frustrated because they cannot prosecute them under the truancy laws.

In Kansas, the law requires that any child who is reported as "not in attendance at school" is automatically turned over to the local social service agency for possible educational neglect. Superintendents who do not recognize children in non-accredited schools which operate in the home as being in attendance at school, routinely refer them to the social services for an investigation.

HSLDA has helped members in virtually every state who have been contacted by child welfare agents. Every one of these situations described above was linked to home schooling and served as a "back door" way of harassing home schoolers. By the grace of God, everyone of these situations was resolved without surrendering to the social workers' frequent demands to enter the house or interview the children.

Fabricated Allegations Against Home Schoolers

Nearly every type of allegation has been raised against home schoolers. Usually it is a combination of factors. For example, a common allegation is neglect of education and an untidy house. Sometimes there are accusations that the children were observed regularly playing outside during school hours or seen playing outside at dusk. Many times there is an accusation of the children having "worn out" clothes. In some instances, spanking has been one of the allegations. Let me give you several true stories that serve as examples of various fabricated allegations against home schoolers I have represented.

A home school father in Michigan was seen picking up his two-year-old child by her arm and taking her into the house while she was crying and was reported for child abuse. I set up a meeting with the social worker and counseled the family on what they should say. I told them to explain their religious convictions concerning raising their children from a "positive standpoint," avoiding Bible verses which spoke about the "rod." Instead, I told them to explain their beliefs emphasizing verses such as Matthew 18:6 which states that if you harm or offend a child, it is better that a millstone be tied around your neck and you are thrown into the deepest part of the ocean. In other words, their religious convictions demand that they do not do anything that will harm their children. When the family began presenting these religious beliefs to the agent, he became visibly uncomfortable and suddenly announced that he would close the case. He then abruptly left. This, by the way, is a valuable lesson to remember concerning what type of information about your religious beliefs you should share with a social worker.

Can We Be Investigated for Spanking?

The answer to that question is *yes!* However, there are ways to reduce the risk. Let me give you some actual examples.

In Colorado, a home schooler was reported after spanking a child in public. Someone had followed them to their car and wrote down the license plate. Based on this situation and many others, I recommend as a safety precaution that you never spank your children in public, no matter what the circumstance. Wait to discipline them at home, or you may find yourself the object of a full-scale investigation.

In Fairfax County, a pastor gave a seminar on child discipline which included spanking. A parishioner had to discipline her child while a neighbor was visiting. She spanked the child in another room and then explained to the neighbor a little of what she learned from the pastor. The neighbor, who was against spanking, reported the pastor to the child welfare agency for "bruising their children and for twenty minute spanking sessions." The social worker who then initiated the investigation told me she thought she might have a religious cult on her hands that abuses children. I expressed my disbelief to the social worker that she was seriously investigating what an anonymous source claimed she heard from a person who heard it from another person. That is thrice removed hearsay! I told her that her evidence was very flimsy, and I set the parameters for a meeting.

In preparation for the meeting, I told the home schooling pastor and his wife not to recount any specific incidents of spanking, since the social worker had nothing on the family that would stand up in court. I told them that they should emphasize the positive verses such as Matthew 18:6. Since the social worker had no evidence, the only evidence she could acquire would be from what information she could gather from the pastor and his wife. Since the parents carefully avoided all specific examples and spoke in general terms, the social worker had to close the case.

Spanking has always been a biblical form of punishment and very successful, when properly and consistently applied to acts of disobedience (e.g., Proverbs 22:15, 23:13-14, and 29:15). It traditionally has been the best form of discipline when administered in love and followed by forgiveness.

Fortunately, no state has completely outlawed spanking, although various state adoption agencies require parents to not spank their adopted children. However, there has been a push by so-called "child rights advocates" to pass legislation to outlaw spanking. For instance, in 1992, HR 1522 was introduced in the U.S. House of Representatives to prohibit corporal punishment or infliction of "bodily pain upon a child as a form of punishment" for any organization or entity that receives federal funding. As of the printing of this book, this bill is still pending. If such a bill would pass, it would send a message across the states that spanking is wrong and should be regulated.

However, some state policies consider "excessive spanking" as abusive. The difference between normal spanking and excessive spanking is left to the discretion of each social worker. As a result, many social workers strongly disapprove of spanking entirely and will manipulate it into an incident requiring a full-scale investigation.

One HSLDA family had just moved to Alabama two weeks earlier and had not yet met anyone in their neighborhood. However, the Department of Human Resources agent received an "anonymous tip" that the children had "bruises" and demanded a strip search! When I refused to allow a strip search, the agent became upset and stammered, "No one else ever refused a strip search before!" She also implied that the family had something to hide. I had the family get a statement from their personal physician who verified that the children were fine, and the situation was resolved. In Kansas, another HSLDA family with similar allegations acquired their personal doctor's statement, but the social worker's supervisor rejected it. The supervisor threatened to get a warrant. We called his bluff and the situation was resolved, based on the family doctor's statement.

The comment of the social worker in Alabama above is a common response I hear from social workers frequently concerning their other demands. They are personally offended that we would refuse to let them into the home or interview the children. Many of them insinuate that the family must be guilty even though they have nothing but an anonymous tip.

Of all the child welfare workers who have threatened HSLDA members that they will obtain a search warrant or a court order to take the children, it is very rare when one actually returns with a search warrant. These social workers are so used to obtaining whatever they want from the families, that our choice to stand on the families' privacy and Fourth Amendment rights shocks them.

False Daycare Center Allegations

Some home school families are turned over to the social service department for running "daycare centers." For instance, in Florida, a social worker investigated a home school family's home, based on an anonymous tip that the family was running an illegal and unlicensed daycare center. It turned out that all six children going in and out of the home were members of the same family! I guess this social worker did not know that home school families tend to have more than the national average of 1.8 children!

In Alabama, a home school mother was reported to a social worker for operating an unlicensed daycare center because she started taking care of one infant, five days a week. She was threatened with a felony and the social worker demanded entry into the home. I discovered, as usual, that the social worker was stretching the truth, since running an unlicensed daycare center was not a felony. However, in Alabama, anyone taking care of a child more than four hours a day and who is not a relative, must get a license! In order to avoid further investigation, the family chose to no longer watch the infant.

The False Allegation of "Lack of Supervision"

"Lack of supervision" or "children outside during school hours" are two of the most common allegations that accompany educational neglect allegations against home schoolers. In Michigan, some particularly nasty neighbors looking for an excuse to get a home school family in trouble saw one of the children run outside one night. The neighbors called the child welfare agency and reported the incident as "lack of supervision." The social worker wanted to enter the home and interrogate the children. We refused and explained that the child had only run out for a moment in order to get the cat that had escaped out the door.

Another Michigan home school family was reported by an anonymous tipster who claimed the children were not supervised, the children did not attend school, the boys ran around barefoot, an old rusty car was in their yard, the boys slept in the attic, and one boy liked to kill mice (can you believe that anyone would want to kill mice?). I talked with the child welfare agent who said she would prosecute the family for neglect and get a search warrant. She also wanted a special study done on the child who killed mice because she thought he might have a psychological problem. We were able to prove to the social worker that the children were being legally home schooled, there was no rusty car in the yard (except their own functional, slightly rusty car parked in the driveway), and the children did not sleep in the attic. As far as lack of supervision, I told the agent the charge was false, and the children have the right to play in their own yard. In regard to killing mice coming from a nearby swamp, we had no apologies but wondered at the competence of the agent. The case was closed.

One home school family had recently moved to Florida. Within weeks, they were visited by a truant officer who questioned the legality of their schooling. The truant officer left and reported them to the Health and Human Services Department. A few days later, an HHS agent appeared at the door and demanded to interview the children within twenty-four hours or he would send for the police. The allegations were that "the children were home during school hours and the children were sometimes left alone." I explained the legality of their home schooling and denied the "lack of supervision" charge (the family only had one car and the father took it to work leaving the mother at home). I then called his bluff and refused to have the children interviewed. After talking with the parents, we allowed him to come by the door and only see the children from a distance. He ended up closing the case, since he had no evidence but an anonymous tip.

One outlandish investigation of a home school family legally home schooling occurred in New Jersey. In the first visit, the agent from the Division of Youth and Family Services accused the mother of kidnapping some of her children because she had so many children. The mother produced birth certificates to prove that all the children were hers. The following year, another agent came by and said someone called and reported that the "children were seen outside during school hours." She demanded to enter the house, but the mother, under my instruction, refused. The agent then said she would be back with the police. She never came back that day, indicating that she was only bluffing. I called her and proved that the family was legally home schooling and the case was closed.

In California, a single mother was contacted by a social worker with allegations that "the children were not in school, the mother was incapacitated, and the caretaker was absent." I talked with the social worker and she admitted the allegations were based solely on an anonymous tip. However, she insisted on interrogating the children separately. When I objected, she said that she would get a police officer, and that she did not need a warrant. We held our ground and she settled for a meeting with the mother and a witness only. The situation was resolved.

One mother in Michigan was visited about a month after her husband died, and the social worker alleged "the children were not in school and the house was a mess." I called the social worker, explained the legality of home schooling, and convinced her to close the case. In Kansas, an SRS worker contacted a home school family and demanded entrance to the home. She alleged children were "locked in basement and deprived of food." After the SRS agent, when asked, admitted that the allegations were made by their former maid, we were able to convince her that the allegations were fabricated by the maid as retaliation for being dismissed for performing lousy work. The social worker dropped the case.

Know Your Doctor!

It is important at this point to give you a warning about doctors. Doctors, like many other professionals, are duty-bound in nearly all states to turn in parents they suspect of child abuse. I have handled several situations in which doctors have reported home schoolers to the child welfare agency, either because they did not approve of home schooling or because the child had a bruise somewhere or a dislocated joint. Of course, children commonly get bumps and bruises that are completely unrelated to abuse.

The best way to avoid this potential problem is to know your doctors. If your doctor knows and trusts you, he will properly interpret bumps and bruises for what they are and use his discretion to not report you to the social service agency. Also use wisdom concerning each injury on whether it is necessary to bring the child to the doctor in the first place. If your child has a bruise that could be deemed suspicious by the doctor, wait another day or so to bring your child in.

I was helping my two-year-old child up the stairs, and her shoulder came out of the socket. I thought of taking her to the doctor but remembered a week earlier when I helped a home school father whose doctor reported him to child welfare agency because he had brought his daughter in for the same reason. I was especially concerned because we were in an HMO program and did not know which doctor would be assigned to help us. As a result, we opted on taking our daughter instead to our chiropractor with whom we were good friends. He quickly popped the shoulder back in and totally understood that it could happen to anybody.

A common allegation raised during flu season, along with educational neglect, is "lingering colds." This is another form of so called abuse, of which I'm sure we would all be found "guilty." It is such a shame that our tax dollars have to pay for social workers who waste their time on such flimsy allegations. In all of these instances, the investigations were closed after we proved to the social workers that the children had visited a doctor recently.

Another allegation involving "health issues" which I will describe is the "thin child" accusation. For example, in Wisconsin, a home school family was reported by an anonymous tipster. I secured a copy of the report by the social worker which said:

> The caller was concerned because the children were all thin and thought that removal of food was possibly a form of discipline. The caller thought this discipline may have been a practice of the parents' religion which was thought to have been *Born Again*. The caller thought that these parents give a lot of money to the church and spend little money on groceries. The caller's last, somewhat passing concern, was that [the mother] home schools her children.

As usual, the anonymous tip was a complete exaggeration. It is apparent from the report that the caller was biased against both the fact that the family was home schooling and that they were Christians. This is a common thread that I see often as I represent home schoolers facing social worker allegations.

Other Outlandish Allegations

A single mother in a low-income apartment in California was reported to the social service agency for a "child not in attendance at school" and a "messy house." The social worker came to her door and demanded entry. When she refused and asked for him to put his questions in writing, he left. Within the hour, however, he was back with a police officer who also demanded entry in order to "see if house was sanitary, child was fed, whether there was food in the house, and to ask the child a few questions." He also wanted to see proof of an education taking place.

The mother handed the phone out the door to the policeman and I told him he had no right to go into the home without a warrant, and he agreed. Over a forty-five-minute period, I kept talking to him and then to the mother to see if the situation could be settled. Meanwhile, the mother and daughter picked up around the house while I talked with the officer. I finally convinced the police officer to agree to not question their home schooling, talk with their daughter, or let the social worker do any searching in the home. Based on my assurances, he promised to only go in the house for one or two minutes and not to scrutinize it very closely. Under those limited conditions, the family let the police officer in, and he was in and out in a few moments finding everything to be fine.

One of the most ridiculous allegations against a home school family that I ever heard was from a child welfare agent in Michigan who received an anonymous tip that the "mother was seen selling all her children's shoes and coats at a rummage sale." I asked the agent if he was serious, and he said it was his job to investigate all allegations. The mother obviously had only sold clothing that would no longer fit the children. The case was resolved after I let the agent stop by and see from a distance the children standing in their doorway wearing shoes and coats.

The last allegation I will mention is another example of how outlandish anonymous tipsters can become. A family in Texas was investigated by a social worker based on the following allegations: 1) children were not in attendance at school; 2) children were unsupervised and running around the neighborhood; 3) children were dirty and abused; and 4) the house may be used for drug trafficking, since people were seen frequently coming in and out of the house. The social worker demanded to interview the children (a six- and seven-year-old) or she would be forced to seek a court order.

The social worker knew nothing about home schooling, and I was able to convince her to not pursue it any further. Concerning the other allegations, the mother was able to convince the social worker that they were false. The children had recess during the day but were always supervised and mostly played in their fenced yard. Occasionally, the boys would catch frogs in a nearby ditch and get a little muddy—hardly abnormal for little boys. The mother was a curriculum supplier and had people occasionally come by to pick up curriculum. So much for being a drug pusher! The mother stood firm and would not let her children be interviewed separately, in spite of threats by the social worker to obtain a court order. Finally, the social worker, having no evidence, closed the case.

How Social Workers Bluff and Intimidate Parents

When I talk to most lawyers, they seem to be afraid of social workers. Many have told me that if a social worker initiates an investigation against a family, that family needs to cooperate fully with those demands. However, I could not and still cannot stomach having the families voluntarily waive their constitutional rights. This is still America, not communist China. Besides, I have heard of too many situations in which families outside of HSLDA let the social worker come into the house or talk to the children, and the social worker ended up gathering additional information which was later interpreted as abuse. The result of some of these situations was the removal of the children from the home.

Bluffing and intimidation are common tactics of social workers. Time and time again, I have been faced with threats by social workers who say that the law gives them the authority to come into the home or requires them to be allowed to interview children. However, not one has been able to show me such a law. Most child abuse laws allow them to interview children without parental consent *if* they obtain a court order, which usually can *only* be obtained *if* they have "good cause shown" or some sort of "probable cause." An anonymous tip, which is usually the only "evidence" a social worker has on a home school family, is neither adequate nor reliable. As a result, virtually all courts will not grant a warrant to enter the house or remove children. No social workers have shown me that they have the right, by their own authority, to enter a home against the parent's wishes.

Of course, if your child is in a public school or away from your home, social workers in most states have the authority to interview those children or remove them without parental consent. In those cases, parents are not notified of anything until the child is already placed in a juvenile home or a foster home. This is obviously another important advantage that home schoolers have over the child who is sent to the public schools.

Another way social workers routinely gain entry into families' homes is to intimidate or persuade the family to "voluntarily" allow them entrance. If they convince you to give them permission to enter, they then can claim that you waived your constitutional rights. We recommend to members of HSLDA that they never let social workers in who are investigating allegations against their family, *unless* they have a warrant or court order signed by a judge. Then the families are instructed to immediately call HSLDA, and I or one of our other staff lawyers will call the social worker.

Many social workers will bring a police officer with them in order to intimidate families into cooperating and allowing them entry into the house. However, these police officers also have no authority to come into the home without a warrant. When I challenge social workers as to why they resorted to using these "strong armed" tactics, they give me all types of excuses. For example, one social worker brought a police officer to the home of an Alabama home schooler to convince her to stop home schooling. When I confronted the social worker, she said she brought the officer along for "protection" since the allegation described the home school mom as a "big woman." In Kansas, an SRS agent tried to gain entry to a home by bringing along a police officer. When I challenged her, she claimed she had only gotten a ride from the police because she was not familiar with the area.

Another problem I have discovered is that many social workers with whom I have dealt have never even heard of the right of privacy and the Fourth Amendment right to freedom from unreasonable searches and seizures. Many do not understand what due process is or that a person is considered innocent until proven guilty. When, on these constitutional grounds, I challenge them in their assertion that they have the right to enter the home or interview the children, they try to deny that such rights even exist.

In Kansas, for instance, I dealt with a Social Rehabilitative Service's agent who insisted she had the right to come into the home school family's home. After I refused, she checked with her superior who admitted that she had no authority to enter the home. The SRS agent then explained that no one had ever refused her entry before.

How Social Worker Contacts Can Often Be Resolved

Below is the average scenario and recommended steps to follow which we explain to members of HSLDA. Each time an HSLDA family is contacted by a child welfare agent, they are first instructed to find out what the agent wants. At this time, we recommend that our members obtain the agent's business card.

The agent will frequently try intimidation to obtain entry. For example, the agent will say: "I have received allegations of child abuse and educational neglect. I need to come into your house right away and talk to your children. I am sure we can clear this all up today." If you refuse entry, the agent will sometimes threaten to obtain a court order. In our experience, it is usually a bluff, but this is not always the case. Then the family will call HSLDA, and an attorney will either talk directly to the social worker outside the door, or if the agent has left, he will call him at his office. We have found that immediately opening the lines of communication will often slow things down and help prevent some of the horror stories that have involved removal of children.

When I receive calls from HSLDA members, I respond by calling the agent, finding out the allegations, and explaining the legalities of the family's home school. If I cannot resolve it over the phone (which I can normally do about 30 percent of the time), I will set the parameters for a meeting with the family. Although I will not allow the child to meet with the child welfare agent, on certain occasions the parents will meet with the agent according to the limitations I set up beforehand. In a few instances, I let the agent "see" the children from a distance but not talk to them. You never can be certain what the most intelligent of children might say or how the social worker could manipulate your child's words against you. It is just not worth the risk.

If a meeting is held, I spend a long time preparing the parents. I recommend that the children be sent over to a friend or relative's house. I always instruct the families to deny the specific allegation, speak in generalities, and keep the social worker on the subject. For example, if the allegation is about a messy house, do not answer questions about child discipline. Or if the agent asks, "Did you spank your child ten times with a belt buckle?" do not reply, "No, I only spanked him six times with a spoon." The social workers love these kind of responses because they did not have evidence to begin with and were "fishing." And now you have admitted to spanking your children with an instrument. You and I know that spanking is not wrong or illegal, but to some social workers it only affirms their suspicions and can be a factor to be used against you. Instead, your response should simply be, "No, that is absolutely false," and you should go on to explain your religious belief from Matthew 18:6, which prohibits you from ever harming your children. As the Bible states, we need to be wise as serpents and gentle as doves.

The reasons we encourage members of HSLDA to not allow their children to be interviewed by social service agents are simply these: 1) parents do not have to let their children be interviewed unless there is an official warrant; 2) such interviews put the children through unnecessary and sometimes damaging trauma; and 3) many social service agents will not limit themselves to only asking about the specific allegations. For example, a family in Texas agreed to have their children interviewed about a simple allegation of "lack of supervision." Although the social worker agreed to limit her questions to only the supervision issue, she asked the children questions such as: "Do you like being home schooled?" "Do you get spankings?" "How often?" "Do your parents touch you in your private parts?" "How do they do it?"

These types of questions are completely offensive and they demonstrate that some social workers are on a "fishing expedition" to get home schoolers into trouble. The best protection parents have is to not let the social workers talk to the children.

More often than not, the child welfare agents are relying more on intimidation rather than any substantial evidence. Nearly every single child abuse investigation of HSLDA families has been resolved without going to court, with every allegation being false or extremely exaggerated.

I should mention that you should carefully teach your children, especially rebellious ones, of the consequences of reporting their parents to the social services department. I have counseled several families over the years who had a rebellious teenager run away and make up allegations against their parents, simply to get attention. However, in every situation, once the teenager found out the tremendous amount of trouble he caused his brothers, sisters, and parents, and saw the conditions he was kept in at the juvenile or foster home, he regretted ever going to the social service department. Therefore, try to prevent such sad scenarios by teaching your children some of the stories above and some of the horrendous statistics below.

The Social Worker at your Door: 10 Helpful Hints

In summary, what can you do when confronted with a social worker at your door? First of all, be certain you join HSLDA in advance. We will represent all our members in conflicts with social workers provided it is related to home schooling.

The home school parent should be very cautious when an individual identifies himself as a social worker. Here are several tips to remember:

1. Always get the business card of the social worker. This way, when you call the Home School Legal Defense Association, the HSLDA attorney will be able to contact the social worker on your behalf. If the situation is hostile, immediately call HSLDA and hand the phone out the door so an HSLDA lawyer can talk to the social worker. We have a 24-hour emergency number.

2. Find out the allegations. Do not fall for the frequently used tactic of the social workers who would tell the unsuspecting victim that they can only give you the allegations after they have come into your home and spoken to your child separately. You generally have the right to know the allegations without allowing them in your home. Nearly every state gives you the right to know the allegations before the investigation goes anywhere. However, you may have to insist and put up with intimidation before they will finally reveal the allegations.

3. Never let the social worker in your house without a warrant or court order. All the cases that you have heard about where children are snatched from the home usually involve families waiving their Fourth Amendment right to be free from such searches and seizures by agreeing to allow the social worker to come inside the home. A warrant requires "probable cause," which does not include an anonymous tip or a mere suspicion. This is guaranteed under the Fourth Amendment of the U.S. Constitution as interpreted by the courts.

4. Never let the social worker talk to your children alone without a court order. In nearly every incident, HSLDA has been able to keep the social worker away from the children.

On a few occasions, social workers have been allowed to talk with children, particularly where severe allegations are involved. In these instances, an attorney, chosen by the parent, has been present. At other times, HSLDA had children stand by the door and greet the social worker, but not be subject to any questioning.

5. Tell the official that you will call back after you speak with your attorney. Call your attorney or HSLDA, if you are a member. In nearly 30 percent of the cases, the problem is solved immediately that day by HSLDA lawyers. Approximately 65 percent of the situations are resolved within the next two weeks. Of the remaining 5 percent, 1 percent goes to court and is handled by HSLDA. The 4 percent that cannot be resolved do not involve home schooling and are referred to other attorneys since they are not covered by HSLDA.

6. Ignore intimidations. Normally, social workers are trained to bluff. They will routinely threaten to acquire a court order, knowing full well that there is no evidence on which to secure an order. In 99 percent of the contacts that HSLDA handles, the threats turn out to be bluffs. However, it is always important to secure an attorney or HSLDA in these matters, since there are occasions where social workers are able to obtain a court order with flimsy evidence.

7. Offer to give the officials the following supporting evidence:
   a. a statement from your doctor after he has examined your children, if the allegations involve some type of physical abuse;
   b. references from individuals who can vouch for your being good parents;
   c. evidence of the legality of your home school program. If your home school is an issue, HSLDA attorneys routinely convince social workers of this aspect of an investigation.

8. Bring a tape recorder and/or witnesses to any subsequent meeting. Often times HSLDA will arrange a meeting between the social worker and the parents after preparing

the parents on what to discuss and what not to discuss. The discussion at the meeting should be limited to the specific allegations, and you should avoid telling them about past events beyond what they know. Usually anonymous tips are all they have to go on, which is not sufficient to take someone to court. What you give them can and will be used against you.

9. Inform your church and put the investigation on your prayer chain. Over and over again, HSLDA has seen God deliver home schoolers from this scary scenario.

10. Avoid potential situations which could lead to a child welfare investigation.

   a. Do public relations with your immediate neighbors and acquaintances regarding the legality and success of home schooling.

   b. Do not spank children in public.

   c. Do not spank someone else's child unless they are close Christian friends.

   d. Avoid leaving young children at home alone.

   e. Avoid leaving your young children alone in your car in a public parking lot, even for a few minutes. I have helped many home schoolers who were reported when their young children were observed alone in their car even though the parents could view the car through the window of the store.

In order for a social worker to get a warrant to come and enter a home and interview children separately, he is normally required, by both statute and the U.S. Constitution, to prove that there is some "cause." This is a term that is synonymous with the term "probable cause." "Probable cause" or "cause shown" is reliable evidence which must be corroborated by other evidence if the tip is anonymous. In other words, an anonymous tip alone and mere suspicion is not enough for a social worker to obtain a warrant.

There have been some home schooled families who have been faced with a warrant even though there was not probable cause. For instance, I handled the Still family's case in Gilmore, Texas, with local counsel Floyd Getz. The social worker refused to tell the family what the allegations were. After the family refused to allow the social worker to talk to their young children alone or let them in the house, the social worker obtained a warrant from the local judge to enter the home, talk with the children, and have the children physically examined by a Child Protection Services doctor!

In her affidavit to the judge to prove probable cause, the social worker said she had "personal knowledge of the allegations and knew them to be true." In other words, she personally knew that hearsay allegations from an anonymous Hotline tip existed and were received in her office. That is not corroboration of evidence or probable cause because she did not know the family and had no idea whether the allegations were true. Yet the judge granted her order! We immediately filed a motion and convinced the judge to "stay" his order to determine if there actually was probable cause.[2]

HSLDA has been able to overturn these in court so that the order to enter the home was never carried out. Home School Legal Defense Association is committed to guarantee legal defense for every home schooler who is being investigated by social workers, provided the allegations involve home schooling. In instances when the allegations have nothing to do with home schooling, HSLDA will routinely counsel most families on how to meet with the social worker and will talk to the social worker to try to resolve the situation. If it cannot be resolved, which it normally can be in most instances by HSLDA's involvement, the family is responsible for hiring their own attorney.

Warning: Every Child Abuse Case Is Different and the Information in this Chapter Is Not Intended to be Legal Advice

Although this information and these stories are true, each social worker is different and each set of circumstances needs to be personally analyzed. I recommend membership with HSLDA or hiring separate legal counsel.

For example, some situations, due to "hometown" justice, have become quite severe. In California, the social workers and the police were so intent on interrogating a home schooled child separately at the police station that they threatened our local counsel with "obstruction of justice," since he insisted on being present with the child. By God's grace, the child never did have to be interviewed.

In Alabama, HSLDA represented a home school family in the *Richards* case before the Alabama Court of Appeals. This involved a low-income home school mother who was contacted by a social worker over some allegations of child abuse and educational neglect. Under my counsel, the family refused to allow the social worker to come into the home or interrogate the children. In order to muscle this family, charges of child neglect were brought, based on no evidence whatsoever, but only on an anonymous tipster who admitted she did not have personal knowledge of the family's situation. Nevertheless, a hearing was held on whether an anonymous tip was enough to require the social worker to enter the home and interrogate the children. Following "hometown justice," the lower court agreed that it was and ordered the family, under contempt of court, to allow the social worker into the home and to interrogate the children.

Attorney Michael Farris of HSLDA appealed the decision to the Alabama Court of Appeals on the basis that the Fourth Amendment to the Constitution requires government officials to have "probable cause" (some kind of reliable evidence) in order to obtain entry into individuals' homes. He also requested a stay to stop the enforcement of the search warrant. On March 10, 1992, the Court of Appeals, by God's grace, miraculously granted that stay which protected the family from additional harassment until the Court of Appeals ruled on the merits of the case.[3]

On August 28, 1992, the Alabama Court of Civil Appeals reversed the lower court decision and ruled in the *H.R. v. Dept. of Human Resources*:

> We suggest, however, that the power of the courts to permit invasions of the privacy protected by our federal and state constitutions, is not to be exercised except upon a showing of reasonable or probable cause to believe that a crime is being or is about to be committed or a valid regulation is being or is about to be violated....
>
> The "cause shown" [in this case] was unsworn hearsay and could, at best, present a mere suspicion. A mere suspicion is not sufficient to rise to reasonable or probable cause.[4]

In short, this case clearly concludes that an anonymous tip is not sufficient for a social worker or court to order the parents to submit to a home visit or interrogation of their children.

Therefore, I recommend you secure legal counsel if you ever find yourself being investigated by a social worker, or call HSLDA if you previously joined as a member.

The Most Significant Court Decision Upholding
4th Amendment Rights in the Face of Social Worker Investigations

HSLDA has handled many cases defending home school parents from unconstitutional investigations by social workers. Below are excerpts from the most significant appellate court case won by HSLDA which clarify the rights of home school parents when faced with an investigation by a social worker.

The Fourth Amendment rights case was originally filed February 24, 1995, by HSLDA on behalf of Robert and Shirley Calabretta in the Eastern District of California federal court, after a Yolo County policeman and social worker illegally entered the Calabretta home and strip searched their three-year-old daughter. The policeman and social worker forced their way in the home over the objections of the mother based simply on an anonymous tip. The tipster merely said she heard a cry in the night from the Calabretta home, "No Daddy no!" After the coerced entry, interrogation of the children, and the strip search of the three-year-old, no evidence of abuse was found and the officials ended the investigation. The police officer and social worker said "thank you" and left.

I do not know about you, but something is wrong with this picture! This type of invasion by law enforcement officials might be routine in a dictatorship but not in America. This is why HSLDA's Mike Farris filed the civil rights suit against the Yolo County Department of Social Services. This type of abuse of innocent families had to stop.

At the trial level, District Court Judge Lawrence K. Karlton ruled that unless there is evidence of an emergency, a social worker and police officer investigating a report of child abuse must have a warrant. The Court clarified that the 4th Amendment applies just as much to child abuse investigations as it does to any other government search and seizure. An anonymous tip or mere suspicion is not enough to reach the standard of probable cause.

The government appealed but the Ninth Circuit U.S. Court of Appeals panel unanimously affirmed the lower court decision on August 26, 1999. Judge Andrew J. Kleinfeld wrote the opinion for the three-judge panel. The court declared that the social worker's act of forcing the mother to pull down the three-year-old's pants "invaded…the mother's dignity and authority in relation to her own children in her own home. The strip search as well as the entry stripped the mother of this authority and dignity. The reasonable expectation of privacy of individuals in their homes includes the interests of both parents and children in not having government officials coerce entry in violation of the Fourth Amendment and humiliate the parents in front of the children."

This landmark decision of *Calebretta v. Floyd, et al* makes it perfectly clear that social workers are bound to obey the U.S. Constitution when investigating child abuse cases. With respect to the Fourth Amendment, the Ninth Circuit settled the social worker question once and for all. No longer can social workers enter a home without either a warrant or probable cause of an emergency. It is a myth that Child Protective Services agencies are exempted from the Fourth Amendment's prohibitions against illegal searches and seizures. We praise God for His protection of His people through this decision.

Social Workers Themselves Expose the Abuse in the Child Welfare Agencies

Occasionally, I will talk with social workers who are fed up with the system and who willingly expose all its problems. When I called one social worker in Chicago who was investigating a home school family, we resolved the false allegation over the phone and then she proceeded to tell me the following information.

Well over 50 percent of all referrals to her child welfare agency are "unfounded." Unfortunately, she complained, many of the cases are deemed unfounded after families are broken apart and children are put in foster homes. She explained that many hospitals and health centers are in the "business" of "always" finding child abuse. She said they would conclude child abuse even if you bring them a salamander!

Expressing her concern about the new training of recently hired social workers, she said that younger social workers are encouraged to go on "fishing expeditions." In the old days, social workers tried to prove a reported family was innocent and considered the family innocent until proven guilty. Now the "system" operates on the principle that a family is "guilty"…period.

After seeing so many families broken up, so many careers destroyed, and so many children harmed by the system, she now refers to the child welfare system as "the child abuse industry." She said she was due to retire in the next year. Her frankness on the abuse of the system is particularly sobering and it confirmed my assumptions that I had developed in dealing with numerous social workers around the country.

I have had several other conversations with social workers from various states who have developed the same opinion of their work. For instance, a social worker with whom I resolved a fabricated allegation concerning a home schooler confessed that 90 percent of all the cases of alleged child abuse she handled turned out to be "unfounded." She explained that she spent most of her time "spinning her wheels." She felt the number of false allegations coming into her office was on the rise.

In Alabama and Florida, I met two recently resigned social workers who were now home schooling their children. Both admitted intimidation was a routine procedure they were taught and always used to get their way. Their goal, in fact, was to get into the house and talk with the children, no matter what the allegation. They would regularly demand entry and act as if they had the right to come in on their own authority. If the parent still was not fooled into voluntarily allowing them in, they would threaten to get a policeman. One ex-social worker told me, "If I ever had a social worker come to my door who acted like I did, I would be scared stiff and probably comply with their demands!" She also said that no judges she knew would ever sign a search warrant or issue an order to take a child based on only an anonymous tip. Both of these social workers admitted 60 percent to 70 percent of their cases were "unfounded."

I will relate one more conversation I had with a social services worker in Michigan who is also a home school father and a member of the local school board. He said that he had been working as a social worker for years, and he has seen much change. He said that social workers have become much more aggressive and eager to go on "fishing expeditions." He agreed with the description of the system that I learned from the other social workers. He said that many social workers use intimidation and deception.

I asked him how long "unsubstantiated" claims stay on the record, and he said sometimes five years and sometimes longer. He said a family whose case was rendered unfounded had a right to have their records "expunged" or erased. However, he warned me not to trust social workers to expunge records, because they usually will not. He recommended going to their office and personally watching the file being destroyed.

I asked him if the individual being investigated has a right to request a copy of their file or to see their file. He affirmed they could do this, but social workers will often refuse on the grounds that the information in the file is "confidential." At that point, he said, the social worker is bluffing. If a person just evokes the "Freedom of Information Act," the social worker is required by law to show him the records in the case file.

However, social workers still have tricks to prevent you from seeing the file they might have on you concerning an "unfounded" allegation. One home school family in Indiana was investigated by a social worker because the mother was home schooling and her children were supposedly left "unattended." After some negotiation, the case was closed. I asked for the records to be expunged and for the mother to get a copy. The mother went down to the social service office to get a copy of the file and to watch the file be destroyed, and the social worker claimed she could not find the file! It is a shame that the social workers are free to damage people's reputations and to keep on file unfounded claims.

As discussed earlier, one of the key problems contributing to the abuse of the child welfare system is the "child abuse hotlines," that can be used anonymously. In effect, the falsely accused person never has a right to face his accuser but still has to suffer through a full-scale investigation by the social service agency, that could result in his children being taken away. You would think this only happens in Communist countries such as China or North Korea!

Studies and Statistics Prove the Widespread Abuse within the Child Welfare System

Some individuals have criticized me for being too "black and white" on this issue, and maybe a little "hyper." My response is that my experience, keeping social workers away from the children of home schoolers and out of their houses, is nothing compared to the horror stories that happen regularly to others outside membership with HSLDA. The statistics, studies, and books exposing this "child abuse industry," are quite numerous.

The San Diego County Grand Jury, for example, issued a fifty-six page report based on a seven-month investigation and interviews with more than 250 social workers, therapists, attorneys, judges, doctors, and families.[5] The discovery was shocking.

The Grand Jury found San Diego's child protection system to be "out of control, with few checks and little balance." The Grand Jury found that the system has developed a mindset that child abuse is rampant and its structure and operation are "biased toward proving allegations instead of finding the truth." The jury declared:

> The burden of proof, contrary to every other area of our judicial system, is on the alleged perpetrator to prove his innocence....
>
> [Social workers rarely try] to find information favorable or evidence exculpatory to the parents. Instead [they] appear to undertake investigations with a bias toward finding facts to support detention or removal and report only that information that justifies detention.[6]

Constitutional rights are ignored and the family has virtually no protection. The Grand Jury reported, "In too many cases, Child Protection Services cannot distinguish real abuse from fabrication, abuse from neglect, and neglect from poverty or cultural differences."[7]

Furthermore, the Grand Jury heard testimony that 20 to 60 percent of the children in the system do not even belong there! After reviewing 300 child abuse cases, the Grand Jury concluded that 250 of the cases need corrective action or reopening.[8] This is a lot of innocent families, as high as 60 percent, whose children should never have been removed from their parents in the first place.

The Grand Jury found that "some social workers routinely lie even when under oath in court." Also numerous times social workers will disobey or ignore court orders.[9]

The jury discovered that every aspect of the system is in the business of confirming "child abuse," even if it is not there. The county counsel, judges, therapists, and hospitals all work together against the parents:

> County counsel, which represents Child Protection Services in court hearings, "has not been screening cases adequately." In fact, the jury said, screening deputies are pressured "to file petitions on cases which are questionable."
>
> The Juvenile Court system, which should be the ultimate check in the system, "is not fulfilling its role." The

jury found that the court does not appear "to offer an even playing field in which the judicial officer serves as a neutral arbiter of the facts."[10]

Rarely, the jury said, does a judge demand a "high standard of performance" from the Social Services staff. The judges "are viewed and appear to view themselves as pro-child which translates to pro-DSS," it said.[11]

Therapists reported that "as long as they are in agreement with the social worker, their reports are given great weight. On the other hand, if they disagree with the social worker, their recommendations may not even appear in the report to the court," the Grand Jury said.[12]

The report also charged that the Center for Child Protection (CCP) at Children's Hospital, which examines most of the local children suspected of being abused, has lost its objectivity." "A highly respected (appellate court) jurist testified that this lack of objectivity within the CCP has poisoned the stream. He felt that much of the bias and even zealotry found in the child dependency system could be traced back to training conferences and meetings at the behest of the Center for Child Protection."

The jury also found that "patently erroneous testimony" by center physicians "played a significant role" in several cases in which children were removed from their homes.[13]

This is a travesty. The child welfare system has turned into a system which literally abuses children. In San Diego, like many other communities, once your children are taken, justice can rarely be found in the system.

The statistics of the abuse of children by the child welfare system go on virtually endlessly. Putting children in foster care is becoming routine, even though the studies show that the children would be better off at home, especially when so many of the allegations turn out to be false.

Professionals estimate that 35 to 70 percent of children who end up in foster care should not be there and can be severely damaged psychologically by the experience. "Research over the past 40 years says that if you remove the child from the home, you traumatize the child more than he is already hurt," says Charles P. Gershenson, former chief of research and evaluation of the Children's Bureau of the U.S. Department of Health and Human Services.[14]

Still increasing numbers of children are routinely being removed from homes with little to no evidence of wrongdoing. A report from the National Commission on Family Foster Care documents that there are presently 340,000 children being raised outside the homes of their natural parents, up from 225,000 in 1985.[15]

There are approximately 2.4 million reports of child abuse each year. Experts conclude that at least 1 million of those reports are erroneous or did not involve risks that could lead to foster placement.[16]

In one county alone—Cobb County, Georgia—I discovered that in 1991, the local Child Protection Services received 4,196 reports of child abuse. Of that total of reported cases only 879 were confirmed. I learned of this information while I was arguing with a child welfare worker who was investigating a home school family. The worker would not understand why we would not allow her into the home or speak with the children. I told her the family was innocent and was being harassed due to false allegations. After she told me the Cobb County statistics, I told her she had just proven my point.

In New Hampshire, the Department of Child and Youth Services (DCYS) data shows that in 1991 there were 6,434 abuse reports. Believe it or not, 5,524 of those reports turned out to be *false!* This means that 86.2 percent of all child abuse reports were false. The statistics over the last eight years show that the number of founded cases is dropping and yet the number of false child abuse reports is rising. In 1984, 54 percent of the child abuse reports turned out to be false. There were 3,855 abuse reports of which 1,814 were founded and 2,041 were false. In 1990, 86 percent of the child abuse reports were found to be false. There were a shocking 5,616 abuse reports, with only 709 which were proven to be founded or legitimate abuse allegations, and 4,907 turned out to be false child abuse reports![17] The system is out of control. Many thousands of innocent families are being abused by the system.

In 1985, a comprehensive study on the abuse of the child welfare system was done by Dr. Douglas Besharov of the American Enterprise Institute for Public Policy Research. His study was published as an article in the *Harvard Journal of Law and Public Policy.* He concludes:

> Much of the present high level of intervention is unwar-
> ranted and some is demonstrably harmful to the children
> and families involved. More than sixty-five percent of all
> reports of suspected child maltreatment—involving over
> 750,000 children per year—turn out to be "unfounded."
> ...The present level of over-reporting is unreasonably
> high and is growing rapidly. There has been a steady
> increase in the number and percentage of "unfounded"
> reports since 1976, when approximately only thirty-five
> percent of reports were "unfounded."[18]

Since Besharov's study, the situation has only worsened with record numbers of families falsely reported for child abuse.

Two important books have been published which confirm much of the reports above and provide important documentation of the frequent abuses of the modern child welfare system: *Wounded Innocents* by Richard Wexler[19] and *The Child Abuse Industry* by Mary Pride.[20] If I had read these books *before* I played "hardball" with social workers, I would have been paralyzed with fear. The thousands of true accounts of the breaking up of innocent families and the mental, emotional, and physical abuse of innocent children by the child welfare system will make it difficult to believe that this really happens in America. However, we must wake up to the fact that this does happen in America, and we need to do something about it.

The Child Abuse Industry begins by documenting that over one million families annually are falsely accused of child abuse. These, of course, are only the ones who had the money and knowledge to fight back. Mary Pride shows how many laws are written so vaguely that virtually anyone could be found guilty of child abuse and many times are. She documents that every state has set up "hotlines" to take calls from anonymous tipsters. These same laws protect malicious callers from lawsuits or prosecution. She demonstrates with case after case that families accused of child abuse are routinely denied the right to due process or a fair trial. She shows that social workers regularly ignore families' constitutional rights and take children from public schools and come into your home, if you will let them.[21]

In the other well-documented book, *Wounded Innocents*, Wexler warns:

The war against child abuse has become a war against children. Every year, we let hundreds of children die, force thousands more to live with strangers, and throw a million innocent families into chaos. We call this "child protection."[22]

That is quite an indictment! He demonstrates that the hotlines have become a "potent tool for harassment." He shows how untrained, inexperienced, and sometimes incompetent social workers are allowed to label parents as "child abusers" and remove the children entirely on their own authority. He states, through the child abuse laws, "We have effectively repealed the Fourth Amendment, which protects both parents and children against unreasonable searches and seizures." He shows that the child welfare system often denies due process to the "accused" child abusers.[23]

When dealing with the question "What is neglect?" Wexler answers: "Anything a child saver [social worker] wants it to be." He gives scores of examples of outlandish allegations that innocent families are confronted with and which result in removal of their children.

Wexler shoots holes in the child welfare system's claims that two million children are abused each year and that is why they must be so aggressive. In actuality, that number represents only the *reported* cases. Over half of the reported cases are false. In fact, in 1987 there were 1,306,800 *false* child abuse reports. Sexual maltreatment, which is commonly argued for the need to increase the power of social workers, only makes up 15.7 percent of all reports! Minor physical injury constitutes only 13.9 percent and severe physical injury only constitutes 2.6 percent.[24]

This means for every 100 reports alleging child abuse:
- at least fifty-eight are false
- twenty-one are mostly poverty cases
- six are sexual abuse
- four are minor physical abuse
- four are unspecified physical abuse
- three are emotional maltreatment
- three are "other maltreatment"
- one is major physical abuse.[25]

After he shows that the "child abuse panic" is a myth and an excuse to give unconstitutional powers to the social service agencies, he documents the terrible abuse children receive in foster homes and juvenile homes. The true accounts and statistics are sobering and shocking. In Kansas City, a study was done showing that 57 percent of children in foster care to have been placed in "high risk of abuse or neglect" situations."[26]

I could continue with more statistics, but I recommend that you read the two books mentioned above for further proof of the abusive child welfare system. Something needs to be done to protect innocent families from this system which is out of control.

Practical Ways to Reform the Child Welfare System

As a result of these abuses of the child welfare system, we at HSLDA are working to reform the child welfare laws in the states. We support legislation which would protect families by forcing social workers to abide by the same laws regular law enforcement officials must obey.

The five areas of state child welfare laws most in need of reform are:

1. Anonymous Tips: Child welfare laws should be amended to require *all* reporters of child abuse to give their names, addresses and phone numbers. This will curtail false reporting and end harassment using anonymous tips.
2. False Reporting: Child welfare laws should be amended to make it at least a class C misdemeanor.
3. Probable Cause/Warrant: Social workers must be held accountable to the same 4th Amendment standards as the police. A warrant must be obtained before a social worker can enter the home without consent of the parents.
4. Access to Records: Many times home schoolers who are investigated by social workers are denied access to the records of their investigation. Child welfare laws should be amended to allow victims of the system to inspect their records in order to seek recourse.
5. Prohibition of the Violation of Parents' Constitutional Rights: Child welfare laws should be amended to specifically recognize parental rights as fundamental. This is

important to create an "even playing field" during child welfare investigations.

Model Legislation

Below is actual model language which may be used to introduce legislation in virtually any state to contribute to solving the five problems listed above:

Penalty for False Reporting.

"Any person who knowingly or maliciously makes a false report of any type of child abuse or neglect shall be guilty of a Class C misdemeanor and shall be fined five hundred dollars ($500) for making a false report. Such person shall also be liable to any injured party for compensatory and punitive damages." [Alabama, S. 679]

Requirements for Social Workers to Obtain a Warrant.

"In the absence of imminent danger, prior to entrance into a home, to remove a child, or for any other reason for which they might seek entrance into a home without consent of the parents, employees of the Department of Human Resources shall be held to the same standard as law enforcement personnel, and shall be required to obtain a warrant, similar in form to a search warrant, issued only on affidavit sworn to before the issuing judge or magistrate authorized by law to issue search warrants and arrest warrants, establishing grounds for issuing the warrant on probable cause, or shall be required to file a dependency petition and receive a pre-adjudication removal order from a judge of competent jurisdiction." [Alabama, S. 679]

Prohibition of Anonymous Tips.

"The division shall not investigate any such report unless the person making such a report provides to the division such person's name, address and telephone number. The division shall not require the taking of a telephone number if the person making the report does not have a telephone." [Missouri, H.B. 30]

The Right to Obtain Investigation Records.

"Any person who is the subject of an unfounded report or complaint made pursuant to this chapter who believes that such report or complaint was made in bad faith or with malicious intent may petition the family court in the jurisdiction in which the report or complaint was made for the release to such person the records of the investigation. Such petition shall specifically set forth the reasons such person believes that such report or complaint was made in bad faith or with malicious intent. Upon the filing of such petition, the court shall request and the department shall provide to the court its records if the investigation for the court's camera review. The petitioner shall be entitled to present evidence to support his petition. If the court determines that there is a reasonable question of fact as to whether the report or complaint was made in bad faith or with malicious intent and that disclosure of the identity of the complaint would not be likely to endanger the life or safety of the complainant, it shall provide to the petitioner a copy of the records of the investigation. The original records shall be subject to discovery in any subsequent civil action regarding the making of a complaint or report in bad faith or with malicious intent." [Virginia Code section 63.1-248.5:1 (C)]

Government Agency Violation of Parents' "Fundamental Rights" Prohibited.

Child protective services "shall not contradict the fundamental rights of parents to direct the education and upbringing of their children." [1997 Tex. Gen. Laws 1022]

(b) No state agency may adopt rules or policies or take any other action which violates the fundamental right and duty of a parent to direct the upbringing of the parent's child. [1997 Tex. Gen. Laws 1225]

As long as social workers continue to operate outside of the Constitution, the privacy and home schooling rights enjoyed by home schoolers and Americans everywhere will be in jeopardy. These amendments to state laws will provide parents with significant protection from child abuse. Your membership with HSLDA enables us to work to enact these amendments. Members will receive regular Urgent Alerts notifying them of the need to contact their legislature about important legislation amending their child welfare laws.

This Is Spiritual Warfare

It is clear that home schoolers are under attack: but it is more than a physical attack, it is a spiritual attack.[27]The Scriptures tell us: "Put on the full armor of God that you may be able to stand firm against the schemes of the devil. For our struggle is not against flesh and blood, but against the rulers, against the powers, against the world forces of this darkness, against the spiritual forces of wickedness in the heavenly places" (Ephesians 6: 11-12).

The home schooling movement is primarily a Christian revival taking place through education of our youth. Satan has a good thing going in the public school system since the courts have censored God and His principles and values from the public schools. But home schooling, as far as Satan is concerned, is out of control. There is no uniform way to censor all God's truth out of the home school textbooks or forbid the home school parents from comprehensively applying God's principles to each and every subject they teach to their children. The home school children are going to be the leaders of tomorrow who not only *believe* as Christians but *think* as Christians and are fully equipped to communicate God's truths in every area of life.

Furthermore, home schooling is strengthening the Christian family. That is also something Satan has been trying to undermine throughout our country. As a result, this attack should be expected. Home schoolers have been making great gains legislatively and have been prospering academically and growing spiritually. Now Satan is lashing back.

Let us remember, "The weapons of our warfare are not of the flesh, but divinely powerful for the destruction of fortresses. We are destroying speculations and every lofty thing raised up against the knowledge of God, and we are taking every thought captive to the obedience of Christ" (2 Corinthians 10:4-5). As we teach our children, let us take *every* thought captive to the obedience to Jesus Christ so our children will make a difference for God in this world. As we face conflict and harassment from the state authorities, let us count it a privilege to suffer persecution for Christ's sake, as we are faithful to God's call. Pray that this spiritual battle with its physical consequences may be won.

I have written this chapter, not to create fear, but to make you aware of a real and growing problem, so that you will be motivated to pray for God's protection for home schoolers and work for legislative change to end the abuse of the social welfare system. An actual example of a family who was overly fearful was a home school family I talked to in Michigan. Since the family was afraid that someone would turn them in to the authorities, they followed a routine every week. Every Sunday evening they would pack one of their cars with empty suitcases, load the children in the car, and the mother would drive the car away to an appointed spot a few blocks away. Then, under the cover of darkness, the mother and children would sneak back into the house and remain there all week without leaving. The father, of course, would still go back and forth to work. The mother covered all the windows with thick black cloth so no light could be seen in the house in the evening before the father would come home. Then every Friday afternoon, the children and mother would sneak back to their car, drive back to their home, and unload the car as if they were just coming back from being on a trip all week. This family apparently did this one whole school year out of fear.

This was certainly an extreme reaction, but it illustrates an important lesson: We should not live in fear. Instead, we need to put our trust in the Lord and act wisely. In 1 Peter 3:13-14, it says:

> And who is there to harm you if you prove zealous for what is good? But even if you should suffer for the sake of righteousness, you are blessed. And do not fear their intimidation, and do not be troubled.

God will honor those who honor Him.

(I encourage you to read the social worker skit in Appendix F for a humorous but effective way to learn what to do if you are ever confronted with a social worker.)

Notes

1. *Families in Crisis: Report #2*, a 56-page report by the 1991-92 San Diego County Grand Jury, after 7 months of investigation of the Child Protective Services.
2. See Roy Maynard, "Unwarranted Invasion," *World* magazine, April 8, 1995, 16-17.

3. *The Home School Court Report,* Vol. 8, No. 2, March/April 1992, 1.

4. *H. R. v. Department of Human Resources,* 609 So. 2d 477 (Ct. Civ. App. ALA 1993). In February 1993, the Alabama Supreme Court upheld the Court of Appeals decision by refusing to reconsider the case on appeal.

5. Okerblom and Wilkens, "Child Protection System Ripped," *The San Diego Union Tribune,* February 7, 1992, A1 and A19. This article summarizes "Families in Crisis: Report #2," A report by the 1991-92 San Diego County Grand Jury.

6. *Ibid.*

7. *Ibid.*

8. *Ibid.*

9. *Ibid.*

10. *Ibid.*

11. Abrahamson, "Child Protection System in S.D. Scored by Grand Jury," *The Los Angeles Times,* February 7, 1992, p. A1 and A28 through A29. This article summarizes *Families in Crisis: Report #2,* a report by the 1991-92 San Diego County Grand Jury.

12. *Ibid.*

13. Okerblom and Wilkens, *San Diego Union Tribune,* February 7, 1992, A19.

14. Daniel Kagan, "Saving Families Fosters Hope For America's Troubled Youth," *Insight,* April 29, 1991, 16.

15. *Ibid.*

16. *Ibid.*

17. "Is DCYS Running Out of Abusers?" *Christian Home Schooling News,* Vol. 2, No. 4, April/May 1992, Manchester, New Hampshire, 3.

18. Douglas Besharov, "Doing Something About Child Abuse: The Need to Narrow the Grounds for State Intervention," *Harvard Journal of Law and Public Policy,* Vol. 8, 1985, 556.

19. Richard Wexler, *Wounded Innocents: The Real Victims of the War Against Child Abuse* (Buffalo, NY: Prometheus Books, 1990).

20. Mary Pride, *The Child Abuse Industry* (Westchester, IL: Crossway Books, 1989).

21. *Ibid.,* 13-14. The rest of the book describes hundreds of actual incidences of abuse of children by social workers.

22. Wexler, *Wounded Innocents,* 14.

23. *Ibid.,* 15.

24. *Ibid.,* 86-88.

25. *Ibid.,* 87.

26. *Ibid.,* 198.

27. For an insightful, though fictional analysis of the spiritual battle taking place for our children, I recommend reading *Piercing the Darkness* by Frank Peretti.

chapter 14

Home Invasion:
The Illegality of Home Visits

It is our view that both the Fourth Amendment and also the constitutionally derived right to privacy and autonomy which the U.S. Supreme Court has recognized, protect individuals from unwanted and warrantless visits to the home by agents of the state."[1]

A frequent problem home schoolers face throughout the country is that in which certain school districts unilaterally impose a "home visit" requirement on home schoolers. Home schoolers who refuse to allow home visits are "disapproved" and often charged with criminal truancy. Usually under a home visit requirement, a school official can visit a home school at anytime, observe instruction in the home, inspect facilities, and demand certain changes.

All of these school districts which have home visit requirements are in states where the education statutes do not mandate home visits. In other words, the various state legislatures have not delegated specific authority to conduct home visits to school districts in the first place. The last state in the entire country, South Dakota, which still authorized school districts, by statute, to conduct home visits, finally repealed this burdensome requirement in 1993 largely due to the efforts of HSLDA. We filed a civil rights suit asserting many of the reasons cited in this chapter. Then we introduced a bill to repeal the home visit law. I testified in both the South Dakota House and Senate explaining the unconstitutionality of home school visits while home schoolers delivered phone calls. Our bill passed repealing home visits, so we dismissed our suit.

The teacher unions, however, are regularly lobbying for heavier restrictions on home schoolers, including home visits. For instance, in the Spring of 1991, L.D. 888 was introduced in the Maine Legislature, which would have required home schoolers to submit to monthly home visits in order to "ensure that a level of academic instruction comparable to in-school instruction is being provided." The bill would have also given the state authority during these "inspections" to "determine whether the equivalent home instruction program should be continued, altered, or terminated." I testified at the legislative hearing along with many home schoolers resulting in the bill being killed in committee.

The purpose of this chapter, therefore, is to demonstrate that home visits of home schoolers should not be practiced or legislated in any state because they are inherently unconstitutional for four basic reasons.

Home Visits Violate the Fourth Amendment and the Right to Privacy

First of all, home visits are a violation of the home school families' *right to privacy* and their right to be free from warrantless searches and seizures as guaranteed by the Fourth Amendment.

On August 7, 1986, in *Kindstedt v. East Greenwich School Committee*,[2] the practice of home visits was struck down, setting precedent for the entire state. This case involved the Kindstedt family who was "disapproved" by the local school board solely because they refused to "bow the knee" and submit to home visits. I talked with the authorities on their behalf, showing them that the family was providing an excellent education and that such mandated home visits were unconstitutional. The school board refused to budge, so we appealed the case to the commissioner of education who held a formal hearing and wrote an extensive written opinion in favor of the family. The Commissioner held,

It is our view that both the Fourth Amendment and also the constitutionally derived right to privacy and autonomy which the U.S. Supreme Court has recognized, protect individuals from unwanted and warrantless visits to the home by agents of the state.[3]

Furthermore, he stated,

In view of the legal and constitutional considerations, we are unable to perceive any rationale whereby a home visitation requirement would be justifiable under circumstances such as these.[4]

It is clear from this decision that home visitation cannot be mandated by public school officials over parental objection. The privacy of the parents, family and home is at stake. Such privacy of the parents was protected in the United States Supreme Court in *Griswold v. Connecticut.*[5]

A school official can only inspect a home schooler's home if the family voluntarily allows them to come in or if the state official has a warrant or court order signed by a judge. Any home school family who does not want to voluntarily participate in home visits cannot be required to do so without violating their Fourth Amendment and privacy rights.

It is a fundamental principle of due process that if a government official comes into one's home for the purpose of making a determination of whether or not a criminal law is being complied with, then such an intrusion into the home is a search within the meaning of the Fourth Amendment. Since violation of the compulsory attendance law is a crime, a home visit by a public school official to determine compliance with the law is a violation of the home schooler's Fourth Amendment rights.

A home visit by a public school official to inspect a home school is equal to a "warrantless search" since it invades the privacy of the home. The U.S. Supreme Court stated: "Except in such special circumstances, we have consistently held that the entry into a home to conduct a search or make an arrest is unreasonable under the Fourth Amendment unless done pursuant to a warrant."[6] It seems apparent that home visits are unconstitutional.

Many school district officials expect their "requirement" for home visits to be complied with readily and without question. If a family will not agree to such an invasion of privacy, the school officials often wrongly assume that the home schooler is trying to hide something. The school officials believe that such a visit is an "inconsequential" request. However, the framers of the Constitution secured, for all citizens, protection from these types of arbitrary state intrusions. The U.S. Supreme Court makes clear their intent:

> Though the proceeding in question is divested of many of the aggravating incidents of actual search and seizure, yet, as before said, it contains their substance and essence, and effects their substantial purpose. It may be that it is the obnoxious thing in its mildest and least repulsive form; but illegitimate and unconstitutional practices get their first footing in that way, namely, by silent approaches and slight deviations from legal modes of procedure. This can only be obviated by adhering to the rules that constitutional provisions for the security of person and property should be liberally construed. A closed and literal construction deprives them of half their efficacy, and leads to gradual depreciation of the right, as if it consisted more in sound than in substance.[7]

Home schoolers are constitutionally justified to refuse warrantless searches such as home visits. There is neither statutory or constitutional authorization for parents to open their houses to public school officials.

Home Visits Violate the Fifth Amendment Right to Due Process

During the last several years, two states, New York and Pennsylvania, engaged in home visits of home schools even though such a requirement was not specifically mandated by law. In both states the practice of home visits was abruptly discontinued by case precedent and subsequent legislation.

In New York, two county court decisions, *In the Matter of Dixon*[8] and *In the Matter of Standish*,[9] both held home visits to be unconstitutional. In *Dixon*, the court held:

This Court firmly believes that the insistence of the Hannibal Central School District authorities to effect the desired on-site inspection was arbitrary, unreasonable, unwarranted, and violative of the Respondents' [home school parents] due process rights guaranteed under the Fifth Amendment of the Constitution of the U.S. The school district cannot expect to put itself in the position of conducting the inspection and then turning around and impartially or objectively determining whether the program subject to that inspection meets the required criteria for valid home instruction.[10]

Regarding protection from self-incrimination, the court explained:

The Respondents, further, cannot reasonably be put in a situation where they in effect are being forced to give evidence that might be used against them at a future date.[11]

The court concluded that the home visit requirement is both "unconstitutional" and "unenforceable." This reasoning of the decision was confirmed in *In the Matter of Standish*.

In order to cure the vagueness in the New York compulsory attendance law, the State Education Department issued "Regulations of the Commissioner of Education" for home schooling. The regulations give the local school boards no authority to conduct home visits (unless a home school is on probation), thereby ending the practice of routine home visits in the state of New York.

In Pennsylvania, at least one quarter of the 501 school districts were mandating home visits although not required by law. The HSLDA, as a result, sued eleven school districts for violating the civil and constitutional rights of the home schoolers. The federal court ruled in favor of the home schoolers in *Jeffery v. O'Donnell*[12] and declared the law "unconstitutional for vagueness." The legislature subsequently passed §13-1327.1 in 1988 which clearly ended the practice of home visits.

It is important to add that certain school districts in South Carolina also sought to impose home visits on home schoolers even though not mandated in the law. On February 27, 1989, the attorney general said that such a practice of mandatory home visits was prohibited by the intent of law:

> Because the amendments do not expressly provide for an on-site visit and because the only reference to the site is the "description" of the place of instruction, a reasonable reading of the whole statute (*Sutherland Statutory Construction,* Volume 2A, sec. K6.05) indicates that the legislature's intent was not to authorize blanket requirements for on-site visits.[13]

In conclusion, where home visits are not clearly mandated by law, local school district policies that have tried to impose such requirements are routinely found to be arbitrary, unreasonable, unwarranted, a violation of the Fifth Amendment, not the intent of the legislature, unconstitutional, and, in several instances, based on unconstitutionally vague laws.

Home Visits Violate Establishment of Religion Clause

The home visitation requirement also violates the First Amendment prohibition of establishment of religion. Approximately 85-90 percent of home schoolers are operating home schools based on their religious convictions. In effect, these families are operating religious schools in their homes.

In *Aguilar v. Felton,*[14] the U.S. Supreme Court held that the establishment clause bars the use of federal funds to send public school teachers and other professionals into religious schools to carry on instruction or to provide clinical and guidance services. The Court further ruled that use of state and federal aid to assist religious schools violated the establishment clause by creating an *excessive entanglement* of church and state, since the aid was provided in a pervasively sectarian environment.

In addition, the aid, which was in the form of public school teachers and professionals, required an ongoing public inspection in order to insure the absence of a religious message. This inspection would require pervasive state presence in the religious schools who utilized the advice of these public school teachers. Justice Powell went so far as to say that such guidance by public school teachers in religious schools constituted direct state subsidy to those schools.

The Court specifically condemned the fact that "agents of the state must visit and inspect the religious school regularly."[15] It also found unconstitutional that religious schools "must endure the ongoing presence of state personnel whose primary purpose is to monitor teachers and students."[16]

Most local home visit provisions give the local public school system the right to come into the religious home school, review their religious instructional materials, discuss the families' religious instructional program, and observe the actual instruction. This service is provided with the use of state and federal money. Since many home schools are pervasively religious schools engaged in pervasively religious instruction, such home visits and their subsequent cost to the state constitute *excessive entanglement with the religious home schools.*

In the sensitive area of First Amendment religious freedoms, the burden is on the school district to show that implementation of home visits will not ultimately infringe upon and entangle it in the affairs of a religion to an extent which the Constitution will not allow.[17]

Furthermore, the home visits are not an end in themselves, but they are part of a regulatory scheme likely to lead to official efforts to alter the operations of that religious home school. In some instances, the home visit results are used to close down the home school. Such entanglement by the school district is excessive and severely condemned by the U.S. Court.

Home Visits of Home Schoolers are not "Essential"

The requirement of home visits effectively denies a majority of parents their *fundamental* rights to teach their own children which is guaranteed by the U.S. Constitution.

First, the Fourteenth Amendment guarantees all citizens the right to liberty. The U.S. Supreme Court in a long line of cases has interpreted this right of liberty to include the concept of parental liberty. The Fourteenth Amendment right is described in detail in chapter 16. This fundamental right of parents to teach their children is guaranteed because they are parents, *not* because they have been specifically "approved" by a local school official during a home visit.

Secondly, the First Amendment guarantees all citizens and families the right to freely exercise their religious beliefs. At least 85 to 90 percent of all home schoolers believe they must home school in order to be faithful to their religious convictions. These families believe they have been called by God to personally teach their own children, applying God's Word to every subject. They believe they cannot delegate this authority to either a public or private school because they would be violating God's command.

All home schoolers who are home schooling for religious reasons, therefore, are prohibited from exercising their First Amendment rights by the requirement of home visit. Their religious convictions will not allow them to be visited in their home by a public school official.

All of the above First Amendment claims demand the application of the well-known *compelling interest test* established by the U.S. Supreme Court, as discussed in chapter 16 of this book. This test demands that the state prove, with evidence, that home visits are *necessary* for children to be educated and, secondly, that home visits are the "least restrictive means" for the state to protect its interest in education.

Not a single study exists that proves home visits are necessary for children to be educated. Hundreds of thousands of parents are doing just fine without them. Not one state out of fifty mandates home visits by statute, and many of those states, such as Wisconsin, Montana, Wyoming, Missouri, Michigan, Alaska, and Mississippi, have no monitoring requirements of any kind. Home visits, therefore, are hardly the least restrictive means of regulating education.

On December 16, 1998, HSLDA scored a major victory in the Brunelle case before the Massachusetts Supreme Judicial Court when the court struck down the public school's authority to conduct "home visits" of home schoolers. *Brunelle v. Lyn Public Schools*.[18] The Massachusetts compulsory attendance law allows for children who are "otherwise instructed in a manner approved in advance by the superintendent or the school committee." For years, home schoolers struggled against arbitrary school committee home school approval policies established in the over 300 school districts throughout the state.

The Pustell family notified the Lynn public school officials in 1991 of their intention to home educate their child. The Brunelles also notified the same school district that they would be teaching their five school age children at home. The school district reviewed both of their curricula and qualifications and found them to be satisfactory. However, they insisted that the families must "allow the superintendent to periodically...observe and evaluate the instructional process and to verify that the home instruction plan is being implemented in the home" in spite of their strenuous objections.

HSLDA challenged this requirement by filing a civil rights suit in federal court. The federal circuit court, however, abstained from making a ruling, declaring that the state issues needed to be resolved in state court first. HSLDA then filed a declaratory judgment that the home visit requirement violates the home school family's rights under Massachusetts law.

In ruling in favor of the home schoolers in the *Brunelle* case, the Massachusetts Supreme Judicial Court recognized that the Massachusetts compulsory attendance law, by allowing home schooling, "protects the basic constitutional right of parents to direct the education of their children."[19] Since this case involved the fundamental right of parental liberty, the court applied a "compelling interest test," which requires the court to determine whether a state regulation or policy is "essential" to fulfill the state's compelling interest in education.

In applying this standard, the court cited an earlier precedent in *The Care and Protection of Charles*,[20] that "the approval of the home school proposal must not be conditioned on requirements that are not *essential* to the state interest in assuring that all children be educated."[21] The court reemphasized, "A home visit is not presumptively *essential* to protection of the state's interest in seeing that children receive an education, and therefore, such visits may not be required as a condition to approval of the plaintiff's plan."[22]

Furthermore, the court found there are less restrictive means of fulfilling the state's interest: "The results of their teaching programs can be adequately verified through testing without the need to visit the home to see a formal schedule is being followed."[23] The issue of privacy was also a concern of the court:

> "Both the United States Supreme Court and this court have emphasized, in connection with the protective right of parents to raise their children, that government may not intrude unnecessarily on familial privacy. *Curtis v. School Committee Falmouth*, 420 Mass. 749, (1995). This concern as well as others dictates, as we said in the *Curtis* case, that home education proposals can be made subject only to essential and reasonable requirements." Nonconsensual home visits are dead in Massachusetts.

The *Brunelle* decision serves as an ominous warning to those school districts across the country which still insist on home visits.

The family's right of privacy, and the recognition that home visits are not essential to fulfill the state's compelling interest, clearly protects home schoolers from these unwanted intrusions.

The Bottom Line: Home Visits Are Unconstitutional

Mandatory home visits are clearly unconstitutional for many reasons. However, if the school official has a warrant signed by a judge that allows him to come into the home, the home schoolers have no choice but to allow him entrance. This, of course, is very rare, since very few school officials or child welfare workers will have warrants. However, there have been hundreds of threats each year.

Furthermore, a home schooler can *voluntarily* allow a school official into the house, but such visits are risky and can cause untold trouble for the family. The public school official may see something in the home schooler's house or in the curriculum which he does not like, and another battle begins. In fact, I know of cases, not involving HSLDA members, where home schoolers voluntarily let the official into their homes. In these instances, the official found something else objectionable, though minor, and referred them to the local child welfare agency. The children were taken out of the home for months. If the official had never been allowed entrance into the home, he would have nothing on the family and would have closed the case. Most of the time, officials are operating on anonymous tips, which in most jurisdictions can never form a basis for a warrant.

The best policy, therefore, is to avoid home visits altogether and keep school officials out of homes of home schoolers. It is also important to fight any legislation that would impose such a requirement. In chapter 13, I provide more information on home visits being conducted by social workers and the importance of keeping social workers who are on "fishing expeditions" out of your home.

Notes

1. *Kindstedt v. East Greenwich School* Committee, slip. op. (Rhode Island Commissioner of Education, August 7, 1986), 5, fnt. 12.
2. *Kindstedt v. East Greenwich School* Committee, slip. op. (Rhode Island Commissioner of Education, August 7, 1986).
3. *Ibid.*, 5, fnt. 12.
4. *Ibid.*, 7.
5. 381 U.S. 479 (1965).
6. *Steagald v. United States,* 451 U.S. 204, 211 (1981).

7. *Boyd v. United States,* 116U.S. 616, 635 (1886).

8. *In the Matter* of *Dixon,* slip. op. No. N-37-86. Family Court of Oswego County, November 21, 1988.

9. *In the Matter* of *Standish,* slip. op., No. N-125-86, Oswego County, December 23, 1988.

10. Dixon, *supra,* slip op. 5.

11. *Dixon,* 5.

12. 702 F.Supp. 516 (M.D. PA 1988). See chapter 18 for more details about the *Jeffery* case.

13. South Carolina Opinion of the Attorney General, 27 February 1989, 2.

14. 87 L.Ed.2d.290 (1985).

15. 4735 U.S., 413.

16. *Ibid.*

17. *Surinach,* 604 F.2d 73, 75-76 (1st Cir. 1979). See also *Committee far Public Instruction,* 444 U.S., 646.

18. *Brunelle,* 702 N.E.2d 1182 (1998).

19. *Brunelle,* at 1184.

20. 399 Mass. 324 (1987).

21. *Brunelle,* at 1184.

22. *Brunelle,* at 1184.

23. *Brunelle,* at 1186.

15

Amalekite Tactics?
Picking on Children with Disabilities

"While these regulations [of the federal Education of the Handicapped Act] define the nonpublic school child's right to participate in public agency services, they do not expand or limit a state's authority to regulate or otherwise set standards for the education of children residing in the state whose parents choose to enroll them in nonpublic educational programs."[1]

U.S. Department of Education

When Israel left Egypt, the Amalekites attacked Israel. However, they would rarely attack armed forces or the main group of the Israelites. Instead they would pick off the stragglers, who were often made up of the sick, weak or handicapped.

Some public school authorities, unfortunately, seem to have adopted the tactics of the Amalekites when they are dealing with disabled children who are being home schooled. When they find it difficult to pick on home schoolers with average or above average students, they turn to harassing the handicapped or special needs home school children. Going after disabled children that are home schooled is somewhat easier since it is harder for the family to prove educational progress. It is also easier to intimidate the families into thinking they are not qualified. Of course, the incentive is greater also, since special needs children are worth nearly twice as much in state and federal tax dollars which will be sent to the local school district.

As a result of discriminatory treatment, many home schoolers with special needs children begin to think they have less parental rights than everyone else. Constitutionally, this could not be further from the truth.

Parents with special needs children are protected by the same Constitution as all other parents. Therefore, they too have the protection of the First and Fourteenth Amendments.

One HSLDA home school family in Colorado had their child in special needs classes in the public school. After awhile, their child basically stagnated, as the classroom atmosphere became unbearable. They decided that they could do a better job themselves so they notified the school district that they were going to home school. Although it was legal to home school in the state, the local school district would not disenroll the child. The district felt the child's IEP recommendation could not be fulfilled by a mere mother. It called the family nearly every week, trying to pressure them back in for more meetings and more conferences with the public school's specialists. The mother could barely stand the intimidation and began to doubt herself. I was called and was able to convince the school district to retreat.

In Illinois, a family disenrolled their child from all special needs programs except speech therapy. Over and over again the school district tried to pressure the family to come into various meetings in which the child would be evaluated and recommendations given. The school district believed the parents were not qualified. Finally, the school district initiated a due process proceeding, pursuant to the Education of the Handicapped Act (EHA, which has recently been retitled "Individuals with Disabilities Education Act" or "IDEA"), since they believed the family was still under the jurisdiction of that act because the child was still receiving speech therapy. The family followed my advice and withdrew their child from speech therapy and provided a written statement to the school district breaking all ties. After further negotiation, the family was finally left alone.

In Indiana, a couple who educated nine adopted handicapped children was harassed repeatedly by school officials. Scores of other families were home schooling in the area, but this family was singled out because all the children had special needs. The school district was losing a lot of money.

The personal experiences I have had with defending handicapped children who are harassed only because they are home schooling could go on and on. In every instance, the situations were resolved, and in every instance, the parents were able to do a better job because they cared about their children and best understood their special needs.

Parents Excel in Teaching Their Special Needs Children

Studies demonstrate that parents do not have to be specially certified to teach their handicapped children at home. In fact, parents in many cases are providing a superior form of education for their special needs children by teaching them at home.

In one of the most thorough studies performed thus far, Dr. Steven Duvall conducted a year-long study involving eight elementary and two junior high students with learning disabilities. He compared one group of five students who received instruction at home with a group of five students who attended public schools. He was careful to match the public school students to the home school students according to grade level, sex, I.Q., and area of disability. Using a laptop computer, Dr. Duvall sat in on teaching sessions and took an observation every twenty seconds, creating tens of thousands of data points that were then fed into a statistical analysis package. Normally his research included a second observer who double-checked Dr. Duvall's readings.

Dr. Duvall recorded and analyzed academically engaged time by students during instructional periods. He also administered standardized achievement tests to them to measure gains in reading, math and written language. His results show that the home school, special needs students were academically engaged about two and one-half times as often as public school special needs students! He found children in the public school special education classrooms spent 74.9 percent of their time with no academic responses, while home school children only spent 40.7 percent of their time with no academic responses. He also found that home schools have children and teachers sitting side-by-side or face-to-face 43 percent of the time, while public education classrooms had such an arrangement for special needs children only 6 percent of the time. This was a tremendous advantage for the home schoolers.

His study further demonstrated that the home school students averaged six months' gain in reading compared to only a one-half month gain by the special public school students. Furthermore, the home school special needs students during the year gained eight months in written language skills compared to the public school counterparts who gained only two and one-half months.

Dr. Duvall summarized, "These results clearly indicate that parents, even though they are not certified teachers, can create instructional environments at home that assist students with learning disabilities to improve their academic skills. This study shows that home schooling is beneficial for special-needs students."[2]

A Theory Concerning Attention Deficit Disorder

In our modern educational system, Attention Deficit Disorder (ADD) is getting a lot of attention. Children are routinely being prescribed Ritalin so that they can perform better in school. ADD children typically have trouble sitting still and are easily distracted. Here is a suggestion that might be of help.

In an interesting analysis by a member of the medical profession, Dr. Matthew James observes that early television exposure is a possible factor in Attention Deficit Disorder. Dr. James states,

> Those of you who know ADD children may realize that the characteristic diversion of their gaze every few seconds or so bears an unmistakable resemblance in pattern and timing to the pattern of camera/scene changes on an ordinary television program. This crippling disability, which prevents them from sustaining concentration and accomplishment, becomes understandable when you consider that early in their lives they had a TV set for a mom. Thus, the frenetic changes in focus of attention that characterize ADD children. It is not genetics that causes ADD; it is not some mysterious and unknown factor in our modern lives. It is our familiar friend, the "boob tube."
>
> It is obvious to me that virtually all variants of ADD, including antisocial behavior, victimization of other children as if they are inanimate objects, and hyperactivity can be laid at the door in whole or in part of the "universal mind," television.[3]

By and large, home school parents take control of their TV set when they begin to realize the massive amount of objectionable material which is shown daily. In my experience, I find more and more and parents eliminating TV altogether. The benefits of taking this drastic step can bring enormous benefits to your whole family, spiritually and mentally. Although some cases of ADD are chemically based and difficult to overcome, I believe taking control of the TV set can only help!

Even though home school special needs children are being taught well by their parents and are being nurtured by the love of their parents, they are still faced with regular legal challenges.

Below is a short summary of the legal rights and conflicts of parents who home school children with special needs.

The Improper Application of the IDEA to Private Home Schools

A common adage, that government controls nearly always follow government money, often rings true with home schoolers who receive public school services for their special needs children. Many times the controls are not immediately visible but they usually surface as soon as the parents begin to disagree with the public school authorities' "recommendations" for new therapy or a different educational approach.

At the very least, home schoolers who receive public school services for their special needs children, place themselves under the jurisdiction of the federal IDEA (Individuals with Disabilities Act) and local state regulations which implement that act. The reader can see this actually being applied in the example of the family from Indiana and the family from Pennsylvania discussed below. The IDEA funding is given to each state, based on the number of special needs children and on how closely the state follows the IDEA regulations. As a result, each state has passed some form of regulations to implement the IDEA requirements.

However, special needs home schoolers who want to discontinue public services or, in some instances, those who never asked for the service to begin with, are faced with an attempt by some state officials, superintendents, and principals to require special needs home schoolers to comply with the IDEA anyway. This action by school districts is, of course, improper because the IDEA was established to make public school services available to all children on a *voluntary* basis.

Parents who do not want the free special needs services, therefore, are not under the jurisdiction of the IDEA and should not have to abide by the federal IDEA regulations, or the state's regulations which implement the IDEA rules.

The purpose and intent of the IDEA, described in 20 USCS §1400(d)1, is:

> (A)...To assure that all handicapped children have *available* to them...a free appropriate public education which emphasizes special education and related services designed to meet their unique needs: (A) and prepare them for employment and independent living; (B) to ensure that the rights of children with disabilities and parents of such children are protected; (C) to assist States, localities, educational service agencies, and Federal agencies to provide for the education of all children with disabilities.

Throughout the entire act, the purpose of making *available* a free appropriate education to disabled children is the central theme. The act defines a "free appropriate public education" as:

> Special education and related services that (A) have been provided at public expense, under public supervision and direction, and without charge, (B) meet the standards of the state educational agency, (C) include an appropriate preschool, elementary, or secondary school education in the state involved, and (D) are provided in conformity with the individualized education program required under section 614(d)(5) [20 USCS §1414(d)].[4]

The intent of the act, therefore, is to provide statutory guidelines for local public schools to make available a free public education to the handicapped. The act is *not* a compulsory attendance statute for handicapped children. Section 1412(a) only allows states to receive federal money for special education services *if* "a free appropriate public education is available for all handicapped children between the ages of three and twenty-one." Most states have compulsory ages set between ages six and sixteen. If the IDEA were a federal mandate compelling all handicapped children between the ages of three and twenty-one to receive special education services, it would be in direct conflict with every compulsory attendance statute in the country.

It is clearly apparent, therefore, that parents who do *not* want to take advantage of a free public education for their handicapped child, are not mandated to do so. Such a mandate would also violate the parents' fundamental right to direct the education of their children, as guaranteed under *Pierce v. Society of Sisters.*[5] In the *Pierce* case, the U.S. Supreme Court declared parents have the right to choose a *private* educational program for their children, and, as a result, the Court struck down an Oregon law that mandated only public school attendance. Parents of special needs children are not required to use any public educational services. To privately educate their special needs child is the parents' choice. By doing so, they avoid the state's controls pursuant to the IDEA.

Example of Misapplication of the Law to Home Schooling the Handicapped.

In Pennsylvania, the Ehmann family withdrew their handicapped child, George, from the public schools in order to instruct him privately, and voluntarily discontinued all state and federal assistance. As a result, they no longer remained under the jurisdiction of the IDEA and were no longer subject to the due process procedures of 20 U.S.C. §1415. Nonetheless, the Philadelphia school district alleged that the Ehmanns were still under the jurisdiction of the federal law and initiated a hearing under the due process procedures of the sec. 1415 to force the family to follow the "recommendations" of the public school special needs experts. The public school, of course, wanted the child to stay in a public school special needs class. The family, as is their right, unilaterally withdrew their child from the special needs program and completely home schooled him privately.

The assistant general counsel of the Philadelphia Board of Education asserted the Ehmanns are *"precluded"* from removing their child from the public school placement and teaching him privately. The counsel stated,

> It is our belief that the Ehmanns by their refusal to comply with federal laws and procedures enacted for the protection of handicapped children, are in violation of Pennsylvania's Compulsory Attendance Laws.

This school district was attempting to make it mandatory that a special needs child comply with federal controls, even though all ties to the public school had been severed.

I filed a brief with the independent hearing officer who was assigned to hear the case pursuant to the due process procedures of the Sec. 1415[6] and requested the hearing officer dismiss the case, since he and the federal law had no jurisdiction.

I argued that the purpose and the intent of the IDEA (titled EHA at the time of the case) is not to *compel* all handicapped children to utilize federally funded special education services, but rather to make available a "free and appropriate" education to those who *choose* to take advantage of such federal services. The Ehmanns are *not* enrolling their child in the public school, so the superintendent has no authority to impose federal public school standards. Furthermore, the superintendent has no legal authority to initiate federal due process procedures pursuant to the IDEA because those due process procedures *only* apply to children enrolled in *public* school programs for the handicapped children, not children being *privately* home schooled, such as the Ehmanns. The only consequence for the Ehmanns in withdrawing their child from the special needs program in order to home school him is that they forfeit all federal and state aid.[7] I also presented the following position of the U.S. Department of Education.

The U.S. Department of Education Supports Special Needs Home Schoolers

The U.S. Department of Education has confirmed that the federal disability laws have no jurisdiction over home schools and private schools. In a letter of June 24, 1988, to Mike Farris of HSLDA, Charles O'Malley, the executive assistant for Private Education stated:

> There is nothing in the EHA [IDEA] statute or regulations that indicates that the free and appropriate public education requirement applicable to participating states was intended to interfere with the right of parents to educate their children at home or in a private school in accordance with their State's provisions for these alternatives.[8]

Furthermore, the letter explains that the IDEA was not intended to regulate schools or families who choose not to participate in public agency services. O'Malley emphasizes that the rights of nonpublic school children and the limited obligations of public agencies for those children are defined in the IDEA regulations.[9] However, O'Malley adds:

> While these regulations define the nonpublic school child's right to participate in public agency services, they do not expand or limit a State's authority to regulate or otherwise set standards for the education of children residing in the State whose parents choose to enroll them in nonpublic educational programs.[10]

In other words, the IDEA standards for an appropriate education do not apply and were not *intended* to apply to handicapped children in home schools and private schools who do not participate in public agency services.

Ehmann Decision in Favor of Parents' Rights

The independent hearing officer refused to grant my motion to dismiss, and ruled against the family and in favor of the public school's definition of an "appropriate" education for this special needs child.

I appealed to the Secretary of Education of Pennsylvania, Thomas K. Gilhool, and he ruled in favor of the Ehmanns, granting the motion to dismiss on June 9, 1989.[11] He ordered that the hearing officer's findings of fact and conclusions of law be rejected and vacated.[12] He also ordered the school district and the family to proceed under the Pennsylvania compulsory attendance act, not the federal IDEA procedures.[13]

Conclusion

Home schooling special needs children takes a tremendous effort on behalf of parents. HSLDA receives regular reports of the consistent success that these parents are achieving, oftentimes far beyond the progress the special needs child made in the public school. In fact, many learning disabilities or handicaps are conquered in the home setting. Thomas Edison, as explained in chapter 7, was labeled "addled" by the public school and lasted only three months. It was through home instruction that he thrived. One of the major reasons for success seems to be the fact that parents know their children best and, therefore, can best meet the needs of their handicapped child.

In order to avoid taking the risk of being subject to objectionable federal and state controls, experience dictates that home schooling children with special needs should be done completely in the private realm. Although some home school families have had no conflict from the school district which provided them with special needs services, the family is taking a risk. HSLDA has even had families turned over to the social services for investigation, since they refused to follow the public school's recommendation regarding the type of educational help the handicapped child should have.

If an HSLDA family withdraws their child from a public special needs educational program, we advise them to avoid signing any IEP forms stating they decline to follow the school district's recommendation. Instead, we tell them to write a short letter clearly stating they are formally withdrawing their child from the special needs program and will pursue private assistance. The parents need to make clear they are no longer desiring to receive any further funding so as to make certain the school district knows they are no longer under the jurisdiction of the federal disability laws (IDEA).

Home schoolers should also carefully watch their legislatures in order to oppose any attempts to create excessive regulations for handicapped children being home schooled. All home schoolers need to stand together to protect special needs home schoolers from being separately and excessively regulated.

Notes

1. Charles J. O'Malley, Ph.D., Executive Assistant for Private Education, United States Department of Education, Washington D.C., Letter to Michael P. Farris, June 24, 1988, 2.
2. Dr. Steven Duvall, *The Impact of Home Education on Learning Disabled Children: A Look at New Research*, August 30, 1994, presented to the Home School Legal Defense Association.
3. Matthew James, M.D., *Early Television Exposure a Possible Factor in Attention Deficit Disorder, The Moore Report International*, Box 1, Camus, WA 98607, Winter 1994.
4. 20 USCS 1401(8).
5. 268 U.S.510 (1925) [Also see *Meyer v. Nebraska*, 262 U.S.390 (1923) and *Wisconsin v. Yoder*, 406 U.S.205 (1972)]. See chapter 16 for a full discussion of this fundamental right guaranteed by the Fourteenth Amendment.
6. The *Ehmann* brief was also expanded and filed with the secretary of education in Pennsylvania.
7. In *Board of Education of the City of New York v. Ambach*, 612 F.Supp. 230, (D.C.N.Y.1985), a family disagreed with the public school's placement of their handicapped child and initiated administrative proceedings. In the meantime, the child was enrolled in a private school. The court held: Section 1415(e)(3) does not act to *preclude parents* from removing their child from an arguably inappropriate placement, but if the parents do violate the status quo provisions of Section 1414(e) (3) and place their child in a private school without the consent of the school agency, they do so *at their* own risk. (emphasis added)
   612 F.Supp. at 234. Also see *Board of Education of Windsor Regional School v. Diamond*, 808 F.2d 987 (3rd Cir. 1986). In the *Stemple, Ambach*, and *Diamond* cases above, nothing was even suggested that the parents had no right to unilaterally remove their handicapped children from the public school placement under EHA (the title is now changed to IDEA). In fact, the disputes only concerned whether or not the local officials had to reimburse them for this choice.
   In *Springdale School District v. Grace*, 494 F.Supp. 266 (W.D.Ark. 1980), parents sued because they

preferred to have their daughter placed in the State School for the Deaf, while the local school district wanted the girl to be placed in their system. The local school district prevailed when the district court held that the program for the girl was "appropriate" and thus satisfied the school's legal duties to offer appropriate special education. However, the court ended its opinion by reminding the parents that if they truly thought the other program was best for the child they could choose that on their own with their own expense. The court said:

We also note that, upon reflection, Sherry's parents may be more desirous that their child receive the *best* instead of a mere "appropriate" scholastic exposure. (emphasis added)

494 F.Supp., at 274. [emphasis in original].

8. Charles J. O'Malley, Ph.D., Executive Assistant for Private Education, United States Department of Education, Washington D.C., Letter to Michael P. Farris, June 24, 1988, 1.

9. 34 CFR §300.403(a), and EDGAR at 34 CFR §§300.651-662.

10. *Ibid.*, 2.

11. In *re the Educational Assignment of George E.*, Special Education Opinion No. 353, Department of Education. of Pennsylvania, June 5, 1989, 3. II

12. *Ibid.*, 3.

13. *Ibid.*

V

A Successful Defense:
The Legal Arguments and the Power of God

The framers of the Constitution, unfortunately, never specifically mentioned in the Constitution the right of parents to educate their children. They took it for granted that parents alone had this right and could *choose* whatever form of education they saw fit. Since biblical theism was dominant in early America, this right of parents was recognized as a God-given right derived from the Bible and codified in English common law.

In the last fifty years, however, the U.S. Constitution has been so twisted in many areas that it no longer reflects the intent of the framers. The most devastating example of the perversion of the original intent of the Constitution is the creation of the "right" to an abortion, which has resulted in the deaths of millions of babies. This has happened in spite of our Bill of Rights which clearly protects life.

Similarly, the right of parents to choose their child's education, as held sacred by the framers, has also been gradually eroded in favor of state intervention and control. The parents are no longer solely responsible for the education of their children as established in the Bible and common law. Now the courts recognize the state having an interest in education and the power to regulate that interest. As a result, prior to the 1980s, home schooling was virtually stifled by the state.

However, the tide is slowly being reversed through the application of the various constitutional or technical defenses in the courts as described in this section or by the legislatures as seen in chapter 20. The ultimate victory will not be reached until the compulsory attendance statutes are repealed in every state. However, at his time, repeal of such laws is a long way off. Therefore, the strategy of this author and the Home School Legal Defense Association, in the meantime, is to push back the interest of the state further and further in education, limiting its power to regulate, until that interest finally evaporates. This will take time, relentless efforts, and a great deal of education of our judges, law enforcement officials, and legislators.

For a more thorough and virtually exhaustive review of home school cases and parents' rights in education decisions, see my latest book *The Right To Home School: A Guide To The Law On Parents' Rights In Education,* published in 1998 by Carolina Academic Press, 700 Kent St., Durham, NC 27701, 919-489-7486 The book is available online at the HSLDA web page: *www.hslda.org*

16

Parents' Rights
and the Constitution

"That some parents 'may at times be acting against the interests of their children' ...creates a basis for caution, but it is hardly a reason to discard wholesale those pages of human experience that teach that parents generally do act in the child's best interest.... The statist notion that governmental power should supersede parental authority in all cases because some parents abuse and neglect children is repugnant to American tradition."[1]

The U.S. Supreme Court

Home schooling is a right, not a privilege. This right of parents to teach their children is guaranteed in the Fourteenth Amendment of the United States Constitution. Parents who are home schooling for religious reasons also have the additional protection of the First Amendment which guarantees them the right to freely exercise their religious beliefs.

Although you will see in this chapter that parental liberty historically was held to be virtually absolute, many state courts and the passage of compulsory attendance laws in the 1900s have gradually eroded this right. These states have used the language of the United States Supreme Court which recognizes that the states have an "interest" in education. During the last seventy-five years, the power to regulate that interest of the state has steadily expanded.

However, home schools have been involved on the cutting edge in pushing back the interest of the state. In 1983, the Home School Legal Defense Association was established for the purpose of shackling the interest of the state by gradually limiting the state's power over parents. Eventually, I would like to see the interest of the state totally erased with the repeal of all state compulsory attendance laws, but that may take some time while we educate the judges and legislators.

Meanwhile, it is important for us to master the history of parental rights, especially as established in the courts, so that we are better prepared for the battle for our children that is presently taking place. We need to work to reestablish the historic foundations of parental rights in our country and restore a respect of the parents' right to choose and control the education of their children.[2]

Early Recognition of Parents' Rights in the Courts

As documented in chapter 6, during the first 250 years of this country, beginning in 1620, education was not subject to the myriads of regulations which presently conflict with the parents' right to control the process of their children's education. Parental liberty was held inviolate, and parents seriously heeded the rights and responsibilities of educating their children. Education was not a government responsibility, and it was left completely under the private control of parents and the churches.

In fact, in *Abington v. Schempp,* the U.S. Supreme Court confirmed that education historically was privately controlled and public schooling, in the modern sense, was nonexistent.

> In the North American Colonies, education was almost without exception under private sponsorship and supervision, frequently under control of the dominant Protestant sects.[3]

Similarly, the modern home school movement is comprised largely of fundamental Christians who hold sacred the biblical view of the family and practically apply God's principles to each and every subject. This fact that biblical theism dominated early American education and culture[4] explains why the present states' attempt to control and secularize private, Christian education and home schooling was nonexistent back then. The Court in *Schempp* further comments,

> Education, as the framers knew it, was in the main confined to *private* schools more often than not under strictly *sectarian supervision*. Only gradually did control of education pass largely to public officials.[5] (emphasis supplied)

Until the 1900s, the Christian concept of parental liberty in education was unquestioned.

This "preferred" position of the parents' duty and right in controlling the education of their children was securely established in the foundation of America's legal system, and its roots were in English common law which was derived from the Bible.[6] One of the most influential common law sources on which the founders of our country relied was Sir William Blackstone's *Commentaries*. Blackstone recognized that the most important duty of parents to their children is that of giving them an education suitable to their station in life.[7] That duty, he admits, "was pointed out by reason."[8]

Building on this traditional liberty of parents as enunciated by Blackstone, the Oklahoma Supreme Court in *School Board Dist. No. 18 v. Thompson*[9] secured the right of parents to control the education of their children, even though the Oklahoma Constitution and Legislature had recently enacted compulsory education.

The attorney representing the school district contended that "the old common law idea that the parent has the exclusive control over the education of the child has long since been abandoned" since the state requirement of compulsory education was enacted.[10] The Oklahoma Supreme Court, however, unanimously *disagreed* with the school district and ruled:

> Under our form of government, and at common law, *the home* is considered the keystone of the governmental structure. In this empire, *parents rule supreme* during the minority of their children.[11] (emphasis supplied)

The Court also quoted Blackstone as strong support for their decision to uphold parents' rights to control their child's education:

> Blackstone says that the greatest duty of parents to their children is that of giving them an education suitable to their station in life; a duty pointed out by reason, and of far the greatest importance of any. But this duty at common law was not compulsory; the common law presuming that the natural love and affection of the parents for their children would impel them to faithfully perform this duty, and deeming it punishment enough to leave the parent, who neglects the instruction of his family, to labor under those griefs and inconveniences which his family, so uninstructed, will be sure to bring upon him.[12]

At this time, Oklahoma is still benefiting from this 1909 decision. This decision clearly established in Oklahoma the presumption that parents act in the best interest of their children, and parents' rights are superior to the public school's authority.

This function of the parent to control the education of his children has been a constitutionally recognized right in a long line of cases beginning with *Meyer v. Nebraska* in 1923.[13] A U.S. Supreme Court decision to protect parents' rights in education was not necessary prior to 1923, because there were hardly any compulsory attendance laws that required children to attend public school. As soon as compulsory attendance laws were passed, however, the attack on parental liberty began. Education became a state responsibility rather than a traditional parental responsibility. As experience teaches, whenever the state takes responsibility of any private sector, controls always follow.

Parental Liberty in Education Is Derived from the Fourteenth Amendment

Even though the Constitution does not specifically mention the right of parents to educate their children, that right is derived from the Fourteenth Amendment. The Fourteenth Amendment guarantees that all citizens have the right to "liberty," which cannot be taken away without due process. The U.S. Supreme Court has determined that this guarantee of "liberty" includes "parental liberty." Based on this application of the Fourteenth Amendment, the Supreme Court has consistently held that parents have the "fundamental right" to "direct the upbringing and education of their children."[14]

The problem, however, is that the Supreme Court, in the same breath in which it reasserted the parents' right to educate their children, also created an "interest" which the state has in education. Consequently, with this "interest" in education comes government controls. The state's interest, as defined by the Supreme Court is that children must grow up to be "literate" and "self-sufficient."[15]

Since the HSLDA was founded in 1983, it has not had a single case, out of hundreds of home school cases, where the home schooled children in question were not receiving an adequate education. In every case, the children were literate and average or above average on their standardized achievement test results. The "interest" of the state in children being educated was being "otherwise served." In fact, the public schools, as demonstrated in chapter 1, comprises the one school system where the interest of the state is *not* being met!

Of course, the state, in order to protect its "interest" in education, tries to impose restrictive requirements on parents who are home schooling, such as teacher certification requirements, curriculum approval, home visits, and countless other controls. The courts then must determine which must give way: the state's interest in regulating education or the parents' fundamental right in educating their children in the manner they choose. Since this conflict involves a "fundamental right," the "compelling interest test" must be applied, which requires that the state prove that its particular regulation imposed on home education is "essential" and the "least restrictive means" to fulfill its interest that children be literate and self-sufficient. This test is described later in this chapter.

The states' attempts to arbitrarily regulate and limit parental control of the process of education result in the infringement of the fundamental rights of the parents as enunciated by the U.S. Supreme Court in the following three cases.

United States Supreme Court Cases
Protecting Parents' Rights

In *Meyer v. Nebraska*,[16] the Court invalidated a state law that prohibited foreign language instruction to school children because the law did not "promote" education but rather "arbitrarily and unreasonably" interfered with "the natural duty of the parent to give his children education suitable to their station in life...."[17] The Court chastened the legislature for attempting "materially to interfere...with the power of parents to control the education of their own.[18] This decision clearly affirmed that the Constitution protected the preferences of the parent in education over those of the state.[19]

In 1925, the Supreme Court decided the *Pierce v. Society of Sisters*[20] case, thereby supporting *Meyer's* recognition of the parents' right to direct the religious upbringing of their children and to control the process of their education. In *Pierce*, the Supreme Court struck down an Oregon compulsory education law which, in effect, required attendance of all children between ages eight and sixteen at *public* schools. The Court declared,

> Under the doctrine of *Meyer v. Nebraska*, we think it entirely plain that the Act of 1922 unreasonably interferes with the liberty of parents and guardians to direct the upbringing and education of children.[21]

In addition to upholding the right of parents to direct or control the education of their children, *Pierce* also asserts the parents' fundamental right to keep their children free from government standardization.

> The fundamental theory of liberty upon which all governments in this Union repose excluded any general power of the state to standardize its children by forcing them to accept instruction from public teachers only. The child is not the mere creature of the state; those who nurture him and direct his destiny have the right and the high duty, to recognize and prepare him for additional obligations.[22]

The Supreme Court uses strong language to assert that a child is not "the mere creature of the State." The holding in *Pierce*, therefore, preserves diversity of process of education by forbidding the state to standardize the education of children, in forcing them to accept instruction only from public schools.[23] This, of course, also prohibits the state from imposing excessive regulations on home schools, which would reduce them simply to "little public schools in the home."

Forty-eight years after *Pierce*, the U.S. Supreme Court once again upheld *Pierce* as "the charter of the rights of parents to direct the religious upbringing of their children."[24] In agreement with *Pierce*, Chief Justice Burger stated in the opinion of *Wisconsin v. Yoder* in 1972:

This case involves the *fundamental interest* of parents, as contrasted with that of the state, to guide the religious future and education of their children.

The history and culture of Western civilization reflect a strong tradition of parental concern for the nurture and upbringing of their children. This *primary* role of the parents in the upbringing of their children is now established *beyond debate* as an *enduring tradition.*[25] (emphasis supplied)

This case involved a family of the Amish religion who wanted to be exempt after eighth grade from the public schools in order to be instructed at home. Furthermore, in *Yoder* the U.S. Supreme Court emphasized:

Thus a state's interest in universal education, however highly we rank it, is not totally free from a balancing process when it impinges on fundamental rights and interests, such as those specifically protected by the Free Exercise Clause of the First Amendment, and the traditional interest of parents with respect to the religious upbringing of their children…. This case involves the fundamental and religious future and education of their children.[26]

The most recent decision which upholds the right of parents is *Employment Division of Oregon v. Smith,*[27] which involved two Indians who were fired from a private drug rehabilitation organization because they ingested "peyote," a hallucinogenic drug, as part of their religious belief. When they sought unemployment compensation, they were denied because they were discharged for "misconduct."

The Indians appealed to the Oregon Court of Appeals, which reversed the earlier decision on the grounds that they had the right to freely exercise their religious beliefs by taking drugs. Of course, as expected, the U.S. Supreme Court again reversed the case and found that the First Amendment did not protect drug use. So what does this case have to do with parental rights?

After the Court ruled against the Indians, it then analyzed the application of the Free Exercise Clause generally. The Court wrongly decided to throw out the Free Exercise Clause as a defense to any "neutral" law that might violate an individual's religious convictions.

In the process of destroying religious freedom, the United States Supreme Court in *Smith* miraculously reaffirmed the fact that the parents' rights to control the education of their children is still a fundamental right. The Court declared that the "compelling interest test" is still applicable, not to the Free Exercise Clause alone,

> but the Free Exercise Clause in conjunction with other *constitutional protections* such as…the *right of parents,* acknowledged in *Pierce v. Society of Sisters,* 268 U.S. 510 (1925), *to direct the education of their children,* see *Wisconsin v. Yoder,* 406 U.S.205 (1972) invalidating compulsory attendance laws as applied to Amish parents who refused on religious grounds to send their children to school.[28] (emphasis supplied)

In other words, under this precedent, the fact that a family is home schooling for religious reasons is not enough to be a defense against a state requirement, such as teacher certification. However, since that religious conviction to home school is *combined* with the fundamental right of parents to control the education of their children, as guaranteed under the Fourteenth Amendment, the home school family battling the restrictive state regulation is still protected by the "compelling interest test."[29] This means that the state must prove, with evidence, that teacher certification is necessary for children to be educated and that it is the least restrictive means.

As a result, a requirement such as teacher certification should not be allowed to prevail over a home school family's religious beliefs, if the state merely proves the teacher certification requirement is "reasonable." The Court in *Smith* quoted its previous case of *Wisconsin v. Yoder:*

> *Yoder* said that "The Court's holding in *Pierce* stands as a charter for the rights of parents to direct the religious upbringing of their children. And when the interests of parenthood are combined with a free exercise claim… *more than merely a reasonable relationship* to some purpose within the competency of the State is required to sustain the validity of the State's requirement under the First Amendment."[30] (emphasis supplied)

Instead of merely showing that teacher certification is reasonable, the state must, therefore, reach the higher standard of the "compelling interest test" which requires the state to prove that teacher certification is the least restrictive means.

Consequently, it is clear that the Constitutional right of a parent to direct the upbringing and education of his child is firmly entrenched in the U.S. Supreme Court case history.

The Free Exercise Defense

Most home schoolers are home schooling for religious reasons as a result of their religious beliefs, as shown by several recent studies.[31] Many of these families believe they are commanded by God to be the primary teachers of their children. In chapter 4, these commonly held religious beliefs and supporting Scripture verses are described in detail.

Since these families have strong religious beliefs that they must home school, they are protected by the First Amendment of the United States Constitution which guarantees to all citizens the right to freely exercise their religious beliefs. This means that a home school family being prosecuted for not complying with a local restriction on their home school, such as the requirement of a college degree or teaching certificate, can use the First Amendment as a defense, as long as they prove that the particular restriction violates their religious belief.

The Four-Part Compelling Interest Test

Whenever the right of parents to educate their children under either the First or Fourteenth Amendments is at issue, a specific legal test must be applied. This test is made up of four parts and is often referred to as the "compelling interest test."[32]

The U.S. Supreme Court has stated that whenever parental rights are combined with a free exercise claim, a heightened standard of review must be applied.[33] This standard of review involves the application of the "compelling interest" test, which requires the home schooler asserting a religious belief to prove two parts of the test and the State to prove the other two parts. This test was originally applied in *Sherbert v. Verner*[34] and has evolved through the years in *Wisconsin v. Yoder*,[35] *Thomas v. Review Board*,[36] *U.S. v. Lee*,[37] and *Hobbie v. Unemployment Appeals Comm'n of Florida*.[38] This test involves four major parts.

First of all, the burden is on the home school family to prove the first two parts of the "compelling interest test": 1) They must demonstrate that their religious belief against the particular state requirement is both "sincere" and "religious." Their belief cannot be only philosophical;[39] 2) the home school family must prove that their sincere religious belief is "burdened" as applied under the facts.[40]

Then the burden shifts to the state to prove, with evidence, the last two parts of the test. The two burdens that the state must prove are that its requirement is "essential" or "necessary" "to accomplish an overriding governmental [or compelling] interest" in education,[41] and that "it is the least restrictive means of achieving some compelling state interest."[42] If the state can prove that its interest in a particular regulation is essential and the least restrictive means, then the religious belief of the home schooler must give way.

This raises the question of what is the state's legitimate interest in education. According to U.S. Supreme Court precedent, the state's interest is twofold: *civic* and *economic*.[43] The state has an interest that children will acquire the necessary reading and writing skills to be able to vote and participate in our democratic system. The second interest of the state is that children will be able to eventually provide for themselves so that they will not become a burden on the state's welfare rolls. Many courts are finding that some of the present compulsory attendance laws are overly restrictive concerning home schools.

For example, a state requiring a college degree for home school parents would fail the third part of the "compelling interest test" since a college degree is not "essential" or "necessary" for a child to be educated. As seen in chapter 12, all available studies prove that there is no positive correlation between teacher qualifications and student performance.

Do Home Schoolers Actually Win under the Free Exercise Clause?

The above described test is what should be applied to home schoolers whose religious beliefs are being violated by a state's education requirement. Unfortunately, few courts properly apply the "compelling interest test."

Convincing a court to actually exempt a home school family based solely on religious beliefs as guaranteed by the First Amendment is not that easy. In fact, it is very rare. Most courts try to dodge the issue or apply an improper "reasonableness" test. In other words, if a particular home school requirement is "reasonable" (virtually all restrictions on home schooling could be deemed "reasonable"), it is upheld against a family's sincerely held religious beliefs. In my book, *The Right To Home School: A Guide To The Law On Parents' Rights In Education,*[44] I summarize many of the cases that have gone against home schoolers or Christian schools who have used as their defense the Free Exercise clause. I also point out the key constitutional flaw in all of those cases.

An example of the difficulty in convincing a court to grant an exemption under the Free Exercise Clause is the initial lower court rulings over an eight-year period in *State v. DeJonge.*[45] In this case, the DeJonge family was opposed to using a certified teacher to teach their children. They proved, in court, that they had sincerely held religious convictions which made them opposed to teacher certification. However, when it came to the prosecution proving, with evidence, that teacher certification was essential for children to be educated, and that it was the least restrictive means of fulfilling the state's interest in education, the judge did not require the prosecution to carry the burden. Instead, the judge, following a whim and an earlier improper ruling against the Christian schools, found the state's interest to override the family's beliefs.

On appeal to the Michigan Court of Appeals, the Court refused to recognize the error that the prosecution never carried their burden that teacher certification is essential and the least restrictive means. The Court merely gave "lip service" to the "compelling interest test" and, instead, applied the "reasonableness test." The Court of Appeals merely ruled, without any evidence, that teacher certification is the least restrictive means of fulfilling the state's interest. The Court also ruled that "teacher certification requirement is a backbone in protection" of quality education. How could the Court of Appeals make such a ruling when we made clear to them the proper test, and informed them that the prosecution never proved that teacher certification is essential and the least restrictive means? I presented studies and facts showing that children can and are being educated better without certified teachers than the children in the public schools. I showed them the studies which indicate there is no positive correlation between teacher qualifications and student performance. I also proved that at that time, forty-eight other states did not require such an onerous requirement, disproving any claim that it is the least restrictive means. Yet, the Court of Appeals ruled against them. However, by God's grace, on May 25, 1993, the Michigan Supreme Court reversed the lower court rulings. It found the teacher certification requirement unconstitutional since it violated the Free Exercise of Religion rights of all religious home schoolers (see chapter 17 for the miraculous story on how God paved the way for this landmark decision).

Although many cases we have handled are won on technicalities or other constitutional defenses, we have won others on religious grounds. For example, in Colorado I worked with local counsel Bruce Lorenzen to win a case for the Main family. In *Hinsdale County School Board v. Main,* the Main family objected to seeking the "approval" of the local public school authorities because they believed that only God can approve their home schooling. The Court ruled that their religious beliefs were sincere and stated, "The state has an important interest in the education of children, but to minimize interference with sincerely held religious beliefs, it must find the least intrusive means to accomplish that interest."[46] Therefore, the Court exempted the family from the approval requirements, stating, "the Mains are complying with the purpose of the compulsory attendance law, even if they have not obtained approval of their home study program."[47]

Similarly, HSLDA has been able to use the combination of the Free Exercise defense along with other defenses, such as the vagueness defense, to win for home schoolers. For example, in HSLDA's civil rights case against school districts throughout Pennsylvania, *Jeffery v. O'Donnell,*[48] the Court ruled in favor of the home schoolers who were all opposed on religious grounds to approval by the public school authorities. The Court declared:

> ...when First Amendment rights are affected by the enforcement of a statute, the state law will be held to a higher standard of specificity than might be the case if purely economic regulation was at issue.
>
> ...the threat to sensitive First Amendment freedoms mandates judicial intrusion in the form of declaring the particular provision of the law [as applied to home schools] unconstitutional for vagueness.[49]

Since the *Jeffery* case was combined with the First Amendment Free Exercise rights of the home schoolers, the Federal Court more strictly applied the vagueness defense to find Pennsylvania's compulsory attendance law unconstitutionally void for vagueness.

Therefore, we regularly raise the Free Exercise challenge on behalf of home schoolers because we never know which courts will want to rule favorably on it.

More importantly, the Free Exercise clause has been very effective in influencing legislatures. Over and over again, I have presented the First Amendment arguments in my testimony before legislative committees who many times have either killed bad bills or passed good bills in response to wanting to protect religious freedom as guaranteed in the First Amendment.

Also, in thousands of correspondence and negotiations with school districts since 1983, the HSLDA legal staff and I have used the First Amendment to contribute to resolving the conflict in favor of home school families.

Conclusion

The First and Fourteenth Amendments are important defenses to families who are home schooling. The "compelling interest test," when properly applied by the court, can carve out an exemption for the home schooler from the particular burdensome requirement. However, many courts try to circumvent this test by applying the wrong test.

Nonetheless, since every court is inclined differently, home schools need to continue to raise the Free Exercise defense with the hope that the Court will properly grant a religious exemption.

Notes

1. *Parham* v. J.R., 442 U.S. 584 (1979), 602-603.
2. For a much more in-depth and thorough look at our parental and constitutional rights in regard to home schooling you may want to obtain my book: *A Guide to the Law on Parents' Rights in Education*, (Durham, N.C.: Carolina Academic Press, 1998) available at HSLDA online at *www.hslda.org.*
3. *Abington* v. *Schempp*, 374 U.S. 203, at 238 Note 7.
4. *Ibid*, 26-29. For example, in 1647, the Massachusetts General Court passed the "Old Deluder Act" that required towns to maintain schools. The object was the defeat of "one chief project of that old deluder, satan, to keep men from the knowledge of the Scriptures." Therefore, the primary goal of education, as defined in the act, was to instruct the child so he could comprehend the Scripture. Although towns had to maintain schools, parents had the ultimate choice of how their children would be educated. [See the Laws and Liberties of Massachusetts, 1648 ed. (Cambridge, 1929), 47.]

5. *Schempp,* 374 U.S. 203, at 238. Even the public schools in existence during the early 1800s were locally controlled and nearly identical to the instruction found in private schools. Thomas Jefferson, as president of the Washington D.C. School Board, established the Bible and the Watts Hymnal as the principal books to be used for reading by the public school students. J.0. Wilson, *Public Schools of Washington* (Columbia Historical Society, 1897), 4. Attendance at these few common schools was completely voluntary.

6. Constitutional scholar, John Whitehead, in his book *Parents' Rights* (Westchester, Ill.: Crossway Books, 1985), 85, explains the Christian foundation of common law:
"Essentially, the common law is an age-old doctrine that developed by way of court decisions which applied the principles of Christianity to everyday situations. Out of these cases, rules were established that governed future cases. This principle, with its origin in Europe…became part of American law."
Whitehead, in the same passage, also quotes law professor John C. H. Wu who stated: "…There can be no denying that the common law has one advantage over the legal system of any country: it was Christian from the very beginning of its history ."

7. Blackstone, *Blackstone's Commentaries,* Vol. II (New York: Augustus Kelley, 1969), 450.

8. *Ibid.,* 450.

9. *Thompson,* 103 P. 578, 24 L.R.A. 221, 24 Okla. 1. (1909).

10. *Thompson,* 24 Okla., 4.

11. *Thompson,* 9.

12. *Thompson,* 8. Lewis' Blackstone, book 1, §451.

13. *Meyer v. Nebraska,* 262 U.S. 390 (1923).

14. See *Pierce v. Society of Sisters,* 268 U.S. 510, 534-35 (1925) and *Wisconsin v. Yoder,* 406 U.S. 205, 232 (1972).

15. *Wisconsin v. Yoder,* 406 U.S. at 221 and *Plyler v. Doe,* 457 U.S. 202, 221 (1982).

16. 262 U.S. 390 (1923).

17. *Ibid.,* 402.

18. *Ibid.,* 401. Also see *Bartles v. Iowa,* 262 U.S. 404 (1923) where the Court reached a similar conclusion.

19 John Whitehead, *Journal of Christian Jurisprudence,* Oklahoma City, Oklahoma: IED Press Inc., 1982, 63.

20. *Pierce,* 268 U.S. 510 (1925).

21. *Ibid.,* 534.

22. *Pierce,* 268 U.S. 510, 535.

23. In *Windsor Park Baptist Church v. Arkansas Activities Association,* (658 F.2d 618 [1981] at 621), the U.S. Court of Appeals cautioned the State of Arkansas not to standardize its children by forcing them to accept instruction from public teachers only. The Court states: "The Fourteenth Amendment forbids the States to prohibit attendance at nonpublic schools, either secular or religious." *Windsor,* 621. In other words, the state must be careful not to overly regulate home schools and Christian schools to the extent that they cannot operate, thereby forcing their children to attend only public schools.

24. *Yoder,* 406 U.S. 205, 233.

25. *Ibid.,* 232. Burger admonishes further, "And when the interests of parenthood are combined with a free exercise claim of the nature revealed by this record, more than merely a 'reasonable relation to some purpose within the competency of the State' is required to sustain the validity of the State's requirement under the First Amendment" *(Yoder,* 233).

26. *Ibid.,* 214.

27. *Employment Division of Oregon v. Smith,* 494 U.S. 872 (1990).

28. *Ibid.,* 881.

29. The U.S. Supreme Court has regularly applied the "compelling interest test" to fundamental rights that arise out of the Liberty Clause of the Fourteenth Amendment. In *Roe v. Wade,* 410 U.S. 113, 155 (1973), the Court said:
"Where fundamental rights are involved…regulation limiting these rights may be justified *only* by a *compelling state interest.*"

30. *Ibid.,* 881, ftn.1.

31. Dr. Brian Ray, "A Nationwide Study of Home Education," November 16, 1990, National Home Education Research Institute, Seattle, Washington. This study of over two thousand home school families found that 93.8 percent of the fathers and 96.4 percent of the mothers describe themselves as "born-again" Christians.

32. See *Wisconsin v. Yoder*, 406 U.S.205, (1972) and *Sherbert v. Verner*, 374 U.S. 398, (1963).

33. See *Wisconsin v. Yoder*, 406 U.S.205, 233 (1972).

34. 374 U.S. 398 (1963).

35. 406 U.S. 205 (1972).

36. 450 U.S. 707 (1981).

37. 455 U.S. 252, (1982).

38. 480 U.S. —, 94 L.Ed.2d 190, 197-198 (1987).

39. *Yoder*, 406 U.S., 216-19.

40. *Yoder*, 406 U.S., 215-19; *Thomas*, 450 U.S. at 713-16.

41. *Lee, op. cit.*, 455 U.S., 257.

42. *Thomas, op. cit.*, 450 U.S., 718.

43. *Yoder, op. cit.*, 221, *Plyler v. Doe*, 457 U.S. 202, 221 (1982) and *New Life, op. cit., 317-318.*

44. My book, *The Right To Home School; A Guide To The Law On Parents' Rights In Education* is published and available from Carolina Academic Press, 700 Kent St., Durham, NC 27701, 919-489-7486 or www.hslda.org

45. *DeJonge*, 179 Mich. App. 225, 449 N.W. 2d 899 (1989).

46. Main, #86 JV 10, District Court Gunnison County, Colorado, May 6, 1987. See "Approval States Cause Trouble," *The Home School Court Report*, Vol. 3, No.2, March/June 1987, 14.

47. *Ibid.*, 3.

48. *Jeffery*, 702 F.Supp. 516 (M.D.A 1988).

49. *Ibid.*, 519 and 521.

17

An Example of
God's Faithfulness:

The Miracle of the DeJonge Case

"Consider it all joy, my brethren, when you encounter various trials, knowing that the testing of your faith produces endurance. And let endurance have its perfect result, that you may be perfect and complete, lacking in nothing."

James 1:2-4

For many years in Michigan, home schoolers faced intense persecution under the restrictive teacher certification law and the hostile Department of Education. In fact, since 1985, I handled scores of successful cases on behalf of member families who were prosecuted by the state each year. In spite of these victories, two 1985 cases, *People v. DeJonge* and *People v. Bennett,* which Mike Farris and I handled, were met with defeat after defeat at every level of appeal. On May 25, 1993, all this changed.

After eight long years of litigation, the DeJonge family and the Bennetts were vindicated by the Michigan Supreme Court which agreed with our arguments and reversed both cases in a 4-3 decision. This resulted in the overturning of the criminal convictions of both families.

This ruling in the *DeJonge* case essentially grants a statewide religious exemption from teacher certification for all parents who are opposed to this requirement on religious grounds. The decision relies heavily on the original intent of the framers, and constitutes virtually the most significant state religious freedom case in the last twenty years. The opinion could easily have been written by James Madison himself since it frequently appeals to the framers and to the *Federalist Papers*. The Michigan Supreme Court held on page 129 of the decision:

> We hold that the teacher certification requirement is an unconstitutional violation of the Free Exercise Clause of the First Amendment as applied to families whose religious convictions prohibit the use of certified instructors. Such families, therefore, are exempt from the dictates of the teacher certification requirement.

Background of the Case

The case began in 1985 when Mark and Chris DeJonge decided to home school their children. When they were contacted by the local school district, they were told that in order to legally home school, they had to use a certified teacher or be certified themselves. Because of their strong religious convictions that God had called them to home school their children and because they believed it was a sin to be certified, the family informed the school district that they could not comply with the teacher certification requirement. As a consequence, the family was charged with criminal truancy.

Dave Kallman, an attorney in Lansing, was secured by the Home School Legal Defense Association to handle the trial. During the trial the trial judge explained that he was impressed with the "very, very favorable report of the education of the children." He also found the DeJonges' religious beliefs to be sincere.

Nevertheless, the DeJonges were convicted and sentenced to two years' probation for instructing their children without state certified teachers. They were fined $200.00, required to test their children for academic achievement, and ordered to arrange for certified instruction. At this point, I handled the case on appeal before the circuit court, court of appeals (three times) and on to the Michigan Supreme

Court. The circuit court affirmed the decision along with three separate opinions by the court of appeals. After eight long years, the Michigan Supreme Court finally agreed to hear the case, and it was argued in November 1992. During this entire time, the DeJonges kept home schooling without a certified teacher since we acquired a "stay" on the sentence while on appeal.

Original Intent of the Framers

As stated earlier, the benefit of the Michigan Supreme Court's reversal of the DeJonges' case is felt not only by the DeJonge family but by every single family in the state of Michigan who objects to teacher certification based on religious grounds. This ruling quickly changes Michigan from the worst state in the country for home schooling to one of the best states. Of course, the practical effects of *DeJonge* for home school families in Michigan is not the only benefit. The case is significant since the Court spent 39 pages carefully explaining the original intent of the framers concerning religious freedom and correctly implying the "compelling interest test" which has been so frequently misapplied by other courts in the country.

In *DeJonge*, the Michigan Supreme Court began by analyzing the "historical underpinnings of the First Amendment." The Court further stated:

> This Court has long held that the Constitution must be interpreted in light of the original intent and understanding of its drafters.... These rules of constitutional construction are indispensable because the literal construction of the words without regard to their obvious purpose of protection is to make the constitutional safeguard no more than a shabby hoax, a barrier of words, easily destroyed by other words.... The Constitutional limitation must be construed to effectuate, not to abolish, the protection sought by it to be afforded.[1]

So that it is not misunderstood, the Court explained, "Adherence to the original intent is crucial to insure that courts do not substitute their own pleasure to the constitutional intentions of the people." This was a quote from Alexander Hamilton in *The Federalist Papers*.[2]

The Michigan Supreme Court emphasized that religious liberty is the "first freedom," and that this religious liberty must be diligently protected by the government. The Court stated, "As our history forcefully attests, the founding fathers envisioned the protection of the free exercise of religion as an affirmative duty of the government, mandated by the inherent nature of religious liberty, not one of mere toleration by government."[3] In fact, the Court quotes Jefferson who held that "religious liberty is a fundamental freedom outside the legitimate sphere of government power unless threatening to harm another."[4] This high regard for religious liberty is evidenced further in the *DeJonge* decision by the Court's statement: "The founders understood that zealous protection of religious liberty was essential to the preservation of free government."[5] In fact, the Court even implied that the Michigan Constitution affords "additional protection to the free exercise of religion" above and beyond the U.S. Constitution.[6]

Furthermore, the Court quoted the U.S. Supreme Court,

> Freedom of worship is not limited to things that do not matter much. That would be a mere shadow of freedom, the test of its substance is the right to differ as to the things that touch the heart of the existing order. (*West Virginia Board of Education v. Barnette,* 319 U.S. 624, 638, 642)[7]

The Proper Application of the "Compelling Interest Test"

Whenever the fundamental freedom of religious liberty is combined with another fundamental right, such as the right of parents to educate their children, a special test must be applied in order to see if the state's regulation will override the individual's free exercise of religious beliefs. As stated above, many courts misapply this test and always find in favor of the state regulation against the religious claimant. However in *DeJonge,* the Court properly applies the four-point test.

First of all, the DeJonges had to prove that they had a sincere religious belief that made them opposed to being certified or using a certified teacher. Secondly, the DeJonges had to prove that their religious beliefs concerning opposition to teacher certification were burdened by the state's requirement. The Michigan Supreme Court found that the DeJonges easily met both of these parts of the "compelling interest test." The Court stated:

As noted, the DeJonges believe that the Word of God commands them to educate their children without state certification. Any regulation interfering with that commandment is state regulation of religion. The certification requirement imposes upon the DeJonges a loathsome dilemma: they must either violate the law of God to abide by the law of man or commit a crime under the law of man to remain faithful to God. The requirement presents a irreconcilable conflict between the mandates of law and religious duty...[8]

According to the U.S. Supreme Court, the second two parts of the "compelling interest test" must be proven with evidence by the prosecution. In the instance of the DeJonges' case, at no time had the State proven these two parts of the test. They did not prove that teacher certification is essential for children to be educated, nor did they prove that teacher certification was the least restrictive means of fulfilling the state's interest that children be educated. Although I pointed this out to the Court of Appeals, the Court of Appeals refused to reverse the decision.

However in *DeJonge,* the Michigan Supreme Court carefully applied this complete "compelling interest test." The Court did not give lip service to the test as did the Court of Appeals and then misapply it. The Supreme Court stated that although education is important:

> Nevertheless our rights are meaningless if they do not permit an individual to challenge and be free from those abridgements of liberty that are otherwise vital to society: freedom of worship...is not limited to things that do not matter much. That would be a mere shadow of freedom. The test of its substance is the right to differ as to the things that touch the heart of the existing order.[9]

In other words, the Michigan Supreme Court was stating that religious freedom does not always automatically lose in face of a conflicting state regulation. To cause it to always lose would render our freedom to freely exercise our religious belief meaningless.

Regarding Michigan's compelling interest in teacher certification, the Court found the state did not prove any compelling interest. The only "compelling interest" the state proved was its interest in education generally. However, the state's interest in education is being fulfilled by the DeJonges successfully home schooling their children. The court ruled:

> Indeed such a searching examination in the instant case is enlightening because it reveals that the state has focused upon the incorrect governmental interest. The state's interest is not ensuring that the goals of compulsory education is met, because the state does not contest that the DeJonges are succeeding at fulfilling such aims. Rather, the state's interest is simply the certification requirement... not the general objectives of compulsory education. The interest the state pursues is the manner of education, not its goals.
>
> Hence, the state's narrow interest in maintaining the certification requirement must be weighed against the DeJonges fundamental right of the Free Exercise of Religion.[10]

The Court emphasized further, "Hence, Michigan's interest in compulsory education is not absolute and must yield to the constitutional liberties protected by the First Amendment."[11] This decision is refreshing in light of the fact that many other state supreme courts have stated that in the reverse. These courts have said that the individuals' free exercise rights are not absolute and must yield to the states' interests in compulsory education. These other states have it backwards.

The court also held that the religious home school family does not have the burden of proving that alternatives exist. It is the state's burden. The court explained:

> Furthermore, the Court of Appeals erroneously placed the burden of proof upon the DeJonges. The Court of Appeals, by requiring that the individual burdened by governmental regulation prove that alternatives exist, while at the same time accepting at face value unsubstantiated assertions by the state, has turned constitutional jurisprudence on its head. Our citizens need not "propose an alternative" to be afforded their constitutional liberties. Lee, Supra, 455 U.S. 257-258...Yoder, Supra, 406 U.S. 233-234.... We are persuaded that the burden of proof

correctly placed in the instant case is fatal to the state's certification requirement.[12]

The Michigan Supreme Court emphasized, "The state, therefore, must establish that enforcing the certification requirement, without exception, is *essential* to insure the education required by the compulsory education law."[13] The Court found that the state had failed to "provide one scintilla of evidence that the DeJonge children have suffered for the want of certified teachers."[14] The Court properly found that the DeJonges were satisfying the state's interest since their children were being educated. Since they were educating without certified teachers, it was clear that teacher certification is not essential. The Michigan Supreme Court relied further on HSLDA's research which was supplied in our brief which demonstrated that Michigan was the last state still to require teacher certification of home schoolers. All other states had changed or abandoned their teacher certification laws.

In regards to the failure of the state to prove in the Court of Appeals' decision that teacher certification was essential, the Court said:

> The Court of Appeals asserted that the teacher certification requirement is a backbone in the protection of state education.... The State's sweeping assertion must be turned aside when it is not supported by evidence. The State's contention is particularly suspect when no other state has such a backbone. To find that, of all the states in the Union, only Michigan meets the aims of compulsory education is untenable and flies in the face of the aforementioned studies.

The Supreme Court relied on studies supplied by HSLDA in order to understand that teacher certification is not essential in order for children to be educated. One study specifically cited in the decision by the Supreme Court is a study by Dr. Brian Ray of the National Home Education Research Institute. Dr. Ray found that there is no positive correlation between the student's performance and the teacher's qualifications. The Michigan Supreme Court made it obvious throughout their decision that the state did not prove that teacher certification was essential in order for children to be educated, nor was it the least restrictive means. In fact, the evidence of the other states and the various studies directly contradict this assertion.

The Court concluded by stating:

> We believe that the DeJonges are the best judges of which regulations are the most burdensome and least intrusive upon their religion. To entertain the notion that either this Court or the state has the insight to interpret the DeJonges' religion more correctly than they is simply an arrogant pretension.[15]

The Court also summarized its decision:

> In summary, we conclude that the historical underpinnings of the First Amendment to the U.S. Constitution and the case law in support of it compels the conclusion that the imposition of the certification requirement upon the DeJonges violates the Free Exercise Clause. We so conclude because we find that the certification requirement is not essential to nor is it the least restrictive means of achieving the state's claimed interest. Thus, we reaffirm that sphere of inviable conscience and belief which is the mark of a free people. We hold that the teacher certification requirement is an unconstitutional violation of the Free Exercise Clause of the First Amendment as applied to families whose religious convictions prohibit the use of certified instructors. Such families, therefore, are exempt from the dictates of the teacher certification requirements.[16]

Needless to say, this decision specifically protects religious home schoolers in Michigan who are opposed to teacher certification requirements. These families are fully exempt. Meanwhile, the religious liberty argument and its appeal to the original intent of the framers is a far-reaching case that other supreme courts throughout the United States can use in coming to similar conclusions in religious liberty cases.

The Miracle

The results of the *DeJonge* case are truly a miracle. In fact, I was informed the day before the decision that one of the Michigan

Supreme Court justices, who had earlier announced he would rule with the three justices who were pro-teacher certification, changed his vote. When asked why by the Chief Justice, he simply replied, "I don't know." This fourth justice then joined with the other three justices, giving the home schoolers the victory. This is due only to God's moving on the minds and hearts of the justices to do His will. As the Bible says, "The kings's heart is like channels of water in the hand of the Lord: He turns it wherever He wishes" (Proverbs 21:1). Certainly He deserves all the glory.

The Bennett Case

The ruling in the *People v. Bennett* case is also very helpful for the state of Michigan since it guarantees a statutory due process right to all home schoolers which previously had been completely ignored by the state. I had argued over and over again before the local school districts and before the various courts in the *Bennett* case that home schoolers are entitled to administrative hearings as guaranteed by the statute before any criminal charges could be brought. Although many lower courts accepted this reasoning, the Court of Appeals stubbornly refused to recognize this due process right of home schoolers. The Michigan Supreme Court, however, reversed *Bennett,* stating that before any home schooler can be criminally prosecuted, the state superintendent must first hold an administrative hearing. A home school is a legal school until an administrative hearing proves it is not in compliance with the law. Home schoolers have the right to appeal this ruling to the Circuit Court and to the Court of Appeals. These hearings will be nearly impossible for the state to use to stop home schoolers since it does not have the resources or the manpower to conduct these all around the state and, since appeals of the administrative hearing can tie up these cases for years.

In *Bennett,* the Michigan Supreme Court reversed this circular reasoning of the Court of Appeals and held:

> It does not make sense that the Court of Appeals itself...applied the Private and Parochial School Act criteria in order to say the defendants had no school, and then told defense that because they were not a school, they were not entitled to the Act's hearing provisions. In fact, they are a school until a hearing produces a determination to the contrary.

The Court further stated that the Department of Education has no authority to approve home schools, but only disapprove them after holding an administrative hearing. Essentially, the *Bennett* case is key since their criminal convictions were reversed as a result of no administrative hearing being held by the state superintendent. This case is vital in protecting the due process rights of home schoolers in Michigan.

By God's grace, these cases comprise a clear vindication of parents' rights to home school in the state of Michigan. These cases also demonstrate God's perfect timing. Although the families and I were repeatedly discouraged by eight years of losses, God intended this case to be ruled on by the highest court in the state of Michigan. If we had won at the trial court like we should have, the cases would only have helped the DeJonges and the Bennetts. Now the cases, by God's grace, protect all home schoolers in the state of Michigan. Praise God for His mercy!

Notes

1. *Michigan v. DeJonge*, 501 N.W. 2d. 127, At 132 (Mich. 1993).
2. *Ibid.*, at 152.
3. *Ibid.*, at 133.
4. *Ibid.*, at 133, Ft 19.
5. *Ibid.*, at 133-35.
6. *Ibid.*, at 134, Ft 27.
7. *Ibid.*, at 139.
8. *Ibid.*, at 137.
9. *Ibid.*, at 139.
10. *Ibid.*, at 139.
11. *Ibid.*
12. *Ibid.*, at 143.
13. *Ibid.*, at 140.
14. *Ibid.*
15. *Ibid.*, at 143.
16. *Ibid.*, at 144.

Hast not thou made an
hedge about him, and
about his house?

—Job 1:10

18

Other Ways to Victory in the Courtroom

"Education ought everywhere to be religious education...parents are bound to employ no instructors who will not instruct their children religiously, To commit our children to the care of irreligious persons is to commit lambs to the superintendency of wolves."

Timothy Dwight, President of Yale, 1795-1817

There are many ways that home schoolers can win in court or avoid court altogether. In this chapter, I will summarize several major defenses of home schoolers which are either based in the rights guaranteed by the Constitution or in the rights guaranteed by state statute.

Technical Defenses of Home Schoolers

Many times we have found that the most successful cases for home schoolers have involved technicalities. For instance, in North Dakota there were a number of occasions where we were able to win cases on behalf of home schoolers who were charged with criminal truancy because the prosecution was not able to prove a very important element of the crime—that the child involved was actually of school age. The Nelson family of Sargent County was charged with criminal truancy since they did not use a certified teacher during the 1988-89 school year. Although the prosecutor made several attempts to introduce evidence to prove the age of the child, I objected to these on procedural grounds. The Court sustained the objections and granted my motion to dismiss the case since the prosecution wasn't able to prove the child was of actual school age![1]

In another situation, God enabled us to successfully win a major victory before the Iowa Supreme Court, based on a mere technicality. In Iowa in 1987, home schoolers had to be certified in order to teach their children at home. The Trucke family was charged in September with criminal truancy. We appealed the case to the Iowa Supreme Court, arguing that teacher certification was unconstitutional. After we submitted our briefs, the Iowa Supreme Court contacted our office. They requested that we submit a supplemental brief concerning the issue that possibly the criminal charges were brought prematurely. In Iowa, children only needed to attend school 120 days, so the court was hinting that a family could have hired a certified teacher later in the school year and still have completed 120 days in compliance with the law. Mike Farris from our office prepared the brief, arguing this point, explaining that the charges were brought prematurely since the family could conceivably have secured a certified teacher in May of that school year and crammed in 120 days of instruction until the end of August when the school year officially ends. The Iowa Supreme Court, as a result, reversed the criminal conviction of the Trucke family and held that the criminal charges were in fact premature. After that decision, for the next several years, school districts did not have any idea of when to file criminal charges against home schoolers, so they didn't![2] This decision protected home schoolers until favorable legislation was enacted a few years later. We cannot claim victory for this case because God alone made the Iowa Supreme Court give us the winning argument!

I will recount one more instance in which a technicality won the day. In the state of Alabama, some school districts periodically attempt to require home schoolers to be certified tutors in order to operate legally. In Fort Payne City, the Johnson family was taken to court since they were not using a certified teacher. In preparing for the case, I discovered that the family lived 1,000 feet outside the city limits of Fort Payne City. I immediately filed a motion to dismiss the Johnson case with the DeKalb County court, based on "lack of jurisdiction." One of the elements of the "crime of home schooling" is that the child has to reside within the boundaries of the school district. The school board attorney was frustrated and hired a surveying team to determine if the family was in fact outside the school district. The surveying team confirmed what we already knew, that the family lived outside the school district. As a result, the motion to dismiss was granted, based on the "One Thousand Foot Rule" in Alabama![3] God works in many diverse ways!

There are many ways for home schoolers to win their cases. Each case must be dealt with in a thorough manner with all potential defenses thoroughly checked. Oftentimes courts will be very favorable towards arguments that raise technicalities.

When many of the compulsory attendance laws were enacted in the early 1900s, home schooling was ignored. In other words, the laws required children between certain ages to attend either public or private school, but no exemption was provided for home schools. When home schoolers in those states tried to operate as private schools, they were prosecuted. However, some of the state courts, as discussed below, properly ruled that since a private school is a "place of learning," a home school could freely operate as a private school and, therefore, legally satisfy the law.

In several of the other states which did not have a home school alternative, the courts followed a different course. They ruled that the compulsory attendance statutes were "void for vagueness" and, subsequently struck down the laws as unconstitutional. These decisions fall into two categories: 1) the definition of the term "private school" was determined by the courts to be unconstitutionally vague, as in Wisconsin,[4] Georgia,[5] and California, 2) some other language in the law such as the term "equivalent instruction" or "properly qualified" was found by the courts to be vague, as in Minnesota,[6] Pennsylvania,[7] Missouri,[8] and Iowa.[9]

Since there are many states which remain where there is no specific home school law, the question arises, "How can someone spot a vague law?"

Identification of a Vague Law

The simplest way to identify a vague law is: 1) after you have read the law you still do not know what you are supposed to do to be a legal home school, or 2) the local school district arbitrarily creates requirements out of "thin air."

Therefore, a vague compulsory attendance law is one in which the local school district or school official is given virtually unlimited discretion to define key terms in the law or generally has the freedom to "legislate" his own home school policy.

For instance, in Pennsylvania before the *Jeffery* decision, 501 different superintendents were given authority, by the law, to determine if home school instruction was "satisfactory." Nearly each of the 501 school districts had different restrictions on home schoolers covering virtually every kind of requirement imaginable. Depending on the particular superintendent in power at a given time, or what school district a family lived in, home schools were either prosecuted or left alone. Many home schoolers had to flee from one school district where home schooling was never "satisfactory" to another school district were home schooling was at least tolerated. In 1988, as the lawyer covering Pennsylvania, I was handling nearly twenty home school cases in court and negotiating on behalf of approximately thirty other families who were being threatened with prosecution. Families were completely confused, and the school districts operated as their own legislatures, regularly adopting new restrictions on home schoolers.

Other states, like Missouri prior to the *Ellis* decision, required instruction to be "equivalent." Similarly, each superintendent arbitrarily created, according to his own whim, a definition of "equivalent." In many school districts it was impossible for a home schooler to satisfy the superintendent's arbitrary definition of equivalent instruction.

Fortunately, the United States Supreme Court has dealt with this issue on numerous occasions and has set clear guidelines for determining whether a statute is unconstitutionally vague under the Due Process Clause of the Constitution.[10] The Court stated:

1. A law is vague if persons of average intelligence, such as home school parents, are not put on notice as to what is required or what is forbidden. Furthermore, "persons of common intelligence must not be left to guess at the meaning of a statute nor differ as to its application."[11] For example, in Pennsylvania prior to 1989, home schoolers were required by law to be "properly qualified," but neither the home schoolers nor the superintendents knew what that meant. Many home school families stayed "underground" (did not notify the school district) because they did not know if the superintendent would interpret "properly qualified" to mean certified, a college degree, high school diploma, or something else.

2. A law is vague if arbitrary and discriminatory enforcement is permitted. In other words, if a superintendent, under the law, is free to discriminate against home schoolers and create his own arbitrary standards for home schoolers, the law is too vague, lacking the necessary explicit standards. In addition, courts have consistently held that a law is vague if the officials charged with enforcement and application of the law are permitted to resolve questions "on an ad hoc and subjective basis." In short, the fundamental right of parents to home school cannot be denied by the enforcement of a vague law which authorizes such a denial purely on the whim of a superintendent or other school official.

The Landmark U.S. Supreme Court which Defined Vagueness

In a landmark case, the U.S. Supreme Court summarized its doctrine on vagueness in *Grayned v. City of Rockford.*[12] In that case the Court said:

> It is a basic principle of due process that an enactment is void for vagueness if its prohibitions are not clearly defined. Vague laws offend several important values. First, because we assume that man is free to steer between lawful and unlawful conduct, we insist that laws give the person of ordinary intelligence a reasonable opportunity to know what is prohibited, so that he may act accordingly. Vague laws may trap the innocent by not providing fair warning. Second, if arbitrary and discriminatory enforcement is to be prevented, laws must provide explicit standards for those who apply them. A vague law impermissibly delegates basic policy matters to policemen, judges and juries for resolution on an ad hoc basis, with the attendant dangers of arbitrary and discriminatory application. Third, but related, where a statute "abut[s] upon sensitive First Amendment freedoms, it 'operates to inhibit the exercise of those freedoms.' Uncertain meanings inevitably lead citizens to 'steer far wider of the unlawful zone'...than if the boundaries of the forbidden areas were clearly marked."[13]

Oftentimes, the problem with state compulsory attendance laws is that the "language [is] so loose as to leave those who have to apply it too wide a discretion," resulting in the arbitrary denial of parental rights in education. Many of these types of vague laws yield discriminatory results: (1) dozens of differing definitions of teacher qualifications, (2) various monitoring procedures such as home visits by school officials, (3) all types, times, and places of student testing, (4) variety of progress reports, and (5) arbitrary periodic meetings.

In many instances, these statutes allow the opinion of the superintendent to control a decision as to whether parents will be allowed to exercise the fundamental Constitutional rights of directing the upbringing of their children and the free exercise of their religion, as guaranteed by the First and Fourteenth Amendments of the U.S. Constitution.

For example, in Pennsylvania, as mentioned above, home schoolers were faced with constant harassment by their local school districts. The law gave the superintendent the power to define if a home school parent was "properly qualified" and whether or not their curriculum was "satisfactory." Since there were 501 school districts, each with its own definition of these terms, the application of this vague law often led to absurd results.

One of the most ridiculous examples involved a member family of HSLDA, the Smeltzers, whose child was designated as having various learning disabilities and in need of special education. For some reason, the superintendent allowed the family to home school for three years. At the end of the third year, the child did so well on her standardized achievement tests, that the superintendent labeled her "gifted and talented." However, he and his specialists also determined that the family could no longer handle her education because she was now gifted. He, therefore, disapproved their home school and demanded that the child be sent to the public schools. When the family refused, he filed criminal truancy charges against the family.

The family called me, and I immediately called the school district, but they would not relent. Michael Farris of HSLDA then prepared a civil rights complaint asserting the family's Constitutional rights, explaining that the superintendent was personally liable for violating their civil rights. A copy of the complaint was sent to the school board's lawyer. By the next day, the school district called and said that they had made a mistake. The Smeltzer's home school program was approved, and the charges dropped, before it was necessary to file the civil rights complaint with the court![14]

Since more and more "brush fires" started across the state with home schoolers being dragged into court, HSLDA filed a civil rights case, *Jeffery v. O'Donnell,*[15] suing school districts throughout the state for trying to enforce a vague statute. This got the attention of the school districts, and some instantly changed their policy and quickly "approved" the home schoolers. These school districts were subsequently dismissed from the suit.

By God's grace, the Federal Court finally ruled in our favor. The federal court declared:

> Disparity abounds [in Pennsylvania]. What can be satisfactory in one school district could be totally unsatisfactory in another. The ultimate conclusion one must reach concerning tutorial education in Pennsylvania is that...the law providing for such an education is unconstitutionally vague...A person of ordinary intelligence cannot reasonably steer between the lawful and the unlawful to avoid criminal prosecution. There exists no standard for determining who is a qualified tutor or what is a satisfactory curriculum in any district. Superintendents of school districts, while exercising a legitimate and constitutional function of managing their districts according to the unique character of each district, nevertheless make their decisions on an ad *hoc* basis which can result in the dangers of arbitrary and discriminatory application...The threat to sensitive First Amendment freedoms mandates judicial intrusion in the form of declaring the particular provision of the law unconstitutional for vagueness.[16]

The court declared the law to be unconstitutionally vague, as applied to home schoolers, and the final result was that the legislature was forced to rewrite the law to specifically protect home schooling, eliminating the school districts' discretionary powers in approving or disapproving home schools.

In fact, the cases in Missouri, Minnesota, Georgia, and Wisconsin, mentioned above, all resulted in their respective legislatures enacting favorable laws, tremendously reducing the conflict between home schoolers and the state. Without the courts striking down the laws relating to home schooling, the new laws, which provided greater freedoms for home schoolers, would never have been passed.

Vagueness Is One of the Most Successful Defenses

Vagueness has continued to be one of the most successful defenses of home schoolers who live in states without specific home school laws. In fact, in June 1991 in Michigan, one of the most difficult states in which to home school, a home school mother had been arrested, fingerprinted, had "mug shots" taken, and was charged with criminal truancy. I, along with our local counsel Dave Kallman, filed a "motion to dismiss" in this case, *People v. Pebler*.[17] During oral arguments, the prosecutor admitted that he did not know what the law required for home schoolers. In fact, he said that although he did not know what the law required, he was sure this home schooling mom was not legal. I capitalized on his statements during my time for rebuttal, and the court ruled in favor of the home schooler. The court dismissed the case and found the Michigan compulsory attendance law "vague and unclear as to what specifically constitutes a violation of that act subjecting a person to criminal prosecution and Laurel Pebler is entitled to fair notice of what conduct is proscribed by the statute."[18] I used this case throughout the state to get other cases dismissed or prevented altogether.

Legislation which gives any amount of arbitrary discretion over home schoolers to the public school system should be opposed to avoid this kind of discriminatory treatment. States that have vague laws at present should be carefully monitored and possibly challenged, if the law is being used to harass home schoolers.

The Private School Defense: A School Is a Place of Learning

Before home school statutes began being passed in the 1980s, most compulsory attendance laws required children to attend either public school or private school. In some states, the only other alternative was for a child to be instructed by a state-certified teacher. No specific statutory option existed for home schools. In at least twelve states, home schools can still only exist as a private school. All of these states are listed below and further discussed in chapter 20.

As a result, home school families who were home schooling based on their religious convictions as guaranteed by the First Amendment, or on their parental rights as guaranteed by the Fourteenth Amendment, were forced to qualify as a private school or, in some instances, become certified to teach as a "private tutor." Qualifying as a public school, of course, was impossible.

The rationale is simple. The right of parents to teach their children at home is a constitutional right guaranteed by the First and Fourteenth Amendments. Therefore, to outlaw home schooling altogether would be a violation of a family's constitutional rights. Since teacher certification (under the tutor option) is an overly restrictive requirement which basically prohibits families from home schooling, operating as a private school is the only option which remains. In states without specific home school laws, home schools need to be able to operate as a private schools, in order for the state to fulfill its duty to adequately protect the parents' constitutional right to teach their own children. Besides, the purpose of the compulsory attendance laws is to have children educated, and that is what home schooling, operating under the private school status, is accomplishing.

Consequently, many of these types of cases have appeared throughout the country, as home school families defend their right to exist as private schools or, in some instances, their right to exist as a "satellite" of an existing private school, I refer to this defense as the "private school defense." Much precedent has already been set, and most of that precedent favors the home schools' right to legally operate as private schools.

Home schools or groups of home schoolers are still successfully operating as private schools in many states, including Alaska, Alabama, California, Delaware, Florida, Illinois, Indiana, Kansas, Kentucky, Maine, Nebraska, and Texas. It is generally to the advantage of home schools to operate under the private school laws since private schools in these states have little to no regulations.

Home Schools Operating as Private Schools Can Face Conflict

Even though I am convinced that it is legal to home school as a private school in these states, I constantly have to deal with school districts throughout many of these states who challenge the right of home schoolers to exist as private schools. For instance, in a small Texas town, a home school family was asked to come to the office of a probation officer, just for a friendly talk on home schooling. When the home school father arrived, the local judge was in the office and proceeded to intimidate him. He flatly declared, "We don't allow home schooling in this town." He did not care if the family met all the private school requirements or not. In fact, he gave the family one week to send their children to public school.[19] After threatening a civil rights suit, I was finally able to persuade the school district to leave the family alone.

In Alabama, home schools are routinely threatened with prosecution, even though they are legally operating as church schools. On one occasion, I was called by a family who was threatened to be arrested that day by a truant officer. When I called that same day, I was told that the officer went to meet with the local judge. I called the number that was given to me, and the judge answered. He stated that when this family would be taken before him in court, he would find them guilty! He said that home schoolers were a bunch of illiterates. When I told him that they had a constitutional right to freely exercise their religious beliefs to teach their own children, he asked me, "What asylum did they escape out of?" By God's grace, the situation was resolved.

In DeKalb county in Alabama, Randy Maas, a home school father, was approached by a truant officer and told to put his children in public school. When he said that he was legally home schooling and refused to enroll his children in public school, the truant officer came back two hours later with a police officer who arrested and handcuffed the father and put him in jail overnight. Even though I explained to the prosecutor that the statute and the Alabama Supreme Court require three days' written notice of truancy before he can be charged, the prosecutor and the judge ignored the statute and precedents and convicted the home school father. I appealed this blatant travesty of justice to the Alabama Criminal Court of Criminal Appeals, and on May 15, 1992, the Court reversed the decision in the *Maas* case and found that the family's statutory due process rights were violated.[20]

In Kansas, home schools operating as private schools are routinely turned over to the Social Rehabilitative Services for investigation.[21] I have talked with nearly a hundred of these SRS agents over the years, and they vary in aggressiveness. Although some insist on inspecting the homes and interrogating the children, we have refused such an invasion of privacy. Furthermore, if a home school family inquires about the legality of home schooling in Kansas, the Department of Education sends them a copy of a memorandum by the Kansas Legislative Research Department which states:

> Is home instruction permitted in Kansas as an alternative to attendance at public schools? Is home instruction, in essence, the same thing as a private, denominational, or parochial school? The answer to both of these questions is "no."[22]

In other words, as far as the state is officially concerned, home schooling is illegal. As a result, some prosecutors have told me that home schooling is illegal and have taken HSLDA families to court. One example involved the Melrose family in Kingman County in Kansas. The local principal did not like home schooling and believed that they had to be state accredited. He convinced the prosecutor to bring charges. After I negotiated with the prosecutor and wrote him a lengthy legal letter explaining the legality of a home school to operate as a non-accredited private school, he agreed to dismiss the case.[23]

In Michigan, in the 1990-1991 school year, I was involved in representing twelve families throughout the state who were prosecuted for establishing home schools even though courts have recognized the right of home schools to operate as private schools. Although we were able to win all of these cases, the families had to put up with much harassment.[24]

Of course, the situations are nearly endless, but the majority of home schoolers in these states are still being left alone. However, it is important to be aware of your rights and to be familiar with the "private school defense."

The Meaning of the Word "School"

As can be imagined, the major contention between the home schools and the state was, and continues to be, in some states, "what is the actual definition of a private school?" Since nearly every state did not define the term "private school" in its statute, some courts, such as two courts in Florida and Arkansas, decided to exceed their bounds and do some legislating.[25] These courts argued that the "ordinary meaning" of the word "school" means an "institution" with a building and children from more than one family. However, both of these decisions were rendered moot (or of no effect) by their respective legislatures in 1984, which passed specific laws legally protecting home schools.[26]

Contrary to the above courts' claims, the ordinary meaning of the word "school" is "a place of learning." This popular definition of "school" is found in many dictionaries and recognized by many other courts around the country.

In Black's Law Dictionary, for instance, "school" is defined as "an institution or place of instruction or education." Funk and Wagnalls Dictionary defines "school" as "the place in which formal instruction is given." Home schooling definitely fits these descriptions because it is a "place of instruction." Many court cases involving home schoolers being charged with truancy found the home schoolers "not guilty" because their home school met all the requirements for a private school.

Cases Which Recognize Home Schools as Private Schools

In Illinois, for example, the Illinois Supreme Court found that a school in the home was a legitimate private school. In *People v. Levisen*,[27] the Court declared that a school is:

> a place where instruction is imparted to the young...*the number of persons* being taught does not determine whether a place is a school.[28] (italics added)

The Court explained further:

> Compulsory education laws are enacted to enforce the natural obligations of parents to provide an education for their young, an obligation which corresponds to the parents' right of control over the child...The object is that all shall be educated not that they shall be educated in any particular manner or place.[29]

Since that decision thousands of home schools, many with only one or two children, operate freely as private schools in Illinois.

In Indiana, the Indiana Appellate Court reached the same conclusions in *State* v. *Peterman*.[30] The Court defined a "school" as:

> a place where instruction is imparted to the young...We do not think that the *number of persons,* whether one or many, makes a place where instruction is imparted any less or any more a school.[31] (italics added)

The parents in the case were vindicated and their home school was considered to be a legal private school.

Home schools in many states do fulfill the object of the compulsory attendance law and meet all of the technical requirements of the law for private or church schools.

In California, thousands of home schools operate as private schools. Each year certain counties take families to court, challenging their right to exist as private schools and stating that their only option is to be certified tutors. However, the courts have sided with the home schoolers. For example, Michael Smith of the Home School Legal Defense Association handled the *People v. Darrah* and the *People v. Black* cases[32] in which two home school families were being denied the right to operate as private schools, even though they met all the requirements of a private school in California. The Court ruled in favor of the families, finding that the law was unconstitutionally vague and that the families could not be prosecuted for operating as private schools. Nothing in the law prohibited them from being private schools.

Although there are many more cases which could be mentioned, there is only one more which will be described. The case is *Leeper v. Arlington Independent School District.*[33] In Texas, thousands of home schools were operating as small private schools. When the private tutorial statute was repealed, home schools continued to operate as private schools. Then in 1981, the Texas Education Agency (TEA) issued a policy declaring that "educating a child at home is not the same as private school instruction and therefore, is not an acceptable substitute." In other words, home schools are not private schools and therefore are illegal. Over the next few years nearly 150 home school families across the state were hauled into court for criminal truancy charges. One HSLDA member family was taken to court even though both parents were certified teachers.

At this point, the home schoolers fought back. The Home School Legal Defense Association joined in with several other home school groups and brought a civil rights class action suit against the TEA and all 1060 school districts in the state for violating the civil rights of thousands of home schoolers. Attorney Shelby Sharpe of Dallas handled nearly all of the litigation. The groups representing the home schoolers sought a permanent injunction to stop the prosecution, a declaration that home schools can operate as private schools, and $4 million in damages. On April 13, 1987, the Court found that home schools which meet the minimum standards of private schools are considered to be legal private schools. He also placed a permanent injunction prohibiting prosecution of these private schools in the home throughout the entire state.

On November 27, 1991, the Court of Appeals of Texas completely affirmed the lower court in the *Leeper* case, recognizing that home schools can operate as private schools.[34] The Court of Appeals reasoned that the TEA "deprived the home school parents of equal protection under the law" since the private schools in the home were unfairly discriminated against "on the sole basis of location in the home," rather than outside the home. The Court further emphasized "that initiation of prosecution of plaintiff parents violates the parents' equal protection rights by establishing an unreasonable and arbitrary classification of parents which is not rationally related to any state interest."[35] The Court found no evidence that the home schoolers were not educating their children. The Court also held that each of the 1060 school districts were not immune from the suit because they were each liable for implementing the TEA's "unconstitutional policy" on home schooling.

This case is a tremendous victory that stands for the principle that parents have the right to be "equally protected" under the law and cannot be prohibited from operating a private school only because it is operated in the home. By God's grace, the Texas Supreme Court *unanimously* affirmed this decision on June 15, 1994![36] After nine long years, this landmark decision is truly a blessing for home schoolers in Texas and in other "Private School" States.

How a Home School Can Operate as a Private School

In conclusion, let us apply these principles to one state, Alabama, where home schoolers have trouble being recognized as private church schools. A thorough search of the Alabama statutes and court cases does not reveal any definition of a school in which it is required to have more than one child or to meet in any type of building. The only definition of a church school which can be found in the Alabama statutes is one that offers "grades K-12 or any combination thereof" and is "operated as a ministry of a local church, group of churches, denomination, and/or association of churches."[37] Furthermore, the statute defines a church school as being operated on a nonprofit basis and not receiving any state or federal funding.

A home school can easily meet the definition of a "church school" as defined by statute. As long as it follows the curriculum requirements, is operated as a ministry of a local church, is nonprofit, and does not receive any state or federal funding, a home school, by statute, is a private church school. In Alabama, a private church school can be a legitimate church school if it has one student taught by his parents in his home or one thousand students taught by hired teachers in a massive building complex.

The Traditional Legal Presumption that Parents Act in their Children's Best Interest

Today many public school officials no longer hold to the tradition that parents act in the best interest of their children. Most of the public school bureaucrats and organizations that make up the educational elite have developed a statist mentality that is repulsed by the idea of individual and parental rights. They have come to believe that they, the state educators, know what is best for the children. They believe that they are the guardians of the children and act in the children's best interest. Parents are considered to be inferior and amateurs in raising and educating children, while the educators are the "professionals." I have talked to hundreds of school officials who genuinely believe this way. A quick look at the teachers' colleges will show the source of this elite and anti-parent mentality.

However, the U.S. Supreme Court still recognizes that parents' rights are supreme in *Parham v. J .R.*[38] This decision presented strong support of parents' rights to control the important decisions which concern their minor children. In that case, Chief Justice Burger wrote for the majority:

> Our jurisprudence historically has reflected Western civilization concepts of the family as a unit with broad parental authority over minor children. Our cases have consistently followed that course; our constitutional system long ago rejected any notion that a child is "the mere creature of the State" and, on the contrary, asserted that parents generally "have the right, coupled with the high duty, to recognize and prepare [their children] for additional obligations." *Pierce* v. *Society of Sisters,* 268 U.S. 510, 535 (1925)...[other citations omitted]...The law's concept of the family rests on a presumption that parents possess what a child lacks in maturity, experience, and capacity for judgment required for making life's difficult decisions. More important, historically it has been recognized that natural bonds of affection lead parents to act in the best interests of their children. 1 W. Blackstone, Commentaries 447; 2 J. Kent, Commentaries on American Law 190.
>
> As with so many other legal presumptions, experience and reality may rebut what the law accepts as a starting point; the incidence of child neglect and abuse cases

attests to this. That some parents "may at times be acting against the interests of their children"…creates a basis for caution, but it is hardly a reason to discard wholesale those pages of human experience that teach that parents generally do act in the child's best interest…The statist notion that governmental power should supersede parental authority in all cases because some parents abuse and neglect children is repugnant to American tradition

We cannot assume that the result in *Meyer v. Nebraska* and *Pierce v. Society of Sisters* would have been different if the children there had announced a preference to learn only English or a preference to go to a public, rather than a church school.[39]

Therefore, school districts cannot automatically monitor home schoolers if the legislature has not specifically granted them such authority. Home schoolers are presumed to be acting in their children's best interest. In other words, they are innocent until proven guilty. This principle is particularly applicable in the "private school states." Also, social workers need to be reminded of this presumption, since they often try to usurp parental authority on a fabricated anonymous tip by attempting to make the parents prove that they are innocent when there is no evidence of guilt.

The Neutral Decision-Maker Defense

Every state has a compulsory attendance law, and generally the local public school officials have the exclusive authority to enforce this law. Many states give the superintendents *discretion,* in some way, over whether or not a home school will be able to operate. As a result, public school officials often treat home schooling as a privilege, not a right, which is subject to their arbitrary approval or disapproval. However, since the superintendent has a financial interest in the outcome of whether or not a home school will be allowed to operate, and has a philosophical bias against home schooling, such discretion is unconstitutional as a violation of due process.

Before 1982, most state superintendents or school boards had unlimited discretion to either approve or disapprove home schools. Since then, at least thirty-seven states have changed their laws to specifically protect home schooling and thereby reduce or eliminate the public school officials' discretionary authority.[40]

The problem of public school officials' discretionary authority over home schoolers is most apparent in the four states which are classified as "approval states" but also in many of the "private school" states.[41] In these states, I have found that home schoolers are often subject to arbitrary requirements that change from year to year at the whim of the local school officials. Home schoolers are frequently disapproved for the flimsiest reasons, such as refusing to allow a home visit or refusing to have their children tested in the public school when they have already arranged for testing privately. Another reason for disapproval is the lack of necessary qualifications that the superintendent personally believes is necessary. Once disapproved, the families will normally face criminal truancy or "child in need of services" charges.

Even in some of the states which have passed home school laws, certain areas of the laws are still left to the discretion of the superintendent. For instance, in Florida, Virginia, Pennsylvania and South Carolina, the superintendents have the discretion to determine if a home school child's test scores or evaluation shows "adequate" progress. In Florida, one superintendent arbitrarily claimed an HSLDA member's test scores of his child were not adequate, even though over half of his public school students in the same grade scored lower. Virginia superintendents that I have dealt with have arbitrarily rejected a home schooler's evaluation, completed by a certified teacher, by simply saying that the progress is not satisfactory and then ordering the home school to "cease and desist."

Public School Officials Are not Neutral
Decision-Makers regarding Home Schooling

Public school officials are not neutral when it comes to exercising their discretion and deciding whether a family should be allowed to home school. One of the most obvious reasons is that they have a *financial incentive* to disapprove a home school and thereby increase the probability that the home schooled child will be placed in the public schools. Since a local school district receives state and federal tax dollars of between $2000 to $4000 per head count, twenty children being home schooled gives the school district a minimum net loss of $40,000 in tax money.[43] This could easily pay for another teacher's salary.

One superintendent, along with a truant officer, visited a home school family in Michigan who is a member of HSLDA and who had pulled four children out of the public schools. The home schooler called me and told me that the superintendent asked her: "How could you do this to our school district? Do you have any idea how much tax money we will be losing for that many children? You need to get them back in school." The family was soon threatened with prosecution. This is by no means an isolated incident. I have record of many superintendents who have admitted to the parents, newspapers, HSLDA lawyers, or in court, that they are concerned about the loss of tax money to their school district, a direct result of families home schooling their children.[44]

For example, in Florida, Dan Wicklund, director of finance for the Columbia County School System, explained to a reporter of the *Lake City Reporter* that he was alarmed by the amount of families home schooling (157) in his county. He said, "The county earns $2,538 per student. The total lost revenue is $398,000 for the students enrolled in home study this year."[45]

In Texas, Pat Whelan, legal counsel to the Texas Education Association, bemoaned the fact that for each home school student not enrolled in the public schools, the public schools lose about $2,800 in tax money.[46]

In some states the financial incentive is even greater. For instance, in Pennsylvania, a superintendent is encouraged by the law to make things difficult for home schoolers. Under chapter 24, section 13,1333 of the Pennsylvania Statutes, he not only has the authority to commence criminal prosecutions, but also under this section all fines imposed are collected "for the benefit of the school district in which such offending person resides." The more truancy fines filed, the more fine money the local public school receives. Or the home school family can avoid prosecution by enrolling in the public schools, in which case the superintendent, on behalf of the school district, receives thousands of dollars per child in increased state aid.

For example, in one case I handled, *Pennsylvania v. Hulls*,[47] a superintendent continued to file charges on a weekly basis during the entire first half of the 1986-87 school year and resumed filing weekly charges during most of the 1987-88 school year, against a family whose mother was a former public school teacher. Over a two-year period, the superintendent accumulated a very large financial interest in the prosecution of the Hulls. He only stopped his harassment when the compulsory attendance statute was ruled unconstitutional in regards to home schooling, in HSLDA's successful federal right suit, *Jeffery v. O'Donnell*.[48]

Another reason that public school officials are not neutral when making a discretionary decision concerning a home school is that many of them really believe that they are the guardians of the children within the boundaries of their school district. They sincerely believe that they know what is best for the children, especially since they have seven years of higher education, and the home school mother, half of the time, only has a high school diploma.[49] With this type of bias, it is hard for many public school officials to approve home schoolers and allow them to operate freely.

The home schools are competitors with the public schools. In North Dakota, the year after the home school law was passed, the number of home schooled children doubled. The more lenient the local home school policy or state law, the more families will home school their children. This is a monetary loss to the public schools, and a threat to the teachers' unions.

This situation in which public school officials have arbitrary discretionary authority over whether or not home schools can freely operate is synonymous with the following hypothetical illustration. Let us say that the legislature in a particular state is concerned over the quality of new cars. As a result, the legislature passes a law requiring all car dealers to be licensed. It then delegates the licensing power to the Ford dealership. Ford is not only given the discretion to decide which car dealers should be licensed but is also given the discretion to draft its own "rules." One of the first rules Ford naturally adopts is that all car dealers, Toyota, Chrysler, etc., can only sell cars built with Ford parts. Is the Ford dealership neutral in determining who should be licensed? Certainly it is no more neutral than public school officials, with a vested interest in public school survival, determining who should be allowed to home school.

The U.S. Supreme Court Condemns Nonneutral Decision-Makers

The Fourteenth Amendment guarantees that life, liberty, and property cannot be taken away from an individual unless he receives "due process." This means that an individual will receive certain procedural safeguards that will ensure that he will be treated fairly. One of the elements of due process is that if an individual's liberty is at stake, in this instance, parental liberty, he has a right to be heard by a *neutral decision-maker,* at the first level. The first level for a home schooler who is being challenged is usually the biased superintendent or school board.

The Supreme Court of the United States has definitively ruled that a decision-maker with a financial stake in the outcome is not a "neutral magistrate" and, therefore, is in violation of the Fourteenth Amendment Due Process Clause. In *Tumey v. Ohio*,[50] a mayor was the decision-maker in a process concerning a liquor law. If the mayor decided in favor of the individual, the city would receive no money. But if the mayor decided against the individual appearing before him, the mayor received a nominal sum of money, while the city received a substantial sum of money.

The Supreme Court held that *both* types of financial incentives violate the due process clause. It makes no difference if the monetary gain goes exclusively to the governmental entity (the public school) and not to the state official (superintendent). *Tumey* clearly stands for the principle that a local government official, such as a superintendent, who has a financial stake in the outcome on behalf of his local governmental unit or public school is not a neutral decision-maker for the purpose of the due process clause.

In another case, *Ward v. Monroeville,* the United States Supreme Court reaffirmed *Tumey* and made even more clear that the financial incentive need not be personal to the decision-maker.[51]

Only two home school cases, at this point, have dealt with this issue of the right to a neutral decision-maker. Both of these cases were ruled on by the Supreme Court in North Dakota. In *State v. Toman*,[52] the North Dakota Supreme Court upheld a truancy conviction of a home school family and avoided the challenge that the superintendent was not neutral. The principle to learn from the *Toman* case is that the non-neutral decision-maker defense may be only applicable if the home school family specifically requested the home school exemption and was denied *before* they were charged with criminal truancy.

In addition, this same Court also considered this due process argument in another case, *State v. Anderson*.[53] The principle to learn from this case is that the function of the decision-maker, who in this case was the local superintendent, must be discretionary and not merely ministerial. In other words, if the legislature enacts a law that requires a home school parent to have a "high school diploma," the superintendent performs a ministerial function in determining whether the parent has a high school diploma. However, if a statute requires a home school parent to be "qualified," the superintendent performs a discretionary function in defining "qualified" and applying his whim to his decision. The latter would violate the due process clause.

School officials cannot be given the authority to decide whether or not families can teach their children at home. They have both a financial incentive and a natural partisanship or bias which precludes them from serving as a neutral decision-maker, as required by the due process clause. The ultimate goal of HSLDA is to repeal compulsory attendance statutes in all the states, which would definitely end this problem because no educational authorities would be needed. However, in the meantime, HSLDA is working with home schoolers and legislatures to remove all discretionary authority of public school officials and reduce their duty to merely gathering information.

Notes

1. "Governor Signs North Dakota Home Schooling Law," *The Home School Court Report*, Vol. 5, No. 3, Summer 1989, 2.
2. *Iowa v. Trucke*, 410 NW2d 242 (1987). Also see "Supreme Court Victory in Iowa," *The Home School Court Report*, Vol. 3, No. 3, September/November Edition 1987, 5.
3. "Case Won in Alabama Due to the Thousand Foot Rule," *The Home School Court Report*, Vol. 6, No. 2, Spring 1990, 9.
4. *Wisconsin v. Popanz*, 112 Wis.2d 166, 332 N.W.2d 750 (1983).
5. *Roemhild v. Georgia*, 251 Ga.569, 308 S.E.2d 154 (1983).
6. *Minnesota v. Newstrom*, 371 N.W.2d 533 (Minn. 1985).
7. Two separate and favorable decisions resulted: *Jeffery*, 702 F.Supp. 513 (MoD. PA 1988) *and Jeffery*, 702 F.Supp. 516 (M.D. PA 1988).
8. *Ellis* v. *O'Hara*, 612 F.Supp 379 (E.D. Mo. 1985). *Ellis*, was "reversed" by an order of the Eighth Circuit. 802 F.2d 462 (8th Cir. 1986). The published decision gives only the word "reversed" as a docket entry. From reviewing the actual opinion of the Eighth Circuit, it is obvious that the decision was reversed to permit the district court to make an inquiry into the issue of mootness, in light of a newly enacted Missouri statute which eliminated the vagueness of the compulsory attendance statute.
9. *Fellowship Baptist Church* v. *Benton*, 620 F.Supp. 308 (S.D. Iowa 1985); aff'd 815 F.2d 486. (8th Cir. 1986).
10. When parents are home schooling for religious reasons under the First Amendment, "special scrutiny" must be applied whenever a vague compulsory attendance statute imposes criminal penalties which tend to operate to inhibit the exercise of those freedoms. See *Kolender* v. *Lawson*, 461 U.S. 352, 358 n. 8 (1983).
11. *Connally* v. *General Construction* Co., 269 U.S. 385, 391, 46 S.Ct. 126, 127, 70 L.Ed. 322 (1925).
12. 408 U.S. 104 (1972).
13. 408 U.S., 108-109.
14. *Home School Court Report*, "Pennsylvania Under Fire," Jan.-Feb. 1987 edition, Vol. 3 No.1, Purcellville, Virginia. This article also documents many other cases pending in Pennsylvania during that time.
15. Two separate and favorable decisions resulted: *Jeffery*, 702 F.Supp. 513 (M.D. PA 1988) *and Jeffery*, 702 F.Supp. 516 (M.D. PA 1988).
16. *Jeffery*, 702 F.Supp. 516, 521.
17. *Pebler*, No. 91-0840-SM, St. Joseph County District Court, July 2, 1991.
18. *People* v. *Pebler*, No. 91-0848-SM, St. Joseph County 3-B District Court, Judge William McManus, Order of Dismissal, July 2, 1991.
19. *"Leeper* Decision Challenged in Texas," *The Home School Court Report*, Vol. 4, No. 4, Fall 1988, 10.
20. *Maas v. Alabama*, 601 So. 2d 209, Alabama Court of Criminal Appeals, 15 May, 1992. Also see "Alabama: Court Ignores Statute," *The Home School Court Report*, Vol. 7, No. 6, November-December 1991, 8.
21. For example see "Kansas School Districts Challenge Parents," *The Home School Court Report*, Vol. 6, No. 4, Fall 1990, 9.

22. The Memorandum is entitled "Kansas Compulsory School Attendance Laws and the Nonpublic Schools," Revised June 1, 1988.
23. "Kansas Tremors," *The Home School Court Report,* Vol. 6, No.1, Fall-Winter 1992, 2.
24. "Michigan: Litigation Proliferates," *The Home School Court Report,* Vol. 7, No. 4, July-August 1991, 15 and "Michigan: More Cases Dismissed," *The Home School Court Report,* Vol. 17, No. 5, September-October 1991, 8-9.
25. For instance, in Florida and Arkansas, two state court decisions ruled that the definition of school did not include a home school. *Burrow v. State,* 282 Ark. 479, 669 S.W.2d 441 (1984), and *State of Florida v. Buckner,* 472 So. 2d 1228, (Fla. Dist. Ct. App. 1985). In both of these decisions, the courts created definitions of private school out of thin air. Since the Arkansas and Florida statutes did not define the term "private school," these courts decided to "legislate" and create a definition that would exclude home schooling. The home school families were convicted even though their home schools satisfied all the statutory requirements for private schools.
26. See Florida Statutes Annotated sections 228.041(34), 232.02(4), and Arkansas Statutes Annotated section 80-1503.
27. 90N.E.2d 213 (1950).
28. *Levisen,* 215.
29. *Ibid.*
30. 70 NE 550 (1904).
31. *Peterman,* 551.
32. *Darrah,* No.853104 and *Black,* No. 853105, Santa Maria Mun. Ct., 10 March 1986.
33. No 17-88761-85, Tarrant County, 17th Judicial Ct., April 13, 1987.
34. *Texas Education Agency et al.* v. *Leeper, et al,* (No. 2-87-216-CV), November 27, 1991. Also see "Texas Home Schoolers Welcome Victory at Last," *The Home School Court Report,* Vol. 8, No. 1, January/February 1992.
35. *Ibid.*
36. *Texas Educational Agency, et. al. v. Leeper, et. al.* (No. D-2022, Texas Supreme Court, June, 15,1994.
37. Alabama Code §16-28-1(2).
38. 442 U.S. 584 (1979).
39. *Ibid.* 402 U.S., at 602-604.
40. See chapter 20 for a list of these states. for a more detailed summary of the requirements for home schoolers in all fifty states see: Christopher J. Klicka, *Home Education in the United States: A Legal Analysis,* Home School Legal Defense Association. Updated annually. To order: www.hslda.org
41. The four remaining "approval" states are Massachusetts, Rhode Island, South Dakota, and Utah. For more details on the "approval" states, the "private school" states, and those states with "home school" laws, see Christopher J. Klicka, *Home Schooling in the United States: A Legal Analysis,* Home School Legal Defense Association, www.hslda.org
42. *Home School Court Report,* Vol. 6 No. 3, Summer edition 1990, HSLDA, Paeonian Springs, Virginia.
43. Theodore Wade, Jr., editor, *The Home School Manual,* chapter 6, "The Battle for the Right to Home School," by Christopher Klicka (Niles, MI: Gazelle Publications, 1995), 68. Also see *The Home School Court Report,* "Denying Constitutional Rights for Money," Vol. 3 No.1, Jan.-Feb. 1987.
44. Home School Legal Defense Association, P.O Box 159, Purcellville, Virginia 22159. The court records where school officials admit the loss of money include cases in North Dakota, Michigan, Pennsylvania, New York, and Minnesota.
45. "Teach Me Mom," *Lake City Reporter,* September 14, 1989, 1B.
46. Mark Schlachtenhaufen, "Home Schooling Under fire," *Bay Town Sun,* Houston, August 7, 1991.
47. See "PA Victory May Come in Legislature," *The Home School Court Report,* Vol. 4, No. 3, Summer 1988, 13.
48. 702 F.Supp. 516 (M.D. PA 1988).
49. This description of the public school officials' mind set is based on over one thousand conversations Chris Klicka has had with school officials, while negotiating on behalf of home schoolers since 1983.
50. 273 U.S.510 (1927).
51. *Ward,* 409 U.S. 57, 60 (1972).
52. *Toman,* Criminal Nos. 880186 and 880187, Slip. Op. 1-2, 10 February 1989.
53. *Anderson,* 427 N.W.2d 316, 320 (N.D.) *cert. denied,* -U.S. -, 109 S.Ct. 491 (1988).

The Military:
Home Schoolers Are Winning the War

"The DoD has a specific statutory authority to operate a school for DoD dependents who are assigned overseas. Our statute, unlike the many State statutes which do not apply overseas, does not compel the attendance of any DoD dependent in DoD Dependents Schools.... Therefore, a defendant may choose not to enroll in our program [DoDDS] and to elect, instead, an alternative enrollment; for example, a foreign language school, a private school, or in a home schooling program."[1]

Nearly two million children in the United States are being taught at home, and that number continues to grow. As home schooling becomes more popular across America, more and more military and Department of Defense (DoD) civilian families are turning to this educational alternative.

Since military personnel are frequently transferred to train or serve at different bases across the country and throughout the world, their children must adjust to a new school with each move. For some children, these moves threaten their sense of security and weaken their self-confidence. Such interruptions in the continuity of life can have a detrimental effect on educational progress.

Home schooling is a logical choice for families in the military, providing a stable environment in the midst of frequent change. More important than the academic continuity is the opportunity to develop close-knit family bonds—the most secure support system children can have.

Military families considering home schooling often have questions. "Is it legal?" The answer is definitely "Yes." "Does their academic program have to be approved or regulated by the DoD?" Thankfully, the answer is "No."

In spite of the advantages to home schooling in the military, some military officials, especially overseas, have challenged the right to home school, and have used excessive restriction or intimidation to deter families from pursuing that course. The Home School Legal Defense Association regularly works on behalf of member families faced with questions or conflicts on military bases.

For instance, in Japan, I helped a home schooling private in the Army who was contacted by his commanding officer, informing him that he was not in compliance since he did not submit test results of his children to him for proof of progress. In Germany, a home schooling major was contacted by his superiors and told he must have his children's curriculum approved and submit to home visits.

In Turkey, an Air Force commander, Colonel Peter Farmer, tried to discourage home schoolers with a memo he issued:

> I've been hearing a number of sponsors here discuss bringing their school aged children back to Incirlik early and having their spouse conduct home schooling to finish out the year. The Defense Department Dependent School recommends against this and their requirements for home schooling are as follows: 1. Instructor must have passed the National Teacher Exam before any period of home school is approved. 2. Student must pass a placement exam prior to the beginning of the next school year before that student will be passed to the next grade.

I could recount many other negative contacts in the military overseas. Of course, such requirements as described above are in excess of the military's authority. As seen below, home schooling is allowed in the military overseas, and the military, under its present regulations, has no authority to regulate it. Military home schoolers in the United States, on the other hand, are required to follow the home school requirements of the state in which they are stationed. Even in the States though, military social workers routinely investigate home schoolers, and I have spent much time convincing them that home schooling is legal.

One of the most blatant examples of harassment of home schoolers occurred on a military base in Germany.

Military Home Schoolers Challenged in Germany

On November 6, 1989, the commander of an Army base in Augsburg, West Germany, Commander Del Rosso, issued a memorandum condemning home schooling. He stated that according to the Status-of-Forces-Agreements, all families had to comply with the "host nation law" which involves choosing one of three options listed in his memorandum:

> They can elect to enroll children in:
> a. A Department of Defense Dependent School (DoDOS).
> b. A locally accredited public, private, or parochial school.
> c. A school accredited by an acknowledged U.S. civil or religious education association, which has applied for local accreditation.
> ...Attendance at schools not meeting the above criteria is a violation of host nation law and therefore strictly prohibited.... Similarly, so *called "home teaching"* (i.e., parent keeps child at home and personally conducts his education) is *strictly prohibited.*[2] (emphasis added)

As a result, home school families were warned that they had one week to enroll their children in a recognized school under one of the options listed above or face disciplinary action for misconduct. "As willful violators of host nation law, repeat offenders will be referred to the Civilian Misconduct Action Authority who can direct appropriate sanctions."[3]

Commander Del Rosso's attempt to prohibit home schooling by instituting this inaccurate policy was immediately resisted by the home schooling families in the community. Several families were planning to request transfers back to the states if they would not be allowed to home school.[4] In an interview, Michael Harris, the military head of recreational services in Augsburg, said that the policy was prompted by reports that Christian schools were operating unofficially on post and "of parents teaching their children at home."[5] He said that they needed to follow the West German mandatory attendance policy at only accredited schools, which was "designed to protect children from abuse." Harris explained further, "When I fail as a parent to educate my child, I might as well be spanking them or beating them."[6] Letters were written to the secretary of defense and the judge advocate's offices, who sent them copies of the actual policy of the military in favor of the right to home school. The commander, after being informed of the Department of Defense policy described below, quickly rescinded his memorandum which prohibited home schooling.

Policy of the Secretary of Defense and Judge Advocate

James Horn, education liaison for the Office of the Assistant Secretary of Defense stated in his reply:

> The DoD has a specific statutory authority to operate a school for DoD dependents who are assigned overseas. Our statute, unlike the many State statutes which do not apply overseas, does not compel the attendance of any DoD dependent in DoD Dependents Schools.... Therefore, a dependent may choose not to enroll in our program [DoDOS] and to elect, instead, an alternative enrollment; for example, a foreign language school, a private school, or in a home schooling program.[7]

While the Department of Defense (DoD) does not have specific regulations to govern home schooling, it allows for it as an alternative to its Department of Defense Dependent Schools(DoDDS). It is not prohibited in any way.

Horn also explained the military's policy regarding military families operating within the states:

> Public education within the United States is a matter which our constitutional system leaves to the discretion of each

state. These laws are binding on all persons within the State's border, including the dependents of the Department of Defense (including the Military Services). The Secretary of Defense does not have the legal authority to issue...regulatory exemption from State education laws.[8]

Military families in the states, as a result, have the responsibility of following the home schooling laws or regulations in that particular state.

Furthermore, regarding the issue of attendance in an accredited German school, Capt. Chris Ambrose, assistant staff judge advocate stated:

> The children of U.S. military and DoD civilian personnel assigned to Germany, however, are *not* subject to state mandatory attendance statutes of the U.S. because the children do not *reside* in any of the fifty states. The children are not subject to German mandatory attendance laws *either* because of NATO Status of Forces agreements which allow U.S. forces to provide for the education of their own children.[9] (emphasis added)

Military home schoolers on foreign soil are not subject to either foreign school attendance law or any of the fifty states' attendance laws provided the NATO Status of Forces Agreement or some similar agreement applies to the specific foreign country. Capt. Ambrose emphasized, however, other nonmilitary "U.S. citizens who reside in Germany (e.g., missionaries), *are* subject to German mandatory attendance laws."[10]

The Judge Advocate's office explained further that the federal law 20 USC Sections 921,932 which authorizes the educational services provided by the DoDDS, does not address mandatory attendance. The implementing directive, DoD Directive 1342.13, also does not require mandatory attendance.[11] Therefore, the DoDDS presently has no authority to prohibit or regulate home schooling.

Capt. Ambrose concluded by stating:

> I have discussed the subjects of mandatory DoDDS attendance and home schooling with attorneys from the DoD

General Counsel's office in Washington D.C., as well as the DoDDS administrators in Germany. They agree that it is not illegal for U.S. Military and DoD civilians to home school in Germany, regardless of whether the family lives on or off post (base). Nevertheless, misinformed commanders occasionally attempt to initiate disciplinary action against home schoolers.[12]

In conclusion, military families have the right to home school. In fact, in 1989, the *Stars and Stripes* newspaper reported that over two hundred military families in Europe were home schooling.[13] Ten years later, the number of home schoolers in U.S. military bases has grown 5 times.

However, occasionally a commander or an uninformed social worker will challenge the right of home schoolers to exist or try to excessively regulate them. HSLDA has been successful in resolving many investigations of military home schoolers.

The educational services for the children of U.S. forces are provided by the Department of Defense Dependent Schools (DoDDS). The law which authorizes DoDDS (20 USC 921-932) is a federal law and does not address mandatory attendance. The implementing directive (DoD Directive 1342.13) for the statute does not require mandatory attendance either. If a military home school family resides in the United States, they must abide by the state's compulsory attendance law. If the military family lives on foreign soil, however, they are not under the jurisdiction of the foreign country's compulsory attendance law. Nor are they under any regulatory authority of the DoD.

Military home school families, therefore, have no obligation to seek approval of the DoD to home school. A family simply needs to secure a curriculum and begin home schooling.

Regarding equal access to DoD school services, I worked through Congressmen John Hostletter's (R-IN) office to craft language to require the DoDDS to make available supplemental education services to home schoolers overseas. The House Armed Services Committee, as a result included the following directive in its report on the FY00 DoD Reauthorization Act:

> The committee believes that military families who decide to home school their children should be supported by

Department of Defense Overseas Schools (DoDDS) to the extent possible. While the committee agrees that a commander's responsibility to manage an overseas community and a family's obligation to observe host nation laws render home schooling overseas more challenging than when conducted in the United States, the committee supports responsible school choice for military families. The committee is aware that the Department of Defense Education Activity (DoDEA) claims that it fully supports home schooling. DoDEA's published material and the actual experience of some parents belie that claim, however. The committee believes that DoDEA should take a more proactive approach in establishing a clear policy and providing parents available information about available DoDEA support for home schooling overseas, rather than merely directing parents to the overseas commander. To that end, the committee directs the Secretary of Defense to develop clear policy on support for home schooling overseas. That policy, which would officially implement what DoDEA representatives state is actual practice, should specify that home schooled students may be supported with library services, music, sports, single classes, and other programs without having to actually enroll in DoDDS. The committee directs the Secretary to provide the Senate Committee on Armed Services and the House Committee on Armed Services with the new policy directive by October 1, 1999.[14]

This simply means that the DoD must create an equal access policy for home schoolers without requiring formal enrollment of home school students in the DoDDS schools.

On September 22, 1999, I met with staff of the House Armed Services Committee and the Director of the DoDEA to offer a recommended equal access policy. After discussing the many benefits and successes of home schooling, I explained the importance of using policy language which prohibited any DoD school from refusing to make auxiliary services available to military dependents educated in a home school. The term "auxiliary services" would include academic classes, access to the library, after-hours use of the facilities, and participation in extracurricular and inter-scholastic activities, such as music and sports programs. Furthermore, home schoolers who registered for these auxiliary services would not have to enroll in the DoD school nor meet any additional eligibility requirements than DoD school students.

The Director of DoDEA, and the Committee staff members were completely receptive and agreed to virtually all these proposals. If any overseas military families have difficulties receiving educational services from DoD schools and if they are members of HSLDA, they should contact our office.

Home schooling is not for everybody—but it is for anyone willing to make the commitment to and sacrifice for his or her children. American military families are thankful to have the freedom to choose home schooling.

The Military Is Looking for a Few Good Home Schoolers

Are you a parent who has a home school student who desires to join the military? We have good news for you! After many years, all four of the armed services have finally removed all obstacles for home school graduates to enlist. Home schoolers are welcome to serve in the armed forces. But this positive atmosphere was not always so.

Before the enactment of new federal law creating a five-year pilot project, discrimination against home schoolers seeking enlistment was the policy. In simple terms, home schoolers were considered by the military as dropouts.

Here is a typical scenario prior to the new law: After being home schooled most of his life, John graduates and decides to follow his father's footsteps and join the Air Force. He sets up an appointment with the local Air Force recruiter where he passes the military aptitude test with a score of 95 percent. He only had to score 40 percent. He passes all other eligibility requirements. The recruiter is excited and tells him he will sign him up for basic training. John sells his car and quits his job. John's parents plan a surprise "going away party" for him to celebrate his acceptance into the Air Force. Then the phone rings. It is the recruiter with bad news. He explains that he checked with his superior and since John's home school diploma is not accredited, there is no place for him in the Air Force. As result, John gives up on his hope of following his father's footsteps and pursuing a promising military career.

This happened hundreds of times during the past decade, as home schoolers were turned away from enlisting in the military simply because they did not have high school diplomas from an accredited school. All four branches of the armed services relegated potential home school recruits to Tier II status, which is reserved for high school dropouts. Tier I was reserved for high school graduates and those with some college. (For most of the armed services, Tier I candidates only have to score 31 on the military's aptitude test while Tier II candidates have to score 50).

This made it very difficult for home schoolers, especially since the Air Force and Marines decided in 1998 that they would accept only Tier I candidates. Only about 10 percent of all Navy and Army enlistees were Tier II candidates. We at the Home School Legal Defense Association were inundated with testimonies from home schoolers who scored over the 90th percentile on the military's aptitude test, met all the military's eligibility requirements, and yet were rejected simply because they did not have an accredited diploma.

Finally, by God's grace, we were able to achieve a solution at the federal level. I contacted Senator Paul Coverdell's office and asked if they would help. They agreed. I drafted language to cure the problem and this resulted in Senator Coverdell introducing an amendment to HR 3616, the Defense Authorization bill to end this discrimination against home schoolers. The bill created a five-year pilot project automatically placing home school recruits into the Tier I status. Each of the four armed services (Marines, Navy, Army, and Air Force) must annually allow up to 1,250 home school diploma recipients to be considered under the Tier I status along with all other high school graduates.

The bill passed the Senate, the conference committee, and subsequently passed both the House and Senate. The President signed the bill into law on October 17, 1998. It became effective immediately.

The most important sections of the new law states:

> **Sec. 571.** Pilot Program for Treating GED and Home School Diploma Recipients As High School Graduates for Determinations of Eligibility for Enlistment in the Armed Forces.
>
> ...(b) Persons Eligible Under the Pilot Program as High School Graduates. Under the pilot program, a person shall be treated as having graduated from high school with a high school diploma for the purpose described in subsection (a) if :

...(2) the person is a home school diploma recipient and provides a transcript demonstrating completion of high school to the military department involved under the pilot program.

(c) GED and Home School Diploma Recipients.

For the purposes of this section:

...(2) a person is a home school diploma recipient if the person has received a diploma for completing a program of education through the high school level at a home school, without regard to whether the home school is treated as a private school under the law of the State in which located.[15]

Under this new law, home schoolers seeking enlistment in one of the four military services must provide a high school diploma, a high school transcript, pass the military aptitude test (Armed Services Vocational Aptitude Battery, ASVAB), and meet any physical and other eligibility requirements for recruitment applicable to all enlistees.

This means military recruiters must accept a home school diploma or transcript regardless of the teacher's relationship to the student. Furthermore, a transcript or diploma prepared by the parent, as well as a high school diploma or transcript issued by a nonaccredited home school correspondence course, satisfies the law's intent. No additional educational documentation is required.

Home school students seeking to enlist in the any of the four armed forces cannot be rejected, as in the past, simply on the basis of not possessing an accredited high school diploma. (HSLDA will continue to assist any member families who have difficulty with local recruiters who may not understand the new law.)

According to W.S. Sellman, Director of Accession Policy, Office of the Assistant Secretary of Defense, all that is necessary to demonstrate academic eligibility is for the home school graduate to produce a "letter from a parent with a list of completed coursework." That is it! No more proof of an accredited diploma is required. This letter carries significant weight since the Director of Accession is in charge of the recruitment policy for all four armed services.[16]

In response to the new federal law, the Army announced, "Young men and women who gain their high school diploma through home schooling can now receive the same Army benefits as those students who graduate from a traditional high school." Home school graduates can now receive an enlistment bonus of $12,000 for enlistment in certain military occupational specialties and up to $40,000 from the Army College Fund for college tuition.

The Navy wasted no time making a new policy. "Effective immediately, a person with a home school diploma will be classified as being in a Tier I status for enlistment purposes.... A home school applicant can score 31 or greater on the ASAVB\AFQT."

In fact, the Navy, during the first year, actually exceeded the 1,250 home schooler enlistment limit, compared to less than 100 home schooled enlistees over the last three years! The pilot project is indeed working.

The other branches are also in the process of opening their doors. Brig. General Sutton, charged with leading the Air Force Recruiting Service, announced, "We want to reach out to home schoolers and let them know they have a place in our nation's Air Force." They are now recognizing home schoolers as high school graduates. The Marines have also changed their formal recruitment policy in light of the new law.

In my role as Senior Counsel at HSLDA, I continue to work with the heads of all four recruiting commands and the Center of Naval Analysis to smooth the transition, solve recruiting problems at the local level and create a uniform enlistment policy for home schoolers.

Home schoolers, by the grace of God, now have the right to compete on equal footing with other high school graduates seeking entrance into the military.

There were many battles to arrive at this point which the home schoolers lost. But now it seems the home schoolers have won the war!

Another favorable development which may contribute to easier access by home schoolers into the military is the academic failure of many public school graduates, as seen in chapter 1 of this book. All potential military recruits need to pass a three-hour Armed Services Vocational Aptitude Battery (ASVAB). This tests math, comprehension, and word knowledge. In order to pass, the person needs to read on at least an eleventh grade level, according to Sergeant Jack Gragg, manager of the Army's Bakersfield, California recruiting station.[17] However, Gragg, in the same interview, stated that half of the graduates of the local public high schools flunk this basic test.

Notes

1. James G. Horn, Ph.D., Education Liaison with the Office of the Assistant Secretary of Defense, Washington, D.C., Letter to Michelle Landers, 1989.
2. Brigadier General Louis J. Del Rosso, *"Memorandum For See Distribution;* Subject: USMCA Augsburg High/Elementary School Attendance, Military Community, Policy Memorandum #31,11 Department of the Army, Augsburg, Germany, November 6, 1989. This policy was later rescinded.
3. *Ibid.*
4. Rosemary Sawyer, "Augsburg Community Takes Action Against Home Schooling of Children," *Stars and Stripes,* November 17, 1989, 2.
5. *Ibid.*
6. *Ibid.*
7. James, *op. cit.*
8. *Ibid.*
9. Chris E. Ambrose, Capt, United States Air Force, Assistant Staff Judge Advocate, Letter to Mrs. Gravelle, July 21, 1989.
10. *Ibid.*
11. *Ibid.*
12. *Ibid.*
13. Sawyer, *Stars and Stripes,* 2.
14. 2000 Defense Authorization Act, House Report 106-162, May 24, 1999.
15. Public Law 105-261, sec. 571 or 10 U.S.C. 520.
16. Letter from W.S. Sellman, dated January 12, 1999 to U.S. Senator Paul Coverdell.
    This was in response to Sen. Paul Coverdell, who had requested on Dec. 15, 1998 that "in order to meet the intent of this new law," Mr. Sellman direct "all recruiting commands to eliminate any reference of 'accredited' when referring to home school diplomas."
17. Gordon Anderson, "Military Wants Literate Recruits," *The Bakersfield Californian,* August 6, 1990, Al and A10.

VI

An Uneasy Peace:
Conserving Our Freedoms

As stated earlier, home schoolers will not be free from conflict until the compulsory attendance laws are repealed. This will remove the public school's legal authority over home schoolers.

However, there is much we can do to gain more freedom for home schoolers in the meantime.

This section will describe how you can make a difference by influencing the media, educating the legislature, and having legal solidarity with home schoolers throughout the country by joining with the Home School Legal Defense Association. The reader will especially benefit from the lessons we learned from battling HR6 in 1994. chapter 22 recounts this story showing how God worked to enable home schoolers to generate one million calls to Congress in eight days.

chapter 20

The Good, the Bad, and the Ugly State Laws

"The competitions of the state for the educating power have been so engrossing that we have almost forgotten the parent as the rightful competitor. And now many look at its claim almost contemptuously. It is vital to a true theory for human rights, that the real independence of the parent be respected."

Dr. Robert Dabney

As demonstrated in chapter 6, home schooling has been operating in the United States since its beginning. However, with the advent of the public schools and subsequent enactment of state compulsory attendance laws in the early 1900s, home schooling nearly died out.

In the 1980s, however, home schooling experienced a rebirth in popularity as hundreds of thousands of families diligently began teaching their own children at home. This rekindling of a historical system of education continues to grow at a tremendous pace in the 1990s, with no sign of slowing down.

The legal road to home school, however, has not been easy since most states did not formally recognize the right of parents to home school their own children. In 1980, only three states in the entire country, Utah, Ohio, and Nevada, officially recognized the right to home school in their state statutes. In most states, it was "open season" on families teaching their children at home, and they were often prosecuted under criminal truancy laws and educational neglect charges.

The Home School Legal Defense Association, from the beginning, realized that litigation was only a "necessary evil" which would yield unpredictable results. Since most courts no longer merely apply the law, but make law, the results would depend on which particular court the case was heard in. Litigation and legal defense has been necessary "to hold back the tide" of legal harassment until the legislatures start changing laws to specifically protect the rights of home schools. Since 1983, HSLDA has been able to help over twenty-five thousand families who were negatively contacted by legal authorities. HSLDA has also provided expert testimony before legislatures to help defeat bad bills or to help pass good bills.

God blessed the efforts of home schoolers with tremendous success in the legislatures across the country in spite of great odds. It is clear that these victories were not the result of families merely home schooling for the sake of home schooling, but rather because families were and are home schooling their children in order to train them up so that they love and obey God, all for His glory. God has honored those thousands of families who have honored Him in the godly training of their children. HSLDA, too, dedicates its work to God's glory. The home school movement, meanwhile, continues to expand.

A Summary of the Home School Laws

A short summary of the home school legislation and case precedent will reveal the national trend to limit state controls over private education in favor of expanding parental liberty. Since 1982, thirty-seven states have changed their compulsory attendance laws or regulations to specifically allow for home schooling, with certain minimal requirements. In addition, two more states, Alaska and Nebraska, amended their private school statutes in 1984 allowing for any private schools to opt out of accreditation and certification requirements by asserting sincerely-held religious beliefs.[1] Home schoolers in these two states can now freely operate under these religious exemptions. It is important to notice that many of these states mentioned above abandoned prior statutory requirements that all teachers, including home schooling parents, be certified, because it infringed on parental rights and offered no guarantee as to the quality of education.[2] A close review of these new home school laws reveals a trend across the nation to lessen state control over private forms of education.

As of January 2000, there are thirty-seven states that *by statute* or *regulation* specifically allow "home instruction" or "home schooling," provided certain requirements are met. These states are Alaska, Arkansas, Arizona, Connecticut, Colorado, Delaware, Georgia, Hawaii, Florida, Iowa, Louisiana, Maine, Maryland, Michigan, Minnesota, Missouri, Mississippi, Montana, New Hampshire, New Mexico, New York, Nevada, North Carolina, North Dakota, Ohio, Oregon, Pennsylvania, Rhode Island, South Carolina, Tennessee, Utah, Virginia, Vermont, Washington, Wisconsin, West Virginia, and Wyoming.[3]

At least eight of these thirty-seven compulsory attendance statutes merely require home schoolers to submit an annual notice of intent, verifying that instruction will be given in certain core subjects for the same amount of days as the public schools. These states are Montana, Michigan, Alaska, Delaware, Wyoming, Mississippi, Wisconsin, and Missouri. In Missouri, home schoolers even have an option not to notify at all. These states' laws tend to be "model" laws since they are properly based on the "honor system" which protects parental liberty and takes all monitoring power from the state authorities.

Colorado and Georgia have laws similar to the eight mentioned above, but the parents are required to have the children tested every other year. The best part of these laws is that the test scores do not have to be submitted to the public schools.

The rest of these home school statutes have an additional requirement that home schoolers administer an annual standardized achievement test or have an evaluation performed which shows that the child has made adequate progress. Tennessee, for example, requires that home schooled children be tested in grades 2, 3, 6, 8, and 10. West Virginia mandates that students be tested annually and achieve above the 40th percentile. Oregon requires that home schoolers score in at least the 15th percentile, while Minnesota requires the 30th percentile and Virginia the 23rd percentile. Colorado requires only the 13th percentile. Arkansas requires that children score no lower than eight months below grade level.

All but two of these thirty-seven home school states allow parents with only high school diplomas or less to teach their children at home. Chapter 12 of this book exposes the fact that, according to numerous studies and experts, such qualification requirements are completely unnecessary for educating children.

For the most part, these states with home school laws have less conflict than before. However, no matter how good the law, some school districts will always add to the law. Many school officials have told me they actually believe the law is the minimum amount of authority to which they can add. Of course, the opposite is true: the law represents the maximum of their authority. In fact, one important case in Michigan, *Clonlara v. State Board of Education*,[4] struck down the Michigan Department of Education's onerous "Home School Compliance Procedures," because it is illegal for the Department of Education to create or enforce requirements *which are not in the law.*

Therefore, every year I have to deal with hundreds of school districts in these states which create "out of thin air" some new policy which illegally restricts the rights of home schoolers. The bimonthly *Home School Court Report,* published by the HSLDA, documents this common abuse in certain school district throughout the country.

Model Home School Laws

I believe the three state home school laws below are model laws which could be used in legislation to satisfactorily protect the rights of home school parents. Michigan's law is one of the best laws to maximize parents' rights:

> Under Michigan state law, "A child is not required to attend a public school if: The child is being educated at the child's home by his or her parent or legal guardian in an organized educational program in the subject areas of reading, spelling, mathematics, science, history, civics, literature, writing, and English grammar." No other requirements apply! This law reflects an honor system where the parents are trusted to act in the best interests of their children. Home schooling is thriving in Michigan without government oversight.

A similar law which was actually patterned after Michigan's home school law is in Alaska. Jack Phelps, a home school leader, called me and said the time was right in the Alaska legislature to pass a home school law. I told him Michigan had just enacted one of the best laws and sent Jack a copy. The Alaskan home school bill proceeded smoothly but the Senate Education committee thought the bill was too restrictive! So they removed the list of required subjects (without Jack's objection, of course) and the law was enacted. So now in Alaska, a child is exempt from compulsory attendance if "the child is being educated in the child's home by a parent or legal guardian." Michigan Compiled Laws Annotated (MCLA) Sec. 380.1561(3)(f).

According to the home school statute from the State of Montana (Montana Code Annotated Sec. 20-5-109), a home school must:

1. Maintain attendance and immunization records which must be available for inspection by the county super-intendent on request;
2. Be in a building that complies with local health and safety regulations (for homes, not schools);
3. Provide 180 days of instruction or the equivalent in accordance with 20-1-301 and 20-1-302 which require a school day to be 4 hours for grades 1-3 and 6 hours for grades 4-12.
4. Annually notify the county superintendent of intent to home school; and
5. Provide an organized course of study according to 20-7-111. The board of public education has the authority to "define and specify the basic instructional program for pupils in public schools." See, Sec. 20-7-111.
6. Neither the superintendent nor the school board has the authority to approve home schools or enforce the provisions above.
7. In Sec. 20-5-111, the "Responsibilities and rights of parent who provides home school - Rights of child in home school," are specifically described. This section of the Montana Code clearly recognizes the parents as being solely responsible for their children's education. The law states:
   "Subject to the provisions of Sec. 20-5-109, a parent has the authority to instruct his child, stepchild, or ward in a home school and is solely responsible for:
   a. The educational philosophy of the home school;

   b. the selection of instructional materials, curriculum, and textbooks;

   c. the time, place, and method of instruction: and

   d. the evaluation of the home school instruction."

The home school law for the State of Wisconsin requires:

1. "A home-based private educational program" is a program of educational instruction provided to a child by the child's parent or guardian or by a person designated by the parent or guardian. An instructional program provided to more than one family is not a home-based private educational program. Wis. Stat. Ann. 115.001(3g).

2. By Oct. 15 each year, the parents must submit a statement of enrollment to the department of education, indicating whether the home school meets all the requirements under Wis. Stat. Ann. Sec. 118.165. Wis. Stat. Ann. Sec. 115.30(3).

3. "Instruction in a home-based private educational program that meets all of the criteria under Sec. 118.165(1) may be substituted for attendance at public or private school" 118.15(4). The Sec. 118.165(1) criteria are:

   a. "primary purpose of the program is to provide private or religious-based education,"

   b. "the program is privately controlled,"

   c. the program provides at least 875 hours of instruction,

   d. the program "provides a sequentially progressive curriculum of fundamental instruction" in the Required Subjects: (which "does not require the program to include in its curriculum any concept, topic or practice in conflict with the program's religious doctrines," or exclude any such topic), and

   e. the program is not operated to circumvent the compulsory attendance law.

These types of specific laws would prevent arbitrary discrimination against home school families by government officials intruding into their privacy through home visits. These are good laws to consider in states where home schooling is more regulated.

States Where Home Schools Can Operate as Private Schools

The rest of the thirteen states have no specific statutes referring to home instruction, although *all states allow home schooling* under certain conditions. For example, in at least twelve states, home schools may presently operate as private schools.[5] In all of these states, home schoolers need only provide instruction in certain core subjects for the same time as public schools. Although each year certain school districts challenge the right of home schools to exist as private schools in these states, home schoolers have thus far been successful.

States Where Home Schools Are Subject to Discretionary State Approval

The remaining four states require that home schools be approved by the local school superintendent or school board in order to legally operate. A couple of the "home school" states cited above should also be included as approval states.[6]

These "approval states," however, have somewhat vague requirements for home schoolers. Of course, each school district in these states creates its own arbitrary definition of these terms, resulting in great disparity between school districts. In Massachusetts, for example, in one school district a home schooler may be completely legal, but when he moves into the neighboring school district with different standards, that same home schooler is prosecuted. Other home school families have legally and successfully home schooled in one district for several years, but a new superintendent comes to office, changes the rules, and criminally prosecutes the family. In fact, the vagueness in these "approval state" statutes has caused several states to abandon their approval requirements altogether, in favor of having home schoolers file notices of intent and take standardized tests.

To illustrate the abuse that often occurs in these "approval states," let me recount one incident which happened in Massachusetts. The Searles family was beginning to home school for the first year and they notified the local school district with the proper information. The school district official responded with a call demanding that they place their child in public school immediately. He said it might be weeks before he could get to "approve" their material. I contacted the school official, telling him that it would violate the family's religious beliefs to put their child in public school, and that they had submitted everything they needed to in order to be legal.

The next day the principal contacted the family, reiterating the demand to put their child in school. This was followed a little later by a visit from a police officer who told them that the child would be "forcibly removed" from the home if the child was not in public school the next day! The mother, badly shaken, called me. While we were on the phone, another knock came on her door. This time a probation officer was there, repeating the threats. She handed the phone to him and he proceeded to tell me that it was in "the child's best interest to go to public school." Although I persuaded him to abandon trying to take the child, he expedited the filing of charges so that the family had to appear in court in just two days, giving us barely enough time to secure a local attorney, Dave Chamberlain. At that hearing, God miraculously brought a substitute judge there who was sympathetic to the Searles, and she ruled that the family did not have to put their child in public school![7] She told the parties of the case to try to settle the dispute.

The school district, however, did not believe the mother's high school diploma was adequate, and they also required regular home visits, testing at least twice a year in the public schools, and meetings eight times a year with a public school official to determine if the family could continue to home school. Of course, none of these restrictive requirements were in the law. The family refused to agree to such terms, and the school district "disapproved." In a subsequent hearing, the court gave us two weeks to prepare, and during the course of that time I was able to convince the opposing attorney (who knew nothing about home schoolers' constitutional rights) that they would not win. By God's grace, the Searles case was settled without the family having to comply with the ridiculous requirements.[8] Obviously, "approval states" do not protect the right to home school but leave it to the arbitrary discretion of biased public school officials.

The "Vagueness Defense" and the "Neutral Decision-Maker Defense," which are discussed in chapter 18, directly apply to these types of "approval states" and are used frequently by HSLDA to defend the rights of parents to teach their children at home.

Trend Toward Lesser State Control of Home Schooling

Finally, all the cases and amended statutes mentioned above, and many dozens more, point to a trend in the courts and legislatures for less state control of home education. Although this author objects to the state having any interest in controlling the education of our children, a long line of U.S. Supreme Court cases does recognize that the state has an interest in education. However, at present, the state only has an interest in the *product* of education, not the *process*. Whenever the state attempts to control the *process* of education, such as dictating teacher qualifications, approving curricula, or requiring home visits, it is in clear opposition with parental liberty.

On the other hand, if the states pass laws concerning the *product* of education, such as various notification requirements or, perhaps, standardized testing or evaluations, the parents' rights and the state's interests can be more peacefully balanced. Of course, this is basically a short-term solution. Ultimately, the long-term goal is to eradicate the state's interest by repealing all of the compulsory attendance laws. But this will not be easily achieved until home schoolers are able to influence legislatures and have their biblically trained home schooled students become judges, legislators, reporters, teachers, and college professors.

Notes

1. See Alaska Statutes §§14.45.100 through 14.45.140 (1984) and Revised Statutes of Nebraska* §79-1701 (2). Prior to 1984, Nebraska had been prosecuting private schools and home schools across the state who refused to use certified teachers. Pastor Sileven of Faith Baptist Church Academy was jailed and his school padlocked. An appointed Governor's Commission investigated the problem and recommended that the legislature pass an exemption for these religious schools to protect the parents' constitutional rights. The legislature adopted the recommendation into law.
2. Some of these states include Colorado, Florida, Nebraska, North Dakota, Iowa, New Mexico, Virginia, and Washington.
3. See, generally, Christopher Klicka, *Home Schooling in the United States: A Legal Analysis*, (Purcellville, VA: Home School Legal Defense Association), for further specific statute citations. This publication is updated every August and is available from HSLDA at 540-338-5600 or online at *www.hslda.org*.
4. *Clonlara*, 496 N.W. 2d 66(Mi App. Ct. 1991).
5. Those states are Alabama, Alaska, California, Delaware, Illinois, Indiana, Kansas, Kentucky, Louisiana, Michigan, Nebraska, and Texas. See Klicka, *Home Schooling in the United States: A Legal Analysis*, published by the Home School Legal Defense Association for an annually updated summary of the cases and statutes in these states which allow for home schools to operate as private schools. Individual state summaries are also available from HSLDA.
6. See *Ibid.* for a complete description of these state laws.
7. In *the Matter of Johnna M. Searles*, No. 903 7CHO01 7, District Court of the Amesbury Division, September 4, 1989.
8. "Major Courtroom Victory in Massachusetts," *The Home School Court Report*, Vol. 6, No. 4, Fall 1990, 2.

Chapter
21

We Can't Afford
Not to Be Involved:
Tips for Influencing
State Legislation

Since 1982, thirty-seven states have passed laws or regulations recognizing and defining home schooling. Some of these new laws passed according to the plans of home schoolers, and others passed leaving home schoolers in disarray.

The enemies of home schooling are just beginning to wake up. From 1982 to 1988, home schoolers, for the most part, surprised the National Education Association and the other public school lobbying groups. Since then, however, the legislative road has not been as smooth.

In fact, in only one year's time, negative bills were introduced in: 1) Kansas, to require home schools to be certified teachers; 2) Maine, to require home schools to submit to monthly home visits in order to determine if they can continue to home school; 3) Montana, to require home schools to be tested by the public school authorities; 4) Illinois, to prohibit spanking in all private schools (which includes home schools); 5) Connecticut, to require two meetings with schools each year, quarterly progress reports, and to limit the number of home school students per household to five; 6) Georgia and Colorado, to require an expansion of ages over which children would be required to attend school; 7) and in Wisconsin and Mississippi legislative study committees were formed to draft more restrictive legislation for home schoolers.[1] In addition to these negative bills, several positive bills were introduced in Iowa (to repeal the teacher certification requirements), in New Mexico (to repeal the college degree requirement), and in Oregon (to put the home school regulations into law).

By God's grace, all of the negative legislation was defeated, and the study committees were disassembled with no recommendations for change to the present favorable laws! The home school organizations worked hard, and HSLDA provided research, gave expert testimony at committee hearings, and sent out legislative alerts to HSLDA members in many of the various states. Concerning the positive bills, teacher certification was knocked out by the Iowa Legislature. The two favorable bills in Oregon and New Mexico were defeated,[2] but subsequently passed a few years later.

However, the point is that, more than ever, it is important for the average home school family to stay informed of the latest legislation affecting parents' rights and to be prepared to participate in the political process. The onslaught of negative bills from State School Board Associations, School Administrator Associations, and State Teacher Associations is just beginning.

The importance of everyone joining together and being involved in legislative activity has been grounded in me for a long time. In fact, for sixteen years my father, George Klicka, was a state representative in the Wisconsin Legislature, so I received much experience and valuable insight from him concerning what the most effective lobbying techniques are.

Since I started working for HSLDA in 1985, I have been directly involved in the passage of eight new home school laws or regulations. In addition, in conjunction with local home school leaders, I have drafted numerous amendments to legislation to protect home schoolers and have fought bills that would have restricted home schools. I have given expert testimony before numerous legislative committees and administrative hearings. I also regularly review newly introduced bills and send out legislative alerts to state home school leaders concerning legislation that may affect home schoolers in their state.

As a result, I have gathered some ideas on how to lobby effectively. Below are some tips and suggestions which the reader may find useful.

The Need for a Vision:
Repeal Compulsory Attendance Laws

First of all, each home schooler and each home school organization needs to decide what the goal is for their state law concerning home schooling. Ultimately, my goal is to see states repeal their compulsory attendance laws, but as I have stated elsewhere in this book, the timing is not right. Much more education of the legislators needs to take place, which may take at least a generation.

It is clear, however, that the public, disgruntled with the failure of the public school system, is beginning to warm up to the idea of repealing compulsory attendance. A national survey was taken on October 22-25, 1998 of 1,012 adults using advanced probability sampling techniques. The poll, conducted by Opinion Research Corporation of Princeton, NJ, found that one out of 4 Americans (25 percent) would support repealing compulsory school attendance and ending tax support for schooling. Those favoring repealing compulsory attendance increased to 57 percent if they were enough private scholarships available so all poor and disadvantaged children could go to school.

A growing number of people are beginning to realize our public school system is academically and morally bankrupt. The goal of repealing compulsory attendance as the ultimate solution to our country's educational crisis should always remain our top priority.

In the meantime, you must first ask the question: Are we, as a body of home schoolers in a given state, satisfied with the status quo? In many states without home school laws, home schoolers, as a whole, are doing pretty well. Although each year some families are harassed, most families enjoy much freedom. Many of the "private school states" fit into this category.

Also several of the states with home school laws already allow maximum freedom and are, therefore, worth protecting. Missouri's home school law, which requires no monitoring of any kind nor any registration, would definitely fit into this category. If it is your position to be content with the status quo, your lobbying strategy should be defensive—keeping the law the way it is. Sometimes it is better to work to contain a few legal brush fires each year, than to open all home schoolers to scrutiny and possibly greater regulation by introducing a bill.

However, if you decide that you are not satisfied with the present law, you need to develop an offensive strategy. This, of course, will involve much planning and coordinating. The most important consideration will be the timing of the legislative bill. Is the legislature ready to deal favorably with home schooling? Or will it make the legal atmosphere worse for home schooling? The bottom line which we must realize is that not every state needs home school legislation.

The Need for Organization

However, home schoolers need to be organized. They should make a determination as to who will spearhead the offensive strategy or who will monitor the legislature for defensive purposes. Most state home school organizations can work together with local support groups to accomplish this task.

Home school organizations in each state should work together on legislative action in order to present a united front and, as a result, be the most effective. This does not mean, of course, that each state must limit itself to establishing only one home school organization in order to appear united. Rather, there can be several independent state home school organizations which each meet the needs of the type of home schoolers they represent. Each of these independent home school organizations, however, should be prepared to work together whenever there is a need for legislative action.

An excellent example of "separate but united" home school organizations working together is in Illinois. There, at least four different home school organizations, representing both Christian and secular home schoolers, have formed the "Ad Hoc Committee." The sole purpose of this committee is to facilitate communication and planning strategy for legislative action. Each home schooling group sends a representative to the periodic meetings in order to participate in setting strategy. Then each representative, in turn, communicates the plan of action to their mailing lists in order to activate the grassroots. In short, each home school organization retains its autonomy and independence but, at the same time, the home school organizations present a united front when battling the legislature. Their effectiveness is demonstrated in the fact that they have killed, in committee, all harmful legislation introduced since the Ad Hoc Committee came together.

The Need for Education

The best investment for a home schooler to make in the legislature is to take time to educate his or her legislative representatives. Most legislators have never met a home school family personally and probably know very little about it.

I recommend that home schoolers write to their state representatives and state senators, even when there is no particular legislation at stake. Even more beneficial is to visit the legislators' office at the capitol (which, incidentally, will be an excellent field trip for your children) or to invite him to speak to a local gathering of home school constituent in his district. Some families I know have invited their legislator over to their house for dinner or for a "coffee" involving local home school parents.

It is a good idea to have information to leave with him that will introduce him to the concept of home schooling and document the fact that home schooling really works. The HSLDA has various concise resources available to its members, which have been frequently used to educate legislators and state officials. Also your state organization may want to consider printing an educational brochure that would summarize what home schooling is, its academic successes, and its legal rights.

One very effective activity is to organize an annual "Capitol Day." One of the home school organizations in Oklahoma, OCHEC, has organized "Capitol Days" for the last several years with good success.[3] This involves advance planning since home schoolers throughout the state must be notified of the date in order to prepare a trip. It is also a good idea for families to contact their legislator in advance and arrange a meeting with him to extol the virtues of home schooling and let him see real live home schooled children. If the legislator is not available, it is important to still stop by his office and leave a message and information on home schooling.

Usually a rally is planned on "Capitol Day," where a few people speak to the crowd of home schoolers and where display tables are set up with free information. These rallies and visits to the legislators' offices tend to draw their attention to the benefits of home schooling. In the future when a bill is introduced involving home schooling, the legislator will remember the home school families and children he has met. It is much easier to vote against the faceless issue of home schooling than it is to vote against people he has met personally. Education of the legislature is something that must take place all year—not just when the home school bill is already introduced.

I might make mention that another effective way of winning a legislator to your side is to work on his campaign, especially when he is a first-time candidate. My wife and I worked for and came to know a local candidate for the Virginia House of Delegates. Many other home schoolers also became involved in his campaign. He won and now is completely supportive of home schooling, although prior to his candidacy he was unfamiliar with the subject.

A few years later, we moved into another legislative district and another opportunity arose. A moderate candidate was trying to unseat a very pro-NEA legislator. Once again, my wife and I and a number of other home schoolers came alongside this candidate and gently educated him on the key issues including home schooling. He was so impressed with our home schooling and the home schoolers' help in his campaign that he took our views in general to heart. He upset the incumbent and is now one of the most conservative statesman and champions of limited government in the House. Of course, he is stalwart defender of home schooling. He is presently considering a run for Lt. Governor. The lesson is obvious. We need to be involved.

Lobbying workshops are also a suggestion. Home school support groups or state organizations can organize workshops in which individuals familiar with the political process can train home school leaders and families on effective ways to lobby. Sometimes these lobbying workshops can take place at the annual state home school conference.

Another way to positively improve the legal status of home schooling is to request the Governor to proclaim an annual Home Education Week or Day. This will improve relations and communications with the Governor to ensure his support for home schoolers' rights. It also creates an excellent opportunity for a "rally day" at the capitol to honor Home Education Week while simultaneously arranging for all the home school families to visit their House and Senate representatives. This promotes goodwill among the Legislature, provides an excellent field trip for youngsters (various tours can be arranged), and serves as an investment in protecting home school freedoms later. More and more states are doing this.

In February 1995, in conjunction with Home Education Week, the Home Education Association of Virginia, under the direction of Anne Miller and Yvonne Bunn, among others, set up a special ceremony over lunch. The state superintendent, secretary of education, and many other government officials attended. Then Governor George Allen gave an excellent address and read the Proclamation. I had the opportunity, along with many home school leaders, to meet and talk with the various officials and government officials in order to secure their support for home schooling.

Governor George Allen proclaimed February 12-18, 1995, to be Virginia Home Education Week throughout the Commonwealth. The Home Education Association of Virginia drafted the proclamation which I reviewed and it was adopted, word-for-word, by the governor. The time and effort to secure such a proclamation is worth its weight in developing a positive relationship with the legislature and governor. This proclamation has been routinely adopted by subsequent governors every year. (For model language to draft a proclamation in your state, see the U.S. Senate's Home School Resolution reprinted in chapter 22.)

The Need for Preparation

Monitoring legislation and the ability to communicate that information to the "grassroots" home schoolers are key elements to successfully defeating negative legislation and passing beneficial legislation. Some of the ways to do this are: 1) hire an actual lobbyist to monitor legislation (who preferably is a home schooler himself or is related to one); 2) start a relationship with an existing lobbying group that is supportive of home schooling and who is willing to watch out for harmful legislation to home schoolers; 3) and/or utilize home schoolers who live in the capitol city who can visit legislators, pick up copies of bills, or "camp out" for a few days in the capitol, monitoring a bill progressing through various amendments.

As an additional support for the states, the HSLDA subscribes to a computer service called "state net," enabling it to monitor legislation affecting home schoolers in all fifty states. During legislative sessions,

HSLDA does a "search" every other day, and all the bills which are found are reviewed by the HSLDA lawyers who cover the particular states. The lawyers, in turn, notify the state home school leaders and normally send out "legislative alerts" to the HSLDA members in the state.

It is also useful to develop a good relationship with a couple of legislators and senators who will keep you informed on bills being introduced, their progress, and chance of passage. If you keep them supplied with favorable documentation on home schooling, they can "lobby" on your behalf and set up key meetings for you to talk with other legislators. One home school mom in Colorado works one day a week for a senator, and her home school son works as a page. That is one way to stay on top of legislation!

State home school organizations also must be able to communicate the information quickly to their members, in order to have them pray, write letters, make phone calls, or attend legislative hearings. Establishing a phone tree can be very effective. In Oklahoma, the Christian Home Educators Fellowship (CHEF) has developed an inexpensive computerized phone system on which they can record a legislative action item. Then the computer program will automatically call approximately two hundred home schoolers and support group leaders, giving them all the same message. The support group leaders can, in turn, contact their local families. In this way news is spread quickly and accurately.

With the advent of the internet, state home school organization communication networks can and are becoming even more sophisticated. At the touch of a keyboard, a legislative alert can be sent, in a matter of seconds, across the entire state to thousands of home school families. A 1997 survey of home school families found that 85.6 percent of home school families owned a computer which is far above the national average.[4] At the Home School Legal Defense Association in January 2000, we had 70,000 member families with over half of them subscribing to our "e-lert" service. God is using the advances in technology to enable home schoolers to better protect their freedoms.

Between HSLDA's e-lert system and the e-lert systems established by the state home school organizations and local support groups, the home schoolers are better equipped with accurate and timely information. Now more than ever, home schoolers are successful in influencing legislation and impacting public policy as they respond to the calls for action they receive by e-mail.

For example, in 1993, Virginia had its organization and communication network tested over and over again to fight two bad bills and pass one good bill.

One bill, Senate Bill 913 was the "baby" of the Department of Education. It would lower the compulsory attendance age from six to five. The Department figured passage would be easy in the completely democratically controlled House, Senate, and governor's office.

However, they underestimated the power of God working through the home schoolers.

Upon the bill's passage in the Senate, HSLDA and the Home Education Association of Virginia got busy. Several Alerts were mailed to thousands of home schoolers three or four times during the course of the battle, and phone trees were humming. The home schoolers were able to convince House member Jay O'Brien to introduce an amendment which would allow any parent to choose to wait a year until his child was six years old.

Due to the pressure of home schoolers, the amendment was passed in the House and then miraculously passed the Senate! It went to the Governor, and he vetoed it. We blitzed the legislature once more, and the Senate voted 39 to 1, and the House voted 87 to 0 to override the Governor and pass the O'Brien amendment! As a result, we now have a *mandatory kindergarten* law in Virginia which is *not mandatory*! One senator commented on the floor of the Senate that based on the number of phone calls and visits and letters that came in concerning this bill, he could only assume every other person in Virginia was home schooling![5]

What Needs to Be Considered When Dealing with Actual Legislation?

When introducing a home school bill or amending an existing bill, always decide how far you will compromise or if you will compromise at all. Concerning harmful legislation, "no compromise" is usually the best policy. Every state organization that has followed this policy has succeeded in defeating bad legislation. As a result, home schooling freedoms are always advancing.

If introducing a bill to improve a law for the benefit of home schoolers, it is suggested that three versions of the bill be drafted, but only submit the "ideal" bill at first. If this bill begins to pass "as is," no need to use any of the other versions. If the "ideal" bill, however, begins to be vigorously challenged by the home schooling opponents, either submit one of your other versions of the bill or, if the risk is too great, abandon the bill altogether. For example, in Alabama a few years ago, I testified in favor of a bill that the home schoolers had introduced. Due to some strings pulled by the Alabama teachers' union and some political maneuvering, the good law died altogether, and a substitute bill was introduced in the same committee that had been considering the home schoolers' bill. The new bill was so restrictive that the home schoolers quickly withdrew all support, and the restrictive bill died.

If a hearing is set for a piece of legislation that will either help or harm home schooling, it is often wise strategy to alert as many home schoolers as possible to attend the hearing. This usually impresses the legislators and gets their attention. Some of the witnesses to have testify are: 1) one or two articulate home school students who will convince the legislators of the excellent product of home schooling; 2) at least one educational expert who can testify to the academic benefits of home schooling, rebuff the lack of socialization claims, and recite various statistics on the success of home schoolers; 3) a legal expert who will testify as to the constitutionality of the bill, the legal conflict it will cure or cause (telling some true accounts of harassment), and the national trend to deregulate home schooling; 4) and several home school mothers and fathers of various educational levels, races, religious backgrounds, and jobs. I have found it beneficial to submit all testimony in writing in case you are cut short, and it also provides the legislators with something to review and pass around as the bill progresses.

Some of the home school leaders may want to target key legislators on the committee before and after the hearing in order to try to influence them favorably. Of course, a rally could also be organized right before the hearing, and the media could be invited to publicize the large crowds.

An Example of the Passage of a Home School Bill

Below is an example of how a bill was passed against great odds. Some of the strategy used may prove helpful in your state.

In the spring of 1988, home schoolers in Colorado were still faced with difficult restrictions. Home schooling had to be "approved" by local school districts which were often quite arbitrary. Families who were disapproved could appeal to the Department of Education which generally affirmed the denial. I was involved in intervening on behalf of dozens of families in various school districts who were having difficulty. Some of the families were already in court.

Bill Moritz, a lawyer and home school father, sent me a draft of an "ideal" home school law which would simply give home schools the same status as private schools, which were not regulated in Colorado. Home schoolers would merely have to notify the school district, and there would be no approval by the school district. The passage of such a bill in Colorado was virtually hopeless, considering the strength of the public school lobbying organizations and the makeup of the legislature at that time. Yet, we talked with the home school leaders and the bill was submitted to the legislature.

Two legislators agreed to sponsor the bill. The House sponsor was very liberal. The Senate sponsor was conservative. The bill was never promoted as a Republican or Democratic bill. I talked at length with the House sponsor and referred to the home schoolers as a "minority" which was getting muscled by the state. He loved the idea of helping a "minority." I then wrote up a letter for him which supported the bill and demonstrated that home schoolers were a minority who were protected by the First and Fourteenth Amendments of the Constitution. He gave a copy of the letter to all the legislators in the House. As you will see, he carried the banner so well for the home schoolers that he was able to get the final version of the bill passed unanimously in the House!

Meanwhile, Rory Schneeberger, a home school mother and home school leader, "camped out" at the capitol for about a week. Many home schoolers wrote in support of the bill and others testified at various hearings.

Rory constantly kept up with the various committees and with the amendments which legislators were trying to get attached. The two sponsors of the bill regularly called me over a two-week period to get my view on various language changes and my suggestions on counter-language.

First, the opposing side wanted some sort of record keeping which could be inspected by the local superintendent. We added the language that he could only inspect records "if he had probable cause that the family was not in compliance." This language applied a constitutional standard of probable cause which can only be used if the superintendent has actual evidence that the family is not educating their children. The language was adopted. (Ever since this law was passed, HSLDA has not heard of a single family who has ever had to have their records inspected!)

Second, the opposing side wanted accountability in the form of annual testing. The home school advocates explained that they only wanted to allow it if it started in the third grade and was administered every three years thereafter. It was finally settled that home schoolers would be tested beginning in third grade and every other year thereafter. The home school advocates also felt that there needed to be a standard, so that families could not be arbitrarily shut down. We suggested the same standard as the public schools, which was the 13th percentile, and the opposing side agreed!

Finally, we explained that many home schooling families were opposed to sending the scores to the public schools and suggested sending them to a private school of their choice. It was agreed. We also made sure that the option was still available for home schoolers who did not want anything to do with the school district to be able to enroll in a private school but to do their teaching at home.

By the end of all this, a very short "ideal" bill became a very long and wordy bill. In fact, the *Denver Post,* which had been against the original bill and wanted excessive restrictions on home schoolers, came out in support of the final, lengthy bill believing it was restrictive.

However, in the final analysis, the bill was mostly unenforceable and hardly restrictive at all. In effect, home schoolers only have to communicate once a year with the public schools in the form of a short notice of intent. This is comparable to some of the better home school laws, such as in Wisconsin, Montana, Wyoming, and Mississippi. The inspection of records never happens because of the "probable cause" protection, and the test results can be sent to a private school. Also the option for home schoolers to enroll in a private school but teach at home was left intact.[6]

Many prayers were offered during this time, and God truly worked a miracle against all odds. Also many valuable lessons in legislative strategy were learned throughout the process.

Believe it or not, we came back in January and February of 1994 and successfully amended the Colorado home school law again to make it even better! I worked closely once again with the state home school organizations, Christian Home Educators of Colorado and Concerned Parents of Colorado, to secure sponsors and organize several statewide letter writing campaigns. I testified twice before the House and Senate education committees, with hundreds of home schoolers in attendance, and the bill passed 33 to 2 in the Senate and the House by a vote of 53 to 9.[7]

The majority leader in the House who sponsored our bill could not believe how organized we were and how many calls we could muster. He said the Colorado Department of Education completely abandoned their attempt to attach restrictive amendments to the bill and told him, "we do not want to mess with the home schoolers!"[7] This should always be our strategy to never settle for a home school law until we achieve maximum freedom. Remember, increasing freedom always involves a risk, but I have found God blesses those who honor Him in such endeavors.

Model Legislation

If you are considering working to expand freedom for home schoolers in your state, review chapter 20 for model language from Wisconsin, Michigan, Montana, and Alaska.

The Price of Freedom Is Eternal Vigilance

The information in this chapter is only suggestions, ideas, and recounted experiences. Each home schooler and home school organization will have to weigh their situation in their state, and act accordingly. Hopefully, one important message will have penetrated the reader: the price of freedom is eternal vigilance.

Notes

1. See, generally, two editions of *The Home School Court Report*, Vol. 7, No. .2, March/April 1991, and Vol. 7, No. 2, May/June 1991.
2. *Ibid.*
3. OCHEC newsletter, Vol. IX, No.1, February-March 1992, p. 1-2, OK Central Home Educators' Consociation, Oklahoma City.
4. Dr. Brian Ray, *Strengths of Their Own, Home Schoolers Across America*, 1997, Salem, OR, www.nheri.org. This was a study of 5,402 home school students from across the country.
5. "Virginia: Home Schoolers Battle Legislation," *The Home School Court Report*, Vol. 9, No. 2, March/April 1993, 18-19.
6. For more details on the home school bill which was passed in Colorado see "Legislative Victory in Colorado," *The Home School Court Report*, Vol. 4, No. 2, Spring 1988, 10-11.
7. "Colorado Passes Home School Bill," *The Home School Court Report*, May/June 1994, Vol. 10, Number 3, 1.

You Can Make a Difference:

Home Schoolers Impact Capitol Hill

Then Jesus told his disciples a parable to show them that they should always pray and not give up. He said: "In a certain town there was a judge who neither feared God nor cared about men. And there was a widow in that town who kept coming to him with the plea, 'Grant me justice against my adversary.' For some time he refused. But finally he said to himself, 'Even though I don't fear God or care about men, yet because this widow keeps bothering me, I will see that she gets justice, so that she won't eventually wear me out with her coming! And will not God bring about justice for his chosen ones, who cry out to him day and night? Will he keep putting them off?'"

Luke 18:1-7 (NIV)

In this day and age the government seems so big and we seem so far away, especially from the Federal Congress, we often wonder, "Will my phone call or letter really matter?" When the cause is just and the Lord is on our side, our involvement does matter. We must remember that God is in control and that the "heart of the King is like rivers of water in the hand of the Lord, he turns it which ever way he wills" Proverbs 21:1.

Even in this day of influential PACs, massive teacher unions, and other special interests, a personal letter or phone call to a congressional office is still the most effective way to influence public policy. This is especially the case when home schoolers are brought into the issue.

I was recently told by a staffer on Capitol Hill, in regard to an upcoming meeting with powerful members of the educational establishment, that we, "came to the table as equals." I said, "How is that since they have over a hundred million dollar budget?" The congressional staffer responded, "They can't deliver the grassroots calls, but you home schoolers can."

Since 1985, I have worked as Senior Counsel for the Home School Legal Defense Association. I have witnessed the home school movement grow from 10,000 families to over 700,000 families. During this time, I have been engaged in hundreds of legislative battles, representing home schoolers at both state and federal levels. Without home schoolers' exceptional activism in political life and ultimate reliance on God's strength, we would have never convinced 37 different states to enact specific home school laws, defeated hundreds of harmful legislative proposals, and influenced the most powerful city in the world, Washington D.C.

There is no doubt, home schoolers comprise one of the most politically active groups, per capita, in the country. I am convinced that it is not an overstatement to say that the home school movement is grassroots politics at its best. The reason for this is simple: the home school movement is future oriented. Home schoolers want to preserve and gain more freedom for their children and their children's children. The home school movement is composed of families—strong, close families—which form the foundation of any nation. Although the movement is decentralized, home schoolers have a tight network with one another.

To say that home schoolers are decentralized is not to say that they are not organized. Most home schoolers are members of local support groups in their community, which range in size from 10 to over 200 families. These local groups are usually linked to state home schooling associations. These state associations often establish phone trees, e-mail groups, and other elaborate communication systems for communicating both news and legislative alerts to their members.

One of the purposes of the National Center for Home Education, a division of HSLDA, is to establish and maintain a network with the state home school associations in all 50 states in order to facilitate instant communication and rapid response to federal legislation. We alert the state home school associations and they pass the alert down to the local level. Because of the home schoolers' commitment to the future, they respond.

In addition, we have created the two-pronged Congressional Action Program (CAP) which is comprised of local home school lobbyists in each of the 435 congressional districts and local home schoolers in the Washington D.C. area. These volunteer lobbyists in each congressional district are simply home school parents who establish e-alert systems or phone trees in order to deliver constituent calls to their congressman at a moment's notice. Thanks to the wonders of modern technology and the internet, when a federal legislative issue which may affect home schooling surfaces, HSLDA can alert our network of home school leaders and CAP volunteers at a moment's notice—very similar to the Minutemen during the War for Independence. These CAP District Coordinators, in response, activate their phones, fax machines, and e-mails enabling us to alert thousands across the nation.

The second lobby prong of CAP consists of volunteer home school parents and teenagers in the Washington, D.C., area who we train to conduct lobbying visits on Capitol Hill as needed. This system, used properly, results in home schoolers becoming the most successful "persistent widows" around.

Lessons from the HR6 Battle

One of the most miraculous examples of God's hand working in a mighty way on behalf of home schoolers was the battle over the Miller amendment, which was attached to HR6. This battle over HR6 also provides us with an example of successful techniques in communicating an emergency "call to action" across the nation in a matter of days. In fact, for two weeks in February 1994, the home schoolers gave Congress a tremendous lesson on the power of grass roots politics that it is not likely to forget any time soon. This is what happened.

Miller's Amendment

It all started when Congressman George Miller (D-CA) introduced an amendment to HR6, an omnibus education reappropriations bill. This amendment stated:

> Each state applying for funds under this title shall provide
> the Secretary with the assurance that after July 1, 1998 it
> will require each local educational agency within the state
> to certify that each fulltime teacher in schools under the
> jurisdiction of the agency is certified to teach in the sub-
> ject area in which he or she is assigned.

At first glance, the provision seems harmless enough, but that is the way bad legislation is usually introduced. The goal of those congressmen who want to limit our freedoms is to make bad legislation look as innocuous as possible.

After looking more closely at this amendment, we discovered that the term "school" was defined elsewhere in HR6 as a "nonprofit day or residential school." In other words, Miller's amendment would require every teacher in all schools—home schools, private schools, and public schools—to be certified to teach in the subject or area in which they are teaching! For home schoolers, the Miller Amendment was the political equivalent of declaring nuclear war.

Of course, this mandate is connected to federal funding. If a state wanted to continue to receive billions of dollars in federal funding, it would have to guarantee to the U.S. Department of Education that all its teachers in the state were certified to teach. Based on experience, nearly every state would change its laws in order to receive the money. Thus the danger was apparent and very real.

Representative Dick Armey (R-TX), seeing the problem, offered an amendment in the House Education committee to protect home and private schools from the certification requirement by simply exempting them. This amendment, however, was soundly rejected in committee on a party line vote. This was further evidence of the seriousness of this attack and the intent behind it.

HSLDA Enters the Fray

At this point, on February 14, 1994, Representative Armey's office contacted Home School Legal Defense Association (HSLDA) for our analysis of the Miller amendment. We immediately contacted Representative Miller's office to express our concern and ask for clarifying language. However, Mr. Miller's staff stated that he would not agree to any amendments. With the vote only nine days away, we were forced to take our next step by preparing and sending out a nationwide Alert.

That evening our "Fax Alert" outlining a six-step plan of action for contacting Congress was sent to our network of home school state leaders in all fifty states. These state leaders, in turn, lit up their phone trees, which were already in place, and got the word spread out further. We also sent our "Fax Alert" to a coalition of conservative and Christian groups representing national organizations throughout the country and to the Christian media. Earlier that day, we were able to send our Congressional Action Program (CAP) lobbyists, including a number of HSLDA personnel, down to the Congress to drop off a prepared packet at each of the 435 congressional offices, which urged the congressmen to vote against Miller's amendment. We asked them to respond within three hours to avoid phone calls. Only a few congressmen took us seriously and responded.

The Second Day: Christian Talk Shows Get Involved

By Wednesday morning, thousands of home schoolers were receiving our information on the dangers of HR6. Tens of thousands of copies of the "Fax Alert" were being photocopied and distributed. On the morning of February 16, hundreds of calls began to pour in to the congressional offices. The onslaught had begun, which was not to stop for the next six days!

Meanwhile, HSLDA contacted home schoolers from around the local area to descend upon the HSLDA offices in order to stuff the mailing to 40,000 HSLDA members. The information for the mailing had been dropped off to the printers the night before and just began arriving from various printers from around the local area.

By Wednesday afternoon, the Christian radio talk shows were beginning to call HSLDA offices and interview Michael Farris, Doug Phillips, myself and many of the other HSLDA attorneys. Marlin Maddoux, who hosts the "Point of View" radio talk show, was one of the first to air the HR6 Alert to a nationwide audience. All that day, while HSLDA was working frantically, the state home school leaders were also frantically spreading the news across the country.

CAP Hits the Hill Again and Misinformation Spread by Congress

On the third day, the local CAP lobbyists hit the congressmen for a second time with a new packet of updated information, urging them to vote against the Miller amendment in order to protect home schools and private schools. Included in that packet was a copy of the

DeJonge decision by the Michigan Supreme Court, which was handled by HSLDA, declaring teacher certification unconstitutional (see chapter 17). Little did the DeJonges know that their case in Michigan and the eight-year ordeal they went through would help stop the teacher certification amendment to HR6. (God's ways are not our ways. We wanted to win that case the first year, but it would have had no precedential value.)

Home schoolers from all around volunteered to deliver the packets to the congressmen. In fact, my eight-month pregnant wife, Tracy Klicka, was one of the home school lobbyists who visited various offices. This time when they visited, many of the congressmen's aides invited the CAP lobbyists to sit down and explain their position. The first time, the CAP lobbyists were basically ignored. It is amazing what a few thousand phone calls will do!

Of course, the Christian talk shows were still cranking out the information and spreading the Alert far and near. In the meantime, home schoolers were continuing to give copies of the Alert on HR6 to their parents and grandparents, neighbors, church members, and people at work. We heard story after story of people who, for the first time, called their congressmen in response to the HR6 attack.

Of course misinformation was rampant from the congressmen's offices. This is a common tactic of many aides to confuse the public and deflect opposition. Many aides said, "There is no such thing as HR6." Other aides stated that "HR6 already passed. Why are you calling us?" Others would say, "HR6 and the Miller amendment are not intended to hurt home schools and private schools." There were also many who did not even know about the Miller amendment.

Remember, what an aide explains concerning the Congress's intention really does not matter, ultimately. We would not be able to defend a home schooler in court by stating, "Charlotte from Representative Smith's office said that this was not intended to apply to home schools and private schools." The courts, instead, would weigh heavily on the fact that when Dick Armey tried to amend the Miller amendment to exempt home schools and private schools, it was soundly rejected, evidencing an intent of the Congress to have this apply to home schools and private schools.

By Friday, the Capitol switchboard was completely shut down! The lines to all the congressmen's offices were completely jammed across the country. In fact, many congressmen were returning home for the weekend and were being besieged in town hall meetings. When the congressmen tried to call back to their aides in Washington, D.C., they could not get through because the phones were jammed! Home schoolers began to tie up local campaign offices and other local offices of the congressman.

Home Schoolers Stir Up State Governments to Fight HR6

Meanwhile, another strategy was being employed by the home schoolers. They were contacting their state representatives and governors in order to get them to oppose the Miller amendment to HR6. In Idaho, the state legislature, in response to an instant rally organized by a home school mom of over six hundred home schoolers on the state capitol steps, passed a resolution condemning the Miller amendment of HR6. The resolution, in part, stated:

> ...WHEREAS, the private schools and home schools of our state are an integral part of that educational delivery system; and
>
> WHEREAS, the State of Idaho recognizes the value of our nontraditional, nonpublic schools and can verify their contributions; and
>
> WHEREAS, private schools and home schools educate and graduate students at a level of academic achievement comparable to and often exceeding state and national averages of academic achievement; and
>
> WHEREAS, the local control of education is vital to the maintenance of our republican form of government; and
>
> WHEREAS, any forced imposition of federal standards jeopardizes the foundation on which our form of government is based; and
>
> WHEREAS, it is the position of the State of Idaho that the role of the state in educating her people, including the preparation and monitoring of those personnel who are responsible for providing that education, is reserved to the state, the local school districts and to the parents.
>
> NOW, THEREFORE, BE IT RESOLVED by the members of the Second Regular Session of the Fifty-second Idaho legislature, the Senate and the House of Representatives concurring therein, that we emphatically urge resistance to and total rejection of any attempt by the federal

government to interject itself into the educational affairs of the nontraditional, nonpublic schools of this state.

In Wisconsin, my father, George Klicka, called the Wisconsin State Superintendent and convinced him that the Miller amendment to HR6 would even mess up the public schools. He ended up having his staff contact the Wisconsin delegation of congressmen to oppose this bill. Many members of the Wisconsin Legislature immediately prepared a document condemning the Miller amendment of HR6. In Virginia, home schoolers convinced Governor George Allen to write a letter to the Virginia delegation of congressmen to oppose the Miller amendment of HR6.

The following week, Doug Phillips and I flew to Texas to hold rallies throughout the state that had been prearranged. As a result of the HR6 phone blitz, over one thousand people showed up for the Dallas rally alone. Also on Monday, James Dobson of Focus on the Family had Mike Farris speak to his twenty million listeners on the importance of calling their congressmen regarding the Miller Amendment of HR6. This caused a second huge wave of phone calls!

February 24: The Miracle and the Victory

Then on February 24, we found out that the Democrats were trying to use a rule called the "Closed Rule" to keep any new amendment from being entertained on the floor. This, of course, would have prohibited Dick Armey's amendment, which we had helped draft in order to specifically exempt home schools and private schools from HR6. Armey's amendment stated:

> Nothing in this act shall be construed to permit, allow, encourage, or authorize any federal control over any aspect of any private, religious, or home school whether or not a home school is treated as a private school or home school under state law. This section shall not be construed to bar private, religious, or home schools from participation in programs or services under this act.

In a miraculous series of events, Michael Farris was able to reach Massachusetts home school leaders in order to get hundreds of phone calls directed to Congressmen Moakley, who was head of the Rules

Committee, to change it to Open Rule in order to allow for an amendment. Within hours, Jayme Farris happened to pick up one of the thousands of phone calls coming into the HSLDA offices. It was an aide from Congressmen Moakley's office asking us what we wanted. Michael Farris took the phone and told him that we wanted him to let the Armey amendment be voted on the floor. Soon the situation was resolved, and a vote on the Armey amendment was going to take place! God worked a miracle.

AT&T estimated that approximately one million to one-and-a-half million phone calls came into Congress over those eight days. Congressmen and aides alike said that the home schoolers set all the records.

CSPAN showed congressman after congressman tripping over themselves to get to the microphone to make a statement to America that they, too, supported home schooling and would do nothing to harm home schoolers! Many of them even stated that it was a constitutional right. Congress voted 424 to 1 to completely kill the Miller amendment, with only Miller himself voting for it. Then they voted 374 to 54 to pass the Armey amendment which would exempt home schools and private schools from every aspect of HR6.

This was a miracle. God was merciful to His people. He answered millions of prayers and blessed the efforts of home schoolers across the country. We "lit the match" to start a "raging forest fire" across the nation. Amazingly, we did an "end run" around the major press. Many of the major television stations called our offices after we had already won the battle, asking what this was about and wanting to do a show or a story. This proves that we can make a difference if we take the time to just call our congressmen on various issues! Ultimately, God is in control, and He reigns.

The Biblical Principle Applied

This also points to some important biblical principles, which the home schoolers used. Luke 18:1-7 explains why so many congressmen who were against home schools and funded by the National Education Association voted in favor of home schools. The Bible tells us in Luke 18:1-7:

> Now He was telling them a parable to show that in all times they ought to pray and not to lose heart saying,

"There was in a certain city a judge who did not fear God, who did not respect man. And there was a widow in that city, and she kept coming to him saying, "Give me legal protection from my opponent." And for a while he was unwilling; but afterwards said to himself, "Even though I do not fear God nor respect man, yet because this widow bothers me, I will give her legal protection lest by continually coming she will wear me out." And the Lord said, "Hear what that righteous judge said, 'Now shall not God bring about justice for His elect who cry to Him day and night and will He delay long over them?'"

The congressmen, many of whom did not respect God or man, gave in to the flood of phone calls because they had been worn out by the home schoolers' tireless efforts. The National Education Association Government Relations Manager, Michael Edwards, in the magazine *NEA Today,* stated that the defeat of the Miller amendment, "probably killed any possibility of any meaningful legislation in the area of national certification and licensure." The agenda of the NEA, with over a $200 million budget, was defeated by the grassroots response of home schoolers faithful to their Lord. We praise God how He preserved us all through the HR6 battle!

Unforeseen Benefit: Home Schoolers Find Favor with Congress

America's home schoolers astonished Congress with this political counter-strike that was quick, effective, massive, and decisive. The Miller Amendment was buried 424 to 1 in eight days by over a million concerned home schoolers and their friends. The whole affair quickly became a permanent fixture in the annals of congressional history.

HR6 put home schooling on the political radar screen in a big way. "Remember HR6" is a phrase repeatedly heard in the corridors of the federal government. As a direct result of the HR6 battle, HSLDA now has working relationships with many offices on Capitol Hill because lawmakers now realize that home schooling is a force with which they must reckon. Congressional staff call us to help draft and redraft major legislation involving education, labor, and parental rights' issues. On a number of education and parental rights bills, congressional staff members, upon hearing our opposition to certain aspects of the bill, told me, "If the home schoolers do not want the language, we do not either. We will remove it." As a result, harmful language has been struck out of many bills—"without firing a shot." Many congressmen and senators go out of their way to include protective home school amendments to bills. This could not have happened if each individual home schooling family did not pick up their phone and call Congress in 1994.

Home Schoolers Wage Fight Against President Clinton's National Test

During the 105th Congress, I obtained a transcript of a meeting the U.S. Department of Education convened with educators from around the country to discuss the creation and implementation of a national test for all students. A university professor from Kansas, John Poggio, made the startling but obvious statement. He warned, "What gets tested, must be taught." A member of the Delaware Board of Education echoed a similar sentiment. She explained that Delaware would have to adjust its curriculum to fit the national test. The danger was clear. If Clinton was able to create and implement a national test, it would, by default, create a national curriculum. The federal education bureaucracy in Washington, D.C. would control the education of our nation's youth in a more profound degree than ever before. We had to fight this test. But how?

After meeting with the president of HSLDA who agreed battling this national test would be a major priority for us, I contacted Congressman Goodling's counsel and told him we would "pull out all stops" if Goodling introduced a bill to cut off funding to Clinton's national test. The counsel said he would talk to Goodling. A week later, he explained Goodling was willing to introduce a resolution expressing the sense of the House opposing national testing. I told him there was no way we could get home schoolers to flood the Congress with calls over a resolution which had no power to stop testing. I asked him to go back to Goodling and explain we could not help him unless he introduced a bill to permanently ban testing. I emphasized, then and only then, could we deliver calls. A week later Goodling agreed!

Over the next year-and-a-half, the home schoolers had the opportunity to prove themselves again and again as we at HSLDA sent out nearly 35 nationwide fax alerts. And the home schoolers responded! Repeatedly the home schoolers flooded the House with calls and we organized our Congressional Action program volunteers to visit every office with packets exposing the dangers of Clinton's national test. In September of 1997, we won the first round in the House; 296 to 125 to stop funding of all national testing. The home schoolers had made the ban on testing viable. A key congressional staff admitted, "Without HSLDA and the home schoolers this could not have happened!"

In October 1997, the Senate sold us out by compromising the bill allowing a national test. This was unacceptable. We told the leadership we would unleash another nationwide alert. In high stakes negotiating in conference committee, we achieved a temporary victory. We won a one-year ban on national testing. This meant the fight would continue in 1998. We hoped the grassroots would not become worn out.

At the beginning of the next year, our champion, Congressman Goodling, introduced HR 2846, a permanent ban on national testing. Riding on a wave of calls from the home schoolers, the testing ban passed in a vote of 242 to 174. The fight, however, was just beginning. We still had to get the bill through the Senate. Our champion in the Senate was John Ashcroft from Missouri. The only problem is that we did not have a "vehicle" to which to attach our testing amendment.

Meanwhile, I attended a meeting with Senator Coverdell's chief of staff where he was recruiting support for the Senator's "A+ Education Savings Accounts" bill. I told him we could not deliver calls unless something was attached which would really motivate home schoolers to call...something like our prohibition on a national test amendment.

A few days later, I received a call from Coverdell's office that they would allow the testing amendment to be attached. The rules, however, required that a separate vote be taken on our amendment. We scheduled a lobby day and set appointments with a majority of senators while simultaneously sending out a nationwide alert to home schoolers to call their two U.S. Senators.

I soon received a call from Senator Lott's office, who was the majority leader, telling me there was "not a chance in ———" that our testing amendment would be successful. They had done a "whip count" earlier in the day and only found 30 senators who would support our testing ban. They urged us not to push for the amendment because we would lose big. Our lobby effort the day before, however, gave us evidence that we were very close to winning the vote. Lott's office told me it was our call. I said we wanted to go forward with the vote. I thought we could win. Besides, it might be our only chance to get a vote that year. In the meantime, the home schoolers were delivering thousands of calls and God's people were praying.

On April 22, 1998, the vote was scheduled. It was amazing to watch. Ashcroft's amendment permanently banning national testing passed in a vote of 52-47! Far more votes than the 30 votes predicted by Lott's office. The Senate leadership was amazed. The home schoolers had pulled it off.

Later in June, we were contacted by the leadership in both the House and Senate, asking us if we would agree to have our testing amendment removed so that the "A+ Education Savings Account" bill could go the president in a "clean" form. (The "A+" bill was subsequently vetoed by the president.) We made Speaker Gingrich and Majority Leader Lott promise, in writing, that our testing amendment would be attached to another bill later in the year. In October 1998, they kept their promise in spite of intense threats from President Clinton. We finally won. A permanent ban on a national test was achieved!

The home schoolers made a difference again. They shaped national policy.

Home Schoolers: "The Most Effective Lobbyists"

The national testing battle and HR 6 have made a big impression on Congressman Bill Goodling, the powerful Chairman of the Education and Workforce Committee in the U.S. House of Representatives. He readily testifies to the exceptional involvement which home schoolers have in the political arena. In an address on March 4, 1998, at the National Christian Home School Leadership Summit in Washington, DC, Congressman Goodling explained to the audience that he often asks other groups who they think are the most effective lobbyists on Capitol Hill. After hearing many responses, Goodling replies, "The home schoolers are the most effective lobbyists." He described their effectiveness even further, "You have heard the saying, 'When E.F. Hutton speaks, people listen.' I have changed that saying around a little bit. I say, 'When the home schoolers speak, you *better* listen!'" This simple testimony speaks volumes.

Home Schoolers Repeal Goals 2000

On November 17, 1999, Chairman of the Education and Workforce Committee, Congressman Bill Goodling along with the House and Senate Leadership, reached an agreement with President Clinton on the 1999 Education/Labor/HHS Appropriations bill. The bill was signed into law by the President on November 30th.

The biggest victory was the inclusion of specific language in this appropriations bill, insisted on by the Home School Legal Defense Association, which officially repeals the worst aspects of Goals 2000, effective September 30, 2000.

Largely because of the efforts of home schoolers, Goals 2000, as a mandate on the states, is dead. This big government failure, representing all that is wrong with the federal department of education's manipulation of our children, is finally and officially dead.

With the federal "seed" money cut off, the troublesome Goals 2000 programs established in the states will likely cease to exist.

Goals 2000 was an attempt by the federal government bureaucracy to set national standards of education which would usher in centralized control of our nation's youth. The emphasis of the Goals 2000 agenda was to create a climate of political correctness focusing on changing the attitudes of children rather than improving academic skills (i.e., reading, writing, and arithmetic). This methodology is called outcome-based education.

Since 1994, we at the National Center of Home Education, the federal lobby arm of HSLDA, lobbied for this repeal. We continued to lobby against Goals 2000 even when the issue dropped off most other organizations' radar screen.

In 1997 and 1998, we lobbied the Congress and orchestrated nationwide alerts in opposition to Goals 2000 by supporting the Gorton Amendment. The Gorton Amendment would have block granted $10 billion of federal education money directly to the states, effectively ending all the federal programs such as Goals 2000. In a surprising turn of events, on April 22, 1998, the home schoolers, almost single handedly, passed the Gorton Amendent in a vote of 50 to 49. Unfortunately, the Congress's session ended before it could proceed any further.

Other lobbying efforts included organizing visits for 1800 home schoolers from around the country with over 250 congressional offices in conjunction with our Proclaim Liberty Rally September 23,

1999. This was one of the largest lobbying events ever organized on Capitol Hill.

Earlier in the year, Congressman Goodling did not reauthorize Goals 2000 in response to a request from HSLDA and the Appropriations Committee would designate any funds for it. However, a month before the signing of the appropriations bill, the National Center received a tip from a congressional contact that Goals 2000 was to be funded regardless. Mike Farris, president of HSLDA, gave the marching orders to the National Center staff to take action.

After contacting several key offices, the National Center was told "Clinton wants Goals 2000. It is his pet project. There is no way we can repeal Goals 2000."

Immediately, I contacted a dozen key members of the Senate on appropriations and education committees and Senator Trent Lott's office explaining home schoolers' uniform opposition to Goals 2000 and insisting on its repeal. I also met with Congressmen Goodling, securing a promise that he would not settle for anything less than the repeal of Goals 2000. At a key juncture in the negotiations between House and Senate leadership, the Congressional Action Program, led by Caleb Kershner, directed a targeted national alert generating hundreds of calls from home schoolers to key leadership offices. Doug Domenech, director of governmental affairs, who works out of our office on Capitol Hill, met with members of the house leadership insisting on killing Goals 2000.

Finally, the word came. Goals 2000, as applied to the states, was specifically repealed in an amendment added during negotiations with the president. This ended all the funding to the states for Goals 2000 programs. The states no longer have to submit reports to the Secretary of Education seeking his approval for their Goals 2000 plans or coordinate their states' Goals 2000 programs with school-to-work programs. No longer are progress reports to be submitted to the Secretary of Education and all federal accountability measures are ended. The states do not have to implement national, federal education standards, giving them back local control.

A staffer of the Educational and Workforce Committee, involved in the final negotiations, remarked, "If HSLDA had not brought up the Goals 2000 issue, it would have never seen the light of day."

The fight against Goals 2000 was a long battle for home schoolers. As one Capitol Hill staffer said, "the home schoolers kept up a constant drumbeat." This constitutes another example of the effective and tireless work of home schoolers—just moms and dads who care and are willing to make a difference. We ultimately thank God for His grace and mercy in all of these situations.

National Home School Week Declared

In January 1999, I was contacted by Senator Ashcroft's office for advice on how to fulfill a request he received from the Missouri Families for Home Education who asked him to try to pass a national home school resolution. I readily agreed to help. We had one senator down and 99 to go!

I worked first on drafting the resolution and chose the week of September 19-25, 1999 to coincide with our planned Proclaim Liberty Rally and Lobby Day on Capitol Hill. I personally lobbied about 35 key U.S. Senators (many members of the Judiciary) and Ashcroft's office lobbied many others. In one of the offices, I was told it was "impossible to pass a resolution anymore."

Undeterred, we moved forward. We called upon four state home school leaders to deliver a few calls to four key Democrats on the Judiciary at a key juncture. Senator Lott agreed with us, along with Senator Hatch, to push this through.

God has once again had the home schoolers find favor with our government. Our U.S. Senate Home School Resolution (Sen. Res. 183) was passed on September 14 by unanimous consent. This means the week of September 19-25, 1999 was officially National Home Education Week. This was truly a historic development.

It is particularly amazing in light of the fact the Senate rarely passes resolutions and liberal senators like Ted Kennedy and Charles Schumer did not object. It only took one Senator to object to kill the resolution. In addition, it had to pass the Senate Judiciary Committee first where we were told they apparently debated a half-hour before passing it unanimously on to the Senate.

Here is the text of the Resolution, which can be used to demonstrate to governors, school districts, congressmen, and media the legitimacy of home schooling.

Senate Resolution 183
IN THE SENATE OF THE UNITED STATES
Mr. ASHCROFT (for himself, Mr. ABRAHAM, Mr. COCHRAN, Mr. COVERDELL, Mr. DeWINE, Mr. GOR-TON, Mr. GRAMS, Mr. HAGEL, Mr. HELMS, Mr.

INHOFE, Mr. GREGG, Mr. SMITH of New Hampshire, Mr. SMITH of Oregon, Mr. THURMOND) submitted the following resolution; which was referred to the Committee on the Judiciary:

September 14, 1999

Designating the week beginning on September 19, 1999, and ending on September 25, 1999, as National Home Education Week.

Whereas the United States is committed to excellence in education;

Whereas the United States recognizes the importance of family participation and parental choices in pursuit of that excellence;

Whereas the United States recognizes the fundamental right of parents to direct the education and upbringing of their children;

Whereas parents want their children to receive a first-class education;

Whereas training in the home strengthens the family and guides children in setting the highest standards for their lives which are essential elements to the continuity of morality in our culture;

Whereas home schooling families contribute significantly to the cultural diversity important to a healthy society;

Whereas the United States has a significant number of parents who teach their own children at home;

Whereas home education was proven successful in the lives of George Washington, Patrick Henry, John Quincy Adams, John Marshall, Robert E. Lee, Booker T. Washington, Thomas Edison, Abraham Lincoln, Franklin Roosevelt, Woodrow Wilson, Mark Twain, John Singleton Copley, William Carey, Phyllis Wheatley, and Andrew Carnegie;

Whereas home school students exhibit self-confidence and good citizenship and are fully prepared academically to meet the challenges of today's society;

Whereas dozens of contemporary studies continue to confirm that children who are educated at home score exceptionally well on nationally normed achievement tests;

Whereas a March 1999 study by the Educational Resources Information Center Clearinghouse on Assessment and Evaluation at the University of Maryland found that home school students taking the Iowa Test of Basic Skills or the Tests of Achievement and Proficiency scored in the 70th to 80th percentiles among all the students nationwide who took those exams, and 25 percent of home schooled students were studying at a level one or more grades above normal for their age;

Whereas studies demonstrate that home schoolers excel in college with the average grade point average of home schoolers exceeding the college average; and

Whereas United States home educators and home instructed students should be recognized and celebrated for their efforts to improve the quality of education: Now, therefore, be it

Resolved,

That the week beginning on September 19, 1999, and ending on September 25, 1999, is designated as National Home Education Week. The President is authorized and requested to issue a proclamation recognizing the contributions that home schooling families have made to the Nation.

Passed the Senate September 16, 1999.

I believe one of the main reasons the Home School Resolution passed against all odds is because home schoolers have stayed involved by regularly and repeatedly contacting Congress.

Study Confirms the Involvement of Home Schoolers in Politics

In the 1996 National Household Education Survey (NHES), the U.S. Department of Education's National Center for Education Statistics surveyed 9,393 parents of school age children. The survey asked numerous questions about the extent of family involvement in a variety of civic activities. Some of the questions asked whether the parent had voted recently, telephoned or written a public official, signed a petition, attended public meetings, contributed to political campaigns, participated in community service activities, worked for a political cause, or participated in a boycott in the past twelve months. The survey differentiated public schoolers from home schoolers and both religious and non-religious private schoolers. Christian Smith and David Sikkink of the Department of Sociology at the University of North Carolina analyzed the data, which was published in 1999.[1]

By comparing differences in family participation in these various forms of civic involvement, Smith and Sikkink found that home school families and private school families are consistently more involved in all of the civic activities examined than are families with children in public schools. In fact, by an average margin of 9.3 percent, the private and home school families are more likely than the public school families to engage in any listed forms of civic participation. Up to 13 percent more private and home schoolers have given money to political causes and up to 15 percent more have voted in recent elections and telephoned elected officials. An amazing 26 percent more private and home school families are members of community groups and volunteer at local organizations.

The researchers conclude that home schoolers and private schoolers are "definitely not the isolated recluses that critics suggest they might be. It is rather the public schooling families that are clearly the least civically involved of all the schooling types." Smith and Sikkink closed the article by stating:

> The empirical evidence is clear and decisive: private schoolers and home schoolers are considerably more involved in the public square than are public schoolers— even when the effects of differences in education, income, and other related factors are removed from the equation. Indeed, we have reason to believe that the organizations and practices involved in private and home schooling, in themselves, tend to foster public participation in civic affairs...the challenges, responsibilities, and practices that private schooling and home education normally entail for their participants may actually help reinvigorate America's civic culture and the participation of our citizens in our public square.

When reviewing both the anecdotal and the empirical evidence, home schoolers clearly are not separating themselves and sheltering their families from their "sociopolitical" duties. Home school families, per capita, are participating at a much higher rate in the life of their communities, states, and nation than their counterparts in the public schools. Home schoolers are simply following Christ's command to love their neighbors as themselves. That love means they must be involved in our culture and government in order to preserve liberty and our God-given rights for all citizens

Home Schoolers Do Make a Difference

All of the accomplishments above would not have been possible without the grace of God working through home schoolers who insisted on protecting their cherished liberties. I encourage each home schooler to continue to fight the good fight no matter how high the odds are stacked against us. Every call, every letter, every personal visit makes a difference. The persistent widow of Luke 18 was able to obtain justice because she refused to give up even though she was the only one fighting. The millions of "persistent widows" in the home school movement of today can accomplish even more. You can make a difference!

Notes

1. "Is Private Schooling Privatizing?" *First Things*, April 1999, 16.

Read All About It:

How to Recruit Your Local Media Support for Home Schooling

Home schooling is considered different, or unusual, to most Americans when they initially hear the term. As stated earlier, most people are only used to institutional schools because that is where they, their parents, and maybe even their grandparents, were educated. However, most people, once they are confronted with the benefits of home schooling, as discussed in chapter 5, are inclined to recognize its legitimacy. Therefore, a process of education must continue to take place so that an accurate picture of home schooling is presented.

This is why recruiting the local media is so important. It can serve as a useful means of not only educating others on home schooling, but also helping to protect home schooling. Let us consider several questions that home schoolers have concerning dealing with the media.

Will the Media Twist the Information on Home Schooling?

This is always a possibility but it rarely happens. In fact, in my experience in dealing with hundreds of newspaper and radio reporters and various talk show hosts, nearly 90 percent of the coverage has been favorable.

I have repeatedly told member home school families that they should participate in media interviews for one simple reason: if home schoolers do not speak out on home schooling, no one is going to do it for them. In fact, only those critical of home schooling will probably be interviewed if home schoolers refuse to participate.

Of course, dealing with the media is not always positive. A few years ago, a couple of home schoolers and I were interviewed in Florida. The resulting article began with something to this effect: "What do ax murderers, rapists, and other parents have in common? They all can home school in the state of Florida." The reporter obviously was very biased and wanted more restrictions on home schoolers. Fortunately, such articles are very rare, and I believe that the benefits of much positive publicity by the media outweigh the risks.

How Should Home Schooling Be Presented to the Media?

Three major points to get across to the reporter is that home schoolers are a *minority,* home schooling *works,* and it is a *right.* The media certainly favors minorities, and since home schoolers are a true "minority," it is very beneficial to represent it as such. It is helpful to portray the home school parent as the "little guy" who is being picked on by the "bully" of the state, school district, or the teachers' union. More often than not, the media loves to defend the underdog.

Secondly, be sure to demonstrate that home schooling works. This is the most powerful argument that convinces most reporters and the public. Describe the average school day at home. Extol the success of your own home school and supply the reporter with statistics and studies which show the academic success of home schoolers in general. By using the information in chapter 6, the academic excellence of home schooling can be easily proved. Lawyers at HSLDA regularly talk with the media and will send the reporter summaries of the academic statistics, so be certain to refer the reporter to HSLDA for further information. The fact that home schooling works silences most critics and embarrasses the public schools. Reporters are generally impressed.

A common question raised by reporters is: "But what about the child's socialization?" One way to be prepared for this question is to study the section on socialization in chapter 6. Summarize many of the activities of your child and emphasize how your child is protected from negative socialization.

Thirdly, try to mention that home schooling is a right. In other words, it is legal. It is a constitutional right, as guaranteed by the First and Fourteenth Amendments, and generally is a right according to the individual state's cases or statutes. You may want to refer the reporter to HSLDA for further information on the legalities of home schooling and what is happening legally around the state.

Could a Home Schooler Get in Legal Trouble by Interviewing with the Media?

In some states, where home schoolers are regularly harassed or legally challenged, a home school family is taking a risk by interviewing with the media. In fact, some families ask the media to only use their first names and thus protect their identity from the school district.

However, HSLDA has found that home schoolers who are more public through the media and who are members of HSLDA will be more likely to be left alone by the school district. The school district figures that it is much easier to try to pick on a lonely home school family without media contacts or legal counsel because they can quietly close them down without public embarrassment.

Therefore a family who is being legally harassed may want to contact the press if legal negotiations behind the scenes fail. This type of coverage is not what the public schools want. Many times I have seen the media indirectly contribute to the resolution of a case and turn public opinion in favor of home schooling.

Conclusion

Developing good relations with the media is important in many ways. The media can both help home schoolers educate the public on the legitimacy of home schooling and indirectly protect home schoolers from harassment. The more the public is aware of the positive aspects, the less likely it is that neighbors will turn families in to truant officers and social workers for home schooling and "educational neglect."

Don't Stay
Home Without It:
Join the Home School Legal
Defense Association

A truant officer is at the door. He pushes his way in. He will not leave until he can take your children to the public school. What can you do?

A police officer is at your door with an arrest warrant to take your six-year-old child. Whom can you call?

A social worker demands entry to your home and insists on interrogating your children. What are your rights?

The local public school official insists that your home school arrangement is not legal and threatens you with criminal charges. Where can you get help fast?

The Home School Legal Defense Association (HSLDA) is the answer. The above accounts all actually happened to HSLDA members in Maine, Michigan, Alabama, and Indiana, respectively. In each situation, the family called me, and I was able to resolve the conflict on behalf of our members by telephone, fax, or Federal Express. This typifies the work of each of HSLDA's lawyers and legal staff on nearly a daily basis.

HSLDA is a nonprofit organization established in 1983 expressly for the purpose of defending the right of parents who choose to home school their children. It was founded by three home schooling fathers, two of whom, Michael Farris and J. Michael Smith, presently comprise the HSLDA Board along with home schooling fathers Judge Ken Johnson of Indiana, and former state legislator, Richard Honacker of Wyoming and Doctor Roger Sayre of Pennsylvania.

Membership in HSLDA Is an Investment

The establishment of HSLDA enables home school parents throughout the country to pool their resources in order to defend in court those home school families who were being legally challenged. Each year HSLDA handles nearly three thousand negative legal contacts on behalf of member-families who are faced with public school officials who attempt to exceed the law. HSLDA handles scores of court cases on behalf of member families each year. HSLDA also gives legal information to thousands or more home schoolers annually. This book summarizes many of the cases and legal threats which HSLDA has typically handled on behalf of home schoolers. In many ways, HSLDA has become the major barrier stopping many legal attempts to infringe on the freedoms of home schoolers.

Membership in HSLDA costs $100 annually per family. If you do not use your $100 in receiving legal representation, another family will. In fact, in one case alone involving a member home school family, HSLDA expended over $75,000 in legal services and representation. You are making an investment in protecting home schoolers throughout the nation. It is a way of having "solidarity" with home schoolers in every state, to work together to protect our commonly shared freedoms.

Although home schooling is "legal" in every state, each state varies as to the manner in which it restricts the right to home school. Each year parents face criminal prosecution for teaching their children at home. Generally, only a few home schoolers in any community are selected for prosecution. When this happens, the family faces enormous legal expense, mostly for attorneys' fees. Families who are not prosecuted are often intimidated into giving up or moving, by the mere threat of prosecution.

HSLDA brings together a large number of those families in order to enable each family to have a low-cost method of obtaining quality legal defense, should the need arise. HSLDA guarantees experienced legal counsel and representation by qualified attorneys to every member family who is challenged in the area of home schooling. The attorneys' fees, court costs, transcript charges, expert witnesses, and attorney transportation will be paid in full by the Association.

HSLDA guarantees legal representation to all our members which, as of January 2000, numbers over 66,000 families. HSLDA's legal team is presently comprised of seven attorneys—all of whom home school their children: Michael Farris, Michael Smith, David Gordon, Dee Black, Scott Somerville, Scott Woodruff and I. Defending home schoolers is not just a job for us—it is our very way of life and our heartfelt conviction.

We are supported by six legal assistants. HSLDA has also established a network of Christian attorneys throughout the fifty states who serve as our local counsel whenever we have to defend our families in court. Normally, one of our attorneys from the national office will travel to the particular court and serve as lead counsel in the case.

Not only will you help protect your own rights, your membership will help others establish their right to home school in difficult states. You can join HSLDA by writing or calling us at:

Home School Legal Defense Association
PO Box 159
Purcellville, VA 20134   540-338-5600
Request an application and a free summary of your state laws. Or you can apply on-line: www.hslda.org

Since 1983, after thousands of legal battles, HSLDA has never had a member home school family who was forced to stop home schooling by the state. If a case was lost, HSLDA has been able to win the case on appeal, find an alternate legal way or change the law through legislation! God and God alone deserves the credit for this extraordinary record!

HSLDA reserves the right to refuse membership to anyone who is already in trouble with their school district—so join before you have any problems. We depend on most of our member families not to be in trouble at a given time, in order for there to be adequate finances to represent all the families who are threatened or criminally charged.

Offensive Litigation

In addition to legally *defending* home school families, HSLDA is prepared to go on the *offensive* and sue local school districts or departments of education which blatantly violate our member's constitutional rights. Your annual fees enable us to take the offensive as needed, thereby sending a message to the public school authorities that we are serious in preserving the rights and freedoms of home school families.

For example, in Pennsylvania, after dozens of home schooling families were in criminal court and many more were threatened, we went on the offensive and filed a civil rights action, suing the school districts for violating the home schoolers' civil rights. We won the case, *Jeffery v. O'Donnell,* and the Federal Court declared the law unconstitutionally vague.[1]

In Texas, many member home school families were being criminally charged for home schooling, so we decided to go on the offensive by joining as plaintiffs in the *Leeper* case. The main attorney handling the case was Shelby Sharpe of Ft. Worth. The case involved suing every school district in the state of Texas for violating the civil rights of the home school families. The trial court, the Texas Court of Appeals and the Texas Supreme Court ruled favorably, making home schooling clearly legal in Texas.[2]

Another example in which we chose to proceed on the offensive occurred in St. Joseph County, Michigan. Four HSLDA families were visited by a local principal and a police officer and threatened with arrest, and in one instance, with having their children removed. These four families and a few others also received intimidating letters from the county school district giving them one day in which to enroll their children in public school.

Later, the local newspaper printed an article based on an interview with the prosecutor announcing that approximately seven home school families would be criminally prosecuted. I contacted the prosecutor to try to convince him not to prosecute, but he would not budge.

As a result, in January, attorney Michael Farris and I filed a civil rights suit, *Amett v. Middleton,* in the St. Joseph County Circuit Court, suing the prosecutor, superintendent, and school district for $200,000 for violating the civil rights of these home school families. We cited five "causes of action" against the prosecutor and school district. They violated the civil rights of the home schoolers by: 1) threatening to prosecute the families under an unconstitutionally vague law; 2) denying the families equal protection under the law; 3) attempting to require an illegal reporting procedure; 4) threatening to prosecute while intentionally disregarding the law requiring the families to first have a due process hearing with the Department of Education; and 5) for making an unconstitutional demand that the children had to attend public school under the penalty of law.

Within weeks, HSLDA was contacted by the school district and prosecutor wanting to settle the suit. Both promised, in writing, that they would not pursue or prosecute home schoolers in the county unless the law changed. They agreed that the law was vague. As a result, we dismissed the suit, since we achieved the protection of our families.[3]

Other Benefits of HSLDA

There are several other functions of HSLDA which your membership dues help to support.

First, HSLDA regularly assists home school organizations to promote good legislation or fight restrictive legislation. Oftentimes, HSLDA will send attorneys to testify at legislative hearings. For example, during one year, Mike Farris testified in Connecticut and Montana, Michael Smith testified in Arizona, Maryland, and Oregon, and I testified in Maine and North Dakota.[4] Regularly, we are also involved in the drafting of favorable amendments to legislation affecting home schooling. HSLDA sends out special mailings to members, urging them to write to their legislators about a specific bills.

Sometimes we will meet with departments of education in order to change their policies to be more favorable to home schoolers' rights. For example, the District of Columbia had adopted one of the most restrictive sets of home school requirements, which included teacher certification and unannounced home visits. I arranged a meeting with the D.C. school administration and presented two memoranda proving the unconstitutionality of home visits and teacher certification requirements. By the end of the meeting, one of the officials ripped in half the D.C. home school guidelines and said, "I guess we won't be needing these anymore!" As a result, all requirements for home schoolers were suspended, and they asked me to help draft new guidelines.[5] The prayers of D.C. home schoolers were answered in a mighty way!

In addition to monitoring state legislation in all fifty states that would impact home schooling, HSLDA, which is strategically based in the Washington D.C. area, monitors federal legislation and alerts state home school leaders and its members to legislation that will hurt or promote parental rights.

Secondly, at least six times per week, the HSLDA legal staff is contacted by newspaper, radio, or TV reporters. As a result, we have the opportunity to "get the word out" on the rights of home schoolers and their tremendous academic success.

Thirdly, HSLDA provides a bimonthly magazine, *The Home School Court Report*, for member families at no extra charge. This magazine covers legal issues and other matters of concern to home schooling parents. It is usually twenty-four pages long and it is filled with valuable information.

Fourthly, each month, HSLDA attorneys speak at home school conferences throughout the country, sharing legal information on the rights of home schoolers, encouraging home school families, and often strategizing with state home school leaders.

Fifthly, HSLDA attorneys routinely help counsel home school parents who are involved in custody disputes where home schooling is an issue. Although HSLDA will not represent the families in Domestic Relations Court, we do provide legal counsel to their lawyers and statistics and research on home schooling.

Sixthly, HSLDA also has a division, the National Center for Home Education (NCHE), which serves state leaders by providing information on the current legal bills and developments, on both the state and federal levels, of concern to home schoolers. I presently serve as the executive director of NCHE. Founded in February 1990, NCHE also works on special public relations projects related to home schooling. It serves as a "clearing house" of major home school research and other news and resources regarding home schooling.

For instance, the NCHE arranged with the Psychological Corporation to voluntarily test 10,750 home school children throughout the country and report their scores. The results of these 10,750 children showed that the home schoolers scored in the top third of the nation. The composite scores on the basic battery of tests ranked 15 to 32 percentile points above public school averages.[6]

NCHE posts a web page with key information, as a free service, to hundreds of home school leaders throughout the country. This information is usually then distributed to home schoolers in each state by state newsletters or home school support groups. In addition, NCHE hosts an annual Christian leadership conference with special speakers, which is attended by many state home school leaders, in order to exchange ideas, learn strategies, fellowship with other state leaders, and provide training. NCHE also hosts several regional conferences for home school support leaders each year throughout the country. These workshops are effective in training support group leaders on the latest legal and legislative developments.

In November of 1992, the Congressional Action Program (CAP) was established as part of the mission of NCHE in response to the anti-family agenda of the Clinton administration. I assigned Caleb Kershner and Samuel Redfern, two home schooling graduates, to run the program.

The National Center for Home Education is set up and functions like a congressional office in order to effectively tackle our federal lobbying work. Mike Farris and Mike Smith fulfill the role of the Congressmen. I serve as Chief of Staff. Doug Domenech, home school father and experienced lobbyist, is our "man on Capitol Hill" who operates our D.C. office and maintains a constant presence for us in D.C. Home school graduates Kevin Koons, Caleb Kershner, Samuel Redfern, and Nathan Richmond serve as Legislative Assistants, each covering several federal issues. This team enables us to monitor and lobby all relevant federal legislation.

CAP is made up of about one hundred home school parents and teenagers from Maryland, Virginia, D.C., and Pennsylvania, who have been trained by NCHE personnel to lobby. Each "lobby day," the CAP coordinators listen to a short briefing from NCHE on the particular issue of the day and they are given professionally prepared packets with information on how the Senator or Congressman needs to vote. They then hit every office, often with personal visits with aides or congressmen.

The second half of CAP is the 435 home schoolers in each of the 435 Congressional Districts. These home schoolers are notified by e-mail from NCHE with the necessary information to start phone trees, "e-lerts" and "fax alerts" within their congressional district. This enables us to dump calls on congressmen from their own constituents.

The CAP system was heavily tested with the HR6 scare in February 1994. The amendment which would have required home schoolers and private schools to use certified teachers was defeated by the ability of NCHE and CAP through its extensive network to generate over one million calls to Capitol Hill, setting all records! Of course, the success ultimately can only be attributed to the power and mercy of God.

CAP immediately began functioning to battle mandatory immunization bills, HR6, the U.N. Convention on the Rights of the Child, and many other sweeping attempts by the federal government to regulate and control our children. (See chapters 11, 21, and 22 for true stories of NCHE's lobby efforts on Capitol Hill.)

How to Become a CAP District Coordinator

To become a CAP District Coordinator you must have e-mail and be able to check it at least once every 24 hours on weekdays. Access to a dedicated fax line is also beneficial, but not required. A CAP District Coordinator builds an alert network by contacting home schoolers, support groups and churches in his district.

In addition to helping defend our home school liberties, there are several other benefits to becoming a CAP District Coordinator: 1) National Center Leader's exclusive access on HSLDA's web site; 2) $50 savings on your HSLDA membership; 3) Legislative information and analysis (CAP mailing, e-mail, fax); 4) Complimentary CAP Congressional Directory and CAP legislative binder; and 5) Free access to CAP events (CAP lobbyist training, tours, etc.).

Learn more about CAP and sign up as a District Coordinator by visiting our web site at http://www.hslda.org/nationalcenter/cap/.

We also have a legislative toolbox that will assist you in finding out information about your congressman and district. The link is: http://www.hslda.org/members/toolbox/ (have your HSLDA membership number available to access this section).

We hope that you will consider becoming part of this important work.

If you have any questions, you can us at 540-338-7600 or cap@hslda.org.

In short, HSLDA is committed to the overall success and advancement of home education in the arenas of education, the media, Congress, state legislatures, churches, families, and neighborhoods.

Home Schooling Expanding across the World

Home schooling is no longer a United States phenomenon. Home schooling is gradually but steadily spreading across the world. The home school movement in many countries is only a fledgling movement but it is beginning to take hold. The first step in many Western and Asian countries is to make it legal.

One of the goals of the Home School Legal Defense Association is to export to other countries the knowledge and lessons we have learned through our struggle as home schoolers to be free here in America. We also want to share the many benefits of home schooling which includes distributing various studies demonstrating the academic success of home schoolers at the elementary, secondary, and college level.

Most important of all is our desire to share the light of Jesus Christ through the vehicle of home schooling. Home schooling enables families to teach what really matters: knowing Jesus as their Savior and obeying Him as Lord. More and more families home schooling on the foundation of the Word of God will bring blessings to the nations around the world.

The HSLDA legal staff at the National Center of Home Education works regularly with home school leaders and home school associations in various countries. The assistance includes recommending legal and political strategies, sending home school studies and materials, corresponding with members of parliament and various government officials, organizing letter writing campaigns to various foreign embassies, talking to foreign press, visiting and speaking in the country, and helping establish national legal defense associations for home schoolers.

I have directed numerous efforts to help the home school movements in South Africa, Ireland, Mexico, Australia, Taiwan, Japan, Canada, and Germany. I presently serve on the Board of the Home School Legal Defense Association of Canada and the Pestalozzi Trust Home School Legal Fund in South Africa.

HSLDA's Goal Is to Serve the Home School Community

HSLDA's only goal is to serve the home school community. We are willing to defend any member home school family who is diligently home schooling their children, regardless of their religious affiliation. An investment in HSLDA of $100 not only guarantees legal defense for your family but also makes it possible for us to wage legal and legislative battles throughout the country on behalf on home schoolers.

However, as an organization and as individuals, we are committed to promote the cause of Christ and His kingdom. We believe that God alone is making it possible for home schoolers to gain greater freedoms and to be successful in the courts and legislatures and in the area of academics and family life. God honors those who honor Him and seek first His kingdom and righteousness. If we have anything to boast in, we boast in the Lord, who deserves all the glory.

Notes

1. "Pennsylvania Law Declared Unconstitutional," *The Home School Court Report*, Vol. 4, No. 4, Fall 1988, 1. Also see chapter 18 for more information on the court's decision.
2. "Texas Home Schoolers Welcome Victory at Last!" *The Home School Court Report*, January/February 1992, 1.
3. "Michigan Home Schoolers Protected by Civil Rights Suit," *The Home School Court Report*, Vol. 8, No. 2, March/April 1992, 3.
4. "The 1990-91 School Year in Review," *The Home School Court Report*, Vol. 7, No. 4, July/August 1991, 7.
5. "District of Columbia: School Board Agrees to Revise Restrictive Policy," *The Home School Court Report*, Vol. 7, No. 5, September/October 1991, 5.
6. This study was released August 9, 1992 and is available from the Home School Legal Defense Association, P.O. Box 159, Purcellville, Virginia 20134.

And all thy children shall be
taught of the Lord; and great
shall be the peace of thy children.

—Isaiah 54:13

VII

Persuasive Handouts
and Home Schooling Resources

Home schooling has proven to be a revival of a time-tested method of individualized education. It reflects a deep concern by parents to be involved in the education of their children. The home school movement is also profoundly religious, for the most part, making the revival more than educational. It is a Christian revival and restoration of the family, with a focus on God's absolute moral values and principles.

Home schoolers can be proud of their great heritage. Many renowned statesman, presidents, economists, pastors, generals, scientists, lawyers, jurists, and accomplished men and women from almost every field were taught at home by their parents. Most of these home schooled leaders of the past were trained in biblical principles by their parents, and they actively applied those principles throughout their lives.

Home schoolers have realized God's commands to parents demand they give their children a comprehensive, biblical education, and that these commands are impossible to fulfill by sending children to the public schools. The home schoolers are not only training the hearts of their children to believe in Jesus, but they are training their children's minds in God's principles, as applied to every subject. The home school children, as a result, will become men and women of godly character who will be able to lead.

Home school parents have become aware of the failure of the public school system, academically, morally, and philosophically. They do not want to take the risk that their children will become functionally illiterate or simply a crime statistic. They want to protect their children from the "vain philosophies" of this world (Colossians 2:8), which are destroying America's youth. The public school children are regularly being indoctrinated in value-free humanism and mind-controlling cultism, all in the name of neutrality. As the public schools continue to slide into chaos, home schooling is steadily achieving success. It is a fast-growing trend and has already proven that it can academically compete with, and nearly always surpass, the present results from conventional schooling.

Furthermore, it is a movement to restore the right of all parents, both Christian and secular, to control and direct the education of their children, with minimal state interference. The home schoolers are informing the state that they do not want "Big Brother" indoctrinating their children anymore. Home schoolers are on the front lines of the battle for freedom, as they counter the attempts of the state to control the minds of our children and to replace the family with "government nannies." Home schoolers are standing up to the monopolistic public schools, the out-of-control and abusive child welfare system, and the agenda of the educational elite. These battles are being fought from house to house, in the legislatures, and in the courts.

Home schooling is working—and it here to stay. Parents are getting serious as they die to themselves and dedicate their lives to training and loving their children in the Lord. Let us all work to save our children!

The following appendices will provide more information on the academic success of home schooling; how to recognize humanistic education from Christian education; reasons why you should home school all the way through high school; and numerous resources for home school families.

The Difference Between Christian Education and Humanistic Education

This simple chart summarizes the basic differences between a biblically based education and humanistic education. Christians should check their public schools, private schools, and even home school curricula to determine on which side of the chart below it best fits. God honors those who honor Him. Let us give our children the best biblical education possible.

Christianity

1. The sovereignty of the triune God is the starting point, and this God speaks through His infallible word.

2. We must accept God as God. He is alone Lord.

3. God's Word and Person is the Truth.

4. Education is into God's truth in every realm.

Humanism

1. The sovereignty of man and the state is the starting point, and it is the word of scientific, elite man which we must heed.

2. Man is his own god, choosing or determining for himself what constitutes good and evil (Genesis 3:5).

3. Truth is pragmatic and existential: it is what we find works and is helpful to us.

4. Education is the self-realization and self-development of the child.

5. Education is discipline under a body of truth. This body of truth grows with research and study, but truth is objective and God-given. We begin by pre-supposing God and His Word.

6. Godly standards grade us. We must measure up to them. The teacher grades the pupil.

7. Man's will, and the child's will, must be broken to God's purpose. Man must be remade, reborn by God's grace.

8. Man's problem is sin. Man must be recreated by God.

9. The family is God's basic institution.

5. Education is freedom from restraint and from any idea of truth outside us. We are the standard, not something outside us.

6. The school and the world must measure up to the pupil's needs. The pupil grades the teacher.

7. Society must be broken and remade to man's will, and the child's will is sacred.

8. Man's problem is society. Society must be recreated by man.

9. The family is obsolete. The individual or the state is basic.

The comparison above was written by R. J. Rushdoony in his book *The Philosophy* of *the Christian Curriculum* (Vallecito, Calif.: Ross House Books, 1981), 172-73. Chalcedon, P.O. Box 158, Vallecito, California 95251. Reprinted by permission.

B

Biblical Principles of Education

by Christopher J. Klicka

Give this to your pastor or Christian friends

Theme: God has delegated the authority *and* responsibility to teach and raise children to the parents *first*. Parents can delegate their *authority* to teach and raise children to someone else, but they can never delegate their *responsibility* to teach their children to anyone else. God will hold parents responsible for what education their children receive (whether from teachers, books, projects, or peers). To whom much is given, much is required. We have a free choice in this country to *not* send our children to an ungodly public school (we will, all the more, be responsible). Remember, our children are dying souls entrusted to our care!

The raising of children is delegated to parents by God:

Psalm 127:3-5 ("Behold, children are a gift of the Lord; the fruit of the womb is a reward. Like arrows in the hand of a warrior, so are the children of one's youth. How blessed is the man whose quiver is full of them; they shall not be ashamed when they speak with their enemies in the gates.")

Gen. 33:5, 48:8-9; Isa. 8:18; Heb. 2:13 ("Children whom the Lord has given me.")

Matt. 22:21 (Render to Caesar that which is Caesar's, and unto God that which is God's (our children are God's). Training of children was *not* delegated to the state. The only biblical accounts of government education were coerced—no choice: i.e., Moses, Joseph, Daniel, Shadrach, Meshach, and Abednego.

Children, however, are still considered by God to be His children:

In other words, children are a gift of stewardship and parents do not own the children:

Ezekiel 16:20-21 ("You slaughtered My children and offered them up to idols...")

Psalm 139:13-16; Job 10:8-12; Isaiah 49:1, 5; Jeremiah 1:5; Luke 1:41, 44 (God's claim to unborn children.)

God has given us certain *conditions* we are commanded to meet when raising children (part of our stewardship responsibility):

Ephesians 6:4 ("Fathers, do not provoke your children to wrath, but bring them up in the nurture and admonition of the Lord.") Fathers have the greatest responsibility in training their children in the Lord and disciplining them. Are fathers "provoking" their children by sending them to public school?

Deuteronomy 6:6-9 (also see Deuteronomy 4:9, 11:18-21) We are commanded to diligently teach our children God's commandments and principles all the time. Sunday school is not enough. Children in public school are taught to *think* as *non-Christians* thirty or more hours a week.

Psalm 78:1-11 (Teach God's principles to your children all the time so they will teach their children and so "that they should put their confidence in God and not forget the works of God.")

Exodus 13:8, 14; Joshua 4:20-22, 24 (Teach your children what God has done.)

Proverbs 6:20-23 (Children's responsibility to obey parents' teachings who in turn, should be teaching God's principles.)

Psalm 1:1-2 (Meditate on God's law day and night); Proverbs 23:7 ("For as a man thinks, so is he.") Children in public school are being taught to think like non-Christians.

2 Corinthians 10:5 (Take *every thought* captive to the obedience of Christ.)

Isaiah 54:13 ("And all your children shall be taught of the Lord;

and great shall be the peace of your children."); John 21:15 ("Feed My lambs" and "Feed My sheep.")

Jeremiah 10:12 ("Thus saith the Lord, learn not the way of heathen nations.") Isn't that what our children are learning in the public schools?

Colossians 3:1-3 ("Keep seeking the things *above*, where Christ is...set your *mind* on things above, not on the things that are on the earth.") The things above are God's words recorded in Scripture. The Bible is the "blueprint" for all areas of life.

Matt. 16:23 (Peter, thinking like a humanist, told Jesus he wouldn't have to die. Jesus said, "Get behind me Satan! You are a stumbling block to me: for you are not setting your *mind* on God's interests, but man's.")

Matt. 22:37 ("You shall love the Lord your God with all your heart, and with all your should, and with all your *mind*. This is the greatest and foremost commandment.") How can our children love God with their mind when public school trains their minds to ignore God?

Luke 6:40 ("A pupil is not above his teacher but everyone after he has been fully trained, will be like his teacher. A blind man cannot guide a blind man, can he? Will they not both fall into a pit?") Are spiritually blind teachers teaching our children and leading them astray?

Romans 12:2 ("Be not conformed to the pattern of this world but be transformed by the renewing of your mind.") Public schools conform our children to the pattern of this world.

Prov. 22:6 ("Train up a child in the way he should go, even when he is old, he will not depart from it.") We need to train our children in God's ways now so they will walk in righteousness as adults.

1 Samuel 15:1-23 ("To obey is better than sacrifice.") Are we trying to make a "sacrifice" to God by sending our children to public school to "save souls" while disobeying God's clear commands to us concerning raising our children?

Parents are responsible for peer pressure:

Proverbs 13:20 ("He who walks with wise men, will be wise but a companion of fools will suffer harm.") What kind of children and teachers are influencing our children in the public schools—day in and day out?

1 Corinthians 15:33 ("Be not deceived; bad company corrupts good morals.")We as parents are responsible before God for the influences of peers on our children.

All true knowledge and understanding comes from God:

Psalm 111:10; Proverbs 1:7 ("Fear of the Lord is the beginning of knowledge.")

Proverbs 2:6, 9:10 ("The Lord gives wisdom; from His mouth comes understanding.")

Colossians 1:16-17, 2:3 ("All things created by Him and for Him, he holds all together.") James 1:5 ("In Christ are all treasures of wisdom.")

2 Timothy 3:15-17 ("...continue in the things you have learned and become convinced of...and that *from childhood* you have known the sacred writings which are able to give you the wisdom that leads to salvation through faith which is in Christ Jesus. All Scripture is inspired by God and profitable for teaching, for reproof, for correction, for training in righteousness; that the man of God may be adequate, equipped for every good work.")

2 Tim. 2:15 ("Study to show yourself approved to God, handling accurately the Word of truth.")

James 3:13-18 (Wisdom *not* from above is earthly, natural, demonic. Wisdom from above is "pure, peaceable, gentle, reasonable, full of mercy and good fruits, unwavering, without hypocrisy.") Whose wisdom are your children being taught?

Psalm 119:97-101 The goal of education is to train children in God's law so they can govern themselves, be wiser than their enemies, have more insight than their teachers, understand more than the aged.

Matthew 18:6 (Whoever harms one of these little ones who believe in Me, it would be better for Him that a millstone hung about his neck and he drowned in the sea.) Are we harming our children if we send them to public school?

Thoughts to remember

God's truth and His principles are the foundation of all knowledge; children must not only be taught to believe as Christians but also to think as Christians; God's principles must be taught to children in a comprehensive manner on a daily basis; God's truth speaks to every academic discipline. Where would Satan like our children to be taught? Sending our children to modern public education is like playing Russian roulette with their souls!

Let us always keep in mind what our ultimate goal is in educating our children—that they will know God and accept Jesus a Savior and Lord. The scripture below says it all:

"I have no greater joy than this, to hear of my children walking in the truth." 3 John 4

Fifteen Reasons to Home School Your Teenagers

1. You get to see the completion of your efforts. Something is lost when you turn over your home discipling to others.
2. You can customize your children's education to provide motivation for their gifts and abilities. No one else will be able to provide the consistent and loving support that you can in weak areas.
3. You can direct them to early college entrance. Even public high schools realize many students are ready for college level courses and have cooperating programs with junior colleges.
4. You can continue the family building process. The teen years continue to be impressionable and formative. This is an invaluable time to cement family relationships.
5. You can be sure that your teens are learning, if they are at home. Studies have revealed that public high school students average 2 hours and 13 minutes of academic work a day.
6. You can continue to have influence over their peer relationships. Teen rebellion is not in God's plan for the family, but it is the humanist agenda for the public schools.
7. You can protect them from pressure to conform to what the other kids are doing. This pressure is so strong in the public high school. You won't need to spend time de-programming.

8. If you send your teens to high school, there will be a diversion away from the academic focus, as well as spiritual priorities. Be aware of the many distractions that won't parallel the home life you have maintained.
9. Your young people will be thrown into things like boy/girl preoccupation, focus on clothes, and pressure to conform in appearance and music.
10. Vast amounts of time separated from the family will affect their relationship with you. We have all put great amounts of our heart and time into our home schooling years, and we want those efforts preserved.
11. Home school is the best preparation for college studies. The home education "style" is closer to college-type instruction.
12. There is greater flexibility for work/study opportunities.
13. The institutional method of public education is designed around "crowd control," not learning. If and when they learn it will be a byproduct of other priorities to maintain classroom order.
14. Home educators have the best available curriculum and greater selection. Public schools offer revisionist history and science that promotes their humanist perspective. The godly commitment of many great Americans has been deleted from public textbooks.
15. Age/grade isolation or segregation inhibits socialization. Public school children are behind their home school counterparts in maturity, socialization, and vocabulary development as demonstrated by available research.

Compiled by Elizabeth Smith, 1992, Home School Legal Defense Association, reprinted by permission.

Do You Know Where You Are Going When You Die?
A Tribute to Kimberly Wray

Some readers may wonder why I took the time to write this book. The major reason is that I believe home schooling is the most effective way to plant the Word of God into the consciousness of our children. In other words, home schooling is a tremendous way to reach our children's souls. Certainly our souls and those of our children are of utmost importance. The time we spend in this world is very short compared to the never-ending time in eternity.

This hit home on May 29, 1994, when Kimberly Wray, my legal assistant at HSLDA, was instantly killed in a car crash along with Angela Yerovsek (another legal assistant in our office). The police said the man who hit them was speeding at least 100 mph and hit them from behind, knocking them off the road into a tree. Both of these girls were in their twenties, and they were expected back to work on Monday, but then suddenly they were gone.

Both of these girls loved the Lord. Kimberly had worked at HSLDA for three years, working as my personal legal and administrative assistant for the last two years. She became a close friend to my family and me. I miss Kimberly very much. She was constantly seeking the Lord's will in everything, and she loved Him with her whole heart, soul, and mind. On her computer were three quotes: "Lord, make me an instrument of Thy peace;" "Trust in the Lord with all your heart and lean not on your own understanding," Proverbs 3:5; and "When I am afraid, I will put my trust in Thee. In God whose Word I praise, in God I have put my trust: I shall not be afraid. What can mere man do to me?" Psalm 56:3-4. Kimberly was so very talented. Her kindness and cheerfulness was well known by all of us at HSLDA and the many HSLDA members she helped. She would agonize over the persecution of innocent home school families by state officials. She gave so much godly and accurate counsel to many families.

God in His wisdom brought Kimberly and Angela home. No doubt, they are where we all want to be and do not want to return. The Scriptures say in 1 Corinthians 2:9, "Eye has not seen, nor ear heard, nor have entered into the heart of man the things which God has prepared for those who love Him." Furthermore, in Revelation 21:4 it says, "And God will wipe away every tear from their eyes; there shall be no more death, nor sorrow, nor crying; And there shall be no more pain, for the former things have passed away."

Kimberly and Angela ran the race and have now received the crown of glory. "Therefore we are always confident in that while we are at home in the body we are absent from the Lord, for we walk by faith and not by sight. We are confident, yes, well pleased rather, to be absent from the body and present with the Lord," 2 Corinthians 5:5-8. However, we continue to experience great sorrow because we miss Kimberly and Angela, yet we know the Bible says in Psalm 116:15, "Precious in the sight of the Lord is the death of His saints."

Do You Know Where You Are Going When You Die?

The important point in all of this for the reader is that Kimberly and Angela were ready. We know they are experiencing unbelievable joy in the presence of God their Father and the Lord Jesus Christ. But where are you today? Have you thought about your soul and about your children's souls? Have you taken the time to consciously train your children in God's Word? Have you taken the time to get your own life ready with God? Do you have hope when you die?

There is so much more to our lives than this life. This life is fleeting and uncertain. I have been diagnosed with multiple sclerosis. Suddenly, my life is changed. I can't run any more, and I have difficulty walking and climbing stairs. My energy has been cut in half. This body is decaying. Some of us are decaying faster than others, but we will all die one day. As I struggle with MS, God has made it clear to me how important it is that we make this life count. The only thing we can do that will last is what we do for Christ. Life is so fleeting and completely hopeless—except for our life in Jesus Christ. God made this clear when we faced the near death of our twin girls. Our relationship with Jesus is the only thing we will be able to bring with us into eternity.

So don't put it off for another day. As we have learned from Kimberly and Angela's lives, we have no idea when we will die. One thing we can all be assured of is that we will all die. There are no exceptions. If you died today, are you sure you would go to heaven? That is a question to meditate upon. If God asked you why He should let you into heaven, what would you say? Would you be explaining to God that you are a good person and deserve heaven? Would you tell God that He owes you something? Would you say that since He is a God of love everyone must be allowed into heaven? Such answers would be useless. God has made it very clear that there is only one way to heaven, and that is explained in the Bible, God's love letter to man.

We Are all Sinners

In Romans 3:23, it says, "For all have sinned and fallen short of the glory of God." In Romans 6:23, it says, "For the wages of sin is death, but the free gift of God is eternal life in Christ Jesus our Lord." In other words, I am a sinner and you are a sinner. Everyone in this entire world has done wrong. We have sinned against the holy and perfect God who created us. As a result, the Bible tells us that the penalty and wages of sin is death. This death, the Scriptures say, is eternal death in hell where the burning and torment will never ever cease.

You are doomed and I am doomed. In order for us to earn our salvation, Galatians 3:10 makes it clear that we must obey all the law which God has laid forth in the Scriptures. This means we must *never* lie, *never* cheat, *never* steal, *never* have bad attitudes and use unkind words, *never* sin in anger, *never* sin at all. Of course, this is impossible. Just look at your own life. Besides, even if we do an extraordinary amount of good works, God says our "works are as filthy rags" (Isaiah 64:6). They cannot save us.

The Only Way to Heaven

However, there is hope because God in His great mercy and love for us has provided one way to heaven. God willingly sent His only begotten son, Jesus Christ, to this world to suffer and be tempted in all the ways we are, yet He did not sin. God went further by having Jesus Christ, who was perfectly God and perfectly man, to be crucified on the cross for our sins. In other words, as my little four-year-old daughter would explain, you and I should have been crucified on the cross and sent to hell, but Jesus willingly did that in our place. He conquered death by rising again from the dead in three days. Now He sits on the right hand of God the Father Almighty. John 3:16 explains:

"For God so loved the world that He gave His only begotten Son, that whoever believes in Him, should not perish, but have eternal life."

God had His only Son suffer untold agony for us! "But God demonstrates His own love toward us, in that while we were yet sinners, Christ died for us" (Romans 5:8). The Bible declares, "He (Jesus Christ) was delivered over to death for our sins and was raised to life for our justification" (Romans 4:25). In other words, Jesus willingly took our place. When we go before God one day, and He looks at us and sees sinners deserving of death, before we are condemned to eternal hell, Jesus Christ will stand in front of us and declare us righteous by His blood which He shed for us on that cross long ago.

There is no other way to heaven. Jesus Himself told Nicodemus in the Gospel of John, chapter 3 that, "one must be born-again in order to enter the Kingdom of Heaven." Jesus explained that this is not where you go back into your mother's womb and be reborn, but this is a new birth of the spirit where we put aside our old man and put on the new. In John 14:6, Jesus says, "I am the way, the truth and the life. No one can come to the Father, but by Me." As I said, there is no other way. Buddha, who is dead, cannot save us; our own works cannot save us. No other god or religion can save us. We must believe in Jesus Christ as our Lord and Savior. He is our Creator. He is the One who made us and the whole universe.

So how can we be saved from our present path straight to hell? God tells us in the Bible in Romans 10:9, "Confess with your lips that Jesus is Lord and believe in your heart that He rose again from the dead. Then you shall be saved!" "Whosoever calls on the name of the Lord shall be saved," Romans 10:13. No matter what you have done, Christ will forgive you. "If we confess our sins, He is faithful and just to forgive us our sins" (1 John 1:9).

Furthermore, the Bible clearly states, "And there is salvation in no one else for there is no other name under heaven that is given among men, by which we must be saved" (Acts 4:12). The road is very narrow. Jesus is the only way. "Enter by the narrow gate: for the gate is wide and the way is broad that leads to destruction, and many are those who enter by it. For the gate is small and the way is narrow that leads to life, and few are those who find it" (Matthew 7:13-14).

We Can't Fool God

It is quite easy to fool men by confessing that Jesus is Lord of your life, and saying that you believe in your heart that He rose again from the dead, and paid the penalty for your sins. It is also easy to fool people saying that you have repented, changed, and put on the new man. However, you cannot fool God. God knows the heart. Jesus warns,

> Not everyone who says to me Lord, Lord will enter the Kingdom of Heaven; but he who does the will of My Father, who is in heaven. Many will say to me on that day, Lord, Lord, did we not prophesy in your name, and in your name cast out demons, and in your name perform many miracles? And I will declare to them, I never knew you. Depart from Me, you who practice lawlessness.

Don't try to fool God because it isn't possible. God knows the heart. Repent from your sins. Accept Jesus as your Lord and Savior. As Paul told the Philippian jailer, "Believe on the Lord Jesus Christ, and thou shalt be saved."

Remember, we will not get a second chance once we die. We know it is easy to die. We could die tomorrow. People die every day. God tells us in Hebrews 9:27, "It is appointed man once to die and after this the judgement." There will be no opportunities for us to confess Jesus as our Lord and Savior after we die. We must do it here, we must do it now.

What more important thing in this life do we have to tend to than that of our own souls ? Once we understand this, how important the responsibility for us as parents to be sure that we have trained our children in God's Word and presented them with the Gospel of Jesus Christ, so they, too, may confess Him as Lord and Savior of their lives. What a glory it would be to be all together in heaven one day.

Caution: Faith without Works Is Dead

One final note involves our lives once we have accepted Jesus as our Lord and Savior. The Bible says, "By their fruits you shall know them," 1 John 5:3, 6. "If you love God, you keep His commandments." If we truly love God, and if we have truly accepted Jesus into our heart as our Savior and are developing a personal relationship with Him, we will want to obey Him and know His Word as found in the Bible. It is in the Holy Bible that God shows us His will and revelation. I challenge you to read your Bible *daily* and meditate on God's law day and night as David encourages in the Psalms. We owe God so much. We owe Him our very salvation, our very life. We need to be "sold out" in our commitment to Him. He deserves no less. We must seek to obey Him in all things and follow His Scriptures. Of course, we must also teach these Scriptures to our children.

Once you are saved, truly saved, you will never lose that salvation. Jesus said,

> I give eternal life to them, and they shall never perish; and no one shall snatch them out of My hand. My Father who has given them to Me is greater than all, and no one is able to snatch them out of the Father's hand (John 10:28-29).

We were all made in the image of God. Only living in His will and knowing Jesus Christ as our personal Savior will we ever have true security in this life and true happiness.

We all know that our bodies are decaying day by day. I know, I am afflicted with the incurable and degenerative disease, multiple sclerosis. Scripture reminds us of this. In Second Corinthians 4:16-18, "Yet we who know God do not lose heart. Though our outer man is decaying yet our inner man is renewed day by day. Momentary, light affliction is producing an eternal weight of glory far beyond all comparison." That is what we must look forward to: the great glory God has prepared for us. That is what Kimberly and Angela lived for. They lived for Jesus Christ. As a result, when they died, they immediately went to be in His presence. They had gotten the most important thing in this life in order: the condition of their souls. How brief our lives are.

Please Accept Jesus as Your Savior

How important it is that we take the steps to accept Jesus as our Savior. "He who believes in the Son has eternal life. But he who does not obey the Son shall not see life, but the wrath of God abides on him," John 3:36. My hope is that every reader of this book comes to the saving knowledge of Jesus Christ. Simply pray to God, confessing your sin and your need for a Savior. Accept in your heart that Jesus died and rose again from the dead, paying the penalty of death for you! Then ask God to forgive you and fill you with His Holy Spirit so you will be saved for all eternity. Repent and turn away from your sins and make Jesus Christ the Lord of your life. Read and obey the Bible, His words and commands to us. God will forgive your sins, but the road will not always be easy, and the race will be hard. But when you reach the finish line, you will be with God in the perfect place He has prepared for you forever!

Jesus is the *only* thing that matters. Remember, "*Today* is the day of salvation," (2 Corinthians 6:2). You do not know what tomorrow may bring. Kimberly and Angela did not expect sudden death that day. But they were prepared. Are you? Eternity is a long time. Can you afford to wait any longer?

Appendix

E

Ten Reasons to Join Home School Legal Defense Association

Your membership:

1. Provides professional legal representations to protect your right to home school against government officials. As home schooling fathers, our attorneys share your commitment to home education as a legal right, educational opportunity and spiritual blessing. One hundred percent of legal fees and associated costs are paid by HSLDA.

2. Helps HSLDA monitor all state legislation that could reduce your home schooling freedoms.

3. Ensures immediate response to attempts to roll back your state's home school law (the army needs to be on the ground when the enemy makes its move).

4. Enables HSLDA to conduct research regarding home schooling and produce literature that presents home education in the best possible light.

5. Allows HSLDA to provide leadership symposiums for support group leaders and the national conference to state leaders to better equip them to serve the home school community.

6. Makes you part of a brotherhood of 70,000+ families who stand together to protect and advance home school freedoms—in the United States and foreign countries.
7. Entitles you to assistance with any social services contact.
8. Entitles you to receive e-mail alerts regarding any federal and/or state legislation that impacts home school and parental freedoms.
9. Keeps you abreast of the latest breaking news in home education through our newsletter and other publications.
10. Ensures a lobbying presence in Washington, D.C., (HSLDA) to remind the federal government that it has no jurisdiction over home schools.

The Social Worker Skit

How to Handle a Visit from a Social Worker

This skit was first presented at the November 1993 National Center for Home Education Christian Leadership Conference in Williamsburg, Virginia. Since then, it has been presented at hundreds of home school conferences across the country.

This skit can be acted out or read before any home school gathering to help educate parents on their basic rights if they ever have to deal with an unwanted visit from a social worker. It provides an easy (and somewhat humorous) way to help parents remember what to say and what not to say if they are surprised by a social worker. Although the principles in this skit generally apply in all states, this does not substitute for independent advice from an attorney.

This skit is a supplement to chapter 13.

Cast:

> Mr./Mrs. Innocent . . . . *an unprepared parent*
> Mr./Mrs. Orwell . . . . *a social services agent*
> Eager-to-Please . . . . *a home schooled child*
> Mr./Mrs. Wise . . . . *a prepared parent*

Scenario 1:

How not to do it, featuring a parent who is not prepared when a social service agent arrives at the door.

[It is 3 o'clock in the afternoon, and a knock comes at the door. Innocent opens the door and finds an agent from Child Welfare Services on the doorstep.]

ORWELL: We recently received a report that your children are being abused or neglected. I need to inspect your home and talk to each one of your children separately to verify or negate this information. *[Innocent hestitates.]*

If you don't allow me to come in, I'll have to get a police officer and a warrant, and things will become much more complicated. I know you don't want that. I'm sure we can resolve this matter today if you'll just cooperate.

INNOCENT: Well…uh…I'm not really ready right now, but I guess so, okay. If we can work this out…

ORWELL: You just cooperate and everything will be just fine. First of all, what are the names of your children?

INNOCENT: Well, we have twelve children!

Orwell: And what are their birth dates?

[The scene shifts to a discussion with one of the twelve children.]

ORWELL: So let's talk about Little Eager. How old is he?

INNOCENT: Six.

ORWELL: Would you call him so I can speak with him?

INNOCENT: Can I stay here with him?

ORWELL: No, I'm sorry. I need you to be out of the room. It's very important that I interview each of your children individually and privately so they can be completely open and honest.

INNOCENT: Well…if it is absolutely necessary…okay…

[Innocent leaves the room, and Orwell begins to interview Eager-to-Please.]

ORWELL: Hello, Little Eager! My name is Orwell, and I work for the government. I visit boys and girls all over the city to find out how they are doing and if they have any problems I can help them with. I'm happy to meet you today. How old are you, Eager?

EAGER: I'm six years old.

ORWELL: Eager, where do you go to school?

EAGER: I don't.

ORWELL: What do you mean, you don't go to school?

EAGER: Well, I stay home here with my mom.

ORWELL: Your parents don't let you go to the public school?

EAGER: No.

ORWELL: Don't they like the public school?

EAGER: No!

ORWELL: Eager, do you have any friends that go to the public school?

EAGER: Yeah, some of my friends who live next door and down the street. They get on the big yellow bus in the morning and drive away.

ORWELL: Do you ever wish you could play with your friends while they're gone all day?

EAGER: Yeah, I do. I get a little lonely. I miss them sometimes.

ORWELL: So, your friends are all gone away to school and you miss them. You wish you could be with them and play with them.

EAGER: Yeah, like Johnny next door. He tells me a lot of fun things about the public school. I'd kinda like to go there some time.

ORWELL: Eager, have your parents ever said why they don't like the public school?

EAGER: They say it's bad cause I'll learn bad things there.

ORWELL: Do your parents let you play with any of the neighborhood kids?

EAGER: Well...uh...there are some kids down the street that I can't play with. One time I tried playing ball with them, but my parents came out and said that their parents don't believe the same as we do, so they didn't want me hanging around them.

ORWELL: So, your parents won't let you play with these other children?

EAGER: No. I get a spank if I play with them.

ORWELL: What do you mean you'll "get a spank"?

EAGER: Well, uh, I get a whupping.

ORWELL: How do your parents "whup" you? Do they use their hands or a paddle or what?

EAGER: They use a paddle.

ORWELL: Like a big wooden paddle?

EAGER: Uh, yeah...It's pretty big!

ORWELL: And they hit you with this wooden board?

EAGER: That's right. Right on my back end.

ORWELL: Eager, when your parents hit you with this paddle on your bottom, do they make you take your pants down?

EAGER: Oh, yeah.

ORWELL: So they hit you with this wooden board on your bare bottom?

EAGER: Yes, I cry a lot. It hurts.

ORWELL: Now, Eager, when your pants are down like that, do they ever touch your bottom with their hands? Do they ever touch you at all?

EAGER: Yeah, sometimes, if they can't find the paddle.

ORWELL: Eager, I'm glad we've had this time to visit. I hope I'll see you again. I'd like to be your friend.

[Orwell sends Eager-to-Please out of the room, and Innocent returns.]

ORWELL: Mr./Mrs. Innocent, I think there's some abuse going on in this home. I have evidence of physical abuse, sexual abuse...

INNOCENT: What...?

ORWELL: ...social deprivation, and educational neglect. I'm need to have your children stripped so I can see if they have any bruises on their anatomy. I'm also going to have to have your children meet with a Department of Social Services psychologist to determine if they are experiencing any emotional abuse from this social deprivation or educational neglect. Mr./Mrs. Innocent, I've have serious concerns about your religious beliefs. And what all this home schooling stuff? Do you have any books?

INNOCENT: We have books. We have some books up here...some over there...uh...and under the table...

ORWELL: Let me see where you do this home school. Do you have desks?

INNOCENT: We sometimes teach our children here, on the couch, and sometimes over here...

ORWELL: At the dining room table?

INNOCENT: Yes...and sometimes on the floor.

ORWELL: You don't have any desks?

INNOCENT: No, we don't have desks for the children. We don't need them.

ORWELL: The lighting in this room is terrible. You don't have a school room; you don't have desks. Do you have a blackboard?

INNOCENT: No, we don't really need those.

ORWELL: What about audio-visual aids?

INNOCENT: Well...uh...we go on field trips. Does that count?

ORWELL: Do you have any test scores for these children?

INNOCENT: Well, we haven't really started testing yet. We have a philosophy...you know...that children should not be tested too young. We are going to wait awhile.

ORWELL: So you have no test scores. Are you certified to teach?

INNOCENT: No...but I do have a high school diploma from the local public school here! That should be worth something!

ORWELL: Now, Eager told me something that really concerned me. He said that you don't allow him to play with other children.

INNOCENT: Yeah, that's true in a number of occasions. We want to protect our children from families who believe very much differently than us.

ORWELL: Tell me about your religious beliefs.

INNOCENT: Well, we believe the Bible is the Word of God, and we have to do what it says.

ORWELL: All right, so what does the Bible say about child discipline?

INNOCENT: Well, it says in Proverbs that...uh..."if you beat your child with a rod, he will not die..."

ORWELL: What do you mean by "rod"?

INNOCENT: Well, we use a paddle.

ORWELL: A wooden paddle?

INNOCENT: Yeah, it's right over here.

ORWELL: May I see it? *[Social services agent takes paddle.]* I think I'm going to keep this for awhile.

INNOCENT: Wait a minute. I think I need to use that right now. Eager!

ORWELL: When you use this paddle on your children, where do you strike them?

INNOCENT: Well, we spank them only on their back end.

ORWELL: Have you ever bruised a child?

INNOCENT: Well...I mean...not recently.

ORWELL: Mr./Mrs. Innocent, I'm afraid I'm going to have to write this up as a case of substantiated child abuse. I'll make arrangements for your children to meet with our psychologist. Mr./Mrs. Innocent, I'll keep in touch with you. Good day. *[Exit.]*

Scenario 2:

In which the agent encounters a prepared parent, an HSLDA member aware of his rights.

[It is 3 o'clock in the afternoon, and a knock comes at the door. Wise opens the door and finds Orwell, an agent from Child Welfare Services, on the doorstep.]

WISE: Can I help you?

ORWELL: Yes, are you Mr./Mrs. Wise? I work with the local social services agency. There's been an allegation made that you've been abusing and neglecting your children...

WISE: Wait a minute. Do you have a business card? We don't just talk to anybody. We want to know who you are, and that, in fact, you work there. Do you have a card, sir?

ORWELL: Uh, yes, just a minute...but, I want you to understand that this is a very important matter. As you can see, I'm from the Department of Social Services...

WISE: Hmmmm. *[Reads name on card.]* "George Orwell." How long have you been working there?

ORWELL: I ask the questions here. You've been turned in for abusing and neglecting your children.

WISE: Well, what are the allegations specifically?

ORWELL: I'm not in a position to share those with you until I have met with each of your children privately for questioning. After I've talked to them, then I'll tell you.

WISE: Well, I appreciate your interest, and I, too, want to get to the bottom of this. I assure you, nothing is going on. There's nothing that we're hiding here. However, I can't even proceed until I know of what I'm being accused.

ORWELL: As I said, I am not going to tell you the allegations until I meet with your children. If you're not willing to cooperate, I'll have to get a police officer. If necessary, we'll obtain a search warrant or court order, and we'll come back and talk to each one of your children privately. It would be much easier though if you cooperated with us here and now, so that we could avoid the unpleasantness of bringing in the police. What's it going to be?

WISE: Well, you obviously have to do what you need to do, and I'm not in a position to stop you. However, you'd be making a major mistake, and I'd hate to see you get in trouble over something like this. As I said, I'm more than happy to work this out.

We'd be glad to meet with you. But I do need to talk to my attorney first. We could possibly set up a mutually convenient time when we could meet to resolve this. But right now, I can't let you into my home. I don't even know what the accusations are!

ORWELL: Good day, then. I'll be back.

WISE: I've got your card here, and I'll call you as soon as I have contacted my attorney.

[After the social worker leaves, Wise calls HSLDA and gets counsel for the next meeting with the social worker. The prepared parent is able to do this because he joined HSLDA as a member in advance! The HSLDA attorney will generally call the social worker on behalf of the member family. He will find out the allegations and try to resolve the situation. If he can't resolve it over the phone, he will set the parameters for a meeting. This meeting is never held in the home, but rather in a designated place away from the home. The HSLDA attorney prepares the parent on what to say at the meeting and recommends bringing a witness or a tape recorder.]

[It is now another day, and Orwell meets with Mr. Wise to follow up.]

WISE: Well, it's good to see you again. I understand now that you can let us know what the allegations are.

ORWELL: All right. We received a telephone call from a person who was "concerned because the children were all thin. This person thought that the removal of food was probably a form of child discipline and was under the impression that this discipline may have been a practice of your religion—some born-again ideology, or something. The caller cited that the parents give a lot of money to the church and spend little money on groceries, and the caller also mentioned that the mother home schools her children." [This comment is in quotation marks because it came from an actual case I handled in the state of Wisconsin.]

Are these allegations true?

WISE: They are not true—except for the fact that we are home schooling our children and we are born again. Do you know what born again means?

ORWELL: Uh...no, but...

WISE: Let me explain. You see, in John 3 Jesus told Nicodemus he must be "born again" in order to enter the kingdom of God. Since the wages of sin is death, we all need a savior. Do you know where you are going when you die?

(I strongly recommend that you share the gospel with the social worker. I had this opportunity when my wife and I were in the hospital the day after my wife gave birth to our twins by C-section. We were in the intensive care unit with Amy, who was only 2 lbs 11 ounces. She was hooked up to every imaginable machine and her survival was in question. Our other twin was being held by a nurse. Our four other children (ages seven and under were two hours away). I was staying in a Ronald MacDonald House. Needless to say, we were considered a family at risk.

There in the intensive care unit, a social worker comes walking up and begins asking us detailed questions about our family. Suddenly, I felt like all the parents I had advised all these years! Do you tell the social worker what she wants to know so she does not get suspicious or do you refuse to answer so she can't twist the facts into a case against you.

I prayed and God made it clear what I needed to do: share the gospel with this lady! I began to tell her the miracle of our little Amy and how the doctors said she would die. I told her about God answering our prayers. I asked her if she believed in God and she said "No, but if you want to believe that, fine." I began sharing with her that she needed a Savior because she was a sinner bound for hell. I pulled out a New Testament to give her but she said she could not accept it because she was on the job. I told her to take off her social worker hat for a minute, but she still refused the Word of God. I asked her if she understood what she was refusing. I said she was rejecting God and she would be hopelessly lost.

By this time, she began looking nervously around for a way out. She abruptly exclaimed, "It was good meeting you but I have some work to do." We were never bothered again! We were hoping she would get saved but the result was good because our family was safe from her scrutiny! God's Word is powerful!

ORWELL: Look, are your children healthy?

WISE: You bet!

ORWELL: Do they eat enough food?

WISE: Yes. We believe children are a gift of the Lord, and as a result, we have to take care of them, giving them the best possible. Part of that is how we feed them—we make sure they have plenty of nutritious food to eat.

ORWELL: Do you ever deprive them of food as part of your religion, or part of your born-again beliefs, or part of your child discipline, or any of that?

WISE: No, we don't. We can, as our attorney has probably told you, offer you references of individuals in the community who would vouch for the good care we give our children.

ORWELL: Now you realize that we're going to have to have your children meet with our physicians so that they can evaluate whether or not the children have been properly fed.

WISE: I've talked to our attorney about that also, and we have already had our children see our personal family physician, and he is putting his report in writing for you. Our children have a clean bill of health.

ORWELL: That report does not remove the need for me to personally interview your children.

WISE: Well, I think we went over this before, but our position is that we cannot take that risk. Besides, we've already provided this other information so that you can really close this file because you're going to have references from individuals, the doctor's report, and our own assurance that everything is fine. The reason we don't want you to talk to our children, frankly, is because we don't trust the system. We're aware of statistics that show that 60 percent of children who are removed from homes by the social welfare system shouldn't have been upon later review. We just can't take that risk because sometimes those children are put into foster homes where they are abused. So it has nothing to do with hiding anything. It's just that we care so much for our children that we can't take this risk. We don't know you.

ORWELL: Everyone else cooperates, Mr./Mrs. Wise. If you have nothing to hide, then why are you hiding so hard?

WISE: As I said, we'd be more than happy to cooperate if you could guarantee that you would find this "unfounded." But since you can't, and we don't know how you're going to interpret this, and the studies show that many, many, many families' statements are misinterpreted, how can we take that risk? Would you take that risk with your children?

ORWELL: *[hesitates in knowing how to respond]*

WISE: Please understand, we appreciate your great interest in our family. We know you're just doing your job, and sometimes that can put a person between a rock and a hard place. But we've got certain rights that we talked to our attorney about. We have the right of privacy which comes under the Fourth

Amendment which protects us from state officials coming into our home at will, and we're standing on that right. Are you familiar with the Fourth Amendment?

ORWELL: Uh…we did not learn about the Fourth Amendment in Social Worker School. However, I am familiar with the Second Amendment…do you have any guns in your house?

WISE: That's really irrelevant. I'll take the Fifth on that one.

ORWELL: Let's talk about your home schooling. I have to see your curriculum and facilities.

I need to verify that you have enough light for these children to read. For all I know, you're ruining their eyesight by reading to them on a couch or something.

WISE: Well, I've talked to my attorney again about this, and we are legal. We're legally home schooling, and in this state, we're allowed to home school. We've followed the necessary requirements under the law. If you have a problem with this, you need to let the school district know because it's not really in your jurisdiction. Meanwhile, our attorney would be glad to send you a letter verifying the legality of home schooling.

ORWELL: Just because you're legal doesn't mean you're not neglecting your children.

WISE: If you have a problem with our educational program, you'll need to contact the local superintendent. We're on file. I can assure you that we're educating our children. It's part of our religious beliefs. We must teach our children to the best of our ability so that they can become productive citizens. Our philosophy is to provide them the best quality education that we possible can.

ORWELL: Look, I have four specific charges against you: you're starving your children, you're giving all your money away, you're neglecting their education, and you're not willing to cooperate with me.

WISE: As I stated, we are going to provide you evidence so that you can find the allegations "unfounded." We're going to provide a statement from our doctor and various references. You have our word on it, and we're known in the community.

Besides, we base our decisions in our family living on the Scriptures, where we are clearly instructed that "if you harm one of these little ones, it's better a millstone be tied around your neck and be thrown in the deepest part of the ocean." That's a responsibility we take seriously in raising our little ones—that God would hold us accountable—in fact, we would be *sinning* before Him if we harmed them in any way in discipline, or food, withholding food as we've been accused of…we would never do those things.

ORWELL: Mr./Mrs. Wise, look, I can tell that you're sincere. I don't know…I'm really concerned about this situation. I wish you would cooperate with us instead of making our jobs so difficult.

WISE: Let me assure you. We care for our children, too, and we appreciate your care. And I believe that you will find this can all be resolved and you can put on file that it is "unfounded." In fact, we'd like something in writing, describing your finding. By tomorrow we should be able to get that statement from our doctor, so we just ask that you hold off any further decision until you can look at this. And if there's still a problem, we'll cross that bridge when we get to it.

ORWELL: It's obvious that you're not willing to do anything more than you've done. So I'll look at your doctor's report…I just want to say, for the record, that this kind of attitude is what makes it so hard for us to protect children. While you may be very sincere, there are real kids out there who are getting hurt. Your way of dealing with this matter ties us up with lawyers and reports when we could be resolving serious crises. Good day, Mr./Mrs. Wise. *[Exit.]*

Home School Organizations and Resources

Alabama

Christian Home Education Fellowship of
Alabama
3325 Crestwood Drive
Semmes, AL 36575-5443
(334) 645-5003
Fax (334) 645-9243
e-mail:hls@prodigy.net
www.ALhome.com

Alaska

Alaska Private Home Educators Assn.
PO Box 141764
Anchorage, AK 99514
(907) 566-3450
www.aphea.org

Arizona

Arizona Families for Home Education
PO Box 2035
Chandler, AZ 85244-2035
(602) 443-0612
e-mail: afhe@primenet.com
www.afhe.org

Flagstaff Home Educators
PO Box 31236
Flagstaff, AZ 86003-1236
(520) 774-0806

Arkansas

The Education Alliance
414 S. Pulaski, Suite 2
Little Rock, AR 72201-2930
(501) 375-7000
Fax (501) 375-7040
e-mail: arfamcouncil@aol.com

California

Christian Home Educators Association
of California
PO Box 2009
Norwalk, CA 90651
(562) 864-2432 or
(800) 564-2432
e-mail: cheaofca@aol.com
www.cheaofca.org

Family Protection Ministries
910 Sunrise Avenue, Suite A-1
Roseville, CA 95661

Colorado

Christian Home Educators of Colorado
3739 E. 4th Avenue
Denver, CO 80206
(303) 393-6587
Fax (303) 393-0924
e-mail: office@chec.org
www.chec.org

Concerned Parents for Colorado
PO Box 547
Florissant, CO 80816
(719) 748-8360
e-mail: treonelain@aol.com
www.members.aol.com/treonelain

Connecticut
The Education Association of Christian
Homeschoolers
282 Camp Street
Plainville, CT 06062
(860) 793-9968
e-mail: teachinfo@pobox.com
www.teachCT.org

Delaware
Delaware Home Education Assn.
PO Box 172
1812 Marsh Road, Suite 6
Wilmington, DE 19810-4528
Phone or Fax (302) 475-0574
e-mail: jcpoeii@juno.com

Tri-State Home School Network
PO Box 7193
Newark, DE 19714
(302) 322-2018

District of Columbia
Bolling Area Home Educators
PO Box 8401
BAFB
Washington, DC 20336-8401
(202) 561-0234
e-mail: haselvid@aol.com

Florida
Florida Parent-Educators Assoc. Inc.
PO Box 50685
Jacksonville, FL 32240-0685
Toll free (877) 275-3732
Local: (904) 241-5538
Fax: (904) 241-5539
e-mail: office@fpea.com
www.fpea.com

Florida Coalition of Christian Private
Schools Association Inc./ Christian Home
Educators of Florida
6280 150th Avenue North
Clearwater, FL 33760
(727)539-1881
CHEFFCCPSA@aol.com
www.flhomeschooling.com

Georgia
Georgia Home Education Association
245 Buckeye Lane
Fayetteville, GA 30214
(770) 461-3657
e-mail: ghea@mindspring.com
www.ghea.org

Hawaii
Christian Homeschoolers of Hawaii
91-824 Oama Street
Ewa Beach, HI 96706
(808) 689-6398

Idaho
Christian Home Educators of Idaho State
7722 Wayside Drive
Boise, ID 83704
(208) 322-4270
e-mail: info@chois.org
www.chois.org

Illinois
Illinois Christian Home Educators
PO Box 775
Harvard, IL 60033
(815) 943-7882, Fax (815) 943-7883
e-mail: ICHE83@juno.com

Christian Home Educators Coalition of
Illinois
PO Box 47322
Chicago, IL 60647
(773) 278-0673
e-mail: ILCHEC@AOL.COM

Indiana
Indiana Association of Home Educators
8106 Madison Avenue
Indianapolis, IN 46227
(317) 859-1202
Fax: (317) 859-1204
e-mail: iahe@inhomeeducators.org
www.inhomeeducators

Iowa
Network of Iowa Christian Home
Educators
PO Box 158
Dexter, IA 50070
(515) 830-1614 or (800) 723-0438
e-mail: niche@netins.net
www.the-NICHE.org

Kansas

Christian Home Educators Confederation
of Kansas
PO Box 3968
Wichita, KS 67201-0081
(316) 945-0810
e-mail: info@kansashomeschool.org
www.kansashomeschool.org

Kentucky

Christian Home Educators of Kentucky
691 Howardstown Road
Hodgensville, KY 42748
(270) 358-9270
e-mail: chek@kvent.org
www.chek.org

Kentucky Home Education Association
PO Box 81
Winchester, KY 40392-0081
(606) 737-3338
e-mail: katy@mis.net
www.viphosting.com/khea

Louisiana

Christian Home Educators Fellowship of
Louisiana
PO Box 74292
Baton Rouge, LA 70874-4292
www.chefofla.org
(888) 876-2433
Fax (504) 774-4114

Maine

Homeschoolers of Maine
337 Hatchet Mt. Road
Hope, ME 04847
(207) 763-4251
Fax (207) 763-4352
e-mail: homeschl@midcoast.com

Maryland

Maryland Association of Christian Home
Educators
PO Box 247
Point of Rocks, MD 21777-0247
(301) 607-4284
e-mail: MACHE@juno.com
web: www.machemd.org

Christian Home Educators Network
PO Box 2010
Ellicott City, MD 21043
(301) 474-9055
e-mail: chenmaster@chenmd.org
www.chenmd.org

Massachusetts

Massachusetts Homeschool Organization of
Parent Educators
5 Atwood Road
Cherry Valley, MA 01611-3332
(978) 544-7892
Fax: (508) 892-3437
e-mail: info@masshope.org
www.masshope.org

Michigan

Information Network for Christian Homes
4934 Cannonsburg Road
Belmont, MI 49306
(616) 874-5656

Minnesota

Minnesota Association of Christian Home
Educators
PO Box 32308
Fridley, MN 55432-0308
(612) 717-9070
www.mache.org

Mississippi

Mississippi Home Educators Association
PO Box 945
Brookhaven, MS 39602
(601) 833-9110
e-mail: MHEA@juno.com
www.mhea.org

Missouri

Missouri Association of Teaching Christian
Homes
2203 Rhonda Drive
West Plains, MO 65775-1615
Phone/Fax (417) 255-2824
e-mail: match@christianmail.net
www.hopewp.org/MATCH

Families for Home Education
6209 NW Tower Road
Platte Woods, MO 64151
(417) 782-8833
e-mail: fhe@microlink.net
www.microlink.net/~fhe/index.htm

Montana

Montana Coalition of Home Educators
PO Box 43
Gallatin Gateway, MT 59730
(406) 587-6163
e-mail: white@gomontana.com
www.mtche.org

Nebraska
Nebraska Christian Home Educators
Association
PO Box 57041
Lincoln, NE 68505-7041
(402) 423-4297
Fax (402) 420-2610
e-mail: nchea@alltel.net
www.nchea.org

Nevada
Northern Nevada Home Schools
PO Box 21323
Reno, NV 89515
(702) 852-6647
e-mail: NNHS@aol.com

Silver State Education Association
888 W. 2nd Street, Suite 200
Reno, NV 89503
702-851-0772
email: SSEA@powernet.net

New Hampshire
Christian Home Educators of New
Hampshire
PO Box 961
Manchester, NH 03105
(603) 569-2343
www.mv.com/ipusers/chenh/

New Jersey
Education Network of Christian
Homeschoolers of New Jersey, Inc.
PO Box 308
Atlantic Highlands, NJ 07716-0308
(732) 291-7800
Fax (732) 291-5398
e-mail: ENOCHNJ@aol.com
www.enoch-nj.org

New Mexico
Christian Association of Parent Educators
of New Mexico
PO Box 25046
Albuquerque, NM 87125
(505) 898-8548:
e-mail: info@cape-nm.org
www.cape-nm.org

New York
Loving Education At Home
PO Box 438
Fayetteville, NY 13066
Phone/Fax (716) 346-0939
e-mail: Info@leah.org
www.leah.org

North Carolina
North Carolinians for Home Education
419 N Boylan Avenue
Raleigh, NC 27603-1211
(919) 834-6243
e-mail: nche@mindspring.com
www.nche.com

North Dakota
North Dakota Home School Assn.
PO Box 7400
Bismarck, ND 58507-7400
(701) 223-4080
e-mail: ndhsa@wdata.com

Ohio
Christian Home Educators of Ohio
117 W Main Street, Suite 103
Lancaster, OH 43130
(740) 654-3331
Fax (740) 654-3337
e-mail: cheo@buckeyenet.net
www.cheohome.org

Oklahoma
Christian Home Educators Fellowship of
Oklahoma
PO Box 471363
Tulsa, OK 74147-1363
(918) 583-7323

Oklahoma Central Home Educators
Association
PO Box 270601
Oklahoma City, OK 73137
(405) 521-8439

Oregon
Oregon Christian Home Education
Association Network
17985 Falls City Road
Dallas, OR 97338
(503) 288-1285
e-mail: oceanet@teleport.com
www.teleport.com/~oceanet

Pennsylvania
Christian Home School Association of
Pennsylvania
PO Box 115
Mt. Joy, PA 17552
(717) 661-2428
e-mail: CHAPKimH@aol.com

Pennsylvania Homeschoolers
RD 2 Box 117
Kittanning, PA 16201
(724) 783-6512

Rhode Island
Rhode Island Guild of Home Teachers
PO Box 11
Hope, RI 02831-0011
(401) 821-7700
e-mail: right_right@mail.excite.com
www.members.tripod.com/righthome

South Carolina
South Carolina Home Educators Assn.
PO Box 3231
Columbia, SC 29230-3231
(803) 754-6425
www.schea.org

South Carolina Association of Independent
Home Schools
PO Box 869
Irmo, SC 29063
(803) 407-2155

South Dakota
South Dakota Christian Home Educators
PO Box 528
Black Hawk, SD 57118
(605) 745-4203
e-mail: lafrance3@juno.com

Tennessee
Tennessee Home Education Association
3677 Richbriar Court
Nashville, TN 37211
(615) 834-3529

Texas
Texas Home School Coalition
PO Box 6982
Lubbock, TX 79493
(806) 797-4927
(806) 797-4629
e-mail: staff@thsc.org
www.thsc.org

Utah
Utah Christian Homeschool Assn.
PO Box 3942
Salt Lake City, UT 84110-3942
(801) 296-7198
e-mail: utch@utch.org
www.utch.org

Vermont
Christian Home Educators of Vermont
214 N Prospect #105
Burlington, VT 05401-1613
(802) 464-0746

Virginia
Home Educators Association of Virginia
PO Box 6745
Richmond, VA 23230-0745
(804) 288-1608

Washington
Washington Association of Teaching
Christian Homes
554 Pletke Road
Tieton, WA 98974
(509) 678-5440
e-mail: Rlisk@aol.com
www.watchhome.org

Washington Homeschool Organization
632 S 191st Place, Suite E
Kent, WA 98032-2117
(206) 546-9483
e-mail: WHOoffice@juno.com
www.washhomeschool.org

West Virginia
Christian Home Educators of West Virginia
PO Box 8770
South Charleston, WV 25303-0770
(304) 776-4664
e-mail: chewvadm@aol.com
www.geocities.com/athens/forum/8045

Wisconsin
Wisconsin Christian Home Educators
Association
2307 Carmel Avenue
Racine, WI 53405
(414) 637-5127

Wyoming
Homeschoolers of Wyoming
PO Box 3151
Jackson, WY 83001
(307)-733.2834
e-mail: mungermtrr@compuserve.com

Australia
The Home Education Research and Legal
Information Network
54 Pilbara Crescent
Jane Brook, Western Australia 6056
e-mail: piffle@tnet.com.au

Canada
Alberta Home Education Association
Box 3451
Leduc, Alberta, T9E 6M2
(403) 320-0924

Association of Christian Home Educators
of Quebec
15-101 Don Quichotte, Suite 374
Ile Perrot, Quebec, J7V 7X4
(514) 425-4267
Fax (514) 425-3515
e-mail: acheq-acefq@uni-signal.ca
www.go.to/acheq

England
Home Service
48 Heaton Moor Road, Heaton Moor
Stockport, SK4 4NX
011-44-161-432-3782

Japan
KANTO Home Educators Association PSC
477 Box 45
FPO, AP 96306-1299

Germany
Eifel Area Home Schoolers
52 SVS/SVA
UNIT 3640 BOX 170
APO AE 09126-0170

HEART for Germany
c/o Bruce & Barbara West
Unit 30400 Box 1584
APO AE 09128
011-49-711-8106-999
e-mail: Batman270@iname.com

Handicapped
NATHHAN (National Challenged
Homeschoolers Association Network)
P.O. Box 39
Porthill, ID 83853
208-267-6246
e-mail: NATHANEWS@aol.com

Military
Eifel Area Home Schoolers
52 SVS/SVA
UNIT 3640 BOX 170
APO AE 09126-0170

Verna Lilly
PSC 118 Box 584
APO AE 09137

Guam Home School Association
1868 Halsey Drive
ASAN, GU 96922
(671) 565- 1360
Fax (671) 477-2838
e-mail: rrb@kuentos.guam.net

New Zealand
Christian Home Schoolers of New Zealand
4 Tawa Street
Palmerston North, New Zealand

Puerto Rico
Christian Home Educators of the
Caribbean
Calle 10, E-19, Villa Universitavia Humacao,
PR 00791
1-787-852-5672
e-mail: JCuret@compuserve.com

South Africa
Pestalozzi Trust Legal Defense Fund for
Home Education
PO Box 31264
Totiusdal, 0134, Pretoria
Republic of South Africa
e-mail: defensor@lantic.net
www.lantic.co.za/~curamus1

Western Cape Home Schooling Association
PO Box 2238
Bellville, 7535, S
Republic of South Africa

Radio
Home Education Radio Network
PO Box 3338-704 Skyline Drive
Idaho Springs, CO 80452
(303) 567-4092
e-mail: HENRadio@aol.com

About the Author

Christopher J. Klicka is Senior Counsel of the Home School Legal Defense Association (HSLDA), a nonprofit legal organization dedicated to protecting the rights of parents to home school in all fifty states, the U.S. territories, and Canada. He also serves as the executive director of HSLDA's National Center For Home Education, the federal lobbying, research, and international branch. HSLDA is based near Washington, D.C., in Purcellville, Virginia, and has over sixty-five thousand member families, as of October 1999.

Klicka earned his BA from Grove City College in Grove City, Pennsylvania, and his Juris Doctorate from O.W. Coburn School of Law, Tulsa, Oklahoma (renamed School of Law, Regent University and relocated to Virginia Beach, Virginia).

Since 1985, he has worked at HSLDA handling scores of court cases and administrative appeals on behalf of home school families throughout the country. He has argued before four state supreme courts and argued before or submitted briefs to appellate courts in Michigan, Alabama, Maine, Colorado, Virginia, Massachusetts, Pennsylvania and North Dakota on behalf of home schoolers.

Also for over ten years, he successfully represented over three thousand home school families with legal conflicts requiring him to deal with thousands of public school officials, truant officers, school board members, social workers, prosecutors, and police officers.

He has provided expert testimony before numerous legislatures (including South Dakota, Virginia, Indiana, Texas, Maine, Pennsylvania, Alabama, North Dakota, South Carolina, Maryland, and Colorado) and state boards of education including Maryland, Iowa, North Dakota and Maine) on behalf of home schoolers.

He is a member of the bars of the Virginia Supreme Court, the United States Supreme Court, the Fourth Circuit Court of Appeals, and the U.S. District Court of Virginia (Eastern Division).

In his role of executive director of HSLDA's National Center, Chris has testified before Congress, drafted amendments, lobbied many congressional offices, and led successful fights against national testing, national I.D. cards, ending discrimination against home schoolers in the military and other issues. Chris also directs a significant part of HSLDA's international effort in South Africa, Canada, Mexico, Ireland, Taiwan, and Germany. He serves on the Legal Defense Association boards of both South Africa and Canada.

He has spoken at over two hundred sixty home school conferences throughout the country and has been interviewed by hundreds of newspapers including the *Washington Times, Chicago Tribune, Wall Street Journal, Washington Post, Newsweek,* and *USA Today* where he was featured as a guest editorial "Face Off." He has been interviewed on many radio shows on the legal and academic aspects of home schooling including "Family News in Focus," Marlin Maddoux's "Point of View," and James Kennedy's "Truths That Transform." In addition to many television interviews, he is a regular columnist for Mary Pride's "Practical Home Schooling" magazine.

Mr. Klicka is the author of *Home Schooling in the United States: A Legal Analysis* published by HSLDA and updated each year since 1985. It describes in detail the legal atmosphere of home schooling in each state. He also authored *The Case For Home Schooling* and *The Right to Home School: A Guide to the Law on Parent's Rights in Education.* He has published articles in the *Religion and Public Education* journal and in the *Ohio Northern Law Review.*

He is married to Tracy and they are home schooling their seven children; Bethany, Megan, Jesse, Susanna, twins Charity and Amy, and John.

The Best of
Catherine
Marshall

The Best of
Catherine
Marshall

Edited by
Leonard E. LeSourd

WALKER AND COMPANY
New York

Library of Congress Cataloging-in-Publication Data
Marshall, Catherine, 1914-1983
  [Selections, 1995]
  The best of Catherine Marshall / edited by Leonard E. LeSourd. — 1st large print ed.
    p. cm.
  ISBN 0-8027-2687-9
  1. Marshall, Catherine, 1914–1983. 2. Presbyterians—United States—Biography. 3. Christian Life. 4. Large type books.
  I. LeSourd, Leonard E. II. Title.
[BX9225.M3515A25 1995]
242—dc20   94-42713
                                                                    CIP

Unless otherwise identified, Scripture quotations are from the King James Version of the Bible.

Scripture quotations identified RSV are from the Revised Standard Version of the Bible, copyright 1946, 1952, 1971, and 1973, by the Division of Christian Education of the National Council of the Churches of Christ in the United States of America.

Verses marked TLB are taken from *The Living Bible*, copyright © 1971 by Tyndale House Publishers, Wheaton, Illinois. Used by permission.

Scripture quotations identified Moffatt are from The Bible: A New Translation by James Moffatt, © 1954 by James A. R. Moffatt. By permission of HarperCollins Publishers, Inc.

Scripture quotations identified NIV are taken from the Holy Bible, New International Version®. Copyright © 1973, 1978, 1984 by International Bible Society. Used by permission of Zondervan Publishing House. All rights reserved.

Scripture quotations identified Phillips are from The New Testament in Modern English, Revised Edition, J. B. Phillips, translator, © J. B. Phillips, 1958, 1960, 1972. Used by permission of Macmillan Publishing Co., Inc.

Old Testament Scripture quotations identified TAB are from the Amplified Bible, © 1965, 1987 by The Zondervan Corporation. Used by permission.

New Testament Scripture quotations identified TAB are from The Amplified New Testament, © The Lockman Foundation 1954, 1958.

Excerpts are taken from the following books:

Section One, "Childhood: Short on Money, Long on Faith," from *Meeting God at Every Turn*, © 1980 by Catherine Marshall LeSourd and published by Chosen Books Publishing Company, Ltd.

Section Two, "The Years with Peter," from *A Man Called Peter*, © 1951 by Catherine Marshall and published by McGraw-Hill Book Company. Rights transferred to Chosen Books in 1978.

Section Three, "The Years Alone," from *To Live Again*, © 1957 by Catherine Marshall and published by McGraw-Hill Book Company. Rights transferred to Chosen Books in 1978.

Section Four, "Second Marriage," from *Beyond Our Selves*, © 1961 by Catherine Marshall and published by McGraw-Hill Book Company. Rights transferred to Chosen Books in 1978. Also from *Meeting God At Every Turn*.

Section Five, "Schoolteacher," from *Christy*, © 1967 by Catherine Marshall LeSourd and published by McGraw-Hill Book Company. Reprinted with permission.

Section Six, *"Guideposts* Writer," from the following articles: "The Protecting Power," "The Man Who Couldn't Stand Leisure," "God's Work Is Where You Are" and "The Healing of Maude Blanford." Reprinted with permission from *Guideposts* magazine, © 1966, 1969, 1968, 1972 by Guideposts Associates, Inc., Carmel, NY 10512.

Section Seven, "The Holy Spirit," from *Something More*, © 1974 by Catherine Marshall LeSourd and published by McGraw-Hill Book Company. Rights transferred to Chosen Books in 1978. Also from *The Helper*, © 1978 by Catherine Marshall and published by Chosen Books Publishing Company, Ltd. Also from *Light in My Darkest Night*, © 1989 by Leonard E. LeSourd and published by Chosen Books Publishing Company, Ltd.

Section Eight, "Prayer Power," from *Adventures in Prayer*, © 1975 by Catherine Marshall and published by Chosen Books Publishing Company, Ltd.

Section Nine, "Dark Night of the Soul," from *Light in My Darkest Night*.

Section Ten, "The Intercessors," from *Touching the Heart of God*, © 1990 by Leonard E. LeSourd and published by Chosen Books Publishing Company, Ltd. Also from the Breakthrough Intercessor, The Catherine Marshall Center, P.O. Box 121, Lincoln, VA 22078.

Section Eleven, "The Flood," from *Julie*, © 1984 by Calen, Inc., and published by McGraw-Hill Book Company. Reprinted with permission.

Section Twelve, "Facing Death," from *A Closer Walk*, © 1986 by Calen, Inc., and published by Chosen Books Publishing Company, Ltd.

Printed in the United States of America
10 9 8 7 6 5 4 3 2 1

To all those individuals throughout the
world whose lives have been touched
by Catherine's writings

Contents

Introduction

From the time she climbed into her backyard "wishing tree" as an eight-year-old, Catherine Marshall dreamed of becoming a writer. As a teenager she began putting her thoughts and observations into journals, a discipline she continued until her death in March 1983. During her twelve-year marriage to Peter Marshall she added research skills, spending hundreds of hours in the library pursuing sermon topics for her husband.

Peter Marshall's death in January 1949 launched her writing career in a way she could never have foreseen or desired. First, a book of Peter Marshall sermons, *Mr. Jones, Meet the Master*, was an astonishing bestseller. Then came his biography, *A Man Called Peter*, a bestselling book and hugely successful movie on the colorful life of this Scottish pastor and U.S. Senate chaplain. Twenty other books followed, with total sales of over twenty million copies, and a hundred or more articles in both secular and Christian magazines.

How do you select the best writing of an author whose subject matter ranged so widely?

Catherine wrote vividly of her childhood; that had to be included. The years with Peter were filled with loving and growing. Ten years of widowhood brought pain and triumph. A second marriage, including stepmothering three small children, was a fresh challenge. This second marriage—to me—moved her into a close editorial relationship with *Guideposts* magazine, during which both of us plunged into the middle of the Holy Spirit movement.

The death of a grandchild triggered a year-long "dark night of the soul." During Catherine's deepening prayer life, a vision was given her of an intercessory prayer ministry, Breakthrough—which could prove her most enduring spiritual legacy. A book of Catherine's best writings would be incomplete without memorable segments from her novels *Christy* and *Julie*. Finally, Catherine turned the approach of her own death into an adventure to be explored in detail.

Putting all this together has revived many memories of our 23 years of marriage, with the low, painful moments in some ways more treasured than the highs. To be sure, there was great euphoria over the birth of a dozen impact-creating books, the extraordinary success of *Guideposts*, the development of meaningful family life through joining together two broken homes.

Yet the low points stand out because God was closer and more real in times of defeat and grief. Thank God for those times! Without them success would have become bland, relationships stereotyped, gratitude and joy never so savored.

By many Catherine Marshall was seen as an unblemished Christian of great maturity and wisdom. Those of us close to Catherine knew better. Catherine was flawed, thank God, or she would have been impossible to live with. Her blemishes made Catherine real. Her weakness forced her to depend on God. So long as she sought His strength, He blessed her—and her readers.

—Leonard E. LeSourd
Evergreen Farm, Virginia
May 1993

Section One

Childhood: Short on Money, Long on Faith

Childhood was not an easy time for Sarah Catherine Wood. Her father, John Wood, was a Presbyterian pastor, struggling to feed and clothe his three children on a small salary. But in frugal living Catherine absorbed the basics of the Scriptures, found childhood joys and developed that special gift of her heavenly Father: creativity.

Our Father, Who Art on Earth

My early childhood was a crazy mixture of exuberant joy interspersed with moments of fear. Assorted odd things alarmed me: mice, spiders, snakes, darkness, the nuns in their flowing black habits in the Catholic school across the street, the page in *The Book of Knowledge* picturing Joan of Arc being burned at the stake. Yet as long as my father was near, my world was invulnerable.

My dad, the young preacher John Wood, was tall and slim, with black hair always combed neatly and soft brown eyes with a glint of mischief in them. And, I thought, very handsome! He was gregarious, full of good humor, fond of teasing and practical jokes.

Until I was seven, I was the only child. Then came my brother, Bob, and fourteen months later my sister, Emmy. Because Dad chose to have his office at home rather than at the church, I saw more of my father than most children do.

Often I would creep into his home office unbidden, but he was never too busy for me. Invariably he would smile and hold out his arms to receive me. "Girlie—my girlie," he would say.

Even when Father had a guest, he would allow me to sit silently on his lap while he carried on a conversation with the church officer or parishioner or the young Catholic priest who lived nearby. Dad's lap always seemed more commodious than Mother's, his arms more firm. For me, those arms were protection and reassurance, warmth, strength and nourishment. In some strange way, the love that flowed between us must have been nourishment for him, too.

The setting for those earliest memories was a one-floor white frame home in Canton, a small mid-Mississippi town. This cottage-manse was dwarfed by the red brick church sitting squarely beside it, and overshadowed by huge old oak trees. The giant oaks also lined Peace Street in front, creating a tunnel of green through which to walk or bicycle—welcome respite from the cruel Mississippi sun.

My shyness might eventually have led to withdrawal and a feeling of inferiority, for I could not easily admit people to my inner self. Fortunately, this pervading reticence was countered by the way my parents treated me. Since I had "discovered" Robert Louis Stevenson's *A Child's Garden of Verses* and enjoyed the sound of the cadences slipping off my tongue, I was encouraged to memorize my favorite poems and recite them to the family.

When Father wanted to chop down the wisteria vine all but smothering the old coal house in our backyard, and I protested loudly, he listened to my pleas. "If you feel that strongly about it," he said, patting my hand, "I'll just give the wisteria a haircut."

When I had progressed enough in my piano lessons to play simple hymns, Father would encourage me to be the pianist for small parlor meetings.

Thus, early was I given a sense of self-worth, the

recognition of my individuality and the surety of being cherished.

Balancing such love and attention to us children, our parents were definitely the authority figures in our home. We were not allowed to give up easily on tasks we considered difficult. Their attitude was always, "We'll help you where help is really needed. Between us, nothing is too hard."

That included a regular Sunday afternoon session of memorizing *The Catechism for Young Children*, followed by the misnamed *Shorter Catechism of the Westminster Assembly*. (Actually, the *Shorter* is considerably longer!)

A futile religious exercise? Not a bit of it! Couched in the chiseled English of another century, these laid a right base for those all-important questions about life and death, about God and our relationship to Him.

Q. What is God?
A. God is a Spirit, infinite, eternal and unchangeable in His being, wisdom, power, holiness, justice, goodness and truth.
Q. What is the chief end of man?
A. Man's chief end is to glorify God, and to enjoy Him forever. . . .

That last idea was startling to me. From some of the pictures and tales in my Bible story books, the Jehovah of the Old Testament seemed stern and unapproachable—unless you were someone like Moses or Abraham. This God thundered from Sinai, demanding sacrifices. His fierce anger destroyed great cities, once even flooded the whole world and drowned everyone in it except for Noah and his family.

Yet here was the catechism telling me that God was to be enjoyed! That I would have to ponder long and deeply.

One day I asked my father, "How can I love God when I'm afraid of Him?"

"Because He loves you," came Dad's reply. "Remember that Bible verse on your Sunday school folder just last week, 'We love Him because He first loved us.' He loved you before you even knew He was there."

"But I don't see a face full of love like I see your face, Dad."

"That's exactly why Jesus came down to earth—to tell us and show us that the Father in heaven is all love, is made of love. Jesus liked to say that even the best human father couldn't be half as loving or kind or generous as the heavenly Father."

Seeing doubt on my face, Dad added gently, "Sometimes I have to punish you or Bob or Em when you've done something wrong. I'd be a poor father to you if I didn't correct you. But that doesn't mean that you're afraid of me, does it?"

Looking into those warm brown eyes, I saw only love beyond measure and, as always, a glint of humor. Certainly I could trust my earthly father. But God was still vague, up in heaven somewhere. I wasn't sure where I stood with Him.

So I went my blithe way reveling in the freedom to roam in an outdoor world of never-ending delights. In the midst of all this, the fact that our family had little money mattered to me not at all. We had each other, and we had fun together. And so, many years later, I have only to turn my memory loose, instantly to recapture the feel of a small child's fresh, sharp joy of sight and sound and touch and smell.

To others, the yard around our cottage-manse may have seemed ordinary enough. To me it was the most beautiful place on earth. How could there be anywhere a more delicious fragrance than the Southern honeysuckle that rioted over all the fences? And not only fragrance, but taste. Pick a blossom, delicately bite off the stem end, suck out the delicious honey. No wonder the bees loved it!

And what bliss in the spring to hunt for the first white bells of snowdrops among the green foliage and to bury my nose in the first hyacinths! How could my eyes absorb enough of the beauty of the purple wisteria vine I had persuaded Father to save? Had anyone before me ever really felt the enchantment of bare feet on the thick carpet of moss under the oaks?

Years later I would read the Genesis account of how the Creator looked with approval on each day's handiwork and "saw that it was good." Reading it was like an echo out of my own deep spirit. Of course it was good— every flower, every fragrance, every drifting cloud and singing bird. Not only "good," but glorious. My child's heart had known it all along.

But my private Eden also bore the unmistakable mark of my earthly father. It was Dad who constructed an outsized sandbox where my playmates and I spent endless hours building elaborate sand castles.

It was Dad who built a seesaw, sturdier and longer than any to be found in a store. Everything he built was big, enduring, meant to last a lifetime.

And the swing! Quickly we learned to stand and pump: begin slowly, bend the knees in rhythm. Make it go higher, higher, up and down. Now again, swishing through the air, until finally the jerk of the chains told us that the swing had gone as high as it could. Then "let the cat die."

There were joys awaiting me inside our home, too. As in many older, deep-South homes, the cool, ten-foot-wide center hall ran the length of our house. This gallery-corridor was the favorite site for games, all revolving around my father. Pure gold were the hours he spent with us children playing Parcheesi, caroms, checkers, dominoes, Rook, Old Maid, jackstraws or jacks or putting together countless jigsaw puzzles.

For some reason, Mother could never get the hang of games, so she would mend or sew or read while Dad and I and anyone else we could pull in battled tenaciously to win. Father was a sharp competitor, never giving us children any quarter because we were small. We liked it that way, for when we won, the taste of victory was all the sweeter.

I also enjoyed just sitting on the floor beside my father, talking to him as I watched him make repairs around the house. He was a good carpenter and painter, even bricklayer and stonemason, with an adequate knowledge of plumbing and electricity.

It must have been the security of Dad's presence that made his office the most lived-in room in successive manse-homes in Mississippi, the Eastern panhandle of West Virginia and the Eastern Shore of Virginia. The study was always lined with open bookshelves floor to ceiling. A comfortable leather Morris chair with wide arms sat in the corner just within arm's reach of *The Book of Knowledge, The Harvard Classics* and *Maclaren's Expositions of Holy Scriptures*, along with novels and reference books.

It was here that the family always gathered after the evening meal while we children worked on our school lessons. Sitting in the Morris chair or at one of the pullout leaves of Father's desk or sprawled on the floor, we were surrounded by plenty of study helps. Dad subscribed to several magazines, and he always had catalogs from which we could order books, for our town rarely had a bookstore. All our *National Geographic*s were saved for schoolwork and a cupboard was crammed full of past issues. We were free to cut and paste them as illustrative material for school papers.

My father had his weaknesses, of course. He could be stubborn. A case in point: the episode of the flamethrower. Fond of tools and gadgets, he was often tempted to spend too much of his meager salary on such things. Since the West Virginia house had a large yard, he treated himself to a power mower. Soon after that he saw a flamethrower advertised. Apparently the War Department had overbought and was offering these items at a discount.

Mother was annoyed when he brought it up. "What on God's green earth do you want such a thing for? You know perfectly well we haven't any money to spend on silly things like that."

Father looked wounded. "A flamethrower is *exactly* what I need for getting rid of the tall weeds in fence corners," he retorted. "And I *am* going to buy it."

Buy it he did. We still have the flamethrower in the family. We also still have the weeds.

Then there was his volatile temper. How vividly Bob remembers the time he was helping Dad string Christmas lights over the front door when Father's thumb accidentally slipped into the live socket.

Out came the thumb and out of Dad's mouth poured forth some very unclergymanlike words. Then Dad glared down from the ladder.

"Son," he said solemnly, "forget that I said that."

Bob never did, of course. Not only that, but in later years he told me, "From that moment, I loved and respected Dad more than ever. He was not too 'good' to be human."

Nor could any of us forget the Sunday morning when Bob and Em got a switching.

During the previous week the two children made the rounds of the neighborhood begging empty fifteen-pound lard cans, neglecting to report to our parents how the empty cans were to be used.

Sunday morning our preacher-father was all dressed for church—black hair slicked down, white suit, white shoes (his only pair of shoes not at the repair shop). Last of all Father went out to the garden to select a flower for his buttonhole.

A half-minute later we heard a howl. Red-faced, Father stomped into the house with a switch broken off the privet hedge to punish the culprits. It seemed that Bob and Em had filled several lard cans with water and sunk them in strategic places in the flower garden, laying twigs and tufts of grass over these homemade booby traps. That Sunday Father preached with a soaked left foot while two of his children listened with smarting legs.

But Dad was always fair in administering punishment. We knew he loved us even while he was chastising us. There was no inconsistency with what he preached from the pulpit and the way he dealt with us as the head of the house.

It wasn't that my father was eloquent in the pulpit. He was an average preacher with only a mild interest in theology. His forte was people. He loved them and enjoyed mixing with them, friends and strangers alike. He had a knack for finding a just-right conversational meeting ground with all manner of folk.

One of my favorite stories is about how Dad went down to the railroad yards near our home in Keyser, West Virginia, to seek out a new member of his congregation. In one of the Baltimore and Ohio's enormous roundhouses, the Reverend Wood found his man at work.

"Can't shake hands with you," said the man apologetically. "They're too grimy."

John Wood reached down to the ground and rubbed his hands in coal soot.

"How about it now?" he said, offering an equalized hand.

But if at an early age I knew I could trust my earthly father, I continued to resist the sermons that urged us to surrender our lives to a faraway God. What would that mean? The idea of spending all my time praying, reading the Bible and talking about God did not appeal to me at all.

When the evangelist Gypsy Smith, Jr., came to hold services in our town, I went with curiosity but little more. A huge tent was pitched on a vacant lot near the town limits—not large enough to hold the crowds that flocked there. On a platform of raw wood from which the resin still oozed sat the massed choirs gathered from all the churches. Their favorite anthem was the spirited "Awakening Chorus":

The Lord Jehovah reigns, and sin is backward
    hurled.

11

Rejoice! Rejoice! Rejoice!

The "rejoicings" vibrated so shrilly that they raised goosebumps along my spine. As the congregation sang, the waving arms of the music director beat out the rhythms of hymns like

Standing on the prom-i-ses of Christ, my King. . . .

or

Sing them o-ver a-gain to me,
    Won-der-ful words of life. . . .

Each time we collectively took a breath, the pianist would run in scales, chords and flourishes marvelous to my childish ears.

Then came the preaching, so dynamic that decades later Gypsy Smith's thundering word-pictures still reverberate in my ears. Samson, succumbing to fleshly temptation, delivered into the hands of the Philistines, his hair cut, his eyes cruelly blinded. Then that final scene in Samson's drama where a repentant Samson, his hair grown back, faces three thousand Philistines gathered in the great hall to make sport of him. With his right hand on one of the two key pillars supporting the roof, his left hand on the other, Samson bows himself with all his might. . . .

The emotion in Gypsy's preaching, mounting steadily, transferred itself to the congregation. What did Samson's story have to do with Keyser, West Virginia? Selfishness and sensuality brought only destruction, the evangelist thundered. It would always be so. Each of us had to decide which road we would travel.

Finally a hush would fall over the tent as the choirs sang almost in a whisper,

Softly and tenderly Jesus is calling, calling for
you and for me. . . .

Soon, at the far edge of the tent, someone would rise and make his way slowly down the aisle toward the front. Then another person, and another, and another. . . .

What impressed me were the faces of the people who went forward. There was radiance and joy on those faces. Most seemed eager to get to the front, where they knelt and wept and prayed and "gave themselves."

At home I asked my parents about the people who had made this act of commitment to God.

"Does this mean they joined the church?" I asked.

I wondered, too: Had not some of them "gone forward" out of the emotionalism of the moment?

Dad understood my wonderings behind the questions. Wisely he answered, "Sure, most of them will join a church. You, too, will want to do that at the right time. But Catherine, joining the church is only the outward part of it. You should not join the church until it really means something. It must mean the gift of yourself to God."

I pondered that statement many times during those preteen years.

I was nine on the Sunday morning when I sat in church beside my mother—my brother and sister were in Sunday school classes—and watched my father conduct the service. My heart was full of love for him in a special way. I can never remember many things he said

13

from the pulpit, but I felt God's love flowing through him for all of us in the congregation.

At the end of the service, rather spontaneously as I recall, Dad issued an invitation for those to come forward who wanted to accept Jesus as the Lord of their lives and to be part of the church fellowship.

And suddenly I felt a stirring inside me. Very gentle. There was no voice, no words, just a feeling of great warmth. I loved my father dearly. And I trusted him with all my heart. I loved him so much that I could feel tears forming behind my eyes.

And then came the assurance. All along God had meant for the love of my earthly father to be a pattern of my heavenly Father and to show me the way to make connection with Him.

Following this inner conviction came the sudden urge to act and the will to do it. To my surprise and Mother's, I rose from the pew and walked down the aisle to the front, joining a half-dozen or so others.

At first Dad did not see me as the group formed a semicircle around the altar. He spoke to us briefly about the step we were taking and was about to pray when he noticed me.

Full recognition flashed into his brown eyes; he knew instantly that my being there was significant. I was presenting the gift of myself, a first step in faith. The resistance to surrender had been broken.

I shall never forget the look on my father's face. Surprise . . . joy . . . sudden vulnerability. He stood for a long moment in front of the altar, looking at me with eyes swimming in tears behind his spectacles. Then he pulled himself together and had us kneel as he prayed.

It was my first encounter with the living God—my

heavenly Father. The catechism had said that He had loved me first. So had my earthly father. He must have loved me even before birth while I was carried in my mother's body.

Not only that, but since I could love and trust my earthly father, how much more could I love and trust my Father in heaven, and without fear place my future in His hands?

Mother Never Thought
We Were Poor

While my father was the one to present God to me as a heavenly Father who cared tenderly about each of His children, it was my mother who showed me how a relationship with Him could change everyday situations.

The lessons God had taught her were indigenous to the poverty of the first eighteen years of her life. Either she had to settle down to lack, or find God's way out of it. The creative approach He gave her has been of help to countless numbers of people, myself among them.

Leonora Haseltine Whitaker was born in 1891 and reared on North Carolina farms. When she was eighteen she volunteered to join Dr. Edward O. Guerrant's mission in the Great Smoky Mountains of east Tennessee as a schoolteacher. Her experiences there with the mountain people in the Cove would later form the basis of my novel *Christy*.

Mother was taller than average, which was accentuated (I see as I leaf through the family album) by the Gibson-girl shirtwaist dresses of her girlhood. She had extremely large, expressive blue eyes and an aquiline nose with a piquant tilt at the end. Her chestnut-colored hair was so long that she could sit on it, though she usually wore it pinned up on top of her head. Later she began braiding it, winding the braids

16

twice around her head in a lovely natural coronet.

Soon after Leonora Whitaker got to the Cove, the mission fell into dire straits for funds. As Mother prayed about this, an idea dropped into her head. She had received an invitation to speak to a woman's group in nearby Knoxville. While there, why not call on a Knoxville businessman with a reputation for philanthropy! What followed was an object lesson in how faith and creativity can blend effectively.

For these engagements she was determined not to look like a dowdy mountain missionary who needed to beg for herself as well as for the mountaineers. She wanted her appearance to say, "I'm having fun doing the Lord's work. Wouldn't you like to have a part in this adventure, too?"

A visit to a beauty parlor was her first step. She emerged with an elaborate hairdo, curls on top, a figure-eight in the back.

Next, in one of Knoxville's best stores, Mother found an enormous black hat with sweeping ostrich plumes. It would be perfect, she decided, with her one good garment—a black broadcloth suit. But the hat was priced at $25, every penny of her salary for one month. She pondered a long time. Shouldn't the $25 go directly into the mission fund? Or would buying the hat actually be an investment in the work?

Mother bought the hat.

Her blue eyes sparkling with the fun of this feminine adventure, Mother swept into the downtown offices of Mr. Rush Hazen, a wholesale grocer and philanthropist. Heads at rows of desks turned to stare. Even Mr. Hazen stared. In fact, he all but whistled.

"You—a missionary! I don't believe it. Why hasn't

somebody thought of sending out missionaries like you before? What can I do for you?"

Mr. Hazen did a great deal. Triumphantly, Mother went back to the mission with enough food and money to keep boarding students all winter, and with the promise of more money for the future. She also went back more secure than ever in the conviction that God would supply our every need if we but asked Him to show the way.

It was at this mission that Leonora Whitaker met John Wood, who had just graduated from Union Theological Seminary in Richmond, Virginia. They were married in Asheville, North Carolina, when mother was nineteen.

My parents spent the next forty years serving Presbyterian congregations in small communities, living frugally. Yet that did not dampen Mother's creativity a whit. I well remember an especially harsh period—the early 1930s. Because his church people in Keyser, West Virginia, were suffering financially, Dad had voluntarily taken three successive cuts in salary. That meant that our family of five barely scraped along.

Dad received his portion of what had been in the church collection plates on Sunday night, and it never lasted the week. The Friday grocery shopping, therefore, included an element of acute embarrassment to us children. Even now I wince at the remembrance of standing beside my father, pretending not to notice while he leaned over the counter and said to the grocer in a lowered voice, "If you'll let us have this list of groceries, I'll drop by on Monday to pay you."

During those lean years our family had no car. We children walked or bicycled. Our parents walked—for all shopping, to church, to call on parishioners.

Bob and Em and I did not mind the fact that we had to go to a neighbor's to read the Sunday funnies, since one of our economies was cutting out the Sunday paper. What we *did* mind were some of the clothes we had to wear.

I've never forgotten one brown velvet dress Mother made for me out of someone's hand-me-down. The velvet was worn in places, and the chocolate brown was wrong for a young girl. I suffered in silence every time I wore it. And my sister was mortified, she tells me, by never having a proper girl's snowsuit of her own, but having to wear an old pair of her brother's pants in wintertime.

We children certainly did not enjoy those Depression cutbacks, yet no tinge of fear about lack of money ever clouded our home. It never seemed to enter Mother's head that we were living through a period of poverty. She went through each difficult day of the Depression as though she had some secret bank account to draw from—and in a sense she did.

Though we did without many things, Mother always provided us with a feeling of well-being. Chiefly, I think, because of the ways she contrived to give to others. Out of our meager pantry she would send a sick neighbor a supper tray of something delicious she had prepared—velvety-smooth boiled custard; feather-light homemade rolls—served up on our best china and always with a dainty bouquet from our garden.

While Mother always tried to provide her family a balanced diet with plenty of fruit and vegetables, we often went without meat, and I cannot recall any luxury foods. The main course for many an evening would be french fries and hot biscuits with honey or jam, or salmon croquettes, or fried mush. But we children didn't mind the mush at all, not the way Mother made it: sliced thin, browned crisp and served with maple syrup.

Mother could turn even fried mush into an occasion by giving some of *that* away. This happened when she discovered that Mr. Edwards, our wealthy neighbor, was fond of mush. Since his wife never served him such lowly fare, he would from time to time be the grateful recipient of our hot, golden-fried mush.

Only unconsciously were we aware of it, but Mother was providing us constantly with an object lesson in giving. The message: No matter how little you have, you can always give some of it away. And when you do that, you can't feel sorry for yourself.

But there was even more to it. For Mother, giving was an act of faith, and the spiritual principle of giving out of scarcity came as easily to her as if she had invented it. Whenever we saw an old-fashioned pump in a farmyard, we knew what she would tell us: "If you drink the cup of water that's waiting there, you can slake your own thirst. But if you pour it into the pump and work the handle, you'll start enough water flowing to satisfy all our thirsts."

She likened the principle of priming the pump to God's law of abundance: We give, and He opens the windows of heaven and gives to us. It is a law of life, she explained to us children, and as certain to work as that the sun will rise tomorrow.

Mother had not been in Keyser long before she had a dream of helping the destitute of Radical Hill, a slum district where people lived in tin-roofed shacks along rutted roads strewn with debris. The "nice" citizens of

20

the town gave the area a wide berth. Yet the children who lived there, often unwashed and with lice in their hair, sat alongside the "nice" children in the public schools.

Mother's first step was to enlist the help of some of the young people of our church to go with her to visit each home and take a survey of the district. Of some five hundred Radical Hill families, she found that only eighty were connected with any church.

At that juncture Mother offered her services to the county welfare board. To our surprise (but definitely not hers!), she was given a job to help improve conditions in any way she could. Day after day she would send us off to school in our hand-me-downs and artfully patched clothing, then go off to help what she called "the poor people."

The first thing Mother managed to do was to get the name of that area changed from Radical Hill to Potomac Heights—a new name for a new start. Then an old, abandoned hotel was remodeled—partitions torn out, repaired, painted; bathrooms and a kitchen put in. This was for meetings of all kinds, a Sunday school and a weekday nursery school. A health clinic, craft classes and Mother's own classes in childcare and Bible study were started. Soon the work was flourishing. Those who had given up hope began to take heart because someone cared.

Then one day Mother was told that county funds had run out and that her employment had to be terminated. For only a moment did she give in to discouragement. Then she approached the director of the welfare board.

"May I go on working?" she asked.

"But we can't pay."

"I understand," Mother said. "But why should I do for money what I would be willing to do for the love of God and humanity?"

The man stared at her. "What do you mean?"

"I mean," she said resolutely, "that the work must go on, salary or not. Shutting down now would be disastrous."

The director looked incredulous. Then, impressed by Mother's determination, his tone suddenly changed. Standing up, admiration and enthusiasm written on his face, he thrust out his hand. "All right, then, of course, go right on working. I'll do something. We'll *all* do something. Somehow we'll get the community behind us."

So day after day Mother trudged on foot to Potomac Heights, receiving not a nickel for her work. And the work not only prospered, it zoomed, as a large task force of enthusiastic teenagers rallied around Mother to help.

Years later I saw on television Kathryn Forbes' warm Norwegian-American reminiscences called "I Remember Mama." Her family of five was exactly like ours—one son and two daughters. Like us, they, too, had lived from weekly payday to weekly payday.

There was another point of similarity. Kathryn Forbes' mama had a bank account. Each Saturday night as the stacks of coins were counted out for the landlord, for the grocer, for half-soling shoes and buying school notebooks, there was great relief when Mama finally smiled.

"Is good," she would say. "We do not have to go to the bank."

Mama's bank account was to be tapped only for the

direst emergencies. By hard work and much coopera-tion, the family made it through year after year. Just knowing that Mama's bank account was there gave them a warm, secure feeling.

Twenty years later when daughter Kathryn Forbes sold her first story, she took the check proudly to Mama: "For you—to put in your bank account."

And at last the truth came out. There never had been a bank account. Mama had hit upon this device because, she explained, "Is not good for little ones to be afraid."

Suddenly in a blaze of revelation it occurred to me that my own mother also had a bank account that kept us, her children, from being afraid. Her bank account was real—as real as the mountain air we breathed and the nourishing bread she baked. Mother's family bank account was her faith in the Lord, her absolute trust that the promise of "Give and it shall be given unto you" was as eternal as the mountains around us.

Even by age twelve I had begun to realize that the secret of Mother's strength was related directly to her daily prayer-conversations with God. I watched her go off alone to talk with Him and wondered what it was like to have a real conversation with God. Could you hear His voice? Were His presence and love something you could actually feel? I had to find out.

At fourteen I was a thin, awkward-looking girl with too long a neck. I had unruly, naturally curly brown hair and large, blue eyes set in a pale face. I was a teenager with a head full of question marks, exclamation points and some ridiculous and implausible dreams. For how could one live with Leonora Wood and settle down to limited horizons?

"You are the beloved children of the King," she

never tired of admonishing us. "Each of you is very special to Him, and He has important work for you to do in the world. It's up to you to find His dream for your life. And take warning, our King doesn't fool around with petty stuff. The sky is the limit!"

By the time I entered high school, I had focused on three major dreams. The first, the oldest, I hugged to myself: Someday I would write books.

I was fifteen when the other two dreams came into view. It happened that spring at the home of Mrs. William MacDonald, with whom I sometimes spent the night when her husband had to be away on law cases.

The MacDonalds' daughter, Janet, had gone to a college called Agnes Scott—glamorous and faraway in Decatur, Georgia, on the outskirts of Atlanta. "Mrs. Mac" talked about how special the college was, how much it had meant in molding Janet's life.

The MacDonald home seemed luxurious to me: real mahogany furniture, a tall grandfather clock whose musical chimes marked the quarter hour, current books, lovely volumes of history and travel lying about. They even received *The New York Times* every Sunday!

When I stayed with Mrs. Mac, it was her custom to serve us ice cream at bedtime—more ice cream than I could eat. Then she would tuck me in under an eider-down in a bed with tall pineapple posts.

How well I remember one particular night when for me time stood still. She had started out of the room when at the door she stopped, half-turned and looked at me. "One of these days a wonderful man, just the right man for you, is going to come and carry you away. Just you wait!"

Her words, shockingly daring to me, yet standing

straight and tall, marched across the room and found permanent lodging in my mind and heart. At that moment two dreams were planted inside me: to go to Agnes Scott College and to ready myself for that wonderful man who would come from far away to marry me.

I did not realize it at the time, but now that I had given my life to God, He was using that perfect time—impressionable adolescence—to reach down and plant in the fertile soil of my immature heart His big, pure, wonderful dreams. The fulfillment of them would be His work, not mine, but I was to learn that none of those gloriously impossible dreams could come true without the pain of self-realization and growth.

By the time I graduated from high school, the Depression was daily dealing our town devastating blows: businesses failing, banks closing, bankruptcies, suicides, almost everyone living on credit. With our family's hand-to-mouth existence, how could there possibly be any money for college?

Already I had been accepted at Agnes Scott. But though I had saved some money from debating prizes and had the promise of a work scholarship, we were still hundreds of dollars short of what was needed.

One evening Mother found me lying across my bed, face down, sobbing. She sat down beside me. "You and I are going to deal with this right now," she said.

Mother took me into the guest room and together we knelt beside the old-fashioned golden oak bed.

"Catherine, I know it's right for you to go to college," Mother said. "Let's ask God to tell us how to bring this dream to reality."

As we knelt together, I knew instinctively that this was an important moment, one to be recorded in heaven.

We were about to meet God in a more intimate way than at bedtime prayers, or during grace before a meal, or in family prayers together in Dad's study, or even in the prayers in church. Mother was admitting me to the inner sanctum of her prayer closet.

In the silence, I quickly reviewed my relationship with this God with whom we were seeking an audience. At the age of nine I had given Him my life. My attendance at Sunday school and church had been regular ever since—little enough to do as the daughter of a preacher, I thought uneasily.

I had prayed many times since my encounter with Him years before, but how real had those prayers been? The truth struck me: Most had been for selfish purposes. I had given so little of myself to Him. I had not taken much part in Mother's work to transform Radical Hill. And with a sinking heart I remembered all the times when I had seen members of the church coming up the front walk, only to flee up the back stairs to my room where I would not have to give myself to others or share their problems.

Scene after scene flashed across my mind's eye of the times I had resented my brother and sister. When they had interfered with what I wanted to do, I had scolded them, avoided them, rejected them. As I thought of the many occasions when my parents had gone without something they needed so that we children could have new clothing, piano lessons, books or sports equipment, I felt more condemned than ever. And my going to college would call for yet more sacrifices from my parents.

I stole a look at Mother. She was praying soundlessly, her lips moving. Then, closing my eyes, silently I prayed the most honest prayer of my life to that point.

"Lord, I've been selfish. I've taken everything from You, from Your Church and from my parents, and given little of myself in return. Forgive me for this, Lord. Perhaps I don't deserve to go to a college like Agnes Scott."

A sob deep in my throat threatened to burst out. I knew what I now had to do. "So Lord, I turn this dream over to You. I give it up. It's in Your hands. You decide."

Now the tears did come!

Those quiet moments in the bedroom marked a new stage in my walk with God. I was learning that the price of a relationship with Him means dropping all our masks and pretense. We must come to Him with stark honesty, "as we are"—or not at all.

Several days later Dad and Mother decided that by faith I should go ahead and make preparations for Agnes Scott. They felt strongly that this was right and that the Lord would soon confirm it. I was not so sure. God had convicted me of my selfishness. Perhaps He wanted me to give up college and serve Him in some other way.

Days passed, then weeks. Then one day Mother opened a letter and gave a whoop of joy. "Here it is! Here's the answer to our prayers."

The letter contained an offer from a special project of the federal government for Mother to write the history of the county. With what I already had, her fee would be more than enough for my college expenses.

Once again, Mother's very real bank account had provided the necessary provision at a time of need. From those hours spent alone with Him each day had come her supreme confidence that He would provide out of His limitless supply. How often she had told us children,

"And don't forget, He will never, never let us outgive Him."

Out of this solid wealth, this certainty, Mother could always afford to give to others, not just material things, but showering sparks of imagination, a gleam of hope, a thrust of courage—qualities that contained more substance than the coin of any realm and which opened the door for fulfillment in many a life she touched.

Section
Two

The Years with Peter

As it turned out, Agnes Scott College was the key not only to Catherine's education, but to meeting the "wonderful man" Mrs. Mac had foreseen entering her life.

Romance

I returned to Agnes Scott College the fall of my junior year, September 1934, to find a report circulating that the pastor of the Atlanta church I had been attending during the school years, Peter Marshall, was engaged to be married.

True or not, this reinforced the resolve I had made: I would be friendly but altogether casual with Peter. There was something ridiculous about a not-yet-twenty-year-old college student fancying herself in love with a 32-year-old bachelor-preacher who had captured so many other female hearts in the Atlanta area.

Peter Marshall was a tall, well-built Scot with the broad shoulders of a football player beneath his Geneva gown. His curly dark blond hair resisted his efforts to slick it down. His face was handsome in a rugged sort of way. There was in it a combination of gentleness and humor along with forcefulness and strength.

He seemed thoroughly at home in the pulpit. The impact of his message came through his voice—an extraordinarily resonant one, flexible, dramatic, with clear, precise diction. The indisputable fact was that, under the impact of this man's preaching, God became real to those who listened. When Peter led them in worship, God was no longer a remote, theological abstraction but a loving Father interested in each individual, who stooped to man's smallest need. So men and women hungry for the love of God came back again and again, as I had done.

Why does he single me out with his eyes so much when he preaches? I asked myself.

A dozen other women probably think the same thing, my logical mind snapped back.

But then why all that special attention after church? Having his secretary, Ruby Coleman, intercept me to tell me Peter would drive me back to the campus in Decatur?

I had no answer to that. Better drop all such ruminations.

That October a young man from Emory began to date me. There was a strong physical attraction between us, and I began to wonder if I could be in love with Fred. But then one day I realized that there was neither spiritual nor intellectual rapport between us. I stopped dating Fred, tried to forget romance and concentrate on my studies.

But soon, inevitably, I was drawn back to Westminster Church and Peter because of an aching void in my life. This notation in my journal is revealing:

There are several reasons why I am attracted to Peter. For one thing, he has so much poetry in his soul. There is such a kinship between poetry and religion. They both try to see into the heart of things. One of the reasons I could never fall in love with Fred is that he has no appreciation for the beautiful.

Peter, however, has such a capacity for affection and tenderness, such a luscious sense of humor sprinkled with an earthy roguishness.

Why must the embodiment of all my dreams be twelve years older than I and as remote as the South Pole?

To my fellow students, I must have seemed on top of things. My grades were good, I was active as an intercollegiate debater, in poetry club and other class activities. Yet underneath it all I was dissatisfied:

Tonight I feel compelled to write until my hand is tired and exhausted. I am restless and unhappy these days because I am neither right with myself nor with God. Why this dissatisfaction with myself? I am driven on and on by an overwhelming sense of some destiny, of some task to be done which I must do. I can never be peaceful and happy and enjoy life until I learn why I am here and where I am going.

Throughout that winter and into the spring my journal notes were peppered with references to Peter Marshall.

The more I hear him talk, the more I realize we have the same ideas and ideals—we like the same things. . . . How I wish I could tell him all the sleep he has made me lose. . . . Dreaming this way about Peter is the most foolish thing that has ever happened to me.

Reading through my journals of this period so many years later makes me aware as never before how tender God was with me, never intruding on my willful self-centeredness, but always there when the heart-hungers inside me cried out. And how beautiful was His timing in the slow—agonizingly slow, to me—way the relationship between Peter and me developed until I, so much younger, was mature enough to meet Peter where he was spiritually and intellectually.

The film version of *A Man Called Peter* indicated that the turning point in our relationship was May 3, 1935, the Prohibition rally (turned into a youth rally in the movie) at which Peter and I and several others spoke.

My journal shows that this rally was an interesting but only an early step along the way. As a group of us drove to the schoolhouse where the meeting was to take place, Peter pointedly squelched the rumor that he was engaged.

"Don't believe everything you hear, my dear girl. I certainly am not even about to be married."

He pronounced the word "mar-rried" with a very broad *a* and a rolling of the *r*'s.

When the meeting began with the singing of some old revival hymns, Peter quickly entered into the spirit of the evening, his fine baritone voice ringing out above all others. One by one then we were elaborately introduced, listened to patiently and given more applause than we deserved. Frankly, I can remember almost nothing about what we said.

On the return drive Peter and I were in the backseat. He tucked his arm through mine and held my hand all the way home. Before we said goodbye Peter asked me if I ever went bowling and said that he would take me out some night.

I was ecstatic. My dream of two long years' standing had at last been fulfilled—Peter was actually going to ask me for a date!

But a week went by, then another, and still Peter did not call. There were get-togethers at the church where he overflowed with warmth toward me. Each time he would go out of his way to drive me back to the college.

On May 12 he asked to return for me at 3:30 that afternoon, after which we walked and talked until eleven o'clock that night—our first real date. Lingeringly, tenderly, he bade me goodnight. His last words: "I'll be in touch with you this week."

But again the days dragged by. No call. What was I to think?

When summer vacation came, I went home to West Virginia more frustrated than the year before. Why did he always seem so interested when I was with him, but never follow up with a note or telephone call?

The ache in my heart continued through the summer and into the fall. I returned to college for my senior year determined to stay away from Westminster Church, convinced once and for all that there was no hope for the one thing my heart yearned for more than anything else. I must forget Peter Marshall.

Meanwhile, three years of college had greatly enriched and broadened the naïve, small-town girl from the West Virginia mountains. Whatever I lacked in ability I made up for in heartfelt desire and intensity and in hard, slugging work.

I must have averaged three hours a day in the college library where I dug into the classics, enjoyed novels, browsed through poetry and dove into history, always enchanted with personalities, lifestyle and human interest data on the men and women who had made history.

My reading ranged widely, from John Calvin's *Institutes* to William Hazlitt's and Thomas Carlyle's essays to the writings of James Madison to Dorothy Wordsworth's journal to Matthew Arnold's prose and poetry. I fell in love with Edna St. Vincent Millay and Robert Frost, who visited our campus via the lecture platform. Apart from studies, I poured my energies into debating, the hiking club and the poetry club. My resolve to stay away from Westminster Church lasted only until October 20 when I made this entry:

> Went to church at Westminster, but got there after 11 a.m. and had to sit in the vestibule and listen to Peter through the loudspeaker. I had planned not to speak to him afterwards, but suddenly changed my mind. He pumped my hand and commented that this was the first time I had been here this year. So he had noticed my absence! He promised to get in touch with me. I shan't hold my breath until he does.

The entries in my journals for the next four months continued the pattern. When he saw me Peter was all interest. He arranged to take me to meals at a friend's where we talked, sang, played games like Monopoly and Parcheesi. Once I was back on campus, however, he seldom if ever called or sought me out.

It is clear to me now that Peter as a bachelor in his early 30s and a preacher of growing importance was reluctant to take the initiative in seeking out dates with a college girl many years younger than he. He knew that to others this would seem improper. And he was right. At the time I could not see this or have any feel for God's timing in the situation.

The crucial turning point in our relationship came a year to the day after the Prohibition rally that the movie-

36

makers fixed on: Sunday, May 3, 1936. I had been asked to review a book at the Sunday afternoon fellowship hour at Peter's church. I chose one entitled *Prayer* by the Norwegian theologian Dr. O. Hallesby. This was an unusual book for any professor-theologian because its content was not theory; what Dr. Hallesby had to say seemed so obviously direct from his own experience.

Such an assignment would have been a challenge to me at any time and place. Since this was to be at Peter's church, and the pastor himself was likely to be in the audience, I did an inordinate amount of preparation. Intuition told me that this was the time and place for something important to happen between Peter and me—if it was ever meant to happen. The depths of Peter's inner being had been revealed to me through his preaching. But there had been no comparable chance for him to catch a glimpse of my inner spirit.

When I arrived at the church that Sunday afternoon, the fellowship hall was filled with people, including Peter Marshall. Just before I was to speak I was stricken, almost paralyzed by tension and nervousness. Did I have anything really worthwhile to say to these knowledgeable people?

"We tend to be superficial in our prayers," I began with quavering voice. "Most of us think of God as a kind of Santa Claus who waits to hear our requests. What He really wants to hear are the hungers of our heart and our confessions of deception and dishonesty."

As the meaning of my words penetrated my stage fright, confidence and strength surged through me. Dr. Hallesby had opened my eyes to my own smugness in certain areas, I admitted, and depicted how I had begun to change my approach to prayer. I confessed my hunger to know God better, to feel the presence of Jesus, to be able to talk to Jesus as a Friend.

Because the book had revealed it to me, I confessed how self-righteous I had been during my college years. Emotion poured through my words as I described how the book had revitalized my prayer life.

Though the audience was quiet and attentive, it was Peter's face that commanded my attention. He stared at me with such intentness that my stomach began churning. There was a moment when I almost felt that only the two of us were in the room.

After my talk Peter was subdued as he closed the meeting. He turned to me, took my hand and squeezed it tightly, a look in his blue-gray eyes I could not fathom. Then we went into the evening service where I made the mistake of sitting within three pews of the front.

My turbulent feelings and the emotion of the previous few hours were too much. The stone pillars and the Good Shepherd window behind the pulpit began to swim alarmingly. I was too sick to be embarrassed when Peter mentioned my name from the pulpit in connection with the talk I had just given. By the time he began his sermon, I knew it would be disastrous to stay.

As I rose to begin the longest walk in my life, the voice from the pulpit trailed off, and there was dead silence, broken only by the staccato clicking of my heels on the stone floor. I could feel Peter's eyes boring into my back every step of the way up the long aisle. Not until I was well out into the foyer did the voice resume over the loudspeakers.

The college infirmary received me that night and attempted to diagnose this strange stomach ailment. The head nurse, properly starched and equipped with a strong nose for sniffing out lovesick maidens, had her suspicions.

In the early afternoon of the following day I was called to the infirmary telephone. The solicitous voice on the other end had a familiar Scottish accent.

"I'm talking from Miss Hopkins' office," the voice said, naming the school's headmistress. "I have secured her permission to come over and see you. May I?"

I gasped. No mere man—unless armed with a medical diploma—had ever, in all the college's history, been allowed inside the infirmary. Male visitors were simply taboo. After all, the young ladies were not properly clothed! How Peter had prevailed on Miss Hopkins I couldn't even imagine.

"I—really don't think you'd better," I said hastily. "I'm well enough to dress and come over. I'll meet you in the colonnade in ten minutes."

I should not have stopped him. Ever afterwards Peter accused me of having thwarted his only chance for fame with future generations of Agnes Scotters. If I had not interfered, Peter might someday have rated a bronze plaque on the infirmary wall as the first male visitor in this off-limits haven.

Almost every day after that my journal records items about the two of us.

Peter was terribly solicitous about my illness. . . . I believe now he wants to be serious. . . . I think Peter is in love with me!! . . . Tonight we went to a play. Afterwards on the front porch he kissed me again and again. . . . Tonight we talked until three in the morning and he proposed. . . .

39

Marriage to Peter

Peter and I were married by my father in a simple church wedding in Keyser, West Virginia, on November 4, 1936. Later that same day my new husband and I traveled by train to Washington, D.C., and spent our honeymoon night at the Lee House Hotel. With considerable chagrin Peter had informed me several days before that he had agreed to meet the morning after the wedding with the pastoral committee of New York Avenue Presbyterian Church.

This prestigious old Washington church had literally grown up with the nation's capital. Located two blocks from the White House, it was where Abraham Lincoln had attended midweek and Sunday services. The President had been scheduled to become a communicant member on April 19, 1865. But five days before, at a few minutes before ten at night, he was assassinated.

It was not Peter's personal preference to move to the nation's capital. He loved Atlanta. Yet our word was that God had some larger plan in the offing. Yes, we were to go.

So at only 23 the young girl who had fled up the back stairs to avoid involvement with people now had to be hostess at a steady stream of social functions at the manse on Cathedral Avenue.

What was the background of this man I had married? Peter Marshall did not grow up wanting to be a minister. That was God's idea, not his. In fact, getting him to accept it took a lot of divine persuasion.

He was born in Coatbridge, Scotland, a city of 45,000 nicknamed "The Iron Burgh" because it was the center of the Scottish iron trade. Coatbridge was only nine miles east of Glasgow, the sea and the famous Clyde Shipyards; as a boy Peter had fallen under the spell of all the color and romance of British Navy tradition.

His father, whom Peter had loved with all the warmth of his affectionate nature, had died when Peter was only four. A few years later his mother remarried. Peter was filled, understandably, with emotional opposition, and nursed a secret, consuming desire to escape to sea.

But it didn't happen. One dark, foggy summer night Peter, a young man now, was walking down an unfamiliar lane when a Voice stopped him just before he would have plunged unwittingly into an abandoned stone quarry. There was never any doubt in Peter's mind about the source of that Voice. From then on he was convinced that God had some special reason for saving his life. His dream changed; his goal now was to become a pastor.

It was a cousin who had emigrated to the United States who encouraged Peter to go to America and gave him money for the trip. His cousin also had this word of advice: "Don't try for a desk job, Peter. Since you want to be a preacher, manual labor will be the best preparation. Most preachers don't know how the other half lives."

On April 5, 1927, Peter arrived in America with just enough money to last for two weeks. He began work as a manual laborer for a New Jersey utility company, getting up at 4 A.M. for ten hours of work with his hands. A job as molder in a foundry followed. Later Peter reminisced, "I thought I'd located the exact site of Dante's Inferno."

Friends steered Peter to Birmingham, Alabama, where he took a proofreader job with the *Birmingham News* and became a lay leader in the downtown First Presbyterian Church whose session sponsored him into Columbia Seminary. Peter's gifts of preaching and teaching developed quickly. His first pastorate was at Covington Presbyterian Church. Then came the call to Westminster Presbyterian Church in Atlanta, a church in deep trouble when Peter became pastor, yet under Peter was soon so revitalized that like a magnet it drew students like me from Agnes Scott.

Peter's ministry in Washington began on October 3, 1937. One observer noted: "At age 35 he seemed to be a sincere, guileless, transparent, naive boy compared to his predecessor, Dr. Joseph Sizoo, a most sophisticated divine."

Another pastor's comment: "At first Peter was a very conservative preacher, clinging rather too tenaciously and defensively to his conservatism. I watched Peter grow during those difficult years here, until he became one of the most thrilling evangelical preachers I have ever heard."

Peter's reputation as a "thrilling evangelical preacher" resulted before long in long lines of people waiting outside New York Avenue Church of a Sunday morning. Often four abreast, not all could get into the sanctuary. Loudspeakers had to be installed in the Lincoln Chapel and the downstairs lecture room to handle overflow crowds. When these rooms were filled, there was nothing left to do but turn would-be worshipers away.

These huge congregations comprised government workers, GIs, ordinary citizens, a constant stream of out-of-town visitors and a sprinkling of Washington's renowned. In our congregation, it was not unusual for a famous judge to worship beside a mail carrier or for a Senator to take the sacrament of holy Communion in fellowship with a government clerk.

Peter's work as a laborer had indeed put him in touch with the so-called common man. The democratic ideal was in his blood. At first, therefore, he was so afraid of paying any servile regard to the capital's notables that he was blinded to their real needs. He soon discovered, however, that the rich and famous have heartaches just like other folks. They cannot escape sickness, pain and bereavement. They and their families need succor and counsel just as the rest of us do. It soon became apparent that serving any of them, from the President of the United States down, was an integral part of ministry in the capital city.

In fact, less than three months after coming to Washington, Peter was asked by the Washington Federation of Churches to preach at the annual Christmas service to be attended by President Franklin D. Roosevelt and his family.

An immense crowd filled the building and overflowed into the streets. I was allotted a choice seat almost directly behind the President's family.

An editorial in *The Atlanta Journal* said:

The Rev. Peter Marshall . . . a preacher who was a favorite among Atlantans a short time ago, awoke last Sunday morning to find his name, and excerpts from his sermon, on the front page of practically every newspaper in the nation. . . .

Peter and I soon saw that God's way of dealing with

43

us was to throw us into situations over our depth, then supply us with the necessary ability to swim.

Along with his growing impact on Washington's leaders and celebrities, Peter had an impact on the young. One area high school serving a cross-section of people had become a battleground for gang warfare. Discipline was quite out of hand and an ugly spirit permeated the school.

During the attempted talks of several guest speakers, peashooters and paper airplanes took over the auditorium. There were hisses and boos. Humming groups held forth first on one side, then on the other. Once a smoke bomb blew off one of the doors in the middle of a talk. More than one speaker had to simply give up and walk off the stage. All of this was so embarrassing to the principal that no assembly at all had been attempted for two months.

Then the principal heard of Peter Marshall and invited him to address the students. Whether or not Peter knew the school's history when he accepted the invitation, I don't know.

The youngsters heard that a preacher was coming and determined to fix him. One girl who wrote me of what happened said, "I fully expected Dr. Marshall to be ridiculed and booed off the stage."

At first the girl was fascinated by the preacher's smile and by his accent. He was talking about gardenias, of all things, her favorite corsage flower.

"You know how a gardenia's petals reveal any telltale fingermarks by turning brown," the preacher said. "Your lives are like that. Purity is like that. . . . Young people, don't give anything to the world to destroy. Don't be ashamed of high ideals, dreams and beautiful thoughts. . . ."

44

Suddenly the girl woke up to the fact that there was dead quiet in the auditorium. No peashooters or paper airplanes were in evidence. The eyes of all the teenagers around her were glued to the speaker.

"I can wish for you nothing better than that God will plant in your hearts a growing yearning to meet the Galilean, to know Him as your Friend. . . ."

As the preacher concluded, the room was swept by a tremendous ovation.

Fourteen years later the woman still remembered the theme of that talk and the gardenia illustration.

"We kids liked to hear Peter Marshall," she wrote thoughtfully, "because he spoke our language. He didn't talk over our heads. And he put the responsibility for what we made of our lives squarely on us."

Peter never "conducted" a service. Instead, he worshiped along with us. This was apparent when he read Scripture. As he read, we, his listeners, were impressed all over again with the timeless beauty of the biblical narratives. Peter's fine voice, his feeling for the rhythm of the King James Version, his almost perfect diction threw that beauty of language into sharp perspective.

To many moderns the Bible is a closed book; it seems dry and unintelligible. But when Peter read it for us, somehow it lived and breathed and throbbed with life. His feeling for the beauty and rhythm, as well as the meaning of the Scriptures, he had acquired as a boy when he read aloud from the Bible for hours at a time to his blind grandmother.

Then there were his pastoral prayers that seemed to make the presence of God almost palpable.

"As we wait in His house to keep this rendezvous with Jesus Christ," Peter might say at the outset, "our

Lord, through the Holy Spirit, is waiting now to hear, to forgive, to strengthen, to cleanse, to bless. Whatever your burden of care, of anxiety, whatever your sorrow or worry, whatever the joy that bubbles within you, whatever impulse brought you here, you may use these moments of silent prayer to make your own prayer, and to seek your own peace with God—for He is here.''

Our son, Peter John Marshall, or ''Wee'' Peter, as his father loved to call him, arrived at 8:53 on a snowy January morning in 1940. His arrival interrupted a sermon. Thereafter he managed to inject himself into many a sermon.

The previous night my mother had arrived to take over the household during my stay in the hospital. Later some friends had dropped in for an evening of game-playing. This sort of impromptu fun in his own home with a few close friends made the kind of evening Peter enjoyed most, and which seemed to refresh him best in preparation for his heavy Sunday schedule. He always tried to reserve Saturday nights for some kind of relaxation.

Part of our regular Saturday night schedule was for Peter to read his Sunday morning sermon aloud to me. He was always apologetic about this, thinking it would surely spoil the sermon for me on Sunday. It never did. On this particular night he read the sermon the last thing before turning in—or so we thought.

In the very middle of it, strange things began happening to me. Remembering the doctor's briefing, I watched the clock on the nightstand and counted the intervals between pains, while listening with half a mind to the sermon.

Suddenly the situation seemed urgent. "I'm sorry, Peter, to have to interrupt you. I hate to do this to you on a Saturday night, but you'd better get me to the hospital right away."

At eight o'clock the next morning the doctor telephoned Peter. "You'll have to come to the hospital immediately if you want to be here when the baby is born."

Mother was watching Peter's face when the doctor told him we had a son. A look of amazement and incredulity, then undisguised delight crossed his features.

It was typical of Peter, however, that he went on down to the church, taught the young people's class and even went through the eleven o'clock service, all without telling a single soul his big news. Several people commented on the fact that he looked very tired, almost as if he had been up all night, as indeed he had.

It was not until a woman came up to him at the close of the service to inquire about me that finally he broke his self-imposed silence. He had simply been afraid that if he told the news to a single person before the service, he would get too excited to preach.

The entire congregation enjoyed this event and considered Peter John their baby, too. "Re-Pete" was immediately enrolled in the cradle roll of the Sunday school, and was flooded with such a supply of silver spoons, booties, sacques, blankets and carriage robes as could have outfitted ten babies.

My Jesus Encounter

The first sign of my illness came as a dizzy spell during a talk to church women. Three days of examinations and laboratory tests followed in a Baltimore hospital. Though the doctor's words were technical, his voice was gentle as if speaking to a child.

"The pictures show definite intrapulmonary markings and heavy linear shadows radiating out into both lungs. There are evidences of a light, soft spotting over both lungs. You are probably running some temperature in the afternoons. We recommend a period of absolute rest, perhaps in a sanatorium. You should not do any housework, or, in fact, work of any kind."

In spite of the diagnostician's studied effort to soften the blow he was forced to give me, I felt my heart pounding; the walls of the room and the doctor's voice seemed to be receding. Tuberculosis! It had always seemed to me the most loathsome of all diseases. I could not even bear to speak the despised word.

"Is . . . is there danger of giving the germs to my husband and child?" I stammered.

The doctor smiled, trying to force a little levity. "I don't think you are a very dangerous woman. We were unable to locate the bacilli. However, your doctor in Washington will undoubtedly want to try again."

"How long do you think it will take me to get well?"

He hesitated a long moment. "Oh, possibly three or four months." Then, seeing my stricken face: "Mrs. Marshall, don't feel so bad about it. People do recover from tuberculosis. There are worse diseases, you know—much, much worse."

I went to bed at the end of March 1943, staying at home because I had a "closed case" of tuberculosis, with no cough and the bacilli never found. Today it would probably be called histoplasmosis. For the first four months I had a nurse in addition to domestic help, while I tried to supervise the running of the household from my bed.

Eighteen months later I was still bedbound, and there had been no change in the X rays. Five doctors, including the best lung specialists we could find, seemed unable to help me. Their only advice: "Wait and rest."

This was a time of great soul-searching. I began reading the New Testament, pondering Christ's healing miracles with my own great need in view. Up to this time I had given no particular thought to the question of whether or not Christ still performs miracles on people's bodies today. The advances made in medicine and surgery had seemed to me quite sufficient.

I was a child of the scientific Age. I knew that God set up this universe to be governed by unwavering scientific and mathematical laws. My generation believed in things we could "prove."

But . . . suppose the spiritual world, too, was governed by laws just as immutable as the law of physics. That would explain why some prayers were answered and some were not. Surely it was not just the caprice of God. The New Testament reveals that Jesus actually expected ordinary men and women in all ages to be able to do the same miracles He did. Wouldn't that point to the fact that those miracles worked for Jesus because He knew the inexorable spiritual laws of the universe, and intends us to learn them, too?

As I pondered these things and read my Bible, I found that Jesus never refused anyone who came to Him asking help. There was no record of His ever having said, "No, I won't heal you. This illness is good for your soul." Instead He was surprisingly concerned with the welfare of men's bodies, and the Bible assures us that not only is this very Jesus alive today, but that He is "the same, yesterday, today and forever." Why, then, could I not ask this Jesus to cure me?

I felt, however, unworthy to ask such a thing.

The practical ramifications of the fact that "God is love" began to dawn on me. I knew that anything unloving in me—any resentment, unforgiveness or impurity—shut out God, just as a muddy windowpane obscures the sunlight. Painfully, in an agony of mind and spirit, I began thinking back over my life, recalling all too vividly my transgressions and omissions.

Through many days I put down on paper all the things of which I was ashamed. Some of it I shared with my mother, some with Peter. To a number of people far away, I wrote letters asking their forgiveness for things they had probably long since forgotten, or never known about. It took me days to muster the courage to mail those letters. Then I claimed God's promise of forgiveness and cleansing.

Peter bore all this patiently, almost silently. He already knew what I still had to learn, that we human beings can never deserve any of God's good gifts, that when we have done the best we can, our best is still not good enough to merit anything from the Lord of all the earth. Peter knew that we can get nothing from God except, as he loved to say, "on the same old terms," always simply "by grace [the unmerited favor of God] through faith."

But he was also wise enough to know that there was a therapy in confession, and that I was traveling a spiritual road that I must travel alone, in my own way.

When this methodical task of confession was completed, I asked God to make me well. Confidently, with what I believed to be real faith, I awaited the verdict of the next X rays. But they were just the same. The shadows were still there—all the soft spotting, the same intrapulmonary markings.

One day as I was leaving to spend a few bedfast weeks with my parents in their Virginia Beach home, Peter slipped a pamphlet casually into my hand. "I found this the other day in the church office. It seems to be about spiritual healing. I haven't had a chance to read it myself."

The pamphlet turned out to be momentous. In it was a nugget of a story about a former missionary who had been bedridden for eight years. During those long years she had persistently asked God why. She could not understand why she should be laid on the shelf when she was doing the Lord's work. There was rebellion in her heart at the lost opportunity to serve. The burden of her prayers was that God should make her well, in order that she might return to the mission field. But nothing happened.

Finally, worn out with the failure of those prayers and with a desperate sort of resignation within her, she prayed, "All right, Lord, I give in. If I am to be sick for the rest of my life, I bow to Thy will. I want Thee even more than I want health. It is for Thee to decide."

Thus leaving herself entirely in God's hands, she began to feel a peace she had known at no time during her illness. In two weeks she was out of bed, completely well.

51

Privately, with tears eloquent of the reality of what I was doing, I lay in bed in my parents' home and prayed, "Lord, I've done everything I've known how to do, and it hasn't been good enough. I'm desperately weary of the struggle of trying to persuade You to give me what I want. I'm beaten, whipped, through. If You want me to be an invalid for the rest of my life, all right. Here I am. Do anything You like with me and my life."

There was no trace of graciousness about the gift of my life and will, nothing victorious, nothing expectant. I had no faith left, as I understood faith. Nevertheless, a strange, deep peace settled into my heart.

In the early hours of the next morning something awakened me. The luminous hands of the clock on my nightstand told me it was 3 A.M. The room was in darkness, that total darkness known only in the country where there are no streetlights. My mind was active, chewing on the spiritual adventure of the day before. I, who had deliberately surrendered all hope of health, now discovered an active, newborn hope in my heart.

My imagination supplied dramatic possibilities. Jesus might tell me, for example, to appear downstairs for breakfast with the family the next morning. I could picture their surprise and mingled delight and alarm.

I had no sooner prayed, "Lord, what would You ask me to do?" when it happened. Past all credible belief, suddenly, unaccountably, Christ was there, in Person, standing by the right side of my bed.

I could see nothing but deep, velvety blackness, but the bedroom was filled with an intensity of power, as if the Dynamo of the Universe were there. Every nerve in my body tingled with it, as with a shock of electricity. I knew that Jesus was smiling at me tenderly, lovingly, whimsically—a trifle amused at my too-intense serious-ness about myself.

"Go," He said, in direct reply to my question. "Go and tell your mother. That's easy enough, isn't it?"

I faltered. What would Mother think? It's the middle of the night. She would think I had suddenly gone crazy.

Christ said nothing more. He had told me what to do. It was clear to me that He would not compel me, and that if I did not obey, the chance might be gone forever. In a flash I understood the real freedom of choice God always allows His human creatures.

"I'll do it if it kills me," I said, climbing out of bed, sensing even as I did so the ludicrousness of my own words. Somehow I knew that Christ's eyes flashed humor as He stood aside quietly to let me pass.

I groped my way into the dark hall to the bedroom at the other end. Naturally my parents were startled. Mother sat bolt upright in bed. "What—what on earth?"

"It's all right. Don't be alarmed," I reassured them. "I just want to tell you that I'll be all right now. It seemed important to tell you tonight."

"What has happened?" Dad asked.

"I'm sorry to have wakened you. I'll tell you all about it in the morning. I promise. Everything's all right."

When I returned to my bedroom, although that vivid Presence was gone, I found myself more excited than I have ever been before or since, and more wide-awake. It was not until the first streaks of dawn appeared in the eastern sky that I slept again.

The question was: Did Christ mean that I had been healed instantaneously, or that recovery would come sometime in the future? I did not know. There was nothing to do but wait for the next X rays.

The healing of my lungs, as it turned out, came slowly, no doubt because my faith grew slowly. But the next X rays showed, for the first time, definite progress. And thereafter there was steady, solid healing, never with the least retrogression, until finally the doctors pronounced me completely well.

Life Is a Vapor

On Sunday, December 7, 1941, Peter was to preach to the regiment of midshipmen in the Naval Academy at Annapolis, Maryland. All the preceding week he had been haunted by a strange feeling that he should change his announced topic and preach a particular sermon. It was a feeling he could not shake off. On Sunday morning he confided it to Chaplain Thomas. .

"If your feeling about it is that strong, follow it, by all means" was the chaplain's advice.

So Peter preached on the text, seemingly a strange text for young midshipmen: "For what is your life? It is even a vapor, that appeareth for a little time, and then vanisheth away" (James 4:14).

In the chapel before him was the December graduating class, young men who in a few days would receive their commissions and go on active duty in a peacetime Navy.

As we were driving back to Washington that afternoon, suddenly the program on the car radio was interrupted. The announcer's voice was grave: "Ladies and gentlemen. Stand by for an important announcement. This morning the United States Naval Base at Pearl Harbor was bombed in a surprise Japanese attack. . . ."

Instantly we knew we were living through one of history's dramatic moments, the "date which will live in infamy."

Within a few months some of the boys to whom

55

Peter had just preached would go down to heroes' graves in strange waters. Soon all of them would be exposed to the risks and dangers of war; and Peter, under God's direction, had preached to them—young, vital, alive as they were that morning—about death and immortality.

Peter Marshall believed in immortality more surely than anyone I have ever known. As a very young preacher he had been curious about the details of the life we human beings are going to live "behind the curtain."

One evening at the manse we received a telephone call telling us that a dear friend, a woman in our congregation, had just died. She had been desperately ill for a long time, so her death was not unexpected.

Peter came away from the telephone slowly and sank down in his favorite chair. His mind seemed far away.

"Gertrude died about ten minutes ago," he said thoughtfully. "I wonder what thrilling experience she's having at this very moment."

Peter's own brush with death came in 1946 at the time of his first heart attack. After that experience, Peter saw precious human life only in relation to time and eternity, which is its true perspective.

Nothing reveals quite so clearly Peter Marshall's own clear-eyed humility about himself than a little incident that took place shortly thereafter. When he had resumed work, a minister friend from Hagerstown, Maryland, dropped in on him at the church office.

"Well, Peter," the friend asked, "I'm curious to know something. What did you learn during your illness?"

"Do you really want to know?" Peter answered promptly. "I learned that the Kingdom of God goes on without Peter Marshall."

* * *

The offer to become chaplain of the U.S. Senate in January 1947 was an irresistible challenge to Peter. Because of his rather severe heart attack, with months of convalescence needed, the prudent step would have been to refuse for health reasons. But prudence was not one of Peter's traits.

At first he was troubled that the official reporters of Senate debates wanted a typed copy of his prayer before it was delivered each day. Peter turned this minus into a plus, asking God to write each prayer through him.

Soon the press all over the United States began to note the brevity of these prayers, their pungency, their sharp relevance. An article in *The Kansas City Star* noted:

> Not without reason are the prayers of the Rev. Peter Marshall, Chaplain of the Senate of the United States, attracting national attention. . . . Even the Senators are now listening to the prayers that open the session. . . .

June 16 was a day of varied business in the Senate, including a brisk argument on a resolution to authorize the Committee on Civil Service to investigate the appointment of first-, second- or third-class postmasters. Dr. Marshall's prayer asked,

> Since we strain at gnats and swallow camels, give us a new standard of values and the ability to know a trifle when we see it and to deal with it as such.

When Secretary of State Marshall left Washington to attend the Council of Foreign Ministers, the Senate chaplain gave voice to the prayers of many when he asked,

May Thy Spirit move them, that there may be concession without coercion and conciliation without compromise.

Commented *The Chicago Sun-Times* under the headline "A New Bite to Senate Prayers":

The least heeded of any of the millions of words uttered in the United States Senate had usually been those of the chaplain, who opens each session with prayer. But now some observers are beginning to urge Senators to get there early enough to hear these utterances, for the new chaplain, the Rev. Peter Marshall, pastor of the New York Avenue Presbyterian Church, avoids the usual platitudes and is handing out some tart advice to the lawmakers. . . .

When Dr. Marshall prayerfully addressed his God, he first took pains to throw the stuffed shirt into the laundry bag. "We confess, our Father," he prayed one day in the chamber of the United States Senate, "that we know we need Thee, yet our swelled heads and our stubborn wills keep us trying to do without Thee. Forgive us for making so many mountains out of molehills and for exaggerating both our own importance and the problems that confront us. . . ."

About 3:30 on Tuesday morning, January 25, 1949, Peter awakened with severe pains in his chest and arms. He had only to speak my name once to arouse me; for some reason I had been lying there awake for some time.

"Catherine, I'm in great pain. Will you call the doctor for me?"

I knew at once from Peter's tone of voice that this was a major crisis. As I sat up and reached for the bedside telephone, I could hear my own heart pounding.

As we waited downstairs for the ambulance, Peter looked up at me and said, "Catherine, don't try to come with me. We mustn't leave Wee Peter alone in this big house. You can come to the hospital in the morning."

Reluctantly I agreed.

After the ambulance came and Peter was on the way to the hospital, I went back upstairs and knelt by my bed. But before I could speak a word, there surged through me, over and around me as a great wave, an overwhelming experience of the love of God. It was as if the everlasting arms were literally enfolding me. It seemed unnecessary to ask God for anything. I simply gave Peter and myself into the care and keeping of that great love.

At the time, I thought this meant that Peter's heart would be healed here on earth. God knew, of course, what I did not know. There in the downstairs hall, just before the ambulance had left, I had seen Peter alive for the last time.

At 8:15 that morning Peter stepped over into the Larger Life. At 8:20 the doctor telephoned to tell me. Little Peter had been making final preparations for school. He was by the phone as I got the news, and burst into a flood of little-boy tears. I was too stunned to weep.

59

Later I sat for an hour by Peter's hospital bed. He had been dozing, the nurse told me, and had slipped away very peacefully.

I felt that I knew just what had happened before I got there. All at once Peter had seen his Lord, and later his own father, whom he had longed all his life to know. There had been moments of glad reunion. Then, suddenly, Peter had realized: He was dead!

"You know, this will be hard for Catherine," I could hear him saying. "What can we do for her?"

And Jesus had smiled at Peter. "She'll be all right. We can supply her with every resource she needs."

So they had waited for me there. That was why, when I opened the door and stepped quietly into the bare little hospital room, it was filled with the glory of God.

Yet the splendor was not to last. In that still hospital room, at a precise moment, the two vivid presences withdrew. Suddenly I saw death stripped bare, in all its ugliness. . . . Carbon dioxide escaping from the sagging jaw. The limp hands. The coldness and white, white pallor of the flesh.

Shivering, I rose to leave the room. Two paces from the door I was stopped as by an invisible hand. As I paused, a message was spoken with emphasis and clarity, not audibly, but with the peculiar authority I had come to recognize as the Lord's own voice: Surely goodness and mercy shall follow you all the days of your life.

It was His personal pledge to me and to a son who would now surely miss his father.

It was not until the following June that I suddenly remembered something, the last words I had ever spoken to Peter. Was it possible that God had prompted these words, seemingly so casual?

The scene was etched forever on my mind—Peter lying on the stretcher where the two orderlies had put him down for a moment while the ambulance waited just outside the front door. Peter had looked up at me and smiled through his pain, his eyes full of tenderness, and I had leaned close to him and said, "Darling, I'll see you in the morning."

I knew now that those words would go singing in my heart down through all the years: See you, darling, see you in the Morning. . . .

Section
Three

The Years Alone

The ten years following Peter Marshall's death was a period of challenge for Catherine. Her gift of writing emerged and provided financial support for her and her son. She was tested painfully as a single parent. Indeed, all of Catherine's weaknesses and strengths came to a head during this period.

Paradoxically, perhaps, one of Catherine's greatest strengths was her willingness to be open and vulnerable about her shortcomings. God was to use this quality to reach and touch the lives of many strugglers.

To Be Comforted

At the death of a loved one, the first need of the bereaved person is for comfort—just plain comfort. In sorrow we are all like little children, hurt children who yearn to creep into a mother's arms and rest there; to have her stroke our foreheads and speak softly to us. But, of course, that is impossible; we are grown men and women.

Or is it?

"For thus saith the LORD. . . . As one whom his mother comforteth, so will I comfort you. . . ."

In my case I had been given that experience of comfort prior to my husband's death.

After the ambulance had gone, I went back upstairs and sank to my knees beside the bed. And there, over the turbulent emotions, crept a strange, all-pervading peace. Through me and around me flowed love as I had never before experienced it—as if Someone who loved me very much was wrapping me round and round with His love.

I thought at first it meant that everything was going to be all right. But when Peter died I knew that my experience of a few hours before had meant something far different. It had been granted so that when the blow fell, I might have the certainty that a loving Father had not deserted me.

After comfort, the next need of the bereaved is for the ability to distinguish between body and spirit. In this age of materialism most of us have had little practice at this.

One recently widowed friend expressed this perfectly. "My biggest need," she told me, "is to believe that Bill is not in that grave. If I could be sure of that, I could stand the personal hurt."

I understood her difficulty. The moment I had stepped into Peter's hospital room after his death, I had known that the man I loved was no longer in the body on the bed. That was a patent, indisputable fact. I had thought I would be able to hold on to that conviction. Yet less than two weeks later, I was having difficulty with it.

One morning about that time I was awakened early by the chirping of birds in the ivy outside my bedroom window. Somewhere in that twilight zone between sleeping and waking it seemed that Peter spoke to me.

"Catherine," he said clearly, "don't think of me as dead."

How could he possibly have known? I wondered. Since the brief committal service I had been unable to think of him except as dead. In my imagination I saw his body lying in the receiving vault (a temporary arrangement until a final decision about burial could be made).

Was this really Peter speaking to me, or was it some sort of subconscious suggestion? I did not know. I wanted to believe that my husband was still alive. But my descent to earth after the funeral had been so abrupt that doubts had come crowding in. At any rate, wherever the brief message came from, it was the precise word I needed at the moment.

In subsequent days I found myself pondering those words. If I was not to think of Peter as dead, how was I to think of him? If he were still alive, then where was he? What was he doing? With no answers to these questions, how could I visualize him or think of him as alive?

66

That brought me to a question my every emotion cried out to have answered: What is my relationship to my husband now?

In marriage I had found my identity, my answer to the question "Who am I?" As a woman, much of my orientation in life had been centered in my relationship to one man. When death cleaves the marriage partnership, the woman left alone feels that her whole basis for living has been washed away. She must begin all over again. "Who am I now?"

These words at Peter's funeral service kept coming back to me:

This morning . . . we are endeavoring to establish a new relationship. We have known Peter Marshall in the flesh. From now on we are to endeavor to know him in the spirit. . . . The fellowship with him will remain unbroken. . . .

Those had been sincere if lofty words. Were they true? For me, the fellowship had certainly been broken.

"Till death do us part," Peter and I had vowed on our wedding day. The fact was that death had now suddenly and ruthlessly parted us. Across that chasm I was to build a bridge to Peter Marshall's spirit.

I could not imagine how to begin. Thus I found my prayers taking a new turn. In a childlike way I began pleading with God for some glimpse of Peter, for some knowledge of his new setting, of what he was doing.

The response came in a vivid dream. Now, years later, every detail is still clear. In the dream I was allowed to visit Peter in his new environment. First I searched for him in a large, rambling house with many rooms and airy porches. There were crowds of people about, but Peter was not among them.

Then I sought him in the yard. Finally, at some distance, I saw him.

I'd recognize that characteristic gesture, that certain toss of the head, anytime, I thought as I began running toward him. I found myself able to run with a freedom I had not known since childhood. My body was light; my feet were sure. As I drew nearer I saw that Peter was working in a rose garden. He saw me coming and stood leaning on his spade, waiting for me.

I rushed into his arms. Laughing, he pulled me close and rubbed his nose on mine.

"I knew it was you," I said breathlessly, "by the way you tossed your head. I've come home to you."

Then, resting there in his arms, I felt something strange. Mixed with the tenderness of Peter's love was a certain restraint. He was not holding me as a lover.

My impression was that Peter was bewildered at what had happened, still surprised at his own death. I wondered if the large, many-roomed house, the yard and the rose garden composed some small part of what the Scriptures call heaven. I had always thought that people in heaven would be extremely happy. Peter's attitude did not quite fit that pattern.

Then I awakened. The feeling of Peter's strong arms around me lingered, and my cheeks were wet with tears.

Days later I was still asking God to reveal the meaning of this strange dream. Certain elements seemed clear. Peter had not expected his life to end so suddenly on that gloomy Tuesday morning. He, like me, had confidently anticipated a different outcome to the problem of his damaged heart.

Five minutes after death he was essentially the same person he had been before death. There had been no dramatic change except that he had shed his physical body as one would take off an overcoat. But the spiritual body in which he found himself—if that's what one could call it—gave him the same appearance as before.

In "heaven" he was being left alone to work in the rose garden to give him time to recover from his bewilderment, to find himself again. It seemed an especially thoughtful and loving touch that, in the meantime, he had been given work of a kind he had especially enjoyed on earth.

But it was that touch of restraint toward me in Peter's attitude about which I thought most. I asked God to tell me what that meant.

When the reply came, it was to have considerable significance for my future. A long time was to pass before I would have the courage to share this bit of insight with other widows, especially when their grief was new. For the dead are so terribly silent. The one whose sorrow is fresh longs for nothing so much as the touch of a vanished hand, the sound of a beloved voice. One in whom the wound of grief is still unhealed yearns for the assurance that, if immortality means anything at all, it means that one's love will be untampered with, will be just as it was here on earth.

Yet will the relationship between husband and wife be the same? From Christ's own lips, as recorded in the Gospel of Matthew, we are given quite another portrait of this. He spoke in answer to a sardonic question put to him by a group of Sadducees, who did not believe in the resurrection of the body. They posed a case about a woman who in this life had had seven husbands, and then asked the pointedly ridiculous question, "Therefore in the resurrection, whose wife shall she be of the seven? for they all had her."

And Jesus answered in part:

In the resurrection they neither marry, nor are given in marriage, but are as the angels of God in heaven.

Matthew 22:30

Christ seemed to be saying, in other words, that after death the woman would not be "a wife" to any one of her former husbands. That is, one's relationship to the person one has loved on earth will be different.

Precisely what the new relationship was to be I did not then understand. I did not know what being like "the angels of God in heaven" would be like, and I was not at all sure I wanted to know. On the whole, I thought it a revolting idea.

In the days following my dream, it was as if God were saying to me, "Because I want you to get this matter straight from the beginning, I am trusting you now with part of this truth. Some of it you will not understand; some of it will be hard for you to take. But I shall never give you more than you can bear."

Single Parent

Peter John had just turned nine when his father died. I can still see his stricken face when he heard the news and feel his trembling body as I knelt to take him in my arms. There were just the two of us now, mother and son.

Still, after the first state of shock, young Peter seemed to be bearing the loss of a father much better than I was taking the loss of a husband. He asked such boyish questions as "Who will help me finish my train set?" "Where will we live now?" "Will I have to change schools?" "Can I still join the Boy Scouts?"

The questions seemed so normal that at the time I did not realize the noxious brew of anxiety, loneliness, desolation and anger the questions were covering up. Few children can articulate the real issue underneath the anger: "If God loves me, then why did He take away my daddy?"

Peter John was included in the planning and in every part of his father's funeral. Repeated attempts were made to explain death and immortality to him. He seemed to understand. Here again, adults often assume a comprehension simply not there.

Too shy and fearful to bare his heart—I, too, had been like that in childhood—my son became quiet and withdrawn. Pictures of him during this period show a sad, strained face. I was not sufficiently aware of his inner desolation during these months and thus failed him at this point.

How should a bereaved mother or father handle such

a situation? I know now that we should never give up easily our efforts at dialogue. At meals I would ask questions about Peter's activities at school and get one-word answers: "Fine." "O.K." "Good." Of course these were phony answers, an effort to head off deeper probing into painful areas.

As time went on during our limping dinner table attempts at conversation, I would get the mental picture of a boy crouching behind a stone wall, peering over now and again but afraid to come out.

I sought the advice of counselor after counselor, had session after session, but we could neither find the way to bring down that wall nor make Peter come out from behind it.

In summer, as the two of us drove the five hundred-plus miles to Cape Cod, I struggled to find subjects of interest to my son. After receiving monosyllabic responses, I would give up and retreat into my own thought world—to Peter's relief, I sensed.

Usually my son would then find a ballgame on the car radio. To me these were interminably boring affairs. "Ball one, strike one. . . ." "Ball two, strike two. . . ." Every now and then there would be a flurry of action, but the litany of balls and strikes and other statistical information seemed to be nine-tenths of the verbiage.

Who cares, I would ask myself, whether the pitcher first scratched his left ear, then his right thigh, then shifted his feet three times while he was winding up? How could such repetitious commentary possibly interest a young boy?

But in an effort to relate, I forced myself to go to baseball games, football games, hockey games with my son.

Baseball to me was excruciatingly slow and boring, with the players constantly chasing after a small white ball. Football seemed to fall into the category of bloody hand combat—men throwing themselves ferociously at one another, sometimes even knocking each other unconscious. The idea that millions of people could go into a frenzy of shrieking excitement about the progress of a melon-sized brown ball down a field was more than I could comprehend.

Ice hockey was more enjoyable, the speed and grace of the skaters exhilarating to watch. But again, the vicious body contact made me wince.

My mistake was in not trying harder to get interested in these sports so that Peter and I could talk about them together. The key to this for me, I discovered belatedly, was the human-interest side of sports—learning the names of the players, their histories, something of their family life.

There were other ways open to me in helping my son grow up without a father. One was to bring him as much as I could into contact with other men in the family. My dad spent many hours with young Peter, trying to teach him to handle tools and do odd jobs around the house. My brother, Bob, could talk Peter's sports language and work on handicraft projects with him.

All of this was to the good, but there was never enough of it. It takes a great deal of masculine companionship to make up for missing a father's steady presence in the everydayness of life.

My experience indicates that our church fellowships fail to pick up a God-ordained responsibility in relation to widows. Many references in Scripture indicate that this ministry—spiritual, financial and help in child-rearing—is important to God. Apparently the New Testament church took seriously their ministry to widows and their children. For instance:

> Now in these days when the disciples were increasing in number, the Hellenists murmured against the Hebrews because their widows were neglected in the daily distribution.

> Acts 6:1, RSV

> Religion that is pure and undefiled before God and the Father is this: to visit orphans and widows in their affliction, and to keep oneself unstained from the world.

> James 1:27, RSV

The need is urgent. Present estimates are that in the United States, over fifty percent of all children will live with only one parent—usually the mother—at some time before they are eighteen.

In my situation the best answers to the sense of helplessness and frustration came through my early morning quiet time, when in prayer I would seek God's guidance for my son. One entry in my journal read:

> Do not be afraid for young Peter. No harm will come to him. He also is My child. I love him more than you do!

But it was hard to overcome my fears for Peter John as he moved into his teens. When I caught him smoking cigarettes at age fourteen, I was devastated. My anger erupted and he retreated into sullen silence. When I stormed heaven about my inadequacies as a mother, I wrote down this answer:

> You have still not completely released Peter to Me. Don't strain too much after it, though. It will come gradually, if you let Me do it. Even as a plant grows under My care, so a child grows.

One day while cleaning Peter's room I found a stack of sex-saturated paperback novels. How was I to deal with this? My first inclination was to let my anger boil over and explode. The inner voice said there was a better way.

Quietly that evening I asked him if there was any real reason he felt it necessary to seek out this kind of reading. He shrugged. "All the kids at school are reading it."

This led into a discussion of peer pressure that he picked up and talked about quite freely. He admitted that being accepted by others was far too important to him, that he was inclined to be a follower of what the crowd did. At the end of our discussion, on his own volition, Peter threw the paperbacks into the trash.

But the problem of peer pressure at school began a new period of fear in me. Not focused fear; more a spiritual unrest that would come to me upon occasion, vague and undefinable, like a splinter in one's soul. One night I asked God what this feeling was all about and what I should do about it. This is the message I got:

> You are fearful for Peter because of deep-hidden

guilt concerning him. Fear usually comes from guilt. You feel instinctively—and rightly so—that where you fail to supply strong enough discipline, then I, Peter's heavenly Father, will have to permit those disciplines to be supplied by hard and difficult circumstances.

In prayer I seemed to receive these instructions:

1. TV and movies: You are to keep a careful check on what he sees. Plan ahead. Be so well-informed about films and TV programs that you will earn Peter's respect in this regard.
2. Tidiness and taking care of his own clothes: Insist that he take responsibility here.
3. Money, allowance, etc.: You have not been handling this properly. You must take time to come back to Me to think these matters through.

For a period of months following this there was a big improvement in Peter's and my relationship. Children thrive under structure, and I was being given daily guidance on how to use consistent discipline.

Then early one morning the telephone rang. "This is Detective C—of the Eighth Precinct, Juvenile Squad. Your son, Peter John Marshall, and three other boys got into trouble last Saturday night. They are being accused of taking school property, two axes and a fire extinguisher, and breaking the headlights of two schoolbuses."

I began trembling as he talked. When he told me that I was to appear with Peter John at the Eighth Precinct station at 3:30 that afternoon, my throat was almost too dry to respond.

No members of my family were nearby, so I called several church friends for prayer support. I asked Peter to stay home from school so that we could talk through what had happened. He was defensive and communicated only the bare details. He and some friends had been messing around the school and a few back alleys nearby. They hadn't meant to destroy any property. "Honest!"

Later, as I prayed alone, I saw that I could be in danger of being too pridefully concerned about what the publicity might do to my reputation as a Christian. So many people had put Peter Marshall's family on a pedestal. Would such publicity hurt Christ's cause?

Peter and I were at the Eighth Precinct station from 3:30 until 6:30. As we waited nervously for the two men from the juvenile board to arrive, I noticed inconsequential details: the dirt in the corners of the room; the sad, shocked face of the father of one of the other boys, his eyes like those of a hurt animal; the luminous brown eyes of the man representing the school, whose name, ironically enough, was also Peter. His black hair peppered with gray, he was wearing tennis shoes on a winter's day.

One of the boys, the son of the man whose eyes revealed so much, put his head down on the table and cried very softly. Since a very little boy, I learned later, he had wanted to get into West Point. If this went on his record, he would never get there.

Peter's face was tense. Not in a long time had I heard him snap to and say "sir." His blond complexion seemed to have a permanent blush. He kept chewing on his fingernails long after there was no bit of surplus nail to chew. When the decision was finally made to let the boys off lightly because they had no previous arrests, he was relieved but deeply sobered.

I was impressed with the way the District of Columbia handled these first offenders. Each boy, with his parents, had to appear before a judge. When Peter and I appeared before a kindly magistrate for our talk, to my surprise the judge raised the issue I had considered too prideful.

"Peter, your father stood for something in the greater Washington community. You have a proud heritage. Don't tarnish it."

In the aftermath of the episode, I saw that the wall between young Peter and me was in part my doing. I had failed to admit Peter to the depths of my spirit. Our whole relationship had been pitched too much on the level of daily schedules, all the superficialities of life between a mother and her sixteen-year-old son.

Was it too late to change this? I would try. The inner voice instructed me to open the deep places of my own life and feelings to Peter and share with him. How much he would understand, I could not know. My business was to obey; God was to supply the communication.

A Christian counselor advised me that Peter needed male authority figures in his life; that, therefore, a Christian boys' school was indicated for his senior year in high school.

As I prayed for God's guidance on this, the Lord responded:

You have done all you can just now. The time has come to relinquish your son. Others will take over the role of parents in his life. You must accept this as natural and trust Me.

My spirit was heavy as we packed the car that

78

September day for the drive to Massachusetts. Peter had obtained his driver's license and insisted on taking the wheel. Now over six feet tall, he so towered over me that I felt almost intimidated by his sheer size.

As we drove there was little conversation between us. As usual, he was listening to a baseball game on the radio.

When the time came to leave our rooms in the inn the next day, I tried to keep my heart from showing—not because I was afraid of the heart, but because I didn't want to embarrass Peter John.

"This is a significant day for us both. Would you be willing for us to have a prayer together and ask God's blessing on it?"

Peter nodded a little impatiently, so I made the prayer brief. The moment hung in space, passed. But I had the unmistakable feeling as we prayed that we were not two but three, with "Big Peter" a part in this intercession around the throne of God, united across barriers that were no barriers.

I was a little disappointed in his room at school— circa 1890, golden oak woodwork, the floor well worn by generations of boys' feet, battered furniture, two small windows almost covered with a summer's growth of ivy.

But Peter did not seem to mind. He had just met his roommate, Bruce, and liked him—as blond as he, also a senior. The room would be their digs, their very own. What did nineteenth-century woodwork and worn floors matter?

I stood on tiptoe to hug my tall son and walked out, down the worn, uneven steps.

Another era was over. I had parted with my husband.

In a very real sense I had just parted with my son. This was the beginning of his life on his own.

As I drove away I was thinking: So to what do I return now? An empty house? Greater loneliness than ever?

A sudden rainstorm came up, the car's jerky windshield wipers keeping pace with my jumbled thoughts. Ten minutes later the rain ceased as quickly as it had come. I was driving into the setting sun, and the sun turned the droplets of rain on the windshield into glittering globules of light.

Then, to my astonishment, a rainbow appeared, every gorgeous color of the spectrum in its wide, perfect arc.

The rainbow of promise. I could forget my dread of returning to an empty house. He would be there.

Into the World

When it was time to deal with Peter's estate, in many ways I was still a little girl. I had adored and leaned on my husband. Like many a sheltered woman who has married young, I had never once figured out an income tax blank, had a car inspected, consulted a lawyer or tried to read an insurance policy. Railroad timetables and plane schedules were enigmas to me. My household checking account rarely balanced. I had never invested any money; I had been driving a car for only three months when Peter died. I would never even have considered braving a car trip alone.

Now I was faced with all these practical matters, plus many, many more.

There was some insurance, but not enough. I had no idea where Peter John and I would live after we left the manse. I was not trained to earn a living. I had married when my college diploma was warm from the dean's hand, before I had even earned a teacher's certificate. The adjustment that faced me, therefore, posed a challenge in every way.

My confrontation with the future took place a week or so after the funeral. Three men, all of them Peter's friends, arrived one evening to give me the grim facts. They were kind, eager to be helpful, but determined that I be realistic about my bleak financial situation. One of them, a knowledgeable insurance agent, had everything worked out neatly on a graph.

"I recommend that you spread Dr. Marshall's insurance over a reasonably long period of time. After all, it will be eight years before Peter John goes to college."

"How much income will we have each month?" I asked.

"One hundred and seventy-one dollars a month for the first eight years. Then the monthly income will take a drop."

"You must be clear-eyed about this, Catherine," chimed in the other businessman. "That won't be enough to maintain your car. You should probably sell it."

"And you're scarcely strong enough yet to hold down a job," the other friend added. "It's only been two years since you regained your health. By the way, what could you do job-wise?"

I began to have a suffocating feeling. "I—I don't quite know. I married right out of college—have only a bachelor of arts degree. I couldn't be a secretary, I don't know shorthand."

The three men were genuinely fond of me. Yet they considered me a poor prospect indeed for a breadwinning widow. I could see it in their eyes, feel it in the way they were approaching the subject of finances."

"I don't think you realize how desperate your situation is," one insisted. "One hundred and seventy-one dollars a month in Washington won't even cover the bare necessities."

"The Cape Cod cottage is a tangible asset," another added. "I think you should sell it quickly."

The three men left that night distressed because I did not seem fearful enough. They suspected that they had failed to convince me I was facing a crisis.

They were right. It was not so much my refusal to

accept their gloomy forecasts; rather, that even as a protective shield had been thrown over my emotions at the time of Peter's death, now I felt that same shield covering my faith regarding the future. It was not my doing; someone else was sheltering me. Their fear-darts, however well-meaning, had simply hit the protective covering and bounced off.

Yet I had not argued with these solicitous friends because facts and figures had substantiated all they had said. There the facts were, all down on paper in neat columns and graphs. How could figures lie? Yet somehow I felt that they did lie. Something was missing.

Alone in my room later, I stared out the window into the moonlight shining on swaying treetops. One brilliant star winked like a solitaire. Suddenly, standing there at the window, I knew what the missing factor was. My three friends who saw my many inadequacies, who had meant to be so kind, had reckoned without God.

I remembered how often Peter had faced this same attitude with his church officers. He would come home from a trustees' meeting sad and grim. "Cath'rine, no matter what's presented for their approval, their litany is always the same: 'But Dr. Marshall, where is the money coming from?' Where's their faith in God?"

But either God was there—I am that I am, a fact more real than any figures or graphs—or He was not. If He was there, then reckoning without Him was certainly not being "realistic." In fact, it could be the most hazardous miscalculation of all.

God had met me in Peter's hospital room the morning of his death. I had felt His presence. And the words He had spoken so clearly to me as I left the room were emblazoned on my consciousness: Surely goodness and mercy shall follow you all the days of your life. It was His personal pledge to me. In the days ahead—and indeed, during all the years to follow—I would cling to that promise.

So now I was facing one of those crises, a crossroads of life. I had to walk on into that new life, but which road should I take?

One decision I could make immediately: I would refuse to be destitute. The thrust of Mother's teaching in this regard had gone deep. Why should any child of the King consent to poverty?

So I claimed for Peter John and for me that great promise that stirs the imagination and sends creativity whirring into action. . . .

And we know that all things work together for good to them that love God, to them who are the called according to his purpose.

Romans 8:28

How often Peter, in quoting this promise from the pulpit, had pointed out that God never meant for this "good" to be limited to spiritual blessing; that He knows perfectly well our need for housing and clothes and food.

But now the Spirit was spotlighting in this promise—His *rhema* for me at this moment—"to them who are the called according to His purpose."

I felt a tingling at the top of my spine. Dared I entertain hope that He could actually be calling me for a purpose of His own; that there was some special work for me to do?

A sense of adventure beckoned. It would be exciting

to see what God wanted me to do with my new life. I was sure that when His design for me was revealed in its entirety, it would include much more than provision for economic needs.

Meanwhile, there were other things I was learning that I would share in the years ahead with those who had lost a loved one, whether through death or divorce. For one thing, no major decisions should be made in the weeks immediately following the crisis. Sufficient time must be allowed for recovery from a state of shock.

I was fortunate in not having to make an immediate determination about where my son and I were going to live. We were able to stay in the manse for almost ten months while the church searched for a new pastor. During those months familiar, beloved and once-shared possessions helped to soothe my sore spirit: Peter's wildly turbulent seascapes on the walls of our home, the well-worn games in the game closet. Being able to walk our cocker spaniel, Jeff, along the same familiar few blocks was, rather than added hurt, balm to my spirit.

Next, I found that the mechanics connected with separation are actually helpful, hard though they seem at first. In the beginning these practical activities come as an intrusion into grief. The wounded person looks out on the world marveling that other people on the streets and in the shops are going on about their business as if nothing has happened. How is it possible, one wonders at such a time, to force oneself to sort out dresser and desk drawers; to put one's mind to business and insurance details; to cope with the dozens of telephone calls and personal messages, and deal with the loving concern of friends and family?

The truth is that the empty heart needs work for the hands to do. I learned that there is a certain therapy in these necessary mechanics, plus a strange, sweet easing of pain.

An entry in my journal at this time charted an avenue of action:

> I must use part of my quiet time to hear what the Lord has for me to do. He has indicated that He does have a plan for my life. Could it be that my dream of being a writer is part of this plan? I must be open to everything that could lead to this: letters, invitations, counsel of friends.

Several days later a friend wrote, "I, along with thousands, earnestly hope that you will see to it that Peter's sermons will be published." Soon these requests for a book making some of Peter's sermons and prayers available were coming at me from all sides.

Since I had no contacts in the publishing field, my response was this prayer: "Lord, if this is Your plan, then You open the door for it. That way I'll know."

Within six weeks I had received letters from three publishers asking the same question: Would I be interested in compiling and editing a book of Peter Marshall's sermons and prayers? It seemed that God's word was "Go."

After conferring with several knowledgeable friends, of the three I chose the Fleming H. Revell Company in New York. A contract was worked out whereby I would edit a minimum of twelve of my husband's sermons for a book to be published in the late fall of 1949. A small advance was provided that helped me with living expenses during the next six months.

Peter had left some six hundred complete sermon manuscripts filed in three worn, black-and-white cardboard boxes. The proposed book could include at the most only fifteen to twenty. The problem was, on what basis should I go about trying to choose from the six hundred?

While the editors at Fleming Revell had caught a whiff of excitement about Peter's preaching, I know now that more deliberate reflection on their part, plus reactions from tough-minded salesmen, had quickly tempered their enthusiasm. "Fond widow editing preacher's sermons for publication" did not exactly herald a bestseller.

A casual or hurried job on my part could have defeated the project or produced a volume with a modest sale at best. But as the editing job progressed, I began to experience the deep satisfaction and inner contentment known only to those who have found just the right vocational spot.

It was not that my adjustment to bereavement was complete. In fact, it had scarcely begun. But in spite of the empty void inside me, it was as if I had finally come home to my natural habitat.

The work of editing, the virility of the sermon material itself, Peter's extraordinary handling of the English language, his intuitive use of the precise word, his humor, his certainty that people would find these messages food for their hungry spirits, the flashing facets of Peter's personality that leapt from the typewritten pages, the feel of paper and pencil in my hands—every bit of it was pure joy. And gradually I began to see that many things done in the years gone by had been preparation for this task.

The first printing of 10,000 copies of *Mr. Jones, Meet the Master* sold out before official publication day. Additional printings sold out as soon as they came off the press. When told the book was on *The New York Times* bestseller list, I was not as impressed as I should have been. Soon I was involved with a biography, *A Man Called Peter*, that would be on the bestseller list for fifty consecutive weeks and then be made into a successful movie.

God's goodness and mercy certainly were following me.

Loneliness

The years immediately after young Peter went away to school (first to Mount Hermon, then to Yale) were the most difficult of my widowhood. The idea of living alone did not frighten me. In fact, like most writers I prefer being alone for long stretches of the day. But there is a big difference between aloneness and loneliness.

Loneliness is the aching need inside one to share one's life with another. There are wholesome relationships for single people outside of marriage where this void can be satisfied. My question was, What kind of life did God want for me?

During the first years after Peter's death I was convinced that it would be impossible for me ever to marry again, that this would violate something very precious that my husband and I had had together. But as the years passed, I began praying about this matter, telling God that I did not even know what it was right to ask for, that I would leave entirely up to Him the decision as to whether I should ever remarry.

But this was a cop-out, a sloppy way of praying. Surely I needed to know myself better than that, what my own deep desires were. Knowing these, I could then at least present them to Him for approval or disapproval.

My growing loneliness was brought into sharp focus the night of a mother-daughter banquet for which I had agreed to make an informal after-dinner talk. Before my part in the program, a young baritone rose to sing a

89

group of semi-classical songs. The last in the group was "Drink to Me Only with Thine Eyes."

I had heard the words from Ben Jonson's poem sung many times. They held no special memories for me, nor had I ever felt in the least sentimental about this song. . . .

> Drink to me only with thine eyes,
>   And I will pledge with mine;
> Or leave a kiss within the cup,
>   And I'll not ask for wine.
> The thirst that from the soul doth rise
>   Doth ask a drink divine. . . .

Toward the end of the song, suddenly without warning I felt myself tighten. I was aware that my hands, hidden under the edge of the tablecloth, were clutching the evening bag in my lap until my fingers ached.

This won't do, I thought. I looked about for something less emotional to focus on. My eyes roamed over the scene before me—the mothers in their finery with their daughters beside them at the round tables, all listening intently to the tall young singer. I noticed a red-headed teenager's hairdo. Deliberately I studied it, trying to decide how some beautician had created the sleek, turned-under effect.

By the time the last notes of the song had died away, the tension in my hands had relaxed, the fullness in my throat had disappeared. I was able to get to my feet and even put some humor into my talk.

But this experience had pointed up a depth of loneliness in me of which I had been only subliminally aware. Years after Peter's death, my journey through the valley was still a running battle with self-pity. Several of the couples on our street would take a stroll in the early evening. Seeing them sometimes, I would think, Were Peter still with me, he and I would be the youngest couple in the neighborhood. Or at the theatre I would see a gray-haired man reach for his wife's hand, and wince with a pang of envy.

There is a price to be paid in reaching out again for a relationship. The first tribute exacted is a modicum of honesty with ourselves. Are we in some perverse way enjoying the pity-parties? How badly do we want to make connection with other people? For, let's admit it, there are pluses in having only oneself to think of.

In the light of honest answers to questions like these, I decided the negatives of a solitary life outweighed the dubious benefits. The first step was to perform a freshening-up on myself. Having to make public appearances forced me to review my clothes situation. I found a specialist who, after studying my current wardrobe, my figure and my features, advised me skillfully on clothes-shopping.

Then came some quiet reappraisal of certain restrictions my parents had placed on me in my growing-up years. Our home had been so full of love that the taboos they had put on activities like ballroom dancing and card games had mattered little to me—then. But now as a widow in sophisticated Washington, I was embarrassed when someone asked me to dance, or I had to decline an invitation to play bridge.

The answer was to develop these social assets—and I did. I enrolled for a series of lessons in ballroom dancing. Then three women friends and I set aside an evening a week to master bridge. We spread out teaching manuals on a second table beside us and learned the game together by playing it.

Seven years after Peter's death a battle was going on inside me. While resigned in my mind to widowhood, emotionally I was preparing myself for a new kind of life. This entry appears in my journal at about this time:

God does want me to be happy. God does want Peter John to be well-adjusted and happy. God has made me the way I am, has made me for happiness and love; I do not believe that He means or wants me to stay by myself for the rest of my life.

Odd, how as soon as I opened the inner door, outer doors began swinging open, too. Men began seeking me out for dates, a procession of men. Widowers—one a college president, one an insurance agent. Older bachelors—a wealthy California citrus-grower, a Washington professor, a Texas investment broker.

Then there was Howard, a tall, slim, distinguished-looking businessman and widower. I liked him immediately. He invited me out for lunch, then dinner, then for a weekend at his large family estate in South Carolina where his sister was the hostess. I was impressed, and Howard's two sons seemed to like me.

Howard was appointed to a government position in Washington and moved into an office in the Pentagon. As we saw each other more often, I became aware of some unsettling qualities in him.

He tended to avoid any discussions about Christianity. I sensed that any faith he had was a sort of inherited social grace with nothing personal about it. He seemed overly fond of the superficialities of life—eating, drinking, clothes, cars and so on. He was restless and ill-at-ease whenever other people paid attention to me in regard to my books. Yet his charm, dignity and statesmanlike approach to issues, and his warm, affectionate nature, appealed to me. Then I didn't see him for several months.

That June a letter came from Howard—a short note, actually. He was to be married again. The woman was the daughter of a general, a widow with three small children.

When the letter came I thought I had already relinquished the whole matter. Apparently not so. There was a surprising emotional backwash. I found it almost impossible to get back to my work. The fact that I was in demand as an author and speaker seemed meaningless. I was a 42-year-old widow whom life was passing by.

I met Jim at church. He was from Wyoming, a plastics manufacturer, married with two young children, but he had to be in Washington frequently on business matters.

Jim was a virile-looking, warmhearted man with a good sense of humor and a fine mind. Though he had dabbled some in Wyoming politics, he was an outdoor man who reveled in hunting and sports.

I was delighted when he invited Peter John for a two-day hunting trip or spent long hours with him in target practice. The two males seemed to enjoy each other immensely.

Then Jim began dropping by our home, and since he was there to see Peter, it seemed natural to invite him to dinner.

As time went on, Jim began asking questions about my life and activities, and I found myself responding quite openly and honestly about how lonely the life of a so-called Christian celebrity could be. He in turn began sharing with me some difficulties in his marriage. In the beginning, Jim's marital problems had not sounded serious; now they seemed to worsen the more he talked about them.

This should have rung alarm bells for me since I well knew that a single, unattached person of the opposite sex should not have been Jim's choice for a marriage counselor. Instead I would listen sympathetically, lulled into a false sense of security by Jim's ability to laugh at himself. That seemed to indicate at least a degree of healthy objectivity.

I will help him see how important it is for him to work out these differences with his wife, I told myself. And I did talk to him almost sternly about how important it was to get back to Wyoming and his family as soon as possible.

Then one evening after Peter had gone to his room, Jim blurted out, "Catherine, I've fallen in love with you."

A kaleidoscope of feelings swept over me: surprise, dismay, concern, fear and, yes, longing. But I knew it had to be squelched—and quickly.

"I'm startled, Jim. And—well, grateful. But it can't be right."

"I think it could be right, Catherine. But not until I'm a free man. I intend to get a divorce."

I protested and he argued. When he left that evening, I could tell he was very determined. I knew what I had to do the next morning: set the alarm, get up at 6:30 and come penitently before my Lord.

With some trepidation I did this, then waited. I felt such kindness and love pouring from Him that my tears came in a flood. I knew I had to be honest with my feelings, ruthlessly so. I poured out the residue of pain about Howard, then took pen in hand to try to analyze how I felt about Jim:

The moments we have been together have had a special flavor, a special character. Maybe that's what often happens when one really lives in the present. But the companionship has the quality of something one may not keep. It's like walking through a garden and catching the whiff of a fragrance one cannot quite capture or identify because one doesn't belong in that particular garden and cannot linger there.

Jim's friendship has done something for me. I have felt more alive during these days than in a long time. It's as if his touch on my life has awakened my emotions, the potential warmth of me, out of a long, long sleep.

But Jim will go back to his family. He must. I must be "hands-off" in my emotional attitude toward him.

Then I wrote Jim a letter that would spell *finis* to the whole thing, stating clearly that God would never honor any relationship between Jim and me that came at the expense of his wife and children.

When I mailed the letter, it was as if I had shed a twenty-pound weight from my shoulders. The next morning I felt a surge of creative vitality I had not experienced in months. Confession and restitution had freed my spirit, and out poured a torrent of words on paper:

For the past year I have felt defeated and frustrated. And this certainly is not as God wishes it. Here are some of the ways I have allowed my loneliness to defeat me:

1. The salt, the savor has gone out of life. Nothing, not even the very great success of *A Man Called Peter*, thrills me much now. "Success" has turned to ashes in my mouth.

2. There has been, over the past several years, a growing coldness in my heart toward other people rather than an increasing love and warmth. Visiting the sick has been a chore—no joy in it.

3. There has come an increasing preoccupation with self. Or perhaps the preoccupation with self is the real cause of the defeats.

4. I have sought satisfaction in material things and have not found anything here that lasts.

5. I have become more irritable in the daily grind of everyday life. Slow drivers, inept sales-girls, parking lot attendants provoke me much more easily than they used to.

6. I have known that God wants me to get up an hour earlier each morning for prayer and Bible reading, yet have not been consistent about this.

7. I have failed almost totally in small disciplines of appetite—small self-denials that, at the time, I knew were right.

8. I have often failed to have the inner strength to discipline or say no to Peter John, when I knew I should have.

9. Along with all these failures, I have often had a feeling of superiority to other human beings, which makes no sense at all.

In my early morning quiet time in my bedroom I even went back to review the Howard relationship in my journals. I saw that what I had written seldom contained any revelations from God about whether He felt we had been right for each other. Most of my notations had amounted to wishful thinking. Too impressed with the man's stature, his appearance, his wealth, I had decided that this was the one.

He was not right for me, and God would have told me, had I come to Him with will and heart wide open to His counsel. Months later, viewing the relationship with God's help, I could easily see how mismatched we had been both spiritually and emotionally.

No wonder, then, that the course of events with Jim had become so tangled.

Jim was not at all satisfied with my letter. Weeks later he flew east to Washington, determined to continue our relationship.

But the morning times had strengthened me and returned clear-eyedness to me. Moreover, I was learning something about how to cope with the temptations that come to the lonely: Admit you are not able to resist on your own strength. Then step aside and let Jesus handle the situation.

When I did this, inner direction came: Call your pastor and meet with him. When I got the pastor, Gordon Cosby, on the phone, I hesitated only a minute. Then I told him the whole story.

"Bring Jim down here and we'll pray about it, just the three of us," he replied.

What a tremendous answer to prayer! Jim agreed to go. So we made an appointment to meet at the Church of the Saviour.

"It isn't necessary for me to preach a sermon to you," Gordon told Jim and me. "You've come here because each of you wants to do what God wants you to do. I honor you both for this. Jesus always has the answer to every one of our needs."

He leaned back in his chair, smiling and relaxed. "How grateful we Christians should be! Without Jesus' agony on that cross, there would be no cleansing for the likes of any of us, no miracle of changing what's wrong on the inside of us to what's right. The blood shed on that cross literally saves our lives.

"That's what the sacrament of Communion should mean to us. I suggest we bring all this to the foot of Jesus' cross through Communion. How about it, Jim? Are you ready to lay there your desires in this matter, what you thought was your will?"

Jim nodded, his eyes moist.

Now Gordon looked at me. "Catherine?"

"Yes, I'd like that."

The bread and wine were there waiting on a little altar-table in Gordon's office. Never had the words been so meaningful: "This is His body broken for you. . . . This is the blood of the new covenant, shed for many for the remission of sins. Drink ye all of it."

We felt the presence of Jesus in that quiet room. At the conclusion of the little service, as we knelt, Gordon blessed us both.

"Jim and Catherine, you are good friends and want

98

to stay that way—friends. God has endowed you both with special talents and has a plan for both of your lives. Jim has responsibilities to his God, his family and his business. God has given Catherine a son to rear and a ministry through her writing. Both need to be protected. Go your separate ways, freely forgiven, restored, refreshed, into new usefulness and creativity."

Then Gordon lifted us to our feet and hugged us both.

Several months later I heard that Jim was back with his wife and children.

Section Four

Second Marriage

As I look back on this event, I am overwhelmed at the supernatural way God brought Catherine and me together. On the basis of pure logic we were a mismatch. Catherine in 1959 was a nationally known author whose Christian stature intimidated eligible males. I was the little-known editor of an inspirational magazine and a single parent trying to rear three small children.

Why would Catherine at age 44, her own son approaching his twentieth birthday, want to take on children ages ten, six and three, and give up her Washington dream house to move to suburban New York?

As for me, I was hoping at age forty to build a new life with an exciting younger woman. I was certainly not looking for a spiritual celebrity, four and a half years my senior, whose romantic first marriage had been depicted in a best-selling book.

Yet there are times when God asks us to throw logic out. Both Catherine and I separately had asked God to be a matchmaker.

Letting Go

A strange thing happened after Gordon Cosby's private Communion service for me and Jim. I stopped thinking about remarriage. Not that the desire for it was wiped out, just that it became much less important to me. My perspective had changed. This was the Lord's doing, of course, and came about because I was able to give the whole matter over to Him to handle.

One morning I wrote this in my journal:

> I am to "seek first the Kingdom of God" in regard to remarriage. Should this be God's will for me, then in any given man I am to seek first those inner qualities of mind and heart that belong to God's Kingdom.
>
> But what about me? What inner qualities should I have to qualify as a wife again?

The next day this is what I wrote:

> Going back to the question I asked yesterday, I would list femininity, warmth of personality, vitality, interest in other people, the desire to give. A big order!
>
> But I am being told this morning that since it is definitely God's will that I have these qualities, I am not to plead for them, but to believe that the prayer is already answered, that God is giving them to me in His own way and in His own time.

Shortly thereafter the president of a Midwestern college telephoned and asked to see me during his forthcoming trip to Washington. I had stayed at his home several years before while giving the commencement speech. Upon hearing that his wife had died, I had written him a note of sympathy.

He telephoned me upon his arrival in Washington and invited me out to dinner. By now I knew men well enough to realize that they usually ask you out for lunch if it concerns business, for dinner if it is more personal.

The college president arrived in a rented Cadillac and held my hand an extra moment when we met at the door. He was a small man, perhaps an inch or two taller than I, about 55, balding, a compulsive talker. During dinner at a fine restaurant I learned everything about his college: the $2 million debt, the growing enrollment, the championship baseball team, the new library, the problems with some of the faculty members.

But the rush of words covered up a rather surprising nervousness for a man in his position. He was obviously interested in me as a person and intended to express it before the evening was over.

He did just that, sitting in my living room later that evening. He proposed marriage. There was no attempt at any romantic buildup; it would be a marriage of convenience and mutual interest. He would supply me a home and security, in return for which I would be the first lady of the college campus.

I was touched and honored by his offer. But as graciously as I knew how, I refused. For me there could be no marriage without romance.

During that same year I declined two more proposals of marriage. What was happening? There could be only

104

one answer. Relinquishment of my intense desire for remarriage, seeking God first instead of a husband, had relaxed me in a way that was now attracting men to me. I could not analyze how I was different except that I could now empathize more with the other person and be much less concerned with myself. And the Kingdom-of-God-first yardstick was enabling me to hear the Lord's word advising me about each person.

A telephone call came one day from Leonard Le-Sourd, the executive editor of *Guideposts* magazine, asking for a luncheon date to talk about an idea for a future article. It had no special significance for me. I had written before for *Guideposts* and had met Len briefly one evening when I spoke to the young adult group of the Marble Collegiate Church in New York City.

Over lunch in a Georgetown restaurant our talk ranged over many subjects. In an easygoing, personal way, Len asked many questions about me—probing, I thought, for a new subject on which to base an article. We found one, finished lunch and he drove me home.

As he stopped the car in front of my house, out of the blue came an intriguing statement: "In my twelve years at *Guideposts* I've learned a lot about the Christian faith. One aspect of it seems both bewildering and challenging."

"What is that?"

"The Holy Spirit. No one talks much about it, especially preachers. There's a mystery here—power, too. Sometime I want to cover it in the magazine."

"The Holy Spirit is a He, Len," I returned quietly.

He looked at me curiously. "You know Him, then?"

"Not as much as I'd like."

The conversation ended and Len helped me out of the car and to the door. Not once during the two hours we were together did it occur to me that there was anything but a professional motive behind his invitation to lunch.

But there was nothing of the professional editor about the letter I received from Len several months later in the summer of 1959.

"I would like to know you better," he wrote. "How do you react to this idea? We'll choose a day, and then you write on your calendar three letters: *F-U-N*. I'll pick you up in the morning in my car and we'll just take off to the beach or the mountains or whatever."

The letter seemed deliberately couched to say, "If you're interested in pursuing this relationship, let's have a go at it. If not, then tell me so right now."

I liked that approach. We set a day in early August. Len telephoned the night before from a Washington motel to say that he would call for me at 10:30 the next morning. He was delighted when I suggested fixing a picnic lunch.

The next morning turned out to be a beautiful summer day, not too hot. When I met Len at my front door, I found myself slipping easily into the adventurous mood he had suggested. I asked no questions about where we were going; he offered no hints. As he helped me pack the lunch into a picnic basket, I could sense his curiosity about my living situation.

"Peter John and I have lived here for several years," I volunteered, "that is, when Peter's home from Yale. This has been a good home for us, but I'm building a new house in Bethesda that will give me a better working situation."

"What's wrong with this?"

"Not enough privacy. Peter's friends are in and out a lot in the summer. I enjoy them, but there are so many other interruptions here, too, and not enough space for my secretary. Anyway, I've always wanted to build my own dream house. It's already about half-built."

"I see." Len was reflective. "Since Peter is at Yale nine months of the year, your dream house could end up being quite lonely for you."

"Yes, it could."

Len put the picnic lunch into the trunk of his car and we climbed into the front seat.

"What do you prefer," he asked casually, "ocean or mountains?"

"I would choose the mountains."

"Which direction?"

I aimed him west toward Skyline Drive. As we drove along, I studied this fortyish editor sitting beside me. He was of medium height; dark hair beginning to gray; lithe, athletic figure. His gray-blue eyes were direct, warm, the lids often crinkling with humor. He was a good conversationalist, probing but relaxed. I relaxed, too. It was going to be a good day.

While driving out Route 193 toward Route 7, we came to a sign: Great Falls Park.

"What's this?" Len asked.

"A scenic spot on the Potomac for picnics and walking on the rocks."

"Let's try it."

We parked, got out and walked along the water. Since it was rocky terrain, Len reached for my hand and continued to hold it. We had lemonade at the refreshment center and then continued our drive west.

By the time we were on Skyline Drive and heading south, it was time to look for a picnic spot. Len chose a grassy knoll under a large shade tree. He took a blanket from the trunk of his car and spread it out for us to sit on. Then, as I began removing the food from the picnic basket, he returned to his car trunk for another item. A ukulele!

Out of the corner of my eye as I watched Len tuning it up, I hoped that I was not about to receive a country music concert. I have nothing against country rhythms. They're fun sometimes. But on the whole, I much prefer classical music.

"I was dancing . . . with my darling . . . to the Tennessee waltz. . . ." Len's voice had a strong nasal quality. I winced a little in spite of my effort to keep an expressionless face.

After a few bars, Len put the ukulele aside and laughed self-consciously.

"You're not a country music fan, are you, Catherine? I taught myself to play—poorly, I'm afraid. And I have no singing voice. Anyhow, I'd rather talk than sing."

I sighed with relief, making a mental note that Len was perceptive or I was transparent—or perhaps a little of both.

It was hard to believe that two people could talk continually for eleven hours, yet feel they had scarcely made a start on subjects of mutual interest. But when Len said goodbye that night, I had no real indication he could be serious about me.

True, I sensed that he was surprised at certain discoveries, especially that I was not the overly sanctimonious, lofty creature some people had painted me. We also knew now that we were both seekers, strugglers, groping toward real growth as Christians. Both of us were reporters, always interested in how to capture on paper scenes, drama, personalities, new discoveries about people in relation to God. We had an open, honest communication at a deep level.

Len's home situation, however, put me on guard. For several years he had been trying to rear three small children alone; he was obviously interested in finding a wife who would be willing to share this load. It was hard to see myself in this role.

He Didn't Mean to Say It

I wasn't prepared for Len's persistence, the frequent telephone calls that followed our excursion to the mountains. When Len invited me to come for a weekend to his little town of Carmel, New York, to meet his children, to my surprise I found myself accepting. The least I can do, I told myself, is be open-minded enough to take a look at this.

On Friday afternoon Len met me at New York's La Guardia Airport. During the drive out to Carmel, he told me that I would meet only his two sons, Chester, six, and Jeffrey, three, that weekend. Ten-year-old Linda was at camp. Mrs. Goutremont, the elderly housekeeper, would serve as our chaperon.

The *Guideposts* property in Carmel included the magazine's business office (formerly a girl's school) and a sprawling, eight-room white clapboard house, once the home of the school president, where Len and his children were living.

A picnic table had been set up on the spacious lawn under a maple tree. Diminutive Jeffrey met me with a wide smile, impish blue eyes and a hug. Chester's big, sad brown eyes stared at me suspiciously; then he held out a tentative hand. During the less-than-gourmet supper of greasy, cold fried chicken, coleslaw, potato chips and watermelon, Chester's suspicion of me seemed to increase. Suddenly his hand knocked over a paper cup filled with milk. Quickly I moved to one side, barely avoiding a lapful.

When Len snapped a sharp rebuke at his son, Chester flounced from the table. With the order to come and sit back down, the small, brown-eyed boy fell on the ground in a wild tantrum of crying and kicking.

With a quick move, Len swept his son up in his arms, threw him over his shoulder like a sack of potatoes and carried him into the house. In a few minutes the annoyed father was back, alone.

"Chester will stay in his room until he's ready to apologize," he explained. "He seems to resent outsiders until he gets to know them, especially all women."

Jeffrey, meanwhile, had snuggled up close to me, obviously hungry for love.

"Well, I've made one conquest, anyway," I said.

"Two," replied Len with a grin.

After dinner a neighboring couple joined us for several rubbers of bridge, and I struggled to cope with three skilled players. I'm about as adept at bridge as Len is with his ukulele, I thought to myself.

The neighbors left, the children were asleep, Mrs. Goutremont had retired to her room. Len suggested we go outside for a walk about the grounds. It was a still, moonlit night. Suddenly his flow of talk stopped as he abruptly leaned over and kissed me gently. Then he chuckled rather self-consciously.

"We're right under Mrs. Goutremont's window, and I'll bet she's looking down at us."

I darted a quick look up at the window. It was dark. "How can you tell?"

"I can't. But she's very, very curious about us."

"Why?"

He did not answer, but led me instead to the other side of the house by the porch. Two lawn chairs were positioned there side by side and we sat down.

"I'm sorry about the episode with Chester," he began.

"It worked out fine. Your son came downstairs while you were in the kitchen and apologized. I think we're friends now."

Len sighed. "That's good. Chester looks to me for almost total security. Anyone who visits here seems to threaten him."

He talked about his two sons and daughter with pride. "They're such good kids. Smart, too. Being without a mother the past few years has been rough. Mrs. Goutremont is the sixth housekeeper we've had."

As Len talked about his children, I saw that he had a father's heart, and I liked what I saw. He was a caring man, affectionate, comfortable to be with, mature. He approached problems calmly, I decided, thought situations through carefully, acted deliberately.

After coming to these flattering conclusions about Len, he promptly blew apart my reasoning. As he was talking about his dreams for the future, suddenly I heard him say, "And I see the two of us together."

"How do you see us?" I asked, surprised.

Even in the moonlight I could see that Len looked startled, too.

"I hadn't meant to go this route." He paused, struggling. "I find myself wanting to say things that will probably seem very impulsive to you. Somehow I have to—I do see the two of us together, Catherine. There's something supernatural involved in all this that I'm not sure I understand."

He stopped again and shook his head with an almost dazed expression. "I was so miserable a few months ago. I told God I didn't see how I was going to make it alone and cried out to Him for help. Immediately after that prayer, your name, Catherine, dropped into my mind. It had to be God's doing.

"Why would you conclude that?" I queried. "I mean, why, necessarily?"

"Because on my own I would never have thought you were—well, my type."

"All you knew about me came through my book about Peter Marshall?"

Len nodded. "What man wants to play second fiddle to a famous Scottish preacher? Surely you must realize that *A Man Called Peter* made yours one of the great love stories of our time."

He paused, struggling again for the right words. "Frankly, I had concluded you were too ethereal and spiritual. But the Lord seemed to be telling me that this was pure assumption, that I'd never really know until I investigated. So I did. That first luncheon was really an effort to probe under that professional veneer of yours. I didn't get very far that day. It was that brief conversation we had about the Holy Spirit just before we parted that kept me from giving up on us."

He reached out for my hand to cradle it in his. "All my preconceptions were exploded that day we spent together on Skyline Drive. When I drove back to New York the next day, I kept thanking the Lord all the way home. I'm convinced He brought us together and that we are right for each other."

There was a long pause.

"But I certainly hadn't intended to tip my hand so

soon," he went on. "I try to approach things carefully, not blurt out my intentions like this."

I said nothing for a moment. My mind was racing furiously. This amounts to a proposal of marriage. By making himself so vulnerable, Len was risking deep hurt.

Finally I found my voice. "Len, you astonish me. This is only the second date we've had. How can you be so sure so soon about us? Don't you realize that with what you've just said, you've walked out on the end of a limb? The limb could so easily be chopped off. Why would you deliberately put yourself in such a position?"

He smiled ruefully. "I don't understand it either. Maybe it's a deep desire for full honesty with you."

"And I honor that and respond to it. But Len, it's too soon for me to know. You're going too fast for me."

Only later did I realize: By following the dictates of his heart rather than the usual, sophisticated, game-playing approach, Len had unwittingly found the most direct route to my love.

A Weekend in Maine

A few days after my return to Washington, Len was back on the phone. He wanted me to come with him to Christmas Cove, Maine, for Labor Day weekend to meet his parents. Almost wondering what would come out, I opened my mouth to reply and heard myself saying, "Yes, I could do that."

Again I flew to New York's La Guardia Airport, where Len was waiting. During the six-hour drive to Maine, Len briefed me on his parents. His father had been a Methodist minister for seven years before he had turned to education. Now he was dean of the School of Communications at Boston University. His mother, while rearing Len and his sister, Patricia, had been very active in women's clubs, Kappa Phi, church organizations.

For some time Len's parents had been conducting a yearly tour abroad and summering in Maine. From Europe his mother would bring home interesting items to stock the "Santa Claus Shop," which she had opened years before. It was a big hit with summer visitors in the Christmas Cove area.

"Mother is impressed that I am bringing you to Maine. She will want you to meet a lot of people," Len said uneasily. "I told her that we wanted to be alone to talk."

Len would be an unusual male, I thought, if he could turn off a socially conscious mother.

We arrived at the gray-shingled LeSourd cottage on

the inlet at South Bristol, Maine. The invigorating salt air brought back nostalgic memories of "Waverly," our Cape Cod cottage. Len's parents greeted me warmly. The confrontation between him and his mother, however, took place almost immediately.

"I know you said you didn't want any parties, Leonard," she began soon after we had unpacked the car. "But Mrs. Stuart insisted on having us all for a lobster dinner tomorrow night. Leonard, there simply was no way I could refuse."

"Sorry you did that, Mother," Len replied quietly. "You'll have to tell Mrs. Stuart we had already made other plans. Tomorrow night Catherine and I are going over to Boothbay."

"But, Leonard, you can go to Boothbay Sunday night."

Len shook his head. "We're going to Boothbay tomorrow night, Mother. I'll explain to Mrs. Stuart, if you like. And please—no more surprises."

Mrs. LeSourd protested a little more, to no avail. Then she swallowed her disappointment and made no further attempts to tie us down socially.

Len's firmness was a relief. The last thing I wanted was a mother-dominated male. His plan was for me to meet his parents, then for the two of us to be alone, to relax in the sun and talk. We started the next morning, sitting on the rocks at Pemaquid Point. At three o'clock in the afternoon we suddenly realized that we had forgotten about lunch and had been in the sun too long. My legs were lobster-red from sunburn.

For the next three days the almost-nonstop exchange went on in cooler places. Though Len appeared to be by nature an easygoing, relaxed person, he could also be determined.

"We're middle-aged adults, Catherine, who have reached a point of maturity where we can make decisions more quickly," he pressed on. "I feel that the Lord has brought us together; He's given me a love for you that overwhelms me, and I am ready and eager to marry you as soon as possible."

"Len, you may have your word from God, but He hasn't spoken to me yet," was my answer. "I think I'm in love with you, but I'm not yet ready to make a decision about marriage. Be patient with me."

Back in Washington after Labor Day weekend, my emotions were in a turmoil. I was facing the ultimate question: Was I going to give the rest of my life solely to a writing career—or did God's plan for me also include remarriage?

If I married Len I would have to move to the New York area near his work. That would mean putting my unfinished dream house on the market. I would have to leave Washington, all my friends, my family and more than twenty years of memories.

One morning that still, small voice in my inner spirit asked me some searching questions:

> You are right to be counting the cost and taking a good look at the major readjustments necessary for another marriage.
>
> Are there not certain areas of your life where some rigidity is creeping in? Did you not realize that My way would be to send you a man not just to satisfy your own needs of love and romance, but because he has gigantic needs himself?

Pondering this, I realized that in a first marriage, in

the beginning, romance usually suffuses and dominates everything. It is only later, deep into the relationship, that commitment to one another and the responsibilities that go along with this become equally important—if the marriage is to succeed.

But in second marriages, when we are older, commitment is writ large even at the beginning.

The question was whether I was ready for that much commitment, not just to a husband, but to three children, too. Part of me was excited and stirred; the other part wanted to flee. Now I began to pray almost desperately for help and guidance.

When Len came down to Washington to meet my family and friends, Peter greeted him suspiciously at first. But I could soon tell that Len's amazing knowledge of sports was making an impression.

Len and I had dinner with my sister, Em, her husband, Harlow, and their two daughters, Lynn and Winifred. We drove to Evergreen Farm in Virginia to meet my parents. There we also met my brother, Bob, his wife, Mary, and their three children, Bobby, Mary Margaret and Johnny. It was a difficult time for Len to be put under such intense scrutiny. I liked the way he handled himself: no attempt to impress, no straining for acceptance.

There were several more trips back and forth . . . to meet Linda, Len's ten-year-old daughter, and to talk to Norman and Ruth Peale, old friends of mine, older friends of the LeSourd family. Len had been at *Guideposts*, which the Peales had founded, for more than thirteen years. Norman and Ruth confirmed all that I had heard already about him: talented editor, devoted father, spiritual seeker.

The time arrived and I knew it. D-Day—"Decision Day."

I was flying back to Washington from New York. As I sat in the hot, stuffy plane waiting for takeoff, flocks of birds darted and wheeled beyond the edge of the runway. Just like my darting, confused thoughts, I mused.

Buckling my seat belt, I realized something: I had thought I wanted love again. But now that love was staring me in the face, I was afraid. Why did I so want to flee? What was my heart trying to tell me? Could it be because this romance was not tailor-made to my dream specifications? Len was asking me to love not only him, but to begin all over again with child-rearing. At my age!

"Lord, You always give it to me straight," I breathed. "What am I to do?"

I thought with longing of the new house being built for me in Washington, almost finished now. Adjoining my bedroom, cut off from the rest of the house, was a step-down room—a sanctuary where I would write. Still, I would live in that house alone except for those brief holiday times when Peter John was home from Yale.

Two roads stretched ahead, and I was at the place where they parted. In that house being built I might produce many articles and books. There I would have a cushioned, sheltered life—yes, and probably a lonely one.

And if I chose the other road, I would plunge directly back into a turbulent life. It meant being a mother to Jeffrey, that mischievous imp; to Chester, with those enormous brown eyes and a passion for baseball; to Linda, approaching adolescence—and I had had no experience in rearing a daughter! I would battle to find enough time for my writing. Someone else would enjoy that beautiful, step-down room off the bedroom.

My thoughts turned again to Him.

"Lord," my plea continued, "aren't You overdoing it? A while back I told You that I was ready to reenter the mainstream of life, but does it have to be quite this much life?"

And then I remembered a sermon Peter Marshall had preached with the intriguing title "Praying Is Dangerous Business." With a clarity I would not have thought possible, several sentences came back to me:

It is dangerous business to pray for something unless you really and truly mean it. You see, God might call your bluff and take you up on it!

Again, God may require something of the one who prays. The answer to a particular prayer may involve some real effort . . . maybe even some sacrifice. God's method in answering almost any prayer is the march-into-the-Red-Sea-and-it-divides technique. You've got to have faith for that sort of venture, and courage, too.

My prayer about remarriage had turned out to be one of those dangerous prayers. My bluff was indeed being called.

I took a deep breath, for there was a luminosity about this moment that I recognized. I had met it before. It had nothing to do with the otherworldly type of inspiration that many people associate with getting a message from God. It was no off-in-a-rosy-cloud vision. Actually, it was more like being slapped in the face with a wet washcloth. Or like being brought to earth with a thud and bidden sharply to stand on one's feet and behave with maturity.

Suddenly the choice God was presenting to me was clear. To say yes meant adjustment, involvement. Yet I saw that if I chose the other road, I would be turning away from the challenge of life. That way would be comfortable, but it would take me further and further from contact with people. It could also mean the slow, softening deterioration of the real person inside, of the spirit God had been molding and shaping and chiseling, often so painfully.

The plane was moving now, gathering speed rapidly. We were lifting off the runway, climbing at a steep angle. The sun glazed off the silvery wings and was reflected back in pinpoints of brilliant light.

At that instant I knew I would say yes, to life.

We were married on November 14, 1959, in the Presbyterian Church in Leesburg, Virginia, with my son, Peter, giving me away. Never have the bonds of matrimony been tied more completely by clergy: my father, a Presbyterian pastor; Len's father, a Methodist minister; and Dr. Norman Vincent Peale, a pastor to both of us— all three officiating at the ceremony, using the memorable wedding service Peter Marshall had always used, part of which he had written himself.

Linda was starry-eyed as she edged up to Peter John, her new six-foot-five brother. Chester had by now accepted me. Jeffrey, Len had decided, was too young to attend, but was eagerly waiting to see his "new mommy" again.

Early that evening after the reception at Evergreen Farm, Len and I would be flying to Los Angeles, then on to Hawaii for our honeymoon.

On our way from the church back to the farm, Len and I learned that Chester had missed seeing the ceremony. Seated beside his Grandmother LeSourd, at a moment when her attention was on the wedding service, he had slid his lithe body off the pew to the floor and disappeared mysteriously from his grandmother's grasp. Chester had spent the remainder of the service crawling under the pews from the front of the church to the back, slithering his way between the legs of the wedding guests, mopping up the floor with his best pants.

At the time we laughed over the ludicrous antics of a small boy.

It should have been fair warning about what lay ahead.

Merging Two
Broken Homes

Upon Len's and my return from our honeymoon, I found it deeply satisfying once again to assume the role of all-out homemaker. We found a home in Chappaqua, New York, forty miles north of New York City, and began blending our two families. First there was the task of combining our possessions, deciding what to take to the new house, what to eliminate, what gaps were left to fill. The decorating job of bringing together this amalgamation was challenging and fun.

The yard dared me to make it beautiful. An outcropping of New York granite in the front yard cried out for a rock garden. A stone wall across the entire front of the property demanded a perennial border. Soon I was poring over nursery catalogs and garden books.

The children watched all this with fascination, Linda enchanted with her own room and the chance to help decide colors and other details, the boys elated over their immediate discovery of playmates next door and of so much space outdoors in which to roam.

But it takes more than a house, no matter how attractive, and possessions, and even a wonderful yard, to make a home. For what is a home but people, the individuals in it and the interaction among them?

The scene of our first dinner together as a new family is forever etched in my memory. We were gathered around the dinner table, two adults and three children; Peter was away at school.

I had lovingly prepared food I thought the children would enjoy—meatloaf, scalloped potatoes, broccoli, a green salad. Len's face was alive with happiness as he blessed the food.

But then as Chester's big brown eyes regarded the food on his plate, he grimaced, suddenly bolted from the table and fled upstairs, slamming the bedroom door behind him.

"Let him go, Catherine," Len said.

Then, seeing my stricken face, he explained ruefully, "I'm afraid my children aren't used to much variety in food. Mostly I've just fed them hamburgers, hot dogs or fried chicken from a takeout place."

Len went upstairs to try to persuade Chester to come back to the table. He found the little boy in bed, covers over his head. When he tearfully refused to come back downstairs, my new husband told his son sternly to undress and go to bed. There would be no supper for him. I was devastated at the thought of Chester going to sleep hungry. The dinner was spoiled for all of us.

And the disastrous evening was not over. Linda's resistance toward her new stepmother surfaced that first night when she refused to wear slippers on the cold hardwood floors, insisting she had always gone barefoot around the house. I understood only too well what it must have been like to be the only female in the family. Now suddenly she was vying with me for Len's time and affection.

The two boys had asked to room together, yet immediately began tussling like bear cubs. When they started scrapping yet again after the lights were out, Len summarily removed Jeff to another room. The little fellow sobbed himself to sleep.

That night as I was sitting propped up in bed reading, my attention kept wandering from the child psychology book to the problems at hand.

"Sibling rivalry," the learned author tagged it. "Parents, remain calm and unperturbed," his advice ran. "It happens in every family. Just remember, this, too, will pass."

Oh, sure, went my rebellious ruminations. It will pass by the time the parents are basket cases.

I could see it so clearly: the bespectacled child psychologist before his typewriter in his cubicle of an office, the door bolted against "siblings" of all ages, cheerfully clacking out his words of wisdom for us beleaguered parents in the thick of it.

It was later that same night, after Len and I, exhausted, had fallen asleep, that the shrill ringing of the telephone awoke us. It was Peter.

"Mom, I got picked up for speeding on the Merritt Parkway. I'm at the police station."

We agreed to post bond for Peter's release.

Yet all these troubles were but surface symptoms, the tip of the iceberg of difficulties. Surfacing day after day were problems relating to our extended family—Len's parents and mine, along with other relatives, together with the children's emotional trauma from that succession of housekeepers over the past two years. Peter, too, was in many ways still suffering from the loss and shock of his father's death ten years before.

How do you put broken families back together again? How can a group of individuals of diverse backgrounds, life experiences and ages ever become a family at all? I did not have the answers, but I knew Someone who did.

So I began slipping out of the bedroom at dawn while Len and the children were asleep for a quiet time of talking-things-over prayers, Bible reading and writing down thoughts in the ever-present journal. For example:

> Our very first step in solving family problems is resolutely to view our particular difficulties as God's schoolroom for the truths He longs to teach us and the immense riches of His glory He wants to pour into our lives—if only we will let Him. He's going to have to be our Teacher all the way. What's required of us is the open-mindedness of the eager learner, plus taking the time day by day to submit practical questions to Him.

During those early morning times there dawned the realization of something I had not wanted to face: Len was one of those men who felt that his wife was more "spiritual" than he, that she somehow had more Christian know-how. Len liked to point out that I was more articulate in prayer. He was assuming, therefore, that I would take charge of spiritual matters in our home while he handled disciplining the children, finances and so forth.

I already knew from my mail how many, many women there are who find it difficult even to talk with their husbands about anything religious, much less look to them for leadership in this area. How could I make Len see that "spirituality" was as much his responsibility as mine?

Lord, what do I do about this one? I hurled heavenward.

Somehow the answer was given me that nagging a man about this would not work. My directive was to go on morning by morning with my quiet time, saying nothing about it but otherwise refusing to accept the spiritual responsibility for the home. The assurance was given me that then God would work it out.

Meanwhile, how desperately I needed that early time with Him! I had been transplanted from metropolitan Washington to typical suburbia, U.S.A. Chappaqua was and still is a sprawling Westchester County community nicknamed "the bedroom of New York City." Every weekday Len and most of the other Chappaqua men caught early morning trains to the city, arriving back in the evening at a weary 6:45 or later. During these long days, the women had to carry all family responsibilities, including seemingly endless chauffeuring of children.

A typical morning for me was this one: A loud yelp from the boys' bedroom took me there on the run. Chester was rubbing his leg. "Jeff bit me!" Sure enough, there were teeth marks on Chester's leg.

"You're going to be punished for this," I told Jeff sternly.

"But Chester kicked me first. Want to see where?"

I really didn't, but Jeff showed me anyway.

At that moment Linda appeared in the hallway in her night clothes, her feet bare.

"Linda, the floor is cold. Put on your slippers."

"Can't, Mom. Can't get my feet in. The washing machine shrank them."

Obviously it was to be "one of those mornings." I went to the kitchen to start breakfast and fix Chester's school lunch. But I had not done my housework properly the night before: It was necessary to empty his lunch box before I could fill it. I extracted two packages of bubble gum, three rocks, a pack of well-thumbed baseball cards and a teacher's note that he had forgotten to deliver.

The doorbell rang with a special delivery letter. The telephone rang. Chester dropped jam on his freshly pressed school pants and had to change them. Peter, who was home between semesters at Yale, called out that he had a dental appointment in New York and couldn't find any clean undershorts. Linda and Chester dashed for the bus, banging the door behind them. Through the window, I saw that they had made it. I turned around to pour myself a second cup of coffee, and there on the kitchen counter was Chester's lunch. So-o-o, yet another errand.

I sank into the nearest chair, sorely needing that cup of coffee. As I sipped it, trying to get back some calmness and perspective, in my mind I was addressing the Almighty. Lord, what is this about, anyway? When You put people together in families, just what did You really have in mind?

Despite myself, I saw the humor in all this. Lord Jesus, are You sure this family bit is not one of Your sneakier tricks? I mean, for hammering and chiseling and molding us into the characters You intend us to be?

Then I remembered that during His time on earth, He Himself had to get along with at least six other children in a humble Nazareth household. What a comfort to know that He has experienced what families are up against, sympathizes and stands waiting and available with the wisdom and help we need.

Spiritual Head

As the days went by, Len was becoming curious about my early arising.

"What are you doing each morning?" he asked one day.

"Seeking God's answers for my day. I know He has them, but I have to ask Him, give Him the chance to give me His perspective and His practical helps."

"That would be good for me, too," was Len's reaction. "After all, we're in this together. Let's set the alarm thirty minutes earlier so that we can pray together."

Thus an experiment began that was to change our lives. The next day at a local hardware store I found an electric timer to plug into a small, four-cup coffeepot. That night I prepared the coffee tray at bedtime and carried it to the bedroom. The following morning we were wakened by the pleasant aroma of coffee rather than the shrill ringing of an alarm clock.

We drank our coffee, and I started to read at a spot in Philippians. But Len wanted to get on with the prayer.

"You start, Catherine," he said sleepily.

"But how are we going to pray about this problem of Linda's lack of motivation to study?" I asked.

A discussion began. It got so intense that time ran out before we got to actual prayer.

After a few mornings of this, Len agreed that we needed more time. Our wake-up hour went from 6:30 back to 6:00 A.M. Discipline in the morning meant going to bed earlier. It became a matter of priorities. The morning time together soon changed from an experiment to a shared adventure in prayer.

By this time Len, always methodical, had purchased himself a five-by-seven, brown loose-leaf notebook. He began jotting down the prayer requests, listing them by date. When the answers came, those, too, were recorded, also by date, together with how God had chosen to fill that particular need. Rapidly the notebook was becoming a real prayer log.

Not only that, but as husband and wife we had found a great way of communication. Bedtime, we had already learned, was a dangerous time to present controversial matters to one another. When we were fatigued from the wear and pressures of the day, disagreements could easily erupt. Yet when we tackled these same topics the next morning in an atmosphere of prayer, simply asking God for His wisdom about them, controversy dissolved, with communication flowing easily between us.

Of the hundreds of prayer requests in Len's brown notebook during this period, these were the most repeated:

1. That household help be found so that Catherine can continue the writing of her novel *Christy.*
2. That Peter will forget trying to be a playboy at Yale and find God's purpose for his life.
3. That Linda will stop rebelling against authority at home and at school.
4. That Chester will learn to control his temper and accept his new home situation.
5. That we can find the way to get Jeff out of diapers at night.

Morning by morning the requests from outside our

home also piled up and up: a neighbor dying of cancer, a close friend involved in adultery, an associate with a drinking problem, parents we knew asking prayers for runaway children, and on and on. We were learning that specific prayer requests yield specific answers, all of them set down in the brown notebook.

I had tried to get help with Jeff's diaper problem from a pediatrician in nearby Mount Kisco. All that netted was: "Mrs. LeSourd"—and the doctor's voice was tinged with sarcasm—"forget it! He'll get over it before he goes to college."

What was the point of reminding this professional about the wasted time, the added daily washload of three to six diapers and sheets? Yet nothing we tried solved this puzzler.

That summer when we went to visit my parents at Evergreen Farm in Virginia, I felt an inner nudge to seek the homely advice of the local country practitioner.

After he had heard me out, the doctor, his eyes compassionate, said, "I meet the bed-wetting problem often and I sympathize. But, Catherine, you've made it too easy for Jeffrey. Nothing's wrong except that he's simply too lazy to get up and go to the bathroom, too well-padded with too many soft diapers.

"So here's the solution I suggest: Waterproof the bed well. Take all diapers off. Steel yourself to let Jeff wallow in wet misery for a few nights.

"But temper that with praise and reward. Put a monthly chart marked off into days on the wall by his bed. Each morning Jeff makes it dry through the night, paste a big gold star on the chart and praise him lavishly."

It worked. And we thanked God and the country doctor for his humor and common sense.

But unless we had been recording and dating both the prayer requests and the answers, we might have assumed these to be "coincidences" or things that would have happened anyway. The prayer log was a marvelous stimulus to faith.

Len and I were certainly being taught about prayer as we submitted the practicalities of daily life to God.

For instance, not all prayers were answered the way we anticipated. We found that prayer is not handing God a want-list and having beautiful answers float down on rosy clouds. Also, His timing is certainly not ours; most answers came more slowly than we wished, and piecemeal. And what God had to say to us in our early morning times was even more important than what we presented to Him.

Out of His direction came some household rules:

1. Meals at regular hours and at least the evening meal eaten together as a family unit whenever possible. Dinner thus to be the focal point of each day. Each child soon learned to say a grace, was encouraged to articulate personal thoughts and needs. At the end of the meal Len or I read something from the Bible and then closed with prayer, again with each child participating, if only one sentence.

2. Regular bedtime, later on weekends.

3. No television for children on school nights. TV and movies on weekends carefully screened.

4. Linda's endless telephone conversations with friends to be limited to one stretch of time, 3:30 to 6 each afternoon. No twosome dates until she is 16.

5. Time reserved for the children on weekends for

family outings and/or home games. (We kept a bulging closet of games.)

6. On Sundays go as a family to church.
7. Len and I to share checking on children's homework. Full interest and participation in the Parent-Teacher Association and school events.
8. Listen carefully to children's complaints about school matters, but stress that the teacher's and principal's authority always to be upheld.
9. Discipline always to be part of our life together; punishment to fit the crime; spankings (administered by Len) by no means ruled out.

The implementation of all this was never easy. In the seventh grade, Linda was bright and freckle-faced with all the instincts of a tragic actress. Like her peers, she was trying to grow up too soon. Len and I became accustomed to the cry "You just don't understand!"

Naturally during those early years the majority of our notations in the prayer log focused on our children. In rearing them, we were gradually learning that God was more interested in our cultivating the patience to wait for His answers than in our rushing ahead of Him with schemes we had devised.

Patience? What could be better calculated to teach patience than trying to drum manners and tidiness into the children? Before dinner on three nights out of five: "Boys, you call those hands clean?" "Jeff, elbows off the table." "Chester, it's no good trying to hide the carrots under the lettuce leaf." From Len: "Linda, are you trying to use your hair for dental floss? Take your hair out of your mouth."

So much practice in forgiveness! There was the matter of Jeffrey repeatedly leaving ink cartridges in his pants pocket and ruining an entire tub of laundry. Each time I put away the family wash, every white garment had the navy-blue measles. Forgiveness. Forgiveness!

Then there was Chester's forgetfulness. He could not wear his P.F. Flyers because he had left them at the public tennis courts; his sweater was abandoned at Donn's house; it was impossible to do his assignment because he had left his book at school.

Late one afternoon I glanced out one of the front windows and did a double-take at Linda kneeling in the newly planted rock garden. My mind refused to believe what my eyes were seeing. Carefully, methodically, she was dragging, first on one side, then the other, newly purchased white sneakers through the garden dirt. My indignant protest brought only a withering "Mom, everyone wears dirty sneakers. I can't go to school in new white ones."

And there was Jeffrey's strange fascination with, of all things, shoelaces. One morning in nursery school the teacher asked him to stand up and recite. Jeff tried to struggle to his feet; he really did. But how could a guy straighten up when he had tied the laces of his Keds securely to his belt?

Then there was the afternoon I put him down for a nap. In no time disconsolate crying was issuing from the bedroom. I found Jeff trapped under the bed, his shoelaces woven in and out of the bedsprings, knotted over and over.

Yet through it all we learned that even though children resist discipline, all of them crave the security of firm structure and are confused and rudderless without it. Years later our children would be admitting that se-

134

cretly they had been relieved at the way we had stood our ground with them.

Linda, as an older girl, would often comment, "I feel sorry for poor So-and-So. She can do anything she wants to. I think her parents just don't care."

As time went on, an especially significant answer to prayer was unfolding before me—my plea that Len would assume his proper role as the spiritual head of our home.

His first insight was the realization that the two boys were going to pattern almost everything after him. This was obvious with something like athletics. Len had begun teaching his sons to swing a baseball bat as soon as they could lift it. He pored over the newspaper sports pages each morning. As soon as Chester and Jeff could read, they, too, were studying the sports pages.

If the Christian faith was to become important to them, he realized, it would happen through their father. Otherwise the two boys would conclude that religion was for the womenfolk and ignore it.

With this revelation, Len did an about-face on turning spiritual matters over to me. He became the one to call the family together for prayer around the table. As the boys witnessed their father praying spontaneously and were called on to follow, they were soon responding, praying aloud with no self-consciousness.

One evening we went to dinner at a crowded restaurant. I had just picked up my fork when Chester remarked quietly, "In school today our teacher was talking about saying grace before meals. He said that we should not skip doing this even when we're eating out."

There was a pause during which Len and I looked at one another.

Len nodded in agreement. "Your teacher was absolutely right, Chester. We should have done that all along."

Around the table we inclined our heads slightly. In a low-key voice Len thanked God for the food. Jeff's chatter started as soon as the soft "Amen" was out of his father's mouth.

We thought we had been exceptionally unobtrusive in the crowded dining room. But when the meal was over a nice-looking young man approached Len, leaned over, spoke several sentences for his ear alone, smiled and left.

"What was that all about?" I asked curiously.

Len was looking bemused. "The man wanted me to know that he thought it was great for a family not to be ashamed to pray in public. I feel I've been given credit for something I don't deserve."

So part of the beautiful answer to this prayer, I sat there thinking, is that Len himself does not realize how far he's come. As he became the spiritual head of the household, I was given the freedom to play the supporting role, as I had in my marriage to Peter. In no way did I consider this a secondary role. Len and I continued as a team, checking and sometimes correcting each other. But the team captain was my husband.

Section
Five

Schoolteacher

During our courtship Catherine had told me a little about the novel she was writing based on her mother's experience as a nineteen-year-old schoolteacher in the Great Smokey Mountains of Tennessee. Although her mother's name was Leonora Wood, Catherine had titled the main character and the novel *Christy*.

"I've never written much fiction," Catherine confessed. "Have you?"

"Not really," I admitted. "But I know something of the techniques."

A few weeks after our marriage Catherine handed me the first 52 pages of the *Christy* manuscript. I read it with a sinking feeling. It contained good descriptions, the mountain people were colorful, but no action. The characters were not confronting each other. Catherine's research was painfully evident in the dialogue, which was hard to decipher.

Our writer-editor relationship was to be tested early, I concluded. Should I be honest? Or tell her what she wanted to hear?

Drawing a deep breath, I pointed out the pluses in her work, but also what it lacked. Catherine didn't like criticism (who does?), but she was a professional. After an intense dialogue, she agreed that drastic changes were needed.

A perfectionist, she rewrote the first chapter of *Christy* eighteen times. Later she said, "Thank you for being honest. We could never work together if you weren't."

Christy, a first-person novel, was a learning experience for Catherine. (It took her nine years from the day she began her research in 1958 until publication day in 1967.) A learning time, too, for me and Elizabeth Sherrill, her editors. *Christy* became an immediate bestseller and has gone on to sell over 8,000,000 copies worldwide.

Smells

Every Monday morning handed me problems in schoolteaching for which no teacher's training course could ever have prepared me. First of all, strangely enough, were the smells. What was I to do about the body odors of children who were disinclined to take any baths during the cold months; who, if they owned any underwear, usually had it sewn on for the winter?

Whenever my pupils and I could stand the cold, we would conduct school with as many windows up as possible. That helped. But on some days the wintry blasts sweeping down from the mountains would whistle through the Cove, shaking the frame building as if it had been a rat in the teeth of some giant terrier, quivering the timbers, shivering us, making it impossible to open the windows.

Of a morning while I was dressing, I came to recognize these bad days by the truculent whistling of the wind: We would have to huddle close to the stove that day. So I would prepare by carrying up my sleeve a handkerchief saturated with perfume. Then when one of my more difficult pupils had to be near me to recite, I could always pull the handkerchief out and dab at my nose. I hoped that none of the children guessed my strategy.

Over and over I rued that too-sensitive nose of mine. Many an evening in my bedroom as I was preparing the next day's lessons, some incident would rise to haunt me: how I had backed away from Larmie Holt when I should have hovered close to check his work. There had been that certain look in the child's eyes, puzzled, a little hurt. Larmie had not understood. How could he!

Then I would chew my pencil and walk the floor pondering my dilemma. I wondered how others trapped in similar situations had managed. All those foreign missionaries, hundreds of them, must have had it far worse than I. Yet I had never heard any returned missionary speak of grappling with poor sanitation and uncleanliness. Perhaps they considered it too delicate a subject to discuss.

Then, in desperation, I would feel like crying out, "O God, it might be funny, but it isn't, really it isn't. Ple-ease—change my nose, or help me get the children cleaned up in a hurry."

This led directly to the idea of including a hygiene or health lesson in each day's curriculum. I sent to Asheville for several hygiene textbooks. These gave me lots of material.

One day we would talk about the skin, how the body got rid of waste through the pores and the necessity of washing perspiration and sloughed-off cells off the skin. But then we had to get down to practical points about how to bathe, since most of my pupils had only a granite tub or pan to use in front of the open fire, and even that was not easy with a large family in a one- or two-room cabin.

Another day the lesson would be about pure drinking water, the dangers of typhoid and hookworm and how to keep a spring clean. It was then I discovered how often the children would go to the bathroom in a mountain stream, and I realized that I had to forget prudishness and speak candidly.

In addition, as I saw how closely the children watched "Teacher," how much they wanted to be like me and in how many ways they were copying me, I tried to be more meticulous about grooming than I had ever been, wearing freshly starched and ironed shirtwaists, always keeping my hair clean and shining.

I hoped that some of this effort would rub off on my pupils—and it did. Soon Lizette Holcombe, Bessie Coburn, Ruby Mae and Clara Spencer were asking me if they could take a bath or wash and iron clothes in the mission house. Since Miss Ida did not take too kindly to this, my room had to be the scene for most of this activity. And when the girls would comment wistfully, "Teacher, you smell so good," I furthered my crusade by keeping a can of violet-scented talc on hand just for them.

Then, as time went on, I made an amazing discovery: The odors ("funks," as my children said, using a sturdy Shakespearean word) were no longer so much of a problem for me. It was not that my hygiene lessons had yet made that much difference, nor that I had grown accustomed to the smells, because in other situations my crazy nose bothered me as much as always.

It was rather that as I came to know the children and think of them as persons rather than names in my grade book, I forgot my reactions and began to love them. I suppose the principle was that the higher affection will always expel the lower whenever we give the higher affection sway. For me, it was letting love for the mountain children come in the front door while my preoccupation with bad smells crept out the rathole.

A problem of a different sort was the plight of those pupils who were far behind their age group in everything. It was not fair that a big boy like Lundy Taylor should have to recite in the primer class with six-year-olds just because he had never before been in school.

But I felt equally sorry about a child like Mountie O'Teale whose real problem was the O'Teale family home. When Mountie tried to speak, she showed a serious speech defect—halted gruntings and croakings like an animal—more like a three- or four-year-old than a ten-year-old.

Also, Mountie wore hand-me-down clothes and her hair was rarely combed. And the little girl never smiled or laughed or showed any emotion whatever. She seemed so dead inside that I could not be sure there was any possibility of helping her.

Then one afternoon I caught Creed Allen and her own brother Smith teasing her. On the playground they bent a sycamore sapling into a bow, lured her by, then released the branch to hit her in the face. It hurt, and when she started crying, they chanted in unison,

"Mush-mouthed Millie,
Can't even speak,
Jabber jabber jaybird
Marbles in the beak."

"Look at her blubber, bawlin' her eyes out. Dare you t' blab to Teacher," I heard them stage-whisper to taunt her. "Only Teacher couldn't understand you if'n you did blab. Cotton-mouth!"

Since I was trying not to interfere too often on the playground, I waited to see what would happen. No, Mountie did not tell on the boys, but I looked at her and saw misery staring out of her eyes. So she was able to feel, feel deeply. Suddenly I glimpsed real intelligence buried behind the wall she had put up to ward off more hurt. There was just a chance that Mountie might turn out to be the white lamb of the O'Teale family. But what to do for her? How to begin?

It may be that my wondering and pondering, and the fact that now I really wanted to help Mountie, constituted a sort of prayer. Prayer (that is, the kind that asks for idea-help with some particular problem life hands you) was still new to me.

However that may be, later on that day, as I was standing before my front bedroom window letting my eyes drink in "my view," the clear thought came to me: Watch for an opportunity to do something special for Mountie O'Teale, something that will please her.

The chance came the next day. For the first time, I noticed that the shabby coat the little girl always wore to school had no buttons. So during recess I dashed over to the mission house, selected some large buttons from Miss Ida's button box, along with needle and thread. As I ate my lunch, I sewed on the buttons, then carefully hung Mountie's coat back on the peg at the back of the room where I had found it.

After school was dismissed, while I was straightening my desk, suddenly I heard a giggle at the back of the room. I looked up and saw that it was Mountie.

"Mountie, what's funny?"

She came bouncing up to my desk, pointing to the buttons, stood there, gleeful and excited. "Look at my buttons! Look at my buttons!"

"Mountie, what did you say?"

"Teacher, look! Look at my buttons! See my pretty buttons!"

I could scarcely believe what I was hearing. In spite of the chortling, the giggles up and down the scale, the child was speaking plainly for the first time. It was like watching something open up inside her. I felt triumphant for her and left school so excited that I wanted to tell everyone about it.

That night as I pondered this breakthrough, the thought came that Mountie's speech defect just might have an emotional base. Perhaps what she needed most of all was to be sure that she was a real person, that someone loved her for herself.

For two days I wondered how best to demonstrate that to her. Finally I decided to give her a gift—that bright red scarf my mother had knitted for me. This had to be presented privately after school the next day so that the other girls would not be envious. The scarf was meant to tell Mountie that she was a very special person to me.

It conveyed the message, all right. This time she not only laughed delightedly but hugged and hugged me, did an impromptu dance up and down the schoolroom, waving the scarf. Then we practiced over and over, "See my buttons." "I like the scarf." "Pretty scarf." "Oh, pretty red scarf." And the child's heart and mind opened up some more.

With every bit of encouragement Mountie received, with each time I could tell her she was doing better, she would try even harder. Teacher cared about her. Teacher loved her. Did she not have the buttons and the scarf to prove it?

Now that the little girl's mind was released, it could function. Mountie O'Teale's reading ability grew astonishingly fast. Later on that year, I gave all my pupils reading tests. I could scarcely believe my own grades when the results showed that in her age group, Mountie had come out highest of all.

Of course, the speech defect was by no means over; the emotional blocks went too deep. But astonishing progress was being made. And this little girl was teaching me a lot about what an adventure schoolteaching is—and, more, that what these children needed most was love instead of lives governed by fear and hate. The adults, hanging on to hatred in the name of virtue, were reaping a bitter harvest in their children.

Part of the harvest was a morbid preoccupation with the negatives of life: sickness, death and dying. An obsession with death was typical of most of the children. This came out in their play.

"Let's Play Funeral" was a favorite game at recess. To me, it seemed bizarre and mawkish play. All that saved it was the spontaneous creativity of the children and the fact that, unerringly, they caught the incongruities and absurdities of their elders.

One child would be elected to be "dead" and would lay himself out on the ground, eyes closed, hands dutifully crossed over his chest. Another would be chosen to be the "preacher"; all the rest, "mourners." I remember one day when Sam Houston Holcombe was the "corpse" and Creed Allen, always the clown of the group, was elected "preacher." Creed, already at ten an accomplished mimic, was turning in an outstanding performance. I stood watching, half-hidden in the shadow of the doorway.

Creed (bellowing in stentorian tones): "You-all had better stop your meanness and I'll tell you for why. Praise the Lord! If you'uns don't stop being so derned ornery, you ain't never goin' to git to see Brother Holcombe on them streets paved with rubies and such-like, to give him the time of day, 'cause you'uns are goin' to be laid out on the coolin' board and then roasted in hellfire."

The congregation shivered with delight, as if they were hearing a deliciously scary ghost story. The corpse opened one eye to see how his mourners were taking this blast; he sighed contentedly at their palpitations; wriggled right leg where a fly was tickling; adjusted grubby hands more comfortably across chest.

Creed then grasped his right ear with his right hand and spat. Only there wasn't enough to make the stream impressive. So preacher paused, working his mouth vigorously, trying to collect more spit. Another pucker and heave. Ah, better!

Sermon now resumed: "Friends and neighbors, we air lookin' on Brother Holcombe's face for the last time. [Impressive pause.] Praise the Lord! We ain't never goin' see him again in this life. [Another pause.] Praise the Lord!"

Small preacher was now really getting warmed up. He remembered something he must have heard at the last real funeral. Hefty spit first, more pulling of ear. "You air enjoyin' life now, folks. Me, I used to git pleasured and enjoy life, too. But now that I've got religion, I don't enjoy life no more."

At this point I retreated behind the door lest I betray my presence by laughing aloud.

"And now let us all sing our departed brother's favorite song:

"I'm as free a little bird as I can be,
I'll build a nest in a weeping willow tree. . . ."

And then later: "Now all of you'uns gather 'round and see how nateral Brother Holcombe looks."

Now it was the mourners' chance for action, mostly the girls. Much screeching, groaning and moaning followed; they pantomimed throwing themselves, sobbing, on the coffin and talking to the dead person.

"Ah, Lordy, he be a sweet bouquet in heaven," someone shouted.

Suddenly from somewhere in the middle of the huddle, the corpse's booming voice was heard: "Stop it, yer ticklin' me. Ground's too hard anyway. Lemme go. I ain't no sweet bouquet in heaven yit. I'm a-gittin' out of here."

The Hunger for Touch

After I had been teaching for a while, I began to realize how hungry my pupils were for love expressed in physical contact. They were forever reaching for me, touching me, squeezing me—like Little Burl, on my first day of teaching, coming up again and again to my desk to crowd his little body close to mine and trace the embroidery on my shirtwaist with a stubby forefinger.

At first I had not realized the significance of this yearning for touch, even as I had not known how far into childhood the need for physical contact is carried. But then I stumbled onto the link between the need for touch and a child's ability to learn. Three of my beginners, Jake and Larmie Holt and Mary O'Teale, were having a great deal of trouble learning to read. When I would take them one by one on my lap and give them a lesson, they learned twice as fast. Loving them up seemed to remove blocks, just as it had with Mountie.

Naturally, with 67 pupils in all grades to teach, it was hard to find time for such individual attention. Nor did it seem right to give most of my time to the dull, slow children rather than to the bright ones. Part of this I solved by appointing Junior Teachers to help me. These were my oldest and best pupils like Bob Allen, John Spencer, Lizette and John Holcombe. They in turn profited from the experience of teaching the younger ones.

In no time at all, being appointed a Junior Teacher became the most coveted honor in school. So much so that I had to design a special badge for these children to wear: a piece of heavy cloth cut in the shape of a shield, each one trimmed differently with bits of fancy braids or beading or shiny buttons or sequins off the dresses in the mission barrels.

Recess provided me with another way of trying to appease this hunger for touch with several children at once. Whenever I would go out on the playground, my littlest ones would swarm to me, each wanting to hold on to a finger.

Gradually the "Finger Game" evolved. Ten children could play, five on each side of me, each holding on to one finger. But in order not to get tangled in one another's legs, fall down and break one of Teacher's fingers in the process, we had to march close together with me at the center of the flying wedge, each child with one hand on the child in front, in a lock-step with perfect rhythm and coordination. If one of the ten got out of step, then all of us fell in a heap. But whether we marched perfectly or whether we tumbled, always there would be gales of laughter.

The Finger Game proved to be perfect for teaching a first lesson in working together in order to live together happily. I was at that time still too new to the Cove to realize how desperately the lesson was needed by the parents of the children, too. For cooperation beyond the immediate family unit came hard to the highlanders.

It was at that point that they showed rather more of their highland Scottish heritage than the typical American frontier pattern. For I had always supposed that in frontier days a high degree of neighborliness and cooperation had been necessary for survival: the "workings" for building cabins or barns, for clearing land and harvesting crops; the drawing together into stockades for protection against Indian attacks; the relay system in pushing westward.

But in the mountains, though there were still a few workings, many factors, including the terrain itself, the isolated coves and the difficulty of travel, bred a self-contained individualism. Set down in its own hollow, each household had to depend on itself—and did. The Cove people were suspicious about joining any group effort or organization. Sometimes I wondered if they yet considered themselves to have joined the United States of America.

Trying to get work done for the school or mission was often like trying to move mountains by shoving against the mountain with one's shoulder. As I struggled to like, much less love, some of the worst of these individualists who wanted no part of accepting anyone's ideas or leadership, I comforted myself with the thought that "Oh well, it's certainly my privilege not to like everyone."

It was Little Burl, of all people, who helped me understand that, rather, it was my privilege to try to like everyone—at least to make an effort to see the good in each individual.

One morning we had interrupted our spelling lesson to watch the birds at our school feeding station. At my suggestion, Mr. Spencer had built this for us and placed it atop a pole close to one of the schoolroom windows. As spring approached, a greater and greater variety of birds were appearing. My pupils were fascinated. This morning we had seen several juncos and some titmice. Now a pair of cardinals, the male with the most brilliant red feathers I had ever seen on a bird, were stuffing themselves on the crumbs and sunflower seeds.

Looking at that glorious red plumage, I exclaimed, "Isn't it great how many different kinds of birds there are, each one so special! God must have cared about them or He wouldn't have made them so beautiful."

Then I couldn't help adding, "He loves everything He's made—every bird, every animal, every flower, every man and woman, every single one of you—loves you extra specially."

Little Burl was not working on spelling at all, but sitting at his desk staring up at the ceiling, his cowlick standing straight up, his funny little face puckered into a look of intense concentration. Something I had said had made an impression on him; I hoped he would let me in on his secret thought.

I had reached down to get fresh papers out of my desk drawer when I felt arms around my neck hugging me fiercely. It was Little Burl. He put his bare feet on top of my larger ones, locked his two hands behind my neck, stretched his head up to look me full in the eyes.

"Teacher, Teacher, hain't it true, Teacher, that if God loves ever'body, then we'uns got to love ever'body, too?"

I looked at the six-year-old in astonishment. "Yes, Little Burl, it is true." Forever and forever and forever.

So once I shut down my privilege of disliking anyone I chose and holding myself aloof if I could manage it, greater understanding and growing compassion came to me, more love for the children and, as time passed, for the older people, too. And suddenly I woke to the fact that smells in the schoolroom no longer seemed a problem.

Troublemaker

It was never clear which of the boys had put marbles in the stove, then scattered them on the floor hoping a barefoot student would step on them and get a hot foot. I suspected Lundy Taylor who, older and bigger than all the other children, was bored by school and constantly creating disturbances.

Then there was the time I went over to the stove to poke up the fire. I had no sooner opened the iron grating and thrust the poker in than a series of explosions like a gun going off spit sparks and flames into my face and onto my hair and dress. With an involuntary cry I backed away, slapping at the sparks.

Ruby Mae, who was sitting in the nearest seat, rushed to me, frantically raking burning pieces of something out of my hair. When we had finally gotten all the tiny conflagrations stamped out, I saw that there were several scorched places and burned holes in my dress, and the way one place on my neck was stinging, I knew it must be burned.

I stood there with flushed face and disheveled hair looking at my schoolroom, so flustered that for a moment I could not trust myself to speak. Finally with a shaking voice I asked, "What was it that exploded?"

There was a long silence. Some of the children would not look at me. Finally Joshua Bean Beck spoke up. "Hit be buckeyes, ma'am. Buckeyes in the ashes. They git hot and then pop and fly all t' pieces when the air hits 'em."

I was opening my mouth for the next obvious question but Joshua Bean was ahead of me. "No, ma'am, Teacher. I wouldn't do that to ye. Not me, Teacher."

I heard a torrent of angry words start to pour out of my own mouth. I bit my lip, choked back the words. In an effort to get control of myself I whirled to the blackboard to get on with the writing of the spelling words that the buckeye trick had interrupted.

But I had written only a few words when a steady noise at the back of the room penetrated my tortured thoughts. I whirled just in time to see Lundy stalking down the aisle, poking a stick into Mountie O'Teale's back, loudly "He-heeing" as he went.

It was deliberate defiance. The sneer on his face and the shifty look in his eyes made me suspect that he was the one responsible for the buckeyes. Yet of course I could not be sure.

"Lundy," I said with an immense effort to speak calmly, "stop that and get back to your seat."

The huge boy stood there gawking at me, stick in his hand, his mouth slack, his eyes empty. Then fire leapt to his eyes.

"No gal-woman's goin' tell me what to do," he snarled. "I'll stop when I'm good and ready."

Momentarily I was startled, then fury took over. The storm inside gave me a courage I would not ordinarily have had. I walked rapidly down the aisle toward the sneering face. The fact that the boy towered at least a head above me mattered not at all now.

"You'll stop when I tell you to," I said, almost shrieking, "and I'm telling you right now."

Then I reached up and grabbed his shock of hair with all the strength I had, dragged him down and shook him as I shoved him into the nearest seat.

The yank of the hair took Lundy by surprise. His watery blue eyes blinked back tears. But then the next moment he was standing up, his fist doubled as if to fight me back. Most of the children were on their feet now. I could feel John Spencer close to me trying to force his body between Lundy and me.

"Lundy-stay-right-there-in-your-seat!" A stern masculine voice spoke from the doorway. It was David Grantland, who had arrived for the mathematics lessons. "One more word out of you, and I'm the one you'll fight," he added.

The boy slunk down immediately. Then I could feel David's eyes riveted to my face. Now that the immediate crisis was over, suddenly I was shaking all over.

The next instant David was by my side propelling me to the front of the room.

"Sit down," he whispered. "I'll take over for a while now. We'll settle with Lundy later."

That week Lundy Taylor did not come back to school. By the second week gossip began to reach me that Lundy's father, Bird's-Eye Taylor, had taken my jerking his son by the hair as an affront to the Taylor clan and was busy plotting revenge for the new "brought-on" teacher. Though I did not believe this, still, the object of discipline was not to alienate pupils from the school. So as one day followed another and Lundy did not appear, I knew that I was going to have to wade into this misunderstanding—and I dreaded it.

One morning my redheaded shadow, Ruby Mae, was waiting for me. "Teacher, ye're in for trouble with Bird's-Eye. More trouble than ever ye saw in all your born days."

It was a beautiful sunshiny day, much too nice to talk

about problems. "What kind of trouble?" I asked unconcernedly.

Ruby Mae hugged herself with both arms and shivered. "Don't know what kind. But he's the awfulest man. Don't take nothin' off nobody."

"But I've never even seen Mr. Taylor."

"Ye seen his son right enough, the way ye yanked Lundy's hair most right out'n his head."

"Lundy deserved it. Probably if we only knew, his father is relieved that somebody could finally discipline Lundy."

Ruby Mae looked at me as if I were a freak. "Y'mean ye ain't scairt?"

"No, I'm not scared."

"But Teacher, his hair or his son's hair, don't make a particle of difference to Bird's-Eye. Talk is that he's sore as a skinned owl at you and is planning his re-venge."

"And my talk is that I think you're getting a big whiz-bang out of exaggerating the whole thing."

Ruby Mae was nonplused at my frankness. Then she said slowly, "But ye see, Teacher, what happened in school ain't lost a bitty-bit in the tellin'."

"I'm sure it hasn't. That's the trouble. And you be careful that you don't—"

"No'm, I won't. But I'm a-feared Mr. Taylor has heerd that ye did things that ye didn't do."

"Oh, I'm beginning to see."

"Yes'm. And he has his head set to believe what ain't true."

"Then that decides it. I'm going to have to go see him and tell him what is true."

Real consternation now constricted Ruby Mae's freckled face. "Oh, no'm, you mustn't do that! Not on yer life, ye mustn't. Teacher, you couldn't stand that man off. He be fractious. He's been known to spill mortal gorm. And them as he don't want t'kill, he may take a notion to rock."

"Rock? You mean he throws stones at them?"

"Yes'm, and if the rock jest happens t' hit a mortal spot, then hit be the rock's fault."

Her face showed that she did not think this funny.

"Ruby Mae, you're a chatterbox for sure. You talk and talk and I haven't the least idea what to take seriously."

She grinned at me. "It's true, Teacher. My mouth don't open jest for feedin' baby birds. But pleas'm, don't ever go to nobody's cabin 'round here without stoppin' at the edge of the yard and hollerin'. Ye should take that serious."

"That a custom in the cove?"

"Well'm, not a custom, exactly. It's jest that if'n ye don't holler, ye mought git shot at."

I could forget all of Ruby Mae's jabber, but if I was going to keep my promise to give school my all, then I could not forget the Lundy matter. Apparently there was no way to resolve it except by seeking out Mr. Taylor.

A Visit to Bird's-Eye

The Bird's-Eye Taylor cabin was the most isolated and freakishly placed one I had seen so far. It had been built between twin shelves of rock planes forming the top of a small mountain and it looked more like a fortress than a home. So steep was the final ascent that I tethered my horse to a tree two hundred feet or so below the cabin to climb the rest of the way on foot. But I paused first to "Hallo" as Ruby Mae had advised.

There was no porch to this cabin perched like an eagle's nest on the rocks. From where I stood, it looked as if one stepped out the front door into space.

No sooner was the call out of my mouth than the doorway was filled with a man's figure, shotgun in hand. It was too quick; he had been watching me all the way up the mountain.

"I want to talk to you, Mr. Taylor," I called. "May I come up?"

"Come up, then," but it was said grudgingly.

The path was steep, hard-packed and slippery. As I came closer I saw that there was a level spot something over a yard wide in front of the door. Bird's-Eye Taylor was not as large a man as I had imagined. Of a different build from his son, he was not quite medium height and slight, though slim and erect. He was dressed in a dirty plaid flannel shirt above a pair of shabby trousers held up by galluses.

"I'm Christy Huddleston, the new teacher, Mr. Taylor."

I tried to sound as if there was nothing unusual about this visit.

"What d' ye want with us?" The tone was churlish. The eyes looking into mine were watery blue, hard eyes. A slit of a mouth was set in the grizzled face that had not known a razor in days. He was wearing a felt hat with the brim turned down all around, holes in the top held together with a large safety pin."

"Just wanted to meet you, Mr. Taylor. And talk to you about Lundy. We've been missing him at school. We wondered why."

"Ye know why."

"May I come in?"

"Ain't no place fer a woman. Jest Lundy and me here."

"I know. I understand. But I'd like to talk to you."

He seemed surprised at my persistence in the face of his deliberate coldness, but finally moved to one side. "Come in and set, then." For the first time I saw Lundy standing behind his father.

The interior of the building was tiny and seemed more like a cave than a cabin. There was a fieldstone chimney at the back with black pots on cranes, no cook-stove in sight. I had the impression that somewhere in the walls there might be an entrance to a cave under the rock ledges. The room was furnished with only bare essentials and had not been cleaned for a long time.

With one foot, Mr. Taylor pushed a straight chair across the floor lazily in my direction, then sat down on another beside the one table.

"Hello, Lundy." I tried to put as much warmth as possible into my voice. The hulk of a boy so much larger than his father had still not moved from Mr. Taylor's side. "When are you coming back to school?"

"Dunno."

The slits of eyes were ogling me so that I felt as if he were undressing me. For the first time I was afraid and realized how foolish I had been to place myself in such a defenseless position. What was worse, no one at the mission knew where I was.

"Mought as well tell ye," Mr. Taylor said, "don't confidence women teachers none."

How was I to answer that?

I started in lamely, "Mr. Taylor, I know you must want Lundy to have some schooling so he can get on in life. I'm not the best teacher in the world. But I think I can teach Lundy something."

He ignored my speech, rubbing his hand over his stubbled chin. "Want t' whop my young'uns my own self. Don't want no gal-woman a-doin' it."

"Mr. Taylor, I didn't whip Lundy."

"Didn't hide him?"

"No, I didn't. Lundy is bigger than I am. How do you think I could whip him?"

Lundy was sidling toward the door. His father's hand shot out to whack at him but the boy ducked. "Consarned fool. Ye lied to t' me."

"Ah, Pap, I jest—"

"I'm a-goin' t' ketch a-hold of ye and smoke yer britches till the fire catches."

But Lundy was already out the door.

"Don't be too hard on him, Mr. Taylor. Lundy was testing me out, that's all. I have had a little trouble with him talking and wandering around the room, changing seats and playing mean tricks on younger pupils. Finally I had to talk sternly to him. And I did jerk him by the hair."

159

For the first time there was something close to a thaw on Bird's-Eye Taylor's face. He did not seem to think yanking Lundy's hair such a bad idea.

"Lundy will be all right. I hope you'll send him back."

"Oh, law! Dunno if schoolin's any use to Lundy. He may be twitter-witted. His maw was."

Cautiously I asked, "How do you mean, Mr. Taylor?"

"His maw was fitified and addlepated. Acrost the line in North Carolina that was. Pulled out from thar. That's why I'm a-raisin' Lundy."

"I see. Well then, seems to me you need help. That's what the mission's here for—to help."

"Ye can't squeeze milk out'n a flint rock."

"No, but don't give up on Lundy. He can learn."

"Maybe. Maybe not. Look-a-here, churches and their goin's-on ain't fer us. Always been a sinner myself. Ain't never been no hypocrite, though. Never lied to the Lord. Ain't no sech can enter the king-dom of heaven. Course I know that ain't the edzact words."

"But I'm a sinner, too. Everybody is. As I understand it, that's what church is all about—to save sinners."

"Don't want savin'. Always been a sinner. Always will be. I disgust churches."

There seemed little point in pursuing this. "Mr. Taylor, I'd better be going. You'll send Lundy back to school, then?"

I'll study on it."

"And drop by the mission house yourself sometime. We'd like to be friends."

He did not respond to that, but then said slowly, "I ain't got no rocks to throw at nobody."

160

What a queer comment, I thought. Then I remembered what Ruby Mae had said about Bird's-Eye Taylor "rocking" his adversaries at times.

"Well, goodbye," I called over my shoulder, and I hurried down the slope as quickly as I dared. I had the feeling that somewhere nearby Lundy was spying on me from behind a bush or tree trunk, but I did not wait to find out.

More than a week went by. Then one day at school I looked up from my desk and there, to my astonishment, stood Lundy looking at me. "Could I clean the blackboard for ye, Teacher?"

He seemed like a new Lundy, not so sullen or obstructive. It was plain that his attitude toward me had changed. He looked at me differently; he came up to my desk as often as he dared; he hung around after dismissal time, talking and ogling.

I sensed the new Lundy would create a new problem for me.

Fairlight

There was a warm touch of spring in the air as I climbed the ridge to the Spencer cabin. The evergreens were tipped with vivid green, and the willows overhanging the streams were a whisper of green lace. Here and there in the fields of the valley, spicewood bushes waved yellow plumes.

It was a site that must have been chosen carefully by someone a long time ago. I felt almost on top of the world. Here with the silent gaze of the mountains upon me, trivialities and pettiness and meanness faded and dropped out of sight. Entering the Spencer cabin was like sticking one's nose into one of those souvenir pillows filled with balsam needles or cedar chips.

Mrs. Fairlight Spencer had arranged galax leaves in two old pewter bowls, the leaves mostly bronze and winey-red from the winter, here and there new green; and in a chipped cup she had put trillium and violets.

"The very first," she told me, and reached out slender fingers unself-consciously to caress the flowers. "The least'uns of the springtime."

The grace of the gesture and the long, tapering fingers (even though they were red and rough with chipped and broken nails) caught my attention. I stood there thinking that these should be the hands of a lady handling an ivory fan or smoothing her skirts of velvet or satin. They were the hands of an aristocrat, and here they were on a mountain woman, buried at the back of beyond.

She was eager to show me everything, including an

unusual quilt stretched on a quilting frame near the hearth. While examining the quilt, I saw it was not the commonplace hit-and-miss patchwork, but a moon-and-star motif. When I asked Mrs. Spencer about it, she pointed to a small window set high in the wall to the right of the fireplace.

"See that lookout? I get a heap of joy from that. When I'm lonesome-like, it perts me up to look up there and see the sun-ball or the moon and stars. So thrice one night I drawed me an idea—three picture-pretties of the new moon and a star."

I looked at her in astonishment. "Mrs. Spencer, you mean you drew a picture of the new moon at three different positions and then copied that onto your quilt?"

She nodded. "Weren't much work. Seems right nice to have the starry heavens on my counterpin."

Then her expression changed. "Look-a-here— you've never handled a school afore. That's a heap of young'uns for one gal-woman. Is there anything I can do to help, like clean up the school yard? I'm a good hand to work. Or wash some of your go-to-meetin' clothes? It's my turn to favor you now."

The words were spoken with a gentle dignity, as if a gift were being bestowed on me, as was indeed the case. Here was a mountain woman with a husband and five children to care for, living in such poverty that if she had any shoes, she was saving them to be worn outside the house, yet thinking of me. Even as I started to answer, I realized something else: There was more to this gracious offer than met the eye. Fairlight Spencer was not just volunteering to do some washing and ironing for me; she was also holding out to me the gift of her friendship.

"Mrs. Spencer, that's the nicest offer anyone has

made me since I left home. You're right. Sixty-seven children are a handful and I do need help."

I paused, groping for words that had no condescension in them. "I'll accept your wonderful offer, if you'll let me be your friend. You see, Mrs. Spencer, I'm a long way from home. Sometimes I get lonesome for another woman to talk to. And maybe there'll be something I can do for you, too."

The face that in repose could look so spartan and pioneer was now wreathed in smiles. "Aye, you can holp, Miz Christy." Suddenly she was shy again, her voice sinking almost to a whisper. "I cain't read nor write. Would—you learn me how? I'd like that!"

The eagerness in her voice added such pathos that at that moment I wanted to teach this woman to read more than I'd ever wanted to do anything before. "I'd love doing that, Mrs. Spencer. Could you come down to the mission house, maybe Saturday?"

"For shore and sartin, I'll be there," she said joyously. "Oh, and would you—handle my front name, 'Fairlight'?"

On Saturday morning Fairlight arrived at the mission before we had finished breakfast. She was wearing a freshly laundered blue-checked gingham dress with a wide white collar and, this time, shoes. I took Fairlight over to the empty schoolhouse, where we started our lesson on two desks pulled side by side before an open window.

I had a box of materials ready and Fairlight was all eagerness to see what was in the box. From magazines I had cut out some pictures of landscapes to use for background scenery; some figures of men, women and children pasted onto cardboard bases so that they could be stood upright (as I used to do with my paper dolls when I was a very little girl); a copy of the alphabet printed in large, clear letters from my first-grade class; a Bible; a fresh ruled pad and some pencils.

Since teaching an adult to read was a new experience for me, I was not sure how to begin. It would not do, I felt, to downgrade the dignity of a human being like Fairlight Spencer by using the primer books for six- and seven-year-olds: "The rat ran from the cat." "Here the boy sat."

Then, too, I believed that Fairlight would learn more readily than the children, and I wanted to give her even in this first lesson the concept of words as ideas. And since I knew from having seen some of her quilt patterns and flower arrangements that she was a creative person, surely she would learn fastest if I could find an imaginative way to teach her. My problem was how to achieve this.

I picked up the Bible. "There are lots and lots of words in this book.

"How soon will I be able to read it, Miz Christy?"

"In no time! And I'll tell you why. Every single word in this book and all the words together use only 26 English letters—these here. So after you've learned just 26 and know how to put the letters together to form different words, then you can read. Easy!"

Her eyes shone. "I'd like that the best in the world." Already she was concentrating on that alphabet.

After we had read it aloud twice, she became so intent on learning it that she almost forgot I was there. So I sat back watching her, feeling instinctively that I should let her set the pace, even do most of the talking, if she would.

165

At last she sighed and looked at me. "Think I've got it—A, B, C, D," and on she went, making only one mistake.

Next we propped up a backdrop picture of a landscape drenched in sunlight. "Now, Fairlight, you pick out one of the paper people from this pile." So she selected a dapper-looking man and stood him up before the landscape.

We learned "man" and my eager pupil practiced saying it and forming the letters. Soon we went on to "tree," "light," "sun," "grass," "sky."

It was at this point that Fairlight stumbled onto her own kind of phonetics—the relation between the way the word looked and how it sounded. She was as thrilled as if she had found a jewel in the dust. She rolled the word "sky" over and over her tongue, spelled it again and again. This went on until we had our first ten words.

Then I opened the Bible to the first chapter of Genesis. "Now, Fairlight, look at this. The words on this page are just ideas marching. Like this one: 'And God said, Let there be light—' "

" 'L-i-g-h-t.' There it is! I see it." Her slender forefinger was on the word. "Oh, I love the light! Don't you? I hate the darkness."

Let there be light. . . . I sat there thinking that I had never seen light dawn so quickly for anyone as for this woman. What an alive mind she had! She scarcely needed instruction, only a chance to let the light come.

I was seeing more and more of Fairlight Spencer. Our friendship was a natural outgrowth of my teaching her.

What the record time is for learning to read, I do not

166

know, but the prize probably belongs to Fairlight. Three long sessions accomplished it. She "practiced" all the time, read everything imaginable—the old newspapers pasted on the walls of the Spencer cabin, the pieces of a tattered dictionary, the family Bible, even the labels on jars and bottles. Within a few weeks, so far as reading was concerned, she had caught up with most of the pupils in my school and was borrowing books two or three at a time.

I wondered if Fairlight's family might not suffer; after all, they could not eat books. I need not have feared. The young Spencers' stomachs were too healthy and clamorous to stand for any neglect.

But Fairlight did invent ingenious ways to do her housework and read at the same time: a book propped on the windowsill while she was washing dishes; a book open on a chair at her side while she was churning or spinning or shelling shucky beans or stringing green beans.

In the beginning I had thought of teaching her to read as just another do-good project. (I admit it, to my shame.) But Fairlight soon changed that with the debt in her favor. Her return to me was, all unknowing, such priceless insights into her heart and spirit that in a few short weeks I had begun to love this mountain woman.

For example, she taught me something important about the use of time and how to enjoy life. With a husband and five children to cook, clean, wash, even make clothes for, and with no modern conveniences at all, not even piped-in water, Fairlight might have felt burdened and sorry for herself—but she did not. Often she found time to pause in her dishwashing to let her eyes and her spirit drink in the beauty of a sunset. She would interrupt her work to call the children and revel with them in the grandeur of thunderheads piling up over the mountain peaks, heat lightning flashing behind the clouds like fireworks.

"It lifts the heart," she would say, and that was explanation enough for any interruption.

There was always time for a story in front of the fire with the children snuggled against her; always leisure for the family to gather on the porch "to sing the moon up."

Fairlight told me how on the first fine spring day, she considered it only right and proper to drop her housework. "The house, it's already been a-settin' here for a hundred years. It'll be right here tomorrow. It's today I must be livin'"—and she would make her way to one particular spot she knew. There she would kneel, and with her long, slender fingers brush aside the dead, sodden leaves and gaze wonderingly on the first blossoms of the trailing arbutus. Knowing her as I did, I could picture her fairly crooning over the flowers.

She and I agreed that never had we known such delight at an end of winter, perhaps because it had been a drab one. Yet I was discovering that spring did not come suddenly in the mountains but on tiptoe, stealthily, with retreats and skirmishes, what Fairlight called "sarvice winter" and sometimes "redbud winter."

Still, the mountainsides were burgeoning at last and I was eager to explore them. Since Fairlight knew just where to take me, she and I were often in the woods, sometimes just the two of us, sometimes like a pair of female Pied Pipers with the Spencer children and some of my other pupils trailing along. They would race ahead of us swinging on the limbs of trees or on wild grape-

vines, "plumb crazy," as Fairlight would say, "cuttin'
shines. Never did see such a doo-raw." Obviously my
pupils considered all of Teacher's excursions "jollifica-
tions."

We were out so often that I began to question Fairlight about whether a proposed lesson or walk would
interfere with her work. I can only remember twice
when there were household tasks she could not interrupt
lest something be spoilt. Her reply was more likely to be,
"It's a fair day. Shorely we'uns can pass the time with
one another." Then, more shyly, "Never have been with
you enough, Miz Christy, to see my satisfaction yet."

The highlanders were often accused of being lazy
and shiftless. As I got to know them better, my conclusion was: relaxed, yes; shiftless, a few of them; greedy,
scarcely ever. Fairlight's "It's today I must be livin' "
summed up their philosophy well, a philosophy that
aggressive people would spurn.

Yet which is right? Human life is short. Each of us
has a limited number of years. So are we going to go
through those so-few years with little time for our family
and friends and unseeing eyes for the beauties around us,
concentrating on accumulating money and things when
we have to leave them all behind anyway? I began to
wonder if the mountain values were not more civilized
than civilization's. At least I found the absence of greed
and pushiness as refreshing as a long, cool drink of
sparkling mountain spring water.

Now I realized why these mountain people were shy
with strangers. They had never learned the citified arts
of hiding feelings or of smiling when the heart is cold.
Friendship was dangerous to them because they had
built up no protection against it. Once they let you in it

must be into the deep places of the heart, as Fairlight had with me. Though I had known her only four months, already I was far closer to her than to members of my own family or girlfriends I had always known.

Through Fairlight's eyes I came to know a quality of friendship that bore little resemblance to the casualness of our relationships back home. The mountain type of friendship was a tie of substance between people with a sort of gallant fealty about it. It had to do with a time in the past when there was no more final bond than a man's pledged word; when every connection of blood or oath was firm and strong, forged in the past, stretching into the future.

Section Six

Guideposts Writer

When Catherine and I were married in 1959, she was the Women's Editor of *Christian Herald* magazine and I was the Executive Editor of *Guideposts*. I had been with *Guideposts* since 1946, working my way up from reporter to the top editorial position. In 1946 *Guideposts* had a few thousand subscribers; in 1960 we passed the one million mark.

There was an enchantment, an excitement, a joyous creativity about the *Guideposts* editorial meetings. One reason: the mix of people—young and old, liberal and conservative, black and white, Catholic, Protestant and Jew. Different viewpoints came together with one central focus: How can every page of *Guideposts* be helpful to the reader?

"What is the takeaway of this piece?" This oft-repeated question at meetings helped the writer decide exactly what he wanted the reader to receive from a particular article.

Some meetings we brainstormed ideas for a new feature or a new series, a *Guideposts* book, a *Guideposts* Christmas card, a *Guideposts* film, on one occasion a *Guideposts* exhibit at the New York World's Fair.

For a while Catherine continued on as *Christian Herald*'s Women's Editor, then was drawn irresistibly to *Guideposts* editorial sessions, developing lifelong friendships with editors John and Elizabeth Sherrill, Starr Jones, Van Varner, Glenn Kittler, Arthur Gordon, Sidney Fields, Dina Donohue, Fred Bauer and Art Director Sal Lazzarotti.

When Catherine became a roving editor for *Guideposts* in 1960, she developed her journalistic gifts in tracking down stories in many parts of the world. Here is a selection from the nearly fifty articles she wrote for the magazine.

The Protecting Power

(*Guideposts,* November 1966)

It is obvious that fear is growing each year among women in our country. Every week we read about some new violence to our sex. We are told what to do: keep away from dark streets, carry a squirtgun filled with ammonia in our purse, put special locks in our house or apartment and so on.

Some of these are wise precautions. Yet there are times when all the safeguards man can devise cannot stand between us and the raw evil loose in this world. At these times we need a surer protection—what is perhaps the only real protection we can have.

Let me tell you how this helped a friend of mine who lives near us in Florida.

On a bright, sunshiny morning last June, Jean Klinger started out in her car for Delray Beach to take her final Montessori teacher's examination. As she turned her car from Military Trail down Fourth Street, she noted the time on her watch. It was 8:50. Good: She would be at school by nine.

Fourth Street near Military Trail is a lonely stretch of road until it runs into the residential area. There are few houses; the terrain is dotted with farms and sand flats.

Just ahead of Jean Klinger was a light-colored pickup truck. It slowed down, then pulled over to the side of the road. An arm out the car window signaled to

Mrs. Klinger to pull over, too. She did so instinctively, wondering if something was wrong with her car.

A big, burly man wearing a sport shirt open at the neck strode up to her window. "Lady, can you tell me how to get to Dixie Highway?"

Mrs. Klinger was unsuspecting. After all, it was broad daylight. "I'm so sorry. I don't live in Delray. I'm just on my way to school here. Afraid I can't give you directions."

The man was looking at her intently. He glanced about him, then suddenly jerked open the car door and pressed a hard metal object into Jean's back. As she sat there, paralyzed, he shoved her to one side and climbed in beside her.

Jean screamed and, reaching over, pressed hard on the horn. But there was not a car or pedestrian around, no one to hear.

"Don't try that again or I'll kill you," the man growled, pressing the metal object harder into her back. Fear, panic, terror washed in waves over her. . . .

Jean admits she has always had many fears. Sensitive, intense, vivacious, she feels deeply. Long ago she determined to face up to her fears and search for ways to eradicate them. Her search led her to God and asking for His help in freeing her from these shackles. She even dared to ask that in certain circumstances He would help her be willing to do the thing she feared.

At her church Bible class she confided to her instructor that she had not yet learned how to deal with her fears. The instructor gave her a copy of a prayer that became part of the fabric of Jean Klinger's life.

The light of God surrounds me.
The love of God enfolds me.

The power of God protects me.
The presence of God watches over me.
Wherever I am, God is.

Upon arising that June morning, she had, as every morning, prayed that prayer of affirmation. Now at the crisis moment, sitting beside the threatening man in the car, when panic and terror almost overcame her, she was forced back on this prayer resource. Jean cannot remember the exact words she used, but she knows the essence of them.

"How can you force yourself on me this way?" she cried. "You are a child of God. You do not want to hurt anyone. God's love is in you. God wants you to be a good man. He cares about you. And I am His child, too. And completely under His protection. His love and protection surround me. . . ."

As she spoke the words, she felt warmed. There seemed to be a kind of aura around her, like a soft light. Then into her mind there came the clear picture of the face of the janitor at her church school, one of the kindest, most gentle men she had ever known, beloved by everyone who knew him. It was as if God were saying to her, "You told the man sitting beside you that he is a child of Mine. True, but now to help you really see that, superimpose the janitor's face and image on this man."

Jean followed directions and, sure enough, after that she could actually sense God's love enfold her abductor.

The result was immediate. The lust seemed to leave the man. He removed the object from Jean's back. Jean saw that it was merely a key case.

The man started Jean's car, drove on in silence for a while, little trickles of perspiration running down his face. He seemed more and more confused. Then he drew over to the side of the road and stopped.

"Get out," he ordered. Quickly Jean opened the door and jumped out. The man drove off, the car careening down the road.

Later Jean Klinger found her car undamaged at the spot where she had first been stopped. The man and his pickup truck had disappeared.

When I met with Jean, she stated to me that she was glad to share her experience because she believes it may point to the most important protection of all for women.

And I agree with her.

"I am the light of the world," Jesus told us. Usually we have thought this to be some kind of Oriental imagery. I wonder! The experience of an increasing number of women would indicate that in His contemporary presence, in His name and His person, there is literal light, protection, power—largely unrealized, untapped, unresearched.

Jesus goes on to make another commonsense observation: "For every one that doeth evil hateth the light, neither cometh to the light, lest his deeds should be reproved." To me it is significant that Jean Klinger felt an aura of light around her and that her attacker either could not or would not penetrate it. By repeating the prayer of protection so regularly, she had bathed herself in this light; it was there the moment she called out for help.

It has probably never occurred to most lifelong Christians that in the light of Jesus Christ there is such help and protection. We tend toward materialism, let us admit it, so we believe in the efficacy of material protection: guns, locks, police, sirens.

While all these means are valuable, obviously they are not enough, for never have assaults on women been so high. There are times when, like Jean Klinger, we may have no protection left other than spiritual. "Let us therefore cast off the works of darkness, and let us put on the armor of light."

The Man Who Couldn't Stand Leisure

(*Guideposts*, September 1969)

During the five years I have been living and writing in Florida, I have become very much aware of the retired couples living about us. At first, retirement seems as good to these people as the advertisements promised. The skies are sunny; the restaurants are fun; there is time for sleeping late, much talk, bridge, tennis, golf, boating.

But then what? Soon a certain lethargy creeps up on them. In its wake, nagging questions arise: Does anyone need us anymore? Is happiness more than leisure and a sunny climate? Isn't there something useful we can do?

Those questions are pertinent to more than eighteen million retired Americans, as well as millions more who are planning for this event.[*]

Paul Pepys is one man, a widower, who is using the last part of life creatively. Paul had had a brilliant career in business—vice-president of one corporation, president of another. He had always been terribly active, flying here and there across the world. But at age 60 he

---

[*] As of August 1992 there were more than 25½ million retired Americans.

began to wonder what there was to look forward to in retirement. His health declined. Then what he feared most came upon him four years too early: involuntary retirement.

"A kind of paralysis set in," Paul recalls today. "It seemed that no one needed me anymore. I began sleeping nineteen hours a day. When awake I could barely drag myself around."

After losing 43 pounds in a few months, he was admitted to a hospital. No serious ailment was found. In desperation, Paul's sister gave him a Bible and several inspirational books to read. It was in the Gospels that Paul saw his first shaft of light. Jesus' words "Follow me" came back to him again and again. What, then, was to be his first step in following?

When the minister of a local church called on him, Paul felt prompted to ask, "Do you have some small job I could do as a contribution of my time—anything, really?"

The pastor thought for a moment. "Yes, we need someone to set up a file system for our church visitation program. Could you begin Monday?"

Paul said he could. He startled his doctor by saying he had to leave the hospital and start work in five days. Reluctantly the doctor agreed to release him, but advised Paul to take it easy.

The advice was unnecessary. Paul discovered that he could hardly stand, much less walk. Somehow he found strength to get up, dress and check out of the hospital.

On Monday at 9 A.M. this former president of a large industrial company was seated at a small table in the church office before a huge stack of 3 x 5 cards. So dizzy he had to cup his chin in his hand to keep his head steady, he forced himself to concentrate on the job at hand. After an hour he went home exhausted.

"Lord," he prayed that night, "please get me going again tomorrow morning."

He was back the next morning and the next. Each day he extended his time one half-hour. At the end of the first week, Paul had made so little progress he apologized to the minister.

"Don't worry about it," he was told. "You're doing fine."

The second week went better. Ideas were beginning to come. One day Paul approached the minister. "I see that a notation is made when a minister calls on a member of the congregation, but there is no record of any laymen making calls on members except during the canvass for the church budget."

The minister hesitated. "You think we should ask laymen to make calls the year 'round? Hmmm. Wonder if they would?"

"I can't speak for other laymen, but I'd be glad to make some calls."

And so Paul had himself another job. This particular church had a large membership. On the calls he made, Paul saw lonely people who needed to know that someone cared. Wasn't the first step to let them know that Jesus cared? And wasn't that the Church's chief business, after all? And how could you do that without personal contact?

Clearly the ministers could not possibly do all that. So Paul sold both the ministers and the layleaders on the idea that all church members had to be responsible for visitation. Yet that idea had no chance of functioning efficiently without careful planning. Paul assumed the task. Those close to Paul could see health and strength and wholeness returning to his life.

One day Paul noticed that the young associate minister missed a call because his ten-year-old car had broken down. Paul went home that night and made a careful study of his financial situation for the first time in three years. The next morning he talked to an old friend who ran a local automobile agency.

That afternoon the associate minister burst excitedly into the church office.

"The most amazing thing," he said to Paul and the clerical staff. "I've got a new car. It's a gift—from some church member who insists he remain anonymous." His eyes filled with tears.

So touched was Paul by the minister's gratitude that he shut himself in his office at home that evening to do some deep thinking and praying.

"The Someone who had called me out of my hospital bed was there giving me the vision of a whole new kind of giving," said Paul, recalling that night. "I'd come close to losing my life. Now Christ was saying, 'I want you to give your life away in My name.' With abandon and in secret I was to give four things: my time, my money, my knowledge and my love."

Meanwhile, Paul began making calls in poorer neighborhoods. One man was out of work.

"Could I see your résumé?" Paul asked.

The man just looked at him blankly.

"If you'll come down to the church this afternoon," Paul said, "I'll help you prepare one."

Paul's counseling on employment problems resulted in an employment clinic held two evenings a month in the church basement. Men and women, members and nonmembers looking for jobs in the community were invited to come have their résumés sharpened and to talk with specialists in various fields, most of whom Paul recruited from among the church's laymen.

Four years passed. Paul awakens now at 5 A.M. eager to get going. After juice and coffee, he reads from the Bible and meditates for an hour to prepare himself inwardly for the day ahead. Next comes a brisk walk, plus work in his garden, then a shower.

By 8 A.M. he is at his downtown office. After dictating letters for an hour, Paul is back in his car to attend a real estate meeting in connection with his new investments. Then to the church for a luncheon meeting on a special program. In the afternoon he drives across town to spend several hours with a ten-year-old boy, his special charge as a member of the Big Brother Movement. If there is time, he will play two sets of tennis.

By 8 P.M. he is due at the university where he takes a two-hour extension course in chamber music one night a week. Paul plays the violin in a 75-piece amateur symphony orchestra several nights a month and fills in as organist for a small church whenever needed.

Paul's finances have improved to the point where he anonymously gives away several cars a year to hardship cases and new suits to as many as ten people. He has given a home to a destitute widow and made the down payment on a house for a man who does not have the faintest idea who the donor is, though Paul sees the man about once a week.

Paul's insistence on secrecy remains; he has learned

that power flows in literal fulfillment of Christ's promise.* Paul made the same condition of secrecy in letting me tell his story, requesting that his name and certain details be changed so that no one would recognize him.

And so the man who once slept nineteen hours a day has, in four years, had his life completely turned around to an active nineteen-hour working day.

"The key to a worthwhile life for the retired person," says Paul, "is not the usual advice 'to get interested in something.' Rather, for me it has been to 'get interested in Someone—Jesus Christ.' How can I ever forget the way He came into that hospital room and told me to get out of bed and start living for other people? I've accomplished more and had more fun in the last four years than in all the rest of my life put together."

---

* "Be careful not to do your 'acts of righteousness' before men, to be seen by them. If you do, you will have no reward from your Father in heaven. So when you give to the needy, do not announce it with trumpets, as the hypocrites do in the synagogues and on the streets, to be honored by men. I tell you the truth, they have received their reward in full. But when you give to the needy, do not let your left hand know what your right hand is doing, so that your giving may be in secret. Then your Father, who sees what is done in secret, will reward you" (Matthew 6:1–4, NIV).

God's Work Is Where You Are

(*Guideposts*, January 1968)

Every time I hear someone complain that he has "no time" for God, I think about our friend Ellie Armstrong. Ellie is in full-time religious work—running a motel.

It is a small but neat motel on U.S. Route 6 in the rolling hills of western Pennsylvania. Ellie was behind the desk when my husband, Len, and I stopped there one night recently. She is in her early 30s and the eyes framed by her dark hair are very blue. It is her eyes that invite you to linger and chat awhile after you have signed the register.

The place, she said, had been named Port Motel after the nearby town of Port Allegany, long before she borrowed the money to buy it three years ago.

"But isn't it the very name you would choose if you were starting a motel new?" she asked. "A name Jesus used about Himself!"

"He did?"

"Of course. 'I am the door'—the portal. 'By me if any man enter in, he shall be saved, and . . . have life, and . . . have it more abundantly' (John 10:9–10). Isn't that the point with everyone we meet, to lead them to that door? And a motel—well, it means a chance to meet new people all the time!"

The blue eyes returned our startled looks with surprise of their own.

"That's why I wanted a motel, you know," she said, as though wondering why else one would be in business. "To meet people who might not have heard about Him."

Like, for example, the unsuspecting pharmaceutical salesman who had stopped for a good night's sleep a few months back. As he registered at the desk, Ellie noticed a large growth on his left eye, almost forcing the lid shut.

"You don't have to have that growth on your eye," she told him.

The salesman stared at her. "What do you mean?"

"I mean Jesus can take it off. He doesn't want you to have it. He'll take it from you."

"Look, lady, I don't believe in magic. I don't even believe in God."

"But," she said gently, "that doesn't stop Him from believing in you."

And with that Ellie gave him the key to Room 3, which she has labeled "the miracle room for unbelievers."

"The miracle room?" I broke in.

Well, Ellie said, in a way all the rooms are miracle rooms. Each of the fourteen motel units had been dedicated to God for a specific purpose: a room for healing, a special room for honeymooners, one for alcoholics, another for the mending of broken relationships, the conviction room, the happiness room and so on.

No outward sign set the rooms apart, she said, just a ceremony held on April 20, 1965, when she had formally offered the motel to God. Ministers and friends came to take part in the service. First came a dedication prayer; then the group walked from room to room claiming each for its special purpose.

"We even anointed the doors and the beds with oil, the way it says in Exodus: 'And thou shalt take the anointing oil, and anoint . . . all that is therein, and shalt hallow it' (Exodus 40:9)."

"Oh, I know it sounds a little crazy," she added hastily, catching what must have been slightly quizzical looks from us. "And of course we don't know what God is going to do with the different people who stay. We just asked Him to be present in each room, to meet each guest."

As in the case of the pharmaceutical salesman. That night some members of Ellie's church were meeting for prayer in her living room. She invited the salesman to join them, but he declined. And so they prayed for him in his absence.

He left the next morning before anyone else was up. A few days later he was back. Even before he got to the desk Ellie could see that both eyes were perfectly normal—no growth.

"Shook me up," he blurted out. "I was driving down the road that morning when I happened to look in the rearview mirror, and that thing was gone! Simply wasn't there! Lady, I told you I don't believe in God, but maybe, if you introduced me . . ."

If the salesman was surprised, Ellie was not. Answered prayer is a common experience here. In fact, keeping the motel open at all requires daily answers. To cut down expenses Ellie, her sister and her mother not only do all the maid work but also the painting, repairs and upkeep.

Even so, there are many debts, for in order to purchase the motel Ellie had to borrow not only the mortgage money but the down payment as well.

186

"I asked God never to let me miss a payment, even by a day, to any of those people who had believed in the idea of the motel. And He never has."

He has, however, tested Ellie often and taught her much through this life of constant financial dependence. There was the time one midwinter when a $300 mortgage payment was due in a few days. She had but fifty dollars. For five consecutive nights not a single car stopped at the motel. And so, as she had done so often when money was lacking, Ellie began to pray. At last an inner voice seemed to tell her, Send the fifty dollars to Dave Wilkerson in New York for his work with young drug addicts.

Ellie was startled, as any of us would have been. Surely this was not the time to give away money! Then she remembered that Jesus had said, "Give, and it shall be given unto you" (Luke 6:38). It took courage, but she mailed off the fifty dollars that afternoon to Mr. Wilkerson.

That same night nine cars came in, one right after the other. The rest of the week the motel was filled to capacity. The mortgage money was paid on time.

Len and I sat silent a moment, digesting this idea.

"And all those customers," Len said at last. "How did you know which rooms to put them in?"

For some, like the salesman, it would be obvious, but most motorists stopping overnight simply pick up their room keys and say goodnight. How often, we asked her, do people stay to talk about their troubles?

Ellie's blue eyes smiled at us. "More often than you'd think. And when they don't, then I simply ask God about them."

One evening God seemed to tell her to put a certain

man in the room where alcoholics had often been helped, although there was nothing in his appearance to suggest this problem. Only the next morning did she learn what happened.

The guest was indeed a recovering alcoholic who had not had a drink in two years. But this night he was despondent because he had just lost his sister to cancer. Life was meaningless, he had decided. He tossed his suitcase onto the bed and was turning to leave the room, intending to get drunk, when he saw a book on the nightstand, *The Cross and the Switchblade* by Dave Wilkerson. He picked it up, curious. Three hours later he finished reading it.

"I knelt down by the bed," he confided to Ellie the next morning, "and once again rededicated my life to God."

The man has been returning regularly for what he calls "refilling."

The literature in each room is part of the ministry, and it goes far beyond the usual Gideon Bible. In our room, besides several books, I spotted the latest *Upper Room* and *Guideposts* and a pamphlet, *The Incomparable Christ.*

But even more important than what travelers read, Ellie is finding, is what they say when they know that someone is listening. She meets many lonely people crushed by problems or isolated in prisons of self, and she is often up half the night hearing their griefs. Indeed, the night we were there she sat up until two, talking and praying with a young couple who had just left their baby in a home for the retarded.

But there Ellie was next morning, bright and early, a stack of clean towels in one hand, a can of scouring powder in the other.

"Isn't it too bad," I said, "that someone else can't do these routine jobs, when God has given you so much work to do for Him?"

"For Him?" Ellie looked puzzled. "Oh, but this is the best time I spend with Him! This is when I go into each room and thank Him for His presence there."

As she sweeps, she said, she asks God to sweep away the fears, angers or doubts that have been left behind. Washing windows, she prays that His light may shine into the room. And making beds. . . .

"I've always had a bad back and making so many beds each day used to be a problem. Then I discovered that if I made beds kneeling, I wouldn't have to stoop over, and now it's the best prayer time I have!"

Stop doing God's work to wash and sweep and clean? Ellie cannot. For as she sees it, floors and beds and motel windows are as much His as church pews and stained glass. In fact, there is no work that cannot be done for Him.

The Healing of Maude Blanford

(*Guideposts*, April 1972)

I t was such a great healing story that I flew down to Louisville, Kentucky, to get the details from Maude Blanford herself.

The woman across the dining table from me had no trace of gray in her reddish hair, though she was past middle age, a grandmotherly type, comfortable to be with.

"My left leg had been hurting me," Mrs. Blanford began. "I thought it was because I was on my feet so much. Finally I went to the doctor. He found several tumor masses on my left side."

A specialist, Dr. O. J. Hayes, pronounced them malignant and prescribed radiation treatment. The treatment was followed by surgery.

After the operation, when Mrs. Blanford pleaded for the truth, the doctor admitted, "It is cancer and it's gone too far to remove. One kidney is almost nonfunctioning. The pelvic bone is affected—that's why the pain in your leg. I am so sorry."

Maude Blanford was sent home to die. Over a six-month period, while consuming $1,000 worth of pain-relieving drugs, she took stock of her spiritual resources and found them meager indeed. She had no church affiliation, no knowledge of the Bible, only the vaguest, most shadowy concept of Jesus.

The first week in January she suffered a cerebral hemorrhage and was rushed back to the hospital. For twelve days she lay unconscious; her husband was warned that if she survived the crisis it would probably be as a vegetable.

But Maude Blanford, oblivious to the world around her, was awake in a very different world. In her deep coma, a vivid image came to her. She saw a house with no top on it. The partitions between the rooms were there, the furniture in place, but there was no roof. She remembers thinking, Oh, we must put a roof on the house! If it rains, all the furniture will be spoiled.

When she came out of the coma, Mrs. Blanford's mind was very much intact, but bewildered. What could the roofless house have meant? As she puzzled over it, a Presence seemed to answer her.

"This Spirit seemed to show me," explained Mrs. Blanford, "that the house represented my body, but that without Jesus as my covering, my body had no protection."

I leaned forward, excited by an insight: Wasn't this what I had always been taught about the Holy Spirit— that His role was to show us Jesus and our need of Him?

"At that time," Mrs. Blanford went on, "I didn't know how to get the roof on my house."

From January until July, her condition worsened. Heart action and breathing became so difficult that she was reduced from normal speech to weak whispers. Even with the drugs, the suffering became unbearable. By July she knew she no longer had the strength to make

191

the trip for radiation treatment. "On July first I told the nurse I wouldn't be coming back."

But that day, as her son-in-law helped her into the car outside the medical building, she broke down and wept.

"At that moment I didn't want anything except for God to take me quickly, as I was. I said, 'God, I don't know who You are. I don't know anything about You. I don't even know how to pray. Just, Lord, have Your own way with me.'"

Though she did not realize it, Maude Blanford had just prayed one of the most powerful of all prayers—the prayer of relinquishment. By getting her own mind and will out of the way, she had opened the door to the Holy Spirit, as had happened during her period of unconsciousness in the hospital.

She did not have long to wait for evidence of His presence. Monday, July 4, dawned beautiful but hot. That afternoon Joe Blanford set up a cot for his wife outdoors under the trees. As the ill woman rested, hoping for the relief of a bit of breeze, into her mind poured some beautiful sentences:

> Is not this the fast that I have chosen? to loose the bands of wickedness, to undo the heavy burdens, and to let the oppressed go free, and that ye break every yoke? . . . Then shall thy light break forth as the morning, and thine health shall spring forth speedily. . . . Here I am.

I stared at Maude Blanford over the rim of my coffee cup. "But I thought you didn't know the Bible."

"I didn't! I'd never read a word of it. Only I knew this didn't sound like ordinary English. I thought, Is that

192

in the Bible? And right away the words came: *Isaiah 58.* Well, my husband got a Bible for me. I had to hunt and hunt to find the part called Isaiah. But then when I found those verses just exactly as I had heard them—except for the last three words, 'Here I am'—well, I knew God Himself had really spoken to me!"

Over the next weeks Maude Blanford read the Bible constantly, often until two or three in the morning, seeing the Person of Jesus take shape before her eyes. It was an amazing experience, without human assistance of any kind—no Bible teacher, no commentary, no study guide, simply reading the Bible with the Holy Spirit.

Along with her hunger to meet Jesus in the Word, the Holy Spirit gave her an intense desire to be out-of-doors, close to His world.

"Joe," she told her astonished husband one day, "I want to go fishing."

This made no sense to him. The terrain to the lake was rough. She would have to be carried down and then back up a steep hill.

But then some kindly neighbors offered to help him take her, so her husband acquiesced. She could not fish, of course, but she could observe: a breeze rippling the water, the wheeling birds and the distant hills. And as she looked, a response grew in her, a response that is another of the Holy Spirit's workings in the human heart: praise. All that day she praised Jesus for the world He had made. That night she slept like a baby.

After that, the lake trip became routine. A month or so later, Maude Blanford was walking up the hill to the road by herself. At home she had begun very slowly climbing the stairs, praising Jesus for each step attained. Or she would sit in a chair and dust a mahogany tabletop, saying, "Thank You, Jesus. Isn't this wood beautiful!"

Next she tried putting a small amount of water in a pail. Sitting in a kitchen chair, she would mop the floor in the area immediately around her, scoot the chair a few inches, mop again. "Thank You, Jesus, for helping me do this!"

Her daughter-in-law, who was coming over almost daily to clean house for her, asked one day in great puzzlement, "Mom, how is it that your kitchen floor never gets dirty?"

The older woman twinkled. "Well, I guess I'll have to confess—the Lord and I are doing some housework."

But their chief work, she knew, was not on this building of brick and wood, but on the house of her spirit, the house in her dream that had been roofless so long. Gradually, as her knowledge of Jesus grew, she sensed His protective love surrounding and sheltering her. Not that all pain and difficulties were over. She was still on pain-numbing narcotics, still experiencing much nausea as the aftermath of the radiation.

"The will to live is terribly important," she commented to me. "It takes a lot of self-effort just to get out of bed, to eat again after your food has just come up. This is when too many people give up."

One Saturday night, when the pain would not let her sleep, she lay on her bed praising God and reading the Bible. About two A.M. she drifted off to sleep with the Bible lying on her stomach. She felt that she was being carried to heaven, traveling a long way through space. Then came a voice out of the universe: "My child, your work is not finished. You are to go back." This was repeated three times, slowly, majestically, and then she was aware of her bedroom around her again.

The rest of the night she remained awake, flooded

194

with joy, thanking God. When her husband woke up in the morning, she told him, "Honey, Jesus healed me last night."

She could see that he did not believe it; there was no change in her outward appearance. "But I knew I was healed and that I had to tell people."

That very morning she walked to the Baptist church across the highway from their home and asked the minister if she could give a testimony. He was startled at the unusual request from someone who was not even a member of the congregation, but he gave permission, and she told the roomful of people that God had spoken to her in the night and healed her.

A few weeks later she insisted on taking a long bus trip to visit her son in West Virginia. Still on narcotics, still suffering pain, she nonetheless knew that the Holy Spirit was telling her to rely, from now on, on Jesus instead of drugs. At five o'clock in the afternoon of April 27, almost two years from the first diagnosis of cancer, on the return bus journey, as she popped a pain-killing pill into her mouth at a rest stop, she knew it would be the last one.

So it turned out. In retrospect, physicians now consider this sudden withdrawal as great a miracle as the remission of cancer cells to healthy tissue.

It took time to rebuild her body-house, nine months for her bad leg to be near normal, two years for all symptoms of cancer to vanish. When she called Dr. Hayes over some small matter, he almost shouted in astonishment. "Mrs. Blanford! What's happened to you! I thought you were—"

"You thought I was long since gone," she laughed back.

"Please come to my office at once and let me examine you! I've got to know what's happened."

"But why should I spend a lot of money for an examination when I'm a perfectly well woman?" she asked.

"Mrs. Blanford, I promise you, this one is on us!"

What the doctor found can best be stated in his own words:

"I had lost contact with Mrs. Blanford and had assumed that this patient had expired. She appeared in my office two and a half years following her operation. The swelling of her leg was gone. She had full use of her leg; she had no symptoms whatsoever, and on examination I was unable to ascertain whether or not any cancer was left. . . .

"She was seen again on November 5, at which time her examination was completely negative. . . .

"She has been seen periodically since that time for routine examinations. . . . She is absolutely asymptomatic. . . . This case is most unusual in that this woman had a proven, far-advanced metastatic cancer of the cervix and there should have been no hope whatsoever for her survival."

No hope whatsoever. . . . No hope except the hope on which our faith is founded.

The miracle of Maude Blanford reminds me again of that scene on the night before His crucifixion when Jesus spoke quietly to His despairing disciples: "Ye have not chosen me, but I have chosen you" (John 15:16). He is still saying that to us today, while His Spirit, always working through human beings, sometimes confounds us, often amazes us and is always the Guide to the true Giver of health and strength.

Section Seven

The Holy Spirit

The brief discussion Catherine and I had about the Holy Spirit early in our courtship was one of many to follow. The third Person of the Trinity was to become increasingly significant in our relationship and in every other aspect of our lives.

Here is how Catherine described her early experience with the Holy Spirit before we met; then His impact on our marriage, family members and friends in the 1960s and early 1970s.

Journey into Joy

It was during my college years and the early years of my marriage to Peter Marshall that I sensed something missing in my relationship to Jesus Christ. I had joined His church, I read God's Word regularly, I prayed to Him, but I sensed there was something more.

In 1943 tuberculosis sent me to bed 24 hours a day for an indefinite period.

Yet God brought good out of this seeming calamity. My search for health became a search for a relationship to God. One spring morning I knew it was time for the plunge—a quiet pledge to God, the promise of a blank check with my life. My healing began with that commitment.

A year or so after this commitment experience, I found myself with a lively curiosity about what seemed an odd subject—the Holy Spirit. Like most people, I had thought of the Holy Spirit as a theological abstraction, a sort of ecclesiastical garnish for christenings, weddings, benedictions and the like. As for the term "Holy Ghost"— that I regarded as archaic, if not downright eerie.

However odd the subject seemed, the fact remained that this was no passing curiosity. As is often the case when something is brought sharply to one's attention, everywhere I turned during those months I seemed to hear or read something about the Holy Spirit.

During our vacation on Cape Cod that summer, the church that Peter and I attended with Peter John included a talk for children as part of its regular Sunday service.

The first Sunday we were there, the guest preacher gave as his sermonette an object lesson on the Holy Spirit as related to the Trinity.

Three glass containers had been placed on a table before the young preacher. One was filled with water, the second with ice, the third with what appeared to be steam, probably dry ice.

"Children," he began, "perhaps you've heard of the Trinity. 'Trinity' means 'three.' When we speak of the Trinity, we mean the three Persons that go to make up God: God, the Father; Jesus Christ, the Son; and the Holy Spirit.

"Now look at these three jars. This one has water. This one has ice. And that one, steam. They all look different, don't they? Yet you know that ice is only frozen water. And when your mother boils water in a pan on the stove, steam rises from it. That means that water, ice and steam are really the same thing.

"Now, the same thing is true of the Trinity. Jesus Christ, the water of Life, is different from the Father— yet the same, too. The Holy Spirit, like the powerful steam that can drive an engine, is different from Christ and the Father, yet the same."

I listened, as interested as any of the children. What the young minister said that morning gave me a new concept and provided a background for approaching the subject that continued to occupy my mind.

About two months later something happened that took this interest out of the realm of theory and placed it on a personal basis. It was in the early fall of that year that my friends Tay and Fern told me of the experience of guidance they had had in Florida the previous winter.

I had known Tay for a long time. Often she had inner nudges and proddings of the kind would send her out to help a friend at a time of emergency that Tay could not, in any natural way, have known about.

Curiously I asked her, "How do you explain these intuitions?"

"Some people call them intuitions," Tay answered promptly. "But I prefer to call the help I get the direction of the Holy Spirit."

There it was again!

Tay was looking at me curiously. "What does the Holy Spirit mean to you?" she asked.

I remembered the sermonette at the Cape Cod church. "Oh, one of the three Persons of the Godhead, the third Person of the Trinity."

"But I sense something in the offhand way you say that—" She looked at me sharply. "Let me guess that in your mind the Spirit has an insignificant and unnecessary place. Isn't that right?"

I nodded. "That's right."

"But I know from personal experience that the Holy Spirit is just as great, just as needed as the other two Persons of the Trinity. Anyway, you still haven't answered my original question. What is He to you?"

Tay's intensity seemed to demand a candid reply.

"I've got to be truthful, Tay," I replied. "The Spirit is nothing to me. I've had no contact with it and could get along quite well without it."

Although at the time I believed my own statement, I was soon to find out that it was not so. As a matter of fact, I could not get along at all well without the Holy Spirit. Some searching in the Bible told me why.

Using a concordance and a notebook, I began methodically looking up all the references I could find on the third Person of the Trinity. Gradually I worked the findings into a logical outline in my notebook.

I learned that the Holy Spirit is not "an influence" but a Person; not "a thing" or an "it" but "He." In a sense, He is both the most basic and the most modest member of the Trinity, for His work is to reflect Christ and to glorify Him.

The obvious meaning of the word "glorify" is "to give homage to, as in worship." But there is a deeper meaning. Dr. Leslie Weatherhead in a 1952 Lenten sermon in the City Temple, London, brought out this richer meaning: "I would define glory as that expression of the nature of a person or thing which, of itself, evokes our praise."

Then the "glory" of a sunrise must be in the beauty of its delicate pinks and oranges reflected in the sky just before the sun itself appears. In this sense, the glory is in the qualities or characteristics of the sunrise that we can perceive.

The "glory" of Jesus Christ lies in the characteristics of His nature that make us want to adore Him. These traits are not kingly trappings or the halo placed around His head by medieval painters. Far from it! Men and women saw His glory in His humanity—His instant compassion, tenderness, understanding, fearlessness, incisiveness; His refusal to compromise with evil; His selflessness that culminated in His ultimate self-giving on the cross.

The apostle John puts it in unforgettable words: "And the Word was made flesh, and dwelt among us, (and we beheld his glory, the glory as of the only begotten of the Father,) full of grace and truth."

But then I found the New Testament declaring that these qualities of Jesus' nature are not apparent to us any more than a sunrise is apparent to a blind man. That is why we need the Holy Spirit—to make Christ's glory perceptible to us. It is as if the Spirit gives us a new way of seeing, with which we can perceive spiritual truth where all has been darkness before.

I found that Jesus had His own preferred names for the Spirit. Christ spoke in Aramaic, the tongue of His own people. This was the dialect of the bazaars and the seaside, replete with colorful idioms, metaphors and probably picturesque humor. There is good reason to believe that the tone of Jesus' speech was quite unlike the English of the King James Version of the early seventeenth century. The King James translators often rendered the Holy Spirit "the Holy Ghost." But Jesus liked to call Him "the Helper," "the Spirit of Truth," "the Teacher," "the Comforter," "the Counselor."

The Gospel of John was especially helpful in giving me more understanding about the Holy Spirit. In Christ's last talk with the eleven (Judas had already left the group), He made it clear that they were to experience Him through the Spirit. On that last night He had important things to say to His apostles, most of them concerning the Comforter.

The disciples knew that their Master was in imminent danger. They were frightened, sorrowful men.

"Do not be frightened about My leaving you," Jesus told them. And the future He promised to them, and to all believers, had these exciting components:

1. When He went away, He would send the Holy Spirit to be "poured out on all flesh," rather than

(as in the Old Testament) on a few chosen people—prophets, priests, kings (Acts 1:4–5, 2:17).

2. He Himself would be the Giver of (or Baptizer with) the Spirit (Mark 1:8; Matthew 3:11).

3. His plan was that this Spirit would dwell actually within our bodies. This would be God coming closer to man than He had ever been before (John 14:17).

4. The apostles and all believers who would follow them down through the ages were, from the moment of Jesus' ascension, entering a new era—the era of the Holy Spirit. This would last until Jesus' Second Coming in physical presence back to planet earth (John 7:39, 16:7).

5. The Spirit would make Jesus' continuing presence and His teachings real to us. He would always turn the spotlight on Jesus and glorify Him (John 15:26, 16:13–14).

6. The chief hallmark of the Holy Spirit would be power for service and ministry to others (Mark 16:15–18, 20, TLB).

7. The Spirit would be our Teacher, Guide, Comforter, Counselor, Prayer-Intercessor, Giver of joy, of freedom, of many spiritual gifts, of eternal life.

8 The Spirit would not ever be totally operative in an individual alone, but only in the fellowship of Christ's Body on earth—the Church (Ephesians 1:22–23).

9. The apostles and those who would come after must expect a degree of resistance, cleavage, even persecution and expulsion from their synagogues (or churches) because "the world cannot receive" the Spirit of truth (John 14:17).

10. After His resurrection and ascension the apostles were "to go into all the world and preach the Good News" (Mark 16:15, TLB). They were not to leave Jerusalem, however, or attempt any ministry of any kind until they had received the Holy Spirit (Acts 1:4).
11. Jesus promised that He would manifest Himself to us (John 14:21) and that the Spirit would lead us into further truth—all truth (John 16:13).

As I put all of this together back in 1945, it shed new light on the account of what happened next. That story is told in the book of Acts—really the Acts of the Holy Spirit. The Spirit's first great miracle was to transform the erstwhile timid, cowardly and contentious disciples into bold men moving with power and authority. Thus the infant Church was born.

Jesus' promise to lead us into further truth began to be fulfilled immediately. Old religious mores and set habit patterns had to be broken.

Virgin truth is always unexpected, often shocking. Though Jesus had spoken often of the Holy Spirit to the apostles, I could find no record that He had mentioned details of the Pentecost to come, such as the sound of a roaring wind or flames of fire, or the sudden speaking of languages they had never learned. Nor were the disciples prepared for the "further truth" that their Jewish food taboos were no longer necessary, or that the Gentiles were also beloved by the Father and chosen by Him to receive the Spirit.

In fact, it seemed to me that Jesus' promise of "further truth" gives us clear reason to believe that not all the truth and instruction Christ has to give us is contained in the canon of the Old and New Testaments. How could it be? He who is Truth will never find the people of any given century able to receive everything He wants to give.

Because the Holy Spirit is a living, always contemporary personality, down all the centuries there must be an ever-unfolding manifestation of Jesus, His personality, His ways of dealing with us, along with new, fresh disclosures of the mind of the Father. I found this concept endlessly provocative . . . and I still do.

At this point in my study some action on my part was clearly indicated. I had already summarized how we receive the Spirit:

1. By going directly to Christ for Him.
2. By asking for the gift of the Spirit.
3. By receiving the Spirit by faith (the only way to receive any gift from God).
4. By entering upon the discipline of hourly, daily obedience to Christ and the Spirit.

So very simply I asked Jesus for the gift of the Helper, thanked Him for granting this and entered upon that fourth step—the daily living out of this new relationship. I experienced no waves of emotion or ecstasy.

When I had asked myself, "Can we expect a manifestation of the Spirit?", I had little idea how to answer. Since the Helper is a Person, I reasoned, then of course He has personality traits, and presumably these traits will show themselves. How or in what way, I could not guess.

Manifest Himself He did, though not in a way I could have guessed. As I stepped out in faith back in 1945, listening day by day to the inner Voice for instructions, the first discipline He gave me was a leash for my tongue. For others the Spirit may give torrents of ecstatic speech; I needed the discipline of not speaking the careless or negative or discouraging word. For weeks I was put through the sharp training of opening my mouth to speak and hearing from the Teacher, Stop! No, don't say it. Close the mouth.

Many other experiences followed, such as the joy of discovering the Helper's concern with guiding us in the details of everyday life, the way He brings us to life at the emotional level. None of this I could have predicted. My experience was rather a solitary one. In 1945 I knew no one who was experimenting along the same line.

I realized that my husband, Peter, had already been given the Helper, along with the Spirit's gift of preaching. Unlike me, he had not been seeking the Spirit per se, rather what God's specific will for his life was. Probably the Helper had come to Peter at the time he was "tapped on the shoulder by the Chief," as he liked to put it, and told to emigrate to America to enter the ministry. Having long known the Spirit's presence and help in so many ways, Peter did not feel the need for conscious search that I did.

Later, at the time of my husband's sudden death, I shall be forever grateful that I was able to know the Spirit as Comforter. Without Him I might have survived, but only as a truncated person and without ever knowing the grace and splendor of the Comforter's presence on this, one of life's starkest frontiers. Not only did He comfort me, but in one practical step after another He showed me how to handle the devastation of widowhood.

By 1950 I was in need of another kind of help. I was under contract to deliver the manuscript of *A Man Called Peter* by May 1, yet had never had a single course in the craft of writing and had almost no practice except scribbling in personal diaries and journals. In that extremity, the Spirit became my Instructor in creative writing.

He took me by the hand, for instance, and showed me that the opening pages must present Peter Marshall in the framework in which the public knew him—through his Senate chaplaincy. Only then could I flash back (I did not even know the term flashback) to Peter's early life in Scotland and come forward.

I tried to outline the book and knew that it was not right. When I asked my Teacher the right way of outlining the book, I was told that Peter's biography would have no lasting significance apart from what his life demonstrated about God—His goodness, His revelation of truth, His ways of dealing with humankind. "Outline the book that way" was the instruction. I did, and the material fell into place.

My Teacher showed me how to construct a book, what to include out of the totality of one man's life, what to omit. All the way through He kept insisting on the importance of the light touch and humor as the way to emphasize greatness.

Now I experienced all the emotion I had not felt when I'd first asked for His presence—plus much, much more.

"No creative work," He told me, "has final impact unless it touches the reader at the emotional level." As I worked on the manuscript, He poured through me a stream of strong emotion, yet permitted me none of the sentimentality into which I was tempted to slip.

So functional and effectual was the Teacher's guidance that I had fewer editorial suggestions, less outside help with *A Man Called Peter* than with any book since, and I wrote it more swiftly.

The Jesus People

Little did I dream that some ten years later I would see the rise of a major surge of the Spirit like a ground-swell across the world.

For me, it began with an encounter I had with John Sherrill, a top editor at *Guideposts*.

As with most of us, it was personal need that brought John to the point of commitment. My need had been a long illness. John's was a more immediate physical crisis. Two years before he had had a malignant mole removed from his ear that had been diagnosed as melanoma, one of the most vicious killers of all types of cancer. Miraculously, everyone felt, it had been caught in time. But now the doctor had discovered a small lump on John's neck that was suspect.

The details of the physical problem and the prayers for healing are not the point I want to make here. Suffice it to say that as soon as I heard about the situation, I knew that John's crisis was also my crisis, part of "my bundle" of responsibility, as the Quakers express it so vividly. Then: How were we who were so concerned to pray about John?

A series of thoughts kept pounding at me and would not be put aside: Healing is not an end in itself; it is a dividend of the Gospel. Physical health is but one part of total wholeness. Then came the inevitable question: Had John ever made an act of turning his whole being over to God?

Who was I to ask John a question like that? He was

an intellectual—an editor and successful writer. Any emotional approach to Christianity, as well as the usual religious clichés and shibboleths, were repugnant to him. Considering all this, would not any question about his relationship to God be gross presumption on my part and anathema to him?

Still, time was running out. Only 24 hours remained until John would enter New York's Memorial Hospital for surgery. After all, what he thought of me did not matter at a time like this. The fact that a life was at stake gave me the courage to telephone John and tell him that I had to see him.

His wife, Elizabeth—Tib—came over with him. The three of us found a quiet room and shut ourselves in. There was no attempt at a subtle approach. I explained what had led up to my telephone call, what I had learned about the process of entering in, and why this seemed important as a foundation for any prayer for healing. My heart was in what I was saying, so that several times my voice broke.

When I had finished, John asked wonderingly, "Do you mean that I can just decide that I am willing for God to take over my life, and tell Him so, as blandly and matter-of-factly as that, and have it work?"

"That's right," was my reply. "Do it as matter-of-factly as you please. You do not have to have all your theological beliefs sorted out. Nor do you have to understand everything. You just come to Christ as you are— questions, complexes, contradictions, doubts, everything. After all, how else can any of us come? You make a definite movement of your will toward God. After that, the next move is up to Him. The feelings, the proof that He has heard and has taken you on, even the understanding, will come later."

At that point John and Tib had to rush away for their last hasty preparations for the hospital. It was not until later that I found out what happened immediately after they left me.

"After we told you goodbye and backed out of your driveway," John told me, "I did the simple thing you had suggested—just said yes to God while driving the car. I can show you the exact spot on Millwood Road where it happened, right by a certain telephone pole.

"Then, because it had been such a quiet, interior thing, I felt that I ought to go on record by telling someone. So I said to Tib, I suppose a bit ruefully, 'Well, I'm a Christian now.'

"And she asked curiously, 'Do you feel any different?'

" 'Not a bit different,' I told her."

Yet John is different now—so different. That quiet transaction at that certain spot on Millwood Road launched John into a series of adventures with the Holy Spirit. But to finish this particular story, when the famous New York specialist operated on John, all he could find was a dried-up nodule, easy to remove. There was no malignancy.

Following his personal commitment to Jesus Christ, John discovered that as a reporter his story interests were switching from the practical and inspirational to the supernatural. That's why David Wilkerson intrigued him.

David Wilkerson was the skinny Pentecostal preacher from the boondocks of Pennsylvania who told his small congregation that God wanted him to go to New York and make the Lord Jesus real to teenage gang members in the inner city.

"But what can one country preacher do in that cesspool?" his church people asked.

David didn't know. He would trust God to show him. And God did. The Holy Spirit moved so powerfully among those teenagers through David's ministry that the media—and John Sherrill—were intrigued.

John proposed a series of articles for *Guideposts* magazine, but there was such skepticism among several editors over the dramatic conversions of tough, crime-addicted teenagers that John suggested that David himself come to the *Guideposts* office and tell his story. He did, and described effectively how the Holy Spirit transforms people. Still, not all were convinced.

Len, as the editor, had to make the decision. He didn't know at the time what a big decision it was. "Let's go with the Wilkerson series," he decided.

The articles had a huge impact on *Guideposts* readers; mail poured in, the great majority favorable.

A book publisher was interested. Both John and Elizabeth worked with David on *The Cross and the Switchblade*, a book that became a huge bestseller worldwide, was made into a successful movie and sparked the growing movement of the Holy Spirit.

John Sherrill was now a reporter on the trail of an even bigger story—the twentieth-century reenactment of the book of Acts. What about this "baptism of the Spirit"? What about tongues?

To a Full Gospel Business Men's meeting in Atlantic City, John came as a reporter. The sponsors asked John if he would like to be prayed for to receive the baptism. John was torn. The skeptical side of him said a firm no. The new believer side said, "Why not?"

He went to a hotel room with a half-dozen charismatic leaders, curious, open. The prayer began with several men laying hands on John. As John himself described it:

"The ceiling split open and this shaft of light poured through. I was thrown to the floor, my glasses flew off, joy welled up inside me. I laughed; I wept. Then I heard strange sounds pouring from my mouth."

Later that night John called Len and me from Atlantic City, urging us to drive down from Chappaqua to share his incredible experience. We couldn't. So a few days later John drove over to our house. He opened his mouth to describe what happened, said the word *Jesus* and began to weep. It was months until he could say the name *Jesus* without shedding tears.

John and Elizabeth had nearly completed a well-researched, objective and very arm's-length book about glossolalia—tongues. Now Len and I urged them to recast it as John's personal search. *They Speak with Other Tongues* captured the imagination of millions. By the late 1960s the Holy Spirit movement had the full attention of America.

Now came the big surprise. Young people who before had been indifferent or even hostile to religion groped their way—some of them through the jungle of drugs or the occult or Eastern religions—to become "Jesus people." They not only carried Bibles, they read them feverishly. They waded into the ocean or into backyard swimming pools to be baptized. All over the world they formed communities.

The Jesus Revolution was marked by highly charged emotionalism—hand-clapping, hugging, singing, religious rock music, exclamations of "Wow!" and "Far out!"

Some of these youthful experimenters, of course,

were not serious and soon drifted away. Yet many had their lives turned right-side-up.

One night at the dinner table Chester was almost too busy talking to eat. He had flown in from Taylor University that afternoon, having just finished his freshman year.

Chester's voice was excited. "Pops, you wouldn't have believed the scene in the Notre Dame football stadium last weekend."

"Football in June?" his father asked quizzically.

"No—singing and prayer and praising the Lord, 25,000 people. It was fantastic!"

"What was the occasion?"

"A big meeting of the Catholic Jesus People. A bunch of us drove up from Taylor. Six hundred priests came pouring onto the field from where the players enter, singing, carrying banners. The whole place was clapping and cheering. I've never seen people so excited."

Later that week we read *Time* magazine's coverage of the event: First, men in business suits or sport coats carrying banners aloft, *The Spirit of Jesus Among Us* emerging from the football team's tunnel onto the Notre Dame field. Then the double line of priests in white robes and clerical stoles singing, their arms raised heavenward, hands open, palms up. The excitement of the crowd building, erupting into applause. As eight Roman Catholic bishops, followed by Cardinal Suenens of Belgium, resplendent in a brilliant red chasuble, came into view, the clapping exploded into a mighty roar.

To the crowd of 25,000 in the stadium, Cardinal Suenens said, "The Pentecostal renewal is not a movement. It is a current of grace . . . growing fast everywhere in the world. I feel it coming. I see it coming."

The seedbed of the Catholic Pentecostal movement was a group of four or five laymen (all members of the Duquesne University faculty) who had begun meeting together in the fall of 1966. A book that fell into their hands led them to ask for the gift of the Holy Spirit for themselves. Yes, it was David Wilkerson's *The Cross and the Switchblade* written by John and Elizabeth Sherrill. Two other books were also key to the movement: John Sherrill's *They Speak with Other Tongues* and Dennis Bennett's *Nine O'Clock in the Morning.*

Like most adults I have watched the Jesus Revolution among our young people with emotions ranging from delight to wonder to perplexity. Yet surely they have been saying something important that the rest of us need to hear: We could use more joy and more love in our spiritual lives. Perhaps we have become so occupied with worshiping God with our minds that we have forgotten that the rest of our beings, including the physical body, need to worship Him, too.

Self-forgetfulness, a sort of joyous, holy abandon, is indeed one of the Helper's trademarks. As Len and I became involved in the movement we formed a prayer group with the Sherrills that met weekly in our homes.

One evening Len shared with the group a problem he had at work and asked for prayer. Two women stood by his chair, rested their hands lightly on his shoulders and head, and prayed that the power of the Holy Spirit would free Len of resentments about the situation. He told me later that he felt warmth coming from their hands. The prayer ended, Len expressed gratitude and the meeting broke up.

Hours later, after we were in bed, Len spoke softly.

"Catherine, I hate to wake you up, but I have the strangest feeling."

A little alarmed, I asked, "How do you mean?"

"There's this rushing, headlong joy inside me! It started in the pit of my stomach after I got in bed, then has kept bubbling up right into my head. I've been lying here thinking how silly it is to be so joyous when I should be asleep, but I can't control it. Catherine, I'd like to pray about it."

"Well, fine," I responded sleepily. "Go ahead—pray."

"But it isn't enough just to lie here. I'd like to kneel."

So both of us knelt beside the bed.

Len's prayer began quietly enough. First he expressed gratitude for the friends who had cared enough to pray for him. Then he thanked God for our life together. After that he expressed love for each member of our family, near and far. In between he kept telling the Lord how much he loved Him. Heartfelt love rose from the depths of his being for each person who had been a human thorn in Len's side. Afterwards he began God-blessing everyone he could think of, as if this love were so great it had to encompass the whole universe.

Always before Len's prayers had been short, even abrupt. Well thought out, words carefully chosen, quite unemotional. That night, in contrast, words poured from him lavishly, exuberantly repetitious, a geyser of deep emotion, unabashedly expressed. Like a bird uncaged, his emotions were darting, wheeling, soaring, wanting nothing so much as to keep on flying forever.

Minutes passed, half an hour, an hour, as love and joy kept pouring from Len. Finally, becoming aware of me kneeling there, too, Len interrupted himself long enough to say reluctantly, "This isn't fair to you, Catherine. I'd like to go on and on, but you need some sleep."

In the morning he reported, "It was the most cleansing experience I've ever had. I got to thinking it was almost like a car engine being overhauled. It's as though negative emotions—my frustrations and anger—had built up a residue in my body just as carbon deposits foul up spark plugs. That love and joy pouring through me was like fresh, warm, sudsy water washing away the bitterness. This morning I have—I don't know—a scrubbed feeling."

Together we praised God for His answer to the prayer of the previous evening. As always He had done "above all that we ask or think."

Walk in the Spirit

In 1970 I received as a gift a very old copy of one of my favorite books, *The Christian's Secret of a Happy Life* by the Quaker Hannah Whitall Smith. As I eagerly turned the yellowed old pages of this 1885 edition—but what was this? A chapter on the Holy Spirit? I had many editions of this book in my library, knew this book practically by heart, and there was no such chapter.

Why the deletion? I wondered.

I couldn't wait to read the chapter. As usual, Hannah Smith turned to the Bible first to summarize what it taught about the Spirit, then took a middle-of-the-road position seasoned liberally with common sense. The gist of her conclusion went something like this. . . .

We make the mistake of looking upon the "baptism of the Spirit" as a single experience rather than a life, as an arbitrary bestowment rather than a necessary vitality. It is plain from Scripture that we cannot possibly enter into a new life in Christ without knowing the Holy Spirit.

There is a big difference, however, between being indwelt by the Spirit and being "filled" with His presence. For years, sometimes a lifetime, a Christian can keep the Spirit at a sub-basement level by the insistence on running one's own life. Then, through teaching or need or both, the person consciously recognizes his divine Guest's presence, opens the hitherto-closed doors into certain rooms in his being so that the Spirit

218

can enter there, too. Thus the individual now deliberately abandons himself to the Helper's control.

"The result of this when done suddenly," Mrs. Smith explained, "is what many call 'the baptism of the Holy Spirit.' It can be, but isn't always, a very emotional and overwhelming sense of His presence."

Hannah Smith's words helped me to understand my own experience 25 years before when, after searching the Scriptures, I had asked God for the gift of the Holy Spirit and in faith thanked Him for granting this. Unlike Len's experience, I felt no waves of emotion or ecstasy. Later, too, when I was given the gift of a heavenly language, it was with no particular fanfare but as a divine quartermaster might casually hand out a tool for a job: "Here, you'll need this."

"In seeking for the baptism," Mrs. Smith continued, "it is not God's attitude toward us that needs to be changed, but our attitude toward Him. He will not give us anything new; rather, we are to receive in a new and far fuller sense that which He has already given at Pentecost. The Holy Spirit is the world's sunlight, its energy and power. Sunlight can be kept out only by erecting barriers against it. All we need do, then, is take down our shutters and barriers and walk out into the sunlight already given."

Though the experience may involve the emotions, Hannah Smith cautioned, it means more than that. "It means to be immersed or dipped into the Spirit of God, into His character and nature. The real evidence of one's baptism is neither emotion nor any single gift such as tongues, rather that there must be Christlikeness in life and character. By fruits in the life we shall know whether or not we have the Spirit."

Nor does this mean instantaneous holiness. The disciples had to learn that after Pentecost, and so do we. Ananias and Sapphira could still lie and cheat, and so can we. In practical fact, our life with the Spirit is a walk, a growth, an unfolding, as we learn to trust Him and open more and more of our being to His presence and control.

To me this seemed such solid teaching that I wondered all the more why the chapter had been deleted from all more recent editions of the book. Intent upon unraveling the mystery, I sought the story behind this chapter. These are the facts as I dug them out of Hannah Whitall Smith's letters and writings, and recent books about the Smith family.

Hannah was born in Philadelphia on February 7, 1832, into a Quaker family, eminently successful glass manufacturers. Though Hannah grew up a lively girl in a happy home, by age sixteen she was writing of "the aching void in my heart." This was in part adolescent drama, but the spiritual hunger was real, so much so that for the rest of her long life she was an eager, open-minded spiritual seeker.

Such eagerness might have led this Quaker girl straying down dead ends and onto paths of heresy. Fortunately she possessed qualities to balance her insatiable zeal—a thorough knowledge of Scripture and a high degree of common sense.

In 1865 Hannah and her husband, Robert Pearsall Smith, and their children moved to the village of Milltown, New Jersey, where Robert took charge of a branch of the family glass business. There Hannah met a group called "the Holiness Methodists." Some of the most penetrating and valuable parts of *The Christian's Secret*, a book helpful to generations of Christians, were to come from what Hannah learned from this group.

One summer the Smiths went to a ten-day Holiness camp meeting at a woodland campsite along the New Jersey shore. The purpose of these meetings, in Hannah's words, was "to open our hearts to the teachings of the Holy Spirit and His coming into seekers' hearts." But it was Robert rather than his wife who received an extraordinary emotional experience. As Hannah later reported it:

> After the meeting my husband had gone alone into a spot in the woods to continue to pray by himself. Suddenly, from head to foot he was shaken with what seemed like a magnetic thrill of heavenly delight, and floods of glory seemed to pour through him, soul and body, with the inward assurance that this was the longed-for Baptism of the Holy Spirit.
>
> The whole world seemed transformed for him; every leaf and blade of grass quivered with exquisite colour. . . . Everybody looked beautiful to him, for he seemed to see the Divine Spirit within each one. . . .
>
> This ecstasy lasted for several weeks, and was the beginning of a wonderful career of spiritual power and blessing.

Naturally this made Hannah renew her efforts to receive similar joy. She described how she "went forward" to the altar night after night in the meetings, then with a smaller group to one of the tents, where they spent hours kneeling in the dark, pleading and wrestling in prayer. For Mrs. Smith all this effort seemed of no avail. Not then or ever did she have an emotional experience of the type that had meant so much to her husband.

At first Hannah was disappointed. Then she realized that what had been given her was a "real revelation of God that made life to me a different thing ever since." She wanted emotions and was given conviction. She "wanted a vision and got a fact."

Later Mrs. Smith came to feel that the difference between her and her husband's experiences was largely a reflection of the difference in their natures: Robert was emotional, inclined to feel response in physical sensations; Hannah was more reserved and analytical.

A year or so later Robert traveled to Germany, where he held highly successful evangelistic meetings before large crowds, always in an intensely emotional atmosphere. "All Europe is at my feet," exulted Robert in a letter to his wife. When engraved pictures of him were offered for sale, eight thousand sold immediately.

Then the blow fell: gossip about Robert Pearsall Smith's improper conduct with female admirers. No one then or now knows the exact truth of the matter. The emotionalism so appealing to Smith had apparently gotten out of hand; Paul's instruction to "salute one another with an holy kiss" had been followed too eagerly.

The rumors got into the press. Meetings scheduled in England were canceled by their sponsors. Hannah stood quietly by her husband. She wrote a friend of the "crushing blow" that had befallen Robert.

And crush him it did. He gave way to discouragement, disillusionment and to a degree of cynicism. Robert sank into a joyless old age, while Hannah went on from strength to strength, her quiet, deep faith carrying her triumphantly over all sorts of trials and difficulties.

What can we learn from this for today? Each opportunity for Christian growth, each step forward, brings new temptations and dangers. In Robert Smith's case, tragedy resulted when he exalted personal experience instead of the Lord Jesus. With Hannah Smith, there was little ecstasy but a quieter joy from the fruitage of her convictions about God.

As for the missing chapter, clearly by the early 1900s editors had grown afraid of the subject. The Holy Spirit is fire. Hadn't Robert Smith been burned? Safer to omit all discussion of it.

As Len and I pondered Hannah's story, we agreed that the modern surge of the Spirit in America may stand poised at the edge of this same problem: too great a love affair with emotion, too little grounding in Scripture, too much wanting in garden-variety discipline, too small an emphasis on purity, honesty, morality—Christ's own life living in us.

What is needed, of course, is balance—plenty of solid teaching, but plenty of joy as well. Let's admit that overemotionalism is the last problem most of us face in our denominational churches. We shall achieve a proper mix of freedom and discipline, however, when we are truly led by the Helper, "always a Gentleman."

It may well be that the missing element in Robert Pearsall Smith's experience was a small corrective fellowship of other Christians like that of the infant Church in Acts 5. What was still missing in the late nineteenth century was a body of wisdom concerning the Holy Spirit movement.

Recent experience is teaching us that as we go adventuring in the Spirit, we must deliberately make ourselves subject one to the other, willing to be checked and corrected as well as encouraged and strengthened.

Section
Eight

Prayer Power

During our first date, that all-day trip along Virginia's Skyline Drive, I expected to find Catherine prim, super-spiritual, self-confident.

She greeted me wearing a casual blouse and a trim skirt that revealed two very shapely legs. More interesting disclosures were to come: She had recently learned to play bridge. She had taken ballroom dancing lessons.

"My life had become too one-dimensional," she admitted.

Most surprising to me: that what came through during our long talks that day was her sense of inadequacy. Despite ten years of success as a Christian writer and speaker, she had strong feelings of self-doubt as a mother and in social situations.

"That's why prayer is so crucial to me. When I go to Jesus with my helplessness, He hears me and responds. He is always adequate when I am inadequate."

After we were married I suggested Catherine write about some of her experiences with prayer for *Guideposts*. She did a series of articles that *Guideposts* eventually put into a booklet entitled *Adventures in Prayer*. Hundreds of thousands were distributed during the 1960s. Later the material was expanded into a book of the same title that has sold over a million copies.

Here are some excerpts.

The Prayer of Helplessness

When I lived in the nation's capital, I used to notice how often the Washington papers reported suicide leaps from the Calvert Street Bridge. This happens so repeatedly, in fact, that the site is often called "Suicide Bridge."

Sensing the human drama behind these brief notices—like the plunge of the Air Corps major's 31-year-old wife with inoperable cancer, or that of the elderly man whose wife had just died—I often thought there was probably a common denominator in all these tragedies. Each person must have felt helpless.

And I have thought, "If I could speak with such persons at the zero hour, I would try to stop them with the thought that helplessness is one of the greatest assets a human being can have."

For I believe that the old cliché "God helps those who help themselves" is not only misleading but often dead wrong. My most spectacular answers to prayers have come when I was helpless, so out of control as to be able to do nothing at all for myself.

The psalmist says: "When I was hemmed in, thou hast freed me often" (Psalm 4:1, Moffatt). Gradually I have learned to recognize this hemming-in as one of God's most loving devices for teaching us that He is real and gloriously adequate for our problems.

One such experience occurred during the writing of

my first book under my own name. As the young widow of Peter Marshall, I was attempting what many felt was the rather audacious project of writing his biography. About midway through the manuscript, I received devastating criticism from one whose judgment I trusted. He told me bluntly, "You haven't even begun to get inside the man Peter Marshall."

And he was right, that was the sting of it. The realization of my inadequacy as a writer was not only an intellectual one. It was also emotional; there were plenty of tears. But out of the crisis came a major realization: In my helplessness, there was no alternative but to put the project into God's hands. I prayed that *A Man Called Peter* be His book, and that the results be all His, too.

And they were. I still regard as incredible the several million copies of *A Man Called Peter* circulating around the world. But numbers are of little importance compared to what I hear from time to time of individual lives changed through this book, of men entering the ministry through the inspiration of Peter Marshall's life.

Years later I saw the Prayer of Helplessness work in an everyday situation—the matter of household help. Before my marriage to Leonard LeSourd in the fall of 1959, I was full of trepidation at the thought of taking on the care of his three young children. My only child, Peter John, had been off at college for over three years, and I had involved myself with a writing career.

In his efforts to reassure me, Len was blithe with promises of household help. But the help situation in Chappaqua, New York, proved unbelievably tight. Months passed. One woman stayed a few weeks, then left. We tried the classified columns without success; persistent prayer brought us no nearer a solution. I finally decided I would have to do it all myself—take care of the family and meet my writing deadlines; but I soon found it was more than a full-time job running a lively household. Week after week I did not get near my desk.

So once again the old familiar pattern: the Prayer of Helplessness—the admission that I could not do everything myself; then the insight that my main responsibility was to our home. If God wanted me to resume my writing, He would show me the way.

After that admission of helplessness, Lucy Arsenault was sent to us. Lucy—steady, reliable, loyal, a marvelous cook, a great person.

Why would God insist on helplessness as a prerequisite to answered prayer? One obvious reason is that our human helplessness is bedrock fact. God is a realist and insists that we be realists, too. So long as we are deluding ourselves that human resources can supply our heart's desires, we are believing a lie. And it is impossible for prayers to be answered out of a foundation of self-deception and untruth.

Then what is the truth about our human condition? None of us had anything to do with our being born, no control over whether we were male or female, Japanese or Russian or American, white or yellow or black. Nor can we influence our ancestry, nor our basic mental or physical equipment.

After we are born, an autonomic nervous system controls every vital function that sustains life. A power that no one really understands keeps our heart beating, our lungs breathing, our blood circulating, our body temperature at 98.6 degrees. A surgeon can cut tissue but he is helpless to force the body to bind the severed tissue together again. We grow old relentlessly and automatically.

Self-sufficient? Scarcely!

Even the planet on which we live—we had nothing to do with its creation, either. The little planet earth is exactly the right distance, some 93 million miles, from the source of its heat and light. Any nearer and we would be consumed by solar radiation; any farther and we would be frozen to death. The balance of oxygen and nitrogen in the air is exactly right for the support of life, the elements in our soil and the water on which we depend, the creation of rare rock deposits. . . . All this goes on quite apart from man—little man who struts and fumes upon the earth.

Did Jesus have any comment about all this? Yes, as always He put His finger on the very heart of the matter: "Without me ye can do nothing" (John 15:5).

Nothing? That seems a trifle sweeping! After all, human beings have made great progress. We have almost eliminated diseases like smallpox, bubonic plague, tuberculosis, polio and most of the communicable diseases of childhood. We have learned to control our environment to quite an extent. We have put men on the moon. How can all that be helplessness?

Most of us do not enjoy that idea. The cult of humanism since the Renaissance has trained us to believe that we are quite adequate to be masters of our own destiny.

Yet not only did Jesus insist on the truth of our helplessness; He underscored it by telling us that this same helplessness applied equally to Him while He wore human flesh: "The Son can do nothing of himself, but what he seeth the Father do" (John 5:19). In this as in everything else, He was setting the pattern for imperfect humanity.

The Scriptures spell out for us point by point how

helpless we are in relation to our spiritual lives as well as our physical ones. . . .

We feel an impulse toward God. We think we are reaching out for Him. Not so, Jesus told us. "No one is able to come to me unless he is drawn by the Father" (John 6:44, Moffatt).

We want eternal life and release from our sins. We think we can earn this salvation. No. The truth is, "It is the gift of God: Not of works, lest any man should boast" (Ephesians 2:8–9).

So far as the virtues and graces we long for in our lives—faith, joy, patience, peace of mind—there is no way we can work up such qualities. Paul tells us in Galatians 5:22–23 that these are gifts of the Holy Spirit; they can be had in no other way. "A man can receive nothing, except it be given him from heaven" (John 3:27).

This emphasis on our helplessness is found over and over in the writings of Christians in other eras. For instance, in that little jewel of a seventeenth-century book, Brother Lawrence's *Practice of the Presence of God*, helplessness was the hinge on which turned the Carmelite lay brother's relationship with God:

> That when an occasion of practicing some virtue offered, he addressed himself to God, saying, "Lord, I cannot do this unless Thou enablest me"; and that then he received strength more than sufficient.

> That when he had failed in his duty, he only confessed his fault, saying to God, "I shall never do otherwise if You leave me to myself; it is You who must hinder my falling, and mend what is

231

amiss." That after this he gave himself no further uneasiness about it.*

Though few of us have Brother Lawrence's maturity, nevertheless sometime in life every one of us finds himself out of control, caught in circumstances he is helpless to change. When this happens, welcome such times! Often it is only then that we lesser spirits enter into the truth of Jesus' statement "Without me ye can do nothing."

Dr. Arthur Gossip, who wrote the exposition on John for *The Interpreter's Bible*, has this interesting comment: "These are surely the most hopeful words in Scripture. . . . For it is on the basis of that frank recognition of our utter fecklessness apart from Him, that Christ . . . gives us His great promises. . . ."

Great promises! Like this glorious one, sweeping enough to make up a thousand times over for our helplessness: "With God all things are possible" (Matthew 19:26). He is telling us that an omnipotent, transcendent and immanent God is above all and through all, far more completely than we realize.

With helplessness alone, one would be like a bird trying to fly with one wing. But when the other wing of God's adequacy is added to our helplessness, then the bird can soar triumphantly above and through problems that hitherto have defeated us.

* Brother Lawrence, *Conversations: The Practice of the Presence of God* (Grand Rapids: Fleming H. Revell Co., 1973), pp. 15, 16.

I have always been impressed by the story of Dr. A. B. Simpson, the famous New York preacher.* Poor health had haunted this man. Two nervous breakdowns plus a heart condition led a well-known New York physician to tell him when he was only 38 that he would never live to be forty.

The physician's diagnosis underscored the physical helplessness that the minister knew only too well. Preaching was an agonizing effort. Climbing even a slight elevation brought on a suffocating agony of breathlessness.

In desperation, sick in body and despairing in spirit, Dr. Simpson went at last to his Bible to find out exactly what Jesus had to say about disease. He became convinced that Jesus had always meant healing to be part of His Gospel for the redemption of man's total being.

One Friday afternoon soon after this revelation, Dr. Simpson took a walk in the country. He was forced to walk painfully, slowly, for he was always out of breath. Coming to a pine woods, he sat down on a log to rest. Soon he found himself praying, telling God of his complete helplessness with regard to his physical condition.

But to this helplessness he added his belief that God was "for health" all the way. It was that majestically powerful combination again, "My total inadequacy, Your perfect adequacy." He then asked Christ to enter him and become his physical life, for all the needs of his body, until his life work was done.

* A. B. Simpson, *The Gospel of Healing* (Harrisburg, Pa: Christian Publications, Inc., 1915), p 169ff.

"There in the woods," he said later, "I made a connection with God. Every fiber in me was tingling with the sense of God's presence."

A few days after that, Simpson climbed a mountain 3,000 feet high. "When I reached the top," he related joyfully, "the world of weakness and fear was lying at my feet. From that time on I had literally a new heart in my breast."

And so he did. During the first three years after this healing he preached more than a thousand sermons, conducted sometimes as many as twenty meetings in one week. His testimony was that never once did he feel exhausted. For the rest of his life he was noted for the amazing volume of his sermonic, pastoral and literary work. He lived to be 76.

Simpson's work, moreover, has lived after him. The Christian and Missionary Alliance, which he founded, is still a potent spiritual force today; his books are still being published and are blessing millions.

Why is prayer so startlingly effective when we admit our helplessness? First, as we have seen, because God insists upon our facing up to the facts of our human situation. In addition, this recognition and acknowledgment of our helplessness is the quickest way to that right attitude so essential to prayer. It deals a mortal blow to the most serious sin of all—man's independence that ignores God.

Another reason is that we cannot learn firsthand about God—what He is like, His love for us as individuals, His real power—so long as we are relying on ourselves and other people. And fellowship with Jesus is the true purpose of our life, the only foundation for eternity.

So if your every human plan and calculation has miscarried, if, one by one, human props have been knocked out and doors have shut in your face, take heart. God is trying to get a message through to you, and the message is: "Stop depending on inadequate human resources. Let Me handle the matter."

Here are three suggestions for presenting to Him the Prayer of Helplessness.

First, be honest with God. Tell Him you are aware of the fact that in His eyes you are helpless. Give God permission to make you feel your helplessness at the emotional level, if that is what is needed. Recognize that this may be painful! There is good psychological reason, however, why it may be necessary. Unless the power of our emotions is touched, it is as if a fuse remains unlit.

Second, take your heart's desire to God. You have accepted your helplessness. Now grip with equal strength of will your belief that God can do through you what you cannot. It may seem to you for a time that you are relying on emptiness, dangling over a chasm. Disregard these feelings and thank God quietly that He is working things out.

Third, watch now for opening doors. When the right door opens, you will have a quiet, inner assurance that God's hand is on the knob. That is the time of action for you, an opportunity for your creativity to join hands with His.

One sunny day in the future, you will look back and your heart will overflow with praise to God that He cared about you enough to shut you up to Him alone. Without that stringently kind providence, you could never have learned firsthand the amazing power of the Prayer of Helplessness.

235

Prayer: Where Are You, Lord?

Lord, I have been so defeated by circumstances. I have felt like an animal trapped in a corner with nowhere to flee. Where are You in all this, Lord? The night is dark. I cannot feel Your presence.

Help me to know that the darkness is really "shade of Your hand, outstretched caressingly";[*] that the "hemming in" is Your doing. Perhaps there was no other way You could get my full attention, no other way I would allow You to demonstrate what You can do in my life.

I see now that the emptier my cup is, the more space there is to receive Your love and supply. Lord, I hand to You this situation, _____, asking You to fill my cup from Your bountiful reservoirs in Your own time and Your own way.

How I thank You, Father in heaven, that Your riches are available to me, not on the basis of my deserving, but on the basis of Jesus and His worthiness. Therefore, in the strength of His name I pray. Amen.

[*] Adapted from "The Hound of Heaven," from *The Complete Poetical Works of Francis Thompson* (New York: Boni and Liverright, Inc.), p. 93. The line of the poem reads: "Is my gloom, after all, Shade of His hand, outstretched caressingly?"

The Prayer That Helps Your Dreams Come True

It was from my mother that I learned about the Dreaming Prayer. She invoked it not only for her family but for neighbors, too—among them a young man from "Radical Hill," a run-down section of our West Virginia town.

Raymond Thomas, who lived with foster parents, had no idea who his real parents were. Dressed in working clothes and clodhoppers, Ray often came to talk with my mother. Of a summer's day he would settle himself on the top step of our vine-shaded front porch talking . . . talking . . . while Mother sat in a wooden rocker shelling peas or stringing beans or darning socks. Mother enjoyed his boundless energy and fine mind.

On one particular afternoon there emerged from Ray the same inner longing I had had—to go to college. Once his dream was out in the open, shimmering, poised in the air, Mother was delighted to see the wistfulness in Ray's brown eyes replaced by kindling hope.

"But how can I manage it?" the boy asked. "I've no money saved. Nor any prospects."

Mother sensed that with Ray, the Dreaming Prayer should involve more than just college, a completely new approach to life.

"Raymond, whatever you need, God has the supply

ready for you, provided you're ready to receive it. And ours is still a land of opportunity, Raymond. The sky is the limit! The money will be there for every dream that's right for you, every dream for which you're willing to work."

For a preacher's wife who had little enough herself, this was a doughty philosophy. But Mother believed it and had often proved it so. And these truths took root in Ray.

There came the day when Ray accepted Mother's philosophy so completely that she could lead him in the prayer that releases dreams to make them come true. Remembering how often she had voiced similar prayers for me, I can easily imagine how it was for Ray. . . .

"Father, You've given Raymond a fine mind. We believe You want that mind to be developed, that You want Raymond's potential to be used to help You lift and lighten some portion of Your world. Since all the wealth of the world is Yours, please help Raymond find everything he needs for an education.

"And Father, we also believe You have even bigger plans for Raymond. Plant in his mind and heart the vivid pictures, the specific dreams that reflect Your plans for him after college. And oh, give him joy in dreaming— great joy."

With a flat pocketbook but faith in his dream, Raymond Thomas got onto a bus and went off to college. How he made it is much too long to chronicle here. It involved Mother's finding a well-to-do woman to start him off with a loan; writing him encouraging letters; praying. And Ray himself accepting responsibility, developing initiative. In four years he had twelve jobs, budgeting time as well as money—so many hours for employer, classes, study, church work, recreation. It was

238

a proud day for Mother when Ray received his bachelor of science degree, cum laude.

Twenty years later Len and I met Ray in Vienna, Austria, where he summed up how much of his dream had been realized: travel in sixty countries, his Ph.D. in physics (taken in German!) from the University of Vienna. Speaking Spanish, passable French, some Italian, Dutch, Swedish and a little Russian, he served his country through a job with the U.S. Atomic Energy Program in Europe.

A story like Ray's reveals the connection between constructive dreaming and prayer. For in a sense all such dreaming is praying. It is certainly the Creator's will that the desires and talents that He Himself has planted in us be realized. He wants us to catch from Him some of His vision for us. After all, this is what prayer is—human beings cooperating with God in bringing from heaven to earth His wondrously good plans for us.

Sadly, sometimes we fail to catch His vision for us because our capacity to dream has been atrophied by some condition that has given us a poverty complex. My first glimpse of this was in a former college friend who had suffered a poverty-stricken childhood.

Dot, as I will call her, was unable to visualize what she wanted in the vocational field. Yet she had come to Washington with idealistic ideas about a government job.

"I don't want just any job," Dot had explained to me soon after she arrived. "I go along with the idea that God has a plan for my life. Only I haven't yet found it, so how do I pray about this job situation?"

"What job would give you the most joy?" I asked her. "Usually that's a key to what one should do."

My friend merely looked puzzled and shook her head.

"Do you ever daydream?" I persisted. "Is there anything you've always longed to do?"

"No-o. Nothing."

The reason this particular girl could not dream constructively was that during financially difficult years, her widowed mother had taught her that those who hope for little or nothing will never suffer disappointment. Actually, this had been nothing less than excellent training in poverty expectation. Sadly I watched my friend fall into a routine government filing job that used but a fraction of her abilities.

I know now that there is healing for such a situation. When we become aware of such damaged areas in the unconscious, we can call on the power of the Holy Spirit. He can walk back with us into the past and drain out the poison, make the rough places smooth and create a highway for our God to march triumphantly into the present with His long-forgotten, oft-delayed plan for our lives.

In fact, there is no limit to what this combination of dreams and prayer can achieve. I have seen amazing results in many areas: finding the right mate or the right job, locating the ideal house, rearing children, building a business

There are those who are wary of this Prayer That Helps Your Dreams Come True because they are dubious about praying for material needs such as bread, clothing, a catch of fish—or, to put it in modern terms, a parking place for a car. Rightly they also ask, "Isn't there the danger of trying to use God and spiritual principles for selfish ends?"

These are valid concerns that need to be addressed.

As for whether God means for us to include material needs in our petitions, certainly Christ was interested in people's bodies as well as their souls. He was concerned about their diseases, their physical hunger. Christianity, almost alone among world religions, acknowledges material things as real and important—real enough that Christ had to die in a real body on a real cross.

And as for the danger that our dreams may spring from our selfish human will rather than God's will, there are tests we can give ourselves. Only when a dream has passed such a series of tests, so that we are certain our heart's desire is also God's before we pray, can we pray the Dreaming Prayer with faith and thus with power.

Ask yourself:

- Will my dream fulfill the talents, temperament and emotional needs God has planted in my being? This is not easy to answer. It involves knowing oneself, the real person inside, as few of us do without prayerful self-examination.

- Does my dream involve taking anything, or any person, belonging to someone else? Would its fulfillment hurt any other human being? If so, you can be fairly sure this particular dream is not God's will for you.

- Am I willing to make all my relationships with other people right? If I hold resentments, grudges, bitterness, no matter how justified, these wrong emotions will cut me off from God, the Source of creativity. No dream can be achieved in a vacuum of human relationships. Even one such wrong relationship can cut the channel of power.

- Do I want this dream with my whole heart? Dreams are not usually brought to fruition in divided personalities; only the whole heart will be willing to do its part toward implementing the dream.

- Am I willing to wait patiently for God's timing?

- Am I dreaming big? The bigger the dream and the more persons it will benefit, the more apt it is to stem from the infinite designs of God.

If your heart's desire can pass a series of tests like this, then you are ready for the final necessary step in the Dreaming Prayer! Hand your dream over to God, and then leave it in His keeping. There seem to be periods when the dream is like a seed that must be planted in the dark earth and left there to germinate.

But the growth of that seed, the mysterious and irresistible burgeoning of life in dark and in secret, is God's part of the process. The very moment a God-given dream is planted in our hearts, a strange happiness flows into us. I have come to think that at that moment all the resources of the universe are released to help us. Our praying is then at one with the will of God, a channel for the Creator's always joyous, triumphant purposes for us and our world.

Prayer: Give Me a Dream

Father, once—it seems long ago now—I had such big dreams, so much anticipation of the future. Now no shimmering horizon beckons me; my days are lackluster. I see so little of lasting value in the daily round. Where is Your plan for my life, Father?

You have told us that without vision we perish. So Father in heaven, knowing that I can ask in confidence for Your expressed will, I ask You to deposit in my mind and heart the particular dream, the special vision You have for my life.

And along with the dream, will You give me whatever graces, patience and stamina it takes to see the dream through to fruition? I sense that this may involve adventures I have not bargained for. But I want to trust You enough to follow even if You lead me along new paths.

I admit to liking some of my ruts. But I know that habit patterns that seem like cozy nests from inside may, from Your vantage point, be prison cells. Lord, if You have to break down any prisons of mine before I can see the stars and catch the vision, then Lord, begin the process now. In joyous expectation, Amen.

The Prayer of Relinquishment

One kind of prayer I learned through hard experience. It is a way of prayer that has resulted consistently in a glorious answer, glorious because each time power beyond human reckoning has been released. This is the Prayer of Relinquishment.

I got my first glimpse of it in the fall of 1943 while bedridden with a "closed case" of tuberculosis. After reading the story of a missionary who had relinquished her own eight-year battle for health, telling God she wanted Him even more than she wanted healing, I did the same.

"I'm tired of asking," was the burden of my prayer. "I'm beaten, finished. God, You decide what You want for me."

Tears flowed. I felt no faith as I understood faith, expected nothing. The gift of my sick self was made with no trace of graciousness.

And the result? It was as if I had touched a button that opened windows in heaven, as if some dynamo of heavenly power began flowing, flowing. Within a few hours I had experienced the presence of the living Christ in a way that wiped away all doubt and revolutionized my life. From that moment my recovery began.

Through this incident and others that followed, God was teaching me something important about prayer. Gradually I saw that a demanding spirit, with self-will as its rudder, blocks prayer. The reason for this, I understood, is that God absolutely refuses to violate our free will; that unless self-will is voluntarily given up, even God cannot move to answer prayer.

In time I gained more understanding about the Prayer of Relinquishment through the experiences of others, both in contemporary life and through books. Jesus' prayer in the Garden of Gethsemane, I came to see, is the pattern for us.

Christ could have avoided the cross. He did not have to go up to Jerusalem at the festival season. He could have compromised with the priests, bargained with Caiaphas. He could have capitalized on His following and appeased Judas by setting up an earthly kingdom. Even in the Garden on the night of the betrayal, He had plenty of time and opportunity to flee. The next morning Pilate wanted to release Him, all but begged Him to say the words that would let him do so. Instead Christ used His free will to turn the decision over to His Father.

The Phillips translation of the Gospels brings Jesus' prayer into special focus: "Dear Father, all things are possible to you. Please—let me not have to drink this cup! Yet it is not what I want but what you want."

The prayer was not answered as the human Jesus wished. Yet power has been flowing from His cross ever since. Even at the moment Christ was bowing to the possibility of an awful death by crucifixion, He never forgot either the presence or the power of God.

There is a crucial difference here between acceptance and resignation. There is no resignation in the Prayer of Relinquishment. Resignation says, "This is my situation and I resign myself to it." Resignation lies down in the dust of a godless universe and steels itself

245

for the worst. Acceptance says, "True, this is my situation at the moment. I'll look unblinkingly at the reality of it. But I'll also open my hands to accept willingly whatever a loving Father sends." Thus, acceptance never slams the door on hope.

Yet even while it hopes, our relinquishment must be the real thing; and this giving up of self-will is the hardest thing we human beings are ever called on to do.

I remember the agony of one attractive young girl, Sara B., who shared with me her doubts about her engagement.

"I love Jeb," she said, "and Jeb loves me. The problem is, he drinks. Not that he's an alcoholic or anything. But the drinking is a sort of symbol of a lot of ideas he has. It keeps bothering me—enough that I wonder if God is trying to tell me to give up Jeb."

As we talked, Sara came to her own conclusion. It was that she would lose something infinitely precious if she did not follow the highest and best that she knew. Tears glistened in her eyes as she said, "I'm going to break the engagement. If God wants me to marry Jeb, He will see that things change—about the drinking and all."

Right then, simply and poignantly, she told God of her decision. She was putting her broken dreams and her now-unknown future into God's hands

Jeb's ideas and ideals did not change, and Sara did not marry him. But a year later she wrote me an ecstatic letter: "It nearly killed me to give up Jeb. Yet God knew that he wasn't the one for me. Recently I've met another man and we're to be married. Today I really have something to say about the wisdom and the joy of trusting God. . . ."

It is good to remember that not even the Master

Shepherd can lead if the sheep do not follow Him but insist on running ahead of Him or taking side paths. That is the why of Christ's insistence on a very practical obedience: "Why call ye me, Lord, Lord, and do not the things which I say?" (Luke 6:46).

Obedience . . . trust . . . are all over the Gospels. The pliability of an obedient heart must be complete, from the set of our wills right on through to our actions.

When we come right down to it, how can we make obedience real except as we give over our self-will in reference to each of life's episodes, as it unfolds, whether we understand it or not, and even if evil appears to have initiated the episode in question?

This was the challenge to Mrs. Nathaniel Hawthorne, wife of the famous American author, as she wrestled in prayer in the city of Rome one February day in 1860. Una, the Hawthornes' eldest daughter, was dying of a virulent form of malaria. The attending physician, Dr. Franco, had warned that afternoon that unless the young girl's fever abated before morning, she would die.

As Mrs. Hawthorne sat by Una's bed, her thoughts went to her husband in the adjoining room and what he had said earlier that day: "I cannot endure the alternations of hope and fear; therefore I have settled with myself not to hope at all."

But the mother could not share Nathaniel's hopelessness. Una could not, must not die. This daughter resembled her father strongly, had the finest mind, the most complex character of all the Hawthorne children. Why should some capricious Providence demand that they give her up? Moreover, Una had been delirious for several days, recognized no one. Were she to die this night, there could not even be the solace of farewells.

As the night deepened, the girl lay so still that she seemed to be in the anteroom of death. The mother went to the window and looked out on the piazza. There was no moonlight; a dark and silent sky was heavy with clouds.

"I cannot bear this loss—cannot—cannot. . . ."

Then suddenly, unaccountably, another thought took over: Why should I doubt the goodness of God? Let Him take Una, if He sees best. More than that: I can give her to Him! I do give her to You, Lord. I won't fight against You anymore.

Then an even stranger thing happened. Having made this great sacrifice, Mrs. Hawthorne expected to feel sadder. Instead she felt lighter, happier than at any time since Una's long illness had begun.

Some minutes later she walked back to the girl's bedside, felt her daughter's forehead. It was moist and cool. Her pulse was slow and regular. Una was sleeping naturally. The mother rushed into the next room to tell her husband that a miracle had happened.

In the realm of answered prayer, the progression of events in Una's recovery was not unique. For in the years since I first read the Hawthornes' story, I keep hearing of strikingly similar experiences from other mothers. The pattern goes like this:

In every case the mother wanted something desperately: life and health for her child. Each mother virtually commanded God to answer her prayer. While this demanding spirit had the upper hand, God seemed remote, unapproachable.

Then, through a combination of the obvious futility of the petition, plus weariness of body and spirit, the one praying surrendered to the possibility of what she feared most. At that instant there came a turning point. Suddenly and unaccountably, fear left. Peace crept into the heart. There followed a feeling of lightness and joy that had nothing to do with outer circumstances. And from that moment, the prayer began to be answered.

Now the intriguing question is: What is the secret or spiritual law implicit in this Prayer of Relinquishment?

Here is part of it. We know that fear is like a screen erected between us and God so that His power cannot get through to us. So, how does one get rid of fear?

That is not easy when the life of someone dear hangs in the balance, or when what we want most in all the world is involved. At such times every emotion, every passion, is tied up in the dread of what may happen. Obviously only drastic measures can deal with such a gigantic fear. My experience has been that trying to force it down by repeating faith affirmations is not enough.

Enter the Law of Relinquishment. Was Jesus expressing this law when He said, "Resist not evil"? Stop fleeing from and denying this terrible prospect. Look squarely at the possibility of what you fear most.

It seems to us at the time that this is the opposite of trust. "Lord," we are inclined to protest, "didn't You tell us to pray with faith? I'm confused. Does relinquishment mean that we can never be persistent about praying for any definite thing?"

To all such pleas for understanding, Jesus always, patiently gives the same answer: "Obey Me. Then—afterward, not before—you will begin to understand."

So we take the first hard steps of obedience. And lo, as we stop hiding our eyes, force ourselves to walk up to the fear and look it full in the face, never forgetting that God and His power are still the supreme Reality, the fear evaporates. Drastic? Yes. But it is one sure way of releasing prayer power into human affairs.

Sometimes the miracle of prayer gloriously answered takes place at that point. With other situations the Good Shepherd leads us from relinquishment on into knowing. Such knowing is different from trying to think positively or making affirmations. It is not our doing at all; it is the gift of God.

Sometimes the knowing is given to us through a verse of Scripture that leaps from the printed page or out of our remembrance and sets the heart afire. Or it may come from a self-authenticating, interior word from the Lord Himself about what is going to happen in our situation. On occasion God may tell us that He cannot return to us what we have relinquished, as in the case of Sara B. Obviously we have not really meant business about the Prayer of Relinquishment until we have faced that eventuality, too.

When, on the other hand, a loving Father grants our wish, gives us the thing we have ceased demanding, we understand that relinquishment and faith are not contradictory. The Prayer of Relinquishment is the child dropping his rebellion against being a child, placing his hand into the big, protective hand of the Father and trusting Him to lead even in the dark.

And if the darkness remains . . . if the cross cannot be avoided . . . our hand is still in His. Our heart is still obedient. But now a fresh revelation comes. We look into the Face beside us with a thrill of recognition: the hand of the Father is Jesus' hand!

All along, our heart told us it was so. Relinquishment? Faith? Just the certainty that Jesus is beside us, whatever comes.

Prayer: I Relinquish This to You

Father, for such a long time I have pleaded before You for this, the deep desire of my heart: _____ _____. Yet the more I have clamored for Your help with this, the more remote You have seemed.

I confess my demanding spirit in this matter. I have tried suggesting to You ways my prayer could be answered. To my shame, I have even bargained with You. Yet I know that trying to manipulate the Lord of the universe is utter foolishness. No wonder my spirit is sore and weary!

I want to trust You, Father. My spirit knows that these verities are forever trustworthy, even when I feel *nothing:*

That You are there. (You said, "Lo, I am with you always.")

That You love me. (You said, "I have loved thee with an everlasting love.")

That You alone know what is best for me. (For in You, Lord, "are hid all the treasures of wisdom and knowledge.")

Perhaps all along You have been waiting for me to give up self-effort. At last I want You in my life even more than I want _____. So now, by an act of my will, I relinquish this to You. I will accept Your will, whatever it may be. Thank You for counting this act of my will as the decision of the real person, even when my emotions protest. I ask You to hold me true to this decision.

To You, Lord God, who alone are worthy of worship, I bend the knee with thanksgiving that this, too, will "work together for good." Amen.

The Prayer
of Joyous Blessing

Some years ago I knew of a home in Washington, D.C., that was full of tension because of an aunt's nagging faultfinding with the children. Ellen R., the mother of the family, did much praying about this situation, mostly that God would take away her aunt's hypercritical attitude. Nothing at all seemed to happen as a result, and Ellen became increasingly resentful of her aunt's attitude and presence in her home.

One afternoon Ellen, whom I had known for many years, dropped by our home to return a borrowed book.

"I know I must look a wreck," she apologized. "I feel like a ball knocked back and forth between the children and Auntie."

In the midst of discussing her problem, I had a sudden inspiration. "You've been asking God to change your aunt's disposition, and you say she's more faultfinding than ever. So why not forget about trying to change your aunt and just ask God to bless her, in anything and everything?"

Ellen looked astonished. "You mean I should ask God to bless Auntie whether she deserves it or not?"

Before I could answer, my friend had a counter-thought.

"I see it," Ellen said thoughtfully. "I guess none of us deserves anything from God, do we?"

"That's exactly my thought," I told Ellen. "Nothing

252

we could ever do would be good enough to earn a scrap or rag from His hands."

"Then, Catherine, let's try your idea. But will you pray with me about it right now?"

"Of course. But remember, Ellen, when you ask God to bless someone, what you're really saying is, 'Make him or her happy.' That's the literal meaning of *blessing* in the Bible—happiness."

Ellen's prayer, as I recall, went something like this:

"Lord, I know it's Your will that we be happier in our house than we have been. And I know that can't happen while any one of us is unhappy. Bless Auntie now in whatever ways she needs. Give her the gift of happiness. Help the children to love and respect her, and show me how I can be kinder to her. Amen."

A week later Ellen telephoned. She said that day by day her prayer was being abundantly answered. "The atmosphere here at home is completely different. You know this blessing business is dynamite! But I still don't understand why that prayer was answered when none of the others were. Why would there be such power in wishing joy for someone?"

Perhaps one reason we are surprised when God moves to bless someone when we ask it is that we have thought of Jesus Christ as primarily "a man of sorrows and acquainted with grief."

But no man with an attitude of gloom could ever have drawn little children to Him. Only an enthusiastic man who went out to meet life with unflagging zest could have attracted rugged fishermen as His disciples. Sadness could not last long when a man threw away his crutches delightedly or a leper went leaping and singing on his way to show his clean new flesh to the priest. And don't forget that the Gospels record Jesus as breaking up every funeral He attended!

Certainly Jesus was unblinkingly aware of life's problems and disappointments: "In the world ye shall have tribulation," He promised His disciples. "But," He added, "be of good cheer; I have overcome the world." In other words: "Cheer up! The worst that the world can do is no match for Me."

The real source of Jesus' joy is given us in unforgettable words first spoken by the psalmist and centuries later by the author of Hebrews: "Thou [Christ] hast loved righteousness, and hated iniquity; therefore God, even thy God, hath anointed thee with the oil of gladness above thy fellows."

He who knew no sin and who is righteousness had a personality sparkling and overflowing with a degree of gladness none of us can match. How could it be otherwise!

That is why the Prayer of Joyous Blessing does not depend on our merit or lack of it. Jesus is the only righteous One; therefore, the only finally joyous One. But this joy He longs to share with all who will receive it.

Now we begin to see why my friend Ellen was on firm ground in not making her aunt's "worthiness" a condition for her Prayer of Joyous Blessing. She knew that Jesus told us, "Love your enemies, bless them that curse you." As soon as we begin to obey Him, we find that blessing those with whom we are having difficulties, and the answer to these difficulties, go hand in hand.

And contrariwise, our refusal to bless may impede God's saving intent. I had this dramatized for me some years ago when a woman came to see me, asking my advice about her marriage. Over a cup of tea she told me her problem. She had just had the hardest blow the feminine ego can sustain: Her husband had announced that he no longer loved her and was going to leave her.

Mrs. B. felt that their marital problems were her husband's fault and she was full of harsh criticism of him: He never went to church; he spent little time with their children; he was unfaithful. "Only God can save him," she intoned gloomily.

"Here's an idea how to pray for your husband," I suggested. "Ask God to rain His blessings—spiritual, physical and material—on him, and leave the rest to God."

My visitor sipped her tea, her lips pursed into a firmer line.

"My husband has prospered too much already," she said. "That's the trouble with him. The only thing that will ever bring him to his senses and back to God is trouble, and more trouble."

She left, saying she was going to pray that God would change her husband, make him good, then bring him back to her and the children. And her prayers fell to the ground. The husband eventually got a divorce and married someone else.

If you and I were running the world, probably we would not allow the wicked to prosper. But the simple truth is that often they do prosper. All through the centuries, this fact has bothered men and women. In what may be the oldest book in the Bible, Job wrestles with the problem. It is mentioned in psalm after psalm.

But Jesus was and always is the Realist. He simply took it for granted that because God is all love, the wicked will often prosper: "He maketh his sun to rise on the evil and on the good, and sendeth rain on the just and on the unjust."

"Therefore," Jesus was saying, "if you are going to be true sons of your Father in heaven, then you'll have to pray for the very best to happen to everyone you know, no matter how you personally may have been mistreated or hurt by them."

Is Jesus saying, then, that goodness or wickedness is of no consequence to God? Not at all! Sin is a serious matter, serious enough to have sent Christ to His cross and our world closer and closer to the brink of disaster. But the point is that self-righteous or accusing prayers do not change men and women from bad to good. Only joyous love redeems.

Long before Jesus' day, the ancient Israelites stumbled onto the truth that gladness is a key to God's empowering presence: "The joy of the Lord is your strength." "In thy presence is fulness of joy." "Serve the Lord with gladness."

Having so often seen the Prayer of Joyous Blessing gloriously answered, I have begun to wonder recently if here we do not have a key to world peace. Even for those who take prayer seriously, it is not easy to know how to pray for other nations. It is especially hard when their ideals are not ours and when they consider themselves our enemies.

Perhaps Christ would say to us, "The people of all nations are My children, too. The more violent, greedy men ignore Me and prey on My innocents, the more they need to be released to My all-encompassing love."

Now obviously, we cannot bless and pray for people who despitefully use others, or pray for people with whom we are at odds, unless we recognize that no self-effort can manage this and until we let Christ living in us love others for us.

But it may be that if even a handful of citizens could pray with that kind of joy for the people of "enemy" nations with the expectation of good, asking for God's all-abundant blessings on them in every sphere, tremendous results would be forthcoming.

Our first reaction to that suggestion may be exactly what Mrs. B.'s was: Too risky! Which of us wants other nations to pull out ahead of our own nation in the sciences, in the exploration of outer space, in military know-how, in the economic sphere?

But it is not a risky way to pray once we see that God's way is to make "his sun to rise on the evil and on the good," and that His sun of joy is the only power in the universe capable of transforming the hearts of men and women, no matter what their problems, their politics or their nationality.

Prayer: Bless Us, Father

Father, I cringe to see myself in that Pharisee in the Temple, for I have been believing a lie: That since I have tried to serve You, I have a right to ask for your blessings; but that _____, so unbelieving and uncaring about You, deserves the difficulties he/she has.

Now I understand, Father, that You must manifest love and joy to us, Your creatures, because You are love and joy; that You, as the Sun of Righteousness in whom no darkness dwells, shine upon us because it is Your nature to shine—not because a one of us is deserving of it.

I now release _____ from my judgment

257

and I ask You to bless him/her abundantly in any and every way that seems good to You.

So live Your life in me, Lord, that from henceforward I shall desire as much good for others as I ask for myself; that I shall never again plead largess for myself and in my heart begrudge Your blessings for others.

Cleanse me of all selfishness and ungenerosity. And O Father, fill me up with the joy of Him who was anointed with the oil of gladness above us all. In His name I pray. Amen.

Section
Nine

Dark Night
of the Soul

From the beginning Catherine felt that she was to be fearless and selfless about revealing to readers her spiritual valleys as well as her mountaintops. Early in her career Catherine also realized that God often used her weaknesses more than her strengths as teaching points.

During the summer of 1971 and the months that followed, Catherine went through a dark night experience that shook her faith and tested all her resources. The following experiences led up to it:

1. MGM had paid handsomely for the rights to film Catherine's bestselling novel *Christy*, then shelved it.
2. After spending three years working on her second novel, *Gloria*, that, too, on the

counsel of her editors and advisers, had to be shelved. This was her first editorial failure.

3. Catherine's relationships with me, with her son, daughter-in-law and stepchildren were strained.

Catherine's chief stumbling block to marrying me was one she had never written about: my divorce. She had prayed about it and felt God telling her that He was in the business of redeeming and restoring broken situations and families, which she felt was a "yes" to our marriage.

Our first five years together in Chappaqua, New York, were creative and fulfilling. Then in 1964 Catherine began experiencing a recurrence of lung problems. When doctors suggested a warmer climate for her, we moved to Florida, with me commuting every other week to my job at *Guideposts* in New York City. By 1971 seven years of this week-at-home, week-away schedule was hurting our marriage.

On July 22, 1971, a third child was born to Peter Marshall and his wife, Edith. Amy Catherine was genetically damaged with cerebro-hepato-renal syndrome (brain, liver, kidney malfunction). Peter and Edith had lost their first child, a little boy, shortly after birth. Then they had a healthy little girl, Mary Elizabeth, now a lively three-year-old. The doctors gave this new baby six weeks at most.

For Catherine this was the worst blow yet—a baby named after her condemned to die. Rebellion exploded inside her as she issued a call to family and close friends to gather at Cape Cod to pray for a miracle of healing for Amy Catherine. When sixteen of us gathered at Cape Cod, Catherine reported that the Lord had told her the baby would be healed.

An extraordinary week of prayer followed. There were healings, sure enough, among the sixteen who came to pray. God used baby Amy Catherine as a catalyst to touch many lives. Then, at exactly six weeks old, she died.

Catherine was devastated, felt betrayed by her Lord. Her dark night of the soul had begun.

These excerpts from *Light in My Darkest Night* reveal how Catherine emerged from the shadows.

The Clouds Descend

Catherine: I believe that Satan won the victory last summer in the Amy Catherine situation. His handwork is all through it.

As I told the family the night before the funeral, there was a vast difference between the day of Amy Catherine's death and that of Peter Marshall back in 1949. I felt Jesus' presence in the room where Peter died. For a week after his death I walked in the glory of the Kingdom of God on earth.

At the time of Amy Catherine's death I could not feel Jesus' presence in her hospital room. On the contrary, I sensed evil there. We did not walk in any glory in the days following. Far from it! There was dissension, blame flung about, nitpicking over various decisions, a sense of failure.

Despite the good things that happened to some of the people who gathered to pray on Cape Cod, I have seen no good come from Amy Catherine's death itself, only misunderstanding and confusion. I have not understood why the results were so negative. I have not understood what was behind all this.

I dreamed last night that I was in my own home, though it was a larger house than our actual one, with several floors. Climbing to the top floor, I found to my surprise six people living there. They were not overtly antagonistic toward me but were obviously intruders; they had moved in secretly and were doing their housekeeping with inadequate equipment, a scruffy broom, etc.

Today, trying to interpret this dream, I sought the identity of my "squatters" so that they could be ousted. The first appeared to be depression, the second unshed tears, the third grief. That's all I've gotten so far.

The fourth one of the "squatters" in my dream of several days ago has to be sleeplessness. On the way to the airport to fly to New York yesterday, I realized that I had left my sleeping pills behind. So last night in the New York hotel I did my usual lying there, hour after hour, waiting for dawn. Just a bit of dozing the last few hours, from which I awoke with a raging headache. And still no feeling of Jesus' presence at all.

Yesterday I was struck by a phrase I read somewhere long ago: We learn humility through humiliations.

Having gone through a humiliation last summer, I should have much more humility today. Yet I don't feel that I've grown spiritually in this area. I don't feel that I've grown spiritually in any area these past months.

Humiliation. The dictionary calls it "a painful loss of pride, dignity and self-respect." I feel I represent every bit of that description and I don't like it at all.

My humiliation, of course, is a paltry nothing compared to the humiliation suffered by Jesus on the cross. Yet somehow Jesus and His suffering seem remote, unconnected with me and my present misery—that's all I seem to think about these days. I'm aware of a fatal self-centeredness here, but seem incapable of breaking free.

I woke up this morning with a Scripture passage running through my head: "No one is able to come to me unless he [or she] is drawn by the Father" (John 6:44, Moffatt).

Does that mean, I asked myself, that I can't have a relationship with Jesus unless God instigates it?

My mind whirled back through the years. Had God drawn me to Jesus as a child? Obviously so. The Father in heaven had drawn me to the Son. But now I feel no relationship with either Jesus or the Father. That seemed to end the day Amy Catherine died. So the Father must be blocking me from this relationship. Why?

I don't want to pursue it further. It's too painful. The hurt over my grandchild's death has to heal. I'm incapable of seeking understanding by going back over the events yet again.

So where does this leave me? Wallowing in my sin? Clearly this is so, but I feel helpless to do anything about it. I'm reminded bitterly of an article I wrote for *Guideposts*, "The Power of Helplessness." I sure don't feel any power in my present state of helplessness. Nor do I sense God coming to my aid. All above me, it seems, is a heaven of brass. My dreams recently have certainly reflected my state:

In one I was the preacher's wife in a church where an elaborate wedding required tickets of those invited. I seemed to have arrived late and not really dressed correctly. There was some discussion as to whether I was to be let in without a ticket.

Whatever was decided, I never saw the inside of the church in the dream. Instead, because something was missing, a whole group of us had to go and get it—whatever it was. As we went on this errand, I kept losing things. First my fur stole, then my gloves. The group grew angry at me; there were even physical threats. I woke with the sense of being odd-man-out, rejected by those who counted.

In another dream I was in an apartment where the plumbing was badly out of order and about to flood the place. I knew where the leak was, but instead of attending to it, I left the apartment to go to a meeting where President Nixon was speaking. I was seated in the front row. Since I had left the apartment while sorting the laundry, I still had in my hands a pair of my dad's old dirty work pants and two dirty socks.

During the meeting, I dropped the soiled laundry to the floor, and to my chagrin, the President came to where I was sitting, picked up the dirty work pants, looked at them wonderingly and handed them back to me. Though humiliated, even in my dream came the thought, But they are not soiled in any shameful way, but through honest work!

When I got back to the apartment, water covered the floor and the plumber had to be called immediately. Here the dream ended. Clearly the overflowing water from the neglected leak represented some situation that my subconscious knew to be wrong, which I was refusing to put right.

And still another dream: I was due to make an important speech, but had no time to go back to the hotel and change my clothes. I was told, "No, you'll just have to wear what you have."

This was dreadful because I had on an old skirt and ankle socks. Behind the stage at the auditorium I started to make up my face while several people watched me impatiently. By now I was acutely aware of an auditorium full of people waiting, too.

The makeup was a process of bungling and stumbling. I could not find a lipstick in the various cluttered purses I had with me. Finally I found it and with shaking hands tried to apply it, while trying to collect my thoughts about what to say in my speech. Thinking about the talk, I absentmindedly applied lipstick around my eyes. Those watching were startled. I tried to wipe off the lipstick, then apply powder on the area. I'll go out there looking like an old hag, I thought. There to my great relief the dream ended.

All these dreams have features in common: clutter, disorganization, unpreparedness, unacceptance of me by those around me, unhappiness with myself, a feeling of being threatened by circumstances and the critical attitudes of others.

And in them all—acute humiliation.

In the Valley

Len: I found Catherine sitting in her chair by the bed, looking listlessly through some catalogs. It was 11:30 A.M., a time when ordinarily she would be in her office hard at work on a manuscript. How do I penetrate the darkness of her spirit? I asked myself.

"We need to talk," I began.

"What about?"

"You cannot go on like this. We're all deeply concerned about you."

Catherine shrugged. Her eyes went back to her catalogs. My concern for her shifted to irritation. "How can you go against the warning you've so often given others about wallowing in self-centeredness?"

For a moment her eyes flashed. I welcomed this, preferring anger to apathy. The sparks quickly subsided, however, and she shrugged again. "Just say that I'm wallowing in my sin."

"You are doing exactly that, and what's more, you're enjoying it."

Catherine shifted about uncomfortably. "What do you want me to do?"

"Put the Amy Catherine matter to rest and get on with your life."

The pain inside suddenly shone through. "I can't put it aside."

"Why?"

"I keep seeing her little mouth crying out for help. I

can still feel her body in my arms, wanting so much to be held and loved, yearning for health. Every time I try to do any writing, these images return to haunt me."

"Why don't we take off for a week? Go down to the Keys, perhaps, or to one of the islands."

Catherine brightened for a moment, then shook her head. "I don't think I'd be good company. It's my problem and I'll work through it." She thought for a moment. "What was the title of that *Guideposts* piece by Joe Bishop? 'The Way Out Is the Way Through'? Maybe I should read it again."

"The point of the article is that you don't duck a painful issue, you meet it head-on. Are you doing that?"

"I'm trying to." She paused for a long moment. "In some ways you know me better than anyone else in the world. In one area you don't know me at all."

"What's that?"

"There's a part of me, deep down, that since my childhood has belonged only to the Person of Jesus Christ. He and I have had some wonderful sharing times together. He has been with me in every crisis—until now." Her lip began to tremble. "Now He just isn't there anymore. Each morning when I awake, I seek Him, to no avail. I must have offended Him terribly this past summer."

I put my arms around her, feeling her pain, fighting back my own tears. "You've been through these dark times before, haven't you? What about those occasions during your widowhood when you felt estranged from God?"

"They were more like dry periods when I was simply unproductive. And they never lasted very long. Sure, I'd be sunk in self-pity for a stretch, but Jesus was

269

somehow close to me even then. For months now there has been real darkness. I feel like I'm talking to the ceiling. And you know how listless my prayers have been."

I nodded. Listless was the right word. "When did you first feel this rejection—if that's what it is?"

For a while Catherine didn't answer. In fact, I had to repeat the question. Her thoughts seemed many miles away.

"I'm not sure," she said at last. "Probably right after Amy Catherine's death. Possibly after hearing about Virginia Lively's prophecy that Amy Catherine would not live. She heard correctly. I didn't."

"And that hurt your pride."

"She should have told me."

"If she had come up to you in Cape Cod and reported this revelation to you, you would have rejected it flat. I've never seen you so convinced, so determined about anything as you were about Amy Catherine's healing."

"I'll never go out on a limb like that again—for anything or anyone, ever," she snapped.

I took a deep breath. "I think it's your anger at God that has shut the door on your relationship with Him."

She shook her head vigorously. "I've been angry at Him before and He still comforted me. I believe God encourages us to be honest, to express anger when we feel it. So I don't think you're right, Len. Sure, I was angry when Amy Catherine died. Rebellious, too. . . ." She stopped, hearing her own words.

I voiced her unspoken thought. "There's a big difference between anger and rebellion. Feelings of anger are often justified, and usually subside fairly quickly. Rebellion is more long-lasting and destructive. Remember that Bible class we taught last year? How you kept stressing that it was the rebellion of the Israelites that kept them from the Promised Land?"

She nodded. "One's words can come back to haunt one, can't they?"

"Think about it, Catherine," I urged. "You're miserable without Jesus. Maybe you should go off somewhere alone and pray it through."

Catherine: Inside I am dry and lonely, unable to accomplish anything, really just going through the motions of life, and barely able to do that. It is more than a dry period. I've been through those before and did not lose the Presence. This is darkness. Deadness. Awful in the way it numbs you, makes you cold and indifferent. You do the very thing, say the very word, you know you should not. Frightening!

I must get down on paper some of the passages I've encountered this week in my reading of Scripture. Though my prayers are hollow and uninspired, I am receiving instruction from His Word. If the Lord will no longer speak to me directly, then I will go this route.

Here are some of the passages I have been led to:

When you spread forth your hands in prayer, imploring help, I will hide My eyes from you; even though you make many prayers, I will not hear; your hands are full of blood! Wash yourselves; make yourselves clean; put away the evil of your doings from before My eyes; cease to do evil.

Isaiah 1:15–16, TAB

271

The Lord is far from the wicked, but He hears the prayer of the [consistently] righteous—the upright, in right standing with Him.

Proverbs 15:29, TAB

You do ask [God for them] and yet fail to receive, because you ask with wrong purpose and evil, selfish motives. . . . You [are like] unfaithful wives [having illicit love affairs with the world] and breaking your marriage vow to God! . . .

James 4:3–4, TAB

During my afternoon nap I had yet another version of a dream that has recurred over and over. I am always in a very large house. I go through corridors and rooms, from one floor to another. There are many people around but they pay no attention to me, and I have nothing to do with them, do not appear to know them. I am searching, searching for my own room, my own place, but cannot find it. I cannot even find which floor it's on. Fear is in the dream, building to panic. Sometimes, in exhaustion, I even stop in someone else's room to take a nap in order to get strength to rise and start searching again.

Usually I awaken from this recurring dream with my stomach hurting and symptoms of severe tension, probably with raised blood pressure.

"In my Father's house are many mansions. . . ." This passage used to comfort me because it promises a place for everyone. I do have a place in the universe. Why am I now so lost?

This terrible feeling of lostness, apparently deep in my subconscious, must reflect my separation from God.

When one has lost one's way and can no longer feel the Shepherd's hand, when the Valley of the Shadow is dark, with the light of faith withdrawn, what does one do then?

Trust God in the dark and wait and hope and hang on as best one can, I suppose.

I have recently received some illumination about this shut-in place in which I have been so confined. It came from a section in *Mysticism* by Evelyn Underhill entitled "Dark Night of the Soul."

She explains that for those who have trod the Christian way for some time, a spiritual fatigue can creep in. In this state one knows anew the helplessness of the human condition. In fact, for a time we can be in a worse state there than at the beginning of our Christian walk.

The reason: When one first becomes a Christian there is, along with new awareness of one's frailty, the sure and wonderful knowledge of God's adequacy. In the darkness that assails the longtime Christian, the skies seem totally deaf; no light breaks through at all. Nothing, inside or outside, seems to work.

This is certainly my state at this time.

According to Evelyn Underhill, if one can ride it through on sheer, blind faith, just hanging on to the rock of salvation, then it has to pass, and we go on to a higher state in the spiritual life.

What was a fresh thought to me was that this dark state is necessary in our Christian growth. It comes when we've reached a kind of plateau of faith where nothing is changing, where certain areas of our life remain uncommitted to Jesus Christ, not being taken over by Him. So we have to find fresh truths in our helplessness and our need, become desperate in a new way, in order to get on with the next stage in our Christian development.

Even many great Christian saints went through a "dark night" experience, some pretty gruesome, according to Underhill, before they came out into the light again. This is encouraging for us ordinary strugglers!

More on "The Dark Night" from Evelyn Underhill: "The most intense period of that great swing-back into darkness . . . is seldom lit by visions or made homely by voices. . . . Stagnation . . . impotence, blankness, solitude, are the epithets by which those immersed in this dark fire of purification describe their pains."

I pause a moment to reflect. Am I being purified? I see none of that, at least not yet. There is stagnation, all right, more like sloth.

Len: After breakfast Catherine would go to her office to write. "How is she doing?" I would ask Jeanne Sevigny. Jeanne, by now a close friend as well as secretary and a participant in our ministry, would just shake her head. "Productivity about zero."

"Nothing at all."

"Nothing for me to type. She keeps reading over parts of the *Gloria* manuscript, but we all know that project is dead. A part of her seemed to die with it. We do get the mail answered, but I have to push and shove and prod her even with that."

"What's your diagnosis, Jeanne?"

"Grief and frustration. Anger, too."

"Aimed at whom?"

"God, mostly. And at us, too. All of us, even her mother."

"Buried anger, isn't it? She doesn't explode as she used to."

"You're right. I think the explosions were a lot healthier."

My efforts toward dialogue with Catherine were mostly unsuccessful. After receiving a series of one-word answers to my questions, I would usually back off. Yet I knew I had to keep trying. If only something would go right for her! The movie version of her novel *Christy* seemed permanently shelved, likewise her novel *Gloria,* though she kept pulling the manuscript from the file drawer and going through the motions of working on it. Amy Catherine had died. Her relationship to Peter and Edith was strained. In fact, none of her relationships was working very well.

The best news I had to give her was about Linda, who continued to astonish me with the changes in her life.

"Linda has found a most remarkable group of Christian friends," I told Catherine one day in our bedroom after I had visited Linda in Washington at the nonprofit organization Cornerstone where she worked. "In addition to her administrative responsibilities and leading a Bible study, Linda writes a newsletter. I think she has a gift for writing."

No response.

"Tell me something, Catherine. Why do you refuse to see the many positive results of Amy Catherine's short life? She was used in a mighty way, you know."

Catherine looked at me wearily. "I'm glad for Linda and for all the others who were helped. It's very self-centered of me not to be more grateful for this, I know. Forgive me."

"You say that, but you don't mean it. Words are coming out of you, but there's no emotion to back them up. It's as if the real you has gone somewhere else and I'm talking to a cardboard figure."

"Thank you for those kind words."

I shifted to another line. "You said several days ago that you felt you were moving about in a dark cage. Do you mean something like a prison?"

"That's pretty close."

"What are you doing to get out?"

"Not enough, I guess. I feel like a dead person. Abandoned."

"Not by those of us here in this house. We love you. We're praying for you."

"Thank you."

I sat down on the bed where she was sitting and reached for her hand. "I've heard you say many times that when a lot of things go wrong in a person's life, the Lord is trying to get that person's attention. I'm sure you've been applying this to yourself."

For the first time, Catherine's eyes met mine. "I sure have."

"What do you think He's saying to you?"

Long pause. "That I'm probably out of His will. That I may have been out of His will for some time."

There was sudden tension between us; a warning light within me cautioned me to cease the probing. Yet another part of me knew I must push ahead.

"How long do you think you've been out of His will?"

The question lay between us for a moment. Both of us knew where we were heading. Catherine's eyes left mine and her lip trembled.

"Since I married you," she finally said.

"You know and I know that everything hasn't gone wrong since we were married," I challenged her. "Forget all the books and articles we've worked on together and their impact on people. Look at the lives of our four children. Has our marriage made things better for them or worse?"

"Better, I guess. But I think you could have married any number of women who would have been better mothers to your children. I just think that I was supposed to stay single after Peter's death."

"And live alone in that comfortable sanctuary you were building, a snug retreat, well away from the action? That's not the guidance you got before we were married. After warning you that it would be difficult at times, the Lord nudged you to say yes to a new life with me."

Catherine nodded. "I remember. But I'm not at all sure about my guidance anymore. I thought I heard the Lord say He was going to heal Amy Catherine. Obviously I heard Him wrong. Maybe I heard Him wrong about us."

I sat there a moment struggling with a decision. How to reach Catherine? Gentleness and patience? Or confrontation? I made up my mind. "Would you like to hear my opinion as to when you began to move away from God's will?"

Catherine stared at me stonily. "Go ahead."

"It all began with the enormous success of *Christy*. I watched the change in you. It was gradual over many months. The plaudits, the adulation, the bestseller lists, the movie sale, all heady stuff. When we flew to New York for interviews, the publisher insisted on providing a limousine. We both loved it. Then came the bowing and scraping by the editors when you described your next book, another novel.

"What they were saying, essentially, Catherine, was

that you could do no wrong. That's when the change in you really began. Deep down inside, you bought it. Every book you'd written, a major success. Magazines eager for articles."

I paused, watching Catherine's reaction. She didn't appear resistant, so I plunged ahead.

"It was at this point, Catherine, that I began to feel the arrogance. Before the success of *Christy* you had what I felt was a delightful sense of inadequacy, especially for one who had been so successful. It was this inadequacy that I related to when we first met. You needed God. Without Him you were incomplete. In a lesser way you needed me. We made a good team in both work and play. On your book projects you needed Tib. Then, after *Christy*, you changed. Ask yourself, Catherine: Did you come to a point where you felt you didn't need God anymore? Or me? Or anyone?"

Catherine flared. "I've always needed God."

"If you've always needed Him, why can't you reach Him now?"

A stricken look clouded Catherine's face. Tears welled up. I tried to embrace her, but she turned away. I patted her shoulder for a few minutes, then left her alone.

Catherine: I am forced to the conclusion that Len is right. I did become spiritually arrogant after *Christy*. I became selfish with the use of my time, not wanting to be bothered with people who bored me or disagreed with me. I forgot too easily what I owed to the skills of others.

God was right to discipline me. I deserved it. Len was right to correct me.

But did the punishment fit the crime? I now feel so completely abandoned, rejected. The pain of Amy Catherine's death still immobilizes me. It's so dreadful to be in a state of darkness that I can understand better the fear of hell. How awful eternal darkness must be!

Reading about the "dark night" in Evelyn Underhill's *Mysticism* both helps and depresses me. Her description of the pain and anguish suffered by St. Theresa of Avila, the sixteenth-century Spanish Carmelite, is agonizingly real to me. And Heinrich Suso's ten years of darkness—ouch!

Is there something inside those great saints that invites, even seeks this kind of suffering? The holy men and women of medieval times seem to have inflicted torture upon themselves as a way to subdue their flesh and thus come to know God better. I confess I'm baffled by this. Life is painful enough without making it more so. Some of these godly people make it sound as if the dark night experience should be deeply relished because it will end up being good for you.

In reading about these Christian saints and mystics, I'm reminded that though the way we talk about our faith changes, the basic truths of Christianity do not. Ego-slaying is a modern term for the process St. Catherine went through. It was a concept I thought I'd come to grips with in *Beyond Our Selves*. I'm forced to the conclusion now that though I may have assented intellectually to this principle, I have done little to live it out.

There are other popular phrases to describe it. "The cross life" is one used today in many Christian groups; "self-abandonment" is another. Whatever the words used, the underlying reality is the same: For there to be more of God in a person's life, there has to be less of self.

The suffering saints—and I should include Job here, too—make my troubles seem small and paltry indeed, but their ordeals continue to frighten me. Is this the kind of "cross life" the Lord wants all of us to live? If so, why does the Bible promise in so many places "good things" for those who love the Lord?

Did those saints have a certain kind of spiritual pride that the Lord found obnoxious and that needed to be demolished? More to the point, do I have this same kind of spiritual pride, and is my dark night experience His way of chastening me?

I find myself with many questions and few answers.

I have never had a problem facing up to the fact that I am a sinner. Since the fall of Eve in the Garden of Eden human nature has been sinful. Glibly I can repeat, "I am a sinner saved by grace."

By saying this, however, I place myself in a general category of sinners, enabling me to avoid facing up to the fact that I have committed, am committing, specific sins. It is much more comfortable to be general than specific. The other day I ran up against this phrase in *My Utmost for His Highest* by Oswald Chambers: "Sin is red-handed mutiny against God."

That hit me like a sledgehammer blow. I am in rebellion against God. I have been for many months now. I am in despair about it but cannot seem to change. All is darkness in my life. Nothing is working. I read books, I go to church, Len and I pray together, but Jesus is not in any of it. My sin is separating me from God—Father, Son and Holy Spirit.

Chambers also says, "If sin rules in me, God's life in me will be killed; if God rules in me, sin in me will be killed." How do I make that switch so that God again rules in me?

I do not want to go through a ten-year period of darkness, as Heinrich Suso did.

A Shaft of Light

Len: One morning in the spring of 1972, two of Catherine's closest women friends, Virginia Lively and Freddie Koch, and I asked Catherine to join us in the living room of our Boynton Beach home. We were all struck by her joylessness, her heavy spirit and by the deep circles under her eyes. Sleeplessness was becoming more and more of a major problem for her.

We talked aimlessly for a few moments, then Catherine, always blunt, cut it short.

"You're here to confront me," she stated. "Let's get on with it."

"We've tried to be helpful to you several times since Amy Catherine's death," Freddie began. "You admit you're in trouble, we pray together and nothing happens. Why?"

Catherine shrugged, then waved her hand in a helpless gesture. "I wish I knew."

"Are you still angry at God?" asked Virginia.

Catherine hesitated a moment. "Who am I to be angry at God? He is our almighty Lord, who knows all, sees all and has His own ways that are mysterious and incomprehensible to us. It would be awfully silly for me to pit my puny anger against the Almighty."

"Yet that's what you've been doing for the past six months," I stated.

For a moment I hoped Catherine was going to deny

281

it, argue back with her old zest. But she quickly subsided into passivity.

"What's happened in the past six months isn't as important as what happens in the future," Virginia enjoined. "We love you, Catherine, and it hurts us all to see you suffering."

Freddie Koch drew a deep breath and said, "Catherine, I feel the Lord is telling me something that He wants me to tell you. It's about your self-pity. You're neck-deep in self-pity."

Catherine nodded unemotionally. "I think that's probably right. I confess to being a mess. So how do I get out of this hole? I'm sick to death of the darkness in my life."

"You could really be sick to death unless you do something about it, Catherine," said Virginia.

"The first step is to confess the rebellion and self-pity to the Lord," I suggested softly. "Confession and repentance."

Catherine shrugged hopelessly. "I've already done this, again and again. I honestly have. It's the complete lack of response that confounds me. I've never, ever lived in this kind of vacuum before. I talk, I pray. Nothing. For most of my life I've felt God's presence, heard His voice, received thoughts that I knew came from Him. No more. He's gone from my life. I know I offended Him terribly last August. I guess I offended almost everybody. But I was so totally caught up in the Amy Catherine battle. It was all-out warfare, you know. Nothing ever like it."

Tears began spilling out of her eyes. "What's destroying me is that I understand nothing about it, nothing about anything that happened. What's wrong with going all-out for something you believe in? God likes single-eyed people, doesn't He? It says so in Scripture. Well, I've always tried to be one hundred percent in everything I do. And always before God honored my efforts. Why not this time? Why have I been flattened so completely?

"I know it's happened to others. Great saints have gone through dark nights a thousand times worse than mine. But they almost seemed to ask for it, seeking some higher plane of spirituality. I didn't ask for anything for myself, only that a tiny baby be healed, and God not only refused that request but turned His back on me. I don't understand."

"Maybe it's that insistence on understanding that's the problem, Catherine," suggested Virginia.

Catherine stared at Virginia for a moment with a hint of surprise in her eyes.

Something stirred in me. Had we made a small breakthrough in Catherine's impenetrable shell?

When the session broke up after a prayer time, I was still not sure.

Catherine: Something happened to me yesterday when Virginia, Freddie, Len and I met. For a moment a shaft of light seemed to break through the darkness. When I awoke this morning, however, the darkness still surrounded me. My prayers still seemed to bounce back from the ceiling.

Then for the first time in months, a new and gentle thought came to rest on my mind: Read Isaiah 53. It didn't come from my thoughts, nor would Satan likely be sending me to Scripture. With a surge of hope, I knew it had to be from the Lord.

I read the 53rd chapter of Isaiah eagerly, struck anew by this foretelling of how Jesus would suffer hatred and rejection, of how alone He would be on the cross. These passages leapt out at me:

He was oppressed and he was afflicted, yet he never said a word. . . . He was buried like a criminal . . . but he had done no wrong. . . . Yet it was the Lord's good plan to bruise him and fill him with grief.

Isaiah 53:7, 9–10, TLB

I had read this passage many times before, even since Amy Catherine's death, but it had not affected me as it did now, particularly the tenth verse. God made His own Son suffer, but it was a "good plan." More than "good," it was perfect, as only something from God could be. It was terribly important to the future of the human race that Jesus Christ have His dark night experience on the cross. Yet what a desperately dark night it had to be for Him, a time of despair and abandonment, for Him to have cried out, "My God, my God, why hast thou forsaken me?" (Matthew 27:46).

Suddenly I was overwhelmed with feelings of remorse, embarrassment, gratitude and relief, all mingled together. Reading about the saints and their trials had not touched or enlightened me the way this sudden realization had. For reasons of His own, God had allowed Amy Catherine to be born genetically damaged. Her death served God's purposes, fulfilled His plan in some specific way not revealed to us, just as Christ's death on the cross baffled and dismayed His disciples at first, but did not destroy their faith.

I heard my own words, "What's destroying me is that I don't understand." I, from my tiny human vantage point, demanding to see into the secrets of eternity!

Virginia had challenged me on it: "Maybe it's that insistence on understanding that's the problem, Catherine."

How many others had tried to caution me? Linda, reading from Isaiah: "Maybe we aren't supposed to understand why God does certain things." Tib, with one of the best minds I know: "Just because I don't understand something doesn't mean it isn't so."

What about the weeks after Peter's death when my plea for understanding was met with something infinitely greater?

Instead of feeling rejected and abandoned, I suddenly felt ashamed. When Amy Catherine died, I demanded that God explain Himself to me, and when He didn't, I proceeded to sulk like a child, a petulant child who had failed to get her own way.

Now, day after day in our Florida home, I shut myself away with my Bible and notebook to work through my new discoveries, seeking a new relationship with my Lord.

Again and again I have read the crucifixion account, feeling the aloneness, the agony, the abandonment Jesus must have felt. I am there in the crowd, looking up into His face.

Flooded anew by contrition one afternoon, I burst into tears and stumbled to my knees. "Forgive me, Lord. Forgive me for my rejection of You, too."

Then came this revelation: When life hands us situations we cannot understand, we have one of two choices. We can wallow in misery, separated from God.

Or we can tell Him, "I need You and Your presence in my life more than I need understanding. I choose You, Lord. I trust You to give me understanding and an answer to all my why's, only if and when You choose."

Understanding. That seems to be the key word in my difficulties. I have sought it from the Lord most of my life and in His gentle tenderness He has often provided it. So often, in fact, that I had begun to take it for granted, assumed I had a right to understanding. What arrogance! What presumption!

Then a new thought hit me like a thunderbolt: Presumption was my sin. During the prayers for Amy Catherine, I took the lead in telling God what He was to do about Amy Catherine: "Thank You, Lord, for healing this tiny, precious baby." Had I really heard Him say what His plan was for her? Or had I wanted the healing so badly I simply imagined that He must, too? Presumption. I had assumed something I had no right to assume. God will always be God. We will never fathom His ways, but I presumed to try. "O Lord, forgive me for my presumption."

Then still another thought struck me. Worse than my presumption, even, is the fact that with Amy Catherine I had really wanted to play God, to be God in her life. Appalled, I tried to detach myself from this sin. There was no detachment. I tried to usurp the power of almighty God. "O Lord, can You forgive me for this abomination?"

And He answered me. At long, long last, I heard the Voice that had been silent for so many months: I, your God, am in everything. The baby died, but Amy Catherine is with Me. And while she lived, she ministered to everyone who prayed for her. You alone, Catherine, were too stubborn to see it.

After this first glimmer of light, Catherine began a disciplined early morning program of a 6 A.M. arising, with Scripture reading, prayer and a focus on praise. It was months before Catherine was ready to resume her writing ministry. When she did, seasoned by her dark night experience, ten of her most productive years followed.

Section
Ten

The Intercessors

As the editor of *Guideposts* from the 1950s into the 1970s, I worked on many prayer articles. The term "intercession" was familiar to me—"praying for others." I remember suggesting once to another editor, "Intercession doesn't exactly roll off the tongue. Wish we could come up with a simpler word for it."

After my marriage to Catherine in 1959, when we joined two broken homes, there were so many prayer concerns in our family that we set aside that early morning hour for prayer. I began listing the specific people and situations, the date we prayed and when and how the prayers were answered. Soon I had a prayer log that served as the basis for a book called *Personal Prayer Journal*, which Catherine and I published in 1978.

By now the word "intercession" had a more familiar ring. Scripture passages using the term were meaningful.

Then one morning early in 1980 Catherine felt led to go off alone to her office to pray. She knelt in front of her reading chair, opened her Bible on the seat of the chair, placed her hands on it and prayed, "Lord, do You have a special word for me today?"

Sometime later Catherine sought me out. Her eyes were shining. "I had an incredible time with the Lord this morning," she began. "He showed me that I knew almost nothing about intercession. Then He gave me a vision for a new ministry."

The pages that follow contain Catherine's description of how the Breakthrough intercession ministry started, plus excerpts from some of her teachings in its newsletter.

The Vision

I have never known a time of such burgeoning need as in our world today. Not just in the lives of those who have never received Christ, but even in Christian families. With so many frantic requests in my mail each day, I ask myself continually, How is it possible to respond adequately?

My mind turns to several organizations that handle such requests by mail or phone. But, my thoughts protest, these groups usually respond with a single prayer petition offered for each need presented, probably with little sacrifice of thought or time given. Surely such a one-time intercession falls far short of the sustained prayer needed.

Then I remember how I was first taught about the awesome power released when a group of people covenant together to pray about a specific need for a stipulated length of time.

On November 10, 1953, I was to leave for Hollywood for two months of daily script conferences as Twentieth Century-Fox began making *A Man Called Peter* into a motion picture. On November 1 I sent a letter to 1,800 friends who had written me after reading the book, asking them for two months of specific prayer that this movie would be protected from "Hollywoodizing" and would be God's project all the way.

The response was overwhelming. I heard from almost everyone who received the letter. And this wave of prayer was gloriously answered! Hollywood proved no match for our sovereign God. *A Man Called Peter* was not only Fox's biggest box office picture for 1955; more important were the lives inspired, even turned around by this movie. For me, this experience was an unforgettable lesson in the power of concerted intercessory prayer.

As I prayed about many concerns one morning, a vision began taking shape in my mind. One part of the vision was a picture of a growing number of Christians—among them the elderly, the handicapped and those in institutions of some sort—dissatisfied with their present level of service.

In the letters I receive, such people ask, "How can I make my life count for more? I'd like to serve Jesus in some way but I'm so limited in movement." Or, "With small children at home, how can I get out where the need is?" Or, "So many appeals come from our church and I have so little money to give."

Recently two parts of the vision began coming together. On the one hand there are His hungry, thirsty, needy sheep who are reaching out, asking frantically for prayer. On the other hand are all those Christians whose intense heart's desire is to be of help, but who are seeking the practical means.

In the vision I saw need and supply coming together. A third part of that vision—a physical location to serve as a coordinating center, to receive the prayer needs and pass them on to intercessors—was already in place in a remodeled school building here in Lincoln, Virginia, currently serving as a publishing headquarters but soon to be vacated.

The passion of Jesus' heart has always been "Feed My sheep." Those asking for prayer often feel so lonely and isolated. They have such a desperate need of knowing that somebody, somewhere cares about them. On the other side are people with time on their hands and un-tapped potential—time to care, time to write letters, time to pray.

During this same period, certain books and pamphlets have come into my hands stressing the fact that intercessory prayer is the most important work there is in the Kingdom. So important, in fact, that the Pioneer and Captain of our salvation, Jesus Christ Himself, "ever liveth to make intercession" for us (Hebrews 7:25).

Having accomplished our redemption on His stark cross, the glorified Lord's chief work before the Father's throne is to intercede as our perfect High Priest (Hebrews 2:10, 17–18). But to complete His work, He also needs some of us on earth to share His concern, His passionate caring, to be His hands, His feet and His voice in co-intercession. Only then is the circle completed from heaven to earth and back to the Father's throne again.

But let's admit it, intercession is work. It means caring about others as much as ourselves, sacrificing time and energy to their well-being.

And if I am anything like the typical Christian, I know all too little about the how of praying for others. So in my vision I saw that some teaching about intercessory prayer would be necessary, including the sharing of fresh insights and discoveries as we made them. All of that would, in turn, take regular communication through something like a periodical newsletter.

"It seems like a big order, Lord," I protested.

"Are not My dreams always big ones?" came the gentle reply.

And being His dream, it would not go away, but

caught fire with others. An article was published in the magazine *Charisma*, inviting people to become intercessors for the non-profit organization Breakthrough that was formed to do this work. Hundreds responded.

[Editor's note: To learn how you might get involved in this intercessory prayer work, see the Appendix on page 365.]

"Old Warhorse"

As we took the first steps toward setting up the mechanism to do the work of Breakthrough, I remembered a chapter in Betty Malz' book *Prayers that Are Answered.* She described one "prayer warrior" nicknamed "Old Warhorse Buckland" as the person her family called on for prayer help in every emergency. As a young girl, Betty had never seen "Old Warhorse," but she imagined him to be a seven-foot giant of a man with booming voice and flashing eyes.

One day Old Warhorse came to dinner, arriving by car. Betty's dad hurried down to the street to help her out of the backseat and guide her tottering steps to the house. She was small, stooped, plainly dressed.

Betty was terribly let down until she looked into Mrs. Buckland's face. Gray hair; firm, resolute chin; patrician nose; character lines creasing her forehead like rivulets. But it was her eyes that held Betty. They flashed determination, tenacity, power. Flecks of fire seemed to emanate from the gray irises of her eyes.

The elderly woman's voice, however, was gentle. She told Betty that as a girl she had been plain; she could not sing, play an instrument or even sew very well. She was too small for sports. But she did love to read.

Stories of courage had fascinated her. She fantasized about riding horses to battle. As an American Joan of Arc, she vanquished the forces of evil in every skirmish. When she became an all-out believer, she transferred her battle to the spiritual realm. And then came the discovery: God had given her the gift of prayer power for others! She rode figurative horses into battle as she fought the forces of Satan.

Her prayers were not loud, but intense and prolonged—in fact, unceasing. As she prayed for people in crisis, she put on the whole armor of God, claimed the power of Jesus, mounted her horse and went "against the rulers, against the authorities, against the powers of this dark world and against the spiritual forces of evil in the heavenly realms."

Old Warhorse did not need to leave her house to wage these battles. Instead, she called upon God to send His ministering angels into action.

This "little" woman did not stop her prayers even when the enemy was in retreat. She kept praying after the victory was won, only too aware that the enemy will return if given a chance.

We need people like Old Warhorse Buckland who know some of the secrets of intercession. We need those who have the willingness and the heart's desire to tithe some time each day for prayer effort on behalf of His lost, hurting sheep. All of us agree that our world is at a crisis stage. Why should we Christians lie down and allow a massive assault of evil to invade our families and our society?

God has given us the total victory of the power of the cross through the weapon of prayer. Isn't it time that we covenant together to pick up that awesome weapon and use it to His glory?

Why Answers Can Be Delayed

Those of us involved with intercession learn patience. If we do not, we are in constant turmoil, railing against the inscrutable quality of the Almighty. A friend tells me, "For eight years I've been praying that my son John will become God's man. I know that what I'm asking is His will. And John's three children need a Christian father. So—why such a long-delayed answer to prayer?"

Another friend writes me, "Ted's affair with that 'other woman' still goes on. I love my husband and this is devastating to our teenagers. I've prayed every way I know to pray and God doesn't seem to hear me. How long will this misery last?"

Is there in your life a cherished desire taken to God over and over in prayer, yet still unfulfilled? Then link hands with my two friends, and with the rest of us, and with all prayer warriors across the centuries! No wonder Jesus had so much to say about persistence in prayer (Matthew 7:7–11, 15:22–28; Luke 11:5–10).

Jesus' actions were consistent with His teaching. As in the story of Lazarus.

We read about it in the eleventh chapter of John. The first few verses set the scene: Lazarus' home in the village of Bethany, less than two miles from Jerusalem. It was the Master's favorite retreat spot where He could relax with His friends Martha and Mary and their brother Lazarus, all three dear to Him.

One day the sisters sent an urgent message to the Master: "Lord, he whom you love so much is desperately ill. Please come quickly."

As I read this story one morning, the transition word between verses 5 and 6 all but leaped off the page: "Now Jesus loved Martha, and her sister, and Lazarus. When he had heard therefore that he was sick, He abode two days still in the same place where he was."

Verse 5: He loved this little family especially.

Verse 6: Therefore He delayed going to them in their distress.

How odd! Why?

Martha and Mary did not understand either. For as Jesus waited, Lazarus died. Separately each sister verbalized the same thought: "Lord, if You had been here, our brother would not have died. You could have prevented it."

Distressed by their grief to the point of tears and groaning, Jesus gave two reasons for His deliberate delay: First, this experience was going to increase their faith—that is, their ability to trust Him in the midst of seemingly impossible circumstances; and second, they were to have an even greater firsthand demonstration of the glory of God.

The Lazarus story has a message for you . . . that Jesus loves you especially. You are His special friend. Therefore He delays. The "therefore" has wrapped in it the limitless love of God, with Jesus experiencing to the full, along with us, our concern, our agony of spirit and sorrow.

Meanwhile, where do we get the needed patience? When the situation shows no change or even grows worse (as with Lazarus), how do we hang on to the faith that God's love is working out our problems?

Marge, a dear friend of mine, was shown how. She and her husband had just learned that he had Parkinson's disease. The entire family gathered, anointed their father and husband with oil, asked the Lord for His healing, then made a deliberate act of turning the situation over to Him.

But Marge's heart questioned, "Until such time as our family sees this prayer answered, how can I keep enough peace of mind not to let worry and fear destroy me?"

God answered her question in an experience Marge had aboard a plane bound for Cleveland, waiting for takeoff. As she settled into her seat, Marge noticed a strange phenomenon. On one side of the airplane a sunset suffused the entire sky with glorious color. But out of the window next to her seat, all Marge could see was a sky dark and threatening, with no sign of the sunset.

As the plane's engines began to roar, a gentle Voice spoke within her.

You have noticed the windows, He murmured beneath the roar and thrust of the takeoff. Your life, too, will contain some happy, beautiful times, but also some dark shadows. Here's a lesson I want to teach you to save you much heartache and allow you to "abide in Me" with continual peace and joy.

You see, it doesn't matter which window you look through; this plane is still going to Cleveland. So it is in your life. You have a choice. You can dwell on the gloomy picture. Or you can focus on the bright things and leave the dark, ominous situations to Me. I alone can handle them anyway. And the final destination is not influenced by what you see or feel along the way.

Learn this, act on it and you will be released, able to experience the "peace that passes understanding."

Marge's sharing is helping me to handle my "meanwhiles." Not one of us finds it easy to put our problems into His hands that completely. But only in that way can our trust in Him grow and our prayer life mature.

The Waiting Prayer

Over the years Catherine learned a lot about patience in prayer, particularly with her son, grandchildren and three stepchildren. Here is a petition she offered up regularly.

Lord Jesus, You want honest words on my lips; no thought of mine is hidden from You anyway. I am puzzled about the Father's timing.

You know how long I have been praying for _____. I have tried to be patient about the answer.

I know that the seasons come and go in majestic sequence. The earth rotates on its axis in a predetermined rhythm. No prayers of mine could change any of this. I know that Your ways are not my ways; Your timing is not my timing. But Lord, how do I, so earthbound, come to terms with the pace of eternity?

I want to be teachable, Lord. Is there something You want to show me, some block You want removed, some change You want in me or in my attitudes before You can answer my prayer? Give me the gift of eyes that see, of ears that hear what You are saying to me.

Come, Lord Jesus, and abide in my heart. How grateful I am to realize that the answer to my prayer does not depend on me at all! As I quietly abide in You and let Your life flow into me, what freedom it is to know that the Father does not see my threadbare patience or insufficient trust, rather only Your patience, Lord, and Your confidence that the Father has everything in hand.

In Your faith I thank You right now for a more glorious answer to my prayer than I can imagine. Amen.

The Mercy Prayer

When you spend a great deal of time praying for others, there is much to learn. Like the Mercy Prayer.

It was my Florida friend Betty who taught me about this way of praying. She had been attending a baptism in an Episcopal church. The baby being christened was not only crying but screaming his lungs out.

"I could see how embarrassed the infant's parents were and I felt such compassion for them," Betty said. "But then the thought dropped into my mind that there was no way I could possibly be feeling more compassionate than Jesus. So I simply prayed, 'Lord Jesus, have mercy on that baby and his father and mother.'

"Catherine, it was remarkable. The crying stopped as if a faucet had been turned off."

Betty went on to explain that she had first "discovered" the mercy prayer when her husband had undergone surgery for cancer. His recovery had seemed threatened some months later when his doctor suspected a return of the cancer.

"It was a time of great agony," Betty told me. "All my praying, hours of it, finally jelled down into a single heartfelt plea: 'Father in heaven, will You have mercy on us simply for Jesus' sake?' "

The result? The finest cancer specialists at Duke University pronounced it a false alarm. There was no return of the cancer.

Since talking with Betty I have spent several of my morning prayer times asking the Lord for insights about the Mercy Prayer. Passage after passage of Scripture was brought to my attention. I saw that many of Jesus' healings, as recorded in the Gospels, came as the result of a prayer for mercy by some sufferer.

There were, for instance, the two blind men sitting by the side of the road one day as Jesus was leaving Jericho (Matthew 20:29–34). Hearing that this was Jesus passing by, the two men cried out, "Have mercy on us, O Lord, thou Son of David."

The crowd following the Master rebuked the men, telling them to keep quiet. But the blind men were so desperate they only cried the louder: "Have mercy on us, O Lord, thou Son of David."

And Jesus, standing still and giving the men His full attention, asked what they wanted of Him. When they begged Him to open their eyes, He had compassion on them, touched the eyes of both men, and immediately each received his sight.

Then there was the time Jesus encountered ten lepers (Luke 17:11–14). Since lepers were ostracized from public gatherings, these ten men stood at a distance crying almost in unison, "Jesus, Master, have mercy on us."

The Master did not question each man about how well he had kept the Law or how righteous he was. Out of Jesus' overflowing, compassionate love, He healed all ten on the spot. "Go at once, and show yourselves to the priests for proof of your healing," He told them. "Your faith has already made you clean."

Faith in what?

The connecting link is our belief that God loves each of us far more than does the most warmhearted person we know; that He heals simply out of that all-encompassing love. "I will have mercy, and not sacrifice: for I am not come to call the righteous, but sinners to repentance," Jesus said (Matthew 9:13).

The apostle Paul expressed the same truth: "Blessed be the God and Father of our Lord Jesus Christ, the Father of mercies and God of all comfort, who comforts us in all our affliction" (2 Corinthians 1:3–4, RSV).

"So then [God's gift] is not a question of human will and human effort, but of God's mercy" (Romans 9:16, TAB).

You and I are altogether dependent, in other words, whether we recognize it or not, on His love and mercy.

From earliest times the liturgical church has incorporated this reality into its essential act of worship, the sacrament of holy Communion:

> Lord, have mercy upon us.
> Christ, have mercy upon us.
> Lord, have mercy upon us.

Cruden's *Concordance* provides an extensive list of Scripture references to the word "mercy." Alexander Cruden's original words of description set down in 1769 are rich food for thought: "Mercy signifies that the essential perfection is in God, whereby He pities and relieves the miseries of His creatures." And, " 'Grace' flows from 'mercy' as its fountain."

The resounding validity of the Mercy Prayer all through Scripture is meant for everyone: "The Lord is good; his mercy is everlasting; and his truth endureth to all generations" (Psalm 100:5).

The Servant Role

The message I am getting today from Jesus is the servant role that He wants to play in the lives of every one of us. Scriptures that affirm this include Matthew 20:28, TAB: "The Son of man came not to be waited on but to serve, and to give His life as a ransom for many"; and Luke 22:27, TAB: " . . . I am in your midst as one who serves."

When Jesus wrapped a towel around His waist, poured water into a basin and began to wash His disciples' feet (see John 13:4–5), Simon Peter objected that this was beneath the dignity of the Master. I want to insist along with Peter that we, as His disciples and intercessors today, are to be the servants.

But Jesus answered him, "If I do not wash you, you have no part in me."

This is a stunning and stupendous thought. Unless I can believe in this much love for me, unless I can and will accept Him with faith as my Servant as well as my God, unless I truly know that it is my good He seeks, not His glory (He already has all of that He can use for all eternity), then I cannot have His companionship.

What an amazing revelation!

Freedom from Bondage

Yesterday as I was praying and lifting up certain people who had written to me of their needs, I was suddenly aware that there had been a gradual change in the type of problems presented in my mail. More and more people seem to be in bondage to something: alcohol, drugs, sex, gambling, money, careers.

Then I was given a fresh viewpoint of what a difficult time the Lord must have had in freeing Saul of Tarsus from his bondage to the Jewish law. For Saul (who became Paul) was a legalist and all-out persecutor of Christians because they were violating the Law.

Yet as we read Paul's letters, we see evidence over and over of how total his freedom became. Paul berates Christians for even considering the need of circumcision, for instance, the very foundation of Jewish Law.

How was Saul freed so totally of his bondage?

The key might well be in the words Saul heard on the road to Damascus: "Saul, Saul, why are you persecuting Me?"

If Jesus considered Himself to be the One persecuted and sinned against, more so even than the Christians Saul had killed or thrown into prison, then is not Jesus the central figure in our present-day problem with bondages?

And if so, then during the period I was in bondage to sleeping pills, I was offending and grieving Jesus more than I was hurting myself.

When our neighbor down the street beats his wife

because of his bondage to alcohol, he hurts his wife, but his greatest offense is to Jesus.

When any of us allow ourselves to be in bondage to the things of this world, we offend and grieve Jesus.

So turn the coin over for the answer. Jesus is saying to us:

> Why do you grieve Me with your dependency on alcohol, pills, sex or sweets? Look to Me for freedom from these bondages. I am the Healer and the Restorer. I am the One to set you free.

Jesus, and Jesus alone, is the Teacher and Corrector and Deliverer from any bondage. Then the old Saul in me, my dependence on [name your bondage], is dead.

Thank You, Lord Jesus, for life and freedom in You.

Pulling Down Strongholds

I s lust one of the strongholds in your life? Is it envy? Or greed? Whatever has a grip on you, know that the Lord is ready to help you be freed. Hold on to this promise:

(For the weapons of our warfare are not carnal, but mighty through God to the pulling down of strongholds;) Casting down imaginations, and every high thing that exalteth itself against the knowledge of God, and bringing into captivity every thought to the obedience of Christ.

2 Corinthians 10:4–5

In intercession the picture often comes to my mind of a strong, fortified castle-fortress atop a steep hill with precipitous cliffs all around. Deep inside a man or a woman is held in chains, a prisoner. Armed guards patrol the area. This is Satan's stronghold. But the above passage tells us that the weapons of our spiritual warfare are able to demolish even such seemingly impregnable bastions.

For Scripture also tells us that Satan's strongholds are delusions, unreal, lies, just as everything he says is a lie and everything he tries to persuade us is real is not real at all. The only real Stronghold is Jesus Himself and the Truth that He is and stands for:

For You [Lord] have been a stronghold to the poor, a stronghold to the needy in his distress, a shelter from the storm, a shade from the heat; for the blast of the ruthless ones is like a rainstorm against a wall.

Isaiah 25:4, TAB

The Lord is good, a strength and stronghold in the day of trouble; He knows—recognizes, has knowledge of and understands—those who take refuge and trust in Him.

Nahum 1:7, TAB

Our refuge, no matter what the assault, is in the light of Jesus' presence. In it we see His truth; in it Satan's lies stand exposed.

Section
Eleven

The Flood

Of all the hundreds of writers I have worked with, Catherine had perhaps the most total absorption with the literary process. As soon as she learned to read, she fell in love with books; they were best friends. As a teenager she began to write poetry. She loved research and always overdid it, whether in a term paper or a novel!

She had researched *Christy* for a year when I married her, having spent weeks in the Great Smoky Mountains, talking to the mountain people, recording dialect and figures of speech and spending countless hours in North Carolina and Tennessee libraries. One reason it took her nine years to write *Christy* was her perfectionism over the small details.

So it was with her novel *Julie*. On three occasions we drove four hundred miles from our home,

311

Evergreen Farm, to Johnstown, Pennsylvania, to research the big floods of 1889 and 1934, the operation of a big steel mill, the inner workings of a weekly newspaper.

Facts and details—Catherine loved to track them down. And she was great with descriptions, character development, bringing out spiritual truths. I loved dialogue, confrontations, plotting the action. With both *Christy* and *Julie* we used our trips by car to talk through the characters, plot the action and suspense.

While the model for nineteen-year-old Christy had been Catherine's mother, Leonora, Julie was eighteen-year-old Catherine herself with her passion for causes. As a reporter for the weekly *Sentinel*, Julie could take on corrupt capitalists, battle for oppressed workers and be delighted and confused by the attentions of three suitors, one of whom was from Great Britain.

And when the big flood occurred, she was right in the middle.

S aturday, September 21, 1935, began in such a normal way.

There had been heavy rain across western Pennsylvania on Friday as predicted. It rained especially hard north of Alderton between midnight and six A.M.

When we gathered for breakfast, Mother outlined for Anne-Marie and me some chores she wanted done.

"They're expecting me at the Fleming farm this morning. Queenie's about to have her puppies," Anne-Marie protested.

My father sighed. "Call and ask if you can come out after lunch. If not, then I guess you can do your chores this afternoon."

Anne-Marie was soon back to report that she was needed this morning. Dad capitulated and agreed to drive her to the farm in the Willys. As Anne-Marie skipped out the front door, she winked at me. I was not amused. I was needed at *The Sentinel.*

Life and death for everyone in Alderton that day hung on such small decisions as to where they would be in the early afternoon.

I carried my lunch to *The Sentinel*, planning to work through the afternoon. When I arrived, Emily Cruley was already there, poring over the subscription list, her

313

black leather case open on her desk with the ledger planted in front of her. She announced self-righteously that it would take her all day to bring it up to date.

Dean Fleming was due in the office after lunch to work on the Goss press.

At 11:30 Rand phoned, very agitated. "Julie, I need to see you. Are you free this afternoon?"

"I'm here all day."

"I'll be there shortly after one."

"Is something wrong?"

"Yes. Things here are in a fright. After he sacked me, Old Man McKeever told me to stay until the club was closed up. But since that official from the railroad stopped by to see him yesterday, he has been in a towering ill humor. This morning he called and told me to clear out by noon today. All my things are in the boot of my car."

"Did you know he is suing *The Sentinel* for two million dollars?"

There was silence, and then a whistle at the other end of the line.

"He's lashing out at everyone in sight," I added.

"The Old Man's not there now, I gather, or you wouldn't be talking so freely."

"He's at the *Vulcania*. But you never know when he'll show up. Can't wait to get out of here. I'll see you in about two hours."

At 12:30 Rand called again. "Julie, I'm not sure when I can make it. The rain last night was so heavy that the lake is rising very rapidly. We've opened the spillways, but it looks as if there'll be an overflow. I'll ring you up later."

Rand telephoned me a third time while I was eating

314

my sandwich. His voice was tense. "I'm leaving right now to see you."

"Is the dam all right?" I asked.

"I can't tell. A lot of men are there working on it."

When he hung up, I had an eerie feeling that I should call him back and ask him to meet me at our home instead. How silly!

When Rand arrived, he walked swiftly back to the editor's office. As he closed the door and turned to me, I was astonished at his appearance. His hair was tousled, his face flushed, his shirt rumpled. I had never seen him so wrought up.

"Dean just called," I said. "Worried about the dam. He's coming down to grease the press. Thinks we ought to clear out."

Rand nodded, flicked a shock of red hair out of his eyes and grinned at me.

"May I kiss you?" he asked.

The look in his eyes made me tremble. "Why so sudden?"

He pulled me to my feet. "No reason. I've been wanting to kiss you for two weeks now—no, three—no, it's closer to four."

I started to resist, but his lips closed over mine. His intensity so overwhelmed me I could scarcely breathe. When we broke apart and I caught a breath, his lips found mine again. Moments later I pulled away and sat down numbly in Dad's chair.

"Rand, please."

He shook his head, sat down beside me and began to stroke my hair. Then he drew my face toward him and kissed each eye and the tip of my nose before he reached my mouth again.

The telephone rang. I was so weak I could barely lift the receiver. "Hello."

A strangled voice spoke, one of Dean's friends. "Get out quickly! The dam broke! A wall of water is heading for Alderton."

Rand saw the fear on my face and grabbed my hand as we ran out of the office toward the front door.

"The dam broke!" I shouted at Emily.

As we reached the door, two people from the street had pushed it open from the outside.

"Too late!" one shouted. "You can hear the water coming. To the top floor!"

We all turned and scrambled frantically up the stairs.

There is no way I can describe the mammoth tragedy of that Saturday, except to put together chronologically the graphic details given me over a period of months and even years afterward by my family and friends, as well as other survivors.

The heavy rain of Friday night covered all of western Pennsylvania. In the mountain area just north of Kissawha Dam there was a torrential downpour that totaled nearly fifteen inches in a three-hour period. The runoff into the lake from the two feeder streams, Bear Creek and Smather's Run, began about 6:00 Saturday morning.

One viewer described these streams at 9:00 A.M. as "going berserk." Smather's Run, seldom more than ten feet wide and two feet deep, was nearly fifty feet wide and stripping branches off trees five feet off the ground.

At 10:00 A.M. a resident of the Hunting and Fishing Club climbed into his small outboard and chugged around the side of the lake.

"The meadowland was underwater in spots almost three hundred feet from the edge of the lake," he reported. "Debris everywhere, mostly logs washed down from a sawmill miles away. The lake was a mass of junk."

All available manpower had been gathered by 11:00 that morning as the lake rose and threatened to spill over the dam. The sluice guards and spillways were opened wide. Then one group of men began to pry away the drift guards and tear up the road to get at the heavy iron gratings in the spillway that kept fish from escaping down Brady Creek.

The panting, gasping workers encountered iron grids rusted and wedged in by years of overgrowth. The heaviest crowbars wielded by the strongest men could not budge them.

By 1:00 P.M. logs, tree branches and other flotsam flowing into the lake from the two feeder streams had reached the dam, adding to the pressure on it. Suddenly workers were horrified to see several large concrete blocks loosen, then tumble thunderously into the stream below. A geyser of water shot thirty feet into the air.

At this point the workers made a final effort to slow the overflow by pouring wheelbarrows full of rocks across the road atop the dam. The heavy rocks were washed off like pebbles.

At 1:30 dam erosion had created a V-shaped notch about six feet wide and two feet deep in the breast of the dam. As it continued to widen and deepen, the workers knew the dam was lost and began a retreat toward the club. Suddenly a big chunk of the roadway over the dam collapsed and was washed away.

Within minutes the opening was so large a yacht could have cruised through it. A sheet of water nearly sixty feet wide was now pouring over and through the opening. So far the concrete buttresses had easily diverted the heavy overflow away from the Sequanoto River into Laurel Run. Onlookers then witnessed an awesome sight. The main part of the earthen dam and the road above it did not burst or crumble, it just moved away. The water, treetop high, exploded over the dam like a living force, sweeping everything before it: trees, other vegetation, rocks, concrete.

The onslaught of water hit the new waterway area with the roar of an express train. Cement retaining walls crumbled, then dissolved into hundreds of missile-like objects and became part of the roaring torrent that joined the Sequanoto River as it thundered toward Yancyville.

It was 2:10 P.M.

It took only 27 minutes for Lake Kissawha to empty more than five hundred million tons of water into the valleys below. Engineers later estimated that 118 tons of water per second pounding away at the dam wall had pushed away 90,000 cubic yards of earth and stone, which went tumbling downstream.

The workers watched, incredulous as the water snapped century-old four-foot-thick trees as if they were twigs and propelled them forward like matchsticks in the swirling torrent. The growing mass of water tore huge boulders from the stream banks and rolled them over and over as if they were marbles.

What had been lake bottom was now eight hundred acres of brown ooze, separated here and there by a few small streams flowing quietly in the direction of the dam. Black bass, pike and trout flopped about in the mud at the bottom of the reservoir basin.

The course of the floodwaters was strangely selective, though it mostly followed the Sequanoto River bed, which flowed through Yancyville, Mills Ford and then into Alderton. Yancyville was the first hit.

Anne-Marie, who had stayed through lunch, was in the kitchen of the farmhouse with Hazel Fleming when she observed Queenie behaving strangely. The usually placid dog, heavily pregnant, was dashing about the yard whining and whimpering. Suddenly the collie sped up the hill toward the small cabin as if in great pain. Anne-Marie, who could not stand to see any animal hurting, hurried after Queenie to see what was wrong.

From her position on the hillside beside the cabin, Anne-Marie heard the flood coming before she saw it. "It was like the roar of a fast freight train," she said later. The noise was obviously painful to Queenie's sensitive ears. Whimpering even more, the dog crept close to Anne-Marie's legs for protection.

Now the booming freight train sound was closer, just around the bend in the river. Anne-Marie stood rooted by the cabin, craning her neck to see. Her first impression was that a dark mist was rolling in. Then she saw a fifty-foot-high wave of debris hurtling forward. She watched in horror as the wall of junk slammed into the right side of the farmhouse. Above the sound of splintering wood and crashing glass, her own screams seemed disembodied.

The roof of the farmhouse tilted sideways. The trunk of a large tree tore through the second-story window above the porch, leaving half of the tree hanging grotesquely outside, swaying in the air. Then the whole building dissolved and was sucked up into the dark mass.

Behind the mountain of trash came the water: huge, churning waves over 75 feet high, carrying along on their swirling surface cows, horses, pigs, trees, sections of fences, boulders.

And, yes, human bodies. A woman's long hair floated on the water. Then the heaving waves thrust a man's body halfway out of the water, only to suck him under again.

Sobbing, Anne-Marie turned her head away. A thunderous crash drew her gaze back. A second wave of water, equally high and spread over a wider front, had crushed two walls of the big red Fleming barn. The ripping, tearing sound of wood, plus the terrified squeals of the animals, sickened her. Just a half hour before, she and Hazel had gone to feed the two Guernsey cows, the riding horses and the beloved old swayback Shorty.

The flow of water continued for about twenty minutes, then stopped abruptly. Because the log cabin had been built on an elevation, the raging water had missed it and Anne-Marie. In fact, the cabin was standing there serenely intact, as though viewing with equanimity the total annihilation of the farmhouse, its mistress and the barn.

Dazed, blinded by her tears, Anne-Marie made her way back down the hill. What had been a gracious dwelling minutes before was litter-strewn ground: a piece of brass, fragments of glass, a kitchen knife, a dented pot, several broken springs, fragments of wood and metal. That mighty body of water had swept away everything else.

Half of Yancyville was demolished by the flood, half was spared. Those farms, houses and stores on the west side of Seven Mile Mountain Road were swept away. Buildings on the east side, on higher ground, suffered only minor damage.

Just below Yancyville the steel bridge over the Sequanoto River took the full brunt of the waters. Said one observer: "The bridge squirted into the air in a crazy L-shape, then exploded into pieces and was gone."

Mills Ford was the next target.

At 2:11 the Allegheny Local, an eight-car passenger train that serviced some twenty stops between Altoona and Pittsburgh, stopped at Mills Ford to discharge and take on passengers, mail and freight. The exchange usually took five minutes.

At 2:13 the railroad clerk received a frantic call from the Yancyville station. He listened for less than ten seconds, then raced outside, shouting at the conductor: "Get the train out of here! The dam broke and the water is heading this way!"

A whistle blew, the loading of freight was stopped and the train pulled out of the station, building up momentum slowly, one minute ahead of the water. A mile south of Mills Ford the tracks turned from the riverbed and climbed to high ground. Would the train reach this spot in time?

With a grade crossing three hundred yards ahead, the engineer pulled the cord of his locomotive whistle. He never let it go for the next two and a half minutes.

The first wall of water hit Mills Ford at 2:16. Warned by the train whistle and shouting word-of-mouth, over half the population had scampered to higher ground. The station clerk, who fled with the others, later described the approaching mass as "a brown hill a hundred feet high rolling over and over."

A flour mill, five stores, eight houses and the railroad station were obliterated by the first onslaught of water. Pieces of railroad track were spinning and flying about "like someone had rained down a shower of steel spikes from above."

The second wave of water collected three more houses, a wooden church and a warehouse. As the roof of one of the houses disappeared down the valley, a naked man was seen on top of it, holding frantically to what remained of the chimney.

Ahead of the water the engineer of the Allegheny Local had pushed his throttle as wide open as he could. But before the lifesaving high ground could be reached, the track bed ahead made a sharp turn around a bend in the river.

A truck driver on Seven Mile Mountain Road several hundred feet above the railroad tracks saw the train's race against death. The water, a tumbling, foaming, debris-clogged mass, closed the gap quickly as the train made its circuitous turn around the bend in the river.

A hundred yards was the difference. The engine had reached high ground, but the rolling water thundered into the last five cars and sucked them up like pieces of kindling, sending them tumbling and bouncing until they broke apart. The engine and three other cars were yanked sideways and flipped over.

In the seconds that passed before the second wave of water struck, seven people scrambled from the first three cars of the train and reached high ground. Then the second force surged into the helpless and prostrate train and lifted up its parts as an ocean wave picks up drift-wood along a beach.

The last view the truck driver had was of engine and cars cartwheeling down the floor of the riverbed like a toy train bouncing down a flight of stairs. Death had won the race.

As the first body of water approached Alderton, the weight of its accumulated debris—trees, buildings, automobiles, trucks, railroad cars—slowed it down. At times it appeared to be an almost solid mass, giving out logs, hunks of metal, bodies and boulders along the way. The second body of water caught up to the first about a quarter-mile north of the turnoff road to McKeever's Bluff.

When the second mound of water hit the first, there was a thunderous roar, as though a bomb had gone off. The whole mass seemed to explode into a thousand multicolored pieces. The rays of the afternoon sun revealed one section of the mass as emerald green, another jet-black, still another an oily brown, while pieces of metal caught the sunlight in a weird pinwheel effect. Then, for no discernible reason, the watery ball veered to the right and ripped a gaping swath through the wooded area behind McKeever's Bluff.

Several viewers lived to describe what then happened to the wealthy steel magnate's private railroad car. "Like a scene in a movie spectacular," said one. "As though the god of water picked up the *Vulcania* like a small toy and threw it over the cliff."

Another said, "It looked from a distance as though the water just nudged the *Vulcania* over the cliff. The *Vulcania* seemed to struggle for a moment as if clawing for its life, then it fell."

The car twisted completely around before tumbling the first hundred feet, where it hit a clump of trees. For a few seconds the *Vulcania* hesitated, then spun, pirouetted and plunged forward end over end.

"It crashed, bounced, slammed into the ground, bounced again as if it had been a pogo stick," reported one witness. "I think it did that four or five times."

At the last crashing impact, a burst of flame shot out one end of the car. Then the *Vulcania* began a slow, rolling, bouncing fall the last few hundred yards down to the outskirts of Alderton. It was a flaming torch when it finally came to rest at the bottom of the hill. Then a wall of water rolled over the *Vulcania*, dissolving it and the hated McKeever inside into a thousand fragments.

When the dam waters hit Alderton, they were about thirty feet high, five hundred feet wide and two miles long.

The time was 2:19.

It takes a moment to react to crisis. When the cry came, "To the top floor," I darted about the *Sentinel* office looking for my sweater. Rand's shout brought me to my senses. He grabbed my hand and fairly propelled me up the stairs. Out of the corner of my eye I saw Emily just behind us, subscription case held tightly to her bosom.

At the top of the stairs I heard a shout and turned to see Dean Fleming coming through the front door. He gave a quick look about and scurried jerkily after us, his bad leg hardly slowing him down at all. In addition to the six of us who raced upstairs from the *Sentinel* office, five others had scampered up the staircase from the side entrance.

The view out the north window of the second floor was frightening. Panicky people were scurrying about in a state of confusion, some heading one direction, some another. The din was growing: dogs barking, women screaming, men shouting, whistles blowing, church bells ringing.

Two comparable scenes flashed through my mind.

The first was a picture I remembered in an old religious book of confused people running about on the Day of Judgment. The second was a sight that had turned my stomach as a little girl in Timmeton: a hen flopping around this way and that after Dad had chopped her head off.

Suddenly we saw the reason for the pandemonium below. A dark, misty wall of water was bearing down upon us, one block away. The sound that preceded it was like rolling thunder.

"Upstairs!" The order came from Dean Fleming.

My last glance at the dark mass revealed all sorts of objects swirling in it: an automobile, a bicycle, a push-cart, street signs, bodies.

Rand held my hand as we rushed up the twisting stairs to the top floor; behind us came Dean and Emily, who still clutched her black case. The third floor contained trunks and boxes scattered about. Old-fashioned clothes trees stood upright, sporting costumes and uniforms.

Rand pulled me aside, placed his mouth close to my ear. "Whatever happens, Julie, I love you."

Grinding, buckling noises shook the floor; the entire building groaned. Rand and I fell onto the floor as the bodies of a brown dog and a half-clothed man burst through a window. Our screams were drowned by awesome noises all around us.

How can I find the words to describe the sounds and sensations of a building breaking up? Swirling waters were hurling assault after assault at the foundation. Timbers cracked, then splintered, mortar crumbled, entire walls heaved and buckled.

A rain of dirt and small particles showered us from

325

the ceiling. When the building suddenly tilted, costumes flew in every direction. Rand and I were back on our feet, arms around each other. Dean was next to us, protecting Emily with his body. I heard him murmur these words:

God is our refuge and strength. . . . Therefore we will not fear. . . . Though the waters roar, though the mountains shake. . . .

Abruptly the floor under us split in two. Next, the seams at the top of the gabled roof ruptured and we could see daylight just above us. Water was pouring through the openings as the floor began to sink under us.

Numbly I stared at the opening above us. Then I found myself thinking that clambering through that space would take no more agility than climbing the cherry tree in our backyard. I jumped on top of a nearby trunk. Rand leaped up beside me, grabbed me with his sinewy arms, strengthened by years of rowing, and propelled me toward the light above.

Desperately I clutched the broken edge of the roof and pulled myself on top. Then I turned to give Rand a hand. He was gone.

The building seemed to explode underneath me. The mass of water catapulted my roof-perch forward as I clawed to keep my handhold. It was tipped at a crazy angle and spun around several times, banging into logs and bales of wire. Dazed, I coughed up brown fluid and clung to a slab of roofing.

Twice my raft almost spun over as I found myself on the crest of a river of debris, cruising through downtown Alderton as buildings on either side of me crumbled. The rushing floodwaters had been slowed by Alderton's stone, brick and wooden structures; we were moving no faster than fifteen miles per hour.

I knew I would not survive on such a wobbly raft. The nearly intact roof of a small house swirled by. In desperation I leaped toward it. My feet went into the water, but miraculously I was able to pull myself up. Then that rooftop was struck by the crest of a wave and began to buck and lurch like a wild bronco. On hands and knees, scrambling and clawing, I clung frantically to it.

I had just a moment to wonder about Rand, Dean and Emily when the branches of a tree swung by and knocked me off my rocking rooftop. Down I plunged into darkness. "This is death," I told myself with surprising calm as blackness settled over me.

Next instant I was catapulted up to the surface. I reached out and grabbed a sodden canvas awning dangling off a piece of house siding. I tried to pull myself up but could not. All strength seemed to have drained from my arms and hands. There was no way I could hang on.

The words Dean Fleming had muttered came back to me: "God is our refuge and strength. . . ."

"Lord, if You have anything for me to do in this life, please save me," I pleaded.

For years afterward I would have the same dream: I was hanging, dangling, gripping that canvas with my fingernails, spitting out putrid water, flinging heavenward my stumbling prayer, knowing that soon my grip would loosen and I would sink down, down. . . .

I felt something brush by. A large tree, torn out by the roots, nuzzled me. With a sudden infusion of strength I pulled myself into the branches and then onto the large tree trunk. Wonderful, protective trees! How I have always loved you!

As I lay there on my stomach, I was able to stare out at scenes all around me—an immense steel girder poking up through the muck; a woman's body clutching a baby and turning over and over in the water; one of the store dummies floating by serenely, hardly distinguishable from other bodies; an entire family—father, mother and two little children—kneeling on the siding of a house. As the current quickened, speeding by me went one dead cow, the bodies of two riding horses, the back of a haywagon and a school of rats swimming smoothly behind a staircase that could have come from our office building.

One hefty woman covered with tar was riding astride a barrel that kept rolling from side to side while she screamed in terror. A man rode past me standing on a large garage door. It was Salvatore Mazzini, the Italian shoe repair man, all alone and totally naked; he raised one hand toward heaven in supplication.

Aware that I was shivering, I looked down and made a shocking discovery—all my clothing had been torn off. I, too, was stripped bare. "Please, let this be a bad dream," I heard myself saying.

But it was not a bad dream. I was astride a large tree, bruised, naked, terrified, as the flood debris merged into one body moved along the riverbed. My tree had slowed down so that instead of holding on to the branches with all my strength, I could sit up a bit and look forward. What I saw was not reassuring. Dead ahead, about three hundred yards, was Railroad Bridge, that stone relic from the past century. People had called it ugly, too small for modern traffic and a transit hazard for all except the smallest boats. It was built to last centuries.

Much of the flood had rushed over, under or around

the bridge, which had resisted an immense tonnage of water power. It had remained firm when assailed by logs, trees and pieces of housing. Trucks, railroad cars and whole houses had not budged it. When a locomotive smashed against two stone pilings, bystanders later reported that the bridge trembled but held.

All these big objects blocked up the passageways underneath the bridge, creating a pileup that had quickly reached the top of the bridge and was backed up hundreds of yards in an area as wide and long as three city blocks.

Then came the most terrifying sight of all. Fire suddenly shot out of a small house that had crunched up against the left side of the bridge. As I watched, the flames leapt high, obviously fed by oil or gasoline. With a brisk breeze now blowing, the entire mass backed up behind the bridge could turn into a fiery torch.

What escape was there? The water had slowed down enough that for a desperate moment I considered swimming for the bank. But it was too far off and the water was churning with debris. Could I steer the tree away from the fire? Several kicks in the water quickly showed me the futility of that approach.

Despairingly I looked behind me for help. Dirt-colored water extended as far back as I could see, floating the wildest collection of objects, living and dead, swimming and drifting, all heading for Railroad Bridge. And all set to pile up on top of me, I thought with horror. I wanted to scream, shout, cry, but to whom? Everyone around me was either dead, seriously hurt or struggling to survive. At least I was astride something unsinkable.

I prayed again, "Lord, are You there?" It was a pathetic plea, a bare whisper, as though I were ashamed to call attention to myself in my nakedness. How ridiculous! I'm about to die and yet still concerned about how I look. Have I always been this vain? Then I laughed. The whole thing was ludicrous. I was stripped down to nothing. I came into the world with nothing on; I was going out the same way. Why was I ashamed of being the way the Lord made me?

The thought freed me. I straightened up, realizing that in my hunched-over state, I had assumed an almost fetal position. I was certainly not ashamed of my body; in fact, in the privacy of my room I had admired it. I looked around me again. Then I stood up to see better.

The sun had gone. The sky was overcast and drops of rain pelted down. I liked the feeling of the rain on my body. I looked up and let it wet my face. Tears came; I don't know why. They poured from my eyes and mixed on my face with the rain.

A new, tingling sensation flooded me. It seemed to start in my feet and work upward. How to describe something I had never felt before? Exhilaration. Joy. Elation. Warmth. A combination of all. But something more, too. Caring. No, stronger than that. Love.

I was being suffused with love. Washed in it. It penetrated every cell in my body. I was being totally, completely loved. By whom? By Someone I did not know, but wanted to know very much.

I stood as straight as I could and reached for the invisible sun.

Nineteen minutes had passed from the time the dam was breached until the wall of floodwater smashed into the outskirts of Alderton. North Bridge took the full impact. Three cars were crossing the bridge at the time;

the cars pinwheeled and somersaulted into the air like toys, then were swallowed up. The asphalt surface on the bridge simply disappeared, leaving the bridge skeleton tilting at a grotesque angle.

The wave of water then separated. One mass roared southwest into downtown Alderton. The other veered to the east side of the Sequanoto River and bore down on the Lowlands.

The first building hit in Alderton was the one-story brick dwelling and office of dentist Harry Froehling. It was smothered by the thirty-foot-high mass of watery debris. Only the foundation was left. Harry had dashed to safety only minutes before.

Next struck was a vacant two-story wooden structure that had once been used as a stable. It exploded in a shower of kindling.

Jordan's Hardware was obliterated before the mass bored into our three-story Sentinel Building. Observers seemed to agree that this structure put up a fight. The dark, broiling wall broke around the building, causing it to shudder violently. As the follow-up waters continued to cascade into it, *The Sentinel*'s home began to totter and tilt. The roof split with a shriek, part of it torn away. People were seen spurting out of the top, spinning, whirling, scrambling, clutching at anything for support.

Then, slowly, the whole building broke apart, floor by floor, and was swept away. Dean Fleming held on to Emily Cruley as they were propelled through the opening in the roof. He managed to get Emily up on a piece of roofing before a tumbling beam knocked him unconscious and he was sucked down into the torrent. Emily was later pulled from the waters, still alive and still clutching her black leather subscription case.

Rand was catapulted into the turgid water and, being a good swimmer, tried to keep himself afloat. Bruised and buffeted, he grabbed a heavy beam as it sped by and hung on to it grimly until his legs were smashed by the pileup at Railroad Bridge. It took rescuers several hours to pry him loose from the debris; by then he was near death from loss of blood.

Of the seven others who scrambled to the top floor of the Sentinel Building with us, only one survived—a woman who was rescued from the tangle at Railroad Bridge.

After conquering the Sentinel Building, the floodwaters roared into the heart of Alderton, looking for bigger challenges. Salvatore Mazzini's shoe repair shop was no obstacle. It was swept up like a piece of flotsam as the old man leapt onto a garage door that was spinning by. Mazzini's body was recovered later, burned almost beyond recognition by the fire.

Onlookers thought that surely the six-story Haslam House Hotel, a solid brick structure, would withstand the roiling waters. At first it seemed to. As the first wave crashed into the brick building, it trembled but held. It resisted the following assaults, too, until a tumbling locomotive gashed a deep hole in the west side of the building at the second-floor level. Waters rushed into the wounds, causing the hole to widen.

Screams poured from the guests as the top floors began to settle. The relentless, flowing mass of debris ricocheted through the hotel, smashing doors, splitting seams, breaking furniture. When the third and fourth floors on the west side collapsed, the whole building shuddered, bobbled, groaned and then broke apart.

* * *

I have two vivid memories from the moments just before plunging into the mess in front of Railroad Bridge. One is of the roaring fire about twenty feet to my left and the hideous screams coming from it. The other is of the huge black horse on my right. He kept popping up out of the water, then disappearing into the muck, only to reappear once again like a monstrous rocking horse. I knew he was dead because his hindquarters had been severed.

As we jolted to a stop I burrowed into the tree branches. Then it seemed as if a whole mountain landed on top of me.

Some time later the shouts of rescuers revived me. "There's one under that dead horse!"

Grunts. Curses. "One big heave. Now!"

The weight lifted. Two men pulled me up. A blanket was thrown around me. Someone brought a makeshift stretcher and I was placed on it. The fire was so near I could feel its heat.

Through pain and shock I dimly remember being carried off the bridge. There I was placed beside the road with other wounded. When I tried to test my body, a spasm of pain shot through my back. Better lie still until a doctor could examine me.

Meanwhile the ambulance shuttled back and forth, taking the injured and burned to the hospital. It was getting dark now, and all about me was turmoil and confusion, groans of pain, sobbing, frantic people searching for relatives. I wondered where my parents were. Anne-Marie? Rand? Dean? Spasms of fear shot through me.

The ambulance was back again. A man stood over me, saw my eyes were open. "How bad you hurt?" he asked.

I just shook my head. He called another man and

333

they lifted me into the ambulance. At the hospital I was carried inside and placed on a mattress on the floor of a hallway already lined with injured. An hour must have passed.

"Julie!"

I looked up to see my father. His face was contorted with a mixture of anguish and joy. Then he was kneeling beside me, clutching my hand, his eyes brimming with tears.

"I think I'm all right, Dad. I was knocked out. My back hurts, but I can move my legs O.K." Sobs choked me.

My father sat down beside me, still holding my hand. "We'll have to wait our turn. Only a few doctors here. So many hurt and burned."

"Mother? Anne-Marie?" I asked.

"Your mother and I were home when the water hit. It missed our house. Anne-Marie was at the Fleming farm." He stopped, his eyes full of pain. "You're the first one we've found."

My head fell back and I closed my eyes to digest this news. My little sister. . . .

"Rand?" I whispered. "He saved my life when the building collapsed."

"Rand's here in the hospital."

Joy and fear jumbled together. "He's badly hurt, isn't he?"

Dad nodded. "Left leg crushed."

"What about Dean? Miss Cruley?"

"Emily's all right. Dean's—" Dad's voice broke. "Dean drowned, Julie."

"No, no." Tears filled my eyes. If only Rand and Dean hadn't come to *The Sentinel*. . . . If only I had followed through on that inner nudge to have Rand meet me at home.

A harried doctor began checking over the patients on the hall floor. He tested my reflexes, then had me wheeled to the X-ray room. Not until the X rays proved to be negative was I given a hospital gown and allowed to get on my feet. "Slight concussion, bad bruises and twisting of the lower lumbar region," was the diagnosis. "Keep her here overnight."

I learned of Anne-Marie's rescue when Dad returned to the hospital later that night. Meanwhile, makeshift wards were set up in every available space; I was moved into the nurses' off-duty room along with seven other women, mattresses lined up on the floor for us to sleep on.

When I questioned medical personnel about Rand, they just shook their heads. There had been no time yet to chart patients by name. Was he still alive? Was this all a bad dream?

No, the moans of the wounded, the sounds of weeping and the hurrying figures in white made it only too real. It was a miracle that I was alive. How had I survived?

Then I remembered. Those last moments before I hit the bridge, something important had happened. I had called out to God and He had responded. Not by voice, but by His presence. The memory stirred me and my lips began to move.

"Please, Lord, help Rand!"

Tears began to roll down my cheeks. So many people drowned. I closed my eyes and sleep came.

Early next morning my father reappeared. I stared at his face, looking for a sign.

"Rand is still in critical condition. He lost a lot of blood, but the doctor thinks he'll make it."

When I walked into Rand's hospital room later that morning, he was asleep. I stood by his bed silently, not wanting to wake him. The gray color of his face frightened me.

Rand stirred and his hand fell off his chest. Timidly I reached over and touched his fingers. Then I cradled his hand in mine; a tear rolled down my face and splashed onto his hand.

I looked back into Rand's face. His eyes were open and his lips slowly spread into a smile.

"We made it, didn't we?" he said.

Section
Twelve

Facing Death

One morning late in our marriage Catherine admitted to me that she feared death.

"But Catherine, all you've written on that subject..."

"I'm not talking about immortality," she interrupted. "I believe everything Jesus had to say about the resurrection and life after death."

"Well, death is simply the doorway to all that."

"I know that, too," she said, her voice tinged with impatience. "But it's all in my head, not in my emotions. Somehow, somewhere back in my childhood, a feeling took root inside me that death is the enemy to be hated and fought every step of the way."

"Catherine, we've been married almost twenty years. Why have you kept this hidden?"

337

"I guess I was ashamed to admit it."

As we prayed together about it, we saw again how Satan uses fear as a weapon to weaken our faith. I had become the spiritual head of our family years before. Now I knew that I needed to go a step further as head of our home and wage all-out spiritual warfare against the enemy.

Though Satan was assaulting us and our family, we were not defenseless. He hates prayer. Our intercession ministry had shown Catherine and me that a wave of prayer renders him ineffective.

Early in 1982 Catherine realized her time on earth was limited. The emphysema in her lungs had been slowly sapping her vitality. Walking up a flight of stairs was a major undertaking. Talking to people, meetings, shopping drained her.

Saddest of all was how her growing breathlessness affected her mornings—the time for the manuscript work she looked forward to so much. I would watch her go resolutely into her office at 9 A.M. Forty minutes later I would hear her return to our bedroom.

Once I confronted her there as she lay listlessly on the bed.

Tears welled up in her eyes. "The inner drive is gone. I don't have it anymore."

Then she railed at herself for being a quitter, got up and tried again.

My dilemma was: Should I prod her into doing what was painful and hard or let her drift into invalidism?

The answer soon became clear. Catherine's basic competitiveness, her battling nature, her spirit of adventure and her curiosity about life could not, should not be allowed to die. Catherine would never have forgiven me if I had encouraged her to let go of all this.

So we waged spiritual war against the forces of darkness and the enemy's subtle enticements to give in to weakness. We ended each day in prayer, when I anointed Catherine with oil, taking a stand against ill health, asking for sharpness of thinking and healing of body and spirit.

Here are some of Catherine's journal entries during her last days.

His Unfinished Work in Me

Dreamed last night about death. I don't relish putting this one on paper, but since it has to be worked through with the Lord, I suppose I must.

I was in a country where certain citizens were being exterminated by order of the state. One got one's notice and came to a special "office" in which were three booths, side by side. In one of these you were given a shot, like a dog being "put to sleep." Afterwards you were carted off to a back room where the bodies were stacked.

Apparently my number had come up. When I got to the office, I noticed that there were stacks and stacks of dirty dishes in the three booths. I sought to stall my death by offering eagerly to wash all the dishes. The attendant said, "Sure, go ahead. I don't blame you. Just don't tell any of the others that I agreed."

I started to wash a stack of plates, saying to myself, "There's always the chance of something happening to intervene, a national emergency or something." Then I woke up.

So now that I have put this dream on paper, Lord, what does it mean—and what do I do about it?

As I waited for some response, a name came to mind—John Wesley. Tuttle's book on Wesley was in the stack of unread volumes on my night table. I picked it up and soon discovered that Wesley and I shared a dread of death as the great enemy.

Wesley's fear surfaced dramatically in 1735 during a crossing of the Atlantic to Georgia. There were heavy storms at sea and the small wooden ship at times seemed doomed. Most on board, including the crew, were terror-struck. The only ones who remained calm were a group of German Moravian Christians.

Seeing the strength of these believers as they faced death, Wesley knew he must work through his problem. In reviewing his walk of faith, he realized he had espoused a life of asceticism that took four forms:

1. Self-denial (he lived frugally in order to give money to the poor)
2. Solitude
3. Works of charity (including visits to the terrible prisons of the time where he prayed with condemned men)
4. Interior prayer life

Wesley had to admit that while each of these disciplines have a place in the Christian life, not one of them dealt with his fear of death. Finally he began to see that this fear was not from God, but from Satan.

Soon after these discoveries, John Wesley had his personal experience of the Holy Spirit at Aldersgate. He was back against the basic New Testament proposition. There is no road to God except by faith in the finished work of Jesus Christ on the cross. Joy flooded in and gradually his fear of death dropped away as the Spirit brought alive these triumphant words of Jesus:

In My Father's house there are many dwelling places (homes). If it were not so, I would have told you, for I am going away to prepare a place for you. And when (if) I go and make ready a place for you, I will come back again and will take you to Myself, that where I am you may be also.

John 14:2–3, TAB

I know that the Holy Spirit has much unfinished work to do inside me about my attitude toward death. I need this, and I will myself to desire it.

Body Language

I beseech you therefore, brethren . . . that ye present your bodies a living sacrifice, holy, acceptable unto God, which is your reasonable service.

Romans 12:1

Reading the Bible yesterday afternoon, I felt an inner nudge to stop and reread the above verse. I was conscious that I resisted this idea of offering my body as a sacrifice. Why? Because I suspected it could mean more speaking and traveling, more stress and pressure, with consequent loss of sleep at night and no chance to recoup with daytime naps.

What is so bad about this is that it is not really trusting the Lord with my physical body, and that's an awful confession. God expects His followers to be willing to be expendable; I have been circling around this point of total trust in a kind of spiritual holding pattern, unwilling to lay down my body as a living sacrifice. I am constantly protecting myself, succumbing too quickly to the temptation to stop my work and lie down for a while.

The conviction then came that I must be willing—and tell God so—to have the self I call "me," the particular bundle of talents, predispositions, preferences, tastes, all that constitutes myself, nailed to the cross with Jesus, to actually die and be buried with Him.

But, a voice inside me argued, didn't I do just this

344

when I became a Christian? Jesus assured me, however, that this was a new step of dying to the self that so loves body comforts and beautiful things, that longs to escape the demands and entanglements of other people.

Much of that self I dislike (Romans 7:15–25). But a lot of what constitutes "me" I like very much. I have been "me," lived with "me" and put up with "me" a long time. To lay this self on the altar would indeed be a death.

I remembered Jesus' words about "counting the cost" (Luke 14:28). Was I really willing to take myself to the cross, die and be buried, not having any idea what sort of person would rise with Jesus on the third day?

I went through agony thinking about this, with a lot of tears.

Scripture says that Jesus resolutely and willingly turned His face to the cross for "the joy that was set before him" (Hebrews 12:2).

I finally told Jesus that I was going forward with this because I knew He was going to have His way with me, now or in the next life.

I got down on my knees in my office by the daybed at 4:40 P.M. and offered up my body to Him as a living sacrifice.

As a result, I must now be obedient hour by hour, day by day, and not hold back. This means seeing the indwelling Spirit so residing in my mortal flesh that I am willing to spend myself totally for others, as He did. It means letting all selfishness go, everything in my desire world, whenever it cuts across His higher priorities.

No wonder we can do no mighty works until the surrender is this complete! Until Jesus has been allowed to come and make His home in me like that, I will be praying for others, doing His work, in my name and in my nature rather than in His.

The apostle John puts it this way:

.. . He laid down His [own] life for us; and we ought to lay [our] lives down for [those who are our] brothers [in Him].

1 John 3:16, TAB

Self-Pity

This morning I took to the Lord a matter that has been troubling me lately: sudden tears. I have never been a person who cries often. I generally keep my emotions in check, perhaps more than I should. Recently, though, bouts of unpredictable weeping.

The Lord has graciously shown me this morning the why of tears being just under the surface these past weeks—self-pity. In reality, I am weeping for myself.

I weep because of what is happening to me physically. First, my energy level has again dropped to such a degree that it is literally a chore to put one foot before the other. Added to that, worse breathlessness than I have ever known. Sometimes even sitting or lying in bed, I wonder if I am going to be able to take the next breath. This makes the stairs and hills at Evergreen Farm an agony.

Most puzzling, after years of battling sleeplessness, suddenly I can hardly stay awake. I must check out with the doctor whether this is an overreaction to the new arthritis drug they are giving me.

Or is it possible that, through lack of oxygen to the brain, I am coming into early senility? Hideous thought! For the first time since early girlhood I have no desire to read at night. During church yesterday, I could scarcely keep my eyes open.

Lord, help!

I am led to this verse:

I know . . . Him Whom I have believed . . . and I am [positively] persuaded that He is able to guard and keep that which has been entrusted to me and which I have committed [to Him], until that day.

2 Timothy 1:12, TAB

Since self-pity is a sin, then clearly it has to be dealt with as a sin. It is a sin because since I belong to Jesus, it is He who has control over my life. Thus He overrules everything that He "allows" to happen to me—overrules it for good.

My part is to trust Him as a loving heavenly Father in each of these adverse circumstances. I am to watch expectantly for the "good"—the new adventure He has for me, the open door I am to go through toward the better way to which He is leading me.

So, given all that, what is there to have self-pity about?

I see that there is a self-discipline to practice during the days ahead: Each time I am tempted toward despairing self-pity, I am to rebuke it, reject it and turn immediately to praise.

Crucified with Jesus

On July 9, 1982, Catherine was so weak we had
her taken by ambulance to the local hospital.
When tests showed an alarming carbon dioxide
content in her body, she was placed in the Intensive Care Unit with respirator tubes through her
mouth to her lungs. The prognosis for her recovery was not good. She could not speak but she
could still write in her journal.

In many ways my 32-day stint in the Intensive Care
Unit of Bethesda Hospital was a crucifixion experience. Soon after I arrived there, the Lord reminded
me of the act I had performed (through Romans 12:1) of
offering my body as a living sacrifice on His cross.

While lying on my back hour after hour, unable to
read or talk, I had plenty of time to reflect on the study I
did a while ago on the humanity of Jesus. Through it I
saw that His humanness for 33 years on earth was real;
that He was as helpless, as "out of control" of circumstances, as we are. All this was in order for Him to be the
Way-Shower, the true and very practical Captain of our
salvation.

I also perceived that during His earthly walk, the
guiding principle of Jesus' life was "never what I want
to do but what pleases My Father in heaven."

In the intervening months since I made this study,
several things have been happening:

1. The Holy Spirit has been doing a steady softening and melting process within me. This has
   meant that the plights of other persons presented
   to me, mostly through correspondence, have
   been laid on my heart with a new urgency.

2. During this same period my own circumstances
   have not only been taken out of my control, but
   also have gone in directions contrary to anything
   I would wish.

At what point in the Christian walk are we actually
"crucified with Him"? At what point is the mortal self
dead on His cross and buried with Him?

In my case, I concluded, dying to self has been going
on for some time. For me it has been a slow, torturous,
lingering death indeed—no doubt because I have been
resisting all the way. I am reasonably sure that it need
not be this drawn out and painful if the believer really
understands what is going on and why and assents to it
in his will. Yet I do think it is something we have to walk
through all the way and feel. Death on a cross hurts.

Early the morning of July 24, fifteen days after entering the hospital, the climax came for me. I was in a
semiconscious, dreaming state when I felt myself literally hanging on the cross with Jesus. There was no pain
from nails in my hands or feet, only a suffocating, crushing weight on my chest as my entire body dragged
downwards. I knew I was close to death, but strangely I
had absolutely no fear.

As the weight on my rib cage grew unendurable, however, I was aware of a dark presence, as well as that of
Jesus. A fierce struggle with some evil force ensued. Again

and again I rebuked the dark power and ordered him to be gone. He didn't leave easily, but leave he did at last.

Then, so gently, Jesus picked me up and removed me from the cross. As He did so, three words came to me: "the great exchange." Later I realized this is what theologians call "the substitutionary atonement," meaning that every sinful thing in our lives was dealt with in Christ's finished work on His cross and exchanged for something wonderful—righteousness for sin, health for sickness, life for death. At the moment I knew only that the crushing weight had lifted from my ribs.

I awoke the next morning very excited, feeling that a miracle had taken place in my body. This is the note I wrote to the nurse, saved by Len:

> Please grant me this one request! I want to see my family, now! My husband first. Please call him. 732-6352.
>
> My husband, my son Peter, my son Jeffrey. I want all of them. I want no medication before they get here. I'll "calm down" to suit you.

When Len, Peter and Jeffrey arrived, I told them through notes about my "death"; that at one point in my struggle with that dark force, it had seemed that my body parts were burnt up and lying in pieces around the room. The turning point came when way down deep I cried, "Jesus! Lord. My Lord." And He came and was with me. And He healed me.

My family was very responsive, but I think they wondered if it was a hallucination brought on by low oxygen levels in the brain. The key would be the next blood gases test.

When the doctor arrived at my bedside the next day, he was all smiles. "The carbon dioxide is way down!" he reported.

And then we all celebrated! On August 11 I was moved out of the Intensive Care Unit. On August 26 I was allowed to go home.

What transpired on the cross two thousand years ago has taken on sparkling new meaning for me. We are accustomed to thinking that Jesus carried only our sins on the cross, but Scripture makes it equally clear that He bore all our sicknesses and diseases there, too.

> When evening came they brought to [Jesus] many who were under the power of demons, and He drove out the spirits with a word, and restored to health all who were sick; and thus He fulfilled what was spoken by the prophet Isaiah, He Himself took (in order to carry away) our weaknesses and infirmities and bore away our diseases.
>
> Matthew 8:16–17, TAB (see Isaiah 53:4)

Len asked me the other night what I considered the chief significance of my crucifixion experience.

"I'm not sure yet," I replied. "I was close to death and the Lord returned me to life. He must have had a reason."

"Do you know what that might be?"

"There are a number of things I'm supposed to do, especially work on some bruised relationships." Then it struck me. "I've had a crucifixion, but not a resurrection."

Len wouldn't accept this. "You emerged from a dark valley into the light. Wasn't that a resurrection?"

"Not entirely. My breathing was restored to what it

352

was last spring, but that's far from normal. My lungs have still not been completely healed."

"Consider this, Catherine," Len replied. "You've operated with little more than half your normal lung-power for almost forty years. But look at all you've accomplished. Maybe, like Paul, God's given you a thorn in the flesh for a reason."

Lord, how much more I have to learn!

This morning I had this word from the Spirit. He tells me to praise and rejoice. He brings to mind the Scripture song we have sung so often at church: "Rejoice in the Lord always; again I will say, Rejoice" (Philippians 4:4, RSV).

Rejoice!

That I can enjoy music again through my stereo record-player. I actually got up and played the piano a bit—"Breathe on me, breath of God. . . ."

Rejoice!

I telephoned T. and confessed my lack of love and understanding about several matters. A time of renewed fellowship and reconciliation.

Rejoice!

For patient Len and faithful family . . . for the Intercessors . . . for all who prayed . . . for my doctors and the hospital personnel.

Rejoice!

Linda and I are so close now. She drove down to be with me for a week, bringing a gift of four placemats and four napkins for the dining room table. "Use them," she urged. The point is that Len and the doctor have insisted on my getting out of bed and eating at the table.

Rejoice!

Praise You, Lord, for Pastor Bob Bonham giving up half of every Saturday to be with me.

Praise You, Lord, for bringing out all the fears that are clinging around the fear of death, so that I can deal with them.

Praise You, Lord, for allowing me to have those experiences in Intensive Care, and for pulling me back from death.

Receiving Love

God continues to heal me here in our Florida home. This morning He gave me a walloping message about the fact that I have not always been able to receive other people's love and so cannot receive Jesus' love. This revelation was sparked by a hassle with Len last night in our bedroom when I was complaining about members of the household who are shielding me about family situations, finances and decisions that involve my manuscripts and affairs.

Len became quite agitated. Finally with tears in his eyes he said, "Catherine, the doctors have told us that you need time to recover from being at death's door. What we're doing is for your protection, out of our love for you. Don't you realize we almost lost you?" With that, his voice broke with a show of emotion such as I have rarely seen in our marriage.

This morning I awoke with the full impact of Len's deep feeling sweeping over me. How often, I wondered, do men in our society shortchange themselves and their families by letting a "macho" front cover up a sensitive nature underneath?

The conviction came, too, though, that I have not been open enough to love. I have often had trouble accepting the feelings Len did express. The affection and gratitude of friends and readers, too.

Read 1 Corinthians 13, the Spirit nudged.

Those verses lay it out for me even more stringently than Len did last night:

Love is patient, love is kind. It does not envy, it does not boast, it is not proud. It is not rude, it is not self-seeking, it is not easily angered, it keeps no record of wrongs. Love does not delight in evil but rejoices with the truth. It always protects, always trusts, always hopes, always perseveres.

1 Corinthians 13:4–7, NIV

I see further that, while my act of laying my body on the altar as "a living sacrifice" was a good first step, it was not enough: "If I . . . surrender my body to the flames, but have not love, I gain nothing" (verse 3).

Now comes further revelation, even as I write. Following the 1944 experience of Jesus' healing presence in my room after I had been bedridden for almost three years, I nevertheless lacked something. I have always supposed it was sufficient faith to make the healing complete.

But suppose it was love that was missing, not faith. Oh, obedience was not altogether there either, but obedience would have followed love.

Lord, I rejoice. Lord, I capitulate. Lord, let Your love—and Len's, and the love of those around me, each member of my family, and all the love of far-flung friends through my books—take over.

Keeping My
Eyes on Jesus

Fell on my face yesterday. Breathing was laborious. Did very little walking. Could not do the exercises. Was discouraged and disheartened and bored.

I knew the cause of all this. A letter came from my doctor, putting names and tags to my "chronic" illness for use in Medicare forms. It sounded so final that I began looking at this, accepting it, settling down to it.

I also opened the door to fear. Not so much fear of death, because I have actually, finally worked through that. This time it was a fear that I would let down the readers of my books who expect me to be an example of victorious faith.

In my session with Bob Bonham I traced the roots of this fear of letting people down back to my childhood. What came out was that my father's praising me so highly when I played the piano for his prayer meetings, or made top grades in school, eventually created in me the feeling that I had to achieve in order to have his love.

As the years passed, this feeling was extended to other members of my family, to friends, even to God. Added to this was my belief that because I have been so public in my life as a Christian, if I did not measure up to what Jesus expected of me, I would not only let Him down, but people "out there" would think less of Him; that Jesus' reputation would actually suffer.

Put in so many words, this is obviously ridiculous! But that's what came out. So yesterday was a total setback for me.

This morning I sought the Lord's forgiveness and was told something like this, most emphatically:

Catherine, take your eyes off yourself, off your symptoms, off your fears, and center your attention on Me. Look at Me. Keep looking at Me.

Allow Me to be your Doctor. This is My will. I do know how to give you health. I made you. I know how to mend you.

Why do you think I healed everyone who came to Me in the days of My flesh? Out of overflowing mercy. I had only to see any human being blind or crippled or sick or in pain to want to set the wrong situation right as quickly as possible.

I have told you in My Word (Hebrews) that as man's High Priest I am able—and want—to run to the assistance of those who cry to Me.

In my answering prayer I said, "Lord, I do cry to You. I give You permission to change me on the inside, to strengthen my flabby spiritual muscles, to reverse the direction of my gaze, to make me eager to look at You only.

"I know You want a resurrection thrust inside me and an end to my doubts and negative thinking. In the wake of this will come new life and health. If not on this earth, then I will go into the next life with the differentness that You want for me."

Then Jesus led me to the sixteenth chapter of John where I was stopped by this magnificent verse:

. . . It is profitable—good, expedient, advanta-

358

geous—for you that I go away. Because if I do not go away, the Comforter (Counselor, Helper, Advocate, Intercessor, Strengthener, Standby) will not come to you—into close fellowship with you. . . .

John 16:7, TAB

These are the blessed functions of the Holy Spirit promised by Jesus:

Counselor—He gives wisdom to the simple
Helper—He lifts us over every obstacle
Advocate—He is our personal lawyer to plead our case
Intercessor—He stands before the throne of grace
Strengthener—He gives us vitality and courage
Standby—He is always at our side

How can any one of us get along without any of those things!
Then glorious verse 33:

I have told you these things so that in Me you may have perfect peace and confidence. In the world you have tribulation and trials and distress and frustration; but be of good cheer—take courage, be confident, certain, undaunted—for I have overcome the world.—I have deprived it of power to harm, have conquered it [for you].

Resurrection

Thanks to her pastors George Callahan and Robert Bonham, plus loving friends and family, Catherine made good progress during 1982. Thanksgiving and Christmas involved healing times with family members.

At the beginning of 1983 Catherine set several goals for herself. An 800-page draft of the novel *Julie* had been completed, but months of work were needed to sharpen characterization. She wanted to resume writing for *The Intercessors* newsletter and do an article about her mother for a *Guideposts* series on aging.

At the end of January she underwent a cataract operation. From her journal:

February 9: I am staggering under what the eye surgeon said to me yesterday during a routine checkup following the cataract surgery: "You are sick from head to toe." I did not have to accept this verdict, but I did. Now I really have to ditch it—with the Spirit's help and by God's grace. This verse has truly helped me:

> If the Spirit of Him Who raised up Jesus from the dead dwells in you, [then] He Who raised up

Christ Jesus from the dead will also restore to life your mortal (short-lived, perishable) bodies through His Spirit Who dwells in you.

Romans 8:11, TAB

February 24: Have hit a new low. I am quite out of breath—indeed, gasping for air—just in walking from room to room. My doctor could find no obvious cause for the trouble yesterday. Today it hit me: Once again the doctors know neither what is wrong nor how to help me. So . . . I am backed up against Jesus' help.

March 9: In my quiet time, this thought: My hospital experience of the crucifixion was centered on the matter of breathing. This morning the Holy Spirit reminded me once again: Jesus took your breathing problem into His own body on the cross so that from henceforth He is your life-breath.

Here is Catherine's last journal entry made from the hospital where she was undergoing tests:

March 12: The blood test yesterday showed the carbon dioxide level in my blood too high, but not dangerous; not enough oxygen in the blood, however. Another problem seems to be anemia.

This morning Jesus told me once again: Keep your eyes off yourself and look steadily at Me. I love you. I know how to mend you.

Shortly after midnight on March 18, Catherine's heart stopped beating. The Lord had come to take her with Him.

Afterword

In the hours and days that followed, the Lord seemed to place all of us in the family under His special love and protection, plus a necessary degree of numbness. The calls, letters, cards, flowers and food that flowed in warmed and nourished us.

Two triumphant occasions followed:

The burial service at National Presbyterian Church, Washington, D.C., conducted by its pastor, Catherine's close friend Dr. Louis Evans, Jr., and her son, Peter John Marshall.

And the memorial service at the New Covenant Presbyterian Church, Pompano Beach, Florida. Pastor George Callahan and Dr. William Earnhart (church elder and Catherine's personal physician) shared their memories of a great lady.

Robert Bonham, the pastor who for so many hours ministered healing to Catherine, spoke these words at this same service:

> During Catherine's funeral in the National Presbyterian Church, my eyes went to some beautiful stained glass windows through which the sun was shining. I thought of Jesus telling His disciples, "You are the light of the world." Catherine as a twentieth-century follower put her light on a lampstand so that all might see.
>
> I looked at the glass in those windows and thought about all the pieces therein. There were

dark pieces and light pieces, all kinds of colors blended together. I thought about the suffering experiences Catherine had early in her life and recently in the hospital. These were deep, deep colors. Her body never was able to keep up with her mind and her spirit. It always hauled her back.

There were, of course, the brighter colors, the rose tints of love and warmth—the giving of her heart to those in her family and to everyone she touched. Those colors went out across the United States and throughout the world.

There were so many pieces in her life—the books she wrote, the articles for *Guideposts* and other magazines. She wrote nothing that did not have all of her heart and mind in it, as well as the heart and mind of Christ.

Starting the Breakthrough intercession ministry not long ago, she and Leonard mobilized prayer warriors across the nation to bring help to many people. The members of her family represent warm, glowing pieces of glass in the mosaic of her life.

A surprising thing about a stained glass window is that when the light is not shining through, it comes across as dull. Have you ever looked at a stained glass window when there is no light behind it? You cannot see what is in it. Catherine always had Christ's light shining through her life. As the light of Jesus radiated through the stained glass mosaic of her life, all of us who were within sight of it got blessed.

When the sun goes down, the horizon stays

bright for a long time. There is going to be a long afterglow to Catherine Marshall LeSourd's life. The books that were written will go on to become classics in Christian literature. The articles will go on helping people. There are things she has written that will yet find their way into print to bless us. Her touches on our lives will live on, ministering to our children, our children's children.

In the last page of her book *To Live Again*, Catherine wrote these words as she faced life without her husband Peter:

"At moments when the future is completely obscured, can any one of us afford to go to meet our tomorrows with dragging feet? God had been in the past. Then He would be in the future, too.

"And with His presence had always come an end to tasteless living. Always He had brought adventure—high hopes, unexpected friends, new ventures that broke old patterns. Then out in my future must lie more goodness, more mercy, more adventures, more friends.

"Across the hills light was breaking through the stormclouds. Suddenly just ahead of the car an iridescent rainbow appeared—hung there shimmering. I hadn't seen a rainbow for a long time.

"I drove steadily into the light."

Catherine is doing that right now—moving steadily into the Light.

Appendix

How the Breakthrough Intercessory Prayer Ministry Operates

It begins with the scriptural promise that the Lord's joyful task as our High Priest is to make intercession for us before His Father's throne.

The prayer needs of individuals are sent to

Breakthrough

The Catherine Marshall Center

Lincoln, VA 22078

Prayer requests for governments, causes or special works are handled occasionally by Breakthrough, but more often forwarded to other groups like Intercessors for America, which specialize in this kind of petition.

Intercessors are the "supply" people who have volunteered to tithe their time to pray for the needs of others. Their names and addresses are known only to the Breakthrough administrators.

Need and supply meet in this way: A summary of each person's need (first name only) is sent to five or more intercessors who have committed themselves to pray for each request for a three-week period. At the end of this time the prayer-requester may ask for an extension of this commitment.

The anonymity of both parties is kept so that the ministry can focus on prayer and not get into personal counseling, which the intercessors are not equipped to do.

When a prayer insight (often a revelation from God) is received by an intercessor, it is forwarded to the prayer-requester via the coordinator in the Breakthrough office.

When an answer to an intercessor's prayer is received by letter or telephone at the Breakthrough office, there is a joyful time of praise.

The Breakthrough newsletter circulates regularly to provide teaching on intercessory prayer and reports on the results of the work. It can be obtained free of charge by writing to the above address.

About the Editor

Leonard E. LeSourd and Catherine Marshall were married for twenty-three years until her death in 1983. Leonard and Catherine, along with John and Elizabeth Sherrill, founded Chosen Books Publishing Company in 1972. LeSourd is a former executive editor of *Guideposts* magazine and is the author of *Strong Men, Weak Men* and *Touching the Heart of God*.

Walker and Company Large Print books
are available from your local bookstore.
Please ask for them.
If you want to be on our mailing list
to receive a catalog and information about our
titles, please send your name and address to:

Beth Walker
Walker and Company
435 Hudson Street
New York, New York 10014

Among the titles available are:

THE WONDERFUL SPIRIT-FILLED LIFE
Charles Stanley

FINDING GOD
Larry Crabb

GOOD MORNING HOLY SPIRIT
Benny Hinn

THE GREATEST STORY EVER TOLD
Fulton Oursler

THE ROAD LESS TRAVELED
M. Scott Peck

**FURTHER ALONG THE ROAD LESS
TRAVELED**
M. Scott Peck

TO LIFE!
A Celebration of Jewish Being and Thinking
Harold Kushner

GOOD MORNING HOLY SPIRIT
Benny Hinn

CATHOLIC PRAYER BOOK

A GATHERING OF HOPE
Helen Hayes

THE PROPHET
Kahlil Gibran

WORDS TO LOVE BY
Mother Teresa

APPLES OF GOLD
Jo Petty

AND THE ANGELS WERE SILENT
Max Lucado

THE POWER OF POSITIVE THINKING
Norman Vincent Peale

LAUGH AGAIN
Charles Swindoll

SOMETHING BEAUTIFUL FOR GOD
Malcolm Muggeridge

THE GRACE AWAKENING
Charles Swindoll

A GRIEF OBSERVED
C. S. Lewis

PRAYERS AND PROMISES FOR EVERYDAY
Corrie ten Boom

GETTING THROUGH THE NIGHT
Eugenia Price

HOPE FOR THE TROUBLED HEART
Billy Graham

MAKING ALL THINGS NEW
Henri J. M. Nouwen

IRREGULAR PEOPLE
Joyce Landorf

CODEPENDENT NO MORE
Melody Beattie

HINDS' FEET ON HIGH PLACES
Hannah Hurnard

NO WONDER THEY CALL HIM THE SAVIOR
Max Lucado

CARE OF THE SOUL
Thomas Moore

A BOOK OF ANGELS
Sophy Burnham

PRACTICE OF THE PRESENCE OF GOD
Brother Lawrence

LOVE IS A GENTLE STRANGER
June Masters Bacher

**MOTHER ANGELICA'S ANSWERS
NOT PROMISES**
Mother Angelica

**TO HELP YOU THROUGH
THE HURTING**
Marjorie Holmes

GUIDEPOSTS TREASURY OF CHRISTMAS

A BOOK OF ANGELS
Sophy Burnham

LOVE'S SILENT SONG
June Masters Bacher

PEACE, LOVE & HEALING
Bernie S. Siegel